Praise for *Gershwin*

"The only book on Gershwin to own."   —**Michael Feinstein**

"The chief virtue of *Gershwin*, which ranks alongside Ira Gershwin's *Lyrics on Several Occasions*, is that Jablonski's approach is scrupulously factual—free from special pleading of any sort and unmarred by bargain-basement psychoanalysis."   —*Chicago Tribune*

"There is a wealth of fresh material derived from letters and notebooks. . . . I would advise addicts to buy this conscientious book."
—*Sunday Times* (London)

"Jablonski's writing is laced with the wry appreciation the brothers brought to their work. His discography is acerbic enough (and as valuable as the chronological list of compositions for both George and Ira) to penetrate any gauze of sentiment."   —*Boston Globe*

"As we read Jablonski's meticulous, year-by-year account of the composer's career, we can only marvel again at the prodigality of Gershwin's gifts—and his astonishing productivity."
—**Michiko Kakutani**, *New York Times*

"[This] sympathetic and revealing biography ought to be required reading not only for Gershwin fans but also for every aspiring young theatrical composer."   —*Daily Telegraph* (London)

"[Jablonski] presents his findings in a straightforward manner, generally avoiding the cliché-ridden psychoanalytical approach that has trivialized so many recent biographies."
—**Francis Davis**, *New York Times Book Review*

GERSHWIN

Edward Jablonski

with a new critical discography

DA CAPO PRESS • NEW YORK

Library of Congress Cataloging-in-Publication Data

Jablonski, Edward.
   Gershwin: with a new critical discography / Edward Jablonski.
     p.   cm.
   Originally published: New York: Doubleday, 1988.
   Includes bibliographical references and index.
   ISBN 0-306-80847-1 (alk. paper)
   1. Gershwin, George, 1898–1937. 2. Composers—United States —Biography. I. Title.
ML410.G288J29   1998
780'.92—dc21
[B]   98-11830
CIP
MN

First Da Capo Press edition 1998

This Da Capo Press paperback edition of *Gershwin* is an unabridged republication of the edition first published in New York in 1988, with the earlier discography replaced by a new one. It is reprinted by arrangement with the author.

Published by Da Capo Press, Inc.
A Subsidiary of Plenum Publishing Corporation
233 Spring Street, New York, N.Y. 10013

Manufactured in the United States of America

Contents

Preface

George Gershwin died on July 11, 1937, but I don't have to believe it if I don't want to.

Novelist John O'Hara characteristically (and rather self-consciously, echoing the hard-boiled romanticism of the American twenties), encapsulated an emotion shared by Gershwin admirers (lovers would not be too strong a word) throughout the world at the time of his death, and since, a half century ago. He remains one of the most fascinating figures in American music—more so now than during his brief, exciting lifetime.

O'Hara's terse, unadorned sentence itself is Gershwinesque, redolent of the Jazz Age when the young composer typified eternal youth in a vibrant, strident America wakening to its potential and power in the arts, business, industry, finance, sports, in a world only recently shocked into the twentieth century. Rural America began moving to the City; the Metropolis fused into a center of finance and art and *the* metropolis was New York: Wall Street, Tin Pan Alley and Broadway. In this setting Gershwin, in less than two decades, would make an indelible impression on his nation's culture.

His contribution extends beyond the obvious one of several hundred memorable songs, an opera and a handful of concert pieces. His influence on popular song and the lyric theater is perennial. This ranges from the musical comedies with gossamer "books"—*Lady, Be Good!,* *Girl Crazy,* the wonderful fiasco *Pardon My English*—to the germinative political operettas, *Strike Up the Band, Of Thee I Sing* and its more brilliant but unsuccessful sequel, *Let 'Em Eat Cake.* As for his one opera, *Porgy and Bess,* it is unique—a failure when originally produced and an extraordinary success when revived in the form in which Gershwin had originally conceived it. While the books of his musicals have not gracefully transcended their time, the songs have. Their discovery and rediscovery have virtually become a musicological cottage industry.

Gershwin was potent, too, in energizing popular interest in the contemporary American composer and his music. When the *Rhapsody in Blue* crackled through staid Aeolian Hall early in 1924, he initiated the first substantial invasion of the "serious" concert hall by a native-born composer, certainly the first since the heyday of Edward MacDowell. Charles Tomlinson Griffes had died virtually unknown, the living Charles Ives was unknown and Aaron Copland was yet to make his debut on the American scene.

It was a time of musical conse.vatism, when in order to have your work performed in Carnegie Hall, it seemed essential to be foreign-born or dead—preferably both. Gershwin, more than any other American composer of the period, helped to ameliorate the situation; his impact on the American musical scene is of social as well as musical significance.

"American composer"—what is it?

Contemporary writings about Gershwin underscored his Americanisms, generally via misguided allusions to what uninformed (and generally unsympathetic) critics and musicologists called "jazz." He too thought of himself as an American composer, though he at times typed himself as "a modern romantic." Gershwin's Americanisms are rooted in popular song and dance, the music of the lyric theater, spiced with superficial borrowings from jazz: rhythmic syncopations, "blue" notes and indigo harmonies. To a greater or lesser degree these same musical characteristics may be found in Jewish and Negro music—and other music as well, including Hungarian and English.

Gershwin's art drew upon these elements, but it took a Gershwin to carry it off. Other composers soon after his advent also more self-consciously adapted the same musical devices. In expressing his own musical personality, his vital, searching curiosity, his delight in musical diversion (improvisation) and invention (composition), he created in the words of his first biographer, Isaac Goldberg, "a new music compounded of grace, vitality and dignity."

To his advantage, besides his musical gifts, were other attractive attributes: youth (twenty-five when he created the *Rhapsody in Blue),* fame (coupled with a disarming capacity for its enjoyment), success in an era that venerated success and, following the furor in the wake of his first rhapsody, an air of controversy about him—and that made for good box office, even at Carnegie Hall.

"A modern romantic" he undoubtedly was, but Gershwin was no innovator in the sense that Schoenberg, Bartók and Stravinsky were. He inspired no school of followers (there were plenty of imitators, however). He was aware of the currents in contemporary music, he attended concerts and recitals of "modern" music, he subscribed to Henry Cowell's avant-garde quarterly, *New Music,* collected scores and recordings, with Stravinsky and Sibelius sharing shelf space with Bach, Schubert and Hindemith. He was receptive to new music but went his own way.

While Gershwin did not sell his talents short, it is unlikely that he saw himself as the great historical figure he has become since his death. He was haunted by immortality; a recurring query was, "Do you think anything of mine will live?" (No rarity in the arts.) Humorist-versifier Newman Levy answered him once, "Yes, if you're around to play it." He was chiding the composer for his well-known practice of holding forth at the piano at parties for hours. This readiness has frequently been dredged up to underscore the Gershwin ego, since the music he performed was invariably his own.

Neglected is the fact that Gershwin's appreciative audience often numbered some of the most illustrious musicians of the time. S. N. Behrman recalled observing Gershwin play to the delight of Leopold Auer, Jascha Heifetz, Fritz Kreisler and Efrem Zimbalist (all violinists, please note; to this can be added Maurice Ravel, among others). His piano technique, his improvisations fascinated musicians, and since his variations were based on his own popular songs, even the layman had no problem with identification. There was some envy, for it gave other composers or pianists little to do but listen, including his friend Oscar Levant, who quipped, "An evening with Gershwin is a Gershwin evening."

Despite the legends, Gershwin did play the works of others. When Kay Swift, a Juilliard-trained musician, once casually dismissed the songs of Irving Berlin, Gershwin played through dozens of Berlin songs, pointing out characteristic ingenuities in that master songwriter's creations. Swift and Gershwin performed not only two-piano Gershwin, but four-hand Bach; Gershwin treasured the complete piano works of Debussy. He was an admirer of Jerome Kern, Cole Porter, Harold Arlen and other contemporaries.

A study of Gershwin's press scrapbooks, particularly of the clippings saved during his lifetime, is fascinating when not ludicrous. Recent writings can be entertaining also. His early critics revealed a range of attitudes from prejudice to envy, not to mention misperceptions and, often as not, uncritical affection.

Only recently has Gershwin been treated by critics and musicologists with some degree of informed seriousness (though many continue to have problems with the larger works). For example, a few years ago an important musicological journal published an article about *Porgy and Bess* by a self-confessed "scholar." He admitted, like so many of his persuasion, that he had dismissed *Porgy and Bess* as a mere collection of "show tunes"—that is, until he finally heard it. Gershwin the tunesmith had actually composed an opera! This scholarly revelation surfaced c. 1978—and *Porgy and Bess* had been an opera since 1935.

During the twenties, Gershwin was usually portrayed as a kind of musical *naif,* who had infused the American musical bloodstream with the illicit colorations of something called jazz. That from his champions; their adversaries regarded him as an untutored Tin Pan Alley upstart who simply did not belong. His wider public did not give a damn. Gershwin's admirers numbered not only average fans but musicians, composers, songwriters. His severest critics most often came from the ranks of the "serious" conservatory-trained composer.

Typical of their approach was that of composer Frederick Jacobi, who had studied with, among others, Rubin Goldmark and Ernest Bloch and was a member of the faculty of the Juilliard School of Music. Writing in *Modern Music* after Gershwin's death, he admitted that Gershwin's music was endowed with "that high attribute of making people fall in love with it," but that there was no future for it.

"It is not in his 'larger' works that George will live," Jacobi stated (which was the common view among his colleagues). "It is in the great number of his songs, every one of which is a gem in its own way. Within the confines of this small structure he was able to mold phrases of considerable variety and in the best of these there is a perfection of an expert craftsman. They are supple, balanced, expressive. His harmony here is equally perfect . . . His rhythms are lively and amusing and in this field he was undoubtedly an innovator . . .

"I believe," he concluded loftily, "that *An American in Paris* will live longer than either the *Rhapsody* or the *Concerto* and that, of the more pretentious works, *Porgy and Bess* will be the first to go."

During his brief creative career, Gershwin read and heard this kind of evaluation often from contemporary "serious" composers: stick to your tunes, George, leave the big stuff to us, your betters."

Virgil Thomson was even harder and more patronizing two years earlier around the time of the production of *Porgy and Bess* (of which more later). Later, writing in his autobiography, Thomson looked back on the twenties, when he felt the nation had been backward in music and the appreciation thereof (especially modern music). Despite that, he admitted that the United States had produced a few "up-to-date" composers, namely, ". . . Aaron Copland, Roy Harris and myself (plus experimenter Henry Cowell) . . ." During that period he conceded that the *Rhapsody in Blue* had been and was very popular and that "none of us could compete with [Gershwin] for distribution, nor he with us for intellectual prestige."

The elements of competitiveness, distribution (as if Gershwin had any control over that) and intellectual prestige might seem irrelevant to music criticism, but anyone familiar with the field and its practitioners (with rare exception) would not find it so. As an evolving artist, Gershwin, conscious of his lack of a conservatory training, found scant counsel in the writings and criticisms of his work, if indeed he ever sought such counsel. It is known that unfavorable reviews may have bothered him but they never upset him. "Maybe they're right," he was heard to say, but preferred his brother Ira's advice, ". . . it's every composer for himself and for the special talents that he has."

Those special talents in his lifetime were widely appreciated by his audience but all too often over- or underassessed by his critics. One other aspect worked against Gershwin: he was a celebrity and was written about and interviewed not only in the popular press but the mass-circulation magazines. Rarely did he receive "serious" consideration in the musical publications of "intellectual prestige" *(Modern Music, The Musical Quarterly)* and then only to be reminded that he did not belong.

Jacobi granted that he did belong with such "demi-gods" as Sullivan, Offenbach and Johann (not Richard) Strauss. So long as he stayed out of the province of such as Jacobi and Thomson, he was fine. Prestigious critic Paul Rosenfeld added to the list, to Gershwin's detriment, Chabrier. Virtually everybody but Gershwin.

Besides referring to himself as a modern romantic, Gershwin often said he was "a man without traditions," claiming that in his work he had no intentions of repeating what had gone in music before. "Where is the sense, and where is the personal satisfaction in doing over again what has been done before, and done better?" When he considered opera, as early as 1929 when he was approached by the Metropolitan Opera, he considered an American theme—his first rejection being the American Indian. A New York City setting seemed most attractive (as it eventuated, the subject was the Jewish folk tale "The Dybbuk" which did not work out because of contractual technicalities).

Whatever the theme or setting, he intended to be no imitation Wagner (who composed in his words, "the overpowering music dramas") or Verdi, "the supreme melodist, [who] wrote the breast-heaving, arm-brandishing orgies of tune that will live on despite the higher-browed critics . . . I want . . . to be myself." And, at an earlier time, "My people are American. My time is today."

When he made that last statement in 1926, it was obvious that he was on the brink of a long, brilliant career. He had only recently acquired a five-story house into which he moved the entire Gershwin family—the fruits of the *Rhapsody in Blue.* Just weeks before he had performed his second extended work, the *Concerto in F,* at Carnegie Hall. He, his family, his friends and the by then ubiquitous press looked forward to an exciting, rich, future, but only little more than a decade remained.

Ironically, at the very beginning of his career Gershwin was asked by *Vanity Fair* (in 1925), along with other luminaries of the time—Dorothy Parker, Michael Arlen, W. C. Fields, et al.—to "Seize the Coveted Opportunity of Saying the Last Word" and write his own epitaph:

> *Here lies the body of George Gershwin*
> *American Composer*
> *   *   *   *
> *Composer?*
> *American?*

In 1931, when he was in Hollywood writing his first film score, the epitaph was reprinted along with those of a number of local celebrities. Six years later he would die in Hollywood, mourned internationally, an unquestionably American composer. Some "higher-browed critics" like Jacobi, Thomson, Rosenfeld might regret that he had not become the American Sullivan, Offenbach or Chabrier. Intuitively, from the beginning, Gershwin had chosen to be himself and achieved a greatness—and perhaps immortality—by being simply and unaffectedly the American Gershwin.

What was Gershwin *really* like, this Lower East Side son of Russian-Jewish immigrants who appears to have evolved into the quintessential musical American? Above average height, slender, dark with pink cheeks (and generally with five-o'clock shadow appearing by three), dapper, expensively dressed—he did not fit the popular notion of the serious composer with long-flowing unkempt hair, indifferent to appearance and to mundane matters. Gershwin was businesslike, he fulfilled contracts and was well-paid for his efforts; he did not suffer from false modesty. Recognition had come early in life and, with varying intensity, stayed with him until the end.

The Gershwin bibliography is extensive, beginning with the newspaper stories in 1924 and Carl Van Vechten's *Vanity Fair* piece in March 1925 and has been growing since. Biographically Gershwin has been portrayed as, indeed, a man of many parts ranging from ". . . a young

Colossus . . ." who "bestrode the musical world of Gotham" with "one foot just outside of Tin Pan Alley and the other planted on Carnegie Hall . . ." (Goldberg, 1931) to being a sleazy opportunist (Charles Schwartz, 1973). Besides the biographies in English, there are those in French, Dutch, Italian and German. There is something about the man and his music that captivates; his music is popular throughout the world. He may be taken more seriously as a composer in Europe than in the United States. The answer may be fairly simple: Europeans take their musical heritage for granted because it appears to have always been there; American composers, musicians and critics are self-conscious about our early musical history and tended to reject our early music as inferior and not European enough. Generations of American composers were educated in Germany and later, when it became fashionable, France.

Gershwin (though he was not the only one) broke the tradition; he grew up in the streets, he made his way in a tough musical marketplace and, a child of his time and place, created a distinctive music—sensitive but unsentimental, sparkling with humor, hauntingly beautiful, underscored by a brooding sense of loneliness, tinctured by a youthful playfulness and swagger, endowed with "that high attribute of making people fall in love with it."

Not long after his abrupt, tragic death, several of Gershwin's colleagues and friends contributed to a memorial collection of reminiscences, articles, assessments and anecdotes. One close friend ended her contribution with a heartfelt but curious apostrophe: "Oh, George, you made your one mistake! It was to die." As if this were his ultimate failure. The final years of Gershwin were dogged by putative failures, the most dismal of the work he called his "labor of love." Thus his story has an almost classic form: success, failure, success—the last posthumous.

GERSHWIN

1

The New American Gershvins

George Gershwin is an enigma to the biographer searching for conventional sources of his genius: heredity or environment? Even the evolution of his name bemuses some writers. And his early musical background, practically nil, is perplexing.

The musicologist-biographer familiar with Bach's extraordinary family tree or Mozart's prodigious childhood (diminutive musical gems composed at the age of four), finds Gershwin unfathomable. He was not reared in a musical or particularly cultured household, nor was he goaded by an exploitive parent into an unnatural childhood. His was, for its time and place, a typical normal childhood: a self-sufficient youngster, he grew up in the streets of New York. During his grammar school years, restless, lively, mischievous, he was more Huck Finn than Tom Sawyer. He exhibited, so far as his family saw, no intimations of artistic talents.

"The only creative ancestry that I have seems to have been my father's father who, he tells me, was an inventor," Gershwin recalled. "His ingenuity had something to do with the Czar's guns." Whether or not this occurred while his grandfather served in the army is not known but is likely; in Czarist Russia twenty-five years of military service was mandatory. Nor is it known what it was that Yakov Gershovitz's ingenuity devised.

Gershwin's maternal grandfather, surnamed Bruskin, was a furrier. This pretty much summarizes the pre-American Gershwin genealogy.

Morris Gershovitz, son of Yakov, worked in a St. Petersburg shoe factory. His father's inventiveness won him and his family the right to move about Russia instead of being confined to a ghetto and subject to periodic pogroms. Morris was able to find work in St. Petersburg, where he met Rose Bruskin, daughter of the furrier; she was then about fifteen and he four years older. Soon after, like so many Russian Jews of the time, Rose's father gave up his business and moved his family to the United States, settling on New York's Lower East Side among family and friends who had preceded them.

Morris was smitten by the attractive Rose and, though ghetto-free, faced the possibility of twenty-five years with the military; he decided to follow the Bruskins.

Sometime around 1892–93, he left St. Petersburg, "seeking," according to George Gershwin, Rose Bruskin's "hand in marriage. She was a beautiful young girl," who, he thought, married his father at the age of sixteen (actually she was nineteen and Morris twenty-three). At the time of their marriage, July 21, 1895, he was a foreman in a shoe factory, having worked his way up from the position of "designer of fancy uppers" for women's shoes.

They joined their relatives and friends on the Lower East Side and were living above Simpson's Pawnshop at the corner of Hester and Eldridge streets, when the first of their four children, Israel ("Izzy"/Isadore), was born on December 6, 1896.

Because he preferred living near his workplace, or later, his own place of business, Morris Gershovitz moved his family around a good deal. Flats and apartments were easily come by in the late nineteenth and early twentieth centuries: cheap, plentiful and often offering a month's free rent. When a new job was offered to Morris, they moved to Brooklyn, where he had found an unprepossessing two-story brick house at 242 Snedicker Avenue, across the street from a synagogue, in a quiet, predominantly Jewish neighborhood in the East New York section. In this house on September 26, 1898, Jacob Gershwine (as George's birth certificate reads) was delivered by one Dr. Ratner. Besides permutating the family name, Dr. Ratner described Morris as a "leather worker" and gave the mother's name before marriage as "Rosa Brushkin."

The name change may have been Morris's idea; it is possible that by the time he married he had streamlined his name to "Gershvin," and so would the doctor have been informed. Gershwine in a Jewish community would still be pronounced Gershvin. When George Gershwin was born, the fact that he was named for Morris's father would indicate that the ex-artilleryman was dead.

Within six weeks of Jacob's birth, Morris Gershvin moved the family back to Manhattan. They moved into a second-story flat above Saul Birn's Phonograph Shop at 91 Second Avenue; here their third son, Arthur, was born on March 14, 1900. Their daughter, Frances, was born December 6, 1906, Izzy's tenth birthday.

Eight-year-old George (no one in the family recalls calling him Jake or Jacob) was developing into a bit of a problem. In recalling his "pre-piano days," he wrote, "There is nothing I can really tell . . . except that music never really interested me, and that I spent most of my time with the boys in the street, skating and, in general, making a nuisance of myself." To some extent this can be attributed to minimal parental supervision; once Morris Gershvin acquired his own business, Rose Gershvin worked with him (especially in his restaurants), overseeing the hard financial side of operations. Izzy, regarded as the family scholar, was a rather serious youngster who behaved himself in school and chose not to roam the streets. A maid looked after the younger Arthur and Frances; that left George pretty much on his own. He played, scuffled, pilfered, skated (he was champion roller-skater of Seventh Street during the family's residence on Second Avenue) and grew up in the streets. In those automobile-free days they provided a setting for much of the socializing in the area.

In the period between the 1880s and the birth of Frances Gershwin in 1906 more than a million and a half Jews emigrated from Europe to the United States, the greater numbers from a virulently anti-Semitic Russia. Most of these émigrés, in turn, settled on the Lower East Side, making it the largest Jewish community in the world. They found work in the tenement-centered, demeaning, sweatshops throughout the area.

The more enterprising or luckier individuals started their own businesses, often beginning as humble pushcart peddlers—Mott Street, between Canal and Broom was known as the "Pushcart Market." Along the Bowery between Canal and Delancey the outdoor jewelry market flourished and the "Thieves Market"—today's "flea market"—ran north from Canal to Houston on the Bowery; it was the outlet for the selling and exchange of assorted objects. The food-vending carts were stationed on Mott Street and the Orchard Street Pushcart Market; it was here that a young nuisance named George Gershvin and his friends relieved the inattentive entrepreneur of a bagel, fruit or other easily transferable, if not always digestible, edibles.

Morris Gershvin, because of his skill as a "leather worker," circumvented the pushcart and sweatshop blight of turn-of-the-century New

York slum life. An artisan, he had little trouble finding work. It was when he struck out on his own that family fortunes waxed and waned as he moved from one enterprise to the other. To a great extent too, the Gershvins suffered little of New York's tenement congestion, finding flats in the less cluttered buildings.

The Gershwins grew up largely in Manhattan, except for the Brooklyn residence and a couple of brief excursions to Coney Island and one to Harlem, then more Jewish than black. The Lower East Side was a self-contained Jewish community, where Old World friends and relatives clustered together and brought their beliefs, customs, language and folk mores with them. In these households the father worked and the mother raised the children, cooked, ran the house.

Mother's Day was not conceived with Rose Gershwin in mind. Gershwin described her as "nervous, ambitious and purposeful." (His father was "a very easy-going, humorous philosopher, who [took] things as they come.") "She never was the doting type . . . She was set on having us completely educated, her idea being that if everything else failed we could always become school-teachers."

Theirs was not the traditional, close-knit Jewish family. Morris and Rose Gershvin were diametric personalities and when he began to prosper as a businessman she participated in running the business; she was not "easy-going." While she was ambitious for her children, she was almost indifferent to them; ". . . she never watched every move we made." But she kept an eye on Morris as he insouciantly shifted from one business to another: a bakery, a Turkish bath, a small chain of restaurants, a pool parlor and, as Ira Gershwin remembered, "bookmaking at the Brighton Beach Race Track for three exciting but disastrous weeks." When such a setback occurred, Rose Gershvin's diamond ring went into the pawnshop for a while.

Even in the New World life was a bit of a gamble—literally, too. Ira Gershwin recalled earning an extra dollar to add to his twenty-five cents' weekly allowance by catering his mother's Saturday night poker parties with "her girl friends." He supplied the new decks, the delicatessen, and dispensed the chips. Both George and Ira remembered being taken to the track by their parents, a practice continued into their adult lives.

"I believe I have more of my mother's qualities than my father's," Gershwin said. But mother and son were not truly close, despite a quote attributed to him later in life (which is generally used to prove a mother fixation). She's "what mammy writers write about, and what mammy singers sing about. But they don't mean it and I do." In his output of hundreds of songs only two qualify as such, "Swanee" (which is more about a place) and *Blue Monday*'s "I'm Going to See My Mother" (the least Gershwinesque song in the opera).

Rose Gershwin and her son often clashed; she had plans for him that did not include music. Even after he had become a successful song-writer-composer she offered unsolicited advice and made demands. After one of their more serious arguments Gershwin announced that he was going to move out (he was then in his late twenties); Rose Gershwin, as was her custom, took to her bed with respiratory problems. As she lay there gasping, Gershwin's wire-haired terrier, Tony, entertained by jumping over her from one side of the bed to the other. As the tension waned, Morris Gershwin took Gershwin aside and asked, "George, why didn't you do it sooner?"

The precise subject of that one argument is not known, it may have been over money or some other material thing. Things meant much to Rose Gershwin. She was candid, pragmatic, even blunt (especially in English); her values embraced objects more than beings. As an illustration: an encounter with Edelaine Harburg, wife of lyricist and longtime Gershwin friend E. Y. Harburg, who had come to visit. One glance at Mrs. Harburg and Rose Gershwin said, "What's the matter with you?"

Mrs. Harburg admitted that she had many faults, "Which one do you have in mind?"

"A fur coat," Rose Gershwin replied, "you got no fur coat."

"But I don't like fur coats and don't wear fur coats."

"If you want to look good," she was informed, "and you want to look rich, you wear a fur coat." That she believed this is evident in one of her favorite photographs of herself wearing a fur coat, staring directly into the camera with obvious pride.

Morris Gershvin, considering his business peregrinations, was also concerned with success but not so much with its trappings. If Rose brought home a fur coat, he brought a phonograph and opera recordings. But it was Rose who managed the household, who watched over the finances; she impressed her children with the importance of education and the success that must follow. She was concerned but not affectionate.

While Arthur and Frances were infants, their older brothers had begun to exhibit personal traits as divergent as those of their parents. George, as he had disclosed, was most like his mother (even physically) and Ira, like his father in his outlook and physically as well. (At maturity he was some inches shorter than George, just as Morris was shorter than Rose, a fact of which she reminded Morris frequently; she made it abundantly clear that she preferred taller men.)

Theirs was not a model marriage, though it lasted a lifetime. The

dominant member was Rose; her husband's not very businesslike handling of his various enterprises led to clashes and family tensions. There
was no fur coat when Morris's string of restaurants went bankrupt.
They had separate social lives; she with her poker evenings and he his
lodge meetings and pinochle games. The preoccupations of the parents
left the children on their own; while the children did not precisely suffer
from parental neglect, family life in the Gershwin household was at once
indulgent and authoritarian. Nor was it unified by a sense of deep religi-
osity; of the three boys only Ira Gershwin was given a bar mitzvah, the
ceremony symbolizing his initiation into the Jewish community at the
age of thirteen. No fewer than two hundred family members and friends
gathered at Zeitlan's Restaurant to mark this rite of passage, an event,
considering the magnitude, that would have impressed Rose Gershvin's
friends.

Writing of his Lower East Side childhood of about the same period,
novelist Samuel Ornitz deftly summarized what could have been the
Gershwin experience as well: "Many of us were transient, impatient
aliens in our parents' home," where tradition-bound immigrant parents
contended with their rebellious first-generation American children. He
described the streets, dense with humanity and encased in concrete,
with few areas for play—a ripe setting for gangs of boys who, "roamed
the streets in search of mischief . . ."

The two older children were distinctly opposite personalities early in
their boyhoods and remained so for the rest of their lives. Ira was
introverted, bookish, an earnest student; not precisely a loner but not
given over to traveling with the pack. True, he cut his literary teeth on
the ubiquitous nickel-novels of the time (to his mother's objections), but
by ten had worked his way up and recalls reading Doyle's "A Study in
Scarlet" three times. Around the same time he began taking piano lessons; his teacher was his mother's sister, Kate Bruskin Wolpin. He
spent some of his allowance at the Grand Street theater, and at the
Unique, a film house. He began compiling scrapbooks of newspaper
clippings from columns, notably the light verse of Franklin P. Adams
and others. He revealed an early aptitude for sketching and watercolor.
By the age of fourteen he was a student at Townsend Harris Hall, a
school for exceptional students, in preparation for entry into the City
College of New York.

George was hyperactive as a boy, light, wiry, competitive and good in
street games and, on occasion, fights. Reading held no delights for him
and school was confining and boring. One experience in grammar
school, P.S. 20, was frequently recalled later in his life. Possibly influenced by Ira, who was drawing copies of pictures from popular maga-

zines, George too began to draw. When he showed a sketch to one of his teachers she humiliated him by ridiculing his attempt before the class.

Ira was often summoned before her to explain his younger brother's frequent absences and infrequent homework. Despite these infractions, George managed to escape P.S. 20 when the family moved from Christie Street to Second Avenue. Then he was enrolled in P.S. 25 where, although he continued as an undistinguished, sometimes delinquent, student, he experienced a "flashing revelation of beauty" that determined the course of the rest of his life.

II

True to form, ten-year-old George Gershvin had chosen not to attend a violin recital in the school auditorium after midday recess. A short, pudgy, dark eight-year-old youngster named Max Rosenzweig had been drafted to entertain and to heighten the musical sensibilities of the students of P.S. 25. But not young Gershvin who, like his gangmates, dismissed music study as only fitting for girls, or effeminate boys; Gershwin's term, he remembered, was "maggie" the diminutive of Margaret.

While playing in the schoolyard George heard the current maggie performing Dvořák's venerable chestnut *Humoresque*. Something in the music captivated him as did the playing; he was determined to meet the artist (who would become renowned as the virtuoso Max Rosen: 1900–56). Gershwin could not return to the school building, lest his absence be noted, so he waited outside for an hour and a half for the prodigy to appear. A heavy rain poured down ". . . and I got soaked to the skin." Since it was safe to enter the school once the performance was finished, he did, only to find that Max had already left.

"I found out where he lived and, dripping wet as I was, trekked to his house, unceremoniously presenting myself as an admirer. Maxie, by this time, had left. His family were so amused, however, that they arranged a meeting. From the first moment we became the closest of friends . . ."

They exchanged letters (the Rosenzweigs lived on the Upper West Side), they played hooky together (obviously George had some influence on Maxie) and "we'd talk eternally about music—that is, when we weren't wrestling. I used to throw him every time, by the way . . ."

As a youngster Gershwin was wiry and slight, but coordinated and, for his size, rugged. "I've always been very strong," he once wrote, "but I can't remember when I've been without some small ailment. When I was young, I had a lot of trouble with my tonsils and with my nose—having once having been kicked on the bridge of my nose by a horse." Another reminder of his street life was the deep scar over his right eye. While not exactly combative, he was assertive as a youngster; he took boyish pleasure in throwing the huskier, heavier Maxie in their wrestling matches.

If the future Max Rosen had "opened the world of music" to the future George Gershwin, he also came close to closing it. Gershwin expressed the hope of one day becoming Rosen's accompanist and was told, "You haven't it in you, Georgie; take my word for it, I can tell!" Whether these disconcerting words ended the friendship or not is not known. Except for a clipping in one of Gershwin's early scrapbooks preserving a souvenir of his attendance at a recital by "Master Max Rosenzweig" at nearby Cooper Union on April 13, 1913, the violinist appears to have slipped out of Gershwin's life. By this time, however, despite his friend's advice, George had begun his own musical career.

Brother Ira had progressed on the piano under his Aunt Kate's kindly but not very authoritarian tutelage (she was very unlike her sister Rose). In fact, he had advanced through all of thirty-two pages of Beyer's method. Rose Gershvin coveted Kate Wolpin's piano and decided such an instrument would enable Ira to study at home. His brother, meanwhile, smoldering under Maxie's dismissal, had befriended one of his street companions whose family owned a piano.

At the time, 1910, the Gershvins were still living in a second-story flat above the phonograph shop at 91 Second Avenue; George was about twelve. One day a van appeared in the street below; the occupants proceeded to unload a piano and hoisted it to the Gershvin flat. Ira observed the process with apprehension; he was, he knew, no music student. But then brother George sprang to his rescue.

"No sooner had the upright been lifted through the window of the 'front room' than George sat down and played a popular tune of the day. I remember being particularly impressed by his left hand. I had no idea he could play and found that despite his roller-skating activities, the kid parties he attended, the many street games he participated in (with an occasional resultant bloody nose) he had found time to experiment on a player piano at the home of a friend on Seventh Street."

To the astute Rose Gershvin, her wayward son's obvious innate aptitude could prove a wise investment. It would, she felt, add a bit of culture to the Gershvin house and, on occasion, he could entertain their friends. Once he had mastered the piano George could concentrate on a serious occupation. Ira was released to read, write—prose as well as verse—and prepare for a respected profession.

The piano lessons began under the guidance of the then traditional local lady piano teacher—"a Miss Green." But the earnest piano student soon exhausted the capabilities not only of Miss Green but of two others, as he breezed through his Beyer's and other instruction books. He was then sent to one Goldfarb, "A Hungarian band leader, impressively moustached," Ira Gershwin remembered him. "Composer of a *Theodore Roosevelt March,* his fancy ran to band and orchestra literature . . ."

He "played the piano with great gusto and a barrel of gestures," George Gershwin said of him. "He gladly took me on as a pupil at $1.50 per lesson. In those days that was a stiff price. He started me on a book of excerpts from grand operas. In six months I had advanced as far as the Overture to *William Tell* when I fell in with a chap, Jack Miller, who was pianist of the Beethoven Symphony Orchestra." (Actually the Beethoven Society Orchestra whose members, young as well as old, lived in the neighborhood of P.S. 63, where they presented concerts; the conductor was Henry Lefkowitz.)

Gershwin met Miller late in 1912 or early 1913, by which time Gershwin had begun regularly attending concerts and recitals that mostly featured pianists (he preserved the programs in scrapbooks). He was then about fourteen. The two embryo pianists discussed music and teachers. Miller spoke glowingly about his teacher, Charles Hambitzer, who had recently come to New York from Milwaukee. Miller offered to introduce Gershwin to Hambitzer.

III

Charles Hambitzer (1881–1918), whose father had owned a music store in Milwaukee, was an exceptional musician as well as an imaginative and perceptive teacher. Besides the piano, he had mastered several instruments. He began his professional life in Milwaukee teaching (piano, violin, cello), playing piano in a theater orchestra and eventually became conductor of the Pabst Theater orchestra.

His talents having outgrown Milwaukee, Hambitzer brought his new wife to New York, where he opened a teaching studio on the Upper West Side near Columbia University. He soon became a member of the string section of the Waldorf-Astoria Orchestra under Joseph Knecht; on some occasions he appeared as piano soloist. Gershwin preserved a record of his teacher's appearance at a Sunday night concert performing Anton Rubinstein's *Piano Concerto No. 4;* the date was April 13, 1913. Hambitzer was then about thirty-one and Gershwin fourteen.

Hambitzer, whom Gershwin called "the first great musical influence in my life," though a composer also, was curiously indifferent to having his works performed. After his death the bulk of his compositions were lost. One of his piano students, Nathaniel Shilkret, who later was a longtime music director for Victor Records and RKO Pictures, remembered that Hambitzer was under contract to the Shuberts to compose musicals for their organization; it was not a compatible affiliation. "He didn't like them," Shilkret told interviewer Milton A. Caine, "disliked taking orders from them, [and] he didn't like their librettos." No Hambitzer operetta appears on the Shubert production roster. Gershwin recalled one, *The Love Wager,* which starred the popular Fritzi Scheff; it never reached New York.

Hambitzer found teaching more to his liking and was beloved by his students. Shilkret remembered him (Shuberts notwithstanding) "as a mild, sweet-tempered man, a little sloppy in appearance . . . relaxed, very likable and very charitable. Pupils of his who had talent, but no money, he either taught free or lent them financial assistance. To him talent was most important.

"He was rather tall—about five ten or eleven, had dark brown hair, big eyes, Liszt-type fingers and a prodigious memory for music. He looked like [Ethelbert] Nevin. He was one of the greatest pianists I ever heard." Then Shilkret added, "And I would say he was a genius."

Another student, Mabel Pleshette (later Schirmer; she was a lifelong close friend of George's), studied with Hambitzer for nearly two years. "He was an extraordinary teacher, unlike any I had ever had before. George, by the way, sent me to him. He had two pianos in his studio on the ground floor of a building, I think, but I'm not sure, on 125th Street, near or on Central Park West. He was not a typical teacher who sat at your side while you played. On his piano he would demonstrate the piece—we did a lot of Chopin—then you would take it home and learn it. He would then listen to you play it on one piano while he just listened from his piano. He was a very kind and sweet man—and an outstanding pianist."

He was astute enough to perceive beyond Gershwin's first demonstration of his piano technique on the afternoon that Jack Miller introduced the boy and the man. "I rubbed my fingers and dived into the Overture to *William Tell.* Hambitzer said nothing until I had finished." The histrionic rendition of the overture led to Hambitzer's suggestion that they hunt up Goldfarb and shoot him—"and not with an apple on his head either!"

The pianist in Hambitzer immediately recognized Gershwin's potential despite the keyboard dramatics; Goldfarb was dropped for

Hambitzer and a regular lesson schedule was arranged. Gershwin was at this time an unhappy student at the High School of Commerce on the Upper West Side (brother Ira was content at Townsend Harris Hall). Hambitzer was impressed with his pupil's avidity, his punctuality and his eagerness to continue lessons beyond the allotted time. His teachers at Commerce would not have agreed; his better moments there came during the morning assemblies when he played the piano. His grades were decidedly poor.

Hambitzer, however, very early called him a "genius" who would "make his mark in music if anybody will." Gershwin threw himself into his piano study as once he had roller skating and street play. He abandoned those childish activities, even hooky, for music. His scrapbooks are replete with recital and concert programs; one of his earliest—a ledger—he filled with pictures of musicians, predominantly pianists. Among the composers: Wagner, Gottschalk, Sullivan.

It was Hambitzer who introduced him to Liszt, Chopin and Debussy. "He made me harmony conscious," Gershwin said years later. "Harmony, up to this time, had been a secret to me. I've always had a sort of instinctive feeling for tone combinations, and many chords that sound so modern in my orchestral compositions were set down without any particular attention to their theoretical structure." Hambitzer did not teach harmony or theory and suggested another teacher he respected in those disciplines, Edward Kilenyi (1884–1968). Despite his enthusiasm for Chopin et al., Gershwin let Hambitzer know about his other musical predilections, what his teacher called "this modern stuff, jazz and whatnot." At this stage in his development Gershwin had discovered the work of Jerome Kern (he especially admired "You're Here and I'm Here" and "They Didn't Believe Me") and Irving Berlin ("Alexander's Ragtime Band"). Hambitzer did not proscribe delving into such music, he merely postponed it, explaining, "I'll see that he gets a firm foundation in the standard music first."

There was a mutual respect and admiration. "I was crazy about that man," Gershwin told a friend. "I went out, in fact, and drummed up ten pupils for him."

His friends at this time in his life were aspiring musicians and he was completely wound up in music when not in school or working in his father's latest restaurant. His Kern-Berlin affinity led him to popular songs and Tin Pan Alley, where he also made musical friends. No one has recorded the length of his study with Hambitzer. In 1926, in an article purportedly written by Gershwin, he stated that he had had only "four years of piano study and those not with teachers of celebrity." (Though popular and admired, Hambitzer was not known to have taught a pianist of virtuoso caliber; Gershwin came closest. Shilkret went on to be a successful all-around musician in concert, radio and films but did not make a career as a pianist.)

Roughly, then, Gershwin was what might be termed a serious student from 1912 to 1916. If in his statement referring to his four years of study included the early phase with Miss Green through the flamboyant Goldfarb, it is possible that he stopped systematic study as early as 1918. Two events occurred that year that may have affected his future: the early death of Hambitzer's wife, which left him with a young daughter and led to his emotional breakdown and heavy drinking, and Gershwin's leaving high school in midterm to take a job as a pianist in Tin Pan Alley.

Although the Alley was heavily populated with composers who played the piano with one finger and untrained pianists who played by ear, a fifteen-year-old boy would have had to have been most proficient at sight reading, transposition and improvisation to have found a place in that competitive setting. Also, by the time of his entry into Tin Pan Alley, George had tried his hand at songwriting while studying with Hambitzer. Hambitzer may even had some influence in this area too, for Gershwin admired his original compositions—he "wrote what I then considered the finest light music."

Gershwin's first known song dates from c.1913. Entitled "Since I Found You," he never completed it (though he never discarded it and played it for his amusement on occasion). The chorus in G wandered off into F, at which point Gershwin found himself incapable of bringing it back into the home key. Around the same time, under the influence of Irving Berlin, he wrote "Ragging the Traumerei"; the lyrics for both were written by Leonard Praskins. After these unfruitful attempts, Gershwin concentrated on his piano technique.

IV

Somehow, through the power of music (for want of a better phrase) and the sympathetic nurturing by Hambitzer, a Lower East Side street boy and accomplished hooky player was transformed in roughly four years into a skilled pianist. But this is too simple. There had to be an inexplicable innate gift, a natural talent, an instinct for music making. Once the flame was ignited it burned with a light not even Gershwin fully understood. "No one expected me to compose music," he said. "I just did."

Nor had his parents invested in piano lessons to produce a concert pianist. They had a more substantial profession in mind—accountant, for example. It upset Rose Gershvin that he spent more time with his music books that his texts and ledgers from the High School of Commerce. Pop Gershvin, on the sidelines, was relieved; he had predicted George would be a vagabond. Even playing piano was better. Hadn't George earned five dollars a week in the summer of 1913 entertaining in a Catskills resort? Not bad for a young boy.

At fourteen he already possessed a self-assurance at the keyboard that was characteristic of his performance style; he loved playing for people. The summer job finished, he reluctantly returned to the classrooms of the High School of Commerce. His brother Ira had graduated from Townsend Harris Hall—where he distinguished himself as cartoonist and editor rather than academically—and barely squeezed into the City College of New York. Here too he was active on the school literary weekly, and wrote in collaboration with a friend from the neighborhood, Isidore Hochberg, better known as "Yip" and later as lyricist E. Y. Harburg, a column they called "Much Ado." But as at Townsend Harris, Ira's encounters with mathematics were dismal. He later confessed that "My career at City College could hardly be set down as felicitous. In my second year I was still taking first-year mathematics and when I heard that calculus was in the offing, I decided to call it an education."

Before that occurred he was instrumental in presenting his brother in his first public appearance as composer-pianist. During his freshman year he joined the school's literary society, the Finley Club (artfully named in honor of the college president). In 1914 he found himself on the committee for the club's annual entertainment to be held at the Christadora House on nearby Avenue B at Ninth Street on March 21, 1914.

Ira placed his brother George in the third spot on the program, following addresses, respectively, by the president and director of the club. The program lists a "Piano Solo" by George Gershvin, the solo being a tango he had prepared for the program. He returned again, following a "Dialogue" entitled "The Interview" to accompany one Chas. Rose in "Vocal Selections." The evening closed with a play (no author attribution), *Lend Me Five Dollars.* The first of the *Dramatis Personae,* as the program has it, onstage was "the best damn little actor on the Lower East Side" (in his own estimation), Isidore Hochberg.

Gershwin the pianist, by the time of his "debut," was known beyond the boundaries of the Lower East Side and the confines of the High School of Commerce. Soon after, he was told by a friend working in Tin Pan Alley, Ben Bloom, that he had heard that there was an opening for a pianist in the "professional department" of the Jerome H. Remick & Company on West Twenty-eighth Street. Bloom (who may have been a pianist; virtually nothing is known about him and his friendship with Gershwin) introduced the then fifteen-year-old pianist to Remick's manager, Mose Gumble, one of the sharpest men in music publishing (he had started out as a seventeen-year-old pianist a quarter century earlier).

Gershwin had two handicaps: his age and no previous experience. Gumble had been skeptical, but Bloom persisted. He brought in "the kid," who obviously impressed the veteran Gumble who offered Gershwin fifteen dollars a week to join his staff as a "piano pounder," demonstrating Remick's songs, accompanying "pluggers" (vocal demonstrators) and pushing Remick songs on vaudeville performers, musicians (many of whom did not read music), dancers—anyone who could advance the fiscal cause of Remick's. In 1914 the weekly wage was considerable and to be associated with the music business—for that is what it was, the art being incidental or accidental—was what he wanted more than anything. He wanted that more than a high school diploma, or life as an accountant, or working in his father's restaurants or the Russian-Turkish baths his father had recently discovered.

After the Gumble hurdle he had to get around the formidable Rose Gershvin; his father, he knew, would accept his decision with his customary equanimity. According to Gershwin's own account, "She was against my becoming a musician, as she didn't want me to be a twenty-five-dollar-a-week piano player all my life, but she offered very little resistance when I decided to leave high school to take a job playing the piano for Remick's."

The family issue settled, Gershwin left the High School of Commerce before the semester ended in May 1914 and became the "youngest piano pounder in Tin Pan Alley." In four years he had progressed from Miss Green's piano student to a Remick's professional.

2

From Tin Pan Alley . . .

Today "Tin Pan Alley" (a colorful writer, Monroe Rosenfeld, is credited with its coinage early in the twentieth century) is primarily a state of mind (dedicated to turning out songs for top-selling recordings); in 1914 it was actually a place—West Twenty-eighth Street, between Fifth and Sixth avenues. Today, though many of the original buildings remain, the street is the center of New York's flower market.

Rosenfeld christened Tin Pan Alley one summer's day, when, with windows open and piano pounders from the several publishers playing simultaneously, he likened the din to sound of striking on tin pans. In the early nineties the music publishing industry had been grouped around Fourteenth Street, near Union Square, then New York's major theater district: legitimate theaters, vaudeville houses, burlesque—and restaurants, including Delmonico's and Luchow's, which provided music with their dinners. When these operations, especially the theaters and vaudeville houses, moved northward, first to Twenty-eighth Street, then to Thirtieth and, finally, Forty-second Street (which spawned the Broadway of Gershwin's productive period), the publishers followed to be convenient to their clientele and outlets.

By the turn of the century, the sale of sheet music was big business; there was no radio, no sound film and no television. The sale of individual hits, as distinguished from the songs of the musical theater—which also generated hits—was assured if placed with an important vaudeville star. This could lead to sheet-music sales and recordings and to the primary objective, profit. When Gershwin entered Tin Pan Alley in 1914 song publishing had become an industry; a contemporary New York *Times* writer put it succinctly: ". . . the consumption of songs in America is as constant as the consumption of shoes, and the demand is similarly met by factory output."

It was a tough, competitive business run by men most of whom knew little or nothing about music, grammar or rhyme. It was risky and often ruthless, characterized by exploitation, cozening of young songwriters, plagiarism and imitation. If a certain type of song—mammy, Latin rhythm, Italian dialect—became a hit, a flood of the same type followed. And, as one publisher put it after a misadventure in Tin Pan Alley, "publishers are not always on the square."

Remick's was a relative newcomer to the Alley, a spinoff from the Detroit-based Whitney-Warner Publishing Company. In 1914 it was not yet in the league with the flourishing Witmarks, Feist, T. B. Harms, Harry Von Tilzer and others, some of which clustered into Manhattan from Chicago, St. Louis and other points to be near the center of musical action.

As an occupant of Remick's "professional parlor" Gershwin's job was to sit in a small cubicle with an upright piano on top of which was piled Remick's most recent publications. There were several cubicles on his floor, with occupants promoting Remick's products; the cubicles were not soundproof. To be able to work in a cacophonous, clamorous environment, to adjust to the many demands of prospective customers of rudimentary musicianship was good practice and kept his fingers nimble. But the repetition of the same dreary, undistinguished songs he found boring: trite melodies, basic harmonies and primitive rhythms. He spiced them up with his own embellishments, which was frowned upon. He had begun keeping original ideas of his own in a little notebook, for he knew pounders were not encouraged to plug their own songs. He bided his time.

His work did not always end at the close of the day. He was often drafted to accompany the pluggers (vocalists, or "boomers" as they were called in an earlier time) who traveled to nearby cities, as well as vaudeville houses in Brooklyn and Manhattan. An important outlet for sheet music in these years was the five-and-ten-cent stores, many of which had music departments, complete with a demonstration piano.

Gershwin stayed with this job from May 1914 until March 1917, admitting later that he "was a most unhappy lad at Remick's." When he approached Gumble with some of his early songs, they were rejected for their "sentimentality." While at Remick's he composed the tunes for the songs that became known later as "Nobody But You" and "Drifting Along with the Tide."

During his Remick's tenure, Gershwin made a few good friends, among them Harry Ruby, a fellow pianist working at Von Tilzer's nearby, an aspiring composer himself; Herman Paley, another composer whose songs Remick's published, and a vaudeville song-and-dance team, Fred and Adele Astaire, then being billed as "the Youthful Brother and Sister." The Astaires, when they met Gershwin, were setting out on their final vaudeville tour and hoping to break into the musical theater. Astaire, about fifteen or sixteen at the time (a year younger than Gershwin) remembered that at times he spelled Gershwin at the piano in trying out a tune and that Gershwin enjoyed his playing (Astaire, in turn, later admired Gershwin's dancing). He recalled, too, that Gershwin said, "Wouldn't it be great if I could write a musical show and you could be in it?"

Even more pivotal at this stage in Gershwin's career was his other Remick's friend, the aforementioned Herman Paley (1879–1955). Paley, almost twenty years Gershwin's senior, was a Tin Pan Alley rarity as well as successful songwriter. A graduate of City College, he taught in New York high schools before launching himself on a career as a songwriter. He was a trained pianist and had studied composition with Edward MacDowell, piano with Charles Hambitzer and theory and harmony with Edward Kilenyi.

Gershwin initially impressed him with his piano playing and, in time, with his songs. Paley invited Gershwin into his musical household where he had been heralding his young friend from Remick's as a "genius." This ménage included his brother Lou, a bookish schoolteacher, and his pretty young niece from another branch of the family, Mabel Pleshette, a music student, among other assorted Paleys and Pleshettes. The Paleys were musical as well as literary—and a close family. Their capacious apartment on Seventh Avenue, near 112th Street, was close to the latest Gershwin address: 108 West 111th Street; Pop Gershwin then being the proprietor of the St. Nicholas Baths (Russian and Turkish), "For Ladies and Gentlemen" on 111th Street and Lenox Avenue.

For Gershwin his friendship with Paley was salutary, enclosing him in a warm bright circle of friends, admirers and giving him a sense of belonging. The literary talk filled in some gaps in his education and in Lou Paley he found an incipient lyricist. When, a couple of years later, Herman and Lou Paley moved to a gracious little house in Greenwich Village on West Eighth Street, they continued their regular Saturday night parties at which Gershwin was a popular guest.

At Remick's, after a year, he was still a fifteen-dollar-a-week piano pounder and was not encouraged to submit songs for publication. Whenever he could he tried to interest other publishers in his work. He approached Louis Muir (famous for his "Waiting for the Robert E. Lee" and "Play that Barbershop Chord") who was encouraging but did not offer to publish what Gershwin called "my first raw pieces." A friend arranged for an audition with Irving Berlin, at the time the most productive partner in the firm of Waterson, Berlin & Snyder Co. Berlin did not recall this first meeting, though Gershwin left the office elated— but still unpublished.

To augment his Remick salary, Gershwin began late in 1915 to cut piano rolls for the Standard Music Roll Co. in East Orange, New Jersey; these were issued, beginning in January of the following year on the Perfection roll. Gershwin's growing reputation as a pianist easily gained him an entrée; in a decade he recorded more than 120 rolls (some duets with others). In a single session on a Saturday he would earn twenty-five dollars for perforating six rolls (or five dollars each if he made fewer). His earliest rolls featured typical Tin Pan Alley products of no great distinction, and it is probably not surprising that one of his first is a Remick's song, "Bring Along Your Dancing Shoes." An exception was a song by Herman Paley, "Sail On to Ceylon." Eventually he would be given the opportunity to make piano-roll recordings of songs by Irving Berlin, Jerome Kern, Walter Donaldson, Louis A. Hirsch, and Richard Whiting, as well as his near-contemporaries, such as Harry Tierney (who would later write such songs as "Alice Blue Gown" and "Rio Rita"), and pianist Harry Ruby (with Bert Kalmar he would produce such songs as "Three Little Words" and "Who's Sorry Now?"). Like Gershwin, they would graduate from Tin Pan Alley to Broadway in the twenties.

Early in his pianola career Gershwin cut some of his own compositions. In the summer of 1916 he produced rolls of his first published song, "When You Want 'Em, You Can't Get 'Em . . ." (of which more later) and his first instrumental (before it was published), *Rialto Ripples.* Later, in 1920, when he had begun to be known as a popular songwriter as well as pianist, he produced many rolls of his own music.

Unlike even the early primitive disc recordings, piano rolls were only approximations of the pianist's style and technique, sound inhumanly mechanical and were frequently tampered with. Additional "fingerings" were often added with a stylus, the effect of which—the characteristic tremolo of the penny arcade pianola—is that of a three-handed pianist. Gershwin's later rolls, those for Aeolian's Duo-Art system approximated a "live" recording with a greater nuance of touch (there was no stylus puncturing). His earliest rolls are interesting primarily because they preserve his own arrangements of those generally trite songs he hawked at Remick's. His later, and better, rolls are important because they feature his own songs and the *Rhapsody in Blue.* The rolls he made during his two years at Remick's were cut to add to his income, not to make history.

Tired of being reminded by Gumble that he was a pianist in the firm, not a composer, he continued making the rounds of other publishers. By early 1916 the publishing houses had begun to move into Times Square. The Harry Von Tilzer Music Publishing Company, once a Remick's neighbor, had taken new offices on West Forty-third Street. Gershwin, having made piano rolls of Von Tilzer songs, knew the Von Tilzer brothers—the other was Albert—and visited their offices on March 1, 1916. Accompanying him was another youngster, Murray Roth, an aspiring lyricist, with whom he had collaborated on "When You Want 'Em, You Can't Get 'Em, When You've Got 'Em, You Don't Want 'Em."

They sold their song to Von Tilzer and a contract was drawn up (that both songwriters were legally minors appears not to have mattered). It began impressively: "Know all Men by these presents" and immediately came to the fiscal point: "that for and in consideration of the sum of $1.00" the company would publish their song. The awesome document —of standard 8½-inch width and 16½-inch length—was replete with such locutions as "And all renewals, benefits, advantages, income and rights of any name and nature, derived or derivable, accrued or which may, might or shall accrue . . ." or "It is represented, covenanted and agreed by said Assignor(s) that . . ." They would learn, if they read the lengthy document that the "representations" they had made were "severally binding upon the heirs, executors, administrators and assigns . . ." All of this for the binding dollar payment and a quarter of a cent each per copy sold.

Roth proved the sharper businessman and managed to talk Von Tilzer out of fifteen dollars as an advance on royalties. Gershwin de-cided he would prefer getting his royalties after a goodly sum had accu-mulated. "After some time," he ruefully recalled later, "I went to Von Tilzer and asked him for a little cash on the song. He handed me five dollars. And I never got a cent more from him."

Encouraged by their first victory, Gershwin and Roth collaborated on another song, "My Runaway Girl," which Gershwin felt would be ideal for the kind of entertainments the Shuberts presented at the Win-ter Garden. These starred such stars as Al Jolson ("The World's Greatest Entertainer"), Nora Bayes, Marilyn Miller, Vivienne Segal and John Charles Thomas before he turned operatic.

The Shuberts' most active major composer at that time was the Hungarian-born Sigmund Romberg (1887–1951). He was some years from the success he would enjoy during the twenties (beginning with *Blossom Time* in 1921, after which, with Rudolf Friml, he dominated the Broadway operetta scene). In 1916 Romberg was considered little more than a dependable journeyman Shubert composer. He had been on the Shuberts' staff since early 1914 and had about a dozen scores to his credit (most for the Shuberts) when Gershwin managed to talk the Shuberts' office manager into arranging a meeting with Romberg. Although Romberg composed most of the music—song and dance—for the Winter Garden shows, the practice of interpolating made it possible for songs by other songwriters to be worked into the score, either on merit or because the show's star insisted.

After Gershwin and Roth performed "My Runaway Girl" for a Mr. Simmons, it was arranged for them to meet with Romberg, who then lived in the Hotel Majestic. Then in his late twenties and a former pianist (before 1914 he earned his way playing in an East Side Hungarian restaurant), Romberg was impressed with the playing and the music of the teen-aged Gershwin. He was more impressed with Gershwin than the song, suggesting that he and Gershwin collaborate on songs for the next Winter Garden production, *The Passing Show of 1916.*

Lyricist Roth was out. Whether Gershwin was a Tin Pan Alley realist who took advantage of an opportunity when he saw one or the Gershwin-Roth collaboration ended for some other reason is not known. They produced only the two songs. Ira Gershwin recalled that he believed their relationship ended when Gershwin and Roth began wrestling in a friendly manner. The match suddenly turned serious and less friendly, and they saw little of each other thereafter. (Roth abandoned songwriting later for a successful career as a Hollywood executive.)

Excited over the chance to place a song in a Broadway revue, starring one of his favorite comedians, Ed Wynn, Gershwin visited Romberg often at the Majestic with ideas for songs. Romberg finally selected one and the show's lyricist, Harold Atteridge, conceived a lyric for "Making of a Girl." Romberg, in the practice of the time, was credited as co-composer. As the catalyst he felt entitled to a share in the royalties should the song catch on (it didn't). Gershwin did not mind sharing credit for the tune, he was too happy over having his name on the sheet music of a "production" (as he called it), meaning a show song as distinguished from the nonproduction Tin Pan alley song like "When You Want 'Em . . ."

Around the time of his Romberg collaboration and Roth's departure, he met Irving Caesar, three years his senior, a graduate of City College, who had worked for Henry Ford as a secretary-stenographer during the First World War before turning to songwriting. He and Gershwin met in a club on Fifth Avenue, talked about songs and decided on a collaboration; although they produced a few they had no luck with them. One was entitled "Good Little Tune" and the other, "When the Armies Disband," an expression of Caesar's (and Ford's) hope for peace in Europe. The songs were neither placed nor published.

Gershwin had better luck with his first instrumental piece, *Rialto Ripples,* written in the late summer of 1916 in collaboration with a fellow Remick staff member, Will Donaldson. The division of labor on this not especially distinguished effort is unclear. It patently reflects Gershwin's tricky piano style and was probably Remick's answer to the current popularity of E. L. Bowman's *Twelfth Street Rag* and Felix Arnt's "Nola." *Rialto Ripples* merged the money-making elements of the two: the traditional rag and the piano novelty number. The piece was published in 1917 and slipped into oblivion. The ragtime era had ended with the death of Scott Joplin in 1917, but the occupants of Tin Pan Alley rarely missed the chance to exploit a trend. *Rialto Ripples* did not make it.

"It was now that the popular-song racket began to get definately on my nerves . . . I was a most unhappy lad at Remick's. I decided to leave after having been with them for over two years." (Later Gershwin gave as his reason his wish to "be closer to production music—the kind Jerome Kern was writing." Ira Gershwin noted in his journal that his brother left Remick's in order to have more time for study.)

Gershwin walked into Gumble's office and simply told him he was through. Unperturbed, Gumble asked Gershwin what he planned to do, assuming he had found a better-paying job.

"I don't know," Gershwin replied candidly. Gumble wished him well and he left Remick's at the end of the week, Friday, March 17, 1917.

"Once out of Remick's I scarcely knew which way to turn," he confessed. He did not want to get back into the piano-pounding grind (even while he worked at Remick's he was offered a job by another publisher at twenty-five dollars a week, but Gershwin rejected it because he felt it would be easier for him at Remick's). His drastic decision in March 1917 momentarily set him adrift. Out of work, he would not be able to contribute, as he was expected, to the budget of the Gershwin household.

In desperation he made the rounds; one stop was at the office of a friend, Will Vodery, a black composer, who did arrangements and orchestrations for Broadway shows. Vodery, who five years later would orchestrate Gershwin's *Blue Monday,* promised to keep an eye out for an opening in the musical theater. He was not successful.

After several weeks, Gershwin heard about an opening for a pianist at the City Theater on Fourteenth Street—a vaudeville house in the old neighborhood. He landed the job of relief pianist at twenty-five dollars a week, playing for the supper show as a soloist while the regular orchestra had dinner. Glad to have a job at last, he attended a Monday morning rehearsal, sharing the piano bench with the regular pianist and studied the performances and the music. He did the same at the matinee. Then came the supper show, a fiasco that made it impossible for him to return on Tuesday.

Slightly nervous, he managed pretty well for a few acts—"I was especially good with a turn that used Remick's songs"—and felt easier until he came up against a skit for six chorus girls, a hero, heroine and comedian, a skit based on what is called "special material" written specially for the act. He now confronted an untidy, sketchy (his word: "cryptic") manuscript. He began the opening chorus of this miniature musical comedy, and felt he was doing well all things considered. Then he suddenly realized that he and the chorus were not together; he played one thing, they sang another. Either the pages had become mixed or he had missed a cue or two. Crimson, he hoped there was no one in the audience who knew him.

The comedian—whose name Gershwin did not remember, but whose face he never forgot: "his looks are forever engrossed on my memory" —could not let the opportunity go by.

Peering down at the mortified Gershwin, he shouted, "Who told you you were a piano player?"

That got a laugh. Encouraged he added, "You ought to be banging the drums!" He laughed at his own wit, the audience joined in and the chorus giggled. Gershwin stopped playing and walked out of the theater, merriment and further comic comments stalking him. It was, he later said, "the most humiliating moment of my life." On his way out he stopped at the box office and informed the cashier, "I was the piano player here this afternoon and I'm quitting." The comedian and company were obliged to conclude their act without music.

And he was out of work again.

II

Both George and Ira Gershwin floundered among the un- and under-employed during the early months of 1917. George continued making piano rolls, but he did not count that as a job (in 1916 a total of forty of his rolls was released; that brought in less than two hundred dollars. In 1917 the same number was issued).

Ira Gershwin clerked in his father's bath ventures; both, eventually went into bankruptcy. Days at the baths being generally dull, Ira had time for penning quips, quatrains, bits of verse, even song lyrics as the day dragged on. He submitted some of his conceits to popular newspaper columnists with occasional success. During his term at the Lafayette Baths in Greenwich Village, which doubled as a hotel, he wrote his first published magazine piece for the now celebrated feisty, irreverent *The Smart Set* edited by the team of Mencken and Nathan. His payment in full was one dollar which was quickly expended on postage for other pieces that were returned with rejection slips.

Unlike his brother George, who concentrated on musical jobs, Ira drifted from one job to another: darkroom assistant to a photographer, the receiving department in Altman's (and before he finally broke into songwriting he worked for several months as a cashier in a cousin's traveling carnival). His literary attempts seemed to get him nowhere. George Gershwin, meanwhile, fretted as a journeyman musician, noted for his pianistic skills rather than his creativity.

Ira Gershwin preserved his thoughts and activities during this time in a mannered Pepysian journal. From this record with its often sardonic remarks and occasional touches of forced humor, it is clear that while they awaited the opportunity to prove themselves, the brothers spent a good deal of time in vaudeville and silent movie houses and the musical theater.

While her two older sons appeared to remain on occupational hold, Rose Gershwin had begun to propel daughter Frances into a stage career. She was ten, sang sweetly in a small voice and had revealed a talent for dance. Mamma (as Rose was called) was the quintessential stage mother: ambitious, protective and willing to travel. Ira Gershwin recorded attending a song and dance recital of his sister's dancing school accompanied by his brothers and a cousin, Henry Botkin, in from Boston (he became best known in Gershwin's phrase as "my cousin Botkin, the painter"). All sat patiently through a long evening—twenty aspiring very young performers—to watch Frances dance (a Russian dance), sing ("M-I-S-S-I-S-S-I-P-P-I") and a duet ("So Long Letty"); the last he had found "very charming indeed."

The next morning Rose and Frances Gershwin boarded a train for a week in Philadelphia, where Frances joined a troupe of talented youngsters in an entertainment entitled *Daintyland.* By June they had begun touring the vaudeville houses (at a weekly salary of forty dollars). The first Gershwin to break into the theater kept the brothers back home informed of her progress (Ira Gershwin copied one of her letters into his journal, preserving her spelling and punctuation). "We got very big write-ups in the papers," she informed "Izzy, George and Arthur." Since they could not come to Boston she described the content of *Daintyland* to them. "The beginning is we all sit up on the piano and sing hellow folks hellow and two girls stand at the foot of the piano. Then a girl sings Lets all be Americans now. Then Honey sings Mississippi. And a boy and girl sings and dances Honalua Hickie Bula Boo. And a boy plays a violin, then after him I come [on] . . ." Following two other numbers the troupe joined in on "There's a Long, Long, Trail" [spelled Trial]. She continued with, "After that we go to the dressing room & wait for the next show. We play in this house four times a day that takes all my time. Then I go to the hotel and go to bed and that is the end of it . . ."

Though exciting for a ten-year-old, this four-a-day grind was exhausting and confining. The tour ended in time for her to return to school. She did not return to vaudeville the next year. Although she dropped out of show business, Frances Gershwin continued to sing, often accompanied in later years by her brother, who loved her interpretations of his songs. She returned to the theater in two Broadway revues, *Merry-Go-Round* (1927) and *Americana* (1928)—and (to sing Gershwin songs) in a Cole Porter revue staged in Paris and in Broadway revue in the thirties. After this she confined her singing to her brothers' parties.

Early in September, George became the accompanist for vocalist Rita Gould. He used the stage name "George Wynne" (it appeared also on some of his early piano rolls—though as "Bert Wynn," along with "Fred Murtha" and "James Baker"). The Gould job appears to have been for a single performance, during which he played a couple of solos (not, however, of his own composition).

In his Broadway rounds he heard that a rehearsal pianist was needed for a Ziegfeld-Dillingham production at the Century Theatre. The revue, entitled *Miss 1917,* had a joint score by Victor Herbert and Gershwin's hero, Jerome Kern. He "was the first composer who made me conscious that most popular music was of inferior quality and that musical-comedy music was made of better material. I followed Kern's work and studied each song. I paid him the tribute of frank imitation and many things I wrote at this period sounded as though Kern had written them himself."

Miss 1917 would provide Gershwin's first experience with a real Broadway production (although the Century was way off Broadway on Central Park West between Sixty-second and Sixty-third streets, a site too far from Times Square to be good for business, as Ziegfeld and Dillingham were to learn). It would be an education in the ways of the theater that so beguiled and beckoned him.

Miss 1917, whose rehearsals began late in September, was scheduled to open on October 21, then October 29 and finally on November 5. Young George Gershwin was surrounded by such glittering theatrical personalities as Jerome Kern, Victor Herbert, author-lyricist P. G. Wodehouse (one of Ira's idols), lyricist Guy Bolton and Ziegfeld's stars. And he observed the production of a musical from the inside. *Miss 1917* was in trouble from the beginning.

Kern had written a song, lyrics by Wodehouse, "The Land Where the Good Songs Go," which brought down the curtain on the first act, a springboard for a nostalgic medley of songs associated with some members of the cast as well as with other popular performers of the then recent past. Kern's song introduced some eight interpolated songs by others, "The Yama Yama Man" (by Karl Hoschna and Collin Davis) which had been introduced by one of *Miss 1917*'s cast, Bessie McCoy; "Be My Little Baby Bumble Bee" (Henry I. Marshall–Stanley Murphy) which had been likewise introduced by the show's Elizabeth Brice and Charles King; Marion Davies, impersonating Edna May, sang "Follow On" (Gustav Kerker–Hugh Morton) and so on, in a medley that included "In the Good Old Summertime," "Sammy" and "Dinah" (not the song associated with Eddie Cantor in the mid-twenties). The act concluded with Herbert's familiar *March of the Toys* and Kern's specially composed instrumental, *Toy Clog Dance.* So far so good.

A newcomer to Broadway (having made her debut only two years before) was a promising singer-actress, twenty-year-old Vivienne Segal. In the "Good Songs" sequence she was to impersonate the great star Fritzi Scheff, who was still active and very popular. She had introduced, and was identified with, songs by both the show's composers. Herbert suggested that Segal do his "Kiss Me Again." Kern countered with his "They Didn't Believe Me," both originally sung by Scheff.

While the two neophytes Segal and Gershwin waited and wondered, the two musical giants, with raised voices, vocalized, each in favor of his own song. Before they stalked out of the theater each suggested that she learn *his* song. Intimidated in the presence of two such powerful figures, Vivienne took no chances: she learned both songs. As she sang them she found herself more comfortable with "Kiss Me Again." She then conferred with co-producer Dillingham, who advised her to stay with her own choice.

The day of the rehearsal, with Gershwin at the piano, Segal managed to get through a couple of bars of "Kiss Me Again" before Kern shot out of his seat in the orchestra, dashed forward and ordered them to stop. She explained to a beet-red Kern that she had permission from Dillingham to do Herbert's song. Whereupon she heard a word or more from Kern, which included unkind references to Dillingham as well as Herbert.

Herbert, who had also been seated in the orchestra, but on the opposite side, stood up. Despite his generally genial temperament, he let it be known that Kern's outburst was offensive. As Kern stalked the aisle on one side of the theater, Herbert paced the other as they shouted "insults and epithets" at one another.

Dillingham was summoned and soon he and Kern were nose to nose, shouting. Kern was adamant—so was Dillingham, and his was a more potent footing, the show's backing; he prevailed. Vivienne Segal would sing "Kiss Me Again." Furious, Kern declared that he was finished with *Miss 1917* and strode out of the theater. Since the entire score was complete, there was little else he could do—and when the show finally opened, Herbert's song was one of the "Good Songs," Kern to the contrary.

Backstage squabbling and feuding was common in the theater, more often between the acting stars than between preeminent composers. Such a public display of ego (plus patent envy) would never be a Gershwin trait.

When *Miss 1917* finally opened (already in financial trouble) on November 5, Ira Gershwin was in the audience with his brother—and, it may be assumed, so was the nettled Kern. Gershwin, who had had a brief career as a reviewer (unpaid) for *The Clipper* (a job his brother George had led him to) found the troubled revue "A glorious show—entertaining every minute."

His was not the consensus; though some reviews were favorable, *Variety* found that it "started weakly and finished worse." *Miss 1917* closed after forty-eight performances, a victim of high operating costs, the out-of-the-way location of the Century Theatre and mixed reviews.

Once the show opened, Gershwin was out of work again, but he was immediately drafted as piano accompanist for the Sunday Night Century Concerts. As there was no Sunday performance of whatever was playing at the Century during the week, the theater was open to variety performances by members of the cast of the show and other vocalists and dancers. At one of his earliest appearances, Gershwin played for a veteran of the stage, Arthur Cunningham (who had appeared in a John Philip Sousa musical, *The Charlatan,* the year of Gershwin's birth).

Gershwin's most significant Sunday was that of November 25, 1917, when he accompanied Vivienne Segal. While they had rehearsed, he had played some of his own songs for her. Even as he moved from one piano playing job to another he managed to find time to collaborate with Ira, Leonard Praskins, his earliest collaborator, and the dynamic, indefatigable Irving Caesar.

Among the songs she chose for her Century Concert, Segal presented two Gershwin-Caesar efforts, "You-oo, Just You" and "There's More to the Kiss Than the X-X-X" (the Xs indicate the imitation of the sound of a kiss). Lyrically the songs are dated (as Caesar explained, "We were kids!"); musically they are well fashioned. "There's More to the Kiss . . ." is graced with a sprightly, arching melodic line and "You-oo, Just You," is distinctive for its humor and wistful harmonies. The songs were well received and Segal brought Gershwin onstage for an extra bow.

In the audience that night was a scout from Remick's who arranged, in mid-December, for the publication of "You-oo, Just You." It was the second Gershwin publication by his former employer. In June of the next year it was interpolated into the score of *Hitchy-Koo of 1918.*

But there was more that came out of the shambles of *Miss 1917* and the Century Concerts. The show's manager, Harry Askins, had been most impressed with Gershwin's songs and spoke glowingly of him to one of the most powerful men in music publishing, Max Dreyfus. In 1904 he had taken over the T. B. Harms Company, which published Herbert and Kern, Rudolf Friml, among others. Askins spoke so highly of the young pianist-songwriter that the astute, shrewd and noncommittal Dreyfus agreed to give the kid a hearing.

III

Max Dreyfus (1874–1964) was another rarity in Tin Pan Alley—a music publisher who could read music. Born in Germany, he had come to the United States around 1888, when he was about fourteen. He sold picture frames in the South before arriving in New York, where he was hired in 1895 as a pianist-arranger by M. Witmark & Sons. His original works, like Gershwin's, were rejected by his employer; he moved on to Howley, Haviland and Dresser, whose major staples were the latter's sentimental or bathetic effusions. When Dreyfus joined the firm, Paul

Dresser's most popular song was "On the Banks of the Wabash"; Gershwin was then about a year old.

One of Dreyfus's functions, as would be Gershwin's years later, was to notate music for nonmusical songwriters. Among these was John Golden, an ex-actor with songwriting aspirations (he was to be better known as a Broadway producer; his one enduring song is "Poor Butterfly," music by Raymond Hubbell). Golden remembered the young Dreyfus of the nineties as small and thin and that he "used to feel a little protective toward him, thinking he was too frail to make the grade." Those songwriters who did not share Golden's feelings, and there were a few, nicknamed him "Chalkie," because of his pallor. Both Gershwins were to be lifelong friends of the soft-spoken but formidable little man.

After a while with Dresser's firm, Dreyfus moved on to join a company founded by Thomas and Alec Harms, initially as a staff arranger. He quietly worked his way up to the position of professional manager with a 25 percent interest in T. B. Harms. In this capacity he chose songs for publication and kept an ear out for promising talents. (In an unusual move, since Dreyfus was generally self-effacing, he published one of his own songs, with a lyric by Bert Timoney. "Cupid's Garden," published in 1903, was much in vogue for a time and was frequently used as background music for silent films. Characteristically, Dreyfus credited the music to a pseudonymous "Max C. Eugene".)

The following year he bought out the Harmses and proceeded to build a rich musical empire; T. B. Harms (for he retained the original company name), would grow to become one of the most active and successful publishers of theater—and later film—songs in the country.

When Gershwin met with Dreyfus in his office on West Forty-fifth Street in December of 1917, he had a sizable portfolio to draw upon to demonstrate his talents, besides his by then four published songs and *Rialto Ripples.* He had "You Are Not the Girl," lyrics by brother Ira, some of Caesar's songs and about ten with lyrics by Lou Paley, including one that Ira considered "surefire," "We're Six Little Nieces of Our Uncle Sam." There was also a Paley-Gershwin lyric to "Beautiful Bird." Dreyfus listened but did not offer to rush any of these efforts into print; however, he offered Gershwin a staff position as composer (no plugging and no piano demonstrations) at a salary of thirty-five dollars a week. If he produced a song Dreyfus deemed worth publishing he would receive, in addition, a fifty-dollar advance plus a three-cent royalty on each sheet-music sale.

Gershwin was all of nineteen when he joined the staff of T. B. Harms on February 10, 1918. Before he could begin, however, he had an earlier commitment to fulfill. In January he had agreed to accompany a popular vaudeville performer, Louise Dresser. They reworked her act and two weeks after he had signed with Harms, opened at the Riverside Theater in New York in her "Song Readings." She featured no Gershwin songs, but did sing his friend Herman Paley's "Cheer Up Father, Cheer Up Mother," and Kern's "It's a Sure Sign."

Ira Gershwin, who met her before she and his brother went off on tour, found her "decidedly congenial." She found her young accompanist lovable, shy and a diligent pianist who practiced constantly. Their tour took them to Boston, Baltimore and Washington, D.C., where they arrived early in March, in time to march in a Preparedness Parade and to perform for President Woodrow Wilson during their run at Keith's Theatre during the week of March 4.

Returning to New York, Gershwin learned that Dreyfus had held on to a handful of his songs, hoping to place them in a show or revue as an "interpolated number." But no promise of publication was forthcoming from Harms. While biding his time, Gershwin took a job with Dreyfus's blessing as rehearsal pianist for the *Ziegfeld Follies of 1918* (with music by Louis A. Hirsch), after which he switched to Kern's *Rock-a-Bye Baby* (in which Louise Dresser sang the role of Aggie). During rehearsals (the show began its tryout in New Haven on April 8), Gershwin and Kern became quite friendly and the older man offered paternal advice. Knowing he was a Harms staff composer, Kern suggested that should a show assignment come his—Gershwin's—way, he should feel free to confer with the veteran composer before taking on the job. The friendship ripened and Kern introduced Gershwin to a complex game of his own devising he called "Guggenheim." It was a word game based on the selection of a category: authors, printers, automobiles, and so on. Then a key word was selected at random and its individual letters served as the first letter of the words the participants were supposed to come up with. All of his life Kern enjoyed this game, which often befuddled his not-so-well-read colleagues. Gershwin, in turn, introduced the game to the Paley circle, where it became popular.

Determined to write for the theater, Gershwin continued adding songs to his notebooks while working with Ira, Paley and Caesar as he waited for something to happen at Harms.

It was Caesar who initiated an idea that catapulted them both, in a phrase, to fame and fortune in Tin Pan Alley. The inspiration, as Caesar tells it, was the popularity of a current hit, "Hindustan," a brisk one-step in two/four time.

"Why don't we write an American one-step, George," Caesar suggested over dinner at Dinty Moore's, a popular Times Square chophouse. Once the Far Eastern one-step had faded, they would be ready with their American version. Besides, it was an established Alley tradition to follow in the wake of a hit with a similar idea, hoping to fill the fiscal void. Gershwin listened, was interested and while they rode a Fifth Avenue bus uptown (the Gershwins then lived in an apartment at 520 West 144th Street, off Riverside Drive), discussed Caesar's plan. Instead of India, the lyric would draw upon a Southern setting. By the time they arrived at the Gershwin apartment they had the song blocked out lyrically, with some concept for the tune (it did not come out of Gershwin's abundant Tune Books, into which he jotted song ideas).

Within fifteen minutes, Caesar recalls, they completed the song over the protests of several of Morris Gershwin's card-playing friends in an adjoining room. But once the song was finished, Pop joined his son in a duet; Morris Gershwin played a tissue-wrapped comb. The title Caesar had devised for their song was "Swanee."

Gershwin was then finishing up as the pianist for the *Follies* at the New Amsterdam. Caesar stopped by during rehearsals, bubbling with enthusiasm over their new creation. They demonstrated it for some of the chorus girls, with great success. Director Ned Wayburn liked it even more and suggested that he would like to include it in a revue he would be staging at the Capitol Theatre, at that time still under construction; though designed as a movie theater it also would have a stage for vaudeville presentations. When it opened in October of 1919 it would be the largest motion picture house in the country. Gershwin played another of his songs, lyric by Lou Paley, "Come to the Moon" and Wayburn took that as well.

Despite the yearlong wait for the Capitol's opening, and the premiere of "Swanee," Gershwin's career as songwriter had begun gaining momentum in mid-1918. Before their "Swanee" collaboration, his and Caesar's "You-oo, Just You" had been interpolated into Irene Bordoni's *Hitchy-Koo of 1918* in June; in September, Harms finally published its first Gershwin song, "Some Wonderful Sort of Someone," with a lyric by Schuyler Greene, a staff lyricist. Nora Bayes, then a leading vaudeville performer, heard it during a scouting visit to Harms's and expressed an interest in interpolating it into her show, *Look Who's Here* (the bulk of the score was by A. Baldwin Sloane). She was also impressed with the pianism of the composer and asked Gershwin to be her accompanist during her midpoint song recital, in which she sang her former hits and introduced songs by other composers. Gershwin had no problem getting leave from Harms and agreed.

He also brought her another song, "The Real American Folk Song (Is a Rag)," with a lyric by Arthur Francis; she liked that too and it went into the show. "Arthur Francis" was in fact Ira Gershwin; he concocted his anonym from the names of two of his siblings. Although the brothers had been collaborating, off and on, for about a year, "The Real American Folk Song" was the first that George had been able to place. Since he did not want to coast into Tin Pan Alley on his brother's reputation, Ira thought it best to hide behind Arthur Francis for a while.

Since his debut as a musical-comedy composer had not materialized, George, like many a blossoming composer at the time, settled for interpolations. Serving as accompanist in his own songs for a star of Bayes's magnitude was advantageous and the experience, as with *Miss 1917*, was to further his education in show-biz deportment.

He had agreed on a six-week stay with the show, which had been retitled *Ladies First*, when the tour began. Both Gershwins were excited over their first theater break—even Ira, who at this phase in his life was affecting a sophisticated detachment, had become what was then called a snappy dresser and preserved his daily thoughts in his journal in a style patterned after one of his favorite columnists, Franklin P. Adams (F.P.A.). When *Ladies First* opened in Trenton, New Jersey, Ira (then working again at the St. Nicholas Baths) took the day off to catch a matinee and to hear—for the first time—one of his works sung by a major vaudeville star.

For the event he dressed in keeping with his part as a professional lyricist as he visualized him—green tweed suit, purple shirt and a blue tie. (Actually in the early Tin Pan Alley years, insofar as dress went, it was difficult to distinguish between a songwriter and a Damon Runyan horse player, especially the type who favored big black cigars.) City-bred Ira managed to get lost, got off at the wrong railroad station, but eventually made it to the theater in time to hear Nora Bayes do "Some Wonderful Sort of Someone" and, of course, "The Real American Folk Song." She also worked in her own song, "Just Like a Gypsy" (lyric by Seymour B. Simons). Brother George was the attentive accompanist.

The *Ladies First* experience began promisingly. Gershwin wrote to a friend, Max Abramson, a cousin of the Paleys, telling him that he thought Bayes was considering putting his name in the program as a composer of the interpolated songs. "If she does, she'll be doing me a justice that I sorely need to get into the select circle of composers in New York . . . I am getting confidence and encouragement from this show, and B. Sloane and his royalties [who] told me he received $400 royalty for Trenton and Pittsburgh . . . He gets 3 percent of the gross . . . Zowie! Why didn't I write the show and let him interpolate? . . .

Seriously," he concluded, "I am thinking of writing a show. I'm going to make an attempt when I reach New York . . ."

Somewhere between Pittsburgh and New York, Nora Bayes and Gershwin had differences. If she made a slip, she blamed it on him, missed cues were his fault; but she went too far when she demanded that he change the ending of "The Real American Folk Song." He refused. She countered with a reminder that if she had asked that favor of Irving Berlin or Jerome Kern, they would have complied. Any other song, he told her, but not this one. He had worked hard on its ending. When *Ladies First* opened in New York on October 24, 1918, Nora Bayes no longer sang the song, which was taken over by Hal Ford, a lesser luminary. It was a success in New York and a tour that followed, but Gershwin had had enough and was happy to leave the terrible-tempered Nora Bayes for the quieter precincts of Tin Pan Alley.

But his ambitions had been fired up by his association with the show and he was eager to tackle the full score of a musical. Thanks to Max Dreyfus, he practically walked into his first show assignment the moment he fled Nora Bayes. It was also his first fiasco.

IV

When George returned to his desk at Harms, Dreyfus introduced him to a young man named Edward B. Perkins. Not yet thirty, Perkins was a Columbia University graduate, with theatrical ambitions. *Variety* described him as "a jazz stage magnet . . . [and] the youngest international stage magnet in the world."

Perkins was in Paris in November 1918 at the end of World War I where he was impressed with the talents of vocalist Ruby Loraine. The scene shifts to London where Perkins saw a show, *Half Past Eight* (actually a revue), which according to him had been running there for nine months. He was apparently also taken with a Welsh member of the cast, vocalist Sybil Vane. The scene shifts again to the office of Dreyfus, where Perkins explained his idea of producing an American version of the hit, *Half Past Eight,* starring his friend vaudevillian-comedian-juggler Joe Cook and featuring the Misses Loraine and Vane. He also needed a composer to fill out the score. Dreyfus was so impressed with the fast-talking Perkins that he offered him an advance (as partial backing) and to even to pay for the orchestrations. He also offered him George Gershwin.

The show went literally on the road. Plans were set to begin in Syracuse, then tour as far west as Chicago before opening in New York.

Before the historic premiere the Syracuse *Post-Standard* heralded the event:

> *When "Half Past Eight" opens at the Empire for an entire week beginning Monday, December 9, Syracuse theater-goers will have the opportunity of hearing a tuneful score written by George Gershwin, a young composer whose melodies are such great favorites with the New York dancing public. His tunes do not soar to comic opera heights. Neither is he of the tin-pan ragtime school. He is said to strike the happy medium—twinkly melodies in one-step and fox trot tempos. His "Hong Kong," sung by Ruby Loraine and her Chinese Parasol girls, is predicted as a big hit. The book and lyrics are by Fred Caryll.*
>
> *Joe Cook, a versatile comedian who made such a success here in "The Red Clock" last season is returning as the featured principal in the production. He is supported by Sybil Vane, the wee Welsh prima donna; Bud Snyder, star pantomist of the New York Hippodrome; Joe Melino, the "happy tramp" comedian; Ruby Loraine from Paris; the Banjo Buddies; Dixie Saxophone quartet and the famous Clef Club Jazz band, twenty expert syncopaters, comprising the biggest jazz band on the American stage.*
>
> *A Broadway chorus is another promised feature.*

To insure such coverage, Perkins took a sizable advertisement in the *Post-Standard* in which he described his show as "A New Musical in Two Acts" featuring "The Biggest and Best Jazz Band in America," the Clef Club Jazz Band. Echoing the paper's article, it was hailed as "Twenty Expert Syncopators," and lest the reader miss the point of the band's expertise, described as "All Spades!"

Gershwin recalled that he had written about five songs for the show and that Perkins as "Fred Caryll" did the lyrics with some assistance from Ira Gershwin. Evidently Perkins had brought some of the songs from London with him. "The show opened in Syracuse and Mr. Perkins was quite delighted over the fact that some organization [the Loyal Order of Moose] bought out the first night for $800," Gershwin wrote of the event.

"*Half Past Eight* had come to its premiere—the curtain went up at a quarter to nine—the first act was over at nine-thirty. Intermission of half an hour and the second act started. The final curtain rang down at a quarter to eleven—not much of a show from the standpoint of running time, you must admit.

"The newspapers came out the next day, and I remember one [Variety] saying 'Half Past Eight isn't even worth the war tax.' "

"On Wednesday afternoon—the first matinee—some of the cast began to worry about not getting paid at the end of the week. One of the acts refused to go on unless they collected. I happened to walk backstage at that moment, dressed in a blue suit and unshaven. Perkins rushed up to me and said, 'You've got to go on—one of the acts just refused to appear and we must have something to go on while we make a change of scene.'

"I said, 'What will I do?'

"He said, 'Play some of your hits.'

"I should have loved to have played my hits—except that I didn't have any.

"But I walked on the stage to a very small and innocent audience, made up a medley right on the spot of some of my tunes. The audience must have thought it was very queer. I finished my bit and walked off—without a hand!

"Another funny incident happened . . . [The show] was advertised as having a Broadway chorus. There was no chorus . . . so I, being the ripe age of around nineteen-and-a-half, suggested to Perkins that in the finale of the show, we send all the comedians out dressed in Chinese pajamas, holding large umbrellas, which would hide their faces from the audience [which] would then say, 'Ah, here's the chorus,'—and, at least, would keep their seats until the finale was over. I hadn't figured that Perkins would get cheap paper umbrellas, though. And what happened the opening night was that three of the umbrellas failed to open, taking away any surprise the audience might have had.

"I managed to get my fare back to New York and the show closed on Friday night of that week. It was a good experience for me and, anyway, I got a thrill out of seeing on the billboards, 'Music by George Gershwin.' "

Variety's review, which did not mention Gershwin, was headed with the comment Gershwin remembered: "$2 Show Not Worth War Tax," which was forty cents. The cast got generally good notices, but Perkins was singled out for reproach as the "gentleman who conceived the idea that the public will pay high prices to see a one-act vaudeville act stretched into a two-act imitation revue." The opening night umbrella blunder inspired this view: "What disappointed the Tired Business Man and the thing he will never forgive is that while somehow the impression had been spread through the city that this was a girly show, there were three of the fair sex in the entire production. This may have been responsible for some hissing as the curtain went down at 10:30." It appears to have gone down on the theatrical career of Edward B. Perkins; he was not heard from or about again.

His musical-comedy-writing career temporarily thwarted, Gershwin settled back into his niche at Harms, adding songs to his file. "Swanee" had yet to be heard, for the Capitol Theatre was still abuilding, but Gershwin and Caesar had two of their songs interpolated into *Good Morning, Judge,* which premiered early in February, 1919. These included the song Vivienne Segal had introduced the previous November, "There's More to the Kiss" and one of Gershwin's finest early songs, "I Was So Young (You Were So Beautiful)," lyrics by Caesar and Alfred Bryan, a Harms staff lyricist. (The bulk of the score was by Lionel Monckton, with lyrics by Adrian Ross and Percy Greenbank).

In March Gershwin produced an uncharacteristic piece, probably the most uninspired tune written by him. The incentive was a contest sponsored by the New York *American* in search of no less than a new national anthem; first prize, five thousand dollars. Gershwin teamed up with another Harms staffer, "Michael E. Rourke" (Herbert Reynolds, who often collaborated with Kern and Sigmund Romberg, among others). The result, "O Land of Mine, America," submitted anonymously, was published in the Sunday edition of the paper on March 2. The judges, Irving Berlin, John Golden, John McCormack, John Philip Sousa and conductor Josef Stransky did not select it as the new anthem, but Gershwin and Reynolds split a fifty-dollar runner-up prize. The winning anthem did not displace "The Star-Spangled Banner," and was instantly forgotten.

Gershwin's progress toward creating a show score was discouragingly slow. Dreyfus found nothing worthy of publication in the *Half Past Eight* songs (though Gershwin salvaged two for later use) and Gershwin was back to interpolations. His few published songs did not bring in royalties of any consequence.

At this moment he and Irving Berlin met again; this meeting was one that Berlin did not forget. After service as a sergeant in the U.S. Army, during which he produced the popular soldier show *Yip, Yip, Yaphank,* Berlin decided to withdraw from the firm of Waterson, Berlin and Snyder and to set out on his own. Before making any final decision, Berlin decided to approach Dreyfus with a song that had been inspired by the Russian Revolution. Dreyfus was interested; the war had taken Berlin out of circulation for a while, but he was still Irving Berlin. Berlin played it; Dreyfus liked it and they were in business.

Berlin then said, "I need someone to write it down for me."

Dreyfus called in Gershwin, who noted down what Berlin called "That Revolutionary Rag"; after which he performed his own arrangement of it. With admiring exaggeration Berlin has said of this treatment, "It was so good, I hardly recognized it!" T. B. Harms published it.

Gershwin then returned to the subject of their earlier encounter. He would like to work for Irving Berlin, knowing that once Berlin had formed his own company (which he did subsequently) he would need someone to take down his music for him. Berlin, still impressed with Gershwin's musicianship, asked him to play some of his own songs. Gershwin did not get the job as musical secretary. Berlin's opinion was that he was too talented to subordinate his talent to that of another songwriter, even Irving Berlin. "Stick to writing your own songs, kid," he was told. Soon after, Gershwin got the chance he had been waiting for.

"Every career needs a lucky break to start it on its way," he told a radio audience years later, "and my lucky break came in 1919 when I was brought to Alex Aarons, a dapper young man who had made some money selling smart clothes [at the time he was associated with Finchley's] and wanted to have a fling at producing a show.

"I was twenty years old at the time, and Arthur Jackson, the lyric writer, was the man who brought us together. After hearing a few of my tunes, Alex Aarons decided to engage me as composer for his first show, *La-La-Lucille!* This was very brave of him, because I was quite inexperienced at the time, never having written a complete score."

Alexander A. Aarons was the twenty-nine-year-old son of Alfred E. Aarons, a major power on Broadway. The elder Aarons had been a sometime songwriter, a manager in the Klaw and Erlanger booking agency and, from time to time, emerged as a producer (most of his songwriting was done around the turn of the century; he had the reputation of being a sharp businessman). Initially the elder Aarons was to have produced *La-La-Lucille!,* with Victor Herbert in mind as the composer. However, once the musical got under way with the production attributed to Alex A. Aarons and George B. Seitz, Aarons senior stepped into the background, all the while keeping a sharp eye on his money and his son's first venture onto the Broadway scene.

Ira Gershwin, writing in his memoir-lyric anthology, *Lyrics on Several Occasions,* recalled Aarons's musicality. When Ira and Aarons met a few weeks later he learned that "Alex was fond at the time of at least twenty of George's tunes which had not been written up lyrically, so he had no means of calling for any of them by numeral or title. But he could request what he wanted to hear this way: Whisking his hand across George's shoulder, he would say: 'Play me the one that goes like *that.*' Or: 'Play the tune that smells like an onion.' Or: *'You* know, the one that reminds me of the Staten Island ferry.' And so on . . ."

Arthur Jackson, who brought the entire project together was to be, in collaboration with B. G. DeSylva, co-lyricist. Of all the participants, DeSylva (1895–1950) was the best known and most successful. He had dropped out of the University of Southern California in his sophomore year to accompany Al Jolson to New York. The star had heard DeSylva perform one of his songs at a club, liked one especially, " 'N Everything," bought half interest in it (meaning he was credited, as he frequently was, as a collaborator) and interpolated it into the mostly Romberg score of *Sinbad,* which had premiered at the Winter Garden in February of the previous year. " 'N Everything" became a great success. When he joined the *La-La-Lucille!* team, DeSylva was half proprietor of a couple of substantial hits. His association with Jolson would soon prove very beneficial to Gershwin and Irving Caesar.

While the score of *La-La-Lucille!* contained several of Aarons's favorite new Gershwin tunes, Gershwin also used the song he and Caesar had written the year before, "There's More to the Kiss . . ." and one written for *Half Past Eight,* "The Ten Commandments of Love." Of the new songs, the most enduring has been "Nobody but You," which proved popular at the time, as did the novelty number "Tee-Oodle-Um-Bum-Bo." Two lesser efforts, "From Now On" and "Somehow It Seldom Comes True," are minor but good Gershwin.

Gershwin's first full-scale Broadway venture excited scant comment on the score and little mention of the composer. After the Boston premiere on June 12, 1919, J. B. Atkinson, the second-string critic and assistant to H. T. Parker of the *Evening Transcript,* found the music "now vivacious and surprising of detail, and again harmoniously pleasing." Gershwin preserved this observation. (The reviewer would eventually become drama critic of the New York *Times* as Brooks Atkinson.) While the New York critics praised the show itself, they pretty much ignored the songs, though the *Globe*'s man mentioned his name in this sentence: "The songs by a new young composer, George Gershwin, are tuneful if in many instances negative, but they retard the action." Burns Mantle, writing in the *Evening Mail,* found *La-La-Lucille!* "much the best . . . of the recent musical plays." It ran from opening night, May 26, until August 19, a success until it was closed by an actors' strike.

Max Dreyfus was impressed enough to publish seven of the songs; in addition to the premature closing, there was another misfortune. Gershwin apparently chose to ignore Kern's invitation issued during their "Guggenheim" playing days of the *Rock-a-Bye Baby* rehearsals the year before. Kern did not forget, however, and felt Gershwin had snubbed him by not coming to him for advice when he did his first musical. According to Ira Gershwin, his brother had conveniently forgotten because Aarons had suggested it. Part of Kern's offer entailed his placing some of his own songs in the score; Aarons wanted to keep it all Gershwin. Kern later even hinted that he was considering retirement—which seems highly unlikely; he was then only thirty-seven and definitely had his best years ahead of him—and planned to turn over his unfulfilled contracts to Gershwin. Eventually Kern got over it; there was no arguing with success. And that, thanks to DeSylva, was just around the corner.

V

Two months after the closing of *La-La-Lucille!* in August, the Capitol Theatre was finally completed. It *was* on Broadway (at Fifty-first Street). For its opening on October 24, 1919, Douglas Fairbanks's new silent movie, *His Majesty the American,* was booked, and Ned Wayburn, whom Gershwin had known since his *Miss 1917* rehearsal stint, had readied a stage show he called *Demi-Tasse*. Finally months after it had been conceived "Swanee" was dusted off for an elaborately staged number employing Arthur Pryor's band and about fifty dancers fitted with small electric lights in the tips of their shoes. "Come to the Moon," with Lou Paley's lyrics, also remained in the show. As was the practice then, sheet music copies of the songs, published by Harms, were on sale in the theater lobby.

To the dismay of Caesar and Gershwin, while the audiences applauded vocalist Muriel DeForrest and the dancers, they ignored the sheet music on the way out. Caesar admitted that he and Gershwin tried to stimulate sales by purchasing copies of their own song, graced with a handsome Art Deco cover, but to no avail. "Swanee" was no "Hindustan."

Meanwhile, DeSylva's friend and alleged collaborator Al Jolson had returned briefly to the Winter Garden while touring with his successful *Sinbad,* which had been around for more than a year. He had returned to New York to do some recording and to make an appearance at one of the Winter Garden Sunday Night Concerts (the then current production at the Winter Garden was *The Passing Show of 1919*). After the concert, Gershwin and DeSylva went to the party for Jolson. As was his wont, Gershwin inevitably got to the piano; among the songs he played was the disappointingly nonpopular "Swanee." Gershwin's kinetic performance immediately caught Jolson's interest: the momentum of the tune, the surprising change of key between verse and chorus, the humor —and the mammy reference in the lyric. On the spot he decided he would sing it in the touring *Sinbad* and, more important, he would record it (which he did on January 8, 1920).

Jolson's interpretation reflected Gershwin's own vigorous, propulsive performance, and the recording became an instant hit. Within a month the frugal Dreyfus bought the entire front page of *Variety* to proclaim "Al Jolson's Greatest Song" and on the back page described it as "the Hit of Hits" from the "Most Successful of All Singers." Unlike DeSylva and others, Gershwin and Caesar did not choose to share authorship (its earlier publication would have precluded that), but Jolson's smiling countenance decorated the new cover. Both sheet music and Jolson's recording sold in the millions; there were other recordings as well.

"Swanee," despite a few characteristic touches, is not exceptional Gershwin, but it served an important purpose: it lit up his name in Tin Pan Alley and literally spread his name across the nation and eventually to Europe. No more could anyone, as did one reviewer of *La-La-Lucille!* refer to him as "someone named George Gershwin."

It was in fact the unexpected success of "Swanee" that gave Gershwin his "lucky break." It brought him to the attention of Broadway producers. His share of the royalty income (reportedly $10,000 the first year) enabled him to concentrate on scores rather than interpolations, although it would be a while before he hit his stride. "Swanee" had catapulted him, after a long wait but then almost overnight, into "the select circle of composers in New York," that he had so fervently hoped to join.

3

. . . to Broadway

I

Considering his identification with a time—the Jazz Age—there is something romantically appropriate in Gershwin's leap to fame (and fortune) at the beginning of a new decade. While it was a biographical-historical accident, it feels right; his story assumes a mythic configuration, a dramatic inevitability: he stepped onstage on cue to become a central figure in American culture during one of its most fertile epochs since the "Flowering of New England." We know this now; he did not know it then. He was, when the twenties began, a gifted, ambitious composer with an eye on Broadway.

Gershwin was twenty-one when "Swanee" brought him closer to the fulfillment of that ambition. He abandoned his earlier dream of becoming a concert pianist—a decision generally attributed to the death of Hambitzer, although there is no record of Gershwin's saying so. He would be a composer, but he would not necessarily confine himself to popular song. He continued to study with Kilenyi even after the success of "Swanee"; the mastery of harmony, counterpoint and orchestration was not essential to the composition of popular song. While this would help him to notate his ideas with greater nuance, it could not teach him how to create a melody; he was born with that gift. It has been suggested that Gershwin had learned how to write catchy tunes that the public would like by assiduously studying the popular hits of others. Would that that were possible. If it were, the nation would be populated with more Gershwins, Berlins, Kerns, Arlens—but there is only one of each.

In the span from his Remick's experience to "Swanee"—roughly the half decade in which he matured from a boy of fifteen to a young man of twenty-one—he had learned a lot, all of it incidental to good songwriting. He became familiar with the inside workings of the music business; he learned that plugging could contribute to the success of an inferior song (on the formulation: "familiarity breeds popularity followed by contempt"). But unless even a superior song was plugged, it languished. He continued to use the term, "plug," all his life and complained as late as 1936 that Hollywood filmmakers had literally thrown "one or two songs away without any kind of plug." He was referring to one of his best, "They Can't Take That Away from Me." This he had learned at Remick's: songs must be heard to become known.

He learned too about business contracts both in publishing and the theater (in this he had additional coaching from Kern). Inside the theater, as a rehearsal pianist, he observed the mechanics of creating, assembling, tightening and revising a musical; he learned structure, timing, what went where: openings, closings, fillers, finales, about "icebreakers" at curtain-up, what went into the opening of the second act (a few musical references to the "plug" song of Act I, for example, hints of songs to come) and how to bring it all to a resounding end, usually with brief medley of the show's hoped-for hits. In short, Gershwin learned the formula of musical-comedy structure; to brighten the formula he was determined to compose nonformula songs whenever possible.

In his work as a peripheral member of the staff of a show, he also had an education in temperament from Nora Bayes and her ultimatums, Romberg and his nonchalant perception of collaboration and authorship, Kern and his lofty concept of the perquisites of success. He learned about producers, conductors, dance directors.

This schooling was enriched by his initiatory ventures into the world of musical comedy, the interpolations which accomplished little except modest publication and once in a while, equally modest success ("I Was So Young" and "Some Wonderful Sort of Someone"). *Half Past Eight* and *La-La-Lucille!* rounded out his primary schooling in the theater and inured him to failure and disappointment.

So it was that the "Swanee" explosion found him with a fairly well-rounded education in the ways and mores of the music business and the musical theater. It afforded him the chance to pick and choose and it enlarged his name enough in the business so that producers even considered coming to him. With Dreyfus solidly behind him, Gershwin was ready for Broadway. "Swanee," his most blatant Tin Pan Alley song, would take him out of the Alley.

And it eventually would bring an end to his regular sessions with Kilenyi—and others. For a time, even with the "Swanee" largess, he continued to meet with Kilenyi for harmony studies. To get ahead of the story a little, but to touch upon his formal music study (more extensive than was generally thought), he noted an idea one day, simply labeled "Melody" in his Tune Book. He also added a memo to himself, that this might be a good tune for a show to be produced by Alex Aarons or Ned Wayburn. The next day, September 28, 1921, he met with Kilenyi for a lesson. Earlier in the year he also attended summer courses at Columbia University with an eminent teacher, Rosseter G. Cole; one of the courses was Elementary Orchestration.

Kilenyi coached Gershwin in orchestration also and for him Gershwin prepared his small and charming study piece *Lullaby* for string quartet (c. 1919), which became a favorite among his string-playing friends, though he had no plans for its publication or public performance. (A later *Piece for Four Strings* has come to light, though little is known about its genesis.) For Kilenyi's class Gershwin arranged a Bach work, *Figured Chorale,* for clarinet, two horns, two bassoons, cello and bass which Ira Gershwin deposited in Gershwin Archive at the Library of Congress.

Much later, in 1923, when his theatrical career had begun to flourish, Gershwin had less time for study; he was too busy to learn how to do what he was already doing. Around this time, however, he had a brief encounter with the best-known of his teachers, Rubin Goldmark. It was not at all productive.

Goldmark was a sought-after teacher of piano and theory then in New York (his most celebrated pupil was Aaron Copland). Some of his fame was rooted in the fact that one of his teachers was Anton Dvořák and that his uncle was the famed composer Karl Goldmark. The nephew's compositions, however polished technically, have not stood the test of time. He later went on to teach at the Juilliard School of Music.

Copland, who had preceded Gershwin as a student of Goldmark, felt that his teacher's one drawback "was that he had little if any sympathy for the advanced musical idioms of the day." Gershwin and Goldmark were not made for each other. Fine and respected teacher that he was, he was not attuned to Gershwin's unorthodox talent; he lacked Hambitzer's vision and understanding as well as Kilenyi's open-mindedness. No documentation has been found dating the Gershwin-Goldmark encounter though it is fairly certain that they met perhaps three times. It can hardly be claimed that Gershwin "studied" with Goldmark.

One anecdote has survived. To acquaint his new teacher with his knowledge of harmony, Gershwin brought him the *Lullaby* for appraisal, an exercise dating back three or four years. According to

Gershwin, Goldmark studied the piece for a moment then said, "It's good. Yes, very good . . . It's plainly to be seen that you have already learned a great deal of harmony from me."

That was Gershwin's last try at regular study until the early thirties. Despite his crowded work and social schedule he confined his study of music to reading recondite books on music and often surprising his friends with arcane bits of information on obscure composers. He regularly attended recitals and concerts, which mystified his Tin Pan Alley colleagues, who associated him primarily with the bestselling "Swanee," and a handful of show tunes.

II

During the peak of "Swanee's vogue, Gershwin called on a former associate, George White, and suggested that he write the songs for *George White's Scandals of 1920.* They had worked together in *Miss 1917,* in which White had appeared as a dancer. Soon after the demise of that show White, who had also appeared as a dancer in a couple of Ziegfeld's *Follies,* decided to challenge the master showman himself. Though he did not have Ziegfeld's access to backers, White did know the theater. He appeared in his first revue in 1910. Nine years later he launched his initial effort, *George White's Scandals of 1919* of which he was producer-director and for which he wrote sketches and appeared as a dancer opposite a former Ziegfeld partner, diminutive Ann Pennington. When the *Scandals* (as White actually and modestly titled his first) opened in June it was not greeted as a threat to Ziegfeld; the songs were by Arthur Jackson (lyrics) and Richard Whiting (whose "Till We Meet Again," published in 1918 sold more copies than "Swanee"). Obviously White had selected Whiting because of "Till We Meet Again," but the songs written for the *Scandals* were undistinguished and served as pallid interludes between the comic routines of Lou Holtz, the White-Pennington dancing and to bring on the girls, as evidenced by some of the titles: "Girls Are Like Weather to Me," "Broadway Belles" and "Girls in My Address Book." They served but did little else. The *Scandals,* incidentally, opened a week after Gershwin's *La-La-Lucille!*

The prime feature of the *Scandals* was its dancing, along with its basic washroom humor, skits parodying Prohibition, the always reliable bedroom farce and scantily clad beauties. One theater historian observed that Ziegfeld had glorified the American girl and White undressed her.

White's venture in Ziegfeld's domain, though hardly auspicious, troubled the great man. Another challenger emerged the same year, John Murray Anderson's *Greenwich Village Follies.* Hoping to protect his product, the story goes, Ziegfeld offered White and Pennington a tidy sum to appear in his next *Follies;* White countered with a better offer if Ziegfeld would agree to appear opposite his star (and wife), Billie Burke in *his* next *Scandals.*

White had not been happy with the music Whiting had written for the 1919 *Scandals* and word got around Broadway and Tin Pan Alley that he was looking for a new composer. Gershwin heard about it (possibly through his *La-La-Lucille!* collaborator, Arthur Jackson, White's new associate) and approached White. With the lucrative strains of "Swanee" ringing in everyone's ears, he was signed to write the music for *George White's Scandals of 1920.* The association, as it turned out, lasted for five years, until 1924; when it began White paid Gershwin fifty dollars a week during the production period (rehearsals and run of the show). He was getting a hundred seventy-five dollars by the time he did the final *Scandals.* During this period he continued the practice of interpolating as well as writing scores for other producers.

In retrospect, Gershwin's *Scandals* scores are transitional between Tin Pan Alley and Broadway. With few exceptions there is a utilitarian quality to the songs, which were either dipped out of the Tune Books to fit a specific need or tossed off for the same reason. There being no plot to White's revues, the songs were tailored to his cast, the point of a skit, even a set (i.e., "South Sea Isles," 1923; "I'll Build a Stairway to Paradise," 1922). Of the thirty-four published *Scandals* songs, only two achieved popularity and longevity—"I'll Build a Stairway to Paradise" and "Somebody Loves Me" (1924). These are distinctive Gershwin songs; the first was given a powerful "plug" by a Paul Whiteman recording. The Whiteman band was featured in the show, and of its rendition Gershwin rightly said, "Paul made my song live with a vigor that almost floored me."

Of the other *Scandals* songs, a few deserve rehearing: the bluesy "On My Mind the Whole Night Long" (1920), the Kernish "Idle Dreams," the sinuous "Drifting Along with the Tide" (1921), the wistful "Where Is She?" (1923), the waltz "Across the Sea" (1922), the typically pianistic, "Throw 'Er in High" (1923), the rhythmic (but hardly singable today because of the lyrics), "Tum On and Tiss Me" (1920) and a song that has a fine show tune feel to it, "Year After Year" (1924).

The *Scandals* scores were stitched together from individual numbers and lack the unity (before the advent of "integration") of the more skillfully fashioned Gershwin scores. The set pieces and topicality of the skits, encouraged such songs as "The Life of a Rose" (with show girls costumed as roses) and two from his final *Scandals* that celebrated a new gadget, radio in "Tune in to J.O.Y." and an imported game sweeping the country, "Mah-Jongg."

Gershwin's association with White is significant not so much for the songs he wrote for the revues, but because for five seasons he was assured of having his name in lights on Broadway.

III

Since his work for White did not require a great deal of time, George worked on other productions during this period, including a few with Ira, who was still disguised as Arthur Francis.

After his tour as treasurer of Lagg's Great Empire Shows in the summer of 1919, Ira decided to turn to song, since he had failed at about everything else. He returned to New York joking about belonging "to the ranks of Brothers of the Great" (a friend had sent him a clipping about the opening of *La-La-Lucille!*).

George had heard through the Tin Pan Alley grapevine that a show then trying out in Chicago, *The Sweetheart Shop*, was searching for a special song for its ingenue, Helen Ford. The Gershwins were familiar with her voice and style; only the year before she scored a success as a replacement for the lead in a Friml musical, *Sometime*. George came home with the news and the brothers went into George's room, closed the door and went to work. The next morning George met with one of the show's producers, Edgar J. MacGregor, who was in New York on the song search and played "Waiting for the Sun to Come Out" for him. He liked it, and though he knew George Gershwin, he admitted that he had never heard of Arthur Francis.

"He's a clever college boy," he was informed, "with lots of talent." An agreement was immediately reached; MacGregor promised to pay two hundred fifty dollars for the use of "Waiting for the Sun" in the Anne Caldwell–Hugo Felix score for *Sweetheart Shop*. The word from Chicago was promising; in May, *Variety*'s reporter described it as "the biggest musical comedy money-maker in America." Of its nine published songs, one was "Waiting for the Sun to Come Out," with an engaging pink-and-gray Art Deco cover.

New York proved less kind than Chicago. One reviewer supplied the consensus when he dismissed the show as "infantile"; it closed in seven weeks. Even as it floundered, Gershwin came to MacGregor to remind him that he and his collaborator had not received their promised fee. The producer reminded him that the New York critics had lambasted the show, business was poor and he and his partner, William Moore Patch, would be forced to close soon.

"I'm working," Gershwin told him, "so I don't mind not being paid myself if things are that tough, but the college boy really needs the money." Whereupon as Ira Gershwin noted in *Lyrics on Several Occasions,* "a most welcome check for $125 was made out to Arthur Francis. 'Waiting for the Sun' was my first published song. The $125, plus, within the year, earnings of $723.40 from sheet music and $445.02 from phonograph records, kept the 'college boy' going for some time."

Not bad for a night's work, but other than this slight boost to the Gershwins' 1920 earnings, "Waiting for the Sun to Come Out" has little significance other than that it was the first published Ira and George Gershwin song. As a song it doesn't amount to much, words or music. It functioned as the show's "Pollyanna song," a cheery reminder to the audience that life was good after all; virtually every show had one.

MacGregor had evidently been impressed with the song. Undaunted by the failure of *The Sweetheart Shop,* he hoped to recoup with a production described as a "novel music-play," *A Dangerous Maid* by Charles W. Bell, based on his novel *A Dislocated Honeymoon,* which pretty much sums up the plot. MacGregor asked Gershwin if he and his collaborator could supply him with the full score. They agreed and came up with ten songs (eight of which were used and five eventually published), more than sufficient for a play with music. The plan was to tour before settling in New York. *A Dangerous Maid* premiered in Atlantic City late in March 1921, then moved on to Pittsburgh in April. En route the maid of the title, Juliette Day, dropped out and her role was filled by Vivienne Segal who, since *Miss 1917,* had scored personal successes in Kern's *Oh, Lady! Lady!* (1918) and Friml's *The Little Whopper* (1919), both of which ran for more than two hundred performances.

But MacGregor had miscalculated again, for after five weeks in Pittsburgh *A Dangerous Maid* closed at the end of April. The Gershwin collaboration produced a few songs intimating works to come: the music for the verse of the otherwise conventional "Some Rain Must Fall" and a duet proclaiming bucolic delights, "The Simple Life," in which Ira Gershwin's wry imagery is an early indicator of his developing talent.

(A half century later he dismissed the song with a characteristic self-criticism: he had used the word "butter" twice in the same stanza. It remains one of the Gershwins' most engaging early songs.) One other song, a quartet for women, "Boy Wanted," would be used by George Gershwin, with revisions, again. It too is a good song and unusual in another Ira Gershwin touch, references to Nietzsche and Freud, whose names must have mystified audiences in Atlantic City and Pittsburgh in 1921. The neglected songs written for the failed *A Dangerous Maid* are in fact the first intimation of the convergence and eventual fusion of two extraordinary talents that would create that unique entity: *the* Gershwin song.

While it seems inevitable now, it wasn't then. Some time before they collaborated on *A Dangerous Maid,* George had introduced Ira to a composer he admired, Vincent Youmans (who had been born one day after Gershwin). He had even spoken to Dreyfus about the promise of this young, very talented composer and went further: he played a number of Youmans songs for his first producer, Alex Aarons. This plugging of another's songs led to Youmans's assignment as composer and Ira Gershwin (still Arthur Francis) as lyricist for Aarons's forthcoming *Two Little Girls in Blue.* The musical, eventually produced by veteran A. L. Erlanger, was a success of the 1921 season—it premiered in New York four days after the expiration of *A Dangerous Maid* in Pittsburgh. Three of its songs sold widely—"Who's Who With You?," "Dolly" and "Oh Me! Oh My!" The first had actually been written the previous year, when George Gershwin brought the two together. Of some significance is the fact that slow-moving Ira had preceded his fast-moving brother to a genuine—though hardly spectacular—Broadway musical hit.

Ira Gershwin was pleased to read in one of the reviews that the "lyrics by Arthur Francis are of the best, and seems to show that there are some lyricists who are still able to write a lyric that rhymes and also means something." He had made it on his own, without depending on his brother's reputation. During the rehearsals of *Two Little Girls in Blue,* director Ned Wayburn had advised the youthful collaborators (Youmans was twenty-one, Ira Gershwin twenty-four) to stay out of sight lest Erlanger fear for his investment (he had paid Aarons one hundred thousand dollars for the show) in the hands of neophytes. They complied, which suited Ira Gershwin perfectly. He was content to leave the spotlight to his kinetic brother.

IV

George Gershwin at the keyboard had become the exciting luminary at those twenties parties that were often as much business as social. Carl Van Vechten put it rather cryptically, but wisely (for he was an inveterate partygoer and -giver) when he observed, "It is impossible to persuade people not to go to parties in New York, particularly if they are uninvited and English."

Despite Prohibition, Van Vechten noted that it was possible to drink from early evening to late at night simply by moving from one party to another, whether or not one had been invited. The more glittering parties were a kind of open house—for celebrities, businessmen, friends of friends, entertainers, producers, society folk. The more gifted guests— they could be singers, dancers or composers—entertained the less gifted but moneyed guests. Such were the parties given by Jules Glaenzer of Cartier's, the exclusive jewelry shop.

Glaenzer's were not the warm, musical-literary gatherings that the Gershwins enjoyed with the Paleys. His gatherings often had an underlying commercial purpose. Although he might push his Cartier wares while a Gershwin, or a Youmans, or a Richard Rodgers played—or a Nora Bayes, a Fanny Brice or Irene Bordoni sang, he did acquire the nickname of "Old Shush" Glaenzer (to rhyme with Old Dutch Cleanser) because of his habit of shushing his talkative guests during some of the gratis performances.

Gershwin referred to him as "one of the most famous hosts on two continents" (Glaenzer entertained in Paris, the home base of Cartier's) and recalled attending a party at Glaenzer's Park Avenue apartment along with producers Aarons and Ziegfeld, French pugilist Georges Carpentier, Paul Whiteman, composers Zez Confrey, Noël Coward and Vincent Youmans, the dancing Duncan sisters and siblings Fred and Adele Astaire, vaudevillians Nora Bayes and Fanny Brice, comedian Charlie Chaplin, Irish tenor John McCormack, and musical-comedy stars Marilyn Miller and Irene Bordoni. These parties were well lubricated with champagne. Ira Gershwin incidentally rarely, if ever, appeared on Glaenzer's guest list; he preferred the quieter evenings with the Paleys.

Gershwin not only entertained at the Glaenzers' but at one he sold one of his latest songs. Its story begins in the Dreyfus office where songwriters dropped by and Gershwin showed up from time to time during his interpolations and *Scandals* period. Early in 1922 DeSylva encountered Gershwin in his office and said, "George, let's write a hit."

"O.K.," Gershwin replied, assuming DeSylva was joking.

At the piano he began improvising a slow, sensuous melody. He developed it as DeSylva listened, interested. Gershwin repeated the phrase as DeSylva sang, "Oh, do it again." It fit and seemed like a good title. Taking it from there they had a complete song; now what to do with it?

DeSylva's lyric, which was considered quite suggestive at the time, beautifully coalesced with Gershwin's sensual melody, under which the cross-rhythms of the accompaniment reflect the tentative invitation of the lyric. "Do It Again" has bar-to-bar modulations, distinctive harmonies and un-Tin Pan Alley long-lined melody that mark it as one of Gershwin's finest creations.

Soon after he was at the piano at one of Glaenzer's star-studded parties and among others of his songs played "Do It Again" Irene Bordoni, then married to producer and sometime songwriter E. Ray Goetz, dashed across the room and said, "I must have that damn song! It's for me!" It was interpolated with some songs by her husband-producer and others into the play, *The French Doll*, a slightly risqué French comedy, and a Bordoni specialty. The play with music opened on February 20, 1922—and, indeed, "Do It Again" became Gershwin's first success of the year.

Coincidentally, on the same night *The French Doll* opened the Gershwins and the Astaires were teamed professionally for the first time. *For Goodness Sake* was not the dream musical they talked about in Tin Pan Alley *(that* was still two years in the future). It was the Astaires' fifth Broadway musical after they had quit vaudeville; not yet full-fledged stars (they were sixth in the billings), they did not get to sing the show's best Gershwin song, "Tra-La-La," which was done by the leads, Marjorie Gateson and John E. Hazzard. The bulk of the score was by Paul Lannin and William Daly (music) with lyrics (except for three Gershwin songs) by Arthur Jackson.

For Goodness Sake was Alex Aarons's third show. While the show did not establish him as the producer of "smart" musicals he hoped to become, it did establish the Astaires. They presented an unexceptional Gershwin song, "All to Myself," but made their mark in Daly-Jackson-Lannin's "The Whichness of the Whatness" and Daly and Jackson's "Oh Gee, Oh Gosh." The critic from the New York *American* called them the show's "principal assets . . . They can speak a little, act a little and dance quarts . . ." After fourteen weeks, *For Goodness Sake* closed down, the victim of a very hot summer. Though hardly epochal, as *Stop Flirting,* starring the Astaires, it would become a London hit in March of the next year.

V

The *Scandals of 1922* was Gershwin's third score for a George White production and it was important in that it would give him his first opportunity to expand his musical horizons in the unlikely setting of a musical comedy revue.

His lyricist for the *Scandals of 1922* was B. G. DeSylva. They had collaborated before on Gershwin's first full-scale musical, *La-La-Lucille!* DeSylva was aware of Gershwin's higher musical aspirations when he suggested some weeks before the *Scandals* was scheduled to begin its tryout tour that they concoct a short opera with a Harlem setting. With the "Harlem Renaissance" then in full bloom—African sculpture, poetry and novels, its uninhibited jazz and dances, it was a natural. One of the most successful musicals of the season before had been the unheralded, underfinanced, all-black *Shuffle Along.* Why not inject a little culture into the *Scandals,* DeSylva reasoned, while exploiting the popular image of the New Negro? Their jazz opera would give the young composer Gershwin the chance to extend himself beyond the thirty-two-bar song. Gershwin had already notated several piano "novelettes"; his student harmony study, a *Lullaby* for string quartet, was performed privately by his string-playing friends. The idea of a miniature opera appealed to him.

Initially White liked the idea also, certain that his audiences would be intrigued by the Harlem setting. It was the place to go; from the intelligentsia to the middle class it represented "a refuge from the dullness, the orderliness, the narrowness of middle-class life," observed historian Geoffrey Perrett. "And it was so convenient—only a taxi ride for most New Yorkers. There, whatever was forbidden elsewhere was easy to find —marijuana, cocaine, sex. When the sun went down Harlem was integrated."

So why not bring Harlem to Times Square?

But then White had second thoughts. In a fast-paced revue, the timing and flow would be interrupted for a long stretch (nearly a half hour) of quasi-opera. He was concerned about how "operatic songs" would fit in with some of the already finished revue numbers, "Oh, What She Hangs Out," "Where Is the Man of My Dreams?" and "I'll Build a Stairway to Paradise." And then there was the problem of makeup, since the *Scandals* cast was all white; how to remove blackface in time for the next number? White told DeSylva and Gershwin to shelve the idea.

"However," Gershwin recalled, "about two or three weeks before the show opened, he came to us and said he would like to try it anyway. So DeSylva sat down with his pencil and I dug down and found a couple of suitable tunes and we began writing.

"After five days and nights we finished this one act vaudeville opera. It was rehearsed and staged and was thought of highly by those in connection with the show, which included Paul Whiteman and his orchestra.

"I can trace my indigestion back to that opening night in New

Haven. My nervousness was mainly due to *Blue Monday.*" (This condition, virtually a Gershwin preoccupation, he called "composer's stomach" and his friends hypochondria.)

"The show opened," he continued, "and the opera went very well—its only drawback for the show being its tragic ending. I remember one newspaper critic said the following day, in a state of enthusiasm, 'This opera will be imitated in a hundred years.'

"*Blue Monday* was kept in the show and played one performance in New York, the opening night of the show at the Globe Theater. Mr. White took it out after that, because he said the audience was too depressed by the tragic ending to get into the mood for the lighter stuff that followed." (It was reported that vaudeville star Nora Bayes was moved to tears by *Blue Monday.)*

If audience depression had not induced White to eject the little opera on opening night, one of the morning's reviews would have given him cause. One critic called it "the most dismal, stupid and incredible blackface sketch that has ever been perpertrated."

Blue Monday was, however, Gershwin's first public offering of what could be called a "serious" work. Although he left the orchestration to Will Vodery, he employed operatic devices to unify the nearly twenty-five-minute piece; the underscoring kept the plot moving with instrumental passages blending into songs.

It opens with an orchestral prelude (Gershwin's marking in the score; on the first page he also wrote "Libretto by B. G. DeSylva"). A recitativelike Prologue follows, informing the audience that it is about to experience a "colored tragedy enacted in operatic style . . ." its theme touching upon "love, hate, passion, jealousy" and "a woman's intuition gone wrong." The set reveals the interior of Mike's Saloon on 135th Street; a musical bridge from the Prologue introduces Sam, the saloon's man-of-all-work. He begins preparing for the opening of the bar with a song, "Blue Monday Blues," which is good if not great Gershwin. Other characters are introduced with appropriate underscoring and *recitativo:* Mike, the owner, Cokey, the pianist, Tom, the ill-tempered villain, Vi, the tragic heroine and Joe, the gambler-hero.

For a work turned out in five days, *Blue Monday,* despite crudities, holds together remarkably well, balancing set pieces (three songs), sung dialogue and orchestral passages—one extended dance sequence is very good, indeed. It made an impression on Paul Whiteman, whose orchestra supplied the music for the opera.

Vi's "aria" "Has One of You Seen Joe?" is first heard in an instrumental introduction of the second scene and then sung by her. Gershwin borrowed the melody from his *Lullaby* in which it served as the main theme as a harmony study for string quartet.

Joe's big closing "aria" is the mawkish "I'm Going to See My Mother." Having cleaned up in a game, he has decided to spend some of his winnings in a trip South to visit his mother and is waiting for a telegram of welcome home after years of absence (and, as it eventuates, no other communication). This song is the weakest in the score, an unabashed "mammy song"; while it may not be "stupid," it is without doubt "dismal," words and music.

Tom, who has designs on Vi, informs her that the telegram that Joe has received "is from a woman!" She wants to see it, but Joe, apparently not wishing to be known as a mammy's boy, refuses. Vi draws the gun he has given her to protect herself from Tom. She shoots Joe, then reads the telegram: "No need to come now, Joe. Mother has been dead three years. Sis."

At this moment, Vi's grief-stricken cry suggests the dramatic writing the Gershwin would fully achieve in another dozen years. "Oh, forgive me!" she exclaims in a soaring lament. She is forgiven and Joe, dying, sings his mammy song. And on this lugubrious note, and in traditional operatic style, the curtain rang down on *Blue Monday*.

Gershwin's music has been better received than DeSylva's "libretto" and lyrics from the beginning (and the revivals since the mid-1950s). By the common attitudes of the time, *Blue Monday*'s stereotypical racism was no worse than the standard treatment of the Negro by white writers. The plot, "freeze-dried Pagliacci," in the phrase of musicologist Wayne Shirley, is cliché-ridden and melodramatic in the extreme. (Was DeSylva parodying the traditional death scene in many operas?) The opera offered no profound statement on life in Harlem or black music; it was designed as entertainment with somewhat serious overtones, a rarity on the musical (or any) stage at the time.

Serious interest in Negroes during the early twenties centered primarily on literary contributions, the works of James Weldon Johnson, Langston Hughes, Claude McKay and Jean Toomer, whose fine but little-known novel *Cane* dates from this period. DeSylva's libretto hardly ranks with their works, and though Gershwin labeled "I'm Going to See My Mother" a spiritual, it hardly qualifies. The jazzier touches in the instrumental sections could have been Will Vodery's; this black veteran composer-arranger had been a friend of Gershwin's since his piano-pounding period in Tin Pan Alley.

When Gershwin's first biographer, Isaac Goldberg, expressed an interest in *Blue Monday*, the composer was rather dismissive. By 1931, when Goldberg had begun work on his biography, Gershwin had come a long way musically from his pseudo-opera. He recalled the titles of the songs but informed Goldberg that the manuscript "disappeared years ago. Where—and how—I do not know. [It has since been found.] The only thing I have left is the orchestration . . . But I am sure this would be of no use to you." When Whiteman later revived *Blue Monday* as *135th Street* with a new orchestration by Ferde Grofé, Gershwin viewed it with objective perspective as a "laboratory work in American music." One reviewer even hailed it as "the first real American opera" despite its "crudities." He found in it "the first gleam of a new musical art."

VI

While hardly either, *Blue Monday* is Gershwin's first step in the direction of what would become the first real American opera and although it made little impression on the *Scandals* first-nighters, it impressed Paul Whiteman. Like Gershwin, he was a man driven by ambition; he also had an uncanny eye and ear for the main chance. The fact that he and his band appeared in the 1922 *Scandals* indicated that his star was ascending.

Whiteman had come out of the West in 1920. After a brief tour of duty in the U.S. Navy during World War I, Whiteman, a trained violinist and violist (with the Denver Symphony, and the San Francisco Symphony), decided in 1919 there was a future in popular music. He began to build a reputation with a dance band playing the hotel circuit on the West Coast. When he shifted operations to the East he brought three of the original members of the band with him: Henry Busse (trumpet), Mike Pingatore (banjo) and Ferde Grofé.

That band played at the Hotel Ambassador in Atlantic City and consisted of nine men, which included Whiteman now and then on violin; by August 1920 they had begun making their first recordings, which served to propagate the band's renown.

The Whiteman band's treatment of popular songs was unaccountably mislabeled jazz by layman and musician alike. Grofé's arrangements afforded the star soloists spots for jazzlike turns—Busse and his muted or growling trumpet, Ross Gorman and his tricky clarinet work—but the real jazzmen of the period, barely known, were generally black and their original improvisations and instrumental tricks were appropriated by such popular white bands as Whiteman's. His recordings became extremely popular beginning with the early Victor Records sessions in 1920, when "Whispering" and "Japanese Sandman" were recorded. A year later, August 1921, the band cut its first Gershwin side, "South Sea Isles" with "She's Just a Baby" worked into the arrangement; both were from that year's *George White's Scandals.*

The next year, Whiteman's band having achieved a profitable following, White contracted the band for the *Scandals of 1922.* It marked the first professional meeting of Whiteman and the show's twenty-three-year-old composer.

VII

By 1923 "Swanee" had become a great hit in Britain and on the Continent, which led to an invitation to London for Gershwin and the opportunity to score a complete show to be entitled *Silver Lining.* Nineteen twenty-two closed with his summer *Scandals* (with its popular "I'll Build a Stairway to Paradise" and unpopular *Blue Monday),* followed by *Our Nell,* with a joint score by William Daly and George Gershwin. That show opened early in December and lingered for a mere five weeks. Archly subtitled "a musical mellowdrayma" and presented by Hayseed Productions, *Our Nell* was an unsuccessful attempt at burlesque (the simple country boy saves the farmer's daughter from a city slicker). The co-author of the book and lyricist was an ex-college instructor (Columbia, Yale), author and literary editor of the New York *Sun,* Brian Hooker. Gershwin and Daly produced one outstanding song, to a good lyric by Hooker, "Innocent Ingenue Baby"; both names appear in the sheet music, but the song has a distinct Gershwin quality in the vein of "Do It Again." The refrain of "Innocent Ingenue Baby," marked "delicately," is characterized by gentle rhythmic lilt. In this melody, Gershwin—and perhaps Daly—created a kind of Broadway art song with a Gallic accent. He took it with him when he boarded ship for London to work on *Silver Lining.*

The projected title seemed apposite when he arrived and was greeted by the customs officer at Southampton, who glanced at his passport and inquired, "George Gershwin, writer of 'Swanee'?"

This gave him momentary pause, which he admitted had made him "very joyful & for the moment very happy I came here . . . Of course I agreed I was the composer." The officer was more interested in Gershwin's plans for his London stay then in his landing card and passport. [One] "couldn't ask for a more pleasant entrance into a country." (It was Gershwin's first trip abroad.)

Glowing, he went ashore and was met by a local reporter asking "for a few words. I felt I was Kern or somebody." And later, after he had

settled in his London hotel a reporter from the *Weekly Dispatch* called
to ask for an interview. "Swanee" had paved the way. In his view, the
English, even cab drivers, were most polite.

Four days after he arrived rehearsals for *Silver Lining* were scheduled
to begin. He met his lyricist, Clifford Grey (1887–1941), a prolific writer
then best known in Britain and for his successful collaboration with
Kern on the songs for *Sunny*. Grey's other American collaborators
would include Sigmund Romberg, Vincent Youmans, Rudolf Friml and
Oscar Levant.

Unlike the *Scandals,* whose scores usually consumed a month of hectic preparation, *Silver Lining* allotted even less. It was, like the *Scandals,* a revue, with the book and sketches the work of producer Albert
de Courville, Noel Scott and Edgar Wallace, the latter correspondent-
turned-novelist and sometime playwright. The final title of their efforts,
which opened in London on April 3, 1923, was *The Rainbow*. Although
he had not expected to be precipitated so quickly into the scoring of *The
Rainbow,* Gershwin was capable of working speedily. As a precaution
he had brought along some possible interpolations, among them "Come
to the Moon" (revised from Paley's lyric into "All Over Town" by
Grey), "Yankee Doodle Blues" (a song he and Irving Caesar had written the year before and which Gershwin had set down in his Tune Book
as "American Blues" in October of 1921). Another song was the hit of
Our Nell, which Grey translated for the English audience into "Innocent Lonesome Blue Baby." Of the three, only the last remained in the
show. In about two weeks Gershwin, probably with the aid of a Tune
Book, tossed off a dozen songs, three of which—the ballad "Sweetheart," the production number "Sunday in London Town" and the
infectious, gently rhythmic "Moonlight in Versailles"—are, if not great,
still not bad Gershwin. Gershwin biographers, following in the trail of
Isaac Goldberg, tend to dismiss the *Rainbow* songs as "insignificant"
(Goldberg's word), intimating that it closed "shortly after opening" (in
truth it ran for more than a hundred performances).

An incident at the premiere undoubtedly colored extra-musically the
appraisals of Gershwin's *Rainbow* score. It gained *The Rainbow* fuller
coverage on the front pages than the amusement pages of the London
papers. A disgruntled comedian, whose part had been chipped away
during rehearsals, stepped out of character on opening night to address
an innocent audience on the subject of detrimental effect Americans had
upon the English stage. In mid-diatribe, he was hustled offstage. This
may have been the show's best performance, but it is unlikely that the
now forgotten comic stayed for the remaining 112 performances.

The Rainbow having been excitingly, if discordantly, launched, Gershwin remained in London briefly before flying to Paris with De-Sylva and Jules Glaenzer (who had an apartment on rue Malakoff). It was Gershwin's first visit to Paris and Glaenzer served as their guide and host for a farewell party on April 27 before they sailed for the States to begin work on the next *Scandals*. Glaenzer became the source of anecdotes in later years which he shared with Gershwin biographers: how Gershwin became airsick on the plane over the English Channel, and his performance in a well-known bordello in which Glaenzer and DeSylva observed Gershwin through peepholes provided by the house. This oft-told tale is the main basis for the legend of George Gershwin as a frequenter of brothels. Glaenzer also took credit for tutoring Gershwin on how to act in company (e.g., to remove the cigar from his mouth when being introduced to someone) and how to dress (an unlikely story, for when they met, about 1921, Gershwin was already a natty dresser, as the many photographs testify). When he was interviewed in 1957 for an earlier Gershwin biography, Glaenzer revealed a remarkable ignorance of Gershwin's compositions, especially the concert works. Gershwin was merely one of the many bright talents who entertained Glaenzer's friends and clients (he once informed the young Morton Gould that he had managed to sell an expensive piece of jewelry as Gould played some of his latest piano pieces).

On April 28, Gershwin, unaware of having diverted his friends that evening in Paris, set off for home where he and DeSylva spent the month of May on their *Scandals* chores. After its June opening, they prepared "I Won't Say I Will" especially for Irene Bordoni for her *Little Miss Bluebeard,* advertised as a "Gay New Song-Play." The still elusive Arthur Francis collaborated with DeSylva on the song. Gershwin about this time reunited with Irving Caesar to write a characteristic rhythm number, "Nashville Nightingale," which was interpolated into a nondescript revue, *Nifties of 1923.*

VIII

That year came to an exciting close for Gershwin. At the same time, Paul Whiteman had enjoyed great success in England. Whiteman, like Gershwin, was ambitious. His British triumphs sparked his aspirations and by the time he left London he had formulated a grand design: "Visions of playing a jazz concert in what a critic has called the 'perfumed purlieus' of Aeolian Hall." As the new year approached the ambitions and careers of George Gershwin and Paul Whiteman were converging. Actually, however, Gershwin got to the hall before Whiteman.

His sponsor in this venture with mezzo-soprano Eva Gauthier was critic-novelist and champion of popular American music Carl Van Vechten (1880–1964). Van Vechten had come East out of Cedar Rapids, Iowa, a devotee of music, the theater and the arts in general (later in his long life he took up photography). After graduating from the University of Chicago, Van Vechten worked as a reporter for the Chicago *American*. In 1906 he joined the staff of the New York *Times* as an assistant to the music critic, Richard Aldrich; in time he became "America's first dance critic."

Van Vechten's enthusiasms embraced the great and not so great singers, dancers, writers and musicians of the pre-twenties New York. He was among the first in the country to write about such moderns as Stravinsky, Leo Ornstein and Erik Satie and about such subjects as film music and ragtime as an art form—all before 1920. He abandoned criticism to write novels (among them the epochal *Nigger Heaven* of 1926) and to contribute to such publications as *The Bookman, Smart Set* and *Vanity Fair*. In the latter, as early as 1917, in an article entitled "The Great American Composer," he maintained that great American art music could be based on popular song; his particular hero of the moment was Irving Berlin.

Van Vechten recalled meeting the very young Gershwin at a party some time in 1919 when the composer played the not yet known, or performed, "Swanee." He considered Gershwin's "I'll Build a Stairway to Paradise" the "most perfect piece of jazz yet written." Van Vechten, in the March 1925 issue of *Vanity Fair*, published the first article devoted to Gershwin in a major magazine. In it he recounted the story of Gershwin's Aeolian Hall debut.

"In the spring of 1923," he wrote, "Eva Gauthier, indefatigable in her search for novelties, asked me to suggest additions to her autumn program.

" 'Why not a group of American songs?' I urged.

"Her face betrayed her lack of interest.

" 'Jazz,' I particularized.

"Her expression brightened. Meeting this singer again in September, on her return from Paris, she informed me that Maurice Ravel had offered her the same sapient advice. She had, indeed, determined to adopt the idea and requested me to recommend a musician who might serve as her accompanist and guide in this venture. But one name fell from my lips, that of George Gershwin, whose compositions I admired and with whose skill as a pianist I was acquainted."

Canadian-born Gauthier (1885–1958) had trained in Ottowa, Paris, London and Berlin; she made her debut as Micaela in *Carmen* in Pavia, Italy, in 1919. A year later she appeared in the London premiere of *Pélleas et Mélisande,* after which she spent five years in the Far East studying the indigenous music of Java and Malaya. This led to her interest in contemporary Western music with oriental overtones, and when she returned, settling in New York, she began a career as a recitalist and attracted attention as a singer of provocative, unusual song programs. In her November 1917 Aeolian Hall recital, for example, she presented the American premiere of Ravel's *Trois Chansons* as well as Stravinsky's *Trois Poésies de la Lyrique Japonaise* and Charles Tomlinson Griffes's *Five Poems of Ancient China and Japan* with the composer at the piano.

For her November 1923 program she promised a "Recital of Ancient and Modern Music for Voice." The ancients included Bellini, Perucchini and Purcell; the moderns, Bartók, Hindemith, Schoenberg, Bliss, Milhaud, Delage, Hennessy—and Jerome Kern, Irving Berlin, Walter Donaldson and George Gershwin. Her accompanist for the standard concert fare was Max Jaffe. As Van Vechten had suggested, Gershwin accompanied her in the American song group programmed between two Hindemith songs and Schoenberg's "Song of the Wood Dove" from *Gurrelieder* in a piano-vocal arrangement by Alban Berg. Ancients and Moderns notwithstanding, Gauthier's group of American popular songs dominated the next morning's reviews.

Van Vechten later suggested that "speaking historically . . . this was the first time in America that a singer had included modern jazz numbers in a serious recital program." That was probably true but the concept dated back some years to 1917. Writer-critic Hiram K. Moderwell proposed in the July issue of *The Seven Arts* that a program of what he called "ragtime" be given in Aeolian Hall and suggested several titles by such songwriters as Bob Cole and James Weldon Johnson, Irving Berlin and Jerome Kern, among others, as well as the traditional "Little David, Play on Your Harp."

Moderwell's ragtime rhapsodizing was as prescient as his hypothetical program. He found something "Nietzschean in ragtime's implicit philosophy that all the world's a dance. I love the delicacy of its inner rhythms and the largeness of its rhythmic sweeps. I like to think that it is *the perfect expression of the American city* [emphasis added], with its restless bustle and motion, its multitude of unrelated details, and its underlying rhythmic progress toward a vague Somewhere. Its technical resourcefulness continually surprises me, and its melodies, at their best, delight me . . ."

He was savaged for his enthusiasms by "serious" composer Daniel Gregory Mason of Columbia University in *The New Music Review.* Mason loathed popular music and jazz and approved only of music of an "Anglo-Saxon" cast. He decried the New York musical scene, dominated as it was, in his view, "by Jewish tastes and standards, with their Oriental extravagance, their sensuous brilliance and intellectual facility and superficiality . . ." (He was particularly incensed over the work of Ernest Bloch and by jazz) and fervently longed for "Anglo-Saxon sobriety and restraint" and in 1920 warned the nation of the "insidiousness of the Jewish menace to our artistic integrity."

Eva Gauthier, when she led a young George Gershwin onto the stage in Aeolian Hall on November 1, 1923, was about to inflict considerable anguish on the likes of the conservative-reactionary Daniel Gregory Mason.

But not on Deems Taylor, who covered the recital for the New York *World.* Having sung a group of "Modern Hungarian and German Songs," Gauthier and Jaffe left the stage to generous applause. She "reappeared," as Taylor described the scene, "followed by a tall, black-haired young man who was far from possessing the icy aplomb of those to whom playing on the platform of Aeolian Hall is an old story. He bore under his arm a small bundle of sheet music with lurid black and yellow covers. The audience began to show signs of relaxation; this promised to be amusing . . ."

Gauthier's recital was divided into six sections: "Ancient," "Modern Hungarian and German," "American," "British" and "French." With Gershwin at the piano in a tuxedo, she faced the audience in a floor-length evening gown, her large diamond earrings sparkling in the spotlight. She had reversed her gown (with décolleté in the back); only her face and neck were visible against the dark backdrop. When she left the platform a generous portion of her back was revealed. She began the American portion of the program with Berlin's "Alexander's Ragtime Band."

"The audience," Taylor reported, "was as much fun to watch as the songs were to hear, for it began by being slightly patronizing and ended by surrendering completely to the alluring rhythms of our own folk music . . ."

Gershwin's sure, inventive, crisp pianistics riveted immediate attention from the audience, which Taylor described as "not average, for

Miss Gauthier makes little appeal to the listener who lacks sophistication and artistic curiosity. It was what might be called a 'brilliant' house, made up for the most part, of people who not only cared for music, but who knew something about it, with a fair sprinkling of poseurs, highbrows and intensely class-conscious cognoscenti."

The newspaper and magazine critics invariably referred to the popular songs as "jazz songs" and one pointed out that Gershwin "diversified them with cross-rhythms; wove them into a pliant and outstanding counterpoint; set in pauses; sustained cadences; gave character to the measures wherein the singer's voice was still . . . In America," he proclaimed, Gershwin had inaugurated "the age of sophisticated jazz."

Having captivated the audience with Berlin, Gauthier and Gershwin swung into Kern's seductive "The Siren's Song" (lyric by P. G. Wodehouse), followed by Walter Donaldson's "Carolina in the Morning" (lyric by Gus Kahn). A Gershwin group came next, beginning with the popular "I'll Build a Stairway to Paradise" (lyric by DeSylva and Ira Gershwin writing under the pseudonym "Arthur Francis"). Next came the graceful, delicately rhythmic "Innocent Ingenue Baby" (written in collaboration with his friend William Daly; lyric by Brian Hooker), followed by his great song hit of a couple of seasons before, the rousing "Swanee" (Irving Caesar).

The audience, Deems Taylor wrote, "behaved like any . . . at any musical show—which is to say that it made so much noise after the group was over that Miss Gauthier had to come back to sing Mr. Gershwin's incomparable 'Do It Again.' Even then her hearers were not satisfied, and she had to do it again."

The closing sections of the recital were rather anticlimactic; it was obvious that it had been the "six jazz numbers" (Taylor again) that had stolen the show. In the celebration after the concert at the home of socialite music lover Mary Ellis Opdycke (who had provided the program translations for the Bartók and Hindemith songs), Gershwin, elated over his successful debut in Aeolian Hall, entertained with further excursions into musical Americana.

Gershwin had little time to reflect on the significance of his debut in one of the city's prestigious concert halls. He had taken a little time away from collaborating with Buddy DeSylva on the score for a musical, *The Perfect Lady,* set to begin its tryout in Boston on December 20. Gauthier had already booked them to repeat their recital in the same city late in January 1924. In February the Gershwin-Whiteman convergence would occur in an event that would set New York on its ear.

4

"Experiment in Modern Music"

A moderately successful songwriter-pianist, at the age of twenty-five, suddenly—or so it seemed—materialized as *the* sensational composer George Gershwin early in 1924.

Overnight, from a composer of a handful of popular songs and a half-dozen musical-comedy scores, he was transmuted into a "serious" composer. He was taken seriously by the musical press, he was discussed at parties, he was interviewed, argued over; he was famous.

No one, certainly no one in his family (with the exception of his older brother, Ira), his friends or his colleagues in Tin Pan Alley and Broadway had expected the triumph, the frenzied reception by an extraordinarily heterogeneous audience and the exciting aftermath of Paul Whiteman's "An Experiment in Modern Music" the afternoon of Tuesday, February 12, 1924.

In a stuffy, overflowing Aeolian Hall there were a few musical friends who were not taken unawares: critic-writer-advocate Carl Van Vechten, Jascha Heifetz, who admired Gershwin's pianistics, composer Victor Herbert, some close friends: Emily and Lou Paley (a teacher who occasionally provided Gershwin with song lyrics), Mabel Pleshette. To these few, and some others, Gershwin's stunning debut that long afternoon was neither abrupt nor unanticipated but inevitable.

Whiteman's "Experiment," according to program annotator (and incidentally the band leader's manager), Hugh C. Ernst, was "purely educational." Whiteman's design was large, if not grandiose: "I intend," he stated, "to sketch, musically, from the beginning of American history, the development of our emotional resources which have led us to the characteristic American music of today . . ." As the self-proclaimed "King of Jazz" Whiteman applied the term warily but loosely. He was not referring to jazz at all. He was obviously ignorant of its history (but then, so was virtually everyone else) and the real thing had, indeed, come from somewhere. The band leader referred to popular song and dance music and the manner in which it was performed by his virtuoso orchestra, its unique instrumental makeup, and the skillfully scored arrangements he employed, particularly those by his pianist, Ferde Grofé.

The "Experiment" was in fact a promotional event to further Whiteman's fortunes, then at a monetary peak.

As soon as the *Scandals of 1922* closed, Whiteman, his new wife and the band boarded the *President Harding* for London and appearances in *Brighter London* at the Hippodrome. As in New York, the newly crowned King was controversial—and successful; he was more than merely impressed by genuine royalty that came to hear the band, especially by "His Royal Highness" (as Whiteman invariably called him), the youthful Edward, Prince of Wales—who proved to be a fine dancer as well as a good drummer who occasionally sat in with the band.

Despite phenomenal success and popularity, Whiteman burned to be more than the leader of a dance band. He appreciated the value of publicity. While in London, he had begun thinking about something truly grand that he might do. He reasoned that many American-born musicians had gone abroad to study and returned, often with a new name of Italian or German derivation, to be applauded and appreciated by a gullible public. "I figured that my orchestra would probably get more serious consideration for what was in the back of my head to do, if we obtained a little of the foreign stamp for ourselves." Thus the hobnobbing with the Prince of Wales, Lord Mountbatten and others "related to the throne."

So it was that when Whiteman and band returned to New York (they were booked to appear in the 1923 *Ziegfeld Follies,* a step up from the racier but less opulent *Scandals),* his publicity mill had begun to grind. The ship was met by a representative of the mayor, the Police Department and several bands. "They serenaded us from the air, from the water and from land." (There is photographic proof.) Five immersed musicians, one a drummer, floated in the bay with their water music. A sign read: "Welcome Home/Paul Whiteman/United Orchestras/Submarine Unit."

In the back of his head Whiteman had an idea that would confirm his regnancy: the Paul Whiteman Orchestra would present a full concert of jazz in one of New York's great music centers, preferably Carnegie Hall, mecca of all aspiring serious musicians. It made sense. "New York is a queer city," he reasoned. "I have a theory that novelty, not luck or ability, is what gets by there. New York doesn't care about merit so much as it does about something new to tickle its eyes, its palate or its ears . . . The bizarre and the unusual get not only the headlines, but the homage and shekels."

His plan was so unique, so adventurous, vendible, Whiteman believed, that he could harvest all three of these desiderata. In his zeal to become a musical harbinger, Whiteman conveniently overlooked jazzman James Reese Europe, who had appeared with his Clef Club Symphony Orchestra in Carnegie Hall on May 2, 1912 and had "astounded the white critics and public who had not yet become acquainted with the sound of syncopated music or 'jazz.'"

The concert "brought a very storm of tumultous applause," Natalie Curtis reported in *The Craftsman,* a Harlem periodical, and that "the musical editors of the New York papers had come in order to give this entertainment serious consideration." And serious, expansive, consideration by the New York press was what Whiteman had utmost in mind. Believing himself to be in the vanguard, he set his plan in motion. He was probably unaware of Europe's concerts (another took place in March 1914), so he overlooked them, but he soon made many aware of his. Whiteman's garrulity, coupled with a passion for ballyhoo, brought George Gershwin into the enterprise. This fortuitous convergent reunion established both of them.

Following the *Blue Monday* disappointment, Whiteman had spoken to Gershwin about their getting together again on a "serious" work in a similarly jazzy vein. Gershwin was interested, but it was only talk with no specific plan as to time, the kind of work or place. It slipped from his mind.

But once back in New York Whiteman talked about it again. He and the band were busy in the *Follies* and in after-the-show performances at a popular Times Square nightclub, the Palais Royal. "Well, we mulled over it," Whiteman recalled later. "And, as young fellows will, I guess I talked too much about it. Another leader got word of it, and reports came that he was going to do the thing we had been talking about.

"I certainly didn't want to see a brainchild of mine ruined, so I called

Aeolian Hall and made arrangements for a concert there within twenty-four days."

The other leader was Vincent Lopez, also a pianist best remembered for an elaborate rendition of the song "Nola," a newspaper astrology column, and for his broadcasts from the Hotel Taft's Grill Room, where his was the band in residence for almost three decades. Lopez too was talking about a "symphonic jazz" orchestra that had been organized to demonstrate jazz as part of a series of Sunday afternoon lectures at the Anderson Art Galleries at Fifty-ninth Street and Park Avenue. It was not precisely in a concert hall, but Lopez beat Whiteman to the concert by two days. The lecture-concert took place on February 10, 1924; the speaker was Edward Burlingame Hill, an eminent composer and teacher (Harvard), who outlined the history of jazz. Lopez and band were on hand to illustrate with "contemporaneous popular music." Clearly, he was invading Whiteman's realm.

Though the Lopez effort antedated Whiteman's, it made no impact. Hill, the *Times* reported, "spoke impressively of jazz," but his *Jazz Studies for Two Pianos* did not impress. Whatever advantage Lopez thought he would have gleaned from precedence was inundated in the blizzard of the Whiteman publicity campaign. (After Whiteman's success, Lopez tried again, this time at the Metropolitan Opera House and succeeded only in losing a thousand dollars; he even tried, during the twenties stock-market boom to incorporate and sell shares in his jazz orchestra. He found it safer after that at the Grill Room.)

Lopez, however, had galvanized the Whiteman forces. As Carnegie Hall was completely booked at that time, Whiteman had to settle for the less capacious Aeolian Hall, 1,300 as compared with Carnegie Hall's 2,800 seats. Lopez's haste had had its effect as well on Gershwin, who first learned about the concert plans in an esthetically unlikely setting of the Ambassador Billiard Parlor on Broadway at Fifty-second Street.

Having returned from Boston, where their show *A Perfect Lady* had opened late in December and was scheduled to premiere on Broadway —as *Sweet Little Devil*—Gershwin and DeSylva were relaxing at a game of pool. Ira Gershwin sat nearby reading the morning's New York *Tribune,* dated Friday, January 4, 1924. Nestled among radio listings, reviews and music columns was a brief item that caught his eye. Its head stated: "Whiteman Judges Named." Next, "Committee Will Decide 'What Is American Music.' " Whiteman's press agent, the indefatigable Stella Karns, had gone into action.

Ira read on, to learn that the concert was set for the afternoon of Lincoln's Birthday—about five weeks away; the committee consisted of a stellar group of musicians whose capabilities as arbiters of American music was questionable: Sergei Rachmaninoff, Jascha Heifetz, Efrem Zimbalist and Alma Gluck. Worthies all: a composer-pianist, two violinists (all three Russian-born and educated) and a Romanian-born, though American-educated operatic soprano (and the wife of Zimbalist). If any of these musical celebrities arrived at any definition of American Music as result of the concert, it has never surfaced.

The final paragraph of the short article surprised Ira:

> *George Gershwin is at work on a jazz concerto, Irving Berlin is writing a syncopated tone poem and Victor Herbert is working on an American suite.*

While George was not quite as surprised as his brother, since he and Whiteman had talked of his writing a special piece for the band, he had not expected to learn about it via the press. What with *Sweet Little Devil* in its final rehearsals, with all the attendant changes to be completed before the opening, plus the impending Gauthier recital in Boston, he would have little time to contrive a "concerto" in time for the concert. Early the next morning, Gershwin called Whiteman to find out what his "experiment" was all about and to explain the impossibility of his participation in the enterprise (only Victor Herbert complied without argument; Berlin produced no syncopated tone poem and Whiteman filled in with a Grofé-arranged Berlin medley).

Whiteman was persuasive, however; after some discussion Gershwin agreed to attempt a piece for piano and orchestra—not a strictly formed concerto, however, but a freer fantasia or rhapsody.

Carried along by Whiteman's enthusiasm and encouragement, Gershwin, in his free moments from the show, pored through his "Tune Books" for some suitable ideas and on Monday, January 7, began writing his *Rhapsody in Blue/For Jazz Band and Piano.* He abandoned his original title, *American Rhapsody,* at Ira Gershwin's suggestion. Ira had spent an afternoon at a gallery studying the paintings of James McNeill Whistler and, influenced by Whistler's descriptive titles—*Nocturne in Black and Gold, Arrangement in Gray and Black* (better known as "Whistler's Mother"), etc.—why not a musical *Rhapsody in Blue?*

The precise chronology of the *Rhapsody*'s writing is somewhat misty, clouded as it is in anecdotal mythology following in the wake of its sensational premiere. Gershwin was uncertain himself; in an article entitled "Jazz is the Voice of the American Soul," he stated, "I wrote it in ten days" *(Theatre Magazine,* June 1926). Later he told Goldberg, "I don't believe that the rhapsody took more than three weeks to write, off and on."

The later (1931) statement is undoubtedly the most accurate; suffice to say the composition was turned out in a remarkably short time. Even as he worked "off and on" Gershwin was on call for any further work on *Sweet Little Devil* and Gauthier requested some polishing up time for their portion of the approaching Boston recital.

II

Sometime between January 7 and early February (in time for rehearsals with the band) Gershwin composed his rhapsody. Most of this was done in the family apartment at 501 West 110th Street, where one room was set aside as his workroom. Since the work was designed specifically for the Whiteman orchestra, and time was short, Ferde Grofé was assigned to orchestrate it. As Grofé recalled: Gershwin "lived with his parents and brothers and sister, all of them children, except Ira, and I practically lived too in their . . . apartment, for I called there daily for more pages of George's masterpiece, which he originally composed in two-piano form. He and his brother Ira had a back room where there was an upright piano, and that is where the *Rhapsody* grew into being."

Ira Gershwin remembered the *Rhapsody*'s genesis: "The newspaper item was the first inkling George had that Whiteman was serious when he once casually mentioned that someday he expected to do such a concert and hoped for a contribution from George. Finding in his notebooks a theme (the clarinet glissando) which he thought might make an appropriate opening for a more extended work than he had been accustomed to writing, he decided to chance it. Three weeks later, with an orchestration by Ferde Grofé, Whiteman was rehearsing *Rhapsody in Blue* in the nightclub Palais Royal."

Grofé's orchestration is dated February 4; it is possible that Gershwin had completed the two-piano version before leaving with Eva Gauthier for their Boston recital set for January 29. There again special critical attention was paid to the "jazz" songs and Gershwin's jaunty interpretations.

Upon his return he became involved with Whiteman's unique rehearsal/luncheons to which music critics and writers had been invited, among them Henry O. Osgood, who wrote for the monthly *Musical America* and other publications; Leonard Liebling of *The Musical Courier;* Pitts Sanborn of the New York *Globe;* two champions of the lively arts, Carl Van Vechten and Gilbert Seldes; conductor Willem Mengelberg and others.

Osgood, later writing in his book, *So This Is Jazz* (1926), reported on the rehearsals: "At the first . . . the score was not yet ready. At the second rehearsal Gershwin played the *Rhapsody* twice with the band on a very bad piano. Nevertheless, after hearing that second rehearsal, I never entertained a single doubt but this young man of twenty-five . . . had written the finest piece of serious music that had ever come out of America . . ."

Also present at the rehearsals was one of the giants of American operetta, Victor Herbert, who had turned sixty-five on February 1 and who composed a *Suite of Serenades* for the concert. One of his major works, *The Fortune Teller* out of which came "Gypsy Love Song," was written the year of Gershwin's birth, 1898. By 1924 Herbert had had a distinguished career as a conductor, composer of concert works as well as the scores for more than forty operettas and dozens of popular and distinguished songs.

Gershwin first met Herbert in the summer of 1917, when he had a job as rehearsal pianist for the Ziegfeld-Dillingham production *Miss 1917.* For Gershwin it was an exhilarating experience as a nineteen-year-old aspiring songwriter and pianist, because the bulk of the songs for the show were composed by one of his idols, Jerome Kern (with lyrics by P. G. Wodehouse, one of Ira Gershwin's idols). For that show Herbert composed some background music, including a "poem choreographic," *Falling Leaves.*

Evidently at that time Gershwin revealed his ambitions to Herbert, for the genial composer offered to teach Gershwin orchestration—without charge. [Herbert was no soft touch, though generous in many instances. When he dined at Shanley's Restaurant one day and found the band was performing his music for the entertainment of its customers although without compensation to him, he instituted a lawsuit, which he won, and as a result helped to found the American Society of Composers, Authors and Publishers (ASCAP) to protect the rights of songwriters.] For some unknown reason Gershwin never took advantage of Herbert's offer.

Whiteman and Herbert had worked closely on the production of the 1923 *Follies,* to which Herbert had contributed a couple of songs and instrumental background scoring, including a spectacular *Legends of the Drums.* It is unlikely that he had been as taken unawares as Gershwin had by the *Tribune* article. If Gershwin had worked rapidly, Herbert worked faster. He turned out his *Suite of Serenades: Cuban, Spanish, Oriental* and *Chinese* between the dates of January 14 and January 20. He undoubtedly orchestrated some miniature pieces he had had in his trunk.

Rehearsals were held mornings in the unprepossessing setting of the Palais Royal nightclub where the band performed after their *Follies* stint. Tables were pushed aside to make room for the enlarged orchestra for the Herbert and Gershwin pieces and the men took their places in the club's gilded chairs. The air was stale from the previous night's revels, which had ended at two; the band returned about noon for the rehearsal. "From outside," Osgood recalled, "through lurchy, half-drawn drapes, leaked a cold, pallid light from the uncomfortable February day."

At the rehearsal attended by Osgood and critics Liebling and Sanborn, Whiteman told them that they were about to hear a new work by a "young man" named Gershwin. Both turned to the obviously more knowledgeable Osgood and asked, "Who's Gershwin?"

He informed them that he was the composer of "several 'song hits' in current revues and musical comedies." As critics of serious music, they had little experience in the musical theater. Puzzled, they waited.

At the conclusion of the rhapsody, Liebling, like Osgood and Van Vechten, was "captivated . . . immediately," but Sanborn was doubtful. "I am not enamored of the themes or workmanship, said he; and then falling into what seemed the appropriate language of the moment, Sanborn blushed a bit and added: 'But the thing certainly has zip and punch.' "

Herbert, too, was present and helpful with suggestions and advice. Whiteman asked him to lead the orchestra in his *Suite,* but Herbert declined. He jokingly explained to an interviewer a few days before the concert why: "The saxophones, I can write for them, but I cannot conduct them. They make me nervous!"

At one hearing of the *Rhapsody in Blue* he made a suggestion that Gershwin gratefully incorporated into the composition. This appears in the published score at the letter F, a four-bar piano passage, *rubato e legato,* that bridges between a long, brilliant piano cadenza into the famous *Andantino moderato* melody. In its original form Gershwin repeated the first bar. Herbert suggested that instead of a simple repeat, he vary the passage, moving upward to the final *pianissimo* chord, played *arpeggio* and held *(fermata).* Gershwin realized that this longer introduction to the work's main theme was more effective than his original conception. Thus did Victor Herbert make a small, but musically cogent, contribution to the *Rhapsody in Blue.*

The preparations, anxieties, tensions and doubts (Whiteman later admitted to many a qualm) came to a climax on the blustery afternoon of February 12, 1924, at Aeolian Hall, 34 West Forty-third Street. Whiteman, according to his own account, slipped out of the hall to check on the box office. "There I gazed upon a picture that should have imparted new vigor to my wilting confidence. It was snowing, but men and women were fighting to get into the door, pulling and mauling each other as they do sometimes at a baseball game or a prize fight, or in the subway.

"Such was the state of my mind by this time that I wondered if I had come to the right entrance. And then I saw Victor Herbert going in. It was the right entrance, sure enough, and the next day the ticket office people said they could have sold out the house ten times over."

Press agent Karns had done her work well; not only had the Lopez jazz lecture-concert of the tenth been swamped in the flood of her promotional outpourings, it also piqued the curiosity of a wide variety of concertgoers. Although the house was full, it was not sold out, it was in fact well papered: tickets were furnished to such as Walter Damrosch, Leopold Godowsky, Fritz Kreisler, Leopold Stokowski, Sergei Rachmaninoff, among others from the world of instrumental music. From opera came Mary Garden, Jeanne Gordon, Frances Alda, Amelita Galli-Curci, Alma Gluck and others. From the world of letters there were, to name a few, Frank Crowninshield (editor of *Vanity Fair)*, popular columnists Heywood Broun, O. O. McIntyre and S. Jay Kaufman (of the *Evening Herald)*. For good measure there were representatives from commerce and industry: banker, opera-lover Otto Kahn (who would one day ask Gershwin for an opera) and professional host and a vice president of Cartier's, Jules Glaenzer.

Many men about the arts were present, some in the official capacity of critic; among these were Carl Van Vechten, Deems Taylor, Pitts Sanborn, Leonard Liebling, Gilbert Seldes, and Henry O. Osgood. Novelist Fannie Hurst attended and so did the eminent Swiss-born American composer Ernest Bloch. It was a glittering audience.

"There was a certain amount of hokum about this . . . concert," Osgood conceded later. In the introduction to the program, entitled "The Why of This Experiment," Hugh C. Ernst, explained, that "Mr. Whiteman intends to point out, with assistance of his orchestra and associates, the tremendous strides which have been made in popular music from the day of discordant Jazz, which sprang into existence about ten years ago from nowhere in particular, to the really melodious music of today, which—for no good reason—is still called Jazz." Ernst then submitted that the "greatest single factor in the improvement of American music has been the art of scoring." And that "Paul Whiteman's orchestra was the first organization to especially score each selection and to play it according to score." Purely "educational" perhaps, but capricious musical history.

The concert began with a demonstration of the "True Form of Jazz" in a performance of "the earliest [sic] jazz composition," "Livery Stable

Blues," which had been a sensational popular recording in 1917 when introduced by the Original Dixieland Jazz Band. This five-man (all white) unit had been organized by Nick LaRocca who, with his New Orleans background knew his jazz. But it "was introduced apologetically [by Whiteman] as an example of the depraved past from which modern jazz has risen," *Times* reviewer Olin Downes reported the next day. "The apology is herewith indignantly rejected, for this is a gorgeous piece of impudence, much better in its unbuttoned jocosity and Rabelaisian laughter than other and more polite compositions that came later." The audience, most of it at least, agreed with Downes.

His description of the Experiment's opening number illuminates Whiteman's flair for showmanship. "The pianist [probably Henry Lange] gathered about him some five fellow performers. The man with the clarinet [Ross Gorman] wore a battered top hat that had ostensibly seen better days. Sometimes he wore it, and sometimes he played into it. The man with the trombone [probably Roy Maxon] played it as is, but also, on occasion, picked up a bathtub or something of the kind from the floor and blew into that. The instruments made odd, unseemly bushman sounds. The instrumentalists rocked about. Jests permissible in musical terms but otherwise not printable were passed between these fiends of music. The laughter of that music and those fellows was tornadic."

The Concert was off to a good lively start. Gorman returned to further divert the audience with his clarinet antics in a Grofé arrangement, "So This is Venice," based on *The Carnival of Venice*. His reception was described by Osgood as "enthusiastic." But as the program continued a pervading monotony set in, the scorings emphasized a defeating sameness. Once Whiteman had dismissed Jazz "in its true, naked form" with "Livery Stable Blues," he proceeded to treat the audience to his by now familiar dance band catalog and discography (with a few exceptions).

The first half of the program closed with No. 7: "Semi-Symphonic Arrangement of Popular Melodies," a medley of three Irving Berlin songs. The second half opened with Herbert's *Suite of Serenades;* the unpretentious, innocuous little work was given a "hearty" reception according to Osgood. The next grouping, No. 9, dance treatments, à la Palais Royal, of Frederick K. Logan's *Pale Moon,* MacDowell's *To a Wild Rose* and Rudolf Friml's *Chansonette* (later popular as the song, "Donkey Serenade"), induced a return of creeping ennui. Only *To a Wild Rose,* Osgood noted, received "moderate" applause. Whiteman's experiment, by late afternoon, was slipping. The caperings of clarinetist Gorman were all but forgotten. The virtuosic highlight of the program's first half, Zez Confrey's humorous piano trickery, faded into the past.

Confrey's popular *Kitten on the Keys* was then regarded by the cognoscenti (who had never heard of James P. Johnson, Jelly Roll Morton or James Lamb) as the epitome of jazz piano.

Confrey's amusing *Nickel in the Slot* parody of a honky-tonk player piano had been received with "wild" applause. But as the second half of the concert drew to a close the novelty had worn away. By the time the final strains of *Chansonette* faded, the audience had begun to stray, some literally toward the exits.

"Then stepped upon the stage, sheepishly," Downes noted, "a lank and dark young man—George Gershwin."

Slender, lithe, nearly six feet tall, Gershwin was the physical opposite of the rotund Whiteman. Both were resplendent in their morning coats, gray trousers, gleaming starched shirts and gray spats. The composer's black hair, like Whiteman's, was combed straight back. Excitement had deepened the color of his cheeks; though swarthy, his cheeks, as friends remember him, were ruddy. His usual five o'clock shadow was gone.

Settled at the piano, Gershwin nodded to Whiteman, who pointed to Gorman, whose clarinet whoop began the *Rhapsody;* the effect was electrifying.

By the time Gorman's clarinet had stirred up the audience with the "outrageous cadenza," as Downes described it, Whiteman's Experiment was a decided success; the hall's deserters hurried back to their seats. Attention was riveted on the dark young man at the keyboard performing a most difficult, and unusually extended, piano part with confidential aplomb. Had they been able to glance into Whiteman's score they would have found several blank pages in that piano part; at the end of several blank bars was the notation (to Whiteman): "Wait for nod." The premiere audience heard a different *Rhapsody in Blue* from the one now so familiar. Gershwin contributed some improvisation and the clarinet cadenza was freely, even mockingly, played by Gorman not as in the printed score.

The major flaw, most critics agreed, was in the work's form. Obviously Gershwin had written a personal showpiece, one which Goldberg pointed out was "top-heavy" in the piano part. The division (or miniature movements) of the rhapsody are clear cut, if not classically proportioned. The opening *Molto moderato* (running to twenty-seven pages of the forty-one-page original two-piano score) introduces the major rhythmic themes of the piece. These are developed at length, giving the piano a good deal to do; the section closes with an elaborate piano cadenza leading into, after the "Victor Herbert" bars, the celebrated slow section, *Andantino moderato.* In the fourteen remaining pages, Gershwin developed the slow theme, trading off with the orchestra and brought the rhapsody to a conclusion with a lively Lisztian finale. Half of the score is devoted to the piano solo part; interest is sustained by Gershwin's handling of the themes (and the motifs themselves) and, of course, Grofé's colorful orchestration, particularly in the original (the first of three) "jazz band" version.

When the final chord marked *ffz* (*fortissimo sforzand* = very loud, accented) was sounded by all hands, it was followed by "tumultuous applause" (Olin Downes), while Osgood found the audience's response "wild and even frantic." The program closed, for no logical reason, with Elgar's *Pomp and Circumstance March*. But Whiteman had triumphed; "At half-past five on the afternoon of February 12, 1924," he crowed, "we took our fifth curtain call." The *Rhapsody in Blue* had done it.

The critics singled it out in their reviews of the concert, some even following their daily comments with subsequent remarks in the Sunday columns. The *Tribune's* Lawrence Gilman was the most negative, entreating his readers to "weep over the lifelessness of its melody and harmony, so derivitive, so stale, so inexpressive." He conceded that the work exhibited a "rich inventiveness of the rhythms" and, in a nod to Grofé, admired "the saliency and vividness of the orchestral color."

In agreement with other critics, composer Deems Taylor, in his Sunday article in the *World,* found that the rhapsody ". . . had all the faults one might expect from an experimental work—diffuseness, want of self-criticism and structural uncertainty; but it also revealed a genuine melodic gift and a piquant harmonic sense to lend significance to its rhythmic ingenuity . . . Mr. Gershwin will bear watching," he concluded.

His opinion pretty much summed up the critical consensus. In the *Sun,* Gilbert Gabriel also described the work as diffuse and felt that the "title of *Rhapsody* was a just one, suitable for covering a degree of formlessness to which the middle section of the work, relying too much on tort and retort of the piano itself, seemed to sag. But the beginning and ending of it were stunning; the beginning particularly, with a flutter-tongued, drunken whoop of an introduction which had the audience rocking . . . Mr. Gershwin has an irrepressible pack of talents . . ."

Pitts Sanborn, who had never heard of Gershwin before the Whiteman rehearsals, remained unconvinced, though he noted that the *Rhapsody* "was applauded stormily" but found that although it began "with a promising theme well stated, it soon runs off into empty passage-work and meaningless repetition." Veteran W. James Henderson, no friend of "modern" music, had found the rhapsody to be "a highly ingenious work, treating the piano in a manner calling for much technical skill

. . . If this way lies the path toward the upper development of American modern music into a high art form, then one can heartily congratulate Mr. Gershwin on his disclosure of some of the possibilities . . ."

In his Sunday column Henderson expatiated, advising Gershwin to "keep to the field in which he is a free and independent creator, and not permit himself to be led away into the academic groves and buried in the shadow of ancient trees." This would become a recurring theme throughout Gershwin's career. Henderson (who had once studied piano as well as voice), appears to be the one reviewer to comment on another aspect of the composer's gifts: "His piano playing," he wrote in his morning review immediately after the concert, "was not the least important feature of the work."

Whatever their criticisms of the *Rhapsody in Blue,* there was a general agreement among the reviewers that a promising, exciting voice— "fresh and new and full of promise," as Downes phrased it—in American music had been heard.

III

Whiteman's Experiment in Modern Music did not answer the question: "What Is American Music?" but it did shake up the metropolitan musical scene. It led to further explorations of contemporary American music although in general New York's concert fare remained as conservative as ever. Then as now the average concertgoer preferred the standard Three B's, with an occasional peppering of Richard Strauss. In avant-garde circles the names of Stravinsky, Schoenberg and Bartók were known, even if few of their works were.

As for the native-born American composer, probably only Edward MacDowell's name enjoyed some currency and for a time he was regarded as "America's greatest composer," but by the mid-twenties his name had begun to fade and his works were rarely heard. Hardly anyone had heard of Charles Ives, who had for years been spicing up his compositions with quotations from popular songs, folk songs, even ragtime. Charles Tomlinson Griffes, who had died young (in 1920), had created a fine but small body of works that was neglected after his death. Except for a slight brush with Americana in his string quartet incorporating Indian themes, Griffes was not self-consciously American. He drew upon oriental scales, impressionism; his fine *Piano Sonata* is abstract in the extreme.

Almost as famous as MacDowell the then still active Charles Wakefield Cadman (1881–1946) who enjoyed a wide popularity with such songs, purportedly based on the music of the Indian, as "At Dawning" and "From the Land of the Sky Blue Water."

The American composer was not well represented in American concert halls in 1924.

As for a "jazz" repertory (using the term imprecisely), there was a considerable one long before Whiteman elected to fill what he believed was a vacuum. Among the earliest composers to base his compositions on authentic American themes was Louis Moreau Gottschalk who, by mid-nineteenth century, was a celebrated pianist and composer whose works evoked Creole and Afro-American songs and dances. Henry F. Gilbert, in the next musical generation, dipped into similar sources for his *Negro Rhapsody,* dating from 1912; even more impressive is the Gottschalkian *The Dance in the Place Congo* which had been performed as a "symphonic poem" by the Boston Symphony four years before Whiteman's Experiment (it had been originally presented as a ballet at the Metropolitan Opera House in 1918). That same year an aristocratic Virginian, John Powell, composed his elegant *Rapsodie Nègre.* In Chicago John Alden Carpenter went jazzy with his ballet based on a popular comic strip, "Krazy Kat" (1921). He came closer with another ballet, *Skyscrapers,* five years later, but by then he had certainly heard Gershwin.

European composers were attracted to American popular songs, folk songs and jazz. Even Brahms, it was once reported, planned a ragtime composition. England's Frederick Delius, after a brief stay on a Florida orange plantation, adapted some of the slave songs he had heard into his compositions. Stravinsky, as early as 1918, had written his *Ragtime* for eleven instruments and the *Piano Rag Music* the following year. The Russian's abstract handling of the idiom would have undoubtedly mystified Scott Joplin.

After a visit to Harlem and a study of sheet music and dance band recordings, the French composer Darius Milhaud created the delightful score for a ballet, *La Création du Monde,* performed in Paris for the first time on October 25, 1923 (on the same program was Cole Porter's "jazz" ballet, *Within the Quota).*

Although Gershwin had been in Paris that year, he did not hear *La Création du Monde,* as has often been suggested—implying that it was the inspiration for the *Rhapsody in Blue.* He had been in Paris briefly in late April and returned to New York in time to work on the *Scandals,* which opened in June. He was not present at the Théâtre des Champs-Élysées in October. Despite the existence of these few "jazz"-inspired compositions, Gershwin was not familiar with them; with his rhapsody he had stepped into what appeared to be a musical vacuum.

His "serious" contemporaries, though active, so far as the American concert hall was concerned, functioned in that same void. Howard Hanson (b. 1896) had written a *Nordic Symphony* (1923). Virgil Thomson (b. 1896) was teaching and conducting the Harvard Glee Club. Henry Cowell (b. 1897) had gone to Europe to startle audiences with his "tone clusters" and other unorthodox musical devices—he was virtually unknown in the United States. Roy Harris (b. 1898) was a late starter and still a student. Randall Thompson (b. 1899) was a student at the American Academy. Aaron Copland (b. 1900) was in France, a student of Nadia Boulanger. He resettled in the United States in 1924, the year of the rhapsody.

Unwittingly, of course, Gershwin had crossed the tracks. He had taken popular music into the concert hall and had opened the doors of that hall to that still unsung rarity, the American composer. From that afternoon on, what with the controversy, the excitement and publicity, the American composer, though his lot was not and would not be an easy one, was heard, respected, commissioned and even performed. Gershwin helped to set that scene, not as a self-conscious crusader but as a vital original talent.

Some years later, in an interview, Gershwin told writer Hyman Sandow a little about his intentions. "In the *Rhapsody,*" he said, "I tried to express our manner of living, the tempo of our modern life with its speed and chaos and vitality. I didn't try to paint definite descriptive pictures in sound. Composers assimilate influences and suggestions from various sources and even borrow from one another's works. That's why I consider the *Rhapsody* as embodying an assimilation of feeling rather than presenting specific scenes of American life in music."

After the concert Whiteman shrewdly capitalized on its notoriety, repeating the concert in Aeolian Hall, with minor changes in the program, on March 7 and, finally Carnegie Hall on April 21 (and repeating in November). Then he toured, performing the same program, beginning in the Rochester, New York, Convention Hall on May 15, and moved on to Pittsburgh, Cleveland, Indianapolis and St. Louis. Gershwin left the tour after the St. Louis concert on May 21 (he was replaced by pianist Milton Rettenberg) to begin work on what would be his final score for George White. During the June rehearsals, after Whiteman had concluded his tour, Gershwin recorded the *Rhapsody in Blue* with the band—the same group that had performed it at Aeolian Hall. The recording, made before the development of the microphone, was done acoustically, i.e., via giant horns; its performance is superior to the later one, recorded electrically with a microphone in 1927, by which time

Whiteman's band personnel had changed. Only the 1924 recording features Ross Gorman's original not-as-actually-written clarinet cadenza.

As the reviewer in the *Nation* had observed, Gershwin (and Whiteman and Grofé) had "added a new chapter to our musical history." For Gershwin it was only the beginning. He had taken a giant step from "laboratory work in American music" to Whiteman's "Experiment."

5

1924

I

Nineteen twenty-four was an active Gershwin year, beginning with the composition of the *Rhapsody in Blue* and its subsequent exploitation. Whiteman literally got plenty of mileage out of it with additional performances in Aeolian and Carnegie halls, a cross-country tour, its premiere recording in June and closing the year with a Boston concert on December 4. Gershwin participated in most of these performances of the rhapsody (he left the tour in May to begin work on his final *Scandals* score).

A sketchy chronology of that year would be:

JANUARY 7	Begins work on the *Rhapsody in Blue*
JANUARY 21	*Sweet Little Devil* opens in New York.
JANUARY 29	In Boston with Eva Gauthier.
FEBRUARY 12	Plays the *Rhapsody,* Aeolian Hall.
MARCH 7	Aeolian Hall.
APRIL 21	Plays the *Rhapsody,* Carnegie Hall.
MAY	*Rhapsody in Blue* tour; begins in Rochester, New York, May 15; also Pittsburgh, Cleveland, Indianapolis; Gershwin leaves after the May 21, St. Louis performance.
JUNE 10	Records the *Rhapsody* with Whiteman's orchestra, New York.
JUNE 30	George White's *Scandals* opens in New York.
JULY 8	To London to work on new show.
SEPTEMBER 11	*Primrose* opens in London.

OCTOBER	Works on new show with Ira for Aarons and Freedley.
NOVEMBER 15	Plays *Rhapsody* with Whiteman, Carnegie Hall.
NOVEMBER 17	*Lady, Be Good!* opens in Philadelphia.
NOVEMBER 27	Performs the *Rhapsody* with Whiteman, Academy of Music, Philadelphia.
DECEMBER 1	*Lady, Be Good!* opens in New York.
DECEMBER 4	Performs *Rhapsody* with Whiteman, Symphony Hall, Boston.

These are the definite recorded dates; the gaps are understandable. Gershwin's own record only consists of his quasi-diary, that year's Tune Book and his occasional letters. In the Tune Book between the dates April 4 and 24, straddling his Carnegie Hall debut, he set down three song ideas; the middle one was not dated. The Gershwins had worked on a ballad, and completed the refrain and began its verse and had nearly completed it, before starting another song on the twenty-fourth. The all-but-complete verse would become the refrain of "The Man I Love." May/June were devoted to the *Scandals* and most of July and August to composing *Primrose* in London; October/November were given over to *Lady, Be Good!* While Gershwin and the Whiteman orchestra were familiar with the *Rhapsody in Blue,* it can be assumed that some time was needed for freshening-up rehearsals. Likewise the musicals required rehearsals, changes, new songs, supervising or preparing orchestrations, etc. As he once phrased it himself, Gershwin was "a fairly busy young composer," and he loved that too.

II

The *Scandals* of 1924 (remembered best for "Somebody Loves Me") was barely launched when Gershwin set out for London to work with lyricist Desmond Carter, a bright young staff lyricist of the Chappell-Harms combine in London. *Primrose* was Carter's first show assignment. Gershwin, then twenty-five, called him "a promising young lyricist." (Carter's birth date is unknown; composer Vernon Duke, with whom he also collaborated, described him as "gentle, sloe-eyed" [and] "a wonderful lyric writer who died young" [in 1939].) Though he worked on more than thirty musicals, Carter's work is virtually unknown in the United States. Gershwin was particularly impressed with his adroit handling of a "lyric song" (in which the point of the words are more important than the tune); within a week after Gershwin's arrival, he and Carter completed such a song, the very British "Berkeley Square and Kew."

During his London stay Gershwin shared "one of the cheeriest flats" with Alex Aarons and his wife, Ella (who often referred to his scores as the latest in "Georgeousness"). It was a busy place. Among the visitors were the eccentric Lord Berners (the composer Gerald Hugh Tyrwhitt, a kind of English Erik Satie), Prince George (the Duke of Kent), Otto Kahn (the American banker, philanthropist, operaphile and backer of musicals), "the Earl of Latham and several others."

With rehearsals of the forthcoming show only two weeks off, Gershwin reveled in the London scene, dining out, attending the tennis matches at Wimbledon, shopping for gifts to send home, playing golf with the show's co-librettist, Guy Bolton, and working on *Primrose* as well as on the future project, then entitled *Black-eyed Susan* for Aarons and Freedley.

Aarons had made the trip to London to arrange for the Astaires to appear in *Black-eyed Susan;* the Astaires had completely won British audiences since opening in the London version of *For Goodness Sake, Stop Flirting* in May 1923. After a year and a half and over four hundred performances, they were ready to return to New York, especially in a Gershwin show.

Gershwin had arrived prepared for work. Besides his Tune Book (which contained the sixteen-bar verse that would, with little revision, become the refrain to "The Man I Love" to which was added a tricky eight-bar idea that would grow into "Fascinating Rhythm") he had brought along seven completed songs, most with Ira Gershwin's lyrics which formed the nucleus of the score of *Primrose*. These were "Some Far Away Someone" (a collaboration with DeSylva, which had begun as an interpolation entitled "At Half Past Seven" in *The Nifties of 1923);* Ira Gershwin is credited with "Four Sirens We," which as "The Sirens" was written for but not heard in *A Dangerous Maid* (1921); he shared lyric credits with Carter (who revised here and there for the English audience) on "Isn't It Wonderful" (lifted out of the 1921 Tune Book), the first-act finale ("Can We Do Anything?"), the delightful "Wait a Bit, Susie" and the skittish "Naughty Baby, for which Gershwin did a delightful orchestration."

Ira Gershwin did not accompany his brother to London, being at the same time occupied with working on two shows, the worthiest of which was *Be Yourself,* music mostly by Lewis Gensler and book by Marc Connelly and George S. Kaufman; it was in rehearsal concurrently with *Primrose* and opened a week before the London show.

Gershwin, writing to Emily and Lou Paley, said he was "optimistic about this show because the book [by Bolton and co-producer, George Grossmith] seems so good." He was happy too with the leading comedian—"the best in England"—Leslie Henson, in his first of three appearances in successful Gershwin London musicals. The work went well in the Gershwin-Aarons flat with its fine view of the Devonshire Gardens. The bulk of Carter's contribution was to provide Henson, and other comic characters, with such "lyric songs" as "When Toby Is Out of Town," "That New-Fangled Mother of Mine" and the Gilbert and Sullivanish "Isn't It Terrible What They Did to Mary, Queen of Scots?" Then, too, there is the first of Gershwin's original, i.e., new, songs, written for *Primrose,* "Berkeley Square and Kew," with the arresting first line by Carter, "Life with you would bore me . . . ."

Gershwin had hopes that the show would one day have an American production, and although it was a hit in London, its very Englishness precluded that. It was however the first of his scores published in full and one of his most expansive—nineteen songs plus a satiric ballet; a dozen songs were completed in the month or so before *Primrose* opened at the Winter Garden on September 11, 1924. It was an obvious hit, for as soon as the first-act curtain went down the ticket brokers (called "libraries" in London) began buying up blocks of tickets; the advance sale the first night was a considerable £21,000 (about $84,000 then; more than double that now). While it never came to New York, it remained in London for 255 performances.

Gershwin, though a mere twenty-five, was taken seriously by the *Primrose* management, George Grossmith and J. A. E. Malone. The former, noted for his portrayals of the monocled, foppish, stereotyped Englishmen, had planned to play the romantic lead, a rather stuffy writer. Grossmith was a fine actor but had no voice and Gershwin pointed out that the leading man had some important songs to sing. When Gershwin insisted, Grossmith (as he admitted in his biography), ". . . retired gracefully and engaged the fine tenor Percy Heming."

It was Leslie Henson and his complex romantic misadventures that set the comic tone of the show. He had no voice either; it was more of a croak. But his raspy way with the Gilbertian patter songs and his bulgy-eyed clowning contributed much to the zaniness of the evening, with a British accent. The plot managed to keep three romances in the air simultaneously, complicated, as was traditional, by misunderstandings. But it was the adventures of Henson as "Toby Mopham," the impecunious, well-born playboy (another stock musical character) who dominated.

Musically, *Primrose* is all of a piece, "composed-through," to borrow a term from musicology. Each of the three acts begins with a musical exposition to establish the setting; there is an unusual degree of integration in a time before integration became self-consciously de rigueur. The score includes three good Gershwin ballads, "Isn't It Wonderful?," "Some Far Away Someone" and "Boy Wanted." There are two fine rhythm numbers, "Wait a Bit, Susie" and "Naughty Baby," and an exceptional waltz, "Roses of France," which sets the scene for the opening of the second act. The last act begins with an extended ballet, a satiric treatment of classical dance, complete with tentative, exaggerated musical pauses, pretty melodic phrases that swoop and fall; contrasting loud and soft passages; all tongue-in-cheek. It is one of Gershwin's least-known instrumental pieces.

In July, soon after his arrival in London, Gershwin wrote to the Paleys and closed his letter with a wishful "Yours for some English hits." *Primrose* brought that, plus the publication of the score and several individual songs—none of which were popular in the United States ("Wait a Bit, Susie" was very popular with British dance bands). Though Aarons and Freedley were slightly involved with the production—under Gershwin's name in the posters was the parenthetical note, "By arrangement with Alex A. Aarons and Vinton Freedley"—they never brought it to Broadway. This may have disappointed Gershwin a little, though they kept him busy over the next few years. He reveled in the good reviews; and one especially amused him when it noted that some of the lyrics were the work of his "sister Ira" (around this time Ira had decided to abandon "Arthur Francis").

With *Primrose* well on its way to a healthy run, Gershwin and the Aaronses (and, incidentally, Otto Kahn) sailed for New York to start work on *Black-eyed Susan*, the Astaire musical. In the ship's lounge Gershwin held forth at the piano, impressing Kahn with the melody of the half-finished "The Man I Love" (although it is unlikely that it had a title then). Later when he was approached by Aarons and Gershwin to put money into the show, Kahn refused, giving his reason that so far as he could see it was destined for success. He only put money into shows that lost money. Gershwin then played "The Man I Love," saying that it would be one of the numbers in *Black-eyed Susan*. Whereupon Kahn invested ten thousand dollars in the show. (As Ira Gershwin reported, he not only had his investment returned but also received a dividend exceeding it. Kahn "wrote Aarons and Freedley thanking them for a unique experience—the first time he had ever received any return from a theatrical venture.")

Gershwin and the Astaires eagerly looked forward to working together in a full-scale musical at last; like the Astaires, Gershwin came home with honors and radiating accomplishment.

III

Guy Bolton and co-librettist Fred Thompson, also English, had preceded them to New York and had begun concocting the book. The Astaires, not surprisingly, were cast as brother and sister, Dick and Susie Trevor. In the opening scene they and all their possessions, under a "God Bless Our Home" sign affixed to a lamppost, are in the street after being turned out of their home. This through the machinations of Josephine Vanderwater (Jayne Auburn), a socialite with her eye on Dick—who, in turn has his eye on another. Another character, patently a tramp, wanders into the scene and introduces himself as "Jack Robinson" (Alan Edwards); he is, in fact, a potential millionaire, who has also been ejected from his home by his disgruntled uncle. All converge on the Vanderwater estate where the Trevors have promised to entertain. Not much of a plot, but it left plenty of room for the Astaires' songs and dances.

At the Vanderwater party the plot thickens somewhat, when the family attorney "Watty" (comedian Walter Catlett) talks Susie into impersonating a nonexistent Mexican widow who he claims is entitled to a large inheritance. Her share would keep her brother from being forced into marriage with the conniving Josephine. (To jumble the plot, it is revealed before the final curtain that the inheritance belongs to the alleged tramp, Jack, who had been in Mexico but had never married.) At the curtain there are no fewer than a quartet of couples who are married to the strains of "Fascinating Wedding" ("Fascinating Rhythm" with changes in lyric). This convoluted and rarely logical tale did not perplex the audiences in the least, nor even the critics. The music and the Astaires rendered it almost superfluous. In the New York *American* Alan Dale had this to say about the Astaires and the book, "They dance, they sing and they have been jellied into some sort of plot which eludes me, as such plots do, and I never worry."

The score of *Lady, Be Good!* (the title had been changed during the New York rehearsals, which pleased Astaire, who had never liked *Black-eyed Susan)* does not have the unity of *Primrose,* consisting as it does primarily of "numbers." While several songs were inserted into *Primrose,* most of the score was fashioned around the book. *Lady, Be Good!* was designed for the Astaires; the only other singer of sorts in the cast was Cliff Edwards, "Ukulele Ike," a popular vaudevillian at the time (so popular and powerful that he was able to interpolate one of his own specialty numbers into the Gershwin score).

With the Astaires in mind, the Gershwins devoted October 1924 to collating the score. They had had their big ballad since April: "The

Man I Love" and an eight-bar fragment that Aarons liked so much in London that he insisted it be in the score. It would give lyricist Ira some arduous moments.

Gershwin dipped into his 1921 Tune Book for a couple of songs, "We're Here Because" (July 26) and "Little Jazz Bird" (November 17); by mid-November they had completed about twenty songs. After the New York rehearsals the show moved to Philadelphia, where it was due to open on November 17 for a two-week tryout.

During rehearsals, Gershwin returned to New York to appear with Paul Whiteman at Carnegie Hall in yet another repeat of the "Experiment," which had begun to wear thin with the critics. Ira Gershwin was pleased to report, however, that the eminent English critic "Ernest Newman knocked the concert but was delighted with the Rhapsody and expressed himself in no uncertain terms."

Two days later, Gershwin was back in Philadelphia as the curtain went up on *Lady, Be Good!* at the Forrest Theatre. When the curtain descended to warming applause and generally good reviews, an obvious problem confronted the company: the show was too long, by more than an hour, and, as Freedley pointed out, the first act dragged. (This did not hurt the box office, which took in more than twenty thousand dollars the first week.)

On Tuesday, the morning after, out-of-townitis was under way. The sluggish first act was tightened by eliminating a song (one of the few that advanced the plot) establishing Astaire as a man about town, "Seeing Dickie Home." Adele Astaire's "The Man I Love" was moved to the second act and before New York went out entirely. Act I then began with the reassuring declaration of sibling fealty, "Hang On to Me," which was also a plot point.

All agreed that a musical highpoint in which the Astaires and Cliff Edwards participated would remain in the first act. It had no plot significance but functioned as the first-act big dance number for the Astaires.

The song was "Fascinating Rhythm" the creation of which affords insight into the Gershwin collaboration. George had returned with the first eight bars from London (the A section of the chorus ending on the word "flivver"); as an instrumental it was truly fascinating. Gershwin was pleased with its "misplaced accents." When he played it for Ira Gershwin, the reaction was, "For God's sake, George, what kind of lyric do you write to a rhythm like that?"

Frances Gershwin was in the room with them and recalls that Ira thought for a moment then mused, "It's a fascinating rhythm . . ."

George thought it to be "a perfect title for the theme. However, it wasn't all as easy as that, for the title covered part of the first bar only and there was many a hot argument between us as to where the accent should fall in the rest of the words."

"It was a tricky rhythm for those days," Ira Gershwin has written, "and it took me several days to decide on the rhyme scheme." This habit of careful planning and deliberation frequently annoyed his brother and was the one major source of their few disagreements. A rhythmic-melodic idea that Gershwin tossed off in a few minutes at a party often engaged Ira Gershwin in days of work. His mercurial brother at times regarded this as simple procrastination.

"I didn't think I had *the* brilliant title in Fascinating Rhythm but A, it *did* sing smoothly, and B,—I couldn't think of a better. The rhyme scheme was a, b, a, c–a, b, a, c. When I got to the 8th line I showed the lyric to George. His comment was that the 4th and 8th lines should have a double (or two-syllable) rhyme where I rhymed them with single syllables.

"I protested and, by singing, showed him that the last note in both lines had the same strength as the note preceding. To me the last two notes formed a spondee; the easiest way out was arbitrarily to put the accent on the last note. But this George couldn't see, and so, on and off, we argued for days. Finally, I had to capitulate and write the lines as they are today:

4th line;	I'm all a-*qui*ver.
8th line:	Just like a *fliv*ver,

after George proved to me that I had better use the double rhyme; because, whereas in singing, the notes might be considered even, in conducting the music the downbeat came on the penultimate note."

This give-and-take, agreement and disagreement, suggestion and countersuggestion was characteristic of their collaboration from *Lady, Be Good!* (and earlier) through *The Goldwyn Follies.* Each freely suggested ideas to the other and each listened with mutual respect. However, as the more assertive, George Gershwin most frequently had the final word.

During the rehearsals before Philadelphia of *Lady, Be Good!* Gershwin even made suggestions to Fred Astaire for the conclusion of his "Fascinating Rhythm" dance routine.

"We had the routine set but needed a climax wow step to get us off,"

Astaire recalls. "For days I couldn't find one. Neither could dance director Sammy Lee."

Gershwin dropped in on the rehearsal and Astaire asked him to take a look at the dance that he and his sister had worked out to a point. Gershwin went to the piano to serve as accompanist. The Astaires went through the routine up to the last step and then had no place to go. Gershwin kept going however and suggested, "Now travel—travel with that one."

Puzzled, Astaire asked what he meant by "travel," Gershwin sprang from the piano and demonstrated.

"The step was a complicated precision rhythm thing in which we kicked out simultaneously as we crossed back and forth in front of each other with arm pulls and heads back. There was a lot going on, and when George suggested traveling [repeating the same step till offstage], we didn't think it was possible.

"It was the perfect answer to our problem, however, this suggestion by hoofer Gershwin, and it turned out to be a knockout applause puller. George threw me a couple for my solo routine, too." Gershwin remembered the Astaires' "Fascinating Rhythm" routine as "a miraculous dance."

The two shakedown weeks in Philadelphia were devoted to paring and shifting. Ira Gershwin remembered that he spent most of that time "writing songs and rewriting verses and choruses." Vinton Freedley prevailed and "The Man I Love" was replaced by a new song, "Leave It to Love" (which too was ejected before the show opened in Manhattan). The changes required new orchestrations so that George Gershwin in the middle of the second week returned to New York to attend to the new orchestrations—then hurried back to Philadelphia to see a special Thanksgiving Day matinee and to appear with Paul Whiteman that evening at the Academy of Music. It was a time of frenetic, exciting, but gratifying activity. Once the changes were made and the first act quickened, *Lady, Be Good!* appeared to have hit potential. Even the usually cautious Ira Gershwin predicted good things: ". . . I think it will take for a nice few months."

During this time, too, an English producer named Saxe approached Gershwin *(Primrose* was still doing well in London) offering him a show, provided he leave for England the next week. Gershwin demurred, admitting that even he was tired. Besides, he wanted to be in New York when his musical opened there. And there was still work to do before that occurred: "Leave It to Love" was eliminated from its spot in Act II—so were the choral numbers "A Wonderful Party,"

"Weather Man" and "Six Little Rainy Afternoon Girls." In place of the last, "Linger in the Lobby" was written to open the second act.

Lady, Be Good! premiered at the Liberty Theatre on December 1, 1924, a Monday evening; on Tuesday the Gershwins read Stark Young in the *Times:* "George Gershwin's score is excellent. It contains, as might be expected, many happy hints for wise orchestra leaders of the dancing Winter months that lies ahead and a number of tunes that the unmusical and serious-minded will find it hard to get rid of. The lyrics, by Ira Gershwin, are capable throughout and at moments excellent." (His critical faculties may have been somewhat impaired, for the rest of his review made it publicly evident that he was hopelessly in the thrall of Adele Astaire.)

The musical was a sweeping success for the Astaires, especially Adele, who came across as being perky, endearing—"piquant," "impish," "charming," were a few of the critical tributes. One critic managed to squeeze her brother into his appraisal: "Fred too gives a good account of himself."

Considering the gossamer plot which they held together with considerable help from the score, the Astaires managed to get away with some outrageous dialogue. In the opening scene in which "Jack," the pseudo-tramp and hypothetical husband, appears, he says to "Susie," "I'm just a poor hobo." To this she replies, "Then I must be in Hoboken."

Another: Lawyer Watkins ("Watty") is explaining to Dick why he has persuaded his sister (to the strains of the title song) to impersonate a fraudulent Mexican widow, Bolton and Thompson concocted this exchange:

WATTY	*The poor thing is in Canto Canto.*
DICK	*What's that?*
WATTY	*That's Mexican for Sing Sing.*

ONE MORE

JOSE-PHINE	*Oh, Lawyer Watkins, do you think me attractive?*
WATTY	*Attractive? You know you're attractive. There have been several complaints about it.*

Because of the Gershwins and the Astaires, as well as to a lesser degree, the popular comedian Walter Catlett, and Cliff Edwards, and despite its skittish but amusing book, *Lady, Be Good!* was the year's most original musical. Though several reviewers made note of the songs they made no mention of the innovative sound, the spare, sinewy melodies, the definitely nonoperetta rhythms, the wit of the lyrics. A score that scintillated and crackled with the unsentimental contemporaneity (once "The Man I Love" was jettisoned, the sole remaining ballad was a lovely tribute to Kern, "So Am I") of such up-to-the-minute, crisp songs as "Little Jazz Bird," "The Half of It, Dearie, Blues" and, of course, "Oh, Lady Be Good!" and "Fascinating Rhythm."

The presence of the two-piano team of Phil Ohman and Victor Arden (Gershwin's idea) in the orchestra and in their own "piano specialty," gave the score a special Gershwin sound. (Ohman and Arden would be heard in three more Gershwin musicals). *Lady, Be Good!* not only brought the Astaires back home for a long stay—the show ran for 330 performances, then toured successfully in 1925—it marked the advent of *the* Gershwin musical.

Lady, Be Good! was the fortieth musical produced in New York in 1924 (and Gershwin's third of the year, not counting London's *Primrose*). Nonmusicals of the year included Maxwell Anderson and Lawrence Stalling's antiwar *What Price Glory?* Eugene O'Neill's *Desire Under the Elms* and Sidney Howard's *They Knew What They Wanted.* Musically, it was a bounteous season, no anomaly for the period, with its usual cluster of annual revues—*Vogues, Grand Street Follies, Ziegfeld Follies, Passing Show,* the Earl Carroll *Vanities, Greenwich Village Follies,* etc., etc., etc.—as well as Gershwin's final *Scandals* and Irving Berlin's *Music Box Revue* (his last in the series also). Inexplicably, besides the Gershwin musical and Berlin's revue, yet another musical, *Princess April,* opened on December 1 but remained for three weeks only. It was a crowded season.

The New York theatergoer had a wide choice of musicals to choose from in 1924: Harry Tierney's *Kid Boots,* starring Eddie Cantor, was a runover from the previous year. Vincent Youmans produced the not very successful *Lollipop;* Kern came up with *Sitting Pretty* and, for two weeks, *Dear Sir.* Victor Herbert's *Dream Girl* was produced posthumously, with discreet finishing touches by the prolific Sigmund Romberg (that year he had three of his own shows on Broadway—*The Passing Show, Artists and Models, The Student Prince*). Noble Sissle and Eubie Blake did not follow the success of *The Chocolate Dandies* that they had known with *Shuffle Along,* and there were lesser, short-lived musicals.

The season's most successful musicals were the operettas of Rudolf Friml *(Rose Marie)* and Romberg *(The Student Prince).* Sentimental, lush, romantic, they appealed to the audiences who preferred the conventional, the expected. They reveled in colorful costumes and grand sets. The new musical comedy with scores by Youmans, Ruby, Gershwin would seem brittle in tone, "smart," characterized by athletic dances, tongue-in-cheek love songs. These musicals represented the beginning of the transition from the traditional musical and operetta to the modern musical comedy. The Gershwins in their sparkling Broadway debut contributed an unpretentious giant step.

IV

The "book" of *Lady, Be Good!,* like most of the now classic Gershwin shows (with exceptional exceptions), was, at best, secondary. It set up the cues for the songs and dances and filled in the time between with work for the resident comedian or the featured performer (in this case Walter Catlett and Cliff Edwards, each of whom was given the chance to shine in his specialty). But primarily the show rested on the work of the Astaires and what the Gershwins created for them.

While the Gershwins did not accept every book that was handed to them, they were remarkably indifferent to the content of the shows for which they wrote songs. Not that these were illiterate or unimaginative, but they could be quite frivolous (who went to a musical to be serious?) and vague. Often as not a musical was concocted around a star. The Gershwins were handed what passed for a book with few questions and spotted their songs in it. Sometimes it worked and other times it didn't and they found their score scuttled by the book no matter who the star. They went to the next assignment with little regret; it was how they made their living.

The kind of "smart" show that Aarons and Freedley aimed at provided them with the chance to compose songs for a knowing, literate, contemporary audience. While the scores abound in hit songs—and the Gershwins did not set out to do this deliberately—some of their best work is found in the lesser-known (often unpublished) songs, the dropped songs and, to spotlight the work of composer Gershwin, the fine choral writing that opened and often closed scenes (this gift flowered in the later political operettas and *Porgy and Bess).*

In the pivotal year 1924 Gershwin unconsciously brought significant though subtle changes to the American musical landscape in the theater and the concert hall. True, many of the critics hailed the composer of the *Rhapsody in Blue* as a promising new voice in American music, but Gershwin, for all that, was practical; he had no plans to desert the theater for the concert hall. Writing for the theater he found "agreeable and remunerative"; he would stay with it. His ambition and training, plus the consciousness of the transitory life of a popular song, impelled him to compose in the larger forms. He was no less "serious" when he composed "Fascinating Rhythm" than when he created a rhapsody or a concerto.

Songwriting, he felt, was not to be taken lightly. Too often he had been told composing a simple song was "an easy affair." He did not agree; the uninitiated or amateur thought that all "a number needs for success, it seems, is thirty-two bars; a good phrase of eight bars used to start the refrain is repeated twice more with a new eight-bar added which is much less important.

"It sounds simple of course, but personally I can think of no more nerve-wracking, no more mentally arduous task than making music. There are times when a phrase of music will cost many hours of internal sweating. Rhythms romp through one's brain, but they are not easy to capture and keep; the chief difficulty is to avoid reminiscence . . . Imitation never gets anyone anywhere. Originality is the only thing that counts."

Inspiration? "When we most want it, it does not come. Therefore the composer does not sit around and wait for an inspiration to walk up and introduce itself. What he substitutes for it is nothing more than talent plus his knowledge. If his endowment is great enough, the song is made to sound as if it were truly inspired."

To Gershwin music was music; he chose to slight the traditional divisions and barriers. "I see a piece of music in the form of a design," he once said. "With a melody one can take in a design in one look; with a larger composition, like a concerto, it is necessary to take it piece by piece and construct it so much longer.

"I've never really studied musical form. That's nothing, of course, to be proud of. But regardless of the kind of music a composer is writing, it must have a definite line of progression. It must have a beginning and an end and a suitable section combining the two . . . In this sense of trying to make my musical compositions each a complete work, I suppose there is a certain form to them."

He was "always composing," he told a friend. If not, it took time to get his stride. "My work is done almost exclusively at night, and my best is achieved in the fall and winter months. A beautiful spring or summer day is least conducive to making music, for I always prefer the outdoors to work"—especially so after he had taken up golf and tennis.

"I don't write at all in the morning, for the obvious reason that I am not awake at the time. The afternoon I devote to physical labor—orchestrations, piano copies, etc." No ivory-tower composer, Gershwin did not always require quiet. "Often I have written my tunes with people in the same room playing cards in the next. When I find myself in the desired mood I can hold it until I finish the song." He worked at the keyboard: "Composing at the piano is not good practice," he admitted, "but I started that way and it has become a habit." This habit often produced songs of a pianistic (instrumental) character that often confronted Ira Gershwin with his own "nerve-wracking, mentally arduous" tasks—only his work had to make literal sense to match the sense and inevitability of his brother's invention. The result: *the* Gershwin song, unique, spare, witty, original and, more often than not, impressing as if "truly inspired."

Having made their auspicious—now historic—musical comedy debut, the Gershwins began preparing for their next Aarons and Freedley production in the spring. For Gershwin the 1924 musical season closed as it had begun, on a note of triumph. He had once boasted boyishly of his "record for industry"; 1925 promised even more.

6

Modern Romantic

In mid-1925 Gershwin was singled out by the youthful founders (Yale graduates Henry Luce and Briton Hadden) as the cover subject of their struggling but vivacious two-year-old publication, *Time* ("The Weekly News Magazine"). Gershwin has the distinction of being the first composer, and American to boot, to make *Time*'s cover. The article, breezy, mannered (Hadden's distinctive touch) and brash, mirrored the ethics of the dynamic twenties and its sundry heroes (three months later *Time* would thus honor its first athlete: halfback Red Grange). Gershwin belonged: he was young, successful and press-worthy. *Time*'s story, "Gershwin Bros." (Ira Gershwin was acknowledged with a small photograph and a paragraph of text), caught Gershwin on the run and underscored his "record for industry"; in a year in which he would compose a piano concerto, three musicals, oversee the revival of his early opera, buy a house, dash off to London and Paris and seem to be a performing guest at all the important musical parties in town.

When *Time*'s interviewer caught him, the Gershwins were still living in the flat on West 110th Street: "Maneuvering around two grand pianos which took up most of the available floor space of a small Manhattan apartment," he began, "a young Jew last week went about the business of packing a suit-case. Old newspapers—the inseparable, useless adjuncts of this operation—lay here and there in crumpled disorder, but two, containing an item which had been circled with a pencil mark.

"The first item related how Composer George Gershwin, famed jazzbo, had recently returned from Europe; the second stated that this Gershwin, when he had finished the piano concerto which Dr. Walter Damrosch had commissioned him to write for the New York Symphony

Orchestra . . . will compose the score of a new musical for the producers of *Lady, Be Good*. Soprano excitement abruptly galvanized the telephone at the young man's elbow: he began to address its black aperture.

" 'Yes,' he said, 'this is Gershwin . . .'

" 'No, no, it's too hot . . . I'm going away for the weekend . . . I can't see anyone.'

"Smiling, he hung up the receiver, tossed a last striped shirt into his bag. It was sometimes a nuisance, but he could not honestly pretend it bored him, this growing public interest in his movements, his past, his plans."

I

The immediate past of the "famed jazzbo" had been more exciting than appearing on the cover of *Time*. He had been introduced to a composer he greatly admired, Igor Stravinsky (1882–1971), then the most celebrated, perhaps notorious, musician of the moment. Stravinsky had arrived in the United States for the first time on January 6 to begin a tour of the United States, conducting his own works, with appearances at Carnegie Hall.

On January 7, the evening before his first concert, Paul and Zosia Kochanski, good friends of Stravinsky and Gershwin, held a reception in his honor. Kochanski (1887–1934), a Polish-born violinist, had made his auspicious American debut in 1921 with the New York Symphony. Settling in New York soon after, he joined the staff of the Juilliard School of Music in 1924. He was highly regarded as an interpreter-advocate of contemporary music; Stravinsky dedicated several of his violin pieces to Kochanski.

Gershwin, as usual, played, and while no one present recorded the details of the first Stravinsky-Gershwin meeting Stravinsky had good things to say about "American jazz" when he returned to Paris after his tour. He stated that the "music of the future will have to take it into account, no matter what the tendency of the composer." Later, he remembered Gershwin as being "nervously energetic."

Their next encounter, the evening of the eighth, came close to being, through no fault of theirs, a confrontation. After Stravinsky's debut at Carnegie Hall—conducting *The Firebird* suite, *Song of the Nightingale* and other pieces (he canceled the announced *Le Sacre*, probably for lack of rehearsal time) there was another party in his honor by Mary Hoyt Wiborg (better known as "Hoytie" to Gershwin and his musical friends). She was a Fifth Avenue society hostess, celebrated for attracting glittering conclaves of stars and future stars, particularly in the world of music. Since her home was situated on lower Fifth Avenue, she borrowed another from a friend more convenient to Carnegie Hall for the Stravinsky celebration. She and Gershwin had been friends for some time; one mutual friend recalled how she had dragooned him, the Kochanskis and monologuist-actress Ruth Draper to see an out-of-town tryout of a musical entitled *The Perfect Lady* late in 1923 in New Jersey (when it opened in New York it was *Sweet Little Devil).*

The group went backstage "to meet a very friendly young man named George Gershwin, whose personality seemed as joyous and rhythmic as his music." The friend, pianist Lester Donahue, remembered too that after the tryout, they all went to Hoytie's apartment, where Gershwin entertained with the score of his new show. Donahue was especially taken with the song "Virginia," which Gershwin played and sang "over and over, with that delightful zest and relish with which he performed his own music, and with that already inevitable black cigar. There was a naïve honesty of enjoyment about him at the piano, which never forsook him. His attitude never approached conceit, and precluded that undercurrent of critical rivalry which usually exists when two or more pianistic prima donnas find themselves at the same party."

Donahue, who was known among his friends and rivals as the "social pianist" (besides recitals in concert halls, like Gershwin he was a regular performer in the homes of the affluent along Fifth and Park avenues), was present at Wiborg's party that night. Apparently, in an excess of *beau monde* zeal, Hoytie was determined to seat these two celebrated composers, the twenty-six-year-old jazzbo and the forty-two-year-old modernist, at the same piano for some diverting four-hand improvisation. (Stravinsky, though he played, was not renowned for his keyboard extemporizing.) It was one of the rare occasions when Gershwin had to be coaxed to play.

"The two unwilling victims . . ." Donahue recalled, "were seated at the piano with a brilliant assemblage of all the leading musicians, Fred and Adele Astaire, and several Mrs. Vanderbilts waiting to hear an inspired moment in musical history. Chaliapin stood benevolently in the curve of the piano, his arms raised to conduct. The two great masters of rhythm studied each other for a moment like prize fighters in the ring and then began to play vigorously.

"Not a sound escaped from the exasperating keyboard."

Neither Stravinsky, nor Gershwin (nor for that matter the tenacious Hoytie) were aware of the mechanics of that special instrument. But

John Hays Hammond, Jr., of the organ and piano manufacturing family did. He saved the evening in a most unique manner: the flick of a finger. Hammond, himself an organist and pianist, was also an inventor; he loved to tinker with keyboard instruments, radios and phonographs. He was familiar with the instrument, may even have installed it but it is not certain. As Donahue remembered it, there was "a curious contraption" that connected the piano to an organ in the same room—obviously a linked sound system. Realizing that both composers were most unhappy with the turn of events, Hammond merely turned off the piano's amplifier—and no sounds emanated from the piano. In Donahue's view, this quick thinking was "an important link in [Hammond's] later friendship with Gershwin and Strawinsky [sic]."

Relieved, Gershwin and Stravinsky retired to their separate corners. The party then settled into the more conventional pattern, Gershwin later taking his place at the reactivated keyboard, the Astaires entertaining with selections from *Lady, Be Good!* and Gershwin captivating with his *Rhapsody.*

That January 1925 he had begun a new notebook on which he had written "Preludes." Since 1919 he had been accumulating fragments and completed little piano pieces in other notebooks he labeled "Novelettes"; the change to "Preludes" suggests a more serious classification and a plan to compose a suite of piano pieces.

About this busy time, Gershwin was visited by violinist Samuel Dushkin (1891–1976). A one-time child prodigy, Dushkin had studied with Leopold Auer and Fritz Kreisler, made an impressive debut in Europe in 1918 and made his New York debut in 1924. Early in February he planned a recital and hoped that Gershwin might have something for him. As they talked, Dushkin picked up one of the notebooks with novelette sketches and found two, in contrasting tempos, that he thought might serve as the basis for a special little violin and piano piece for him.

Gershwin had no objections, so Dushkin added the violin part and had it ready in time for his recital at the University Club on West Fifty-fourth Street on February 8, 1925. The Gershwin-Dushkin work was published as *Short Story* in 1925, by Dushkin's publisher, B. Schott's Sohne, a German-based firm. Gershwin is credited as composer and Dushkin as arranger. While it is a winning piece, *Short Story* is rather flimsy Gershwin, even in its solo piano form. The earliest "novelette," *Allegretto scherzando,* Dushkin selected as the conclusion, has a swinging ragtime quality. It dates from around 1919 (Gershwin recorded it for the Welte-Mignon piano roll company that year as *Novelette in Fourths).* The opening *Andantino con fantasia* was dated August 30, 1923.

Once *Short Story* had been launched, Gershwin pretty much dismissed it as he did the early "novelettes"; he admitted writing some but added, "they have never been published and are not worth bringing up." They represent the pre-*Rhapsody in Blue* Gershwin compositionally and the pre-*Preludes* Gershwin pianistically. As for the *Prelude* dated January 1925, he would find a likely spot for it later in the year.

II

Gershwin's winter partying came to a close with a March 24 evening at the home of author-critic Alexander Woollcott, then writing drama criticism for the New York *World.* Woollcott had an evening celebrating the arrival of English novelist Michael Arlen, whose popular novel, *The Green Hat,* then being transformed into a play for production later in the year. Among the guests besides columnist Franklin P. Adams, who, taking a cue from *Time* had begun to keep track of Gershwin's movements and plans in his "The Diary of Our Samuel Pepys," which appeared in the *World.* He proclaimed his colleague's party as a "great" one and that Gershwin and "I. Berlin played some melodies." By the end of March, Gershwin would be pre-auditioning at parties the new songs he and his brother had written for the forthcoming *My Fair Lady,* then in rehearsal.

The Gershwins had little to work with in the plot of *My Fair Lady,* by William K. Wells and Fred Thompson. It proved to be yet another reworking of the rich girl disguised as a shopgirl to test the good intentions and integrity of her wealthy suitor. A subplot utilized the talents of Yiddish dialect comic Lou Holtz as a poor young man in pursuit of a wealthy young woman. Still another plot layer was contributed by another comic team, Andrew Tombes and Emma Haig. The attractive leads were Phyllis Cleveland in the title role as "Peggy Van De Leur" and Alexander Gray. Vaudevillian Holtz was essential enough to the show to be able to interpolate a non-Gershwin song in the important next-to-closing scene, his then very popular "Oh, So La Mi!" It didn't help.

Coming so soon after the effervescent *Lady, Be Good!, Tell Me More* (its title when it opened at the Gaiety on April 13), suffered critical comparisons. While it was not precisely a tossed-off score, its seventeen songs (of which thirteen remained) were produced under pressure; Ira Gershwin was assisted on the lyrics by DeSylva for that reason. Gershwin had no trouble keeping up with them and when necessary, as he told writer Charles G. Shaw, he could "work for twelve hours without stopping, during which time he becomes so engrossed that he suffers from a nervous indigestion," the "composer's stomach" he attributed to the rushed writing of *Blue Monday* three years before. This condition was apparently one of Gershwin's favorite topics of conversation. "Beyond these spells," Shaw noted, "his health doesn't trouble him. For relaxation he visits an osteopath."

February and March were devoted to work on *My Fair Lady/Tell Me More* to meet the April 6 tryout opening in Atlantic City. While it is not generally regarded as one of the outstanding Gershwin scores, it contained some characteristic and finely wrought songs, several of which were popular with dance bands of the period. Gershwin recorded a piano roll of one of the most popular, "Kickin' the Clouds," a typically athletic rhythm number that was danced with show-stopping acrobatics by Vivian Glenn and Mary Jane and Dorothy Wilson. Another lively song, "Baby!" is a delightful vintage twenties show tune. The first and final title songs merely served; "My Fair Lady" alludes to words from the old English song "London Bridge Is Falling Down"; "Tell Me More" enjoyed current popularity probably because of its catchy and (unusual for Gershwin) repetitious refrain.

Though the show was not favorably reviewed, it managed to remain for a run of a hundred performances in the aftermath of a brief but sharp depression the year before. Even *Lady, Be Good!* had begun to falter by June. As Ira Gershwin put it, "Business all over town has taken a nose dive . . ." By September the Astaire musical would begin its national tour in Newark.

Even as *Tell Me More* floundered at the Gaiety Theatre, Gershwin was on the move again. Because an almost simultaneous production had been planned for London, he and Alex Aarons sailed for Britain in mid-April to prepare the English version for a May 26 opening. Then, too, there was a secondary reason for his being in London. The indefatigable Eva Gauthier had managed to time her appearance there to coincide with his trip. In her first spring recital she had decided to "introduce English audiences to her famous program "From Java to Jazz," and she had talked Gershwin into serving again as her accompanist. On May 12 a reception was given them by Lord and Lady Caribrooke, cousins of King George V, at which were assembled members of London's cultural elite (the guest list ranged from archaeologist Leonard Woolley to composer Herbert Howells, among the assorted conductors, critics, composers and artists—but no popular English songwriter. Gershwin had the evening to himself).

The recital took place at London's Aeolian Hall on May 22, (only four days before the premiere of *Tell Me More);* its American Popular

Song section ("jazzed by George Gershwin") repeated their New York Aeolian Hall program of two years before. The inclusion of "jazz" ruffled some of the daily critics, but the anonymous reviewer of *The Chesterian* (who was well disposed toward contemporary music) found Gauthier's renditions of the moderns "sensitive" and the jazz interpretations "spirited." Pianist Ivor Newton was reported as "accompanying with insight the non-ragged numbers."

On the twenty-sixth the modified *Tell Me More* opened at the Winter Garden to begin a long successful run. What plot there was was twisted to expand what had been the Lou Holtz role to fit the comic talents of the popular Leslie Henson. Opposite him were Heather Thatcher and Claude Hulbert (all three were veterans of the previous year's *Primrose*). With additional lyrics by Desmond Carter the show was easily transformed into a vehicle for Henson although one of the most jocular songs, "Murderous Monty and Light-Fingered Jane" was cut before the opening.

His London chores done, Gershwin left for Paris to visit Mabel Pleshette, who had married Robert Schirmer (of the music-publishing family), and to party with the Glaenzers before joining Aarons on the ship for New York at the end of June. They had begun talking about the next Aarons and Freedley production, *Tip-Toes*, scheduled for a September premiere. Somehow during the two months abroad, what with his diverse comings and goings and parties, the rehearsals and three new *Tell Me More* songs, and the Gauthier recital,—he had already begun jotting down ideas for a "New York Concerto."

III

Early in 1925 Walter Damrosch, the genial and venerable conductor of the New York Symphony Society, had approached the society's president, Harry Harkness Flagler, with the suggestion that they commission a Gershwin piano concerto. The young composer was then regularly in the news, his comings and goings noted, and his rhapsody and songs ubiquitous. While the society was not noted for its sponsorship of the contemporary composer, George Gershwin was good box office. Flagler readily agreed with the conductor, who then called Gershwin one spring day with the proposal.

"This showed great confidence on his part," Gershwin admitted, "as I had never written anything for symphony before." Considering this fact, he himself showed no little confidence when, four days after *Tell Me More* had opened and he was preparing for the trip to London, he stopped by the society's office in Steinway Hall on West Fifty-seventh Street to sign contracts. The date was April 17, 1925, and in agreement with manager George Engles, for a consideration of five hundred dollars, he promised to deliver the score and parts of a New York concerto to the society one week before the rehearsals were scheduled to begin for the first concert, set for the afternoon of Thursday, December 3. Gershwin agreed to appear as piano soloist in seven performances of the work with the New York Symphony. One of the stipulations of the contract was that the December 3 date in Carnegie Hall "will be [the] first performance of the work in New York." Engles was not familiar with the Gershwin method of composing in public and performing works in progress all over town.

With the contract in hand, he left for London where he fortified himself with "four or five books on musical structure to find out what the concerto form really was!" He brought with him his copy of Forsythe's *Orchestration* dating back to his student days with Kilenyi. From the beginning he planned to do all the work on the concerto himself. His tongue-in-cheek comment about finding out what a concerto really was, was published in the *Tribune* a week before the first performance of the concerto. While an exaggeration, it reflects Gershwin's self-consciousness about his lack of a conservatory training. It haunted him to the end of his life.

For all that, he was a self-assured young composer ready to tackle a formidable and ambitious undertaking for a standard symphony orchestra perhaps three times the size of the Whiteman band. And no whooping clarinets, no banjos—no "jazz band." In London with Aarons and between rehearsals, parties and other activities, he began jotting down a few sketchy ideas for his concerto.

When he returned to New York late in June, Gershwin had a few ideas in mind and some on paper. The Tune Books provided some more. Because the production of *Tip-Toes* was postponed (from September to December), he had time to assemble his ideas and to begin concentrating on the concerto by mid-July. In his preperformance *Tribune* article he wrote "It took me three months to compose this *Concerto,* and one month to orchestrate it." Toward the close of this work he was concurrently occupied with *Tip-Toes* and an operetta collaboration, *Song of the Flame.* December 1925 would prove to be a Gershwin month in Manhattan; all three of these works premiered within days of each other. Gershwin's record for industry was intact.

To escape the New York summer heat, he and Ira, plus friends—one being the writer S. N. Behrman, whom they had met at the Paleys'— fled to New Hampshire for a while. In mid-July they returned and

Gershwin began working on the concerto, playing some of the themes at Edwin Knopf's apartment on July 18. The inveterate diarist Carl Van Vechten was there to record the incident. On the twenty-fourth Gershwin had dinner with the Van Vechtens (she was the actress Fania Marinoff), after which he "played some of the themes from the *Concerto in F.* He has had some of these in mind for months, as he intended using them in Black Belt, but many of them are new. George started this concerto two days ago and has already written five pages." He had by then decided to discard the contract's descriptive title, "New York Concerto."

Black Belt was a reference to a tone poem for symphony orchestra that Van Vechten had mentioned in his article on Gershwin for *Vanity Fair,* published earlier in the year. Another was a plan for twenty-four preludes. Neither of these ambitious projects were carried through; however, the prelude that had been dated January 1925 served as the opening for the concerto's last movement.

It was a month before the Van Vechtens encountered Gershwin again at a party given by publishers Alfred and Blanche Knopf for playwright-songwriter Noël Coward, who had come to New York for the production of his comedy *Hay Fever.* Coward entertained with his witty, satirical songs and Gershwin played several of his own songs, an abbreviated *Rhapsody in Blue* and, Van Vechten believed, "a long passage (possibly a complete movement)" from the *Concerto in F.* It was a good guess; by August 27, the date of the party, Gershwin had finished the first movement.

It had been a hot July, and besides working on the concerto George had to begin thinking about working with Ira on *Tip-Toes* and with Oscar Hammerstein and Otto Harbach on songs for *Song of the Flame* (his co-composer was Herbert Stothart, who took some of the musical work load off Gershwin and vice versa). To escape the commotions of the household—virtually a community center what with the comings and goings of Rose Gershwin's friends, Pop Gershwin's card games, and well as Arthur's and Frances's activities—Gershwin rented two rooms in the Whitehall Hotel on Broadway and 110th Street. There he met with his collaborators and worked on the concerto away from the human traffic. "But even here," S. N. Behrman discovered, "the 'privacy' he achieved was only comparative; here, too, the rooms were generally full of admirers, voluntary secretaries who asked nothing further than to be allowed to copy out a score—and relatives."

Ernest Hutcheson (1871–1951), a friend and admirer, came to Gershwin's rescue. The Australian-born pianist-composer was then Dean at the Juilliard School of Music. In the summer he taught master classes in piano at the Chautauqua Institute, in the western part of New York State near Lake Erie. Hutcheson had given up a promising career as a pianist for teaching. (In 1915 he dazzled musical New York by performing the concertos of Liszt, Tchaikovsky and MacDowell—at a single concert.) In July of 1925 he offered the somewhat beleaguered Gershwin sanctuary in the woodsy setting of Chautauqua, where he arranged for him to have his own cottage for work.

Even away from Manhattan, Gershwin's celebrity shadowed him. His cabin became the focus of attention for Hutcheson's young piano students until their teacher placed it off-limits until four in the afternoon. "Promptly at that hour," Hutcheson recalled in his autobiography, ". . . a group of students invaded the room, when George would good-naturedly play and sing for them. George was a wonderful friend and companion, ever reliable, sympathetic and unshakably well-tempered."

One of Hutcheson's most gifted students of that summer might have disagreed, for he had once encountered Gershwin in a rare display of ill temper. He was Abram Chasins, regarded, along with Gershwin's friend Josefa Rosanska as a Hutcheson star student. Four years Gershwin's junior, he was very serious about serious music, especially as a teenager, when he and Gershwin first met. The Gershwins were then (1919) living on West 144th Street and the Chasinses a few blocks away.

"I was a sober sixteen, he an exuberant twenty-one," Chasins recalled. "The age difference was dissolved by mutual interests; girls, tennis, but mainly music . . . The things that made him so special to me were his confidence, force, and love for music; his incredible ease, joyous spontaneity, and originality at the piano. He was the only pianist I ever heard who could make a piano laugh, really laugh.

"We soon got into a fight. My nose was stuck to the musical grindstone. George was having a love-affair with music; no slaving away at theory, harmony, counterpoint, orchestration, or form [this may be an error; if Chasins's date is correct, Gershwin was studying with Kilenyi at the time].

"One day on the corner of Lenox Avenue and 113th Street in 1919 he confided more of his big ideas."

"George," Chasins told him, "Don't you think it would be a good idea to take some lessons from Goldmark?" [Chasins was a Rubin Goldmark student.] "Nobody can do what you do without basic training."

Gershwin stopped in his tracks, glared at Chasins, then in a loud voice exclaimed, "You're just the kind of person who's keeping me from my great work!" He strode away leaving an abashed Chasins standing in the street.

By the summer of 1925 the misunderstanding on Lenox Avenue had been forgotten and, like his fellow students, Chasins complied with Hutcheson's rule and did not keep Gershwin from doing his "great work" (if that is the term he had used). In the sylvan but qualified privacy of Chautauqua, Gershwin completed his two-piano version of the concerto's first movement and began work on the second.

So it was a complete first movement that Van Vechten had heard at the Knopfs' party in late August. The party season had begun in early September. Gershwin met Van Vechten at a party given by producer Edgar Selwyn, where they discussed the new work. Later in the month Gershwin phoned Van Vechten and invited him to his new quarters—a five-story house at 316 West 103rd Street, near Riverside Drive. On the second floor, where his parents' bedroom was situated, there were also the dining room and a large living room with two pianos (Gershwin had the fifth floor to himself and a Steinway grand).

Gershwin was anxious to perform the two completed movements of the concerto, with himself in the solo part and William Daly, on the second piano, substituting for the orchestra. Daly, then conductor of the current *Scandals* (score by DeSylva, Brown and Henderson) was an all-around musician, composer, arranger, pianist, conductor. Daly had studied piano as a boy and achieved a reputation of child prodigy. He abandoned music temporarily after graduation from Harvard to work as a magazine editor. He returned to music as a conductor around 1915; subsequently he was active in the theater, primarily as a conductor. In the 1930s Daly conducted the orchestras for radio programs.

He and Gershwin became good friends from the time of their collaboration on *Our Nell* (1922), after which Daly conducted several Gershwin musicals beginning with the *Scandals* of 1924 through Gershwin's last Broadway show, *Let 'Em Eat Cake* (1933); six in all. He made special arrangements of Gershwin songs for concert and radio; likewise the concert works for radio. From 1922 until his premature death in 1936, Daly was one of Gershwin's closest friends, a trusted interpreter and advisor. He undoubtedly advised Gershwin during the composition of the *Concerto in F.*

Some weeks after the two-piano pre-audition, Fania and Carl Van Vechten encountered Gershwin in early October at a dress rehearsal of Coward's *Hay Fever*. "He tells us," Van Vechten noted in his diary, "that he has completed the Concerto lacking two bars." The balance of the month and a little more than a week of the next, was devoted to orchestration. Gershwin marked the entire work finished on "November 10, 1925." The *Concerto in F,* discounting whatever preliminary sketches were done in London, was written, as Van Vechten carefully recorded, between July 22 and November 10.

Eager to hear his creation two weeks before rehearsals were scheduled, Gershwin arranged for a reading of the concerto one afternoon at the Globe Theatre. "I enjoyed it," Gershwin admitted, "not as one of my fair and mischievous friends said, as the mad King Ludwig enjoyed Wagner, being the sole audience in the theatre, for Mr. Damrosch was there, and about a dozen others who wished to hear it. Four of these were music critics. The rest were personal friends."

Among the friends was Ernest Hutcheson, whose advice on the role of the piano in the concerto Gershwin respected. For this event, a musical equivalent to a theatrical tryout, Gershwin had hired some fifty experienced musicians and had asked Daly to conduct. During the run-through Gershwin inserted some revisions. Daly had suggested six quite extensive cuts; Gershwin assented to three. This tightened the structure of the work.

Damrosch's markings also appear in the manuscript (although these may have been added later during the Carnegie Hall rehearsals). His annotations are in German: *Pos(aune)* for trombone, *Fliessend* for "flowing," etc. During the tryout Damrosch may have asked Gershwin to employ the piano as a kind of filler in some orchestral passages; Gershwin complied, although these did little more than to thicken the texture with little effect. By the close of that exciting November afternoon, Gershwin had experienced a "peak of my highest joy in [a] completed work"; he had written a real piano concerto.

Two weeks later the Damrosch rehearsals were held. It was a gray, dank morning when the orchestra assembled onstage and a small audience gathered in the auditorium at Carnegie Hall. As usual, a number of Gershwin's friends and relatives were present, along with musical acquaintances, critics and writers, among them Henry Osgood who observed, that "for the most part [the audience] was made up of gentle, gray-haired ladies, longtime subscribers of the New York Symphony who lose no opportunity, even mornings, to sit at the feet of their beloved conductor."

Damrosch (1861–1950), though a musical pioneer, was an unlikely Gershwin exponent; he was never really comfortable with "modern music." Born in Breslau, he was brought to the United States in 1871, when he was about nine. His father, Leopold, was an eminent violinist and conductor; his younger brother, Frank, was a choral conductor and teacher (in 1925 at the Juilliard School). All three became major figures in New York's musical life.

By the time he was twenty, Walter Damrosch had made a reputation as a choral and orchestra conductor; in 1885 he succeeded his father as leader of the Symphony Society of New York. Ten years later he organized the significant Damrosch Opera Company, which introduced major European singers to America and premiered important operas in the United States. As conductor of the New York Symphony, Damrosch was one of the first to broadcast "serious music" via radio. As early as 1927 he led the NBC Symphony in a network concert; from the late 1920s until 1942 he presented a popular weekly music-appreciation hour over the National Broadcasting Company's stations throughout the United States and Canada. In addition to some of Wagner's operas, Damrosch conducted the first United States performances of Brahms's last two symphonies and Tchaikovsky's Fourth and Sixth symphonies.

He was a friendly, stolid man in his sixties, leonine with fine white hair. He was most popular among his symphony subscribers whom he frequently invited to his rehearsals, a rare cultural treat, and they adored him for it.

When Gershwin arrived, Damrosch had already spent nearly an hour rehearsing Alexander Glazunov's Fifth Symphony [also programmed with the Gershwin concerto: Gluck's overture to *Iphigenia in Aulis* ("with close by Richard Wagner") and Henri Rabaud's arrangement of Elizabethan music, *Suite Anglaise*. This was an unusual program for the Symphony: three of the composers were still alive].

During a short break, Damrosch left the stage to greet his guests; Gershwin entered from backstage, was introduced to the patrons and subscribers, then took his place at the piano. With him was a young musician friend, pianist and aspiring songwriter, Philip Charig, who had been rehearsal pianist for *Lady, Be Good!* and *Tell Me More*. He had offered to carry Gershwin's briefcase and scores. (Two years later he wrote the music for his first show, *Yes, Yes, Yvette;* in 1928 he collaborated with Ira Gershwin on a London show, *That's a Good Girl.* Their most successful collaboration was the song, "Sunny Disposish" from the 1926 *Americana*. Charig's greatest success was his World War II musical, *Follow the Girls.)* His coveted role as Gershwin's aide was soon taken over by a brilliant, bumptious ex-Pittsburgher, then not quite twenty—Oscar Levant. Earlier in the year Charig, a friend of Levant's, then a pianist in the Ben Bernie band, introduced him to Gershwin. This introduction eventually led to his being supplanted by Levant as aide, rehearsal pianist, official interpreter and second piano in trying out new Gershwin compositions. This ejection from what he called the Gershwin Circle embittered Charig.

In late November 1925, however, Charig was still a member in good standing and he placed the concerto manuscript on the piano.

Damrosch returned to the podium and the rehearsal began. One news-man present was quite taken with one extra musical prop. Gershwin played with a pipe clenched between his teeth. It "wandered in and out of his mouth all through the rehearsal. In particular, he used it to point accusingly at members of the orchestra who were not solving their jazz problems successfully."

That label again: "jazz." Gershwin was not, in fact, attempting to compose a sequel to the *Rhapsody in Blue*. But word had begun to spread, and in the *Times* Olin Downes had dubbed it the "Jazz Concerto in F." But Gershwin did not agree, asserting that "Some people go so far as to affix the jazz label to my *Concerto in F*, in which I have attempted to utilize certain jazz rhythms worked out along more or less symphonic lines." His most obvious debt to popular folk forms are heard in the first movement's Charleston motif and the muted trumpet blues that opens the second.

With tryout and rehearsals over and final revisions set, the *Concerto in F* was ready for the official première performance on Thursday after-noon, December 3, 1925. Despite a cold, winter downpour, Carnegie Hall was filled to capacity. Gershwin was indeed good box office. (One disgruntled member of the orchestra, violist-composer Allan Lincoln Langley, intimated that that was precisely why Damrosch had commis-sioned the concerto; no Gershwin fan he. Langley would later insinuate that Daly did much of Gershwin's orchestration.)

The *Concerto in F* is cast in the traditional fast-slow-faster three-movement form of the contemporary concerto. The first movement is formed along the lines of a modified first movement sonata form: expo-sition, development, recapitulations, connected with proper modula-tions. The middle movement is one of comparative serenity: nocturnal repose between the more agitated outer movements. The third move-ment, which Gershwin described as "an orgy of rhythm," is in the form of a rondo, introducing a new theme and reintroducing motifs from the first two movements. Gershwin, evidently, had learned "what a con-certo actually was." But there the orthodoxy ended; while the orchestra employed was not an augmented Whiteman band, Gershwin put the New York Symphony through some unusual paces, what with his Charleston, blues and syncopated "orgy." Damrosch's faithful Thurs-day afternoon audience was in for a number of surprises; so were some of Gershwin's followers and friends—those few who had not already heard the work at recent parties.

"To judge by the enthusiasm displayed," reported Henry O. Osgood, who had attended the New York performances, "the audiences heartily enjoyed" the *Concerto in F*. In the Green Room, after the concert,

Gershwin thoroughly enjoyed the excitement and clamor of congratulations from family and friends. Even celebrated musicians "paid me compliments on my efforts as a composer. What caused a surprised smile, however, was that all of them, Rachmaninoff, Heifetz, Hoffman, complimented me upon my piano execution."

Before the official reviews were in, there were two celebrations, one in the afternoon given by Jules Glaenzer and one in the evening at the home of the Damrosches. Glaenzer presented Gershwin with a gold cigarette case engraved with the signatures of more than two dozen musical and theatrical friends and the inscription:

To
George Gershwin
and His
First Concerto

"He was very happy that night," recalled Lester Donahue of the Damrosch party, "pleased with the reception of his concerto and also over his first appearance as pianist with Damrosch at Carnegie Hall.

"The heated controversy started that evening as to whether George should abandon Broadway and the brilliant shows he had given it or continue with concertos, a symphony or two, an opera for the Metropolitan. He remained less upset by it than some of his friends . . ."

Gershwin had heard it all before, of course, at the Paley parties in Greenwich Village, when he was still regarded as a fine pianist and a good songwriter. After the *Rhapsody in Blue* these discussions of his future became more public. Damrosch believed that he had started it at the concerto party. "To tell the truth," he admitted, "I tried to wean him, so to speak, from Broadway, as I felt that he had it in him to develop on more serious lines than the Broadway shows demanded or even permitted. But the lighter forms in which he had become a master, proved too strong.

"Perhaps I was wrong and his own instinct guided him towards what he felt most able to do."

"But it's every composer for himself," Ira Gershwin once told his brother during a discussion of this same topic. "If you went ahead and became too self-conscious with your writing, and packed it full of counterpoint and all those other things I know nothing about, you might achieve a certain academic standard, you'd kill much that is spontaneous in your gifts."

"You may be right," Gershwin countered. "But I maintain that a composer needs to understand the intricacies of counterpoint and orchestration, and be able to create new forms for each advance in his work . . ."

Damrosch was right in one respect, Gershwin followed his instinct: he neither deserted Broadway nor ignored study. "Actually," Ira Gershwin recalled with apparent pride years later, "I can't recall a period in George's life when, despite all his musical creativity, he didn't find time to further his academic studies—whether analyzing Schoenberg with Edward Kilenyi, Sr., in the twenties or, in later years, exploring cerebral areas like 'Rhythmic Groups Resulting from the Interference of Several Synchronized Periodicities' with Dr. Joseph Schillinger."

The premiere of the *Concerto in F* served to stir up the old (but not very) "heated controversy." It even surfaced in the press the next month in Franklin P. Adams's column in the *World.*

The morning-after press was, as usual with Gershwin, mixed. The *Tribune*'s Gilman found the concerto "conventional, trite" and "at its worst, a little dull." Some reviewers anticipated Ira Gershwin, saying that in constricting himself with the conventional concerto form Gershwin had sacrificed the spontaneity so obvious in the *Rhapsody in Blue.* Chotzinoff of the *World* was the friendliest and most perceptive. Brushing aside the work's "shortcomings," he proceeded to lecture his readers (and undoubtedly his stuffier colleagues): "He alone actually expresses us. He is the present, with all its audacity, impertinence, its feverish delight in its motions, its lapses into rhythmic exotic melancholy. He writes without the smallest hint of self-consciousness . . . And here is where his genius comes in, for George Gershwin is an instinctive artist who has a talent for the right manipulation of the crude material he starts out with that a lifelong study of counterpoint and fugue never can give to one who is not born with it."

In assessing the "much-heralded piano concerto" in the *Times,* Olin Downes managed, as did so many critics in Gershwin's lifetime, to be at once perceptive and condescending. "Mr. Gershwin chose the form of the classic piano concerto in three movements, and there was great excitement about it," he began. "There would not have been as much excitement if Brahms had come to town, although Brahms also wrote piano concertos. But then, he did not employ 'jazz.' The writer of these lines believes strongly, seriously, in 'jazz.' He thinks it has a future as well as a past, and marked possibilities for the serious composer. So he, too, repaired with curiosity and anticipation to Carnegie Hall.

"The rhythms employed by Mr. Gershwin are principally those of popular dances and songs, including the 'Charleston' of recent rage and various aspects of the 'blues.' Lusty blows upon the drum announce the rhythms and pace of what is to follow. There is considerable orchestral preparation before the piano enters. The piano is given an important part, but its role is not vainglorious. Mr. Gershwin played the piano, as need hardly be said, but it was plain that he had written for it as one of a number of instruments with something important to say. Two of the three movements, the first and last, are in a lively vein. The middle movement is more tropical and nocturnal, a stopped trumpet playing a 'blue' melody against a sensuous harmonic background, and this passage is perhaps the best part of the concerto.

"Throughout Mr. Gershwin has tried earnestly and sincerely to compose a work of symphonic dimensions. But it cannot be said that he had succeeded. He has not succeeded because the form he employs is not native to a composer of his experience, and he has neither the instinct nor the technical equipment to be at ease in it; and also because of the rather obvious limitations of his orchestral scheme. Sometimes the color scheme turns from classic symphonic standards toward 'jazz' orchestration that is so striking a feature of our popular music today. But this is done half-heartedly, in such a way that the instrumentation is neither flesh, fowl nor good red herring. And this is in turn the prevailing character of the composition.

"The *Rhapsody in Blue* was slangy, sentimental, audacious and vulgar in its essential ideas. It was not responsible and did not aspire to be. It had a cheerful Broadway insouciance and a certain raciness and ginger in its principal ideas. Moreover, these ideas were well contrasted. There is no such effective contrast in the themes of the concerto."

Downes found the concerto's themes "denatured," the harmonies "forced and dry," the development flagged. He suggested that Gershwin should not have attempted a concerto at all. "Another rhapsody or one movement concerto—Liszt wrote one-movement concertos—might have been a marked step in advance whereas the three-movement concerto is a new and dubious experiment."

He deplored its "evident lack of technical resource"; he found it "not only immature—which need be no crime—but it is self-conscious, lacking the esprit and felicity of touch that he shows when he is truly in the creative vein."

Downes's conclusion was that "in essence" the *Concerto in F* was "a more ambitious and less original piece of music than" the *Rhapsody in Blue*. He found virtually nothing to say about the other works on the program though he appended an extramusical note: "At the end of the performance the popularity of the composer was attested in long and vehement applause, so that Mr. Gershwin was kept bowing for some minutes from the stage."

Gershwin read this and the other reviews Friday morning and afternoon; that evening he was back in Carnegie Hall for another performance to bask in the same glowing reception by the audience that he had enjoyed the previous afternoon. While most of his critics agreed with Downes that the *Concerto in F* was technically a step (though not totally successful) forward but inspirationally a step backward, the audiences loved it. And that is what Gershwin wanted. Five years earlier, when he had only "Swanee" to his credit, an interviewer for *The Edison Musical Magazine,* after noting that Gershwin's "words seemed more suited to the learned lecturer than to a composer of popular hits," inquired about his ambitions at the time.

"Operettas that represent the life and spirit of this country are decidedly my aim," Gershwin replied. "After that may come opera, but I want all my work to have one element of appealing to the great majority of our people.

"I am one of those," he reflected on the same point years later, "who honestly believe that the majority has much better taste and understanding, not only of music but of any of the arts, than it is credited with having. It is not the few knowing ones whose opinions make any work of art great, it is the judgment of the great mass that finally decides."

One of the important knowing ones, Paul Rosenfeld, who virtually made a hobby of scourging Gershwin's "serious works," actually found something to admire in the *Concerto in F*—the principal piano theme of the first movement and the bluesy opening of the second, but little else. He went so far as to admit that the concerto was "the juiciest and most entertaining of Gershwin's concert works," but that "the main honors for the symphonic exploitation and idealization of jazz have gone to Milhaud for *La Création du Monde* [1923], to Honegger for his Piano Concerto [1925] and to Copland for his Piano Concerto [1926]."

Of these contemporaneous compositions, only Gershwin's concerto is regularly heard in the world's concert halls today.

IV

That double life that perplexed George Gershwin's critics, but in which he reveled, came to a near-frenetic climax during December 1925 following the premiere of the *Concerto in F.*

By the late summer of 1925, while working on the final movements, he worked simultaneously on the next Aarons-Freedley musical comedy, *Tip-Toes,* with his brother Ira and on an Arthur Hammerstein operetta *Song of the Flame* in collaboration with Hammerstein's nephew, Oscar, Otto Harbach and co-composer Herbert Stothart. Around this time too the Gershwins moved from the 110th Street flat into their own five-story house at 316 West 103rd Street, near Riverside Drive, which in the winter, one friend found, was "the coldest spot in the world . . . when a northwest wind ruffles the Hudson." In this splendid symbol of achievement, Gershwin completed the concerto and the songs for *Tip-Toes* and *Song of the Flame.* The street may have been chilly but inside the house there was bustling warmth. When he needed a temporary period of privacy, Gershwin ducked out and took rooms in the still handy Whitehall Hotel.

The entire family settled into the house on 103rd Street. On the ground floor (where the kitchen was located) was a largish room, once a modest ballroom, in which a billiard table had been installed. It was later supplanted by a Ping-Pong table. Family, friends, neighbors and strangers gathered around one or the other for friendly if animated games.

The second floor was often the setting for the elaborate Gershwin parties of the later twenties. Reached by a self-service elevator, a rarity at the time, were the main dining room, a large living room with its twin Steinways, Rose and Morris Gershwin's bedroom and small sitting room. Rose Gershwin also entertained in this area.

The third floor served as the sleeping quarters of the younger Gershwins, Frances and Arthur; the fourth was taken over completely by Ira Gershwin in 1926, when he married Leonore Strunsky.

The fifth floor belonged to George: a music room with a third Steinway, a book-lined study, his bedroom. The floor was recessed from the building front and screened from the street by a grill fence. While the top floor was ostensibly his, the house was a lively one. S. N. Behrman came by one evening and found Gershwin working on the orchestration of the *Concerto in F* in a room "in which there were must have been six other people talking among themselves, having tea and playing checkers." It was time to head for the Whitehall again. Under these convivial conditions he managed to complete *Tip-Toes* in time for rehearsals and a November 29 tryout in Newark, the concerto for its December 3 first performance at Carnegie Hall and for the December 9 premiere in Wilmington of *Song of the Flame.*

The second week of December can best be described in the worn word *hectic. Tip-Toes* moved into Philadelphia on the seventh; on his way to Washington, Gershwin looked in on how it was going and found it doing well. The next day he played the concerto with Damrosch and the New York Symphony in the capital. The day after, December 9, they introduced the *Concerto in F* to Baltimore. That evening *Song of the Flame* began its tryout tour in Wilmington.

It was a memorable occasion for Frances Gershwin, who had turned nineteen three days before and was her brother's guest in a box at the Playhouse. "George's Russian musical," as she remembers it, was rendered even more memorable when she saw sections of the overhead scenery crashing to the stage (it was a ponderous production), fortunately without injury to anyone. The show went on.

Gershwin had taken rooms in a hotel in Wilmington to see *Song of the Flame* launched and to be near to Philadelphia, where he, Damrosch and orchestra were to perform the *Concerto in F*. This was their final stop of their tour with the concerto (two more performances were scheduled in New York: a "by popular request" appearance at the Mecca Auditorium on Sunday afternoon of January 3 and another in Brooklyn on the sixteenth).

Frances remembers, too, a telegram her brother received during their stay in Baltimore. For several years he had been seeing Pauline Heifetz, the attractive sister of the violinist. He had escorted her to musical parties and there was some assumption among their friends that it was a serious thing. But during the same period Gershwin had been seeing others. His practice generally was to take the young women to an Emily and Lou Paley party; if they fit into this special group he saw more of them. However, he was not at the time thinking about marriage.

In her telegram Pauline Heifetz informed him that music critic Samuel Chotzinoff had just proposed—what did he think?

With *Tip-Toes, Song of the Flame* and the next performance of the *Concerto in F* on his mind, Gershwin's initial reaction was a bemused "Wonderful!" He telegrammed good wishes to his two friends, then dashed off to Philadelphia to play the concerto. On his way homeward he checked into Washington to look in on *Song of the Flame*. Back in New York in mid-December, he spent his time alternating between rehearsals of his two forthcoming musicals. December closed with a dramatic Gershwinesque flourish: on Monday (the twenty-eighth) *Tip-Toes* premiered at the Liberty; on Tuesday his one-act opera *Blue Monday*, retitled *135th Street*, was revived at Carnegie Hall; *Song of the Flame*'s first curtain went up on Wednesday at the Forty-fourth Street Theatre.

Tip-Toes is the true successor to *Lady, Be Good! Tell Me More* lacked the sparkle and zest of the earlier musical that *Tip-Toes* displayed. The score, one of Gershwin's most endearing, was conducted knowledgeably by William Daly. And, as he had with *Lady, Be Good!*, Gershwin wove his characteristic sound of two pianos into the orchestration. These parts, as in *Lady*, were played by the team of Phil Ohman and Victor Arden.

Queenie Smith appeared in the title role; she had begun her professional career as a dancer at the Metropolitan Opera. She switched to Broadway, making her debut at the age of seventeen in something entitled *Roly Boly Eyes* (1919). Four years later Smith garnered critical and audience attention in a secondary role in George S. Kaufman and Marc Connelly's *Helen of Troy, New York* (songs by Bert Kalmar and Harry Ruby). In *Tip-Toes* she appeared as the young female member of a vaudeville team, "The Three K's," the others being her conniving uncles, portrayed by two comedians, Harry Watson, Jr., and Andrew Tombs. Romantic interest was provided by a veteran musical comedy song-and-dance man, Allen Kearns, as a wealthy glue magnate in the first of three leads in Gershwin musicals. The plot, by Guy Bolton and Fred Thompson, set the penniless "K's," in Palm Beach, Florida, where the other K's try to pass off Tip-Toes as a wealthy young woman, hoping she will meet a wealthy, marriageable male.

She does of course, but upon learning of her part in her uncles' scheme, he decides to put her, and some of his friends, to the test. He invites them all aboard his yacht and announces that he himself is penniless. All desert the sinking ship except *Tip-Toes*, for the requisite happy ending. This plot, suffice to say, did not go over very well with the reviewers.

The anonymous critic from the *Times* chose to ignore it; in fact he concentrated more on Gershwin than either the performers or plot. Like Olin Downes, he commented on Gershwin's musical double life. "Drawn chiefly by the fact that its own George Gershwin," he began, "still its own despite the excessive temptations being put in his way by the stranger gods of Fifty-seventh Street, had written the score, a large and prominent Broadway audience sat in attendance upon the new 'Tip Toes' at the Liberty last night. It found pleasure," he concluded, "of course, in everything with which Mr. Gershwin provided it . . ." He predicted that three of the songs, "Looking for a Boy," "Sweet and Low-Down" and "It's a Great Little World" were "destined to be restaurant pests this Winter."

He was right about the first two, although it was the distinctive "That Certain Feeling" that was taken up by the "potted palm" bands of the cafés and hotel tea dances. "Looking for a Boy" is notable for its melodic-harmonic charm and the not too sweet whimsy of the lyric. This song and the tongue-in-cheek duet, "Nightie-Night," has evoked a comparison of the *Tip-Toe* score to the Kern Princess Theatre classics of pre-twenties Broadway. But that could be over done. The wistful

"Looking for a Boy" and the silly-sweet "Nightie-Night" are Gershwin-esque variations of the operetta love ballad and the sentimental boy-girl duet. The first is a tribute to Kern with Gershwin overtones—a bitter-sweet blue note, the rich harmonies, the engaging lilt of the melody.

The more characteristic songs were those in which Ira Gershwin revealed himself as a master lyricist (and which inspired a fan letter from a brilliant peer, Lorenz Hart). These were not the songs one heard in restaurants: the social satire of "These Charming People" (the title borrowed from a current Michael Arlen play) which skewers the pretensions of the newly rich. In it Ira employs some wonderfully dreadful rhymes: "blokes pass" with "faux pas"; "enjoy it" with "De-troit." It was one of his own favorite efforts. Another was "Harlem River Chanty," a choral number that had originally opened the second act. When the show's setting was shifted from New York to Palm Beach, the number was eliminated from the score. It is a mock pirate song, a sly comment on the Prohibition law that the nation chose pretty much to ignore. Out of *Tip-Toes*, it became a popular Gershwin party song, like "Mischa, Yascha, Toscha, Sascha," the fiddler parody and the *Lady, Be Good* reject, "The Man I Love."

George Gershwin's characteristic "jazz age" creations were the sin-ewy rhythm songs "That Certain Feeling," an unsentimental love duet, and the compelling "Sweet and Low-Down," with its typical Ira Gersh-win lyric and title (a portmanteau, combining the title of the old song and a current slang phrase). Another good but lesser-known song is the lively "Nice Baby" (one of its vocalists was Jeanette MacDonald in her pre-Hollywood phase). "When Do We Dance?" is very characteristic Gershwin in its rhythmic propulsion and a remarkable chromatic pas-sage in the last four measures of the verse, serving as an intriguing bridge between verse and chorus. Also delightful is the sprightly 2/4 defiance of the Volstead Act "It's a Great Little World!"

Only eight songs of this bountiful score were published (fewer than half written for it) and most of them have gone out of print. It was not customary to publish full scores in the twenties, a hangover from hit-oriented Tin Pan Alley. Many a fine idea—and, in Gershwin's case, choral piece—went into the limbo of publishers' warehouses and was lost.

This business practice was taken for granted by the songwriters, who —no matter what their stature—settled for what they got; that was the way it was. Ira Gershwin explained this to a friend. "Naturally," he wrote, "as in the case of all show writers where no *complete* score is published there are many, many songs by George which remain unpublished.

"If, as in the case of, say, a George White "Scandals" where George would write 15–20 songs and incidental things like opening choruses, short ballets, etc.—only 6 or 7 of the songs were published—obviously there would be a wealth of songs. But since most of these would be songs for special personalities or dancers or were minor efforts—my brother never bothered keeping copies of these."

Tip-Toes, despite some critical reservations, was honestly proclaimed by Aarons and Freedley in their Tuesday advertisement THE UNDISPUTED HIT! The show joined an array of current popular musicals— *Sunny* (Kern), *No, No, Nanette* (Youmans), *The Cocoanuts* (Berlin), *Dearest Enemy* (Rodgers and Hart), and the operettas *Rose Marie, The Vagabond King* (both Friml) and Romberg's *The Student Prince of Heidelberg* for a healthy stay.

V

The next night Gershwin stepped from Forty-second Street to the precinct of "the stranger gods of Fifty-seventh Street" for the first of two presentations of a refurbished *Blue Monday* by Paul Whiteman at Carnegie Hall. It was the same one-act "opera" that had run for a single performance in the *Scandals of 1922,* with a new orchestration by Ferde Grofé. Whiteman's advertisements gave Gershwin top billing and promised a "one-act jazz opera by Gershwin and DeSylva, *135th Street* (It happened on Blue Monday)." The same program featured, besides the usual and latest Whiteman novelties, new works by Deems Taylor, *Circus Day,* and Grofé, *Mississippi Suite.* The opera was presented onstage with minimal props and no set except the entire Paul Whiteman Orchestra.

The *Times* dispatched its Fifty-seventh Street authority, Olin Downes, to cover the Tuesday night event. In the light of what he had written about the concerto on December 4, his views on Gershwin's "jazz opera" are curious: his was the most favorable review and, predictably, a little patronizing. And as with the concerto, he also reviewed the audience "in which hundreds had stood for two hours before [the Gershwin work was performed], while many restless feet kept time to the changing jazz rhythms . . ."

This was followed by Downes's view: "Twenty minutes of as vivid 'grand opera' as has yet been provided from native and local materials by an American composer . . . Mr. Gershwin's music, whether or not it proves to be the 'grandest' was certainly the first in an opera premiere to be whistled within an hour on Broadway.

"On a stage dedicated once by Tchaikovsky [in 1891, when it opened], under the remembered Paderewski lights and in the presence of a typical [soprano Maria] Jeritza house, Blossom Seeley and Charles Hart acted the swift tragedy of Harlem Mike's saloon, with its 'prologue' by Jack McGowan 'just like the white man's opera.' . . . Half a dozen short songs, as many spoken retorts in the dramatic action, and then a pistol shot cracked noisily. Hart as the cheap gambler died game, with the dancing chorus and the bar attendants, Benny Fields and Francis Howard, taking up the tenor's refrain, 'I'm Going South in the Morning.'

"The song was sung by a crowd applauding out in front. It echoed later in the lobbies and was still in the air when a street full of limousines came surging to the carriage calls." Downes noted too that Walter Damrosch and composer Henry Hadley had been present and visited the Green Room to congratulate "all concerned."

The *Sun*'s reviewer was not that impressed or amused, finding that the "music, with the exception of two clever songs [he neglected to name them], served simply as an unimpressive accompaniment for an old hokum vaudeville skit."

Gershwin did not quite agree, although he felt that once again *Blue Monday (135th Street)* had not worked. Although "the opera sounded well," that night, he felt that "the performance was marred by the fact that the stage within a stage idea, as Whiteman had originally planned, was found impractical and, at the last minute, he switched the thing around so that the performers sang and acted in front of the orchestra, without any scenery. They used some props, such as a bar, tables and chairs to give the effect of a Harlem nightclub. The thing really didn't come off, and I'm sure that the reason most of the critics were very nice about it was the fact that they had listened to the orchestra rehearse the music before the actual performance . . ." After these two Carnegie Hall performances Gershwin chose to abandon *Blue Monday;* in the three years since its hurried creation, he had grown beyond it.

The next night, Wednesday, he temporarily left Fifty-seventh Street for Forty-fourth Street. Advertised by producer Arthur Hammerstein as "a romantic opera," *Song of the Flame* was out-and-out operetta and one of Gershwin's least characteristic musicals.

Mysterious, too, is why he became involved with yet another production when he was occupied with the *Concerto in F* and *Tip-Toes.* Conjecture would suggest that producer Hammerstein, hoping to mine the rich lode opened by his own still running *Rose Marie* of the year before and the more recent Shubert production of *The Student Prince,* contracted his nephew, lyricist-librettist Oscar Hammerstein II, and Otto Harbach to concoct a romantic musical with a Russian Revolution setting. He assigned composer Herbert Stothart, who had contributed several pieces to the predominantly Friml score of *Rose Marie,* the job of scoring the operetta. Stothart was a good, solid, all-around musician—a conductor as well as arranger; he had worked with Hammerstein and Harbach before, as well as on joint scores with Vincent Youmans and others. He was mildly successful on Broadway and in 1929 left for Hollywood where he supervised important film musicals at Metro-Goldwyn-Mayer—his own Broadway shows transcribed for the screen and originals, most notably Harold Arlen and E. Y. Harburg's *The Wizard of Oz* (1939). He also composed a good deal of background music for films.

Gershwin may have been called in for two reasons. His name had been current during virtually all of 1925 and would, as at Carnegie Hall, prove to be good for the box office. If for some reason Stothart had bogged down, an extra musical hand would have helped Hammerstein bring his production in on schedule. That Gershwin was a kind of afterthought is evidenced by an early advertisement for *Song of the Flame* that gave Stothart top billing.

But this is speculation. Still, by the time he agreed to fill out the score of the operetta, Gershwin needed neither the fame nor the fortune. But he loved the excitement and the activity.

The Hammerstein-Harbach libretto told the story of a Russian noblewoman (sung by Tessa Kosta) who, disguised in her fiery scarlet costume, incites the proletariat to revolt against their leaders and landowners. Her theme song is the musical's title song. Unaware of her double identity, a Russian Prince (Guy Robertson) falls in love with her. The Revolution separates them, by which time The Flame's heart has been enkindled by the Prince, despite political-social differences. But, like so many from the Czarist upper classes, both end up in Paris after the Revolution (apparently The Flame's contribution was not appreciated by the Bolsheviks), where they reconcile and marry.

Hammerstein did not stint on the production: there was an enormous cast augmented by the eighty-member Russian Art Choir, the American Ballet with a company of seventy-five and an orchestra of sixty, under Stothart's direction. These features were prominently displayed in the advertisements; on opening night, this boxed item appeared in the *Times:* "Owing to the importance of the Opening Scenes, Arthur Hammerstein Requests that the audience attending the premiere of "Song of the Flame" at the 44th Street Theatre Tonight be seated before 8:25 P.M."

The facts as to who wrote which song are not completely known. Only two of the published songs, "Midnight Bells" and "The Signal," are attributed solely to Gershwin. Neither is particularly distinguished, though the first is a passable ballad and the second, without the lyric, might have been one of the early novelettes. The program noted that several songs were based on Russian folk songs, among them the title song and "The Cossack Love Song." "Vodka" too is folk-flavored and graced with an amusing lyric. One song, though credited to both composers, is almost certainly all Gershwin—"You Are You." Its linear melody and off-beat rhythm stamps it as more of a musical-comedy ballad rather than song for a quasi-opera. Though printed, it was eliminated from the score before the opening.

The seriousness of the production is explicit in the program note to a ballet (probably by Stothart) that opens Scene 2 of Act II. Entitled *The First Blossom,* it was "Symbolic of Russia's long winter of adversity and the arrival of the first blossom of victorious ideals." The solo dancers in this were Ula Sharon and Leonard St. Leo.

The critics, generally, were not impressed with the Hammerstein touch. Though he found *Song of the Flame* "a romantic spectacle" (the scenery was designed by Ziegfeld's master artisan, Joseph Urban), Brooks Atkinson, in the *Times,* felt that "the size of the production makes the opera generally heavy." Percy Hammond (the *Tribune)* pronounced it "a large, beautiful, and serious feast." Still, despite all that, he feared that it lacked "that something." The reviewer of the *World* described it as "the most gorgeous entertainment in New York . . ." But he found the libretto to be "pretty hopeless," although "George Gershwin and Herbert Stothart obliged with a score of richness and variety."

Whatever the dramatic shortcomings, something kept *Song of the Flame* going. Of his two December shows, *Song of the Flame* had a longer run than the more Gershwinesque *Tip-Toes* (219 and 194 performances).

That out of the way, Gershwin began the New Year with typical energy; Carnegie Hall for another performance of *135th Street,* the concerto in the Mecca Auditorium on January 3 and in Brooklyn on the sixteenth. Then off to Connecticut to reprise his Eva Gauthier "Recital of Ancient and Modern Music," beginning in Derby on the twenty-first. As one year fused into the next, Gershwin was as usual on the go.

7

Interlude and Preludes

Though his life was as animated as it had been the year before—concert performances of his works, parties, travels—Gershwin composed only one show score in 1926, *Oh, Kay!* There would be a three-year gap between the *Concerto in F* and his next large orchestral work. This creative hiatus was a kind of response to the cocktail party discussions of his future, as Franklin P. Adams quaintly reported in his column about one party Gershwin had attended, given by broker Harry Cushing: "Then G. Gershwin the composer come in, and we did talk about musique, and about going ahead regardless of advice, this one saying, Do not study, and that one saying, Study; and another saying, Write only jazz melodies, and another saying, Write only symphonies and concertos. But the thing to do is what you want to do, for all advice is of no moment."

What Gershwin did, in fact, was to spend the next several months searching for a suitable teacher—and produced the scores for five musicals and only one small "serious" work. Three nights later F.P.A. encountered Gershwin at a party given by a darling of the Algonquin's notorious "Vicious Circle" (later the Round Table), commercial artist Neysa McMein (she had changed her first name from Marjorie on the advice of a numerologist). Gershwin had brought Bill Daly, and Adams reported that the two held forth at the two pianos for three hours. It

was a social period: a few evenings later, they arrived at the Adamses'
and performed both the *Rhapsody* and the *Concerto*.

I

Gershwin, by this time, had begun holding his own regular Sunday
evening gatherings at 103rd Street that commingled his circle of friends
and colleagues from the worlds of publishing, art, business, music. Dazzled by such brilliant company, twenty-year-old Frankie Gershwin sat
quietly in the background. "I remember sitting in a corner and looking
on as if I were an outsider, overwhelmed. It never occurred to me to
talk to anybody—I was too shy."

Gershwin, however, drew her out, for he liked her interpretations of
his songs. Hers was a small but true voice, a light soprano and, in the
phrase of the time, she knew "how to put over a song." Gestures, small
graceful steps, expressions: Frankie Gershwin underscored the point of
the music as well as the words, and both Ira and George loved it. With
George at the piano, she blossomed at the Gershwin parties and was in
demand as a singer of her brothers' songs at other parties as well.

George, however, was protective and not happy about her theatrical
ambitions. Despite this he paid for her new dance routines when she
needed one (these came as high as a hundred fifty dollars). He especially
admired her dancing and told her he felt she had as great a talent for
dance as he had for music. "He danced beautifully," she recalled, "and
would show me new steps" that he had picked up from the Astaires or
other dancers he knew in the theater—or he would contrive steps of his
own. He often challenged her with tricky rhythmic improvisations, but
she kept up with him.

The house on 103rd Street, despite its community-center bustle (one
writer likened it to a Kaufman and Hart play), was the first truly home-
like Gershwin home. The family was closer than during any other period since their childhood. Although there was a maid to help with the
housework and to answer the door (when the spirit moved her—the
door was never locked), Rose Gershwin did the cooking. Gershwin was
especially fond of her borscht; another favorite was double lamb chops.

Morris Gershwin by 1925 had retired from the uncertainties of the
restaurant business and enjoyed being around the house, meeting his
sons' famous friends, riding the self-service elevator and gently delight-
ing Gershwin's friends when, poker-faced, he delivered his wry quips.
One of Gershwin's favorite Pop Gershwin stories came about during an
impromptu tour of his son's art collection. George had become an avid,

and astute, collector of contemporary art—a collection that eventually became one of the most impressive private collections of its kind.

One day a group of women—"some of George's society friends"—came around to view the growing collection—early Picasso, Derain, Chagall, Utrillo, others. Gershwin was guiding them through the paintings when he was called to the telephone; Pop Gershwin had unobtrusively attached himself to the group, listening to the exclamations of the expensively dressed women. Their appreciative speech was enlivened with a tough, colorful, post-*What Price Glory?* Marine barracks vocabulary.

During a momentary silence Pop Gershwin asked, "Tell me, ladies, whatever became of 'Oh fudge'?"

Ira Gershwin, when not working, enjoyed his own quarters in the house. He read and generally skipped the partying except at home or at the Paleys' in Greenwich Village. Arthur Gershwin enjoyed being a Gershwin brother and man-about-town and was trying to find his way in some business or other. He frequently invited his young friends over to use the pool table. Most of them were unknown to the other Gershwins.

S. N. Behrman captured the rhythms of that house in his *New Yorker* Gershwin profile. He had telephoned ahead and had arrived around nine o'clock in the evening. He rang the doorbell but no one answered. Through the curtained door he saw people moving about inside. He rang again, with no result, then pushed the door open and walked in. "Three or four young men were sitting around the hall smoking. Off the hall was a small reception-room which had been converted into a billiard room. I peered in—there was a game in progress but I knew none of the players. I asked for George, or his brother Ira. No one bothered to reply, but one of the young men made a terse gesture in the direction of the upper stories."

One flight up he encountered another group, one of whom he "vaguely recognized from 110th Street" and asked where George and Ira were.

"Upstairs, I think."

On the third floor he found Arthur Gershwin, who admitted that he did not know anyone below. Behrman climbed to the fourth floor and found no one, but he called out. Ira answered, inviting him up to George's part of the house, where it was cooler and uncongested.

"Who under the sun," Behrman demanded, "are those fellows playing billiards on the first floor?"

"To tell you the truth, I don't know."

"But you must, they looked perfectly at home."

"I really don't," Ira assured him. "There's a bunch of fellows from down the street who've taken to dropping in here every night for a game. I think they're friends of Arthur's. But I don't know."

Another member of the Gershwin household not yet mentioned was George's wire-haired terrier, Tony. He too was very popular on 103rd Street. In an era before the automobile dominated Manhattan's streets, Tony was permitted out on his own. One afternoon one of the neighborhood youngsters, eleven-year-old Joseph Zahler, spotted Tony seated obediently on the curb in front of the Gershwin house. Seeing no one about, he whistled, and the friendly—and to him strange—dog scampered over and followed him home.

Zahler senior was curious. Wire-hairs were a fancy breed; in addition, this one had a collar and license. He made a phone call and was informed that the dog belonged to George Gershwin on the next block. Joseph was then ordered to return the dog to its owner.

George Gershwin answered the door and was delighted to see the missing Tony. He asked where Joseph had found him. Evasively Joseph merely told him that Tony had followed him home. A grateful Gershwin gave him a five-dollar bill, saying, "Strange, he never did that before."

Dogs appear to have been a favorite Gershwin pet. Oscar Levant liked to tell about the time that George Gershwin presented Pop Gershwin with one as a birthday gift. The dog did not appear to be very friendly, and Pop Gershwin studied him skeptically, then said to his son, "Thanks for the present, George—so far."

During the period of settling in the new house and into its family rhythms, Gershwin took on no new assignments. He had already agreed to go to London to work on the British versions of *Lady, Be Good!* and *Tip-Toes.* Kay Swift, a composer-pianist herself, recalled how he made a characteristic exit from one of her parties.

They had met fleetingly the year before when her friend (and Gershwin's) cellist Marie Rosanoff came to a party given by Swift and her financier husband, James Paul Warburg. Swift, whose musical training had been thorough and classical—she recalls writing a fugue a week when she was a student of Percy Goetschius—had rather looked down on popular song for years. It was her brother Sam who introduced her to recorded versions of "Do It Again" and "Stairway to Paradise," that stimulated her respect for and an interest in the music of George Gershwin.

When Rosanoff (with whom Swift had formed a performing trio before she married Warburg) brought the intense young composer to the

Swift-Warburg home, Swift was also impressed with his remarkable piano playing.

They did not meet again for several months, until some time in March 1926, when the Warburgs had a musical evening to which Gershwin was invited. He arrived, bubbling with the success of the *Concerto* and happily played songs from his December shows. Swift never forgot his exit line. Casually, as if he were leaving to catch the crosstown bus, Gershwin left the piano and said, "Well, I've got to go to Europe now."

II

For Gershwin the trip was mostly recreational, for there was little work to do on the London *Lady, Be Good!* The Astaires had preceded him after a tour of the show that had begun in Newark in September and ended in Boston in December.

There were minor but necessary adjustments to accommodate British tastes: some of the jazzy Manhattan pacing was tempered and slight lyric changes were required. One troublesome word of dialogue was altered. The word "bum" was freely applied to the show's poor rich man, Jack Robinson. In Britain it is a vulgarism referring to the human posterior. As Freedley recalled, "William Kent [in the Walter Catlett part of the conniving lawyer, Watty] did absentmindedly use it one night, when nobility was in the house, and the effects were rather electrical."

The opening scene was extended "in order to get Fred and Adele Astaire on the stage later than they appeared in New York. Like George Gershwin, the Astaires have a large society following, and as these people come to theatre even later than they do in New York, we felt it would be better to hold off the entrance of our stars until the house was in."

Working again with Desmond Carter, Gershwin contrived a new opening choral number, "Buy a Little Button," and, to provide the Astaires with sprightly comic song and dance, "I'd Rather Charleston." In addition he interpolated the 1919 song he had written with Lou Paley, "Something About Love." Once this was done in time for the opening of *Lady, Be Good!* in Liverpool on March 29, Gershwin was free for the London social whirl.

Vernon Dukelsky (later Duke), Gershwin's excitable, gossipy, class-conscious composer friend, was then in London working on a musical and hoping for a production of one of his ballets (under Gershwin's influence, the classically trained Dukelsky moved between the theater and the concert hall). He described Gershwin as "the darling of May-fair. He was showered with invitations, including those of Prince George and the Mountbattens." Lady Mountbatten—Edwina to Gersh-win—was the willful, rather spoiled wife of Louis Mountbatten (great-grandson of Queen Victoria). She had contributed to the London, and later Paris, popularity of "The Man I Love" when she had returned the year before with a copy of the sheet music after it was dropped from the original production of *Lady, Be Good!*

"When not busy with a London production of *Lady, Be Good,*" Duke later wrote, "Gershwin accepted these invitations with joy, because he loved to play piano for people who loved to hear him. George's superb piano playing took London completely by storm . . ."

Among those Londoners was Beverly Nichols, who wrote for the trendy magazine *The Sketch.* He had begun in music as secretary to the Australian soprano Nellie Melba, then branched out on his own as a writer. His autobiography, *Twenty-Five,* established him as a Bright Young Thing in London's art world. He was also an aspiring song-writer, a good pianist and a drama critic. His mannered, glittering *Sketch* pieces deftly profiled London's current celebrities.

Before *Lady, Be Good!* left for Liverpool, Nichols called on Gershwin in his Pall Mall flat in central London. It was dusk and, for March, an unseasonably mild early evening.

"The twilight was fast fading when [Gershwin] sat down [at the pi-ano], and by the time he had finished it was almost dark, and the street lamps were lit. Yet in that brief period I had passed through one of the most singular experiences I have known. I ought to be slightly drunk to be able to describe it properly, for it was the music of intoxication."

Nichols described Gershwin as "a swarthy young man of twenty-seven, seated at the piano by the open window." At the writer's request, Gershwin played portions of the *Concerto in F,* which had not yet been performed in Britain. Nichols found it "beautiful, *really* beautiful," but admitted he could not verbally delineate its complex rhythms. Though he loathed "people who make pictures out of music" especially those "to whom the Preludes of Chopin mean nothing more than rain drip-ping on a roof or George Sand having the vapours," Nichols envisioned "the whole of a new America . . . blossoming into beauty before me" . . . the stern unfaltering grace of a skyscraper . . . chattering of Broadway chorus girls drinking mint juleps at Child's . . ." not to mention "something of the mystery of vast forests . . ." and ". . . tunes that clashed and fought, degenerated, were made clean again, joined together, and scampered madly over the keyboard in a final rush which was as breathless as the thundering herd over the prairies of the West."

When Gershwin finished, there were some moments of silence until Nichols became aware of the street sounds bringing him back to Pall Mall. "I felt the occasion was one for repeating what Schumann said after hearing Chopin for the first time: 'Hats off, gentlemen—a genius.'" Instead, not wishing to be "embarassed by so un-English a display of emotion," he began turning pages of the concerto score, then selecting "one of the most complicated," asked Gershwin, "quite bluntly, how it was done."

"I don't know," Gershwin told him.

"Play this bit very slowly."

Gershwin did, and Nichols detected three different rhythms "fighting each other—two in the treble and one in the bass. I began to laugh."

"What are you laughing at?" Gershwin asked.

"All those rhythms—scrapping. How *do* you make them fight like that?"

Shaking his head, Gershwin said, "I feel things inside, and then I work them out—that's all."

He continued playing; syncopation and polyrhythms were no mystery to him. As his hands moved over the keyboard fragments of a melody began to form. Gershwin repeated it, then rejected it with a discord. He tried another—not so bad—and tried it again.

"I say," Nichols said, "I rather like that."

"So do I," Gershwin said and began to expand it. "It's got possibilities. But it's really a Charleston tune, and it hasn't got a Charleston rhythm." He proceeded to shape the tune, variation after variation, until Nichols "felt that I never wanted to hear it again." Gershwin then played it through and stopped, saying, "Well, at any rate, that's a beginning." (Nichols would hear it again when he saw *Lady, Be Good!* the next month as "I'd Rather Charleston.")

Some time later Dukelsky visited Gershwin and found him working with Desmond Carter on the song. Dukelsky described the two at work: young Carter, "a model of tact and reticence," sat comfortably in an armchair with a pad and pencil, while Gershwin, "a big cigar in his mouth and eyes shining, played 'I'd Rather Charleston' over and over in every existing key."

He was excited about *Lady, Be Good!*; it had a special significance. He told Nichols about his piano pounding at Remick's. "Every day at nine o'clock I was there at the piano," he said, "playing popular tunes for anybody who came along . . . Chorus ladies used to breathe down my neck. Some of the customers treated [me] like dirt. Others were charming. Among the latter was Fred Astaire.

"It was at a time when Fred and Adele were doing a little vaudeville show of their own. Fred used to come in sometimes to hear the new songs. I remember saying to him once, 'Wouldn't it be wonderful if one day I could write a show of my own, and you and Adele could star in it?'

"We just laughed then," he said against the sounds of London's nighttime traffic, "but it came true."

Before leaving for Liverpool (where their show began its pre-London run on March 29), Gershwin received a letter from Mabel Schirmer in Paris. He was delighted to learn that she and her husband "were as close to London as you are & not off somewhere in Greece studying Gods." He outlined his plans, informing her that between the Liverpool and London openings he planned to visit Paris for several days. She replied immediately inviting him to stay in the Schirmer flat; he in turn accepted, provided he did not inconvenience them, adding that he hoped they could return to London for *Lady, Be Good!* "It ought to be exciting," he promised her, "as everyone is looking forward to see the Astaires."

Pleased with the show in Liverpool, he arrived in Paris early in April for his visit with the Schirmers, who put him up in their small spare room. Their mornings were devoted to breakfast, the phonograph, Gershwin at the piano and singing—mostly Gershwin songs. They partied evenings, or saw a musical (one was so bad Gershwin walked out); they went to the races in the Bois de Boulogne and to boxing matches. There were also reunions with several friends—Irving Berlin, Edwin Knopf and novelist Michael Arlen, whom Gershwin had met at an Alexander Woollcott party the year before.

The Schirmers had a musical evening for Gershwin to which they invited Knopf, a woman friend and the young self-styled "Bad Boy of Music," George Antheil and his wife, Böski Markus. The Trenton-born Antheil had been in Europe (mainly in Paris) since the early twenties, following a tour during which he had demonstrated his exceptional piano technique in performances of his own ultramodern compositions. Just the year before he had composed a "Jazz Symphony" and had recently completed the soon-to-be-notorious *Ballet mécanique*. Antheil and Böski were members of the group of artists, writers, musicians and intellectuals that congregated at Sylvia Beach's Shakespeare and Company, the bookstore where one might meet James Joyce, André Gide, Gertrude Stein or Ezra Pound.

After dinner Antheil attempted to give Gershwin some idea of his latest composition, but with little success. The solo piano did not do justice to his original scoring: a battery of pianos (eight, ten or more), assorted percussion instruments and, ideally, an aircraft engine. Robert Schirmer found it not "a very fair test," since "most of it is scored for 16 grand-player pianos, with an obbligato by a boiler factory . . ."

Gershwin came off better in a recital of songs, excerpts from the *Concerto* and the *Rhapsody in Blue;* the last Antheil considered "a marvelously flamboyant piece full of breathtaking Americana." Of Gershwin's well-schooled contemporaries, Antheil was one of the few who admired him and his work and considered him "a great composer."

On April 10, three days before the scheduled premiere of *Lady, Be Good!,* Gershwin and the Schirmers boarded the boat-train for London, which they found as Gershwin-conscious as it was Astaire-expectant. On Sunday afternoon, the eleventh, they took a box at the Royal Albert Hall for the publicized London debut of the Paul Whiteman Concert Orchestra. Though sold out and popular with the audience, it was not warmly embraced by the critics. Nor by Gershwin. He was unhappy with Whiteman's tempo tampering in the *Rhapsody;* in Schirmer's view, it was "murdered." Whiteman had begun taking his title of Jazz King seriously and since the success of the *Rhapsody in Blue,* had begun distorting tempos, speeding up (i.e., "jazzing") the work beyond recognition. This would later lead to a dispute between composer and conductor. The afternoon was further marred when Gershwin found that someone had stolen his overcoat and hat.

Back at his flat, he presented the Schirmers his form of thank-you note "for a wonderful week in Paris": a dramatic photo portrait of himself at the piano, signed with a few bars of music. On the right he had sketched the main theme from the *Rhapsody in Blue;* on the left there were three and a half sprightly bars of something new under which he wrote "An American in Paris."

That evening all three went off to the Hotel Metropole to attend a rehearsal of a ballet based on the *Rhapsody in Blue;* on the twelfth they saw the premiere. The scenario was peculiar. "Truly," Robert Schirmer later informed the Paleys, "the Rhapsody makes a splendid ballet—a Greek classic idea—nymphs and satyrs, Pan, etc., all the costumes and lighting in bright blue." Musically, like Whiteman's rendition, this one was off; the orchestra was drastically reduced, which left the soloists particularly exposed, "the pianist stumbled thro the solo passages, the clarinet cracked and from time to time the trombonist came through with sour notes." The Schirmers and Gershwin were uncomfortable but the audience loved it.

The next two days were devoted to the last-minute preparations for the Wednesday night opening of *Lady, Be Good!* at the Empire Theatre in Leicester Square. It was mobbed. When the Astaires arrived in their limousine, they needed a police escort to get into the theater.

"It was a triumph," Schirmer reported. "When it was over the audience sat in their seats for a full ten minutes after the final curtain—speeches by the Astaires and Billy Kent [the popular English comedian]—the greatest enthusiasm you can imagine—every entrance and exit was greeted by literal cheering such as I have only heard previously at football and baseball games." He predicted that the musical would "be packed for almost a year." He was close; *Lady, Be Good!* remained at the Empire for nine months until the theater was closed for demolition to make way for a movie house. The Astaires then toured Britain with it until the spring of 1927, when they returned to New York for their next hit Gershwin musical.

The Schirmers accompanied Gershwin to an opening night party at the Embassy Club, the "most fashionable club in London," according to Schirmer. The hosts were Lord and Lady Butt (Alfred Butt was the managing director of the Empire, and made a practice of importing American musicals). It was a triumphant celebration, replete with stars, show people, lords and ladies. The Schirmers decided to call it a night at two in the morning, but Gershwin remained until eight, joyously playing *Lady, Be Good!* past dawn.

The Schirmers then returned to their more placid life in Paris and Gershwin remained in London to record several of the show's songs with the Astaires on the nineteenth and twentieth of April. Soon after, he and Aarons boarded ship for home. During his stay in London the producer had signed up their star for the next Aarons and Freedley Gershwin show, then tentatively entitled *Mayfair*. Gertrude Lawrence, whose performances in the London and New York productions of *Charlot Revues* had agreed to appear in *Mayfair* when she heard that George Gershwin would write her songs. Two of her most devoted admirers, Guy Bolton and P. G. Wodehouse, had begun devising a whimsically improbable plot for her in an unlikely corner of Worcestershire named Droitwich.

III

Though they had no libretto, the Gershwins began blocking out possible songs for Gertrude Lawrence's exquisite voice; the bulk of the work would be done after the summer, when, it was hoped, Wodehouse and Bolton would deliver a finished book.

Practically off the ship, Gershwin began his usual round of parties with Bill Daly; at one, at the end of May, they dropped in one late evening on Franklin P. Adams, who was entertaining Aldous and Laura Huxley (the British novelist was then known in America for his cynically ingenious *Crome Yellow* and *Antic Hay)*. Gershwin and Daly performed their two-piano specialties, the *Rhapsody in Blue* and *Concerto in F.*

At an earlier musical party Gershwin again encountered Kay Swift Warburg. Her husband was away on an extended business trip, leaving Kay with time on her hands and many party invitations. Gershwin began squiring her around during that pleasant May. This marked the true beginning of a friendship, a unique personal-professional association, that lasted until Gershwin's death.

There still being no *Mayfair* book, Gershwin returned to London in early July (he recorded songs from *Tip-Toes* in preparation for the show's opening there on August 31). By early September he and Ira Gershwin began working systematically on the Gertrude Lawrence score. There was an interruption, Ira Gershwin recalled.

"George and I were well along on the score of *Oh, Kay! [Mayfair* had been transmuted into *Cheerio,* then finally became *Oh, Kay!]* when one morning at six A.M. I was rushed to Mt. Sinai Hospital for an emergency appendectomy. I was there six weeks—this was long before antibiotics shortened stays. When after great insistence ('They're waiting for me to finish the lyrics!'), exit was finally permitted. I was still weak but able to work afternoons.

"Then, with rehearsals nearing, and myself a bit behind schedule, a friend and many-faceted talent, Howard Dietz, showed up one day and offered to help out, and did. We collaborated on two songs (the title song, "Oh, Kay!," and "Heaven on Earth) and he was helpful on a couple of others. Also, one day when he heard the slowed-up ex-jazz tune he ad-libbed several titles, one of which stuck with me and which, some days later, I decided to write up (as "Someone to Watch Over Me")."

George Gershwin had originally conceived the tune as a quick rhythm number. One day as they were working, he began playing "at a comparatively slow tempo . . . half of it hadn't been sounded when both of us had the same reaction: this was no rhythm number but rather a wistful and warm one . . ."

Howard Dietz (1896–1983), a press agent and hopeful songwriter in 1926, had not yet formed his successful partnership with Arthur

Schwartz. In his autobiography, *Dancing in the Dark,* his account of his contribution to *Oh, Kay!* approaches the churlish. "George needed a substitute and selected me" because he "wanted Ira to retain as much credit as possible. He chose me because I would be least demanding on both credit and money and I showed promise." Gershwin's story has Dietz offering to help; a curious omission is the fact that P. G. Wodehouse was very much around and was a skilled lyricist. Besides the two songs for which Ira Gershwin shared the lyric credits with him, Dietz also claimed the verse to "Clap Yo' Hands."

"While the doctors were sawing away at Ira's midriff," Dietz related, "I was submitting a variety of ideas to George. One of the more successful was the title of the best song in the show, 'Someone to Watch Over Me.' "He also wrote something called 'That Certain Something You Got' but Ira changed it to 'Oh, Kay, You're O.K. with Me.' It was the title song of the show and the least distinguished. Ira made me a present of the credit for it. It was the opposite of plagiarism; we'll call it donorism."

Dietz suggested that he and George Gershwin completed "That Certain Something" and that Ira Gershwin jettisoned the Dietz lyric to write his own title song. Since Dietz had worked on the song, Ira considered it only fair that he should retain some of the credit and his share of the royalties. Dietz, looking back nearly a half century later, did not see it that rosily.

"George," he elaborated, "realizing that any sum paid me would have to come out of Ira's royalties, paid me next to nothing [he neglects to define this "next to nothing"]. It was decided I was to get 1¢ for every copy of sheet music that was sold. When Ira sent me my first paycheck it was for 96¢."

This is a curious assertion, since royalty statements originate with publishers (unless this brief collaboration was even more peculiar than it seems). Since the standard royalty rate on sheet music at the time for the songwriters was three cents, it was an equitable arrangement: a cent each. Despite his disgruntlement, Dietz said, "I was very proud to work with the great Gershwin and would have done it for nothing, which I did." He never worked with either Gershwin again.

IV

The Wodehouse-Bolton book for *Oh, Kay!,* despite its earlier English titles and English star, was set in contemporary social Long Island. Bolton was familiar with it, for he had a home in Great Neck. They

selected as their theme the timely subject of rum-running and bootlegging. Thanks to these two profitable industries, liquor of varying, often
deadly, quality was readily available despite Prohibition. Wodehouse
and Bolton attributed their inspiration to "the liquor fleet off Mon-
tauk," the sight of which brought out a poetic third-person trait:
"Scores of launches and fishing boats darting back and forth like nest-
ing swallows. It's a heartening sight for those of convivial kidney. I use
the word playfully. Most of us old-timers have only half a kidney left
after a seven-year bout with Prohibition."

They worked in Gertrude Lawrence, in her first book musical, as the
sister of a titled yacht-owning but needy English bootlegger, who stored
his product in the home of an American playboy. They then tossed in a
couple of bumbling assistants for the bootlegging duke to keep an eye
on the "stuff" and a dim-witted revenue agent. One of the assistants was
portrayed by Victor Moore.

The librettists thickened the plot to a sometimes bewildering degree,
touching it with Wodehousean whimsy. Unexpectedly, playboy Jimmy,
who has an affinity for nuptial complexity, returns to his liquor-laden
home with a new bride, unaware of the fact that his previous marriage
is still on. After the Lady Kay rescues him from the waters of Long
Island Sound, he proposes to her. During the course of the play Lawrence alternated between the roles of the maid, complete with Cockney
accent, and that of Jimmy's alleged wife, to the consternation of the
judge, his daughter, and the revenue agent. But not, inexplicably, the
audience, for *Oh, Kay!* became a solid Gershwin hit.

For a time it had not looked so promising. The musical was set to
begin its pre-Broadway run in Philadelphia on October 18. The three
Gershwins—Ira Gershwin and Leonore Strunsky had married on September 14—set out a little early to attend a birthday party for producer
Edgar Selwyn, who had acquired a libretto by George S. Kaufman
lampooning war and warriors. Hoping to produce it in the following
1927 season, he also hoped the Gershwins would provide the words and
music. They were interested, but there was much to be done in Philadelphia.

While in Atlantic City, Gershwin met with a man with whom he
wished to collaborate on an opera based on the novel *Porgy*, which he
had read during the *Oh, Kay!* rehearsals. DuBose Heyward and his
wife, the dramatist Dorothy Heyward, met briefly with Gershwin to
explain that since Dorothy had converted the novel into a play which
was under consideration for production by the Theatre Guild, it was
not available. This did not disturb the composer, who felt he had a lot
to learn before he would compose a full-fledged opera. He could wait.

This meeting—of which more later—resulted in one of the most re-markable collaborations in the history of the American musical theater. The Heywards then excitedly left for their conferences with the Guild and the Gershwins for Philadelphia and a show in trouble.

Songs for *Oh, Kay!* were written and rejected. No fewer than eight were either dropped or redone. One published song, "Show Me the Town" was eliminated and replaced with one of Gershwin's finest, "Dear Little Girl." Another good song, "Ain't It Romantic," went into the trunk never to emerge again (it is Gershwin Melody No. 44 in the Library of Congress Gershwin Archive).

The Gershwins obliged co-producer Vinton Freedley's demands with their customary composure. He was uncertain about Victor Moore as Shorty, the unlikely bootlegger and inept butler; Moore's hesitant, un-derstated style, Freedley felt, would spoil the pacing and mood of the show. While Aarons and Freedley had declared that they wished to carry on the tradition of the unpretentious Princess Theatre shows, they did not want to become too traditional and genteel. They wanted some-thing more grand and zesty. They provided a large dancing chorus and, in Philadelphia, had no fewer than two more vigorous less languid comics on hand to replace Moore if necessary. As they hopefully stood in the wings on opening night, the audience reaction made it clear that they were not needed.

In Philadelphia *Oh, Kay!* was finally set; the cast, despite Freedley's anxiety, was perfect. To round out the perfection, Ohman and Arden were in the pit and Bill Daly led the orchestra. The company opened at the Imperial Theatre the evening of November 8, 1926, and stayed for eight months—256 performances; not as long-lived as *Lady, Be Good!* but longer than *Tip-Toes* and *Song of the Flame.* Like *Lady,* it moved on the strength of its score and the performances of Gertrude Lawrence and Victor Moore; the entangled gossamer plot did not impede the flow of the show. In the *Times* Brooks Atkinson attributed the show's suc-cess to the blend of all the contributors, calling *Oh, Kay!* "intensely delightful."

He found "Mr. Gershwin's score . . . woven closely into the fun of the comedy. Sometimes it is purely rhythmic as in 'Clap Yo' Hands' and 'Fidgety Feet'; sometimes it is capricious as in 'Do-Do-Do.' Mr. Gersh-win also composes in the familiar romantic vein of "Someone to Watch Over Me.' In this plaintive number Miss Lawrence embellishes the song with expressive turns on the stage; she employs none of the artful rheto-ric of musical comedy singing." The conventional presentation of a solo ballad like "Someone to Watch Over Me" would have had Lawrence, center stage, singing directly at the audience; this generally worked.

Instead, dressed in her maid's uniform, alone onstage, she sings in her wistfully uncertain voice to a rag doll.

This prop Raggedy Ann was Gershwin's idea. During the Philadelphia trials he spotted "a strange-looking object" in a toy store window, acquired it, presented it to Gertrude Lawrence and suggested she use it in the scene. (The idea may have been suggested to him in recollection of her affecting rendition of Noël Coward's "Parisian Pierrot" when she sang it in *André Charlot's Revue of 1924* to a Pierrot doll.) Whatever the source of the inspiration, it truly worked, for Percy Hammond in the *Tribune* claimed that Lawrence's singing of "Someone to Watch Over Me" had "wrung the withers of even the most hardhearted of those present." One of the Philadelphia reviewers had been especially prescient when he declared with uncritical enthusiasm: "Hell, it's almost perfect!"

V

Oh, Kay! can serve, as well as any, as the typical Gershwin musical of the twenties. It began with the premise that Gertrude Lawrence would star and that the Gershwins would write the songs before Wodehouse and Bolton started on their plot concoctions. There had to be a lead comic, dancers and a female chorus—these were requisite conventions in virtually every musical of the period. In keeping with the Aarons-Freedley hopes for smart, crisp, contemporaneity, structuring the plot around the infant growth industry of bootlegging (then in its sixth year and grossing three billion dollars tax-free) was inspired. To justify Gertrude Lawrence's British accent, the librettists were further inspired to fall back on another musical-comedy type (especially in Britain), the upper-class "silly ass." This was her brother the duke, of whom the musical's hero says, "No doctor would ever dare give that fellow chloroform, they'a never know when he was unconscious."

How to explain a member of Britain's nobility masterminding a rum-running operation? That is done simply in a single expositional sentence when his sister explains, "You see, what with taxes and super-taxes and inheritance taxes all my brother had left was his yacht," which is put to use transporting booze. Since *Oh, Kay!* was a musical comedy, neither the duke nor his inept henchmen are portrayed as much of a menace to society.

Add to these a pompous judge, his spoiled daughter, a confused revenue officer (who is not what he seems) and assorted "girls." The most unconventional aspect of *Oh, Kay!*'s plot is that its most lovable characters flout the law. The 1926 audience had no trouble with this, an often favorite Wodehouse device. A line that got a laugh was Victor Moore's: "The difference between a bootlegger and a federal inspector is that one of them wears a badge."

The musical structure conformed to the conventions also: an overture employing the hoped-for hits, a title song and a finale. While the term "integrated" was not then in vogue, the score has its share of expository songs. One of them is a fine choral number, the "ice-breaker" (i.e., opening number after the overture) "The Woman's Touch." It served, too, to bring on the girls, another musical-comedy convention. They sing of the impending arrival of Jimmy while they clean his house for the night's party; no thirty-two-bar popular song, "The Woman's Touch" establishes several plot points: that, despite his marriage, Jimmy has several women admirers, that he is expected home, that they are willing to clean house for him and that there will be a party.

They leave, and the duke and one of his henchmen enter. In a few lines of dialogue the audience learns of the duke's new trade, that the spirits are stashed in the cellar and that Jimmy is coming home unexpectedly and they have to do something about it. The duke wanders off, leaving henchman Potter (the dancer Harland Dixon) to flirt and dance with twin sisters who have come in. This is all the cue required for the song, "Don't Ask" and a dancing specialty by Dixon and the twins (who are, in fact, dancing sisters, the Fairbanks twins Marion and Madeleine).

The rest of the show is spun out of this wispy material, but with whimsical, illogical ingenuity. The plot does not intrude on the flow of the musical numbers, the pacing is lively. Closing the act is the fast "Mammy song" (as it is called in the script), the quasi-spiritual "Clap Yo' Hands." The general musical character of Act I is one of youthful high spirits with ingratiating melodic interludes: "Dear Little Girl" and "Maybe." Gershwin's score is thought out, not a random collection of numbers.

The second act's opening number is "Bride and Groom," which begins the final act brightly, engaging the hapless Jimmy, the bride-to-be he does not want to marry and the chorus. The rest of the act is devoted to getting him out of the clutches of "Constance" and, of course, attending to the cache of liquor. The one slow ballad was Gertrude Lawrence's only solo, "Someone to Watch Over Me." In the Philadelphia version the song had been placed in the first act, but the cutting of a scene led to its being put midway in Act II, between the contrasting rhythm numbers "Do-Do-Do" and "Fidgety Feet," the first a duet between the principals and the second a complex production number for the dancers. If libretto and songs are not integrated in the contemporary sense—songs like "Fidgety Feet," "Clap Yo' Hands" and "Heaven on Earth" have nothing to do with the plot and would serve in any score as production numbers—Gershwin's score is a study in unity and contrast. They are carefully plotted and placed to keep the show moving.

This structure may very well have been the result of a team effort with suggestions (and demands) from Aarons and (especially) Freedley, accounting for the eight discarded songs. The Gershwins respected their producer's theatrical instincts and readily complied when a song went out and a new one was needed. Some of the stress of the reshaping in Philadelphia is implied in a note Gershwin sent off to a friend, Mrs. Berthold Neur (her husband was an American Piano Company official). She had invited him to a party at her New York home. Gershwin's reply (actually written and signed by Ira) was: "I'm here in Philly with a new opus—*"Oh, Kay!,"* and will have to remain and help nurse it for some time to come."

This nursing required writing a new lyric for "Guess Who," which became "Don't Ask." "Show Me the Town" was tossed out and "Dear Little Girl" substituted; ditto "Bring On the Ding Dong Dell" for "Bride and Groom." "Fidgety Feet" went in for "Stepping with Baby," and so on. Such revisions were frequently dictated by plot changes or if director John Harwood sensed the need to spice up the pace with another dance. (The dance sequences were staged by Sammy Lee; Harwood "staged" the book.) The small army of many cooks did not spoil the froth.

As with all the Gershwin musicals of this period, only the songs survive; revivals of *Oh, Kay!* in its original form are rare. Some of the book's flavor may be suggested by a nonmusical scene, the first in Act II which follows Lawrence's "Someone to Watch Over Me" and "Fidgety Feet" sung by one of the rum-runner's assistants. The cue for this dance number is ingeniously obvious. "Potter" (Harland Dixon) is trying to talk one of the twins into marriage. She responds with: ". . . you'd be like all the rest of the men. After you get married you'd be too tired to take your own wife out stepping in the evening."

Potter's reply sets up the cue: "Not me. A nightclub is a health resort for me. It's the only place I can find the cure for what ails me." She: "What ails you? Why, Larry dear, aren't you well?" He: "No!" And the song begins, "Something is the matter with me . . ." He then sings "Fidgety Feet."

At the close of the number, Potter and Phil (Marion Fairbanks) leave and Gertrude Lawrence (in her maid's disguise) and Shorty (Victor

Moore) enter. They are trying to find a plan that will get Constance, the quasi-wife planning her second marriage to Jimmy, to throw him over so that Kay can marry him. They are interrupted by the revenuer, to whom Kay had been introduced as the new Mrs. Winter the night before. He is confused, for the maid resembles her uncannily. When he inquires, and asks if they weren't introduced the night before, she denies it.

"Then who was it?" he asks.

"How the 'ell do I know?" she snaps in her best Cockney.

Shorty tries to be helpful. "What time was it?" he asks. "He's had several wives around here since he got back." The agent leaves in a state of befuddlement.

Then the fake maid and butler prepare a special prewedding lunch for the judge and his daughter; they begin their plot by perpetrating a havoc of domestic sabotage. Loud noises come from the (offstage) kitchen, crockery clatters, things break. The final touch: Kay serves them and says, "It's a shame about that fish. The cat gave me such a nasty look the last time I took it aw'y from 'im." Exeunt Constance and the judge.

The antic, at times hard-boiled, capriciousness of the book, plus the performances of the entire cast, but especially those of Lawrence and Moore, assured Aarons and Freedley their new Gershwin hit musical. That the songs were a significant factor is evident in the sheet-music sales figures Gershwin received at the end of the year. The song sheets were probably available in time for the Philadelphia run; eight songs in all, including "Show Me the Town," which was not in the New York version. Roughly from mid-October until December 31 "Do-Do-Do" sold more than 20,000 copies, "Clap Yo' Hands" 13,388, "Someone to Watch Over Me" 10,107 and "Maybe" 7,099. Including the other songs, each of which averaged over 1,000, the sheet-music sales for the short period totaled 57,230.

The success of "Do-Do-Do" pleased Ira Gershwin, since it had been his idea to begin with. Inspired by a current catchphrase, the humorously emphatic, "Oh, do! do! do!" (throughout his career, he continued this borrowing from popular speech: "Half of It, Dearie, Blues," "That Certain Feeling," "High Hat," "Sunny Disposish," and so on).

The brothers were working on the song while waiting for Leonore Strunsky, Ira Gershwin's fiancée to join them for dinner (in the summer of 1926, before his appendectomy). "Maybe we can do something with the sounds of 'do, do' and 'done, done,'" Ira suggested. George agreed and they went upstairs to his studio. As they were about to begin, Leonore called to let them know she was on her way by cab from

Greenwich Village and should arrive at 103rd Street in about half an hour (she later maintained it was less than that).

By the time she arrived the refrain was complete, a milestone for Ira Gershwin, who habitually worried over a lyric for days. It was the first of only two lyrics that he completed so quickly (the other was "A Foggy Day," a decade in the future).

George Gershwin, too, was pleased with the *Oh, Kay!* score, many of whose songs were recorded by several bands and taken up by tearoom and hotel orchestras around town. With *Lady, Be Good!* and *Tip-Toes* doing well in London and *Oh, Kay!* even better in New York, he was ready to turn again to the concert hall.

VI

This modest return was a sequel to the Eva Gauthier recitals and had begun, as had the Gauthier experience, at the prompting of Carl Van Vechten. His friend the contralto Marguerite d'Alvarez had attended the Whiteman Experiment and, as Van Vechten told Gershwin, she ". . . was reduced to a state of hysterical enthusiasm . . . especially your contribution. She wants to sing at the next one! You might tell Whiteman this: she would certainly give the audience a good time."

D'Alvarez was British-born (Liverpool), of Peruvian parents and was billed during her career as a Peruvian contralto. She had sung with the Manhattan Opera Company as early as 1909; she was also with the Chicago Opera Company in the twenties. By 1926 she was more active as a recitalist—and also about forty (she was reticent about her birth date). She and Gershwin had met at Van Vechten's musical parties; he admired her rich, dark voice and frequently accompanied her in his songs. One of these parties had occurred early in the year and one of the guests—blues singer Bessie Smith—upon hearing D'Alvarez sing, embraced her and exclaimed, "Don't let *nobody* tell you *you* can't sing!"

Whether Gershwin mentioned Van Vechten's suggestion to Whiteman is not known, but D'Alvarez did not sing at the next Experiment. However, in planning her 1926/1927 recital tour she succeeded in talking Gershwin into serving as her accompanist in a group of popular songs, in addition to performing in the two-piano *Rhapsody in Blue* (the second pianist was Isidore Gorin). Further, he agreed to compose a new serious solo piano work for her recital.

For this he turned to his Preludes January 1925 notebook and novelettes. The front pages of that notebook today have been torn out and only sketches for the later *Rumba* remain. One of the leaves, in Gershwin's hand, is labeled "Prelude" and dated January 1925; Ira Gershwin later identified it as having been used in the third movement of the *Concerto in F.*

The creation or evolution of the collection published as *Preludes for Piano* is shadowy. The pieces Gershwin performed at the first of the D'Alvarez recitals at the Hotel Roosevelt on Saturday afternoon, December 4, 1926, numbered five. Since the opening of *Oh, Kay!* on November 8 and after a brief rest, he could have composed the three he eventually published. Kay Swift, of whom he was seeing a good deal at this time, recalls his composing the last prelude (which he referred to as the Spanish Prelude) in her apartment and that she put it down on paper for him. The two additional preludes played at the Roosevelt are conjectured to be the two pieces that make up the 1925 piano-violin piece *Short Story* reverted to their original solo form.

In 1926 Gershwin was still talking about the twenty-four preludes *The Melting Pot,* which Van Vechten had mentioned was a work in progress in his March 1925 *Vanity Fair* article. In his review of the recital, Richard L. Stokes of the *Evening World* noted that "the musical smart set clustered at the Hotel Roosevelt to hear George Gershwin to play his five new preludes for the piano. It was the first public performance of these pieces, which are still in manuscript and which are to be joined with others as yet unwritten in a series called 'The Melting Pot.'

"They proved brief and glowing little vignettes of New York life. The first was a vigorous bit of syncopation; the second, lyrical in vein, resembled a nocturne; the third combined a jazz melody with a rolling, Chopinesque bass; the fourth was of the 'blues' variety, and the fifth stirred together a Charleston for the left hand and a Spanish melody for the right."

Abbe Niles, critic for *The New Republic,* described the pieces so: "One was a frank salute to Chopin; one criticized the crudity in Debussy's Golliwog's Cake Walk in just the way one clog-dancer would choose to criticize another's step; one was built on a theme written but not used for the famous blues movement of the *Concerto in F;* one might be a song deprived of its words; one started on the docks of New Orleans, to find itself joyously footing it in Madrid."

Subtracting some highly impressionistic writing, it is possible to identify the three published preludes and the two sections of *Short Story.* But then Gershwin further added to the puzzle, for when he and D'Alvarez repeated the recital in Boston on January 16, 1927, he played yet a sixth prelude. For years this has been sought by pianists wishing to enlarge their serious solo piano Gershwin repertoire—the so-called "lost prelude."

And for almost as long it has been thought to be a piano piece in the Gershwin Archive, "Gershwin Melody No. 17"—"Sleepless Night." Ira Gershwin contributed something to the myth when he wrote a friend who had inquired about *Short Story* and the missing prelude. "There is an actual 4th prelude, however unpublished. Since it is in 32 bar song form I'm going to put a lyric to it some day." Unfortunately, he never did. In fact, "Sleepless Night" though, in fragmentary form, was noted in a 1925 Tune Book, was completed a decade after the *Preludes* were originally performed. It was composed in Beverly Hills as a possible song sometime after the Gershwins settled there in the summer of 1936. Although it is an effective piano piece, as are most Gershwin songs, it is a song, not a prelude. The "lost prelude," then, is the sixth one Gershwin played in Boston; since no manuscript or sketch have materialized, it is highly probable that Gershwin simply improvised a finished "Sleepless Night" prelude—he was capable of it.

Having abandoned the elaborate *The Melting Pot,* he chose to publish a well-balanced suite of only three preludes—two dances enclosing a night song (which Gershwin once called "a sort of blue lullaby"). The dedication reads "To Bill Daly."

8

Hits and Misses

Following his tour with Marguerite d'Alvarez (besides Boston, their last
stop, they also performed in Buffalo on December 15, 1926), Gershwin
took a little time out late in January and early February 1927 for diversified vacationing: skiing in Canada and golfing and deep-sea fishing in
Florida. In March he performed the *Concerto in F* with the Cincinnati
Symphony, Fritz Reiner conducting. His work load for the next several
months was set: he and Ira had agreed to write the songs for Edgar
Selwyn's production of George S. Kaufman's antiwar musical. That
was the first work on the agenda. Aarons and Freedley already had
plans for two follow-ups to their success with the Astaires (still in London with *Lady, Be Good!*) and with Gertrude Lawrence (after *Oh,
Kay!*). Yet another offer would come out of left field, but at the beginning of 1927 Gershwin was unaware of that. Of these four shows two
would be successes and two utter failures.

By mid-March even *Oh, Kay!* had begun to run down. "Aarons and
Freedley," Ira Gershwin told a friend some years later, "asked George
if he would appear some night to help the box office. He agreed and
spent a good deal of time arranging a 15 minute intermission program
for two pianos (Bill Daly was the other pianist). This was announced in
the papers several days before the appearance. That it was a good idea
for the management can be attested to by the fact that that Monday
night's (March 28) receipts were eleven hundred dollars over the previous Monday.

"George and Bill didn't use Ohman and Arden's pit pianos—two
Steinways were pushed onstage and it made for an exciting fifteen or so
minutes. Of the program itself all I can remember now is a three chorus

plus coda of 'Do-Do-Do.' C'est ça." (To date this elaborate Gershwin arrangement has not been found in the Gershwin Archive.)

One newspaper reported the rather unusual event and headlined it "Gershwin delights audience at Oh, Kay!" It was not repeated and the show closed on June 18 as preparations for an English production were already under way. Gershwin by June was well into work on his first political operetta, *Strike Up the Band,* for producer Edgar Selwyn.

I

On April 4, 1927, the Ossining *Citizen Sentinel* announced that "George Gurshwin (sic)" had leased the "Shubart house" (Shubert was misspelled too, but no matter). It was in this house, situated on the forty-acre Chumleigh Farm in Westchester County, New York, that the bulk of the songs for *Strike Up the Band* would be written. The farm was within easy driving distance, less than thirty miles, from Manhattan. The house was roomy, with plenty of space for visitors—a two-story stucco-and-brick structure. There was a lawn for croquet, trees, one with a swing, and rugged rock outcroppings in the yard. The excitable *Citizen Sentinel* reporter predicted that "without doubt some of the Broadway hits for next season will have been conceived at the Schubart (sic) estate." He was wrong again.

By the end of April the Gershwins were settled in the house and planned to remain through the summer. Like the house on 103rd Street, Chumleigh Farm became a social center as well as a workplace. Over the summer the Gershwins entertained the Schirmers in for a visit from Paris, the Paleys, Bill Daly, collaborator George S. Kaufman, columnist Franklin P. Adams (a croquet aficionado) as well as songwriters Howard Dietz, Harry Ruby and others.

Before getting down to serious work on the songs, Gershwin returned to the recording studios of the Victor Talking Machine Company in New York's Liederkranz Hall to re-record the *Rhapsody in Blue* with Whiteman on April 21. Since the first recording of June 1924 had been done acoustically, it had been decided to redo it electronically; the microphone had been developed in the meanwhile and Victor was in the process of modernizing their catalogue.

The recording sessions proved disagreeable for Gershwin. Ever since his experience at the Albert Hall in London in 1926, when he had been upset by Whiteman's distorted performance of the *Rhapsody,* he had quietly smoldered. During the prerecording rehearsals, he found that Whiteman had not improved since London. Jazzing up certain passages by speeding them up ruffled Gershwin; it seemed that he was playing one work and Whiteman and the band were playing another. (By 1927 the Whiteman orchestra was not the same one that had premiered the *Rhapsody* three years before; many of the original musicians had gone on to other bands or had struck out on their own.)

Gershwin and Whiteman disagreed and then argued. An irate Whiteman stalked out of the studio. Victor's Director of Light Music, Nathaniel Shilkret, was present, so that Whiteman's angry defection had no effect on the procedure. Shilkret took up the baton and led the Whiteman Concert Orchestra, and the recording session began. A cooler Whiteman returned, saw what was happening and left again. The released recording credits Whiteman as conductor. The earlier recording, though acoustic, is superior not only because of the presence of most of the original musicians, including clarinetist Ross Gorman, but because Gershwin's performance is freer, more relaxed. The argument with Whiteman had slightly disturbed him.

Eventually the two patched up their differences, though Gershwin never again produced a work for Whiteman. He did, three years later, appear with Whiteman on the stage of the Roxy Theatre in conjunction with the showing of the film *King of Jazz*. Perhaps by May 1930 Whiteman had returned to Gershwin's original tempos, for Gershwin joined him in performances of the *Rhapsody*. (In the film the work was also performed with Roy Bargy, who strikingly resembled Gershwin, at the piano. For its use in the film Gershwin received fifty thousand Depression dollars.)

The recording completed, the Gershwins were ready to begin work on George S. Kaufman's lampoon of war. This was done, as in Manhattan, primarily at night. Days were spent with their family and guests or driving around the pleasant countryside. George Gershwin had acquired a secondhand Mercedes, and Ira, who had also just learned to drive, bought an automobile but found the experience disconcerting and left the driving to Leonore. His reason: he gave up driving because of the stern looks he inadvertently garnered from fellow motorists because of his conservative driving. (He never drove again, even after settling in Beverly Hills where a set of wheels was more essential than legs.) George, on the other hand, enjoyed speeding around Westchester County and to and from Manhattan when necessary.

II

Kaufman's libretto for *Strike Up the Band* gave the Gershwins, for the first time, the opportunity to produce a fully integrated score. It was literate, at times scathing, not at all typical of the musical designed for the tired businessman. It was, in its time, doomed (as we know now) because it was—book, music and lyrics—ahead of its time. The songs were written to the plot—there were no planted potential hits for the stars; even the dances were at one with the story: patriotic rallies, military drills, a parody march. The title song, Gershwin later recalled, was one of the few—possibly the only one, for he never mentioned another —that came to him in a dream. "Occasionally compositions come in dreams," he said, "but rarely can they be remembered when you wake. On one occasion I did get out of bed and write a song."

It had not, in fact, come quite that easily. The Gershwins had gone down to Atlantic City that spring for discussions with producer Edgar Selwyn. It being the off-season, the hotel obligingly put a piano in George's room, since, as Ira put it, there "were no guests to disturb within ten rooms of us."

He went down late Saturday night to get the Sunday papers and when he returned noticed no light under George's door in the adjoining room and assumed that he had gone to sleep. He had not finished the first section of the paper when a slit of light showed from his brother's room. The door opened and his "pajamaed brother appeared."

"I thought you were asleep."

"No, I've been lying in bed thinking," George replied, "and I think I've got it."

"Got what?"

"Why, the march, of course. I think I've finally got it. Come on in."

Ira dubiously took a chair near the upright and said, "I hope you've *really* finally made up your mind." To date his brother had written no fewer than four different marches. After hearing each, Ira approved and offered "to write it up." George then cautioned him, agreed that the march was "not bad," but to wait before writing a lyric, explaining that it was for "an important spot, [the first act finale] and maybe I'll get something better."

He now felt he had it and played the refrain to "Strike Up the Band" virtually as it is known today. Did Ira like it?

"Yes, but . . ."

"But what?"

"Are you sure you won't change your mind again?"

"Yes, I'm pretty sure this time."

"That's good," Ira told him. "Don't forget it" (meaning both the tune and the promise).

By mid-June the score was virtually complete (rehearsals were scheduled to begin in New York early in July). On one of their last Sundays at Chumleigh Farm, on June 19, they entertained a few guests from town. In the afternoon they played croquet, George and Ira teamed against Bill Daly and Franklin P. Adams. F.P.A. noted that his team did better when "H. Dietz was one of our opponents." In the evening Gershwin went to the piano to play the score of *Strike Up the Band.*

July found them back at 103rd Street in time for rehearsals and for Gershwin's first appearance at a Lewisohn Stadium concert, July 26. This was the summer quarters of the Philharmonic: a football stadium converted into a concert "hall" for eight weeks (it was located on Amsterdam Avenue between 136th and 138th Streets, adjacent to the City College of New York, and has since been demolished). For his debut, with Dutch conductor Willem van Hoogstraten, Gershwin played the *Rhapsody in Blue.* He took pride in the fact that that evening's concert had brought in one of the Stadium's largest crowds, about eighteen thousand.

A month later the Gershwins were in Long Branch, New Jersey, where *Strike Up the Band* premiered in preparation for six weeks at the Shubert Theatre in Philadelphia for final polishing before New York. On September 5 it opened there and closed after two weeks.

This failure is generally attributed to the bite of Kaufman's unmusical-comedy-like book; *Strike Up the Band* was definitely not an Aarons-Freedley or a Ziegfeld musical. It underscored man's often trivial and venal rationale for going to war; Kaufman scourged profiteering, jingoism, diplomacy, business manipulations—it was not a conventional song-and-dance show. Nor was it devised around musical-comedy stars (the best known were comedian Jimmy Savo, the veteran Edna May Oliver and ex-Paul Whiteman tenor Morton Downey). Nor were there potential song hits, for the songs were embedded in the plot (producer Selwyn had insisted, however, on finding a place for the *Lady, Be Good!* reject "The Man I Love"; in a revised version Downey sang it as "The Girl I Love"). Once again, though already popular out of the theater, it was lost in the shambles of the show's failure.

Political satire, apparently, was not the stuff of a successful musical comedy. Though the show was critically acclaimed, audiences did not grasp its theme and were not amused by its long expository musical sequences (there were inevitable comparisons to Gilbert and Sullivan—which did not upset the Gershwins, for their Savoyard employment of words and music, particularly in the patter songs, was deliberate).

By the middle of the second week, Selwyn had decided to close and

Morris and Rose Gershovitz around the time of their marriage, July 1895. (Gershwin Collection)

George Gershwin's birthplace: 242 Snedicker Avenue, Brooklyn, New York. Though an attempt was made to preserve it, it failed, and the house has since been demolished. (Museum of the Borough of Brooklyn, Brooklyn College; courtesy of Shelly Mehlman Dinhofer)

Rose Gershwin (right), Prospect Park, Brooklyn, c. 1901, with a maid and her sons: Arthur, George and Ira. (Gershwin Collection)

George Gershwin, c. 1913, during a summer when he worked as a pianist in the Catskill Mountains resort area. (Gershwin Collection)

Charles Hambitzer, Gershwin's piano teacher and most important musical influence. He guided his young pupil through the classic as well as contemporary repertory and encouraged Gershwin to enlarge his musical horizons by studying harmony and counterpoint. (Gershwin Collection)

Edward Kilenyi, Sr., Hungarian-born composer and teacher and colleague of Hambitzer. Gershwin studied counterpoint, harmony and some orchestration with him. (Gershwin Collection)

Gershwin at eighteen, about to graduate from his profession as "piano pounder" and accompanist for pluggers. Soon after he got his chance to write songs for his first musical, *Half Past Eight;* it was also his first failure. (Gershwin Collection)

George reporting for work as a staff composer for Max Dreyfus at the T. B. Harms Publishing Co., on West Forty-fifth Street. (Gershwin Collection)

Veteran music publisher and astute judge of songs Max Dreyfus, who not only discovered Gershwin but was noted for furthering the careers of such composers as Jerome Kern, Richard Rodgers, Vincent Youmans and Cole Porter. (Gershwin Collection)

Albert Sirmay, who gave up a career as a Hungarian operetta composer to serve as chief editor of music for Dreyfus. He worked with Gershwin on virtually all his shows from the earliest through *Porgy and Bess* and the final films. (Gershwin Collection)

Early formal portrait of George, c. 1923. (Gershwin Collection)

An Experiment
in
MODERN MUSIC

AEOLIAN HALL

Program for Whiteman's Aeolian Hall concert, February 12, 1924. (Gershwin Collection)

The expanded Whiteman orchestra that premiered the *Rhapsody in Blue*. Directly behind the conductor, with banjo, is Mike Pingatore, who was with Whiteman for years. In the back row to the right (second from right) is Ferde Grofé, orchestrator of the *Rhapsody*. He also played second piano in the work. (Gershwin Collection)

George Gershwin, with his first "serious" publication. Both he and Ira Gershwin were mystified that Dreyfus took a chance on publishing such a composition, since Harms specialized in popular songs and musical theater music. Dreyfus was right again. (Gershwin Collection)

George Gershwin's second hit of 1924 and his first full-scale collaboration with his brother Ira, was *Lady, Be Good!* Starring two friends from his Tin Pan Alley days, the show was an immediate smash. Fred and Adele Astaire, as usual, played a brother-sister team. In this scene Adele is disguised as a fake Mexican widow. This afforded the chance for the Gershwins to write the song "Juanita." (Gershwin Collection)

The success of the *Rhapsody in Blue* inspired a commission for a piano concerto from the New York Symphony Orchestra. To escape the hustle-bustle of his house on 103rd Street, Gershwin took an apartment at the Whitehall Hotel on Broadway and 100th Street. At this time he worked simultaneously on the *Concerto in F* and the scores for *Tip-Toes* and *Song of the Flame*. (Gershwin Collection)

Gershwin: *Time* Cover Story

Producer Alex Aarons and Gershwin aboard ship returning from England after launching the London production of *Lady, Be Good!*, 1926. They had also gotten an agreement from Gertrude Lawrence to star in a new Gershwin musical. (Gershwin Collection)

Gertrude Lawrence and Gershwin, 1926.
The show, one of his best, was *Oh, Kay!*
(Gershwin Collection)

Gertrude Lawrence, 1926. (Gershwin
Collection)

Fred Astaire leads the men's chorus in the "High Hat" number; *Funny Face,* 1927. This was the last Gershwin show for the Astaires. (Gershwin Collection)

On a London visit Gershwin chats with singer-dancer Olive Brady. (Gershwin Collection)

Gershwin and conductor Fritz Reiner in Cincinnati, February 1929. The Cincinnati Symphony, under Reiner, was to perform *An American in Paris.* (Gershwin Collection)

Gershwin, "hornist" James Rosenberg and tenor Richard Crooks contemplate the French taxi horns the composer had found with the help of Mabel Schirmer in Paris. (Gershwin Collection)

Adele Astaire, comic Leslie Henson and Fred Astaire in a scene from the London production of *Funny Face*. (Gershwin Collection)

Frances Gershwin, who accompanied her brothers on their trip to England and France, 1928. In Paris she met her future husband, Leopold Godowsky, Jr., son of the great pianist. (Gershwin Collection)

Gershwin at the racetrack, Paris, 1928. (Courtesy of Mabel Schirmer)

Mabel Schirmer and Gershwin, Ossining, New York, 1927; the Gershwins were then working on the first version of *Strike Up the Band.* (Courtesy of Mabel Schirmer)

Kay Swift and husband, James Paul Warburg, of the banking family. Both, under Gershwin's influence, became fascinated with songwriting and collaborated on several fine songs, among them "Can't We Be Friends?," "Fine and Dandy," "Can This Be Love?" Warburg wrote under the pseudonym of "Paul James." (Courtesy of Katharine Kaufman Weber)

George Gershwin took up painting after Ira presented him with a set of watercolors. Here he completes an early self-portrait, *Me,* dated April 7, 1929. He later presented it to his friend composer Harold Arlen. (Gershwin Collection)

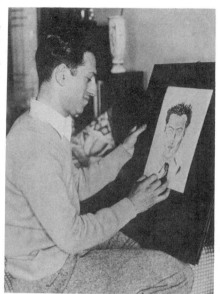

As a painter George Gershwin quickly developed a style of his own and in time was regarded by art critics as a better than amateur artist. This oil, *Self-Portrait in an Opera Hat,* was done in 1932. (Gershwin Collection)

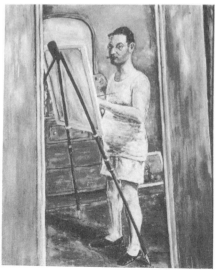

Ira Gershwin's self-portrait *My Body,* a wry commentary on his brother's more formal portrait. (Gershwin Collection)

Portrait of George Gershwin, c. 1929. (Gershwin Collection)

Bust by Isamu Noguchi, 1929. (Gershwin Collection)

forget about New York. There was a drastic drop in ticket sales—good reviews had not helped and word of mouth did the rest. Ira Gershwin remembered overhearing a brief exchange during one performance as he sat in a small audience in the large theater.

"Awful!" snapped a man's voice behind him.

A feminine voice retorted, "Father, I think it's just wonderful." Philadelphia was not ready for Gilbertian social satire with a decided American accent. War as entertainment had worn thin. One of the most successful Broadway treatments of the theme—disillusioned yet romantic, brutal yet comic—was *What Price Glory?* Its realistic view of life in the trenches, its sexual overtones, its strong language shocked and delighted audiences in 1924. But by the mid-twenties the War to End Wars sentiment seemed old hat—and, in 1927, hardly an appropriate subject for a musical "comedy."

Had this version of *Strike Up the Band* survived it would have been one of the first important "book" musicals of the pre-Rodgers and Hammerstein era. It closed in September; in December Kern's *Show Boat* arrived on Broadway to qualify as one of the first truly integrated musicals (one of its principals was Edna May Oliver, who went directly from the cast of *Strike Up the Band* into the Kern operetta).

Except for the title song, no song from the 1927 version of *Strike Up the Band* was added to the Gershwin catalog of standards ("The Man I Love" was already included by then). Unfortunately, at least two fine songs were lost—for when the show was revived and revised three years later they would be eliminated. One, a tongue-in-cheek duet, "Seventeen and Twenty-One," was published but dropped from the show; another is the lilting miniature nature poem "Meadow Serenade." Undoubtedly inspired by the setting at Chumleigh Farm, it too is a duet, a ballad whose lyrics invoke the mating of rural fauna: "Where the whippoorwill is wooing,/And the katydid is cooing to his Kate." ("Meadow Serenade" is Melody No. 72 in the Gershwin Archive.)

Such songs as the opening "Fletcher's American Cheese Choral Society," "Typical Self-Made American," "The Unofficial Spokesman" and "Patriotic Rally" are patent tributes to Gilbert and Sullivan but with a strong Gershwin touch, words and music. The sequence combining "The Knitting Song" and "O, This Is Such a Lovely War" plus "Homeward Bound" and "The War That Ended War" are so closely tied to the plot that they could hardly make sense out of the show's context. They are, however, inventive and like the rest of the score reveal Gershwin in a step closer to that opera he dreamed of.

Despite its untimely closing in Philadelphia, *Strike Up the Band* would be heard again. Selwyn was certain that he had the makings of an important musical; he and the Gershwins would come back to it another day.

III

There was no time to fret over the fate of *Strike Up the Band;* the Gershwins immediately went to work for Aarons and Freedley. Following the successful run of *Lady, Be Good!* in Britain the Astaires had returned to the United States in June and bided their time. The producers had contracted *The New Yorker* drama critic-humorist Robert Benchley and veteran Fred Thompson to supply the book, temporarily entitled *Smarty.* [Thompson had collaborated with Guy Bolton on *Lady, Be Good!, Tip-Toes* and, that same year (1927), on the non-Gershwin musical hit *Rio Rita.] Smarty*—later to be known as *Funny Face*—promised to be surefire.

To the Gershwins' dismay, *Smarty* threatened to be a reprise of the *Strike Up the Band* disaster. Less than a month after surviving the trials of their antiwar operetta, George and Ira Gershwin were back in Philadelphia where, when *Smarty* opened on October 11, 1927, it "looked" to Ira Gershwin "like a failure. We were on the road six weeks, and everyone concerned with the show worked day and night, recasting, rewriting, rehearsing, recriminating—of rejoicing there was none."

Fred Astaire called it "agony. We were playing one version while rehearsing another."

In those six turbulent weeks *Smarty* was practically rewritten: book, score and title. In recasting, the second leading man Stanley Ridges (opposite Adele Astaire) was replaced by the more musically experienced Allen Kearns, who had sung the leading male role in *Tip-Toes.* (Ridges moved on to Hollywood and a long career as a character actor in films.)

There was a further casting change, the creation of a new character, a fainthearted jewel thief, Herbert, to be played by Victor Moore. By this time, Benchley had decided to bow out; he was replaced by play doctor and Broadway veteran Paul Gerard Smith. Even so, Benchley's name remained to taunt and haunt him on the *Smarty* as well as the final *Funny Face* sheet music. (Later in the year he observed, with some chagrin, that abandoning *Smarty/Funny Face* had cost him quite a lot in royalties.)

Though Aarons and Freedley insisted that the score was not up to standard, that they called in Smith and Benchley fled, says little for the book, a bit of fluff about jewel robbery, an aviator (a bow to the current

Lindbergh fever), Adele Astaire in her usual role of charming ingenuousness and Fred Astaire as her suffering guardian. Her wildly imaginative diary gets him in a good deal of trouble when the diary is stolen along with the jewels.

Whatever the "recriminations," the Gershwins composed twenty-four songs for this single production, enough for two shows; of these, eleven were casualties of the hard six weeks on the road (three, "How Long Has This Been Going On?," "The World Is Mine"—as "Toddling Along"—and "Dance Alone with You"—as "Ev'rybody Knows I Love Somebody"—would be heard again in future shows). A hint of the strain between producers and songwriters is suggested by the fact that Freedley insisted that Gershwin defray the cost of copying the new orchestrations, not the usual friendly practice. The Gershwins made little of this, at least in public, and it was generally not known until Ira Gershwin mentioned it to his secretary, Lawrence D. Stewart, years later.

Two final changes were made; the title: *Funny Face* and the last new song went into the score in time for its run in Wilmington. This was the comic "The Babbitt and the Bromide," Ira Gershwin's commentary on platitudes and casual friendships. "It went in on a Thursday or Friday night in Wilmington," he has written, "when the audience consisted of no more than two hundred mostly pretty and young and pregnant Du Pont matrons (my wife's observation). The number was introduced at 10:50 and concluded with Fred and Adele doing their famous 'run-around'—to show-stopping applause—and suddenly, with all the other changes, the show looked possible . . . The following week we opened at the new Alvin Theatre in New York . . ." (The "runaround" to which Gershwin refers was an Astaire specialty—also sometimes called a "nut dance"—dating back to an unsuccessful musical, *The Love Letter* (1921), in which they had had a small part. Conceived by the show's director, Edward Royce, it was an amusing way for the Astaires to exit after a dance routine. Royce suggested that Adele put out her arms, as if grasping the handlebars of a bicycle and, with a blank face, begin circling the stage as if looking for a place to go, around and around. At about the third circuit, Fred would join her, also expressionless, to reiterative *oompahs* from the pit. After several runarounds they would trot into the wings to great applause. This must have been the one high point in *The Love Letter,* for it closed within weeks, but the runaround proved so successful that the Astaires used it for the rest of their theatrical career (except in their last joint appearance in *The Band Wagon* ten years later). In 1937 the Gershwins created another runaround for

Astaire, "Stiff Upper Lip," which he did with George Burns and Gracie Allen, in *A Damsel in Distress.*

With *Funny Face* looking promising, the Gershwins were happy to pack up and leave Wilmington after a hard six weeks. En route Gershwin discovered that he had left behind two Tune Books containing some forty songs. As soon as they got to 103rd Street he called the hotel, but with no luck. The Tune Books were never found. He did not fret, for, as he said, there were more where those had come from.

The Alvin Theatre (now the Neil Simon) an Alex Aarons–Vinton Freedley enterprise, was especially designed for their kind of musical productions. Fittingly, it opened with a Gershwin musical, having in part been underwritten by the profits from *Lady, Be Good!, Tip-Toes* and *Oh, Kay!*

Funny Face premiered the evening of November 22, 1927. Contemporary critical consensus suggests that the extended tryout did little for the book ("scrambled," "perishable," "flat"). George Jean Nathan spoke for most when he wrote in *Judge* magazine that "the Astaire team lifts the evening as they have lifted equally dubious vehicles and sends the show gaily over. If there are better dancers anywhere I must have been laid up with old war wounds when they displayed themselves." Alexander Woollcott underscored the Astaire-Gershwin affinity with "I don't know whether George Gershwin was born into this world to write rhythms for Fred Astaire's feet or whether Fred Astaire was born into this world to show how the Gershwin music should really be danced."

The *Sun*'s Gilbert Gabriel rhapsodized the Astaires and made a passing reference to the "winsome Gershwin tunes." The Astaires, with the Gershwins' help, had captivated New York again. *Funny Face* would stay for a substantial 244 performances and did better the following year in London. The nonplot, bordering now and then on quasi-Wodehousean whimsy, did not deter the audiences; the songs were readily taken up by dance bands, were recorded and heard at tea dances and in nightclubs.

The *Funny Face* score is prime Gershwin. Besides the title song, which was popular immediately, there were also two that belong on the list of Gershwin standards still in print and still performed. One, "How Long Has This Been Going On?," was rejected when Kearns replaced Ridges and "He Loves and She Loves" was substituted. Both have become evergreens and were revived in the 1957 film, starring Astaire, also entitled *Funny Face* (except for Astaire and a few songs it had nothing to do with the original).

"He Loves and She Loves" has a curious history and sheds some

light on the Gershwins' working methods. In 1919, George had collaborated on "Something About Love" with Lou Paley which was initially
interpolated into the short-lived *The Lady in Red* and later into the
London production of *Lady, Be Good!* Except for publication, not
much came of it.

"Something About Love," whose lyric evinces Paley's profession of
grammar school teacher, is a good if not exceptional song. The melody
is passable early Gershwin. In the final eight measures he created a tag
to Paley's lyric employing the classroom conjugation in the present
indicative. In this section the melodic line rises and falls alternately on
the subject and verbs (the word "and" serves as a step between): "I love
(and) you love (and) he loves (and) she loves . . ." The otherwise passable tune takes on a perky character overshadowing the rest of the song.

While they labored over the *Funny Face* changes the Gershwins recalled that final phrase of "Something About Love." With Lou Paley's
delighted blessing, Ira Gershwin lifted the words and George created a
new song based on the original music of that eight-year-old motif. The
character of the song was changed slightly in the tempo, marked
"Slowly, with sentiment." Years later Ira Gershwin told Lawrence D.
Stewart that, although he was not absolutely certain, what is now the
chorus to "He Loves and She Loves" may have been the refrain to the
song to which "The Man I Love" was initially the verse.

There is another song that was stitched together in the score, the
complex wedding of a waltz and a fox trot, "Let's Kiss and Make Up."
It was initially titled "Come! Come! Come Closer!" and its verse began
with "Let's kiss and make up;/We mustn't break up . . ." and the
chorus, "Come! come! come closer!/Don't say, 'No, no, sir!'" Unhappy
with the verse, they decided (or were pushed by Aarons and/or Freedley) to revise it. The music of the chorus was largely retained and all but
the first line of the verse was scrapped. It became the title and first line
of the chorus—the second is "Come on!/Let's wake up . . ." A new
verse was written and another fine Gershwin song had been pieced
together.

If something seemed good to the Gershwins, despite the producer's
objections, they preserved it for another time. There was another,
"Those Eyes," which was also known as "Your Eyes, Your Smile," via
the usual revisions. It was never published, but the brothers remembered the bridge (the B section between choruses) five years later when
they were asked to write a new song for the first (1932) film version of
the successful *Girl Crazy.* From the bridge, Gershwin developed the
main strain of the chorus of "You've Got What Gets Me."

Other songs written for *Funny Face* would surface for time to come:

in their next musical, *Rosalie,* and as late as the posthumous *The Shocking Miss Pilgrim* (1946), when the propulsive "Blue Hullabaloo" from 1927 was rewritten as "Demon Rum."

Another musically distinctive song is "High Hat," sung and danced by Astaire with the chorus—all the men were formally dressed and wearing top hats. Though published, the song is hardly popular song material. Obviously it was a production number, and the stage version is remarkably orchestrated. Although no orchestrator is credited, it is likely that Gershwin had much to do with it. Once sung—the point being that the best way "to win a girlie's hand" is to treat her "high hat"—the song builds to an exhilarating dance with complex variations from the two pianos (Ohman and Arden in New York; Jacques Fray and Mario Braggioti in London), percussion, chorus and orchestra.

Another obvious nonhit, "The Babbitt and the Bromide" was also published; its satiric point and patter-song melody precluded popularity, but it served beautifully as the Astaires' runaround. They met, exchanged trite greetings and clichés deadpan, apparently not listening to each other. It pleased lyricist Gershwin when editor Louis Kronenberger included it in his *An Anthology of Light Verse* (1934).

Even with *Funny Face* solidly on its way the Gershwins had very little free time. Some time before their *Smarty/Funny Face* exertions they had agreed to write songs for a Florenz Ziegfeld musical that would star the popular, exquisite Marilyn Miller, who had triumphed at the age of twenty in *Sally* and *Sunny,* both Ziegfeld productions and both scored by Kern. When the brothers agreed to work on the show, they had no idea that *Funny Face* would use up so much of their time and, during the tryout, put Ziegfeld out of their thoughts.

The first reminder of their Ziegfeld commitment came while they were hard at work on *Funny Face* rewrites in the Sylvania Hotel in Philadelphia around the end of October. They received a cryptic telegram from Edgar Selwyn (though *Strike Up the Band* had failed, he continued to plan for another attempt at its production). The message informed them, somewhat to their mystified surprise, that he was releasing "The Man I Love" and that they were free to use it in the next Ziegfeld musical. It was Ira Gershwin's guess that Ziegfeld had "worked on Selwyn," so that Marilyn Miller could sing the song in the new show.

By late 1927 the Gershwins were quite tired of "The Man I Love," which had been doing fine on its own for the past three years, and they agreed it really was not a show song; for his part, Ira was "bored" with it. Still, Miller was the most luminous of Broadway musical stars, and it seemed like a reasonable idea. (True to tradition, despite revisions, it was not used in the show.)

On October 26, the *Times* announced that Ziegfeld was starring Marilyn Miller in a new musical, *Rosalie,* and that the music would be by George Gershwin and Sigmund Romberg, lyrics by Ira Gershwin and P. G. Wodehouse. It was set to begin the tryout in Boston early in December.

IV

Rosalie was already in rehearsal when the Gershwins were free of *Funny Face.* Originally the plan had been to have Romberg and Wodehouse collaborate on the operettalike plot (by Guy Bolton and William Anthony McGuire). But the composer, like Gershwin, was at the time working on another musical (it turned out to be *The New Moon,* one of his most successful shows). Romberg agreed to do the Miller musical, provided they could get the Gershwins to help on the score. It was a peculiar collaboration.

Romberg and Gershwin did not collaborate on the music, but Ira Gershwin and Wodehouse collaborated on some songs and worked independently on others. The Gershwins dug into their trunk for the consistently rejected "The Man I Love," and five additional songs: from *Primrose* (1924) they borrowed "Wait a Bit, Susie" and called it "Beautiful Gypsy"; from *Oh, Kay!* (1926) they lifted "Show Me the Town"; from the temporarily closed-down *Strike Up the Band* they took "Yankee Doodle Rhythm," and from their nicely running *Funny Face* they salvaged "Dance Alone with You" (relyricized into "Ev'rybody Knows I Love Somebody") and one of their best, "How Long Has This Been Going On?" Before *Rosalie* opened, "The Man I Love," "Beautiful Gypsy" and "Yankee Doodle Rhythm" were cut. So was the Gershwin-composed title song, one of the several originals he contributed to the score.

Other new songs included "Say So!," "New York Serenade" (with an Ira-only lyric), "Oh Gee!—Oh Joy!," the Romberg-like "Follow the Drum" and an instrumental, *Setting-Up Exercises* (Gershwin Melody No. 43, *Comedy Dance,* and published as *Merry Andrew).* A handful of other Gershwin songs, five, were also dropped.

Romberg's contribution consisted of stock operetta numbers with titles like *Entrance of the Hussars,* "West Point Bugle," *West Point March,* "Kingdom of Dreams" and "The King Can Do No Wrong." It is likely too that he composed Marilyn Miller's *Ballet of Flowers.*

If ever a score was a musical hodgepodge it was the one for *Rosalie*—and yet it worked. The Bolton-McGuire book had been inspired by a 1926 visit to the United States by Queen Marie of Romania (in the show Miller is a mere princess). Her regal progress cross-country was lavishly covered on the front pages of newspapers, feeding on the American fascination with royalty. Brought over at government (U.S. Government, that is) expense, she traveled to several states and into Canada in an attempt to marshal good will for her husband's unpopular reign and to persuade the United States to prop up their financially troubled country.

Queen Marie's visit was marked by grand gestures—she wrote notes to the governors of forty states, she made speeches ("Life could be very glorious if people loved each other a little more and hated each other a little less . . .") and wrote copious articles of her impressions of the country. She was fair game for a musical comedy.

The attention she excited was enough for Bolton and McGuire. They came up with a plot about a visiting princess who falls in love with a commoner, a West Point lieutenant. They cannot marry unless her father, the king, abdicates, which by the *finale ultimo,* he conveniently does—joining several real-life ex-kings then in exile. Another convenience was the hero's duplication of Lindbergh's solo Atlantic flight by flying from the United States to the princess's country, Romanza, to prove his steadfast love.

The spectacle was dangled from this improbable plot. *Rosalie* was lavishly designed by Ziegfeld's Viennese artist-designer, Joseph Urban. Some idea of the production's abundance is evident in Alexander Woollcott's description of Marilyn Miller's entrance: "Fifty beautiful girls in simple peasant costumes of satin and chiffon rush pell-mell onto the stage, all squealing simple peasant outcries of 'Here she comes!' Fifty hussars in a fatigue uniform of ivory white and tomato bisque march on in columns of fours and kneel to express an emotion too strong for words. The house holds its breath. And on walks Marilyn Miller."

Obviously the blend of operetta and musical comedy and pageantry worked. Marilyn Miller was reigning female star of the moment in musical theater; her dancing partner was the popular Jack Donahue (her love interest, the West Pointer, was portrayed by Oliver McLennan). After the tryout, which began in Boston on December 5, *Rosalie* moved into Ziegfeld's New Amsterdam Theatre on January 10, 1928; its run (335 performances) would prove to be even longer than that of *Funny Face.* While it is generally dismissed as one of Gershwin's lesser efforts, a mere collection of scrapings from the trunk, it is notable for having saved "How Long Has This Been Going On?" and was the source of other worthy songs.

Gershwin fared better than Romberg in the reviews. Woollcott waspishly suggested that teaming Gershwin with Romberg was comparable to a collaboration on a novel by Ernest Hemingway and Harold Bell Wright (a then bestselling writer of pulpish Western romances). Nor was he kind to Romberg in noting that "Brother Romberg has written his usual thunderous choruses which you enjoy while they are being roared at you and you forget by the time you reach the lobby." As for "Brother Gershwin," Woollcott declared that he had "written at least two jaunty songs which follow you up the street." (These were probably "Oh Gee!—Oh Joy!," which became one of Frankie Gershwin's most popular party songs, and the elegantly exquisite duet, "Say So!" both with Gershwin-Wodehouse lyrics.)

With two hits running simultaneously, the Gershwins agreed it was time for time out. Not only was a vacation in order, but George Gershwin was itching to cross the musical tracks again. Despite concentrating on the three musicals completed in 1927, he continued working on an idea for an orchestral work when he could, and also studied whenever possible. Sometime in 1927 he met informally and irregularly with Henry Cowell. The iconoclastic modernist, according to Gershwin biographer David Ewen, found that conventional rules "exasperated" Gershwin, "but not because he was incapable of mastering them. With no effort at all he rattled off the almost perfect exercise, but would get side-tracked into something using a juicy ninth and altered chords he liked better, and would insert these into [a] Palestrina-style motet."

What had begun as weekly sessions dwindled to one a month and for some reason stopped (Gershwin seems never to have mentioned Cowell as one of his teachers; or the names of others who supposedly taught him: Wallingford Riegger, a friend and colleague of Cowell's, conductor Artur Bodanzky, and Lajos Serly, father of American composer Tibor Serly).

Soon after *Rosalie* opened Gershwin was interviewed on the run (he was on his way to some Florida sunshine) by Hyman Sandow of *Musical America* (the result appeared in the issue of February 18, 1928). Sandow reported that Gershwin, "jazz composer of the *Rhapsody in Blue* and other successes, hopes to complete a second rhapsody and an orchestral ballet, *An American in Paris*, before the end of the coming summer . . .

"Early in March," he continued, "Mr. Gershwin will sail for Europe. After visiting London and Paris, he plans to take a house in Southern France, where he will work and study—he does not now know with whom or what . . . I asked Mr. Gershwin if it were true that he might soon undertake to compose an American Opera. He said he did not contemplate any such work, just now, nor did he expect to attempt so arduous a task until he could devote at least two years entirely to it."

Sometime before this interview Gershwin had completed, in pencil, nine pages of thematic ideas for projected orchestral work; also, despite the distractions that had begun with the summer rehearsals of *Strike Up the Band* and ended with the December premiere of *Rosalie,* he had begun sketching out a solo piano version of the complete *An American in Paris* as well as another for two pianos. The first, in its final form runs to sixty-four pages and is undoubtedly his initial sketch. In pencil on the last page it bears the date, "August 1, 1928"; both versions, however, are dated—imprecisely—January 1928 on the title pages. The two-piano *American* is seventy pages in length. Both were used as the basis for the orchestration. Obviously, before he set out for Europe, Gershwin had blocked out the work quite thoroughly so that, despite musicological legend, he did not go to Paris to write *An American in Paris;* it was virtually complete, except for the orchestration, before he sailed from Manhattan.

As he told writer-artist Charles G. Shaw, he loved Paris for its beauty, London for its calm and that "New York is the greatest city in the world for work."

9

Americans in Paris

Late in February, 1928, Gershwin wrote to Mabel Schirmer in Paris telling her that he was "glad you are going to be excited" over his coming visit and promised to cable details about "the time of our departure, arrival, etc." as soon as they were definite.

He outlined their preliminary plans. The first stop would be London for a week or so to see *That's a Good Girl,* a musical starring Jack Buchanan with some songs by Ira Gershwin and Phil Charig. They would also see *Oh, Kay!,* which was nearing the end of its run at His Majesty's Theatre. After which "we are coming to Paris, and from then on our plans are rather vague. I expect that we will stay in Paris for about two weeks and then go someplace where the climate is right, and where I can do some work. If, however, I find somebody to study with in Paris, I may take a place on the outskirts of Paris and stay there most of the time."

On the other hand, "If I go to the south of France, the kind of place I would like to take would be a house surrounded by a few cottages, where we could all live together and yet be separated if I wanted to work. In looking over some places . . . I wish you would keep this in mind. Also, I'd like to find, when I get to Paris, a valet who speaks several languages, and possibly drives a car."

While the trip did not turn out quite as planned, it proved to be productive and, for Gershwin, exciting since, as he put it, "it is the first time I have ever gone abroad without having to put on a show, and I will have much more time to myself." Nor did he have a deadline for his projected new work; there was no commission for him to compose *An American in Paris* (though with his box-office record he could hardly have doubted a quick performance once the job was done). Before leaving, about a week after he had written to Mabel, he had an experience that stimulated his search for a teacher.

I

Early in January, 1928, composer Maurice Ravel had arrived in the United States to begin a four-month tour as lecturer, pianist and conductor across the country and into Canada. Like Gershwin, he was a good friend of Eva Gauthier, who celebrated the French composer's fifty-third birthday (March 7) with a dinner party. When asked if he had any special request, Ravel told her he wished to meet George Gershwin and to see one of his musicals (it was *Funny Face*).

The party was formal (black tie) and, except for Gauthier, all male. Besides Gershwin and Ravel, at least two conductors were present, Oskar Fried, who led the Berlin Symphony, and who had made musical history by performing Ravel's *Rapsodie Espagnole* twice during a single concert; the other conductor was one Tedesco of Naples.

Gauthier recalled that after dinner "Gershwin played the *Rhapsody* and, in fact, his entire repertoire, and fairly outdid himself. It was an unforgettable evening, the meeting of the two most outstanding composers of the day, the young man just beginning to scale the heights, the other at the very pinnacle.

"The thing that astonished Ravel was the facility with which George scaled the most formidable technical difficulties and his genius for weaving complicated rhythms and his gift for melody."

She acted as interpreter and through her Gershwin told Ravel that he wished to study with him. As Gauthier remembered it, Ravel told Gershwin he did not think it a good idea, that, in her words, "it would probably cause him to write bad 'Ravel' and lose his great gift of melody and spontaneity." Instead, Ravel provided Gershwin with a letter of introduction to the great French teacher Nadia Boulanger. Ravel was impressed with Gershwin and his jazz experiences in New York. (Gershwin had taken him to Harlem to hear authentic jazz.) His tour took him to Houston in April, where he spoke on American music at the Rice Institute. He referred to "the gradual formation of a veritable school of American music" and had no doubt that "this school will become notable in its final evolution . . ." He addressed the audience directly and hoped "this national school of yours [may] embody a great deal of the rich and diverting rhythm of your jazz, and a great deal of the sentiment and spirit characteristic of your popular melodies and songs, worthily deriving from, and in turn contributing to, a noble heritage in music."

By April, as Ravel spoke in Texas the Gershwins were comfortably, and excitingly, settled in Paris.

II

Ira Gershwin succinctly synopsized their three European months with: "In the spring of 1928 George took his fifth and last trip to Europe. With *Funny Face* and *Rosalie* running in New York and *Oh, Kay!* in London, a vacation was in order and my sister, my wife and myself accompanied him. I did little other than see sights and drink beer, but George, despite all his social activities, his meetings with many of Europe's important composers, the hours spent with various interviewers and musical activities, still found time to work on *American in Paris* in the hotels we stayed at. The entire 'blues' section was written at the Hotel Majestic in Paris."

The journey began festively with a bon voyage party given by Kay and James Warburg on the night of March 9, which lasted until around five the next morning in time for the travelers to board the *Majestic* bound for Southampton.

The crossing proved to be musical. Besides Gershwin the passengers included the American pianist George Copeland, a celebrated interpreter of Debussy, and a violinist, also American born, Albert Spalding. Aboard, too, was lyricist Leo Robin, whose *Hit the Deck,* written with Vincent Youmans, was running in New York and London. He and Ira Gershwin, two of songwriting's least demonstrative men, became good friends. Years later, after both had settled in Beverly Hills, their rejection of Hollywood mores (petty criticisms, backbiting, gossip) won them the permanent presidency (Gershwin) and vice-presidency (Robin) of the "Sweet Fellas Club" founded by composer Harry Warren.

While his brother talked with Robin or read, George spent a great deal of time at the ship's piano. In the afternoon of the day before docking, at the request of a pretty passenger he had met the night before, he played for over an hour in the restaurant lounge. The audience, Ira cited in his diary, "was very enthusiastic, especially Spalding and his accompanist—Benoit [sic., François Benoist]." Later that evening, Copeland entertained with Debussy and Spanish moderns for a small, appreciative audience. "Then," the diarist noted with fraternal pride, "George Gershwin played with his usual success, people coming in from on deck to hear him."

The *Majestic* docked on March 16 after which the Gershwins headed for London for a full week of sightseeing, socializing and a little business. Gershwin immediately called Gertrude Lawrence to let her know they had arrived and would see her in *Oh, Kay!* on closing night. Then the two went shopping, Lawrence guiding Gershwin along Savile Row for a supply of suits, then to Hawes and Curtis's for ties and shirts and to Scott's for lunch.

March 18 was spent seeing London—it was the first visit for Frances, Leonore and Ira. The next evening they saw the opening of *That's a Good Girl* at the Hippodrome in nearby Lewisham. On the twentieth George and Ira visited the London offices of Chappell for what turned out to be a virtual reunion and Manhattan-like convocation.

As they were about to enter the building, they encountered Phil Charig (one of the composers of the *That's a Good Girl* songs) admiring Vincent Youmans's new Mercedes, imported from Paris the day before. Upstairs they found Youmans in conference with Max Dreyfus. They were joined by Jerome Kern and arranger-orchestrator Robert Russell Bennett, the latter two in town for a new Kern musical, *Blue Eyes* and the London production of *Show Boat.*

From Youmans, to their surprise, the Gershwins learned that he had been asked by Ziegfeld to write the songs for a musical to be based on a successful 1918 play set in the Orient, *East Is West.* Diplomatically they did not, in turn, inform Youmans that Ziegfeld had also asked them to score *East Is West.* The idea of doing a musical with oriental overtones had interested the Gershwins enough to have sketched some ideas for such a score. As with many of Ziegfeld's grandiose projects the musical did not come off, a casualty of the Depression, the producer's stock-market misadventures and his mercurial whim.

But they had other things to do. George, particularly, seemed to be in constant motion; the evening of the twentieth he had dinner with the Mountbattens, after which he went to the Embassy Club for a long chat with the Prince of Wales. Two nights later, George escorted his sister to the premiere of Noël Coward's *This Year of Grace* at the London Pavilion, after which they attended a party in Gershwin's honor at the Kit Kat Club. It rather upset George that Ira preferred the quiet of his hotel room to the smoke and din of the trendy club, especially for a Gershwin evening.

The London stay was climaxed with dinner with Gertrude Lawrence and a small group of friends. Ira pronounced it a "lovely meal with plenty of wine and cocktails, smoked salmon, consommé, filet of sole, duck, applesauce, asparagus, sweet, coffee, cigars, brandy . . ." In a word: "swell."

After dinner they returned to their rooms to dress to attend the final performance of *Oh, Kay!* at His Majesty's Theatre. They were a little apprehensive, for Kern had told them that he had found the show "poor." Worse, there were other friends who agreed with Kern. When one of her shows ran too long, Lawrence had a tendency to get bored with it and turn in indifferent performances.

Instead, the Gershwins were agreeably surprised and all "rather liked it—wasn't bad at all, though Gertie did clown too much." After the curtain, Gertrude Lawrence appeared to make a tearful speech before joining the Gershwins and others backstage where "[Bert] Taylor [her beau] was drenching everyone with magnums of champagne." Ira's entry ends, "Home—packed—Goodbye to Phil [Charig]. Looking forward to tomorrow and Paris. To bed about 4 A.M."

III

When they arrived at the Gare St. Lazare, in central Paris, on March 25, the Gershwins were greeted by Mabel and Bob Schirmer and Josefa Rosanska, who was then concertizing in Europe. They settled into the Hotel Majestic, where they would stay, except for a couple of side excursions, from late March until early June. Gershwin had a Steinway piano moved into his room, unpacked his *American in Paris* sketches, music paper, reference books and other materials and settled in to do some work. Excitedly he showed Mabel Schirmer the letter from Ravel to Boulanger and asked her to accompany him when he presented it to the renowned teacher. Since he spoke no French and Mabel did, he wanted to be certain Boulanger would understand what he wanted. (Boulanger spoke English, but he was not aware of it.)

Most of the celebrated American composers of Gershwin's generation had studied, or would, with Boulanger, among them Aaron Copland, Virgil Thomson, Walter Piston, Roy Harris and David Diamond. When they met, Boulanger was aware of Gershwin's accomplishments, fame and success—and an endorsement by Ravel was an impressive compliment. But she seconded Ravel's view, particularly after hearing Gershwin play. Gershwin was Gershwin; his natural gift might very well be inhibited by her strict academic approach. So the answer was another "No." For Gershwin it was a kind of disappointing flattery.

The encounter with Nadia Boulanger has been the subject of controversy, suggesting that Gershwin was rejected because she did think much of his musicianship and promise as a student and was not worth wasting her valuable time on him. But Mabel Schirmer does not remember it that way; she talked about it in 1928 and has been interviewed ever since and recalls vividly how the meeting went.

Ira Gershwin evoked the name of Boulanger in a response to an attack on his brother's musicianship in 1945: "I found [the article by Metronome critic Barry Ulanov] a malicious outpouring rather than an analytical criticism and therefore too special to be much concerned about. Generally, an unfavorable notice of my brother's music doesn't bother me too much. So someone doesn't like the 'Rhapsody' or 'American in Paris' or whatever it is. So someone is entitled to his opinion. So all right.

"What does bother me is when I see phrases like 'naive orchestration' or 'structural ignorance' as though my brother were just a terribly talented fellow (which they grant) who somehow stumbled into the concert hall, was impudent enough to take advantage of it, put on a high pressure sales talk—and got away with it.

"With these critics there is an utter disregard of the facts that George from the age of 13 or 14 never let up in his studies of so-called classical foundations and that by the time he was 30 or so could be considered a musicologist (dreadful word) of the first degree besides being a composer. When, in 1928, he went to see Nadia Boulanger in Paris about studying with her she turned him down on the grounds that there was nothing she could teach him. And she wasn't kidding because she was quoted in 'Time' on the matter four or five years ago."

Gershwin took the complimentary dismissal with good grace; there were other composer-teachers in Paris. Maybe Stravinsky or Milhaud. Ravel at the time was still on his American tour.

They were more successful the next week, when Gershwin made a peculiar request. Where, he asked Mabel, could he acquire some of those taxi horns that suffused Paris with one of its most indigenous sounds. She took him to the Grande Armée, where she knew there were several automotive part shops. They didn't miss one, as Mabel translated and George squeezed until he found the "honk" or "squawk" that suited his purpose; some were wonderfully off-key. They then took several back to the Majestic.

Soon after, the sight of these (now) "instruments" startled two youthful music students (and unabashed Gershwin fans) who, in turn, had surprised him by appearing unannounced at his door.

They were Mario Braggiotti, Italian-born, American- and French-educated, then an eighteen-year-old student at the Paris Conservatory. His equally young friend and colleague was Jacques Fray. When the two strangers presented themselves as fellow musicians Gershwin invited them in despite the fact that, as Braggiotti sensed, they had interrupted him. He ushered them into his room "with that vague and stunned manner of one who is holding tightly to the threat of a creative mood."

Looking around, Braggiotti saw some card tables near the piano on which several taxi horns had been placed. Nothing was said, then suddenly Gershwin went to the piano, "sat down in front of his manuscript and quickly finished a musical sentence that my bell ringing had interrupted . . ." Gershwin then stood and noticed that his guests were staring at the horn collection.

"I'm looking for the right horn pitch for the street scene of a ballet I'm writing," he told them. "Calling it 'An American in Paris.' Lots of fun. I think I've got something. Just finished sketching the slow movement [the "homesickness blues" section]."

He had an idea. Gesturing to Braggiotti, he said, "Here, I want to try this accompaniment. Won't you play the melody in the treble?"

Braggiotti, "Flattered and eagar . . . moved swiftly beside him at the piano. He started the two-bar vamp and I joined in, reading the single-note lead from his fresh manuscript. And, for the first time anywhere, there echoed the amazingly original and nostalgic slow movement of *An American in Paris,* undoubtedly one of George's most brilliant works. George chewingly switched his perennial cigar from mouth left to mouth right and said, 'How do you like it?' "

They liked it very much.

He explained the taxi horns. He hoped to evoke the sounds of Parisian traffic by using real taxi horns in his "ballet." He then conscripted the delighted pianists as "hornists." He turned to the opening of the piece and played it, cueing them in on their parts with a nod. On that first and audaciously impromptu meeting with their musical hero, Braggiotti and Fray found Gershwin approachable, relaxed and remarkably modest for one they considered to be one of Paris's most popular celebrities of the moment.

Considerate, too, he asked them to play for him; they were, in 1928, a neophyte two-piano team specializing in the standard classics as well as popular songs in two-piano arrangements. All three left for Fray's flat with its unique twin keyboard piano, a Pleyel. Impressed, Gershwin offered to get them work in London playing the Ohman and Arden parts in *Funny Face* when it opened later in the year—and he kept his promise. (Later, when they came to the United States as the team of Fray and Braggiotti, making their debut in Carnegie Hall, Gershwin was one of their most helpful champions and a friend.)

Finding Gershwin when he was alone was rare during his Paris stay. In his journal, Ira Gershwin recorded a regular flow of callers, old friends and new. On their second day in Paris he dropped in on George and found that Rosanska had come by with four young men, one of them the left-handed violinist Rudolf Kolisch whom she later married (and divorced). The Kolisch Quartet treated them to performances of Schubert and Schoenberg (Kolisch's former teacher and husband of his sister). Ravel's friend Alexandre Tansman dropped by the same day; he spoke of musical parties and would be Gershwin's guide when Mabel Schirmer was not free. Dmitri Tiomkin, a concert pianist, and his wife, dancer Albertina Rasch, also visited Gershwin to tell him he was preparing an all-Gershwin concert soon (actually the only Gershwin was the *Concerto in F* in its European premiere). Tiomkin eventually abandoned his pianistic career for one as a successful film composer in Hollywood *(High Noon, The High and the Mighty,* etc.).

When not being interviewed or visiting, Gershwin managed to get into the streets of Paris to absorb ambiance. The other Gershwins acted like typical tourists. On the day that Gershwin and Mabel Schirmer searched for the taxi horns, Leopold Godowsky, Jr., son of the famed pianist (whom the Gershwins had just met), escorted Frankie, Leonore and Ira Gershwin to the Louvre. Ira was especially taken with the work of the early Flemish artist Hans Memling. Unlike George, his tastes leaned more toward the classic or conservative masters.

That evening Tansman had a Gershwin gathering with an impressive guest list. Among those present were composer Jacques Ibert, the young Italian modernist Vittorio Rieti, pianists E. Robert Schmitz, Dmitri Tiomkin and others, including the wives of Ibert, Schmitz and Tiomkin. "George played about 2 hours without stopping to the success and enthusiasm he is accustomed to . . ." Ira wrote in his diary.

Gershwin was equally enthusiastic, for when he was visited by Vernon Duke he recounted the evening. Duke had arrived at the Majestic dramatically attired in a self-designed conception of what a rising intellectual songwriter-composer should wear, which gave Gershwin slight pause. (Duke later admitted that, on looking back, he was reminded of the remark Degas had made to the dandyish Whistler: "You dress as if you have no talent"; he recalled too that the Gershwins "had good enough manners not to laugh out loud.")

Duke, like Gershwin, was then moving back and forth through the imaginary barrier between "serious" and popular music. A member of the Russian colony in exile (among them Stravinsky), he was still one of the lesser lights who fed on envy, competitiveness and knowing the right people. In 1928, Dukelsky-Duke had not yet made his mark, except among the modern music clique in Paris and his popular songs were not yet popular (later he would produce "April in Paris" with E. Y. Harburg and "I Can't Get Started" with Ira Gershwin). He had very strong, nonnegotiable views on the Parisian cultural pecking order.

When Gershwin told him about the Tansman party, Duke demanded a résumé of the guest list; the host was immediately dismissed as a "second rater who will never amount to anything."

"Rieti," George told him, "the Italian."

"Very good."

"E. Robert Schmitz."

"Very good."

"Ibert."

"Second rate."

"[Raymond] Petit, the critic."

"Not important, third rate."

Duke's final verdict was, "You shouldn't have gone to that party. It will hurt you, people like that. A dozen people there, but only two really, Rieti and Schmitz."

He extended further commentary. As Ira noted in his diary, Duke argued "with George about parts of 'American in Paris,' saying that George was 1928 in his musical comedies and in most of his concert music but that in 'A.I.P.' he allowed himself to become somewhat saccharine in spots."

After a heated, opinionated hour, Duke left an unconvinced Gershwin; besides, George was pleased with "blues" he had created for his homesick American. Duke dashed off, a fulgent figure with his gun-metal cloth suit, yellow shirt, an orchid in his lapel, "the whole structure supported by a magnificent eighteenth-century walking stick, a present to myself . . ."

He was succeeded by the young British composer (then twenty-six) William Walton, who was then celebrated for his orchestral piece *Portsmouth Point* and notorious for his setting of Edith Sitwell poems, *Façade*. Ira Gershwin was unimpressed with his piano technique as he performed excerpts from a new symphonic work and a "parody waltz" (probably from *Façade).*

Gershwin took his turn at the keyboard to play from his work in progress, then told Walton of Duke's criticisms. Walton told Gershwin, Ira noted in his diary, "to disregard Dukelsky's advice as Duke was influenced by Prokofiev and thought anyone who wrote in another style old-fashioned; also, that nothing of Duke's had become popular, etc., etc. Most interesting what they all think of one another."

It was a new experience for the Gershwins, this envious in-fighting;

not even backstage and out-of-town Broadway tryouts were so marked by envy and hostility. The London-Paris musical axis was especially competitive (with Paris a particular hotbed in itself)—one composer's success was considered another's failure. The jousting for performances, the wooing of conductors, soloists, the rejections, reactions and criticisms often led to lifelong feuds (in later years Duke's and Stravinsky's became nastily virulent). In 1928 both Stravinsky and Prokofiev were in Parisian exile, in mutually opposed musical camps. Gershwin tended to avoid these internecine squabbles; he was fortunate in that any announcement of a new composition of his brought bids from conductors and orchestras for its premiere. Though he did not feel himself in competition with his fellow composers, he suffered occasional Parisian-like nettles from the critics (some of whom were composers, more or less).

The same morning's mail brought a cheering message from Edgar Selwyn. He had returned to *Strike Up the Band* for the 1929/30 season and had humorist Morrie Ryskind at work revising the Kaufman book. After assuring him by cable that they would be ready when he was, the brothers decided to take a stroll. Ira's weather report read: ". . . sunshine at last."

They set out from the hotel, strolling along the Avenue Kléber, picking up a large sack of fruit and some bottles of Cointreau and "a quart bottle of wonderful Spanish port—all for $6." They crossed the Seine and, packages in hand, stood in line for fifteen minutes in order to squeeze into an elevator that would carry them to the top of the Eiffel Tower. The 984 feet height was the highest Ira Gershwin had been at that time; his record to date had been achieved atop a twenty-two-story New York skyscraper (he had yet to take his first flight in an aircraft; George was a veteran, having flown as early as 1919 in an old World War I two-seater).

Their Eiffel Tower experience was different. "I was afraid to walk the few feet to the railing, but finally did. George complained about peculiar sensations in his stomach and other portions. We walked around kidding one another, but really impressed."

Emboldened, they chanced leaning slightly over the rail, as most other spectators did so casually, to view Paris spread before and around them in the bright sunlight. A caricaturist sketched George (at twenty-five francs, Ira found it "not bad"). They took the elevator to the landing below and decided to walk down, a descent that Ira estimated to be thirty-eight New York flights. The most sedentary of the young Gershwins, he suffered. " . . . boy how my legs trembled when we finally got to the street. It took me three blocks to get them straightened out."

Besides sightseeing and meeting with assorted visitors, there was also music and, since word that Gershwin would be in Paris had preceded them, they were treated to a great deal of Gershwin.

Within a week of their arrival they attended an afternoon concert at the Théâtre Mogador (the regular tenant was Friml and Stothart's *Rose Marie,* then in its second year). These Saturday Concerts Pasdeloup were led by Rhené-Baton (born René Baton)—in Ira's description, "a large, bearded man with a ring on his left hand." The piano soloists were Jean Wiener and Clement Doucet, famed for their jazzy nightclub performances as well as their sponsorship of the avant-garde—Wiener was especially active in this—Schoenberg, Darius Milhaud, Stravinsky and Alois Hába.

Their program that afternoon ranged from Bach to Gershwin—two harpsichord concertos by Bach and the *Rhapsody in Blue,* all performed on two pianos with orchestral accompaniment. They were fine pianists, proved by the Bach, but they were ill prepared for Gershwin, whose work concluded the program.

"I alternately giggled & squirmed," Ira wrote. "It was at times almost unbelievably bad. The solo part had evidently proved too hard for M. Wiener, the premier soloist, so he got an assistant to oompah. Some of the fast tempi were taken at a funereal pace, and the rhythms were terrible in spots. A banjo played the same chord almost all thru the piece.

"The middle theme couldn't be spoiled of course and came like a violet ray on a bald spot. And yet I realized that since probably 95% of the audience had never heard it before they might take the occasional sour notes as a true reading and find it all interesting. Sure enough at its conclusion there was real spontaneous applause all over the house and lots of cheers and bravos."

Not among the unenlightened "95%" was George Gershwin, who had fled the hall to the bar to wait for the more resilient Gershwins.

Ira noticed that Wiener stood on the stage "looking anxiously over the audience and gesticulating to the conductor," and realized "they wanted G. So I called him and he was rushed backstage—and on his appearance the house gave him another big hand. So the 2 pianists played for an encore 'Do-Do-Do,' a verse & 3 choruses they had evidently arranged and practiced for it went with great éclat and the house wanted more. It was the first time I had heard of an encore by soloists at a symphony program.

"In the lobby G. told us Baton had apologized for the performance saying they had only rehearsed the piece ½ hour. At any rate, despite the almost laughable performance George was thrilled by the reception." In an appreciative gesture, George, accompanied by Tansman, called on Baton and Madame Baton, which reassured the conductor.

The next evening they were treated to the *Rhapsody* again. At the Théâtre des Champs Élysées they saw yet another ballet based on *La Rapsodie en Bleu de George Gershwin* with *Chorégraphie d'Anton Dolin* (born Patrick Healy-Kay) in which the English-born dancer-choreographer performed as *Le Jazz;* his partner in the company, Vera Nemchinova, represented *"La Musique classique."* The "plot" of the ballet was current: the clash between classical music and jazz. Ira Gershwin apparently was more impressed with the design of the theater and the "jazz band of 5 girls" that played in the bar between the acts than the ballet. He did not record George's reaction.

Another Gershwin, sister Frances, too was popular in Paris; she was regularly squired by Leopold Godowsky, Jr., while her brothers competed at poker. Further, she was discovered by the professional hostess Elsa Maxwell, who had settled in Paris where she subsisted by engineering elaborate, very social parties.

Elsa Maxwell had a Gershwin evening to which she invited her regular convocation of celebrities, assorted exiled dukes, musicians and her good friend Cole Porter, just returned to Paris from New York after contributing several good songs to a musical entitled *Paris* (he would not learn of its success until its opening in October). He was then working on a score for a nightclub revue. Porter later said that the highlight of that evening was hearing Frankie sing her brother's songs with Gershwin at the piano. It gave him an idea.

A couple of days later they met at lunch—Frankie, Ira, Porter, the Tansmans and violinist Samuel Dushkin (who had induced Gershwin to let him arrange two piano novelettes for violin and piano as *Short Story).* Porter felt it would be proper to present his idea to Ira Gershwin, the older brother. He asked Ira if he thought his sister would want to go on the stage. Gershwin's reply was straightforward, "Ask her."

"Of course," was Frankie's equally to the point response.

The next day, April 22, when the other Gershwins left for Berlin, Frankie remained in Paris for rehearsals. For Porter's revue *La Revue des Ambassadeurs* (also *In the Old Days and Today),* he wrote her a special verse leading into a medley of her brothers' songs: "I happen to be the sister/Of a rhythm twister/ No doubt you know him as Mister/ George Gershwin." Porter went on to rhyme "orgy" with "Georgie" and then Frankie announced "I'll try to sing some fav'rites/ Of the Man I love."

Even as she rehearsed her Gershwin Specialty—"It was so exciting—suddenly all this glamour happening"—the Gershwins, accompanied now by a friend of Leonore, Henrietta Malkiel, arrived in Berlin and registered at the Esplanade. In the evening the three Gershwins walked to the Bechstein Salle where Josie Rosanska presented an "exceptionally well played" and "most interesting" recital (Bach, Chopin, Berg, De Falla, Ravel, Stravinsky). In Berlin, too, they met the young "radical" composer, Kurt Weill (who would years later collaborate with Ira); he was still best known in Germany for a rather atonal violin concerto, the jazz-inspired song collection, lyrics by Bertolt Brecht, *Das Klein Mahagonny,* both unknown to the Gershwins. Not long after they left Berlin, Weill and Brecht began collaborating on their bitter *Die Dreigroschenoper (The Threepenny Opera),* which would make them world famous as well as unpopular with the German Government. Weill too was attempting to fuse popular song with classical forms and musical devices.

After Berlin came Vienna, the birthplace of operetta. Appropriately, their stay began (on April 28) with a luncheon at the Café Sacher with one of operetta's eminent composers, the Hungarian-born Emmerich Kálmán. The entrance of the Gershwin party was signaled by the café's band playing an excerpt from the *Rhapsody in Blue.*

The next day Kálmán came to the Bristol Hotel, enjoyed a full hour of Gershwin at the piano, after which they went to Kálmán's home for lunch with writer Ferenc Molnár and Gershwin's musical editor, also Hungarian-born, Albert Sirmay. He too had tried his hand at operetta before settling in the United States to work for Dreyfus. Besides Gershwin, he was editor to Cole Porter, Richard Rodgers and virtually every great American popular songwriter. His responsibilities included preparing their songs for publication, simplifying them for the general musical public without damaging the original.

In the evening the Gershwins saw Ernst Krenek's notorious and popular "jazz opera" (it was not his description, but that is what it became in the public's mind), *Jonny Spielt Auf (Johnny Strikes Up the Band).* The two-act opera had achieved international renown since its premiere the year before in Leipzig (it came to the Metropolitan in 1929). Besides musical allusions to American jazz, the lead character was a black American musician (the role was sung by a baritone in blackface). He is an amoral womanizer who steals a priceless violin.

The libretto by Krenek made little more sense than most Broadway musicals (or operas, for that matter) of the time. Max, the composer-hero, for example communes with a convenient Alpine glacier when he has difficulties with his sweetheart after she takes up with Jonny. The glacier proved to be of little help, but the score was brilliantly orchestrated, sometimes mixing Schoenberg and Weill. The point of the libretto and the musical symbolism might best be described as vague. Did Jonny represent an America on the make? Was "jazz," as Krenek had gleaned it from recordings, a force for evil? Was he making a statement on race?

By coincidence, in the audience that same night were pianist Lester Donahue, touring Europe with a Hammond piano, and John Hays Hammond, Jr., the inventive savior that evening when Gershwin and Stravinsky had been coerced by Mary Hoyt Wiborg into taking their places at her keyboard.

Donahue had not been at all impressed by Krenek's opera. "Aside from the remarkable scenic and ballet resources of the famous Vienna Opera House," he concluded, "it was completely 'phoney.'" In the lobby he voiced a rather undiplomatic protest. If anyone should attempt a jazz opera, he stated, it should be George Gershwin.

"Oh yeah!" a voice interjected. Donahue turned to see three smiling Gershwins. "George was very fair about *Jonny Spielt Auf,*" he admitted, "and contended that it was a worthy effort, but I was quietly pleased the following winter when it was produced at the Metropolitan and several of the critics claimed they had never sufficiently appreciated Gershwin."

Donahue and Hammond joined the Gershwins after the opera for a round of tourism and drinking in the cafés. One afternoon, which began at five and lasted until ten in the evening, was spent in the home of the widow of Waltz King Johann Strauss, Jr.

"She was a fascinating old lady," Donahue wrote, "full of anecdotes about her husband, Rubinstein, Liszt, Tschaikovsky and many other great names which seemed too far in the past for even her living memory." When asked about Brahms, she dismissed him as "just a Hamburger," his works as "too modern" for her and totally lacking in "musical beauty."

A Brahms admirer, Gershwin was disconcerted by her opinion. Before the party left, Frau Strauss tried to sell them the manuscript of *Die Fledermaus* "for quite a healthy sum, but our enjoyment of the afternoon did not reach that peak."

Yet another Manhattan friend turned up in Vienna. Richard Simon, one of the founders of the publishing house Simon and Schuster, had arrived to arrange for the American publication of a new book by Felix Salten, *Bambi.* He too was registered at the Bristol. One evening after dinner, Gershwin invited him up to his suite where he played portions of his burgeoning *An American in Paris.* (In a letter to his musical brother, Alfred, Simon told him that he did not agree with Duke at all on the bluesy "Homesickness Theme," which he found superior to "The Man I Love.")

Later, over Gershwin's protests, Simon insisted on hearing some Viennese waltzes in a café. Gershwin felt that he had been neglecting his work—besides, he hadn't shaved (Simon nicknamed him "Bluebeard") and felt a little queasy. But Simon and others persisted and Gershwin went along and had a fine time, mastered his composer's stomach and "was glad" Simon and company had "kidnapped him." By midnight they were back at the Bristol and Gershwin went happily back to the keyboard.

For Gershwin the peak of the Vienna visit occurred on May 3. After lunch with composer Franz Lehár *(The Merry Widow,* among other popular operettas) he met with one of Schoenberg's star pupils, Alban Berg. Two days later Rosanska invited him to the Kolisch apartment, where the quartet played Berg's string quartet with the composer present. The Viennese atonalist and the American rhapsodist took warmly to one another. Gershwin was asked to play and Berg was delighted, but then suddenly Gershwin stopped; he felt uncomfortable playing show tunes, even the *Rhapsody,* after Berg's cerebral quartet. Berg encouraged him to continue playing, reassuring him with, "Mr. Gershwin, music is music."

Gershwin and Rosanska returned to the Bristol; he was happy with a signed photograph of the Viennese composer, complete with an autographed excerpt from the *Lyric Suite* and a pocket score of the quartet. (He later had the photograph carefully framed and in time acquired a rare French recording of the suite by the Galimar Quartet from his favorite record shop in New York, the Gramophone Shop on East Forty-eighth Street.)

After the memorable afternoon with Berg, George made plans to return to Paris for sister Frankie's debut in the Cole Porter revue. Leonore, Ira and Henrietta Malkiel continued their tour into Hungary, after which they would drive through the South of France before returning to Paris later in the month.

Gershwin arrived in Paris in plenty of time for the May 10 premiere of *In the Old Days and Today.* Among the other known Americans in the cast were Morton Downey, who had left Paul Whiteman to work as a single in nightclubs, Evelyn Hoey (who would introduce Vernon Duke's "April in Paris" later in her career), dancer Georgie Hale (who would later stage the dances for several Gershwin musicals), comedian Buster West and the Fred Waring Orchestra. Porter, at Hale's urging, agreed to look in on rehearsals and help with the staging.

All seemed to be going well as the excitement over the show spread through Paris so that the manager of Des Ambassadeurs, Edmond Sayag, felt justified in setting the price of admission for opening night at seventy dollars per person for dinner and show, champagne extra. The first night glittered with parties, Elsa Maxwell's usual gathering of dukes; William Randolph Hearst, Jr., his new bride and guests; Mrs. Porter in a sapphire blue gown and a spectacular Cartier bauble. The Schirmers were there with Gershwin.

Mabel has said that Frankie's Gershwin Specialty "literally stopped the show." Her brother accompanied her in her debut, then took over at the piano for a time. While he played, Frankie sat on the steps of the platform as she had often done at parties on 103rd Street.

The revue's success quickened the management's greed; soon the enterprise was spoiled when, in subsequent performances, more tables were moved in, overcrowding the floor. Other changes caused several members of the cast to look for work elsewhere. To fill some gaps, Porter's friend Clifton Webb came in as a replacement, as did vocalist Dorothy Dickson (who had starred in *Tip-Toes*). Frankie Gershwin found that her small voice was barely audible above the clatter of the kitchen crockery. When Leonore and Ira returned on the twenty-second, she had already left the show.

She had made a fine impression nevertheless and there were offers for her to sing in London and Madrid, but "George wouldn't let me stay on. I was his kid sister, and he wanted me to return home."

During this period Gershwin worked on the piano versions of *An American in Paris* and partied. One evening he once again encountered Stravinsky at the home of violinist Paul Kochanski. It was there that a famous exchange occurred, one that Stravinsky continued to deny for years, despite a witness—composer Richard Hammond. (Later, Stravinsky would admit he had met Gershwin and that it had, in fact, taken place.)

Gershwin could not let the opportunity slip. He told Stravinsky that he wished to study with him. The Russian—now *très Parisiene*—composer looked up and inquired, "How much money do you make [a year] Mr. Gershwin?"

Off guard, Gershwin told him, a sum that ran into six figures.

"In that case," Stravinsky told him, "I should study with you."

This characteristic Stravinsky quip terminated Gershwin's quest for a teacher in Paris.

The next event on the agenda was the European premiere of the *Concerto in F*. On May 22, when Ira Gershwin noted in his diary that his brother was doing nicely on *An American in Paris,* they attended a grand party given by the Tiomkins. The concert was scheduled for the following week, with Tiomkin at the piano and Vladimir Golschmann conducting. Ira was present at the party with a distinguished guest list that even Vernon Duke would approve. Even Dukelsky came, happy to be among such as Arthur Honegger, Lazar Saminsky, the Robert Russell Bennetts, the Glaenzers and Maurice Chevalier as well as close Gershwin friends, Mabel Schirmer and Josie Rosanska, among others. Even the presence of the "second rater" Tansman did not spoil Dukelsky's evening. And "George, as usual, knocked them for a goal and we left about 3:30."

Virtually the same group attended the concert at the Théâtre de l'Opéra on May 29; Gershwin shared a box with Elsa Maxwell, who had already planned a post-concert celebration in the garden at Laurent's on Avenue Gabriel, assisted by Metropolitan soprano Grace Moore. Duke arrived in stellar company, with ballet impresario Sergei Diaghilev and Sergei Prokofiev; all three were critical of the concerto. Diaghilev dismissed it as "good jazz and bad Liszt." Prokofiev, however, was "intrigued by some of the pianistic invention" and "asked me to bring George to his apartment the next day."

The performance particularly irritated Duke; he concluded that French musicians were "notoriously allergic to jazz" and Tiomkin was "no Gershwin." The audience, however, did not agree with the three Russian jazz authorities and French critics commented on the work's "flowing melodies," "verve" and the composer's "feeling for the orchestra." Gershwin was "highly pleased" with the reading of the concerto, the first he had heard performed by a pianist other than himself. He was also pleased with the review by the eminent Émile Vuillermoz, a pianist himself and once a composition student of Gabriel Fauré: "By the character of [Gershwin's] style and also by the dignity of Tiomkin's playing, this very characteristic work made even the most distrustful musicians realize that jazz, after having renewed the technic of dancing, might perfectly well exert a deep and beneficient influence in the most exalted spheres."

After the concert, some thirty Maxwellian luminaries congregated under a colorful awning at Laurent's. Gershwin arrived, Ira logged in the diary, with "some countess" (de Ganny, whom Maxwell often implied, though it has never been substantiated, Gershwin had wanted to marry). Also gathered were Cole Porter, Clifton Webb, Beatrice Lillie, the Glaenzers, Tansman, Honegger, et al. The evening closed with entertainment in the ballroom: a two-piano performance by Gershwin's new friends, Fray and Braggiotti, who were followed by Porter, Lillie, Grace Moore—and Gershwin. It was past two-thirty when the Gershwins returned to the Majestic.

After some rest, the next day Gershwin accompanied Duke to the Prokofiev apartment where, as Duke put it, "he played his head off," including passages from the concerto. Prokofiev was still critical and told Duke later he found the *Concerto in F* a succession of "32-bar choruses ineptly bridged together." But he was impressed even so with Gershwin's gift as composer and especially as a pianist and predicted he'd go far if he left "dollars and dinners alone."

After dinner that same evening the Gershwins took in another party —no dollars involved—at Samuel Dushkin's apartment. Vladimir Horowitz diverted the company with his pyrotechnical transcriptions of themes from *Carmen*. Gershwin followed with a piano medley of Gershwiniana and joined host Dushkin in a violin-piano recital: *Short Story* and a piece entitled *Blue Interlude* (in his diary entry Ira does not identify the composer; it is probably Gershwin).

More parties the following day, Thursday, May 31; the tempo quickened as their Paris adventure began winding down. Hosts and hostesses vied with one another to send the Gershwins home in a memorable haze. The first reception was given by a Baron Rothschild ("which one I don't know," Ira admitted). The second was impressive indeed.

The avant-garde American bookshop proprietor Sylvia Beach wrote of it in her memoirs: "In 1928 an American in Paris dropped in at Shakespeare and Company [her celebrated shop on the rue de l'Odéon on the Left Bank] to buy a copy of Ulysses: George Gershwin. A very attractive, lovable fellow was Gershwin. A lady I had never met [Gladys R. Byfield] gave a party for the Gershwins and invited me.

"You didn't have to shake hands with the hostess because nobody could point her out in the throng that kept pouring into the apartment and shoving their way toward the grand piano at which George Gershwin was seated. His brother, Ira, and his sister, Frances, a very pretty girl, were standing by him, and his sister sang some of his songs. George, too, sang and played his piano pieces."

It was *très chic,* even the *moderne* invitation, all in lower case. It read: "please come thursday the 31st of may at 10 p.m. to 179 rue de la pompe to meet the gershwins. medgyes will shake a wicked cocktail [he also drew the Art Deco design on the invitation]."

While Gershwin hobnobbed with the Rothschilds, Leonore and Ira arrived around eleven at the Byfields' with Mabel and Bob Schirmer. Frances came a little later and Gershwin around midnight. Ira, the family chronicler, was impressed. "It was a large party," he wrote, "200 easily being present and a mixture of Mayfair, the Rialto and Left Bank." The musicians included Deems Taylor, Robert Russell Bennett, Samuel Dushkin, Nadia Boulanger, Alexandre Tansman, Dmitri Tiomkin, Josie Rosanska and Rudolf Kolisch, Jacques Fray and Mario Braggiotti. A slightly bemused Sylvia Beach was accompanied by her friend painter-photographer Man Ray, a founder of the Dada movement.

There were swarms of caterers, a band, "some counts and barons" and "a couple of guys with monocles and dirty shirts." In short, a most successful, if teeming, farewell to the Gershwins. While his brother and sister entertained, Ira consumed "lots of champagne and didn't feel it." Day was dawning when they found a cab to take them to the hotel.

One of the more inconspicuous guests at the Byfield celebration was Alex Aarons, who had come with his wife, Ella. The time was approaching for the preparation of the next Aarons and Freedley musical. On June 3, Ira stopped by his brother's room, where he found Leonore and Mabel Schirmer busily packing Gershwin's luggage for his return to London with the Aaronses. While the rest of the Gershwins remained in Paris (they were to join Gershwin in Southampton on the thirteenth to board ship for home), Gershwin spent the closing days of the trip in London discussing the next show with its star, Gertrude Lawrence, and with Aarons. It would be the tuneful but ill-fated *Treasure Girl.*

By this time the *Times* in New York announced that his new composition, *An American in Paris,* would be given its premiere by the New York Philharmonic Symphony Orchestra later in the year. Although Gershwin and Walter Damrosch had missed each other during the trip (when Damrosch was in Paris, Gershwin was in Vienna), the conductor told Gershwin he "would love to arrange with you to do your new work at a Philharmonic Symphony this winter!" Even as he worked, between interruptions, Gershwin was also approached by Diaghilev, who wanted to produce a ballet around it (this was a few days before the impresario heard the concerto), and Leopold Stokowski of the Philadelphia Orchestra. But Gershwin fended them off, saying he had promised the first performance to Damrosch.

Gershwin's London stay ended with a party and a recording session; Gertrude Lawrence gave one of her elaborate parties which Gershwin attended with Ella and Alex Aarons. On June 8 he recorded the *Preludes for Piano* and the *Andantino moderato* (the slow theme) from the *Rhapsody in Blue* for the Columbia Gramophone Company.

Arriving in Southampton on June 13 to reunite with Frankie, Leonore and Ira, he was weighed down, along with gifts for his parents and friends, by a conglomerate of taxi horns, an eight-volume collection of the piano works of Debussy, and two versions of *An American in Paris,* neither yet complete. He had had a Mustel reed organ shipped separately from Paris.

Having "vacationed," he had plenty of activity in his future: *Treasure Girl* for Aarons and Freedley, *An American in Paris* for Damrosch, perhaps a show for Ziegfeld and the revised *Strike Up the Band.*

Five days later, when the ship docked in New York, the Gershwins were greeted by assorted Gershwins, Strunskys, Paleys and other friends. They traveled uptown for a welcome-home party on 103rd Street. Among the shore party was a cousin of Emily Paley and Leonore Gershwin's, seventeen-year-old Rosamond Walling, a lovely Swarthmore College student. She and Gershwin had first met at the wedding of Emily Strunsky and Lou Paley. She had then been all of nine and Gershwin twenty-one.

Over the years, when she visited her cousins or he passed near Swarthmore (convenient to the tryout cities of Philadelphia and Wilmington), he presented her with tickets to his musicals. On this day, she wandered through the reverberating Gershwin house. Like Pop Gershwin, she was fascinated by the self-service elevator—wherein Gershwin eventually found her. On one of his shopping excursions with Mabel in Paris, they had come upon an Art Deco cigarette case, with a striking design in black and white, and in an antique shop an exquisite, jeweled gold bracelet. These he had acquired for Rosamond.

As they descended to the kitchen Gershwin teased her; the teenaged beauty was notorious for her voracious appetite but retained a slender figure. In a short time, Rosamond Walling became one of the few women with whom Gershwin seriously discussed marriage, children and home. They chatted, munched, then took the elevator upstairs to the party. Gershwin took his place at the piano, surrounded by family, friends and admirers. With Gershwin back in town, it promised to be a lively, exciting season.

IV·

Treasure Girl was scheduled for rehearsals around the end of August. While working intermittently on his *American* sketches, Gershwin began blocking out songs with what little book had been supplied by Fred Thompson and Vincent Lawrence. This was a common practice at the time. Songwriters frequently worked from the merest sketch of a book, and it was not unusual for a show's final act to be written even as its first was in rehearsal. By the middle of July the Gershwins hit their stride and felt comfortable with what they had. This gave them a little time to turn again to the songs for *East is West,* based only on a vague telegramed message from Ziegfeld that brought the nebulous project back to life.

Damrosch too had begun to question him about the status of the new work. Gershwin was able to inform him that on August 1 he had completed the solo piano version and had perhaps a couple of days' work on the two-piano arrangement, after which he would begin the orchestration. Damrosch even tried to entice him to his summer home in Maine, with the promise of "numerous charming and altogether exquisite creatures," whom he said were asking about Gershwin and looking forward to his visit. He was less subtle when he added ". . . and of course bring the score, finished or unfinished . . ."

With *Treasure Girl* nearing completion and rehearsals impending, Gershwin could not get away, though he promised Damrosch that, if he could, he might "wend my way Bar Harborwards." During late August and September and until mid-November, Gershwin did work on the orchestral piece while simultaneously occupied with the Gertrude Lawrence musical. It was ready to go by early October and began its tryout run in Philadelphia on October 15. There are no records of the usual out-of-town problems; apparently when it came to the Alvin on November 8 all were satisfied with the production—all but the critics and, eventually, the theatergoers.

Gertrude Lawrence was peculiarly cast in the role of a lying, avaricious, clothes-conscious schemer. She and her fiancé, portrayed by Paul Frawley, spent most of *Treasure Girl* squabbling when not racing for the prize of one hundred-thousand-dollars on a Pirate's Party buried treasure hunt. They end up on a desert island, where he abandons her, which brings her to her senses in time to sing the beautiful, haunting "Where's the Boy?" But not soon enough to save the show.

The astringent characters of the leads alienated audiences; the disagreeable tone of the book was lightened by the comedy of Walter Catlett and the dancing of Clifton Webb and Mary Hay (both of whom also sang; one of their songs was the now standard "I've Got a Crush on You," presented at an *Allegretto giocoso* tempo and not the slow version that has become known since). Brooks Atkinson called them "the brightest pair in this production" which he branded "an evil thing."

British reviewer St. John Ervine, writing for the *World,* began his critique with "A fear filled my heart as I left the Alvin Theatre that the run of this piece would be over before my notice could be printed." He went further. "The notoriously tone-deaf Ervine was so carried away by his anger that, after demolishing the book," Lawrence D. Stewart has written, "he accused the Gershwins of plagiarizing two of the production's songs: certainly the first time anyone charged this in print. The Gershwins immediately sent the critic copies of the attacked numbers and asked for details. No reply was forthcoming."

Chagrined, as the show floundered in December, Gertrude Lawrence sent Gershwin a copy of the W. C. Handy's anthology of *Blues* with a note: "Dearest George! This is with much love and appreciation for all the lovely tunes you have let me sing(?) and with many apologies for my countryman St. John Ervine. Best of everything for next year and many to come."

By the birth of the new year *Treasure Girl* was gone after sixty-eight performances, taking a substantial score with it. The Gershwins would salvage a couple of ideas, as usual. "I've Got a Crush on You" would find a spot in the revised *Strike Up the Band* and, as Isaac Goldberg recalled, a slow number when speeded up became "I Got Rhythm." It may date from this period since it was also intended for Ziegfeld's *East Is West.*

Among the outstanding songs is the quasi-waltz, "Oh, So Nice," a rare harmonious Lawrence-Frawley duet (more in keeping with their stage personalities is the splendid "I Don't Think I'll Fall in Love To-day"). Before the show opened Gershwin told an interviewer, "The waltz will always be in vogue. By that I mean the three-four time. I find it interesting to experiment with. My number 'Oh, So Nice' is an effort to get the effect of a Viennese waltz in fox-trot time." As was often the case, this experimentation presented his brother with a word problem. "Sometimes I work days and days on a lyric," Ira Gershwin added.

Among the other worthy efforts in the score were "Got a Rainbow," "Feeling I'm Falling," "What Are We Here For?," a fine rhythm number added after the opening, "What Causes That?" and, worth mentioning again, "Where's the Boy?," which was sung by Lawrence and chorus, with Gershwinesque pianistics by Ohman and Arden. (When Clifton Webb and Mary Hay moved from the Alvin to the Palace for a vaudeville stint, they adapted the song as "Where's the Girl?") The score was very well received by all except the tone-deaf Ervine. "But," as Ira Gershwin philosophized, "some songwriters to the contrary, numbers alone do not make a show."

Ten days after *Treasure Girl* began its abbreviated run at the Alvin, Gershwin completed *An American in Paris* in plenty of time for its Carnegie Hall premiere in December.

V

Back in August Gershwin had been inverviewed by Hyman Sandow with whom he spoke about his just completed European trip and the new work he had under way. He had just completed the two-piano version. Sandow's article appeared in the August 18, 1928, issue of *Musical America*. As the elevator took Sandow to Gershwin's studio on the top floor of the Gershwin house, he heard "the sonorous notes of an organ," which Gershwin explained was the Mustel that had arrived the day before. "Here's something else I prize very much that I bought in France," he told him and took down a "handsomely bound" volume of Debussy.

"One of the high spots of my visit," Gershwin told Sandow as he walked across the room to a music cabinet from which he took a pocket score, "was my meeting with Alban Berg, an Austrian ultramodernist composer almost unknown in this country, who wrote this string quartet."

Gershwin showed him the score, with an inscription by Berg (who, the writer explained to his readers, was forty and a pupil of Schoenberg), telling him that although "this quartet is dissonant to the extent of proving disagreeable to the average music-lover's consonant-trained ear, it seems to me the work has genuine merit. Its conception and treatment are thoroughly modern in the best sense of the word." (Another favorite was a Hindemith quartet of which he told a friend, "I'm the only one in the gang that likes it.")

Of his own work in progress he told Sandow it was "really a rhapsodic ballet . . . written very freely and is the most modern music I've yet attempted."

He had its form and development—even an extramusical scenario—well thought out. Before Sandow's interview he had completed the sixty-four-page pencil sketch begun in January and finished just days before on August 1. Within the week he completed the seventy-page two-piano arrangement from which he would orchestrate. When the Gershwins left for Paris Gershwin had some seven pages of thematic sketches and was about half through the work by early April. Despite the travel, guests, visitors and partying, he continued work on both the sketch and arrangement during the European trip in order to complete both by early August.

During the rest of the month, when the demands of *Treasure Girl* gave him time, he proceeded with the orchestration through September and October. Part of this time he spent on the Warburg farm in Connecticut, where he had his own guest house and the services of a cook and where he could work in country quiet. Kay would come up for a visit and they spent time on horseback, a sport to which the composer did not take as readily as he had to tennis and golf.

From mid-October until *Treasure Girl* opened in New York on November 8, he was preoccupied with the show. On November 5 Damrosch told him that December 13 had been set for *An American*'s premiere and that he was anxious to hear the work. Gershwin had already told him that the playing time was about twenty minutes and the conductor was anxious to get a little coaching from the composer regarding "your tempi and the proper spirit." Two weeks later Gershwin inscribed the title page of his full orchestration (104 inked pages): " 'An American in Paris'/ a Tone Poem/ for Orchestra/ Composed and Orchestrated/ by/ George Gershwin/ Begun early in 1928./ Finished November 18, 1928."

While *An American in Paris* is indeed written freely, even rhapsodically, its formal structure is tighter than that of the *Rhapsody in Blue,* more flowingly logical than that of the *Concerto in F.* The orchestration, only his second on a large scale, is more adventurous than the concerto's, even eloquent, and free of the concerto's occasional stitchings. Primarily self-taught though he may have been, Gershwin had learned a good deal about orchestration between July 1925 and July 1928, despite social and creative diversions.

The design was carefully worked out from sketch to arrangement to orchestration. There are minor differences between the arrangement and the final orchestration; there are cuts, one of twenty-one measures, but these are minor and perhaps judicious (these interesting but not essential musical passages may be heard in the two-piano arrangement). Whether a "rhapsodic ballet" or a "tone poem," *An American in Paris* is lucidly organized in a one movement (actually three minimovements plus recapitulation/coda) form.

"As in my other orchestral compositions," he said of it, "I've not endeavored to present any definite scenes in this music. The rhapsody is programmatic only in a general impressionistic way, so that the individual listener can read into the music such episodes as his imagination pictures for him."

Despite the disclaimer, he did have a fairly definite "plot" in mind. "The opening part will be developed in typical French style, in the manner of Debussy and the Six, though the themes are all original." The reference to Debussy is apposite but that to the Six is curious. Still, there is a saucy perkiness to the opening "walking themes," which are close in spirit to some of the more lighthearted, impudent pages of Poulenc, Milhaud and their leader (though not a member of Les Six),

Erik Satie. The Six, however, was militantly opposed to the Debussy aesthetic; this Gershwin blithely ignored. No musical partisan, he drew upon Debussyian harmonies for the quiet, impressionistic passages in the work.

"My purpose here," he explained about the opening, "is to portray the impressions of an American visitor in Paris as he strolls about the city, listens to various street noises, and absorbs the French atmosphere.

"The opening gay section is followed by a rich 'blues' with a strong rhythmic undercurrent. Our American friend, perhaps after strolling into a cafe and having a few drinks, has suddenly succumbed to a spasm of homesickness [In the two-piano-arrangement score he had scrawled a word 'drunk' over this passage; he omitted it in the orchestration]. The harmony here is both more intense and simple than in the preceding pages.

"This 'blues' rises to a climax followed by a coda in which the spirit of the music returns to the vivacity and bubbling exuberance of the opening part with its impressions of Paris. Apparently the homesick American, having left the café and reached the open air, has downed his spell of blues and once again is an alert spectator of Parisian life.

"At the conclusion, the street noises and French atmosphere are triumphant."

This was Gershwin's scenario; a more detailed "analysis," as it was termed in the *Times* when it was announced on December 9, was prepared by Deems Taylor for the concert's program notes. Well written, entertaining—almost a short story—it is nonetheless superfluous to an understanding of *An American in Paris,* which musically stands on its own.

Nor did composer or annotator agree on the "meaning" of some of the passages. In the orchestral score (Cue 23–25) there is a quiet moment—*calmato*—of Delius-like lyricism and fragility. Gershwin suggested to Taylor that maybe his American, at that point, had passed a cathedral—but Taylor held out for "the Grand Palais—where the Salon holds forth." He took a cue from Gershwin in a passage that followed, immediately preceding the blues. After four bars featuring the celesta accompanied by strings, a dialogue for violins leads directly into the blues.

Taylor put it so: "And now the orchestra introduces an unhallowed episode. Suffice it to say that a solo violin approaches our hero (in soprano register) and addresses him in the most charming broken English; and, his response being inaudible—or at least unintelligible—repeats the remark. This one-sided conversation continues for some little time."

In the two-piano arrangement Gershwin had written at that point: *"sees girl—meets girl—back to 2/4 (strolling flirtation)—into cafe—mix love theme with 2/4—conversation—leading to—slow Blues."*

Having "downed" the blues, the orchestra breaks into a jazzy, boisterous, very American fast dance (Taylor labeled it a Charleston though Gershwin did not employ its very characteristic rhythm; whatever the precise terminology, it is a brash contrast to the blues). A return of the walking themes brings the work to a busy, clamorous close. In passing, it might be noted that although the score calls for a piano (doubling briefly on celesta), it is not employed as a solo instrument.

VI

An American in Paris received its first public performance in Carnegie Hall the evening of Thursday, December 13, 1928, preceded by Franck's *Symphony in D Minor* and Guillaume Lekeu's *Adagio for Strings*. The Franck was followed by an intermission after which came the Lekeu, *An American in Paris* and Wagner's Magic Fire Scene from *Die Walküre.*

The entire Gershwin family attended the concert that night, as did many friends, among them Kay Swift and Rosamond Walling. Morris Gershwin distinguished himself with yet another typical aphorism. After the final chord had sounded, he checked his watch and said, "Twenty minutes, a very important piece."

After taking his bows, and radiant from the applause of an enthusiastic audience, Gershwin went to a party in his honor at the Glaenzers'. He was presented with a silver humidor on which had been inscribed:

To
George Gershwin
and His
American in Paris
December 13, 1928

It came with a heartfelt but magisterial speech by financier-impresario Otto Kahn. The sermon began: "George Gershwin is a leader of young America in music, in the same sense in which Lindbergh is the leader of young America in aviation." He went on to compare the two disparate heroes, underscoring attributes they shared, ". . . the same unspoilableness—if I may coin a word—the same engaging and unassuming ways, the same simple dignity and dislike of show, the same absence of affectation, the same direct, uncomplicated, naive, Parsifalesque outlook upon life and his task."

He dilated on the theme of contemporary youth, whom most pundits of the time were certain were jazzing their wanton way to Hades. Kahn, though professionally a financier, knew the arts, the theater, opera and the world of music, and saw promise in this flaming youth. "There is no better raw material found anywhere," he told the Glaenzers' by now bemused guests. "Below their apparent 'hard-boiledness' and sophistication, there is a groping, unadmitted, sometimes uncouth, often unconscious prompting of idealism—a note welcome and needed in the in the midst of the colossal sweep of the nation's material occupations . . .

"And George Gershwin, without self-seeking or self-consciousness, and just because of that, is one of their typical examples, and in his art, thoroughly and uncompromisingly American as it is, one of their foremost spokesmen. In the rhythm, the melody, the humor, grace, the rush and sweep and dynamics of his compositions, he expresses the genius of young America."

Kahn quoted several lines from Thomas Hardy, then adapted one to underscore his theme.

"The 'long drip of human tears,' my dear George! They have great and strange and beautiful power, those human tears. They fertilize the deepest roots of art, and from them flowers spring of a loveliness and perfume that no other moisture can produce.

"I believe in you with full faith and admiration"—he spoke directly to the composer now—"in your personality, in your gifts, in your art, in your future, in your significance in the field of American music . . ." And because of this profound faith and admiration Kahn concluded that he wished "for you an experience—not too prolonged—of that driving storm and stress of the emotions, of that solitary wrestling with your own soul, of that aloofness, for a while, from the actions and distractions of the everyday world, which are the most effective ingredients for the deepening and mellowing and the complete development, energizing and revealment, of an artist's inner being and spiritual powers."

Unfortunately there is no record of Gershwin's reaction to this peroration, but some of his friends interpreted as an opaque proposal that Gershwin, after a short-term course in voluntary anguish "to deepen his art," he might be ready to compose an opera for Kahn's Metropolitan.

Whatever Kahn's intent, Gershwin ignored the invitation, if any. Only months before, after his return from Paris, he had told an interviewer who had brought up the topic of a "jazz opera," that he hoped "some day to write a jazz opera, but before undertaking it, I want to write more orchestral music so that I can get into the mental swing of serious composition and improve my technique.

"I realize that I have so far written very little music for symphonic performance, but I plan to spend more and more time on such work from now on."

To Gershwin *An American in Paris* was another step in the direction of that opera he hoped to compose "some day."

After the party and the fervent speech, lightened by Gershwin at the piano, there were the Friday morning reviews. They were the mixture as before, ranging from Chotzinoff's assertion that *An American in Paris* was "easily the best piece of modern music since Mr. Gershwin's *Concerto in F*" to Herbert F. Peyser's petulant dismissal: "Nauseous claptrap, so dull patchy, thin, vulgar, long-winded and inane that the average movie audience would be bored by it . . ." He found it a "cheap and silly affair . . . pitifully futile and inept." He even objected to some members of the audience, who looked as if they did not belong in Carnegie Hall.

Henderson of the *Sun* did not agree. He believed that the opening "walking theme" was "one of the genuine inspirations of our native music. It is without doubt the sassiest orchestral theme of the century." The dour, humorless, Peyser missed what Henderson called the work's "unbuttoned humor . . . There is much cleverness in the score, and some rudeness of manner."

It remained for Olin Downes in the *Times* to point out the place of *An American* in Gershwin's development. Gershwin's "technique, and especially his orchestration, was more solid," he wrote. "He was obviously seeking a new form germane to the nature of his ideas . . . There is material gain in workmanship and structure."

Gershwin clipped the reviews, the good, the bad, the in-between, for his scrapbook. He read them with curiosity, and, as his family and friends attested, unfavorable reviews did not particularly bother him. He had done his best, was aware of his weak spots and went on to the next thing. *American in Paris* went on to join the *Rhapsody in Blue* and the *Concerto in F* as a standard repertory work in Europe and the United States.

This could hardly have been attributed to Damrosch's interpretation. Though a Gershwin enthusiast and champion, he could not grasp *An American*'s complex rhythms and breezy tempos. After rehearsals and the premiere Gershwin had become familiar with the conductor's podium style.

Gershwin invited Kay Swift to the Friday afternoon concert to hear *An American in Paris* again. They stood unobtrusively in the rear of the hall. As the walking theme began Gershwin whispered in a mock moan,

"Oh no—he's starting to bend his knees." To Gershwin it signaled that Damrosch was about to conduct his piece at too slow a pace.

Before the Wagner they slipped out of Carnegie Hall into a brisk December twilight and walked east on Fifty-seventh Street to Madison Avenue, where Gershwin spotted "two lovely bracelets" in a shop window. Whatever the reviews, despite Damrosch's less than ideal performance, he was filled with the accomplishment of *An American in Paris.* He celebrated by going into the shop, then presented the bracelets to Kay, ". . . thanks to Walter Damrosch and his bent knees."

10

Transition:
Broadway
to Hollywood

Otto Kahn, though no seer, was more prescient than he might have imagined—or hoped—in his *American in Paris* speech. In one of his digressions he had said that the "path of America . . . has been all too smooth perhaps, too uniformly successful . . ." and had "been spared . . . the ordeal of deep anguish, besetting care and heart-searching tribulations . . ." The "nation's material occupations" to which he had alluded in December of 1928, with the Big Bull Market thriving in Wall Street, seemed destined only to go up. But by the end of 1929 those occupations would unleash a prolonged—and often tragic—"chastening" of the nation's "soul": the Great Depression. For nearly a decade (until another period of prosperity was initiated by a war), its drastic effects touched virtually every aspect of American life and culture, from business to the arts, from farming to the production of Broadway shows.

In this transition from the Jazz Age to the Depression the Gershwins managed quite well. Ira Gershwin recalled some stock losses, and it is possible that his brother did likewise, but they had work, unlike millions of their countrymen. When 1929 began, ten months before the Crash, they had already agreed to score a musical film, a new form of entertainment that flourished since the birth of the sound film, especially after the premiere of Al Jolson's *The Jazz Singer* in 1927. George and Ira were promised one hundred thousand dollars, and Hollywood had already handed George fifty thousand dollars for the use of the *Rhapsody in Blue* in a projected film starring Paul Whiteman and band, *The King of Jazz.* Then too there were their existing agreements with Ziegfeld on the *East Is West* extravaganza and the revised *Strike Up the Band.*

Gershwin's 1929, a year that ended dismally for so many, was stimulating: he became seriously interested in art, took up painting and sketching in addition to collecting the art of others; he blossomed as a conductor—symphony orchestras and theater pit bands—he signed a contract with the Metropolitan to compose an opera and would round out the year with the score of a hit musical.

I

The precarious year began felicitously for Gershwin early in January when the *Times* reported that he was being paid for the first radio performance of *An American in Paris.* A broadcast premiere, a rare event in 1929, especially of an American work, was Nathaniel Shilkret's idea; it was to be followed soon after by recording sessions at the Victor Talking Machine Company's studios. For both the broadcast and recording Shilkret would conduct the Victor Symphony—a hand-picked group of the finest musicians in town. Shilkret invited Gershwin to the recording sessions set for February 4.

Shilkret recalled the event of that day, years later, for interviewer Milton A. Caine:

> Gershwin got in the way of Shilkret's rehearsal prior to the recording . . . Gershwin had come to play the celesta—neglecting to tell Shilkret a celeste player was needed. [A curious statement since Shilkret had already conducted the work twice on the Mobile Hour and the Hall of Fame broadcasts, for which incidentally Gershwin had received $2,500. As the score calls for a pianist, who could easily double on celeste, any conductor should have known about this.] He continually interrupted until Shilkret told him to get lost. Gershwin was hurt and surprised that anyone should want to play his music without his being there to help. But Shilkret told him that the orchestra couldn't learn it with him there, and to come back in half an hour. Gershwin did, obligingly. He was delighted with the way Shilkret played it. During the record-

ing, Gershwin was so enrapt with this rendition that he forgot to come in with the celesta.

This is yet another example of anecdotic enrichment (the arts, especially show business, is rife with it); Gershwin is heard on the recording
and at the proper cue. The one error associated with the fine idiomatic
recording appears on the label which reads: *George Gershwin, pianist.*

Shilkret was no Damroschian knee bender, and he and his orchestra
captured the spirit and tempo of *An American in Paris,* its swagger and
humor. Few recordings since equal it—nor can they feature the original
taxi horns and Gershwin at the celesta. Later that month Gershwin
went to Cincinnati with his battery of horns to hear the symphony
conducted by the distinguished Fritz Reiner.

In the spring of 1929 the Gershwins closed their house on 103rd
Street. Rose and Morris Gershwin had begun spending most of the
winter months in Florida and their summers away from the hot city in
upstate New York. Arthur Gershwin, then twenty-nine, was testing his
skills and luck in Wall Street (that luck would run out by year's end).
Frances Gershwin, in her early twenties, lived with her parents and
despite her mother's objections was seeing handsome young Leopold
Godowsky, Jr. Rose Gershwin had been wrong about George and his
future; she was mistaken about Leopold, whom she saw as an impecunious musician (a violinist) with few prospects. He would in fact one
day become her son-in-law in an episode of familial chicanery.

George and Ira Gershwin rented adjoining penthouses in a seventeen-
story apartment building at 33 Riverside Drive on the northwest corner
of Seventy-fifth Street. The view was spectacular, across the Hudson
River to the Palisades of New Jersey. George's apartment had this view;
Ira's, on the east side of the roof, had a view toward Broadway and
Central Park West. To the south, they saw only as far as the architec-
tural bastions of West Seventy-second Street; in between was the mansion of industrialist-financier Charles M. Schwab, director of various
companies, ranging from Bethlehem Steel to Loew's Incorporated. A
Victorian structure, described in a 1932 New York Guide Book as "one
of the most palatial homes in America," of some four stories, it was set
back from Riverside Drive, by an elaborate, carefully kept expanse of
lawn, through which curved a driveway. The view inspired Ira Gershwin, and resulted in his oil painting irreverently entitled *Charlie's Lawn.*

Under his brother's influence, George began dabbling in art, beginning with a set of watercolors he had received from Ira on his last
birthday. Gershwin's interest in drawing and painting, the first since the
withering humiliation from a grammar school teacher, had been rekin-

dled during their stay at Chumleigh Farm in April 1927. Ira had regularly sketched and did so during time off from work on the first *Strike Up the Band;* George joined him in attempting some early pencil sketches.

From the Riverside Drive terrace he followed Ira again; the subject of his first watercolor was Charlie's lawn. A couple of days later, on April 4, he tried portraiture, the first being *Margaret* (Margaret Wolfe, the Countess Ricci) and his cousin the artist Henry Botkin, *Harry.* Encouraged, he tried another on April 7, the self-portrait *Me,* which he presented to his friend composer Harold Arlen.

Neither primitive nor really polished, these early drawings and watercolors reveal an innate talent that developed over the years. Unlike his brother, who abandoned this pursuit because "it became too interesting" (i.e., it took time away from writing lyrics), George, once started, sketched and painted for the rest of his life. Two of his finest portraits date from his last year, *Jerome Kern* and *Arnold Schoenberg* (his last oil). By that time he was taken quite seriously as an artist by collectors and some critics. The only instruction he had came from his cousin Botkin, to whom Gershwin consistently referred to as "my cousin the artist."

Gershwin had by this time begun collecting art; in a 1928 interview a writer mentioned his collection of George Bellow lithographs, ranging in subject from *Dempsey Through the Ropes* through *River Front* and *Prayer Meeting.* He became a devoted, even avid, discerning collector of art, especially modern and contemporary works. Botkin, himself an admired painter, advised him on his collection and served as alter ego after Botkin settled in Paris in the early thirties. In three years the Gershwin art collection had grown to the point that it excited the attention of the elegant monthly *Arts and Decoration.*

Gershwin's letter to Botkin upon receiving the first shipment from France reveals him as a knowledgeable and shrewd collector. "The pictures are as you said they would be," he wrote, "much more beautiful than the photographs could possibly show—and, from now on, I appoint you my official framer of pictures, because I think the frames are beauties.

"I believe that each picture is a fine example of the artist. The two favorites of most of the people who have seen them so far, seem to be the Modigliani and the Rouault.

"The Rouault is a gorgeous painting, although it is a little darker in tone than I thought it would be. The Rouault gives me great pleasure as a painting and I hope you will find some more of his work to send to me.

"*The Suburbs* of Utrillo is painted with a much more vigorous brush than some of the ones I have seen in America. It is a very luminous picture. It seems to throw out its own light. I am crazy about it, and it fits perfectly in my living room.

"The Derain is a masterpiece of simple color and the Pascin, while the least exciting of the five, has a strange quality that seems to grow on me.

"Before the pictures arrived I sent you a cable which, unfortunately, did not reach you as you had already left for Nice. I wanted you to find out how much I would have to pay for the Renoir picture of two women in the doorway. In the cable I believe I made an offer of $1,500, plus the Pascin as a trade-in.

"Last week I met [artist] Maurice Sterne at the Lewisohns' country home, and I had the photographs with me. He complimented me greatly on my selection and your advice. He urged me to get this Renoir that I speak of.

"Well, the pictures are all hung in my living and dining rooms and will give you a big welcome when you come over the next time.

"I am extremely happy that I have finally gotten started on a collection, although it has been rather expensive, I feel that I am off to a flying start."

When an *Arts and Decoration* writer toured the collection, it had grown. Besides the paintings mentioned in the letter, Botkin had shipped him works by Gauguin, Rousseau and Picasso.

Arts and Decoration was impressed. The unsigned article, entitled "A Composer's Pictures," began with "It is a moot question in Mr. Gershwin's mind whether he collects the moderns because he wants to learn to paint; or whether he wants to learn to paint in order to better understand the moderns. But he buys paintings for a fairly simple reason—because he gets pleasure out of them. And he can study them during the interludes from composing, not in brief tours to the art galleries, but at leisure.

"He surrounds himself with the works of men he admires because they say something to him through a technique he wants to master. But Mr. Gershwin has made some humble beginnings in painting. And just as he is studying music all the time—he has three lessons a week [with Joseph Schillinger]—so he is studying painting when the moment allows."

Besides the European paintings mentioned, the writer pointed out some American works by Max Weber, Alexander Brook, Thomas Hart Benton, Louis Michel Eilshemius, Maurice Sterne, others. "Knowing the scarcity of buyers in this day and age," the author commented, "he makes every effort to assist the struggling painter." Among them was his cousin Botkin.

"The walls of his living room are hung with paintings. Over the mantel is an Utrillo *[The Suburbs]*, to the right of this is the beautiful *Absinthe Drinkers* by Picasso. On the opposite wall the little Rousseau *[Île de la Cité].* In the dining room is hung a large Derain still life. A Thomas Benton decorates the barroom. The upstairs hallway [this was written after Gershwin had moved from Riverside Drive to a duplex on East Seventy-second Street] is thick with fine paintings, but to come out into Mr. Gershwin's working room is to come out on stark simplicity and a piano—with one small woman done by Matisse (from the collection of the late Arthur Davies) and two African wood images.

"Of the Modigliani *[Cariatide]* . . . Mr. Gershwin said as we stood before the canvas, 'Those who like the art of the moderns, like this painting especially. If they heartily dislike the moderns, they hate this particularly.'

"Of his whole collection Mr. Gershwin gets the most pleasure out of his big Weber *[Invocation].* The painting hangs in a place of honor in his living room . . . [He] sees in it a deeply wrought picture, tremendously felt. To him the distortion increases its feeling and adds to the design. Technically, he points out, it is a composition of triangles, and in it there is a strict absence of line, only color against color. And in the whole there is great movement.

"As Mr. Gershwin points out, music is design—melody is line; harmony is color, contrapuntal music is three or four lines forming an abstraction or sometimes a definite shape; dissonance in music is like a distortion in a painting, and as Alice Toklas adds, like the egg shell in the coffee."

Gershwin told the interviewer that he felt it was "too late [for him] to become a painter of distinction," though he believed that his attempts at painting had "considerably enriched his musical background."

He enjoyed the collections of others as well. He heard that the eminent collector Chester Dale had some very interesting paintings. One evening, when they met, Gershwin said, "I understand you got a lot of swell paintings. I'd like to see them.

"O.K. with me, George," Dale replied, "come over anytime it's convenient for you."

A time was immediately set and in his unpublished biography, Dale wrote: "So George, and I think his brother and somebody else, I don't remember, came in for cocktails. Just where we were in the morning room there happened to be a Cézanne, right near the door called *Es-*

taque. Well, there were a lot of other good pictures, but George said, 'My God, Chester, that's a wonderful picture!' "

"What the hell do you know about pictures?" Dale asked in his affected tough-guy manner.

"Well, it's a Cézanne isn't it?"

"Sure it's a Cézanne—George, are you interested in art outside of your great art?"

"Yes, Chester, I'm crazy about pictures."

"Well, George, I don't know much about pictures but I happen to like 'em. Music and pictures aren't they more or less the same?"

"He looked at me and he said, 'Yeah,' and he began to tell me some things about Cézanne that I didn't even know. Well I said now look George if you feel like that why don't you play me a Cézanne."

"Sure I will," Gershwin said and went to the piano.

"I haven't got any more idea than the man in the moon what he played," Dale wrote, "but there was Cézanne to the both of us.

"I was thinking over what George had said and to this day I still don't believe there is a hell of a lot of difference between music and art. They are the same thing. To people that love either one of them what is the difference? They are both emotional. We came back, had another drink, and I was humming and happy as a lark."

II

Gershwin's spring artistic interlude was interrupted by Florenz Ziegfeld; he had decided to "postpone" the musical *East Is West* (for which the Gershwins by now had completed seven songs). He planned to shift to a simpler, less opulent (i.e., less costly), more commercially feasible production of J. P. McEvoy's *Liberty* magazine tales (and later a bestselling novel) about Dixie Dugan, a hopeful flapper-actress who dreams of starring in the "Zigfold" Follies.

On an impulse Ziegfeld decided to glorify one of his own creations, the Ziegfeld Girl. McEvoy's book treated the world of show business satirically, providing song and dance spots and wise cracks. Ziegfeld summoned Gershwin to his office one spring afternoon.

"George," he began, "I'm going to produce J. P. McEvoy's *Show Girl* and you must write the score for it. We go into rehearsal in two weeks."

Gershwin protested; not even he could turn out a full score in so short a time.

"Mr. Ziegfeld smiled up at me," Gershwin recalled some years later, "and said, 'Why, sure you can—just dig down in the trunk and pull out a couple of hits.'

"Flo Ziegfeld had a way of getting what he wanted . . . Well, the show went into rehearsal with half the score finished and about one third of the book [by William Anthony McGuire and McEvoy] completed.

"The show opened in Boston [on June 24]—and I think the last scene was rehearsed on the train going up."

Ira Gershwin remembered their final Ziegfeld experience with gentle acerbity: "In his hypnotically persuasive manner (always great charm until a contract was signed) Ziegfeld managed to have us postpone the operetta *[East Is West]* and start on *Show Girl. Show Girl* wasn't much —it cost much and lost much—and, unfortunately, *East Is West,* whose production would have cost much more, never happened."

Ziegfeld assured the Gershwins they would return to the operetta. "We were most enthusiastic about this project *[East Is West],*" Ira recalled, "which was to star Marilyn Miller and [Bobby] Clark and [Paul] McCullough. Approximately one half of the score" [most of which had oriental overtones] "had been completed when, alas, Mr. Ziegfeld read J. P. McEvoy's snappy *Show Girl.*"

Because, as he explained, Ziegfeld owed an assignment to lyricist Gus Kahn (who had contributed to the Eddie Cantor–Ziegfeld hit, *Whoopee,* the year before), would Ira mind working with a co-lyricist? He "welcomed the opportunity because *Show Girl* had to be done quickly to make a much too soon Boston opening date."

One of the minor leads of the still running *Whoopee* had been the dancer-singer Ruby Keeler, celebrated mostly for her buck-and-wing. She left the musical before its New York premiere to spend time with her new husband, Al Jolson. The honeymoon over, Ziegfeld cast her as Dixie Dugan and billed her with Ziegfeldian perspicacity as Ruby Keeler Jolson. McGuire, who had served Ziegfeld well with his books for *Whoopee, Rosalie* and *The Three Musketeers,* was drafted to convert McEvoy's patchy novel into a libretto. He failed.

On that point, Brooks Atkinson had this to say in his review: "Doubtless you recall Mr. McEvoy's effervescent novel of last season as the breathless and wryly amusing chronicle of Dixie Dugan's career on Broadway. Composed of telegrams and letters, scattered and spotty, with a satire of the greeting card business as a minor embellishment, Mr. McEvoy's novel seemed hardly suitable for the musical stage unless, as is the custom, the adapter straightaway forgot it. But William Anthony McGuire, author of the dialogue, has been faithful in his fashion not only to the novel, but to the whole tradition of musical plays of backstage life."

Ira Gershwin described the McGuire method. "Including openings and finalettos and several songs written during rehearsal, George, Gus and I wound up with twenty-seven musical items. Many of these were for imagined spots, as we were as vague about what most of the scenes would be as librettist William Anthony McGuire."

When rehearsals began, the Gershwins and Kahn had a script for the first scene only. "Genial Bill McGuire," as Gershwin remembered him, seemed unperturbed by deadlines or opening dates. He "loved listening to anything new we played him."

"You never can tell," he told them. "Maybe I'll get a good idea for a scene from one of the songs."

If so, they were few, for the final *Show Girl* was long on musical and comedic activity and short on continuity and simple logical sense, even for a musical. Of the twenty-seven musical items, about half remained. Skeptical about the drawing power of his lead, even with the name of Jolson tagged on, Ziegfeld backed her up with the popular nightclub act of [Lou] Clayton, [Eddie] Jackson and [Jimmy] Durante, Duke Ellington's Cotton Club Orchestra, ballerina Harriet Hoctor, plus the Albertina Rasch dancers (to dance to *An American in Paris)*, eccentric dancer Eddie Foy, Jr., comedian Frank McHugh, guitarist-vocalist Nick Lucas, "The Singing Troubadour," out of vaudeville, nightclubs and recording studios. Joseph Urban provided them all with lavish settings.

The problem was that virtually the entire cast was a "specialty act," noted for certain routines, even their own special material songs—which trammeled the Gershwin score.

Lucas, for example, had little to do; he appeared near the end of the final act to join Keeler in the show's best-known song, "Liza," a song no one would ever associate with either. Ziegfeld had contrived a bit of business for this scene that he believed would assure him an ace in the hole.

Lucas, as Ira Gershwin recalled, as did the other "specialties," did one of his current popular numbers, besides Gershwin; the Ellington Orchestra performed some of their own latest hits; Clayton, Jackson and Durante did their act and songs, moving through *Show Girl* as if they had nothing to do with the plot (though Durante was cast as a property man). Then too there was the virtually complete *American in Paris* ballet whose "homesickness theme" was lyricized as "Home Blues."

After a study of the show's program and its succession of specialties,

Ira Gershwin observed that he "wouldn't be surprised if *Show Girl* set a record for sparseness of dialogue in a musical."

The single surprise of the show was not that it was graced with a quasi-book for the Boston first night, but an unexpected and unadvertised (though not unplanned—Ziegfeld's ace in the hole) contribution from the audience.

As George Gershwin remembered it, Ziegfeld had ordered "a minstrel number in the second act with one hundred beautiful girls on steps that cover the entire stage." Gershwin obliged with "Liza."

Then came Boston. "Imagine the audience's surprise, and mine," Gershwin said, "when without warning Al Jolson, who was sitting in the third row on the aisle, jumped up and sang a chorus of 'Liza' to his bride!" Keeler was caught off guard, but proceeded with her tap routine. Jolson's gesture had not been contrived, as was later intimated in his film biography, to hearten a nervous teenager in her first starring role. She was not in the least jittery and stardom was not one of her objectives. Jolson's studied noble deed—he had been away from Broadway since 1927 making films—was good for him and good for Ziegfeld.

"It caused a sensation," Gershwin exclaimed, "and it gave the song a great start!" From that night on "Liza" was associated, like "Swanee," with Jolson for the rest of his professional life. The "sensation" was restaged for the July 2 premiere at the Ziegfeld in New York. Brooks Atkinson reported that "Mr. Jolson, sitting in Row C on the aisle [same as Boston, an interesting coincidence] last evening, rose in the audience toward the end of the performance and lifted up his voice in a general jubilee. It was a touching episode." It was also just about the best thing he could say about *Show Girl.*

A few more of Jolson's appearances did not help. The critics were generally kind, if a bit patronizing, to Keeler. Burns Mantle described her as "a nice child and agreeably modest. She speaks her pieces with a good understanding of their meaning, presents a picture of youth and good looks that few eighteen-year-olds [she was nineteen and Jolson forty-two] command, and goes periodically into tap dancing at which she excels."

By the first week of the run gossip columns intimated that she might leave the show; during the third, she collapsed in her dressing room. The *Tribune* reported that "Although she is seriously ill and needs an operation, Miss Keeler will continue in her role, according to her physician, until Dorothy Stone arrives from California to replace her." Jolson is supposed to have told one reporter that his wife was so anxious to be at his side that she deliberately fell down a flight of stairs in order to get out of the floundering *Show Girl.* Other column items had her undergoing an appendectomy on August 1, but on the seventh she was seen, after a miraculous recuperation, at her husband's revue, *Say It with Songs*.

Out of the show, she and Jolson spent further recuperative time in Florida, after which they returned to California, where she did better than her husband in thirties film musicals.

For the Gershwins the experience had been intense, if brief. But with the box office doing badly, the agony was prolonged. With Keeler— and, from time to time, Jolson—gone, it had become dismal; by September Ziegfeld was forced to close. The next month he was wiped out in the stock-market crash.

He blamed the Gershwins for the show's failure. He dictated long letters and protracted telegrams to them—and refused to pay their royalties during the run (III performances) of *Show Girl*. For the first and only time in their lives the Gershwins sued a producer to no avail; the great showman was broke.

Duke Ellington had observed the preproduction shambles and was impressed with Gershwin's equanimity "when cuts and adjustments were being made . . . He was not the kind of guy who would be in Row A, ready to take a bow on opening night. In fact, when several of his most successful shows opened, he could be dressed like a stagehand, who could get in the front or back stage door. In a sports shirt, with no tie, he would humbly take his place in the standing-room area. If you didn't know him, you would never guess that he was the great George Gershwin.

"He once told Oscar Levant that he wished he had written the bridge to 'Sophisticated Lady,' and that made me very proud."

Besides "Liza" the *Show Girl* score was graced with other good songs. Atkinson, in his *Times* review dismissed the score as second rate, but mentioned two songs he liked, "Do What You Do!" and "Harlem Serenade," both sung by Ruby Keeler, the first as a duet with Frank McHugh. She had an amusing number as a none-too-bright show girl in "I Must Be Home by Twelve O'Clock."

One of Gershwin's finest creations, "Feeling Sentimental," though published, was eliminated before the New York opening. Whether it had been drawn from his "hit trunk," as Ziegfeld had suggested, or a Tune Book, or written in the heat of a compressed period of preparation, is not known. It is one of his most perfectly realized songs; the B section, the bridge is especially affecting. Of the score, only "Liza" became popular.

After *Show Girl*'s July opening and as the columns kept track of Mrs. Jolson's condition, Gershwin had already moved on to other things.

The *Times* announced that *An American in Paris* was to be given its Lewisohn Stadium premiere in August and that Gershwin would make his debut as a conductor.

III

Two days before the first rehearsals of the Stadium concert George wrote to Isaac Goldberg, then preparing a series of articles about Gershwin, explaining why he had had little time to spend with Goldberg's researcher, John McCauley, and a questionnaire Goldberg had prepared. Another meeting was set for the following week. "The reason I cannot see him any sooner," Gershwin wrote, "is because on Monday next I am playing *Rhapsody in Blue;* and conducting a performance of *An American in Paris* at the City College Stadium, for the very first time."

To prepare for this new venture, he went to his old teacher Edward Kilenyi for pointers in podium technique ("composure" was Kilenyi's term). For all his customary composure, Gershwin was a bit nervous at the prospect. The summer Stadium orchestra was the New York Philharmonic.

Under Kilenyi's avuncular supervision, Gershwin practiced conducting with the score while Shilkret's recording of *An American in Paris* sounded from the phonograph, interrupted only when a side ended (there were four in all) and Gershwin had to flip the disc. After the Saturday afternoon rehearsal with conductor Van Hoogstraten, he was ready for Monday night's concert.

Lewisohn Stadium was packed—as an oversized panoramic photograph taken that night attests—to the aisles as a new attendance record was set. Gershwin was second and fourth on the program, which began with the overture to Weber's *Der Freischütz.* Gershwin appeared to play his part in the *Rhapsody in Blue.* Van Hoogstraten then conducted three Brahms *Hungarian Dances.* After intermission Gershwin led the orchestra in *An American in Paris.* He appeared to be poised and in control of the orchestra, whatever composer's stomach twinges he may have had. The *Times* reviewer wrote that "he could hardly contain his enthusiasm" but still managed "a clear and admirable sense of rhythm."

Kilenyi described the debut simply as "a triumph."

Gershwin enjoyed this new avocation so much that when composer-conductor Henry Hadley of the Manhattan Symphony asked him to repeat a performance of *An American* at the Mecca Auditorium in November, Gershwin did not hesitate. Of that rendition, the *Times* reviewer found the tone poem "as fresh and novel as if it were being heard at a premiere . . . The composer-conductor was recalled many times and prevailed upon the orchestra players to rise and share the honors with him."

This marked the beginning of Gershwin's conducting career. He returned to the podium the next summer to conduct *An American* again and often led the pit bands on the opening nights of his musicals, beginning with the second version of *Strike Up the Band*. Having, in a sense, mastered the orchestra Gershwin believed he was ready for that opera he had been talking about for years. That could be yet another "first."

IV

Since reading *Porgy* in 1926, the subject of opera intrigued him, although as late as 1928 he had rebuffed the rumor twice (in February, before he left for Paris, and in August after he had returned) that he was considering opera. But after his successful Stadium appearance in August and the close of *Show Girl* in September, he became fascinated in adapting the Central European Jewish folktale "The Dybbuk" as an opera. This story about a lost, restless spirit that enters the body to possess (and destroy) it, was presented in an English version at the Neighborhood Playhouse, an early experimental Off-Broadway (the term did not exist then) theater on Grand Street in the Lower East Side. Gershwin was familiar with the production, as he may also have been with a 1926 version in Yiddish by the Russian playwright-folklorist S. An-Ski (Solomon S. Rapoport) that opened in New York about a month after *Oh, Kay!*

On October 11, 1929, Gershwin wrote to a friend, "I have been doing a lot of thinking about the 'Dybbuk,' and have had a few chats with [Henry] Ahlsberg, the gent who did the Neighborhood Playhouse production and who, I believe, has the rights to the piece . . . I have also spoken to Otto Kahn about my idea and he is very eager to have me do the opera. I think something will come of it. I will let you know first hand if something does. In the meantime do not mention it to anyone."

Someone mentioned it; a few days later Gershwin wrote that "The 'Dybbuk' news broke out on the front page of the 'Morning World' . . . and has caused quite a bit of excitement. [The head of the article read: GERSHWIN SHELVES JAZZ TO DO OPERA.] Other papers writing the news afterward.

"My arrangement with the Metropolitan Opera House is, I believe, as good as settled. I am seeing Mr. Kahn this week."

A week later, on October 30, he was issued a contract as "party of the second part" in which he agreed "to compose the music of a new opera, the libretto and title of which are to be known as 'Dybbuk,' this opera to be ready for performance by April 1, 1931." The librettist of the opera was to be Henry Ahlsberg, who had made the English translation and adaptation of the play.

According to the terms of the contract, Gershwin was to meet the April deadline with a piano-vocal score, a full conductor's score, all orchestra and choral parts. He would supervise the preparation and corrections, if need be, of these materials "gratis," although the Metropolitan agreed to underwrite the expenses, provided the composer had it done "at the most reasonable figure."

For this—a year or more of work, making and copying parts—the party of the first part agreed to pay Gershwin "the sum of Two Hundred Fifty ($250) Dollars for each and every performance of said opera and further promises to give or pay for not less than four (4) performances; this payment to include the rights for the use of the material, of the libretto and the plot." In short, Gershwin was guaranteed all of a thousand dollars, which he would divide with Ahlsberg.

Unlike many of his contemporaries, Gershwin could afford to take time out from earning popular-song money to work on an opera. He began setting down ideas in a Tune Book. He spoke of spending a couple of months abroad to study Jewish folk and liturgical music. He played some of his early ideas for both Kay Swift and his future biographer, Goldberg, at the time working on his series of Gershwin articles for the *Ladies' Home Journal.*

On one of Goldberg's visits from Roxbury, Massachusetts, Gershwin showed him some of his Dybbuk themes. Taking the notebook, Goldberg saw a "few melodic phrases unsupported by any harmonic structure; they suggested a slow lilt and might have been anything from a buck-and-wing to a dirge.

"He glanced at the notes and was soon constructing not only music but a scene. This slow lilt gradually assumed a hieratic character, swinging in drowsy dignity above a drone. The room became a synagogue, and this was the indistinct prayer of those to whom prayer has become a routine such as any other. The lilt had acquired animation; it was the swaying bodies of the chanters.

"An upward scratch in the notebook suddenly came to life as a Khassidic dance. And those who know what Khassidic tunes can be like in their wild, ecstatic abandon, know that the Khassid, like his brother under the skin, can grow wings and walk all over God's heaven."

Unfortunate realities cut the project short. When the rights were researched Gershwin learned that, while Ahlsberg had been granted permission to translate the play, the musical rights had been previously granted to Italian composer Lodovico Rocca. (Presented as *Il Dibuc* at La Scala, Milan, in March of 1934, it was not heard in the United States until 1936, when it was presented in Detroit. Gershwin did not see either production.)

And when the news came that "The Dybbuk" was not available, he was at work on the revised *Strike Up the Band.*

V

Producer Edgar Selwyn did not want to take chances the second time around. He turned over George S. Kaufman's caustic 1927 book to part-time lyricist-librettist Morrie Ryskind. Some years before Ryskind had worked with Kaufman, though he was not credited, doctoring the book of the Marx Brothers revue *The Cocoanuts.* They followed that with a collaboration, again for the Marxes, the Irving Berlin revue, *Animal Crackers.*

Kaufman, though he worked on several musicals as librettist and sometime lyricist or director, was notorious for resenting the intrusion of song in his books. He agreed to let Ryskind work over his original libretto.

The revision extracted much of the cynical Kaufman bite, rendering it a lesser commentary on war, but resulted in the first musical success of 1930.

The Gershwins completed their part of the work during the final months of 1929 in time for the Boston premiere on Christmas night. They kept seven songs of the original's fifteen; they lifted "I've Got a Crush on You" from the hapless *Treasure Girl,* an unusual practice, for they rarely reused a song that had already been heard in a previous show. An additional thirteen numbers were written to the revised book.

Unfortunately discarded were a bittersweet satire of the love duet "Seventeen and Twenty-One," a lovely pastoral nature poem (with tongue in cheek), "Meadow Serenade" and the droll "Knitting Song," during the singing of which soldiers are seen knitting for the folks back home.

Ryskind diminished the Kaufman sting by setting the war with Swit-zerland in a dream. The war was fought over a tariff on imported chocolate (in the first version it was cheese). This necessitated a different ending; in the 1927 version the final curtain went down as the United States prepared for war with Russia over caviar. In his rewrite Ryskind simply has the dreamer awaken for the happy ending.

The title song was retained as a satire on military marches and the first-act finale. (Since, and particularly during the Second World War, it has become a stirring martial air, provided the verse "We don't know what we're fighting for" is omitted or changed. After the Gershwins settled in California, Ira Gershwin adapted the lyric to a march for the University of California; for the rest of his life he received two season passes for all home football games in exchange.)

Among the notable new songs written for the 1930 edition was the winsomely caustic "I Want to Be a War Bride," which was eliminated early in the show's run. "My recollection," Ira told a friend, "is that it was acceptably, if not excitingly, sung by a charming young woman who somehow, even after the market crash, had access to enough money to become the principal backer of the show. Not in her ken though was that unwritten theatrical law: 'The show must go on.' During the second week in New York run she eloped with a Hollywood director without giving notice to the management. Neither she nor the song ever returned . . ."

Also memorable are the flippant "Mademoiselle from New Rochelle," the diffident ballad "I Mean to Say" and the exceptional "Soon."

The main strain of that song was used in the earlier *Strike Up the Band* in the recitative conclusion of Act I. In the original the melodic fragment (two lines of lyric, eight bars of music) underscored an embittered upbraiding of the hero by the heroine. Friends of the Gershwins suggested that it be developed into a complete song; they agreed, and "Soon" was the result.

Remarkably there were few of the tryout problems that had afflicted the Gershwins during the gestation period of some of their previous musicals. *Strike Up the Band* was in good shape and ready for Boston.

Selwyn, having noticed that Gershwin had received attention as a conductor in the months before, suggested that he lead the orchestra on the official opening night. After attending one of the rehearsals, Goldberg wrote, "To watch him is to see with what ease he gets most of the men under his baton [among whom were Benny Goodman, Glenn Miller, Jimmy Dorsey, Gene Krupa, Jack Teagarden]. Baton, did I say? George conducts with a baton, a cigar, with his shoulders, with his hips, with his eyes, with whatnot. Yet without any antics for the eyes of the audience. It is, rather, a gentle polyrhythm of his entire body—a quiet dance. His infinite patience with the ladies and gentlemen of the ensemble, when teaching them a new number, is as remarkable as it is, by those selfsame ladies and gentlemen, appreciated."

After the Christmas premiere in Boston (Gershwin conducting), *Strike Up the Band* opened at the Times Square Theatre on January 14, 1930—Gershwin again conducting the overture. About midway through, he turned to Kay Swift, seated in the first row directly behind him and said, "April and Andy." He referred to her two young daughters who had choreographed a song-and-dance routine to "I've Got a Crush on You," one of the songs in the overture. "It seemed remarkable to me then," Swift has written, "and it still does, that any composer, on the first night of one his shows, as well as during his initial stint of conducting in the pit, could feel easy enough in his mind to remember the children and their routine."

The second time around the antiwar operetta worked; both critics and audiences approved. Columnist William Bolitho (remembered now for his book *Twelve Against the Gods)* later observed with wonder, "Of all things in the world, here is a bitter, satirical attack on war, genuine propaganda at times, sung and danced on Broadway to standing room only."

Kay and James Warburg gave a midnight party in celebration of the opening. Gershwin sat at the piano until the reviews came in—"All excellent," according to Vernon Duke, who had returned to New York. He brought along his friend Sergei Prokofiev, who had recently arrived in the country (Gershwin had given both opening-night tickets).

After the glowing reviews were read and reread to joyful exclamations from the guests Gershwin "resumed his recital with renewed vigor," as members of his family mingled with show people, musicians and the show's cast.

Russel Crouse, an ex-newspaperman turned publicist for the Theatre Guild (before he began collaborating on librettos with Howard Lindsay), encountered Morris Gershwin among the guests and inquired, "How did you like the show?"

"What do you mean how I like it? I *have* to like it."

Duke overheard another exchange. Gershwin took Morris around to meet the cast. When he was introduced to Jerry Goff, the lead singer-hero, Pop Gershwin said, "Oh yes, you were on the American side."

Strike Up the Band was more than the Gershwins' first hit musical of the new decade; it was the harbinger of the political musical satires of the Depression. Though less acerbic than the first version, it had sufficient bite—warriors, diplomats, politicians were its targets—to make its point. The Gershwins had been given the opportunity to work with a fully realized book in which they began moving toward a new form of American musical; the next in this genre would prove to be even finer and more successful. But before they got to that, they took a step backward in a simple-minded but highly successful conventional musical comedy for Aarons and Freedley.

VI

Having recovered from the *Treasure Girl* debacle with two mildly successful musicals by Richard Rodgers and Lorenz Hart—*Spring Is Here* produced in March 1929 and *Heads Up* in November—Aarons and Freedley felt solvent enough to bring out another Gershwin show in the fall or winter of 1930. (Both Rodgers and Hart shows echoed Gershwin somewhat: Ohman and Arden played in the orchestra of the first and Victor Moore appeared as a comic villain in the second, whose plot revolved around rum-running.)

With *Strike Up the Band* settled into the Times Square Theatre, Gershwin attended to several small chores while awaiting the new musical's book, by Bolton and John McGowan. McGowan had worked on the *Heads Up* libretto; ex-actor-singer, he had appeared in vaudeville and several musicals. In blackface he had sung in Gershwin's *Blue Monday* in the *Scandals of 1922.*

By this time Gershwin was cooperating actively with Isaac Goldberg, who was finishing up his series of articles, "Music by Gershwin" for the *Ladies' Home Journal* (they would not appear until early 1931, but were the foundation of Goldberg's biography that followed). He took a little time out in February 1930 for a Florida vacation for, as he put it, "some sunshine, some fishing and perhaps a little gambling."

In the meantime, also at liberty, Ira Gershwin collaborated on a few songs with Vernon Duke and Harry Warren; some of these efforts were interpolated into *The Garrick Gaieties* ("I'm Only Human After All," with Duke and co-lyricist E. Y. Harburg) and *Sweet and Low* ("Cheerful Little Earful" and "In the Merry Month of Maybe" with Warren and alleged co-lyricist Billy Rose, who happened to be the producer of the show).

On his return from Florida Gershwin lent Goldberg an additional hand with a book the latter was writing about Tin Pan Alley. In a letter dated May 1, 1930, Gershwin offered some suggestions: "There are so many people connected with Tin Pan Alley that it is difficult to give you the names off-hand. I suppose you have the obvious ones, like: Harry von Tilzer, Gus Edwards, Max Dreyfus, John Golden, Ray Goetz, etc.

You see different names are connected with different aspects of Tin Pan Alley and as I don't know from what angle you are attacking the subject I am at a loss to name just the ones you want. I should think if you got hold of a former song plugger you can get an interesting line on Tin Pan Alley. I mean one of those people who use(d) to go from café to café singing their publisher's songs."

Goldberg's book, published later in the year as *Tin Pan Alley,* with an introduction by Gershwin, was dedicated to him "for the *Rhapsody in Blue,* the *Concerto in F,* and not least for . . . his unaffected friendship."

He told Goldberg, in that May first letter, about "a very hard week" that would begin the next day at the three-year-old Roxy, advertised as the "Most Magnificent Motion Picture House in Any City, or Any Country, Anywhere." The occasion was the world premiere of *The King of Jazz,* one of the earliest star-studded—and in color in spots—musical films. Whiteman and his orchestra were booked for the initial three weeks of its run; Gershwin agreed to appear during the first week, anticipating four or five appearances a day and "a lot of hard work." He performed in the *Rhapsody in Blue* onstage; in the film the work was done, purportedly, on an enormous grand piano (large enough to hold the entire orchestra—and Paul Whiteman). Roy Bargy was piano soloist in this sequence.

The King of Jazz turned out to be yet another in a series of filmed variety shows (not unlike vaudeville, then expiring), a plotless series of skits, musical numbers, dubious comic turns and even a cartoon in which Whiteman was crowned King of Jazz in an African setting. In the wake of such ponderous efforts as *Fox Movietone Follies, Show of Shows, Paramount on Parade* and *Hollywood Revue* (all pretty much the same show, only the names were changed), *The King of Jazz* was not welcomed; the novelty had worn thin.

After the first screening on May 2, Whiteman came onstage, resplendent in tails, to conduct his orchestra as well as the Roxy Symphony, an aggregate of over a hundred. While an unruffled Gershwin waited in the wings, Whiteman led an introductory medley of popular songs. Then the opening strain of the *Rhapsody* was Gershwin's cue. He extinguished his cigar, executed a neat dance step to the laughing delight of an unidentified "charming companion," and sat at the piano; the clarinet cadenza began.

While the newspaper criticisms were mixed rather than bad, *The King of Jazz* did poorly after the first week, which might suggest that Gershwin had been the major draw. The second week was one of the worst in the Roxy's brief history. Manager S. L. (Roxy) Rothafel canceled the entire stage show that week and withdrew the film before the planned run had gone the course.

Gershwin's third appearance at Lewisohn Stadium on August 28 with Van Hoogstraten marked the summer 1930 high point; on the program were Weber, Debussy, Tchaikovsky (one work each) and Gershwin (three: the *Rhapsody, Concerto* and *An American in Paris,* which he conducted). He was then free to concentrate on the Aarons and Freedley show which Bolton and McGowan called *Girl Crazy.*

"We didn't do George justice," McGowan later said of their book about a New York playboy who is sent off to an isolated village in Arizona by his father to sequester him from the temptations of Manhattan night life (bootleggers, nightclubs and especially women). "Danny Churchill" (Allen Kearns in his third Gershwin musical) is, in short, "girl crazy" and is shipped off to Custerville, nationally famed for an all-male (cowboy) population, an Indian and some livestock.

A musical without "girls" was unthinkable, so Bolton and McGowan skirted that handicap by casting Ginger Rogers as Molly, the town's postmistress, who lives elsewhere (her second show). One ingenious touch was to have Danny arrive in Custerville by cab; the New York cab driver was called Gieber Goldfarb (Willie Howard in a role fashioned for Bert Lahr, who was then doing well in *Flying High* and whose management would not release him). Howard, ordinarily teamed with his brother Eugene, was a clowning master of Broadway Yiddish. In one scene, disguised as an Indian, he speaks Yiddish to elude some bad men; the only one who understands him is a college-educated Indian.

Danny is smitten by Molly, who spurns him as a girl-crazy, effete Easterner. With the help of the resourceful Gieber, he converts the town's only hotel (owned by his father) into a dude ranch, complete with gambling, drinking and entertainment. Soon Custerville is filled with women and song; among the former are a number of Danny's former flames and a vindictive rival, who also fancies Molly.

Among the new arrivals are a not very sharp gambler, Slick (William Kent) and his long-suffering wife, Kate (Ethel Merman in her Broadway debut). The actions of the first act occur in and around Custerville; the second changes the scene, transporting all to Mexico for some musical spice. All ends well.

While *Girl Crazy* represents a literary (i.e., libretto) retreat for the Gershwins after *Strike Up the Band,* it remains one of their most inspired scores, including as it does the classic "I Got Rhythm" (which Merman introduced and which thrust her to instant stardom); "Bidin' My Time"; "But Not For Me"; "Embraceable You" (written originally for *East Is West);* two lesser-known but superior bluesy numbers, "Sam and Delilah" and "Boy! What Love Has Done to Me!"; "Could You Use Me?"; "Treat Me Rough"; the book may have been mid-twenties, but the score was of the moment—and has yet to date.

Among the lesser songs are "Goldfarb, That's I'm," a parody of a George M. Cohan song, the minor "When It's Cactus Time in Arizona," which Ira Gershwin recalled as "a throwaway during which Ginger Rogers did rope tricks or something." This was performed "in one," in front of the curtain while the scenery was changed to move the locale back to Arizona from Mexico.

Especially interesting is the opening of the second act, a choral-dance piece, "Land of the Gay Caballero," which leads into a fiery instrumental, *Mexican Dance* (Ira Gershwin's title; in the score it is simply marked *Dance*). Also notable is the opening of Scene 2 in Act I, "Bronco Busters," a syncopated choral number for male voices.

Worth mentioning is the fact that there were no real "names" in the cast of *Girl Crazy;* Kearns and Howard were veterans, dependable but not names-above-the-title stars. Rogers was little known, while Merman was unknown—until after opening night.

Merman was Freedley's discovery, an ex-secretary singing in a Brooklyn vaudeville theater. In her "Sam and Delilah" scene she was supposed to be accompanied onstage by her regular pianist, Al Siegel, who backed out when he realized he would have to play in full view of an audience. He called in sick and was replaced by a young, talented arranger-pianist (and later, composer and producer of films), Roger Edens.

An audience never daunted Merman, however. "Although this young woman was appearing for the first time on any stage," Ira Gershwin said of her, "her assurance, timing and delivery both as comedienne and singer—with a no-nonsense voice that could reach not only standees but ticket-takers in the lobby . . . [which] convinced the opening-night audience that it was witnessing the discovery of a new star."

Equally assured that first night was the composer in his new avocational role of conductor. The Red Nichols orchestra is credited in the program; its members then included Benny Goodman, Glenn Miller, Jimmy Dorsey, Jack Teagarden and Gene Krupa, fresh from the *Strike Up the Band* pit. The show's conductor was Earl Busby.

Girl Crazy converted the Alvin box office into a gold mine after the opening on October 14, 1930. The critical consensus was expressed by Brooks Atkinson who found the "book serviceable, rather than distinguished. It gets its characters in and out of the proper entanglements and tears its hero and heroine apart at the end of the first act as every orthodox musical show libretto should.

"Not the least important item in these [good] tidings is the part played by the brothers Gershwin . . . The premiere performance was conducted by George Gershwin, and he got as much applause as any one on the stage." Atkinson concluded that *Girl Crazy* was "an agreeable diversion," and predicted it would be around for a long time (it was: 272 performances).

VII

"I am just recuperating from a couple of exciting days," Gershwin wrote to Isaac Goldberg after reading the *Girl Crazy* reviews. "I worked very hard conducting the orchestra at the rehearsal and dress rehearsal and finally at the opening night, when the theatre was so warm that I must have lost at least three pounds, perspiring.

"The opening was so well received that five pounds would not have been too much. With the exception of some deadhead friends of mine, who sat in the front row, everybody seemed to enjoy the show, especially the critics. I think the notices, especially of the music, were the best I have ever received . . .

"The show looks so good that I can leave in a few weeks for Hollywood, with the warm feeling that I have a hit under my belt . . . Ira, Guy Bolton and I leave definitely on November 5 . . ."

He had a minor criticism of his own; apparently Goldberg had revised Gershwin's *Tin Pan Alley* introduction. "I objected," he told Goldberg, "to so many personal pronouns and I asked [the editor] Rimington to cut out several paragraphs which I thought didn't belong. As it is I feel that there is a little too much about me in it."

Before the Gershwins left for California they participated in a quite hectic wedding when Frances Gershwin married Leopold Godowsky, Jr., one Sunday afternoon.

When he returned from Europe on Saturday, November 1, Godowsky learned from Frances that her parents were leaving for Florida on Sunday and that her brothers for Hollywood on Wednesday. While they had been quitely planning to be married for some time, Godowsky felt they should be married immediately—say Sunday—with her family present.

There were obstacles: where to find the license, the ring, a clergyman (all on a Sunday in New York)—and especially Rose Gershwin. She did not feel that Godowsky would ever amount to anything, the son of a great pianist who lived in his father's shadow, a violinist of no special talent with an inexplicable scientific bent. He was handsome, charming, witty, but to Rose Gershwin a young man of little promise. She attributed her asthmatic attacks, which forced her to take to her bed, to her daughter's choice of a husband.

When she considered all the impediments, Frances called Leo early Sunday morning suggesting they forget the whole thing. But he was reassuring, persistent and resourceful.

Through a friend, a judge, he managed to acquire a marriage license somewhere in the Bronx; he found a jeweler who made house—or rather street—calls. Frances found the jeweler's black limousine early Sunday morning awaiting her on the corner of Broadway and 103rd Street. After exchanging identifications, she got into the auto to select her ring.

With further assistance from the judge, they selected someone from a directory to marry them. They felt he should live somewhere nearby and have a name Jewish enough for him to be a rabbi. By this time it was four in the afternoon; Rose and Morris Gershwin had reservations on the six o'clock train.

The clergyman they found fulfilled the two stipulations. The rabbi—a music lover, they learned—was delighted to join such musically distinguished names.

Meanwhile, hasty preparations for the wedding and a celebration had been under way at Ira Gershwin's penthouse apartment. And by late afternoon Rose Gershwin finally learned about the wedding; for some moments she had thought Leonore and Ira had planned a farewell party for herself and Morris. By this time it was too late for histrionics; there was nothing she could do. Family and friends assembled in the Gershwin apartment: Gertrude Lawrence, Bill "Bojangles" Robinson, Kay Swift with a bouquet for Rose and Morris. George Gershwin wandered in from his apartment in pajamas and robe, smoking a cigar. He then learned it was his sister's wedding day. Everyone was there but the rabbi, who had mistakenly gone to the wrong Gershwin penthouse apartment.

As train time neared, he found the right apartment. A bridal bouquet was improvised from Kay Swift's present and Morris Gershwin conspicuously glanced at his watch, reminding all they had a train to catch.

Still in pajamas and robe, with cigar, Gershwin sat at the piano and played the wedding march as well as an excerpt from the *Rhapsody in Blue*. After the ceremony the rabbi made a point of discussing music with Gershwin, a musicological disquisition checked when assorted Gershwins and friends accompanied the senior Gershwins to the station. That evening Gertrude Lawrence and Bert Taylor had a party for the departing songwriting Gershwins; for the new Mr. and Mrs.

Godowsky it was virtually a wedding reception. George circulated among the guests, obviously more excited by his sister's marriage than the imminent trip to Beverly Hills.

The three Gershwins and Bolton boarded the train at Grand Central Station on November 5; the Gershwins brought along some Tune Books and fourteen pages of an outline to a Kaufman-Ryskind political satire, in the event that Hollywood did not keep them busy enough. Also aboard was happy producer of *Strike Up the Band,* Edgar Selwyn, who also doubled as a film director, and others. All gathered in the dining car evenings to while away the time at poker.

VIII

Before they left Gershwin had told an interviewer that "I go to work for the talkies like any other amateur, for I know very little about them. I am not a film fan, a movie addict . . . [composer Burton Lane remembers a time when Gershwin invited him to see a movie in a theater across the street from the house on 103rd Street; it was a documentary about the life of a bee] . . . Because I am inexperienced with films, I am approaching them in a humble state of mind."

The three Gershwins rented a house on Chevy Chase Drive in Beverly Hills that Gershwin described as "most comfortable, although it gets quite cold at night." The brothers had been assigned a cottage on the Fox lot, but they did most of their work in their house—which Gershwin learned had once been occupied by Greta Garbo. "I am sleeping in the bed that she used," he wrote to Goldberg. "It hasn't helped my sleep any."

He also told Goldberg that "Hollywood is okay, despite what Mr. George Kaufman has to say about it [he was referring to the scathing play, written with Moss Hart, *Once in a Lifetime*]. I am really liking it out here—my face is tanned—I still have indigestion—there are many beautiful women out here—I shot an eighty-six at the Rancho Golf Club the other day . . .

"Our picture is practically written, with the exception of a Manhattan Rhapsody—or Fantasy—which I am going to write for it. We had a meeting with Winnie Sheehan [Winfield Sheehan, assistant to studio head William Fox] the other night and read and played him what we had written. He and the director [David Butler] of our picture seemed more than pleased."

Within six weeks of their arrival the Gershwins had written a half-dozen songs, and an extended dream sequence. Life in Hollywood was serene compared with Manhattan—and writing for films was free of the hectic periods of tryout rewriting. While George worked on his Manhattan Rhapsody, Ira had "nothing to do but get up at noon, read the papers, see pictures, and dine in or out. A pleasure!"

Among the many beautiful women he had met, George was attracted to silent screen star, Aileen Pringle, then making her first sound films. (She made a great impression in the silent adaptation of the Elinor Glyn novel *Three Weeks;* her last film was *The Girl From Nowhere* in 1939.) During January and February 1931, they saw a good deal of each other. Her home was in Santa Monica, where Gershwin worked on his rhapsody and made several sketches of her.

The finished film was entitled *Delicious,* with a screenplay by Bolton, with adaptation and dialogue by veteran onetime attorney Sonya Levien. Starring the very popular team of Janet Gaynor and Charles Farrell, it told the story of a Scottish immigrant (Gaynor) who spends most of the film fleeing from a persistent immigration officer; she had come into the country illegally, hidden in a horse van belonging to a wealthy Long Islander (Farrell). Most of the action takes place in Manhattan, however, which afforded Gershwin the opportunity for his rhapsody. (In the script it was called *Manhattan Rhapsody;* in the production list of works issued on January 8, it is entitled *Rhapsody in Rivets.)* A young Russian composer-pianist (Raul Roulien) formed the final section of the film's triangle. He provided several of the song cues and composed the rhapsody (his piano playing was dubbed by Marvine Maazel).

As was the practice, the Gershwins conceived a title song, though with a twist, "Delishious," which was Ira's nod to his father-in-law's frequent after-dinner pronouncements. In the film it is Gaynor who mispronounces it in the Strunsky manner, to the composer's amusement—which inspires him to write the song. It is a song of some charm, particularly in the verse, though the lyric of the bridge is one of Ira's least inspired: a count from one to ten.

One song, "Blah, Blah, Blah," was one of the several written for Ziegfeld's never produced *East Is West,* where it was entitled "Lady of the Moon." It was revised for *Show Girl* as "I Just Looked at You," but again dropped. In its *Delicious* reincarnation it was a spoof of theme songs and Tin Pan Alley balladry. Theme songs were often fashioned even for nonmusical films; the best example being Mabel Wayne and L. Wolfe Gilbert's "Ramona." Some peculiar, if that's the word, examples are "Dynamite, Dynamite, Blow Back My Sweetie to Me" (for *Dynamite)* and "Woman Disputed, I Love You" (for *Woman Disputed).* When Dorothy Parker was asked to suggest a theme song title for

Dynamite, she suggested, with some malice, "Dynamite, I Love You." The Gershwins bit the hand that fed more gently.

The refrain to "Blah, Blah, Blah" is one of Gershwin's best—and the lyric is composed of numerous "blahs" and assorted popular-song clichés: "moon," "above," "croon," "love," a "merry month of May," a few "tra-la-las," "clouds of gray" and even "a cottage for two." Some of their friends accused Ira of spoiling one of his brother's finest ballads with his satirical lyric, which precluded its chance for popularity. Perhaps, but the brothers were pleased with it.

Other songs included the folkish "Somebody from Somewhere," "Katinkitschka," also folkish, and the excellent "You Started It," wasted as background music under dialogue. The "Dream Sequence" also known as "Welcome to the Melting Pot," is a miniature musical complete with a brief overture and several snatches of song. On-screen it is stiff and pretentious as Gaynor imagines being welcomed to the New World by reporters, eight Uncle Sams, "Mr. Ellis of Ellis Island" and even the Statue of Liberty. In some respects, the recitatives and choral sections point toward the work of the Gershwins in *Of Thee I Sing,* which they had begun working on even as they polished up *Delicious.*

By January 1931, Gershwin had completed his rhapsody (contrary to popular belief, the original, eight-minute work remained in the finished picture). In this sequence a despairing, about to be deported Gaynor leaves her happy, singing Russian friends and wanders alone through the streets of Manhattan; there is minimal dialogue with the music blending with street noises which range from the shouting of newsboys to the hammering of riveters.

Photographically, it is the most imaginative aspect of *Delicious,* as much the contribution of cameraman Ernest Palmer as that of director Butler. Dramatic camera angles, lighting and fluid movement of the camera capture the apprehension of the young woman as she moves almost balletically through the clamorous, crowded streets, dodging cabs and mashers and even contemplating suicide before deciding to give herself up to the police.

Gershwin's music for this sequence is restless, pulsating; interspersed are quiet moments but with the rivet theme serving as a *ritornello.* As in his first rhapsody, Gershwin conceived a long-lined middle melody for the second. It is not in the romantic, Tchaikovskian mood of the *Rhapsody in Blue* andante. It is spare though memorable, but hardly as eminently accessible as that famous andante.

Gershwin fashioned this form of the rhapsody in the time between late December and the end of January 1931. To judge from his other activities during this period it is obvious he did not spend all his waking moments on it. Besides the time spent with "Pringie," as he called Aileen Pringle, there were dinners and parties, a New Year's trip to Caliente, Mexico, a return to Los Angeles to hear the Philharmonic, under Artur Rodzinski, perform *An American in Paris* on January 15, with a celebration party after. Ira reported that the Philharmonic had had its "biggest house of the season," which he attributed to *An American* and the programming of Stravinsky's *Le Sacre du Printemps.* "George got his usual big reception," he reported to friends in New York.

The next day George was off to spend a weekend at the Hamilton Fish ranch, some 350 miles distant, near San Francisco. On his return he came down with influenza and spent January 24 in bed, but occupied himself by doing a watercolor of his friend George Pallay (a cousin of the Paleys). By this time the Gershwins had begun working on the Kaufman-Ryskind musical that was to be produced by Sam H. Harris; they had also heard from Aarons suggesting another show for the Alvin. They decided to do the Harris show first.

When they boarded the Pullman for their return to the East on February 22, they were finished with *Delicious,* and already had some ideas for their next show, including the title song, "Of Thee I Sing." Initially Gershwin planned to return to Hollywood in May, then July, to oversee, Broadway-wise, their work. Because of delays, however, it was September before *Delicious* went before the cameras. Gaynor and Farrell did three films that year, the most important being *Daddy Long Legs* for her and *Liliom* for him. Besides, it was becoming obvious that the musical film market had begun to shrivel and there may have been some hesitation about it; the popularity of Gaynor and Farrell and the name of Gershwin made a great difference. But once shooting began, Gershwin was too involved with *Of Thee I Sing* to return to Hollywood.

In July he appeared on an early historic television broadcast performing "Liza." Others seen on the program were Mayor Jimmy Walker, Kate Smith and the Boswell Sisters. In August he returned to Lewisohn Stadium to perform the *Rhapsody in Blue* in an "All-American Program," with his "good-looking Irish pal, Bill Daly," conducting. Also in August he went on the air with the Philharmonic, conducted by Damrosch and performed the second movement of the *Concerto in F,* which was broadcast by short wave to Germany.

By September he and Ira were deep in their work on *Of Thee I Sing.* From California they heard from Sheehan that "great things were expected of the picture." This was encouraging news and might "mean another picture contract next year, which would be pleasing to Ira & me . . ."

Had he returned for the *Delicious* filming it is unlikely that Gershwin would have been pleased. Word had already begun to drift back to New York that filmmakers preferred not to take advice from songwriters. Sheehan, the producer, was not noted for his musical taste. The Gershwins' friend S. N. Behrman, who had worked on Sheehan films, made that point in a single sentence. Sheehan had engineered a divorce from his wife (he had all their furniture removed from their apartment while she was at the movies). Then, as Behrman put it, "Winnie promptly married Maria Jeritza, the famous opera diva. As he was tone-deaf, this marriage showed signs of promise."

The rumors filtering back to Manhattan about the poor working conditions for songwriters in Hollywood prompted one studio head to hold forth on the Good Life in California. "We give them about everything they want," he said in referring to songwriters. "They have big, beautiful rooms to work in. There's a nice quiet atmosphere; some of the boys have windows with a view of the mountains—just the atmosphere for the composition of melodies. Why, we even let the boys do their work at home if they want to. We don't expect too much from them, either. When they've done two or three songs I make them go off on a vacation and do some fishing.

"I usually give them about six weeks in which to do an assignment. They don't have to turn in anything until three or four of those weeks have elapsed. Then they show what they've done and I criticize it. I'm sort of a song doctor myself, and I make suggestions to help the tunes along." The Gershwins would encounter his kind of mentality again.

By curious coincidence, *Delicious* and *Of Thee I Sing* opened in New York on the same day—the film at the Roxy in the afternoon and the political operetta that evening of December 26, 1931. Only one was greeted to dancing in the streets.

The *Sun*'s critic lamented over the "union of the rather squeaky but appealing Miss Gaynor and of Mr. Farrell, the Adonis with the Calvin Coolidge method of delivering lines . . ." In the *Times* Mordaunt Hall wrote that he found Bolton's book "a conventional piece of sentimentality with dialogue that is scarcely inspired." He made passing reference to a "New York Rhapsody" as being "played on the piano," ignoring the orchestra. It was very well played by Maazel, who also provided the very Gershwinesque accompaniments for the songs.

Delicious was publicized as opening simultaneously in no fewer than 162 movie houses across the country, but its ultimate fate at the box office brought no new contract to the Gershwins in 1932. The first film musical cycle had ended; the Winnie Sheehans of Hollywood had much to learn about producing this kind of film. The really memorable movie musicals would come in the second cycle.

The single Hollywood assignment of the next year, 1932, was one song, "You've Got What Gets Me," for the film version of *Girl Crazy*, starring the team of (Bert) Wheeler and (Robert) Woolsey. The studio's "song doctors" by not very deft surgery eliminated most of the Broadway score (although inexplicably retaining "Barbary Coast" and the *Mexican Dance* as instrumental pieces). "But Not For Me," "Bidin' My Time" and "I Got Rhythm" were all that remained of the original.

Hollywood was not ready for the Gershwins; first *Delicious* and then *Girl Crazy* proved that. Nor did they put in much work on the new film song (writer Lawrence D. Stewart found that they received twenty-five hundred dollars for this effort). They lifted the release (the middle, B section) from a song written for but not used in *Funny Face*, "Your Eyes, Your Smile." They then proceeded to concoct a new verse and a chorus to enclose it and literally mailed it in.

The Depression had begun to insinuate subtle changes into the music business as well as Broadway. The studios, to assure a cooperative and reasonable attitude from songwriters, had quietly begun to buy out the major publishing houses. This assured a proper flow of "product" (songs) when it was essential to a "property" (the film musical). The takeover had started when sound was introduced and before the end of the first cycle which was induced by a glut of bad material. Excluded from this outpouring were the early efforts of such directors as Ernst Lubitsch, King Vidor and Rouben Mamoulian. Their camera sense and feel for music made even their initial musicals exceptional and it is obvious that their peers learned something from them before the second cycle got under way.

Meanwhile, however, the Gershwins remained in Manhattan; it would be a half decade before they returned to the Coast.

11

Manhattan Rhapsody

Upon their return to New York from Hollywood late in February, 1931, the Gershwins learned that they had no more to work from on the Kaufman-Ryskind political musical than the fourteen page outline they had taken to California the past November. This time off did not disturb Ira, but George as usual was anxious to keep busy. In April there was talk about Aarons and Freedley coming up with a book that could be scored before Kaufman and Ryskind completed their work. Gershwin hoped to complete the Aarons-and-Freedley musical by July, when he planned to return to California for three weeks to look in on the filming of *Delicious.* But no libretto materialized, and there were delays in shooting the film. While he waited, George devoted the spring of 1931 to working on a new rhapsody and assisting Isaac Goldberg in his Gershwin biography—and reveling in his burgeoning art collection.

I

The *Second Rhapsody* is a curiosity among Gershwin's concert works in that it was not given a premiere immediately on completion (as had George's previous "serious" compositions). Its genesis, too, is unique for it was not originally designed for the concert hall, being an expansion of the "Manhattan Rhapsody" sequence written for *Delicious.*

In his letters of this time Gershwin frequently refers to its progress, especially in the letters to Goldberg, whose work at Harvard kept him confined to the Boston area and his home in Roxbury, Massachusetts. He consequently accomplished a good deal of his research on his Gershwin biography by proxy or mail. In his replies, Gershwin interspersed the answers to Goldberg's queries with a section-by-section report on the rhapsody.

"I wrote it mainly," he told Goldberg, "because I wanted to write a serious composition and found the opportunity in California to do it. Nearly everybody comes back from California with a western tan and a pocket full of moving-picture money. I decided to come back with both . . . and a serious composition—if the climate would let me. I was under no obligation to the Fox Company to write this. But, you know, the old artistic soul must be appeased every so often."

He may not have been obliged to compose a large, full-scale work for Fox, but the studio certainly planned to exploit the composer of the *Rhapsody in Blue* (a snatch of which is heard during the film's opening credits). As heard in the film, the rhapsody runs for a bit more than seven minutes (not the minute or two as has been generally believed); all the themes of the final composition are heard. Gershwin's artistic soul merely set to work expanding the film's music.

"There is no program to the *Rhapsody,*" he explained. "As the part of the picture where it is to be played takes place in many streets of New York, I used a starting-point what I called 'a rivet theme,' but, after that, I just wrote a piece of music without any program."

Working from the *Delicious* version, he plotted the fuller work for two pianos and from that worked out the final orchestration. The work consisted primarily of developing the existing themes. As it grew he considered the title. "In the picture for which it was written," he wrote Goldberg, "it may still be called *Rhapsody in Rivets* . . . [When the film was released it was listed as "New York Rhapsody"]. I am calling it just plain *Second Rhapsody* and, although the piano has quite a few solo parts, I may just make it one of the orchestral instruments, instead of solo." (The title page reads: *2nd Rhapsody for Orchestra with Piano.)* As he informed another friend, he felt the final title was "much simpler and more dignified."

By the second week after the return from the Coast he began expanding the rhapsody; at the end of April he told Goldberg that he was devoting all the time he could to the new orchestration and that "last night [April 28] I finished up to the slow theme, which means I have little less than half of it completed." He was still awaiting word on the Aarons-Freedley project and mentioned the July trip to Hollywood. He concurrently gave some time to the special arrangements of eighteen songs for Simon and Schuster's *George Gershwin's Song Book,* set for publication the following year. Goldberg was lending a hand on the preparation of the introduction.

With no word from Aarons, Freedley, Kaufman, Ryskind or Hollywood, George concentrated on the rhapsody. In mid-May he wrote to his friend George Pallay, then in business in San Francisco that he had been "a very g-b (good boy) and have finished fifty-five pages of the orchestration of my Rhapsody, and, in about another week, I expect to finish the entire thing. I have an idea it is going to sound very good as I made quite a rich orchestration." In mid-June, as the orchestral parts were being copied, he wrote Goldberg to tell him that the composition was complete with "the exception of two piano cadenzas."

On June 26, he was given the use of the National Broadcasting Company's Studio B in Radio City to try out his *Second Rhapsody.* He was happy with the outcome, for as he wrote "America's most beautiful girl" (as he called her), Rosamond Walling in London: "I won't bore you with a long description of the rehearsal except to tell you it sounded better than I hoped it would . . ."

He was less reticent with Goldberg: "And now for some good news— I hired fifty-five men last Friday to play my orchestration of the new Rhapsody, and the result was most gratifying. In many respects, such as orchestration and form, it is the best thing I've written. It was a bit longer than I expected, lasting about fifteen and one-half minutes.

"The National Broadcasting Company, whose studio I used, are connected by wire with the Victor Recording Laboratories so the studio, as a great favor to me, had a record made of the rehearsal. I shall get it tomorrow. Good idea, eh?"

Not only did he get a reference recording of the rehearsal, but also several copies pressed onto sixteen-inch transcription discs, which enabled him to study the work in order to make some final changes; these were minor, i.e., in the opening, he extended the piano's rivet theme from four bars to six.

Gershwin's letters during this period (an unusually prolific yield for him), have four recurring themes: work on the rhapsody, awaiting a book from Aarons and Freedley, the Hollywood trip and delight in his growing art collection. There was also a growing disaffection with the producers, saying that he and Ira "are biding our time, waiting for Aarons and Freedley to deliver a book, which always seems like a difficult thing for them to do."

Simultaneously Fox slipped further behind schedule with *Delicious,* which canceled out that excursion. When his friend Ev Jacobs called suggesting they take a trip to Europe in August, George begged off. He did it reluctantly, for it would have given him the opportunity to see Rosamond Walling in London, but as he wrote her, he had decided to remain in New York because of "the show I must write for Aarons and Freedley." And, as he told another friend, the California trip was off too, "It would be unfair to leave Aarons and Freedley flat when the picture company is the one who is at fault."

When the producers' book finally materialized the following year, it proved to be no book at all—the first of his three final Broadway failures.

Despite the exhilaration the *Second Rhapsody* experience had given him, and the enjoyment of his paintings, helping Goldberg with his biography, and other activities (a week in Canada for the Canadian Open golf tournament and "playing some lousy golf myself"), he was restive, not happy, not working.

The delays in New York caused a bothersome ripple in his personal life. "I just got a wire from [Aileen] Pringle," he wrote Pallay, "in which she says she expected me out there around the fourth of July but had just heard that I had no intention of coming out—and never did. Which, of course, is untrue. I was—and am—most anxious to go out to California again, but am at the mercy of the moving picture gods that be. If the picture had been done on schedule, I should have been in California now. But I always knew that if they kept postponing it, it might be a little more difficult on account of the shows I have contracts to do."

His many letters to Rosamond Walling at this time reveal loneliness and a longing to join her (but he had the same excuse not to: Aarons and Freedley). "Things are very depressing around here," he told Pallay. "All my relations are in terrible shape. There is not a rich one in a carload. I'm trying my best to do what I can, but it isn't very pleasant."

Several letters written to Pallay during this time reveal a rather casual approach to those "relations." "Met up with a very attractive blonde recently—by the name of Roberta Robinson. I believe she was on the Coast some time ago. Did you ever meet her? She is in *Band Wagon* and is young and beautiful."

Or, while in Chicago for the opening of the touring *Girl Crazy,* "There is a cute little girl in Chicago that I knew in New York. She is a lot of fun—and as cute as she can be. If you ever go to Chicago, let me know and I'll put you in touch with her."

Pallay reciprocated: "Received a telephone call from Barbara Briston," George wrote him, "who said you had told her to call me. I had her up for dinner one night and found her very nice. She accompanied

Mosbacher and myself to one of my broadcasts and seemed to get a big thrill out of it. Who is she, by the way?"

He had news about another mutual friend: "I don't know whether you've read in the papers the very sad item concerning our little friend Grace Brown," he wrote Pallay. "A few days ago she jumped out of the window of [address illegible] Riverside Drive after a misunderstanding with her mother. I was terribly shocked to read it and know you will be shocked to hear about it. Poor kid! I wonder why she did it."

When Pallay's brother, Max Abramson, a newspaper writer from Gershwin's Tin Pan Alley years, got married, George reacted enthusiastically: "Will you congratulate your brother Max very heartily for me, on his recent marriage? That was really exciting news and I hope it will be an inspiration for some real hard work on his part."

As usual he was serious about his health. He believed that Pallay would be interested to know that in late May 1931, "I have given up smoking and . . . have not had a puff of any form of tobacco. I have done this in an attempt to perhaps help my stomach disturbances. I intend to keep it up indefinitely. Some will, eh, George?"

By October he began to falter. He wrote Pallay: ". . . as for that picture you saw of me with the cigar in my hand, it was taken just before I swore off. It has been about four months now since I have touched tobacco—but as I don't feel any better or different, I am liable to hop right on again at any time." He did.

Earlier, in August, he had tried something else besides. "I am feeling much better of late because I have started taking yeast again. (Fleischmann didn't pay me to say that)."

Not occupied with work, he fretted. On August 15, 1931, he wrote Pallay that "Unless the managers come through a little better than they have been, I'm afraid I'll have to produce my own show next year, provided I find a great book. I have a friend who is practically begging me to produce a show with his money, but I've fought shy of it because I figured that writing was tough enough. But one of these days I might take a fling at it."

He never did, but in the same letter he did say, "Now I've got to settle down to work again on some new shows to earn some of that well-known currency. Aarons and Freedley, as usual, are late with their book, so I'm doing a little work on the book George Kaufman has written, which will be produced later in the season."

In an earlier letter Gershwin appeared to be worried about money and Pallay offered to lend him some. "I am glad," he wrote in reply, "you are doing so well at a time like this and appreciate your generous offer to send me some money. But, fortunately, I don't need any. I just feel financially low because I'm not used to having months go by without those weekly checks coming in." (A couple of years later, it was Pallay who needed, and asked for, help. This came at a bad time for Gershwin, who explained, ". . . my funds are fairly low at the present time. I don't like to go below a certain bank balance so if $500 will help now I will be glad to send it to you and if you need the other $500 a little later I will let you have that also.")

During that summer too he helped Goldberg with long autobiographical letters, clearances of reproduction rights for the music and photographs; he even offered to go to Brooklyn to photograph his birthplace on Snedicker Avenue. His letters to "Dear Far-away Rosamond," were affectionately filled with news, professional and family, and playful flirtation. In July he wrote "By this time I imagine you are settled comfortably in jolly London & perhaps already trying on your court dress. The Prince has probably danced with you at the Embassy & has pronounced you America's most beautiful girl. (If he hasn't he should have.)"

There had been a new move in the Gershwin family. "Frankie & Leo left for Rochester where they will reside for the next two years," he told Rosamond.

"I shall miss my sister very much as I have great fondness for her as a person as well as the usual brotherly love. I hope she will be happy there & think there is a good chance for it as Leo is a most interesting fellow & will take her mind off Rochester . . ." Godowsky had finally proved himself to Rose Gershwin. Working with another musician, Leopold D. (for Damrosch) Mannes, he had invented what is known as Kodachrome film, which made him financially comfortable. He and Mannes would spend several years with Kodak. Rochester is also the home of the Eastman School of Music.

In early August Gershwin wrote Rosamond: "How lucky to be where you are. Away from hot, depressing America where high temperatures & low stocks seem to hold sway over a helpless people . . ."

Early in September he wrote again to tell her he had given up "smoking three months ago & not one puff of smoke has passed through these lips." (Only two years before this he had appeared in an advertisement endorsing Lucky Strike cigarettes.) But, he wrote, "I may start smoking again someday if only to live up to those caricatures of me with a corona-corona in my face."

He mentioned meeting Otto Kahn, who had asked about her. "You certainly made an indelible impression on my friends," he continued. "Only last night Billy Seeman said you were the nicest girl he had ever seen me with. Often when I think of you I get the desire to fly over to where you are, swoop down like an eagle & steal you & bring you to a big rock on a mountain & there have you all to myself. And I may do it some day."

He wrote too that shooting had finally begun on *Delicious* but that his supervision would be confined to telephone conversations with Sheehan and company. And finally on September 5, 1931, he told Rosamond that "Ira & I have been working on a George Kaufman book—a satire on 'Politics & Love'—called Of Thee I Sing. It is most amusing & we are looking forward to writing a score for it."

II

During the summer Sam Harris finally raised the backing for the show and Kaufman and Ryskind had come up with a libretto. It has been reported that they went to Atlantic City, holed up in a hotel and sent the Gershwins a complete first act within sixteen days.

The irreverent libretto, in the words of theater historian Stanley Green, "Sharply and deftly skewered . . . such institutions as political conventions and campaigns, beauty pageants, marriage, the Vice-Presidency, the Supreme Court, foreign affairs and motherhood."

The book is peopled with vulgar, scheming, unprincipled characters, i.e., politicians. It is riddled with gags, some right out of the Catskill Borscht Belt (a chambermaid enters a smoke-filled room with towels over her arm and announces, "I brought some towels. I'm just going to the bathroom." One of the politicos answers with, "First door to the left").

The political stereotyping, while broad, with often incisive. This was particularly evident in the character of the Vice President, Throttlebottom, in an endearing portrayal by Victor Moore as he suffers with blundering innocence, general uselessness, exploitation by his own party members and anonymity (he is denied a card at the Library of Congress because, though he is Vice President, no one knows who he is).

Kaufman's sour view of love and marriage is evident in the party's selection of love as the platform for their campaign. The decision is made in the smoke-filled room. When the politicians are stuck for the theme of their campaign, someone asks the chambermaid what is most important in life to her. After money, she tells them, love. They have their platform—and proceed to cheapen it further by holding a beauty pageant in Atlantic City to select the First Lady for their candidate, John P. Wintergreen, in a portrayal based on the slick James Walker, Mayor of New York, who was then in deep trouble. Wintergreen, however, betrays his own committee when he decides to marry his new secretary instead. The reason, he explains, is that she bakes superior corn muffins. This brings on international complications with France, for the pageant winner was one "Diana Devereaux," technically French (though she speaks with a lush magnolia-laden Southern accent), because she is the "Illegitimate Daughter," and a direct descendant of Napoleon. The crisis deepens later when the French Ambassador learns that the President's wife is about to become the mother of twins (the joke here is that France was then troubled by a low birth rate, part of the legacy of the First World War), which nearly leads to war.

An attempt is made to impeach Wintergreen, but all is saved by the birth of the twins; never in history had a father been impeached. The diplomatic problem is resolved when Throttlebottom marries Diana Devereaux in compliance with the Constitution: if the President cannot fulfill his obligations, they become the responsibility of the Vice President.

Both libretto and score have been—since the beginning—compared to the Gilbert and Sullivan operettas, with some justification. The songs, and the choral passages are particularly similar. Gershwin even quotes from *The Pirates of Penzance* ("The Pirates' Chorus," known better today in an adaptation, "Hail, Hail, the Gang's All Here") in his sprightly overture.

It is unlikely, however, that even Gilbert could have come up with as scathing a book, a fusion of jaundiced realism and Marxian (the brothers, that is) zany surrealism.

Unlike the scores of the twenties, *Of Thee I Sing* was not studded with planted (or hoped-for) hits. Such songs as "Of Thee I Sing," "Love Is Sweeping the Country" and "Who Cares?" have achieved out-of-show popularity, but equally distinguished songs have not. There was little demand for such a song, a near aria, as "I'm About to Be a Mother," lovely waltz though it was decidedly not for radio exposure. Another soaring melodic invention is the satiric interruption of the presidential wedding by the jilted Diana, "I was the most beautiful blossom in all the southland." A mere three bars, it might have readily served as the theme for an impressive song. The Gershwins elected to set a unique libretto to music, not to write song hits; what they did accomplish was a hit operetta. The entire score pulsates with rhythmic rhymes carrying the plot along. It breaks out in melodious celebration of dimpled knees, working from nine to five, kissing one's former girlfriends good-bye—all fitting seamlessly into the book. The humor and lilt of the songs render the show's cynicism as well as the venality and political shallowness of the characters less obnoxious.

On the subject of love, Ira Gershwin had this to say about it and Kaufman. They were in Boston for the tryout of *Of Thee I Sing*.

"Funny thing about Kaufman," Ira has written. "It's very funny, considering he did so many musicals—he hated music, you know. I remember standing at a performance of *Of Thee I Sing* . . . George and I and Kaufman. Kaufman turned to George and said, 'How do you account for the success of this thing?' "

Gershwin replied, "George, you don't like to be sentimental. You hate love, and so forth. But the people *believe* that the President of the United States, even though he's going to be impeached, is *not* going to give up the girl he loves."

Ira Gershwin concluded: "But Kaufman could not understand that. He was very cynical about those things. But, God knows, he was a clever craftsman."

It was in Boston that they realized that, despite the acrid tone of the libretto, they had a hit. The tryout began there on December 8. Until curtain time Kaufman, ever the pessimist, was sure *Of Thee I Sing* would go the way of the first *Strike Up the Band*. He was wrong. The *Transcript's* H. T. Parker, a true Bostonian, anointed it with the highest possible praise by noting that the operetta ". . . rejects all things Broadwayish . . ."

When the show left for New York, scheduled to premiere there the day after Christmas, the Boston *Herald* objected in the editorial page: "The reviewers were so flattering about the play and it was advertised so effectively by those who had been delighted by it that all seats were sold out for every performance several days before it left town," thus depriving Bostonians in the "hundreds, perhaps thousands, who would have liked to see it but were unable to get tickets." That kind of word quickly spread to Manhattan.

The reception convinced Kaufman, who suggested that Ira buy into the venture. He was sure that producer Harris would be willing to sell him a 5 percent interest for only twenty-five hundred dollars. Ira agreed, but like so many of his countrymen at the moment, he was short of funds, victim of the Crash. "So," he told interviewer Max Wilk years later, "I borrowed [the money] from my brother George and I got five percent of *Of Thee I Sing*. I was able to pay George back in a few months because I eventually got $11,000 from my little $2,500 investment!"

Gershwin once again conducted the opening night performance (December 26, 1931) at the Music Box in New York, in place of the regular conductor Charles Previn (uncle of conductor-pianist André Previn). The reception was even more enthusiastic than in Boston. George Jean

Nathan proclaimed *Of Thee I Sing* "a landmark in American satirical musical comedy . . ." Brooks Atkinson, in the *Times,* praised virtually everyone connected with the enterprise, especially that night's composer-conductor.

"Best of all," he wrote, "there is Mr. Gershwin's score. Whether it is satire, wit, doggerel or fantasy, Mr. Gershwin pours music out in full measure, and in many voices. Although the book is lively, Mr. Gershwin is exuberant. He not only has ideas but enthusiasm. He amplifies the show. Satire in the sharp, chill, biting vein of today needs the warmth of Victor Moore's fooling and the virtuosity of Mr. Gershwin's music. Without them *Of Thee I Sing* would be the best topical travesty our musical stage has created. With them it has the depth of artistry and the glow and pathos of comedy that are needed in the book."

Gershwin ascribed the operetta's success simply to the fact that it was "one of those rare shows in which everything clicked . . ." though he admitted that it was the "one show that I'm more proud of than any I have written."

It was also his most successful: a run of 441 performances, and a second company that began its profitable tour in Chicago. The libretto and lyrics were awarded the Pulitzer Prize in the drama category.

Such acclaim and success attracted trouble: the France-America Society, offended by the caricature of the Ambassador, the acute references to unpaid war debts and "the Illegitimate Daughter," demanded revisions. Kaufman's rejoinder was to invite them to submit equally amusing situations and dialogue; he would be happy to fit them into the script. They were not heard from again.

A more serious complaint was filed by one Walter Lowenfeld who accused all concerned with plagiarism and sued. Lowenfeld claimed that, in February 1930, he had copyrighted a revue, also a political satire with music. On December 28, 1932, Judge John Woolsey, U.S. District Court, finally dismissed the case, and like the France-America Society, Lowenfeld was not heard from again.

III

When the new year, 1932, dawned, Gershwin could look ahead knowing he had another "hit under his belt," and—finally—to the first performance of his *Second Rhapsody.*

This rhapsody is an anomaly among Gershwin's works; while its abbreviated form was heard in *Delicious,* the composition he ultimately completed on May 23, 1931, was not immediately grabbed up by an enterprising conductor. Word about his activities got around however. Some time in the spring, as he worked on the orchestration, his friend Samuel Chotzinoff, then writing for the *Post,* arranged to introduce him to Arturo Toscanini, then principal conductor of the recently formed (1928) Philharmonic-Symphony Society of New York (a merger of the Philharmonic Society of New York and the New York Symphony Orchestra). While Toscanini was regarded as a great conductor, he was not noted for his advocacy of contemporary, let alone American, music.

One evening Toscanini had dinner with the Chotzinoffs; the critic suggested that the maestro might perhaps be interested in meeting the young American composer. Toscanini acceded, and Chotzinoff called Gershwin, who arrived with friends, among them Oscar Levant, now a regular in the Gershwin entourage who frequently joined Gershwin in two-piano performances of Gershwin works, including the *Second Rhapsody.*

Gershwin was honored to meet the great conductor, though disconcerted to learn that Toscanini was totally unfamiliar with his work. "Imagine," he said of this meeting later, "a man living in the last seven years—being connected with music—and never hearing the *Rhapsody in Blue.*"

Gershwin, with Levant's assistance, proceeded to enlighten the maestro—to what appeared to be the older man's delight. They played both rhapsodies and Toscanini expressed his admiration but did not offer to program either. William S. Paley, founder of the Columbia Broadcasting Symphony, had heard Gershwin perform the *Second Rhapsody* at a party and was so impressed that he also offered to speak to Toscanini about launching the new composition. Nothing came of that either; it was simply not Toscanini's kind of music; he never programmed any Gershwin during the composer's lifetime. Gershwin's only memento of his encounter with Toscanini was a large, boldly signed photo portrait which he had framed.

The first performance of the *Second Rhapsody* took place in Symphony Hall, Boston, January 29, 1932, under the baton of Serge Koussevitzky. Gershwin had met the adventurous conductor of the Boston Symphony during the Boston tryout of *Of Thee I Sing.* As early as October 1929 Koussevitzky had approached Gershwin to compose a work for the Symphony in celebration of its fiftieth anniversary. Through Vernon Duke (Dukelsky in Boston) the conductor had heard that Gershwin wished to hear a Koussevitzky performance of one of his works. During the celebration period (1930–31), Koussevitzky was anxious to program special, newly commissioned works rather than already performed compositions. Gershwin at the time was too occupied with

Strike Up the Band to comply. (The best-known of these anniversary pieces and a Gershwin favorite was Stravinsky's *Symphony of Psalms.)*

Though the festal season had passed, the subject of a new Gershwin work came up in Boston in December of 1931, and it was agreed that Gershwin would return the following month to appear as piano soloist with the Boston Symphony. Eight months after its completion, the *Second Rhapsody* was given its first public performance in Symphony Hall, Boston, January 29, 1932 (followed by its New York premiere on February 5).

The reception in both cities was perplexing; while the critical consensus agreed with Gershwin's own perception that the rhapsody represented a forward step in his growth as a composer, they found it less spontaneous, less original than the *Rhapsody in Blue.* There was general praise for the orchestration and form, but some critics suggested that it was little more than an uninspired reworking of the first rhapsody.

Still the Gershwin name was good box office, as before. There was standing room only at Carnegie Hall when he appeared as soloist, with Koussevitzky conducting. The audience responded enthusiastically and he was called back to the stage for extra bows. But unlike the *Rhapsody in Blue* and *An American in Paris,* the *Second Rhapsody* did not become an immediate repertory piece. Like the *Concerto in F* it has taken time (even longer in fact); its frequent performances and several recordings (most, unfortunately, with a doctored score; of this, more later) are all quite recent.

Some critics waxed nostalgic, longing for the jazzy romanticism of the twenties; the rhapsody did not provide that. The orchestration was more studied, less effervescent, than that of *Rhapsody in Blue;* one reviewer found it "generally too thick." Another, Olin Downes, found it "too long for its material," a fair criticism. In expanding the rhapsody, Gershwin tended toward attenuation of the two main themes—the rivet motif and the broad, not quite bluesy "Brahmsian melody," as he called it. And yet, the *Second Rhapsody* is a fascinating composition; it is Gershwin around the corner. He had left the twenties; the self-styled "modern romantic" created a work that is more modern than romantic.

Its Gershwinisms are set with harsh overtones carried along by an insistent percussive motion interspersed with reflective quiet moments and the slow ("Brahmsian") section. It is a restless, even somewhat disturbing composition reflecting Gershwin's Manhattan (as seen through the eyes of the film's lonely immigrant). Despite his saying he had used the film's score merely as a starting point to write "a piece of music without a program," the atmospheric touches evoke the film's balletic sequence in which at times the city exudes a menacing air. In

Art Deco-like portrait of George Gershwin by an unknown photographer, c. 1930. (Humanities Research Center, University of Texas, Austin)

The *Rhapsody in Blue* sequence from the film *The King of Jazz* (1930). The entire Whiteman band covers the piano top; four pianists are at the keyboard. The piano on the soundtrack was played by Whiteman's pianist, Roy Bargy. (The Whiteman Collection, Williams College, Courtesy of Carl Johnson)

George and Ira in the ground floor of the Gershwin house on West 103rd Street with a tennis table behind them, c. 1930, while working on *Girl Crazy*. (Gershwin Collection)

Scene from *Girl Crazy;* Ethel Merman, in her Broadway debut, with chorus; the song is "I Got Rhythm." (White Photo)

Ginger Rogers and the Foursome, *Girl Crazy* (1930). The Foursome sang "I'm Bidin' My Time" all through the show. Ginger Rogers sang "But Not for Me" and "Embraceable You," among other songs. (White Photo)

When the Gershwins went to Hollywood late in 1930, they rented a house in Beverly Hills; Gershwin enjoyed telling people that Greta Garbo had once lived there. (Gershwin Collection)

Ira, George and Guy Bolton, who collaborated with Sonya Levien on the screenplay for the first Gershwin film musical, *Delicious*. (Gershwin Collection)

Janet Gaynor and Charles Farrell, a popular screen team at the time, were the stars of *Delicious*, one of their least successful films. (Gershwin Collection)

Scene from the Pulitzer Prize winning *Of Thee I Sing* (1931), (the first Pulitzer for a musical). "Mary Turner" (Lois Moran) has just promised to marry "John P. Wintergreen" (William Gaxton) *if* he is elected President of the United States. Wintergreen is running on the Love ticket, of course. (Gershwin Collection)

Boston, January 29, 1932, with conductor Serge Koussevitzky for the premiere of the *Second Rhapsody,* Gershwin's expansion of the music composed for the orchestral (with piano) sequence in *Delicious.* (Gershwin Collection)

At a musical-theater gathering with writer Sigmund Spaeth (standing) and producer Daniel Frohman. (Gershwin Collection)

On the terrace of the Gershwin penthouses at 33 Riverside Drive, where the brothers lived in adjoining apartments. The young woman is film actress Florence Rice, daughter of sportswriter Grantland Rice. (Gershwin Collection)

Inside Gershwin's penthouse with William Daly, pl ning an All-Gershwin Concert, the first, at Lewis Stadium, August 1932. At this concert the *Cuban O ture* (then called *Rumba)* was introduced. (Gersh Collection)

After an intense period of work, Gershwin took time out, often in Florida, where he went deep-sea fishing (not one of his favorite "sports"), golfed (a favorite) or sat around waiting for good weather. (Gershwin Collection)

Rehearsing for a broadcast of his radio show, "Music by Gershwin," in 1934. The program began as a fifteen-minute, twice-a-week feature on NBC; after a summer break it returned as a half-hour Sunday show weekly on CBS. (Gershwin Collection)

Gershwin's-guest on his new half-hour series on CBS was his friend, and his brother's collaborator, Harold Arlen. This occurred on Sunday, September 30, 1934, four days after Gershwin's thirty-sixth birthday. (Gershwin Collection)

Kay Swift (in a photograph by Gershwin) helped him during the composition of *Porgy and Bess,* playing over passages, discussing the work, making copies, etc. (Gershwin Collection)

one section there is an unsettling blend of brass and woodwinds accompanied by *misterioso* flickers from the flute, or xylophone or woodblocks (it would be interesting to know what Gershwin had in mind at this point—he may have simply been playing with the orchestra). Another passage is martial, as the piano plays to an accompaniment of side drums. The *Second Rhapsody* is not a soothing, dreamy work to hear while holding hands. This is not to imply that there is some deep message embedded in the *Second Rhapsody,* but it is a revelation of the darker side of Gershwin.

What were other contemporary American composers doing around the time Gershwin composed this rhapsody? Howard Hanson, who had received a Boston Symphony Anniversary commission fulfilled it with his aptly named "Romantic Symphony" (his second). Aaron Copland submitted the uncompromising *Symphonic Ode,* a little late for the anniversary season (its premiere took place in Boston a month after Gershwin's *Second Rhapsody).* Around this time Randall Thompson produced his Second Symphony, a fine work suffused with the melancholy of the Depression. The unpredictable Virgil Thomson also composed his Second Symphony, an orchestration of his first Piano Sonata. Roy Harris was just beginning his symphonic career (which would reach its high point with his Third Symphony in 1939) with the *Symphony 1933.*

About the only thing these compositions have in common is that they were written by American composers—and, in most instances (excepting Thomson and Thompson), for Koussevitzky. With the *Second Rhapsody* Gershwin joined their company as a maturing craftsman and a master of the orchestra with a composition that, like many of theirs, did not win instant popularity. No composer sets out to write an unpopular work; but some compositions need time for assimilation and appreciation.

IV

The *Second Rhapsody* was not much appreciated in 1932; it has since been rediscovered in its two-piano version (most notably by the two-piano team Frances Veri and Michael Jamanis) and the orchestra-with-piano version, this last unfortunately and unaccountably, as the score reads, "Arranged by Robert McBride." Only Gershwin's not-too-well-recorded rehearsal and the Oscar Levant–Morton Gould performance, dating back to the pre-longplaying fifties, preserve the authentic orchestration. So does a 1985 recording by Michael Tilson Thomas, which lacks the Gershwin touch, however (recordings are covered more fully in the discography). All other currently available recordings and performances of the *Second Rhapsody,* have been tampered with.

After Gershwin's death, his publisher's music editor, Frank Campbell-Watson, took it upon himself to revise (by which he meant improve) the concert works with, as he claimed, Gershwin's approval and cooperation.

This is hard to swallow, considering how many times Gershwin performed these compositions under all possible conditions: in concert halls of all description, in outdoor stadiums, in radio studios. It is inconceivable that he did not make his own adjustments at the time. Campbell-Watson, who regarded Gershwin as "a great man who had his faults" (he never fully explained, at least to one interviewer, whether these "faults" were professional or personal), himself tampered with the *Concerto in F* and *An American in Paris.* (Since Ferde Grofé was still around, Campbell-Watson kept his hands off the *Rhapsody in Blue,* though he lusted to fix that too.) Gershwin, incidentally, told an interviewer that he once considered reorchestrating the *Rhapsody,* but decided to stay with Grofé's Whiteman "jazz band" version and the one for symphony orchestra, also by Grofé.

Campbell-Watson assigned the *Second Rhapsody* to McBride and the *Variations on "I Got Rhythm"* to William C. Schoenfeld. Curiously, he left the *Cuban Overture* alone, erroneously calling it the "Rumba Rhapsody." The published orchestral score credits no revisionist, yet he claimed that this work "required more 'housecleaning' than anything else." This was accomplished in "the 'short' period of a year." He neglected to define housecleaning—perhaps this meant catching slips or mistakes in the score and parts. Why it would require a year is another question; also, the work had been performed frequently during Gershwin's lifetime, at its Lewisohn Stadium premiere, on his radio show and he himself conducted it at a concert in the Metropolitan Opera House. Why a year's "housecleaning"?

"The *Second Rhapsody* (or 'Rhapsody in Rivets') presented a tough problem," Campbell-Watson wrote in 1953. "The score was not completely finished. (From what then had Gershwin and Koussevitzky performed in Boston and New York? And Gershwin and Albert Coates at Lewisohn Stadium later that year? And Oscar Levant in concert and on records?)

"It was temporary and in its existing form there were but few pianists and orchestras close enough to the work to negotiate the hurdles offered by many structural barbed wire fences. The task of revision, leaving the solo piano part intact, was effected by Robert McBride, who followed the preconceived plan with meticulous care and understanding." Another curious statement. Oscar Levant was currently active—and, in fact, performed the rhapsody at the Stadium with conductor Alexander Smallens around this time. Roy Bargy had no problems with the work; as for the orchestras, the Boston Symphony and the New York Philharmonic were familiar with the work. What the "preconceived plan" was is another mystery.

The result, like all of Campbell-Watson's "recasting and 'revoicing' [as he called it] each score" is pointless. His rationale was an inexactitude, to say the least. "As is well known, the composer scored many of his masterpieces for jazz band or heterogeneous instrumental groups which later made it impossible to satisfy the ever increasing performance demands by symphony orchestras." All untrue, even the *Rhapsody in Blue* is not scored for a true jazz band; all other orchestral works, except the *Variations on "I Got Rhythm"*, are scored for full symphony orchestra—by Gershwin.

In his startlingly self-serving and not especially veracious "Preamble," written as an introduction to the published score of the *Variations,* Campbell-Watson makes another peculiar statement: "I have said that the composer and I worked out all of the details involved in these revisions. Actually there were three of us. The third member was responsible for an important decision—his name was Tinker, a wire-haired fox terrier [a gift from Kay Swift]." That decision was that the orchestration of *Rhapsody in Blue,* though "far from ideal," would not be touched. He says that Gershwin brought this up, but that he convinced the composer that the "work belonged to the world *as it stood."* He also claimed that even before their discussion he had decided that this "first successful bridge from Tin Pan Alley to Carnegie Hall" should "remain exactly as it was."

"While struggling to give voice to my various arguments and making a quick prayer that George might agree," he wrote, "Tinker sensed something of unusual importance was about to be decided. He gave me a belligerent look of a harassed prosecuting attorney, and snapped in the most un-canine sound I ever heard a clearly articulated 'WELL?' We both laughed. The day was saved! I told George how I felt about the *Rhapsody in Blue* in every detail. He merely gave me one of his rare smiles and took Tinker out for a stroll—or a conference. I never knew."

Campbell-Watson was a classically trained musician, organist and not very successful composer. He had studied with Karl Straube, the celebrated German organist, and composer Max Reger in Leipzig. Author of several theoretical works on music, he regarded Gershwin with condecension. Luckily all of Gershwin's original manuscripts, carefully and handsomely bound, are stored in the Music Division of the Library of Congress; these contain whatever revisions he himself made or authorized. To restore them to their original state would be no large undertaking.

V

With *Of Thee I Sing* well on its way at the Music Box and the launching of the *Second Rhapsody,* Gershwin felt he had earned a rest; if the early weeks of 1931 had made him restive because of the comparative inactivity, the year closed and the next began with the pressures and excitement that nurtured his temperament. With the rhapsody premiered, he agreed to join some of his friends for a couple of weeks in Cuba; none, interestingly, was musical. As Oscar Levant noted, with a hint of rebuke, "He had a curious partiality for successful, well-to-do people of the stockbroker type, with whom he could play golf and go on weekends, but there were always other people around who were attracted by his enormous vitality, the worth and genuineness of his accomplishments."

In a cold mid-February, Gershwin shipped out for Havana, accompanied by financier Everett Jacobs (who frequently invested in musicals), Adam Gimbel (of the department store family), Daniel Silverberg and publisher Bennett Cerf. From Havana George wired broker Emil Mosbacher, then at his Palm Beach winter home, to join them, which he did. Like boys on the town, they spent their days golfing or at the race track and their nights nightclubbing. (Gershwin did not keep up with "the boys" in drinking; he was not, however, a teetotaler, as recorded by one interviewer with an affinity for trivia: "He likes ice cream sodas and Scotch highballs, with a casual cocktail on the side, but rarely touches loganberry juice. Don Sebastians are his favorite cigar.")

According to Mosbacher and Cerf, Gershwin evinced a decided interest in Cuban beauties other than cigars. As Mosbacher remembered, both Gershwin and Cerf "were chasing after the same girl."

The composer's most humbling moment of the trip occurred when he encountered a "lovely Cuban miss" and reproached her for standing him up for a lunch date. Her reply, according to Cerf was, "Oh, I meant to phone and tell you, but do you know something? I simply couldn't think of your name."

"George," Cerf gleefully reported, "didn't recover for days."

Cerf imagined that the inspiration for Gershwin's next composition could be traced to a small crisis he inadvertently caused. "In Havana," the publisher remembered, "a sixteen-piece rhumba band serenaded him en masse at four in the morning outside his room at the old Almendares Hotel. Several outraged patrons left the hotel the next morning.

"George was so flattered that he promised to write a rhumba of his own."

Gershwin's recollections of stay was slightly different. "I spent two hysterical weeks in Havana," he wrote Pallay soon after his return, "where no sleep was had, but the quantity and quality of fun made up for that . . .

"Cuba was most interesting, especially for its small dance orchestras, who play most intricate rhythms most naturally. I hope to go back every winter, if it is possible, as the warm climate seems to be just the thing my system requires for relaxing purposes." Before the merrymakers returned to New York, Gershwin sought out some authentic Cuban instruments: a bongo drum, gourd, maracas and claves (sticks) he proposed to work into a future composition.

Disappointed on his return to find that Aarons and Freedley were floundering around for a musical book, he returned to an idea he had set aside five years before. On March 29, 1932, he again wrote to DuBose Heyward reviving his idea of turning *Porgy* into an opera. Still restless, even after Havana and its "relaxations," he advised Heyward that he was planning to "go abroad" and hoped they might meet there. Heyward, severely hit by the Depression, was not planning a trip to Europe, though in his reply he expressed his pleasure in Gershwin's return to the idea and looked forward to their collaboration.

Gershwin's reply was delayed for more than a month. Between April 12 (the date of Heyward's letter) and May 20 (when Gershwin finally wrote), all considerations of an opera and any trips were overshadowed by the death of his father.

By early April it was obvious that Morris Gershwin was seriously ill. His children visited him in the Gershwin suite in the Hotel Broadmoor; Frances Godowsky came in from Rochester. She learned that her father was terminally ill with lymphatic leukemia. Pop Gershwin, to the end was as George had described him, "the happy philosopher" who "goes along uncomplainingly, taking things as they come."

Frances found him in the bedroom, from time to time breathing with the help of an oxygen mask, very thin, and, she also found, "objective" about the fact of death. When Rose entered, he removed the mask for a moment to say, "Well, Rose, when you marry again, will you marry a tall man?" (Rose had often let it be known that she preferred tall men, which Morris was not.) An hour later, on May 14, 1932, Morris Gershwin died. Rose never remarried.

Six days after his father's death, which affected him deeply, Gershwin wrote to Heyward. There is no mention of Morris, or explanation for the gap. He told Heyward that he was happy to learn that "the operatic rights to *Porgy* are free and clear." Then, to Heyward's consternation, told him that he could not begin work on the opera before January of the next year. The rest of 1932 was fully booked. He was scheduled for a Lewisohn Stadium All-Gershwin Concert (the first) in August; for that special occasion he planned to write his promised rumba.

In addition, Aarons and Freedley had come up with a book spoofing psychiatry entitled *Pardon My English.* The Gershwins were not impressed and tried to beg off. Aarons beseeched them: he had promised his backers the Gershwins. No Gershwins, no show—and he would be finished on Broadway. Out of loyalty to Aarons (Freedley was not at first involved with the production), the Gershwins agreed to do the show.

Further, because of the extraordinary success of *Of Thee I Sing,* then in its sixth month, Sam Harris was seriously talking about a sequel. What with a new composition and two musicals in the offing, Gershwin was forced to postpone work on *Porgy.* The postponement stretched out to two years, not the eight months he had initially predicted.

12

Song Book

Early in May of 1932, a handsome limited edition of *George Gershwin's Song Book* was published by Bennett Cerf's Random House. Illustrated by Constantin Alajalov's interpretive drawings illustrating the eighteen songs in the collection, it was dedicated to Kay Swift. The special edition was limited to three hundred copies, was signed by Gershwin and Alajalov (an admired *New Yorker* illustrator) and included the never-before-published early party song "Mischa, Yascha, Toscha, Sascha."

The main feature of the book was the special arrangements Gershwin had made of each song, ranging chronologically from 1919 ("Swanee") to 1932 ("Who Cares?" from *Of Thee I Sing*). Each of the songs appeared in its original printed form after which came Gershwin's variation, or as he called them, "transcriptions."

In his introduction Gershwin wrote that "America, in the last twenty years, has become a veritable hot-bed of popular music. In the same fruitful period it has mothered some of the best music to be found in the musical comedy of the time." He touched briefly on the history of popular song in America, the contribution of the minstrel show and early "popular composers, not to speak of the faint beginnings of jazz bands and Tin Pan Alley methods long before the pavement of Tin Pan Alley was laid."

He suggested that "American popular music, since its origin, has been steadily gaining in originality; today it may truly lay claim to being the most vital of contemporary popular music. Unfortunately, however, most songs die at an early age and are soon completely forgotten by the selfsame public that once sang them with such gusto. The reason for this is that they are sung and played too much when they are alive, and cannot stand the strain of their very popularity." This he attributed to phonograph records and especially radio.

"When the publishers asked me to gather a group of my songs for publication I took up the idea enthusiastically, because I thought that this might be a means of prolonging their life."

He explained the transcriptions: "Playing my songs as frequently as I do at private parties, I have naturally been led to compose various variations upon them, and to indulge the desire for complication and variety that every composer feels when he manipulates the same material over and over again. It was this habit of mine that led to the original suggestion to publish a group of songs not only in the simplified arrangements that the public knew, but also in the variations that I had devised."

He rationalized the music publisher's point of view: "Sheet music, as ordinarily printed for mass sales, is arranged with an eye to simplicity. The publishers cannot be blamed for getting out simplified versions of songs, since the majority of the purchasers of popular music are little girls with little hands, who have not progressed very far in their study of the piano."

He credits some of his "predecessors" for the evolution of his own piano style: Mike Bernard, Les Copeland, Lucky Roberts, Zez Confrey and Ohman and Arden, among others. "There was the habit of Les Copeland," he wrote, "had of thumping his left hand onto a blurred group of notes, from which he would slide into a regular chord; it made a rather interesting pulse in the bass, a sort of happy-go-lucky *sforzando* effect. Then there was Bernard's habit of playing the melody in the left hand, while he wove a filigree of counterpoint with the right; for a time this was all the rage, as it sounded pretty well to the ears not accustomed to the higher musical processes. Confrey's contribution has been of a more permanent nature, as some of his piano figures found their way into serious American composition . . .

"As American popular song has grown richer in harmony and rhythm, so has the player grown more subtle and incisive in his performance of it."

Gershwin offered a "hint: To play American popular music most effectively one must guard against the natural tendency to make too frequent use of the sustaining pedal. Our study of the great romantic composers has trained us in the method of the *legato,* whereas our popular music asks for *staccato* effects, for an almost stenciled style. The rhythms of American popular music are more or le*s brittle; they should be made to snap, and at times to cackle. The more sharply the music is played, the more effective it sounds.

"Most pianists with classical training fail lamentably in the playing of our ragtime or jazz because they use the pedaling of Chopin when interpreting the blues of Handy. The romantic touch is very good in a sentimental ballad, but in a tune of strict tempo it is somewhat out of place."

The excitement over the publication of the special edition of the *Song Book* was blunted by the death of Morris Gershwin less than two weeks later. A standard edition was released by Simon and Schuster later in the year, in time for Gershwin's thirty-fourth birthday. It came complete with the illustrations but without "Mischa, Yascha . . ."

Gershwin's introduction is his own. Initially, Goldberg had ghosted it; Gershwin, though he found it "very good," believed it "should be of a much more personal—rather than technical—nature. And so, I wonder if it would not be a good idea for me to sit down and dash off an Introduction, and then show it to you, for criticism."

I

Around this time, in the spring of 1932, Gershwin began to study with theorist-teacher Joseph Schillinger, who had come to New York from Russia in 1928, and taught at the New School for Social Research and at Columbia University's Teachers College (mathematics, music, fine arts). By 1932 he had made himself a reputation as one of New York's most cerebral teachers.

How Gershwin found him goes back a few years. According to a former music critic with Russian friends, David Platt, Gershwin first heard of Schillinger some time late in 1929. Platt related how the celebrated Russian composer Alexander Glazunov, then in his early sixties, had come to the United States as a guest conductor. After an appearance in Detroit he came to New York, where he again met a former colleague, composer-pianist Vladimir Drozdoff, who had been a professor of music under Glazunov before emigrating to the United States in the early twenties.

Glazunov expressed an interest in hearing a performance of the *Rhapsody in Blue,* programmed by the Philharmonic, with Gershwin at the piano and Ernest Schelling conducting. He asked Drozdoff to accompany him as interpreter.

He was one of a group who attended the concert, including Mrs. Schelling, the conductor's wife. After the performance of the *Rhapsody,* Mrs. Schelling asked Glazunov what he thought of it.

The very conservative symphonist, according to Drozdoff, replied, "It's part human and part animal."

The group then assembled in the Green Room to meet Gershwin. "That such an eminent composer had come to listen to his *Rhapsody* brought a 'radiant smile' to Gershwin's face. 'Please tell him,' he said to Drozdoff, 'it has been the dream of my life to go to Russia to study orchestration under him' [actually Glazunov was then living in Paris, arriving there after Gershwin's 1928 visit]. Glazunov's response was to shrug his shoulders coldly: 'He wants to study orchestration but he hasn't the slightest knowledge of counterpoint,' he whispered to Drozdoff in Russian. For what seemed a long time neither composer spoke. Finally, Glazunov himself broke the ice. Summoning all the English he knew, he slowly but precisely told Gershwin the bitter truth that he lacked theory—that that defect had to be remedied before he could begin to think of studying orchestration.

"By the end of their backstage meeting it was obvious that Gershwin was feeling pretty low. Nevertheless, overnight apparently, his crest-fallen mood had changed. Two days later a phone call from Glazunov to Drozdoff revealed that the American composer, much to their surprise, had called the Russian composer at his hotel to tell him how grateful he was for Glazunov's not pulling his punches. Gershwin asked the older man to recommend a teacher closer to home. Drozdoff's suggestion was Joseph Schillinger."

(Other sources, including Schillinger himself, maintain that it was another Russian emigré, violinist-composer Joseph Achron, who brought composer and teacher together. It is likely that both Drozdoff and Achron spoke of Schillinger with Gershwin, the former in 1929 and the latter in the early thirties. The Gershwin story abounds in claimants: who introduced him to whom, on whose piano he composed "Summertime" or the andante from the *Rhapsody in Blue,* etc. etc.)

The conversation between Platt and Drozdoff occurred some years later in the wake of the Moscow debut of *Porgy and Bess* (December 1955). Drozdoff's final comment was, "Though Gershwin was a very famous man even in the 1920s, he had the strength and wisdom that accepts criticism and goes on learning."

Gershwin studied with Schillinger from about the spring of 1932 until he left for California in the summer of 1936. According to Schillinger they met three times a week. He later claimed that when Gershwin came to him he was desperate, he felt he was written out and had begun to repeat himself. "Can you help me?" he is supposed to have pleaded.

"I replied in the affirmative," Schillinger wrote in his book *Kaleidophone,* published in 1940, intimating that once Gershwin saw some of the materials in this book he "became a sort of Alice in Wonderland." He is also supposed to have exclaimed, "You don't have to compose music any more—it's all there."

If he said that to Schillinger, there is no record of his repeating it to anyone else, though he spoke enthusiastically of what is now known as the "Schillinger System." Oscar Levant, also a Schillinger student around the same time, was not quite so enthralled. He found Schillinger's approach to be virtually "a reduction of all musical procedures, from the most formidable to the least imposing, to a mathematical system which he contracted to impart in a definite calendar period—a compositional equivalent of playing the piano in six easy lessons. Surprisingly enough this was thoroughly efficacious if taken with the considerable mixture of application that George contributed to the studies."

In short, the system was strong on technique, weak on originality (or that elusive thing, "inspiration"; if the gift is missing, not all the mathematics in the world is a substitute). Levant saw Gershwin's fascination with and enthusiasm for the Schillinger methodology as "but one reflection of George's broadening horizon about this time." The lessons were done on graph paper with such titles as "Rhythmic Groups Resulting from the Interference of Several Synchronized Periodicities" and "Groups with the Fractioning Around the Axis of Symmetry." What he learned technically from such studies about the application of complex contrapuntal devices in orchestration Gershwin applied in composing the works he wrote after he began working with Schillinger—the *Cuban Overture, Variations on "I Got Rhythm", Porgy and Bess,* and in his final show scores. However, Schillinger's claim that the opera was composed under his supervision is but another of the exaggerated allegations he made after the composer's death. Though Schillinger taught many well-known musicians—arrangers and orchestrators, mostly—none, including Schillinger himself, developed into a celebrated composer. Gershwin was Schillinger's most famous student and it is understandable that the teacher would claim some credit for that fame. All the claims, however, were made when Gershwin could no longer comment on them.

His first work, composed under the influence of the Schillinger system, was his experiment with the Cuban rumba and instruments.

II

He called it *Rumba* and worked out his piano version in July (not a two-piano version, but for a single piano and two pianists: this he tried

out during composition with either Kay Swift or Oscar Levant). According to the manuscript score, he began orchestrating on August 1
and finished on the ninth. Some of this work was done at the Mosbacher's home in Westchester to escape the summer heat. Kay Swift
would frequently visit to lend a couple of hands. Gershwin finished
eight days before the All-Gershwin Concert was scheduled. Of this
work musicologist Frank C. Campbell has written after a study of the
manuscript, "Gershwin may not have considered the work a major
effort, but from the rapidly written full score to the brilliant sounds of
its complex orchestra, it reveals a command of superb orchestral technique, now capable of choosing more consistently those materials that
express his own musical nature."

Levant accompanied Gershwin to a rehearsal in the afternoon before
the concert; the conductor was Albert Coates, who was English. On the
title page Gershwin instructed that the players of the four Cuban instruments "should be placed right in front of the conductor's stand," i.e.,
between the conductor and orchestra and visible to the audience, not
hidden in the percussion section. This was also good showmanship; in
1932 the instruments, as well as the rumba, were little known in the
United States.

The rhythms and the stretto passages (in which the orchestra plays
overlapping themes rapidly) in the coda (the section leading into the
close of the piece) presented problems to the conventionally trained
musicians. Coates lost his temper and scolded the orchestra, but with
Gershwin's guidance the work was in shape for the evening's performance.

That night, August 16, Gershwin later said, was "the most exciting
night I have ever had." The first All-Gershwin Concert was not only
sold out (some eighteen thousand attended), but thousands reportedly
were turned away. It went like this:

I.   *Of Thee I Sing,* overture
     William Daly, conductor
II. *Concerto in F*
     Oscar Levant, piano; Daly, conductor
III. *An American in Paris*
     Albert Coates, conductor
IV. *Rhapsody in Blue*
     Gershwin, piano; Daly, conductor
V.   "Wintergreen for President"
     Daly, conductor

VI. *Second Rhapsody* (first time at Stadium)
    Gershwin, piano; Coates, conductor
VII. *Rumba* (premiere)
    Coates, conductor
VIII. Medley of Popular Tunes (Arranged by Daly)
    "Fascinating Rhythm," "The Man I Love,"
    "Liza," "I Got Rhythm"

    Gershwin, piano; Daly conductor.

For the concert Gershwin prepared a sketchy analysis (which pretty much followed his initial outline of the *Rumba,* ten lines in pencil on a yellow sheet). The composition, he wrote, had been "inspired by a short visit to Havana . . ." and in it he had "endeavored to combine the Cuban rhythms with my original thematic material. The result is a symphonic ouverture which embodies the essence of the Cuban dance."

In his analysis Gershwin employs such technical terms as "three part contrapuntal episode," "developing canon in a contrapuntal manner," "climax based on an ostinato," etc. For all this, it is a straightforward easy-to-take (but not necessarily easy to play) little piece. Requiring about ten minutes' performance time, it is in Gershwin's typical fast-slow-fast form. His use of polytonality adds the spice of dissonance and his writing for the orchestra is sure. The slow middle theme, introduced by a solo clarinet, he marked "plaintively"; it is not as memorable as the slow melodies of the *Rhapsody in Blue, Concerto in F* and *An American in Paris.*

In *Rumba,* as in the *Second Rhapsody,* his writing is more spare, even austere. It didn't distress him that these latest compositions did not become immediately popular; they represented experimental explorations of new means of expression. Later he said of *Rumba* to Merle Armitage, a West Coast impresario, that he saw in it "a manner in which he wished to work in the future."

He celebrated the success of the first All-Gershwin Concert with a short vacation in the Adirondack Mountains. On his return on September 9, he found a letter from DuBose Heyward, informing him of a new twist in the continuing saga of *Porgy* (of which, more later). He continued working with Schillinger and agreed to participate in a benefit concert at the Metropolitan Opera House in November. It was this gesture that would lead to a flurry of disputation and acrimony.

III

The beneficiary was the Musicians' Symphony Orchestra, organized to provide work for two hundred musicians. In the first of a series of twenty Tuesday evening concerts, Gershwin and Bill Daly appeared as soloist-conductor and conductor. The first half of the program was devoted to Franck (the D Minor Symphony), conducted by the Hungarian-American conductor-violinist Sándor Harmati. After intermission Gershwin and Daly came on to present the *Concerto in F, An American in Paris* (Daly conducting), *Cuban Overture* (formerly *Rumba,* Gershwin conducting) and a suite programmed as *Four Tunes* for piano and orchestra (which Daly had prepared for the Stadium's All-Gershwin Concert in August and now conducted). It was this medley that led to heated exchanges in the press.

During rehearsals of *Four Tunes,* Daly stopped the orchestra and checked the score; he thought one of the instrumentalists had played something wrong. Peering at the score he was heard to say, "Did I write that there?"

The rhetorical comment perked up the ears of violinist-violist and sometime composer Allan Langley, who was obviously not a Gershwin fan. This galvanized him to produce an article for George Jean Nathan's *The American Spectator* entitled "The Gershwin Myth." In the short, vitriolic piece, Langley assailed Gershwin and his work, dismissing the concerto as disgusting, reviling the orchestrations of all Gershwin's concert pieces and implying that they were the work of others anyhow.

During the rehearsal, Langley claimed that "any member of the orchestra could testify that [Daly] knew far more about the score [of *An American in Paris]* than Gershwin.

"The point is," he concluded, "that no previous claimant to honors in symphonic composition has ever presented so much argument and so much controversy as to whether his work was his own or not."

Since Grofé orchestrated the *Rhapsody in Blue* in 1924, each new concert work incited insinuations in the "serious music" community that its true orchestrator was not Gershwin. This was especially true among those who considered themselves his betters—except in the enviable spheres of fame and fortune.

Langley had a good, solid, if conservative, musical background. Among his teachers at the New England Conservatory were George Whitefield Chadwick, Arthur Shepard and Daniel Gregory Mason. The last was especially upset by the "corruption" of American music by black jazz and the "insidiousness of the Jewish menace to our artistic integrity . . ." It is likely that Langley shared Mason's views. Since he found the concerto "disgusting," he was undoubtedly nettled by the Charleston rhythms, the bluesy harmonies and pianistic syncopations.

Gershwin's success and popularity contributed to Langley's indignation. In 1932 he was not too happy playing in the Musicians' Symphony Orchestra, whose program ran a line reading "Benefit of Unemployed Musicians," after a promising beginning with the Boston Symphony, and then a move to New York and the Philharmonic. (Langley, Gershwin and Daly had come together for the first time in public at the 1931 Lewisohn Stadium All-American Program, when Gershwin and Daly performed the *Rhapsody in Blue* and Fritz Reiner conducted Langley's orchestral *Waltz.)* Langley was envious and excitable (he died of a heart attack while traveling from New Jersey to New York in the Hudson tube).

Gershwin was accustomed to criticism, and he had grown used to the rumors about his orchestration (even some of his close friends were not aware that, from the *Concerto* on, he did his own). But Langley's allegations infuriated him (he even suggested that Gershwin had others write his music for him). Gershwin decided to sue and sought legal advice. Word got to Nathan, who offered Gershwin all the space in *The American Spectator* he wanted to rebut Langley's allegations.

"Why bother?" was Gershwin's reaction. Nathan thrived on controversy; charge and countercharge would only bolster the *American Spectator*'s circulation (It floundered three years later). A courtroom drama would prolong the issue and there was too much to do. In fact, Gershwin was then preoccupied with the Aaron-Freedley *Pardon My English,* which was in deep trouble.

It was his "Irish friend," Daly, who chose to set the record straight. Instead of writing for Nathan, he wrote a piece for the New York *Times,* whose circulation greatly exceeded that of Nathan's little magazine.

"Mr. Langley's asseverations," he wrote in the article entitled 'George Gershwin as Orchestrator,' "are of importance only through the fact that they are now published and are sent abroad in the world to influence those who have no means of checking up on the facts, and to give support to those who want to think that Gershwin is a myth.

"In fine, the fact is that I have never written one note of any of his compositions, or so much as orchestrated one whole bar of any of his concert works."

As to the insinuation that he knew *An American in Paris* better than its putative composer, Daly said, "I thank Mr. Langley for the compliment, but I neither wrote nor orchestrated the *American.* My only contribution consisted of a few suggestions about reinforcing the scoring here and there, and I'm not sure that Gershwin, probably with good reason, accepted them. But, then, Gershwin receives many such suggestions from his many friends to whom he always plays his various compositions, light or symphonic, while they are in the process of being written. Possibly Mr. Langley feels that we all get together (and we'd have to meet in Yankee Stadium) to write Mr. Gershwin's music for him.

"I would only be too happy to be known as the composer of *An American in Paris,* or any of Gershwin's works, or as the orchestrator of them. But, alas! I am by trade a conductor (and because Gershwin thinks I am a good one, especially for his music, maybe Mr. Langley has been thrown off the scent).

"It is true that I orchestrate many Gershwin numbers for the theatre; but so does Russell Bennett. And I have reduced some of his symphonic works for smaller orchestra for use on the radio. And it is true that we are close friends—to my great profit—and that I use that relationship to criticize. But that is far from the role that Mr. Langley suggests."

Daly saved the coup de grace for the conclusion: "I suppose I should resent the fact that Langley attributes Gershwin's work to me, since Langley finds all of it so bad. But fortunately for my amour propre, I have heard some of Langley's compositions.

"He really should stay away from ink and stick to his viola."

IV

Ten days after the provocative rehearsals at the Metropolitan Opera, Gershwin made his first appearance on the "Rudy Vallee Show," an excellent, adventurous radio program that featured scenes from current plays and musicals, important guests from the arts and the latest songs from films and theater.

When Vallee asked Gershwin what he was working on at the time (November 10, 1932), the composer told him that he and Ira were working on *Pardon My English* and that "the thing is already in rehearsal and we're trying to finish the score."

Vallee then asked the inevitable question: which came first, the words or the music? "Usually the music," Gershwin replied. "I hit on a new tune, play it for Ira and he hums it all over the place for a while till he gets an idea for a lyric. Then we work the thing out together."

When asked about influences, he immediately named Irving Berlin and Jerome Kern and said that he believed Kern's *Show Boat* score to be "the finest light opera achievement in the history of American music."

What he did not say was that *Pardon My English* was a troubled show; one good reason the score was unfinished was because its several assorted writers and directors introduced a mélange of changes. According to the printed music sheets and the program, Herbert Fields was credited (blamed might be the more appropriate word) with the book. But during the show's out-of-town tryout period (Philadelphia, Boston and Brooklyn) several play doctors were known to have left town, among them Morrie Ryskind and Jack McGowan. Georgie Hale is credited with staging the musical numbers but attempts at direction were made by George S. Kaufman, Ernst Lubitsch and Worthington Minor. Vinton Freedley also lent a hand and George Gershwin contributed an idea or two to the shambles.

"*Pardon My English* was a headache from start to finish," Ira Gershwin wrote in *Lyrics on Several Occasions.* He felt, because of the Depression, that they were lucky to be making a good living from *Of Thee I Sing.* There was unemployment, wrecked businesses and poor theater attendance. "In addition, I disliked enormously the central notion of the project—duo-personality or schizophrenia or whatever the protagonist's aberration was supposed to be; so why toil and moil for six months on something we didn't want or need?"

English musical-comedy star Jack Buchanan was signed to portray the gentleman-kleptomaniac. The comic idea was to get him involved with the daughter of the police commissioner of a German city (Dresden, according to the song "The Dresden Northwest Mounted"). After two weeks with the tottering show Buchanan bought his way out for a reputed several thousand dollars. He was replaced by George Givot, whose specialty was a Greek accent.

In the cast as the bumbling police commissioner was the popular comic Jack Pearl, radio's "Baron Munchausen," whose tall tales, when questioned by anyone, was challenged with catchphrase, "Vas you dere, Sharly?" His specialty was a German accent. To round out the international mishmash, there was bouncy, curvy, blond Lyda Roberti, whose specialty was a polyglot of Polish, German, and near-Hungarian. (The two Americans the commissioner mistakes for criminals, of course, sang and spoke in standard Broadway English). It is unlikely that in the history of the musical theater was a show more appropriately titled than *Pardon My English.*

"Opening night in New York (January 20, 1933)," Ira recalled, "I stood among a few standees, but only for twenty minutes. A bad cold and a lukewarm audience had me home by nine thirty." His brother too had a severe cold and passed up the opportunity to conduct the first-night performance; instead the regular conductor, Earl Busby, opened the show's brief run. The critics united in a total condemnation of it. Percy Hammond had good words for Pearl whose "comic sorceries changed the pasty book into what seemed to be gems of humorous bon mots and badinage."

That one good sentence did not help; *Pardon My English* had the double distinction of being the first musical of the year—and the first failure. It hobbled on for five weeks, closing on February 27, the date, too, of the Reichstag fire in Berlin. There is no connection between these two events, although it has been suggested that the setting—Hitler's New Germany—might have worked against the show.

This is unlikely; few Americans in 1933 realized the threat of Hitler and no one would have mistaken Jack Pearl for a Nazi. The trouble with *Pardon My English* was the disjointed book.

It was a disaster for Aarons and Freedley; both left town, Aarons fled to California (where he would work on musical films) and Freedley, who had undoubtedly been responsible for a good portion of the backing, left the country with creditors on his heels. This misbegotten musical finished one of the most productive, and often imaginative, producing teams of the musical theater. After the heat died down, Freedley returned to production with Cole Porter's *Anything Goes* (1934), the first of a series of successes, most of them with Porter scores. Dispirited and not very active, Aarons died in Beverly Hills in 1943 at the age of fifty-two.

Despite initial doubts about *Pardon My English,* the Gershwins did not stint on their score. There are twenty-one documented songs, of which fifteen remained in the show and seven were published. An eighth, "Tonight," was published in 1971 as the theme of the contrapuntal *Two Waltzes in C.* In the show it had a lyric, of course, but also served in an instrumental sequence. Gershwin and Kay Swift played this often on two pianos, first "Tonight," then a countermelody and then the two together (Ira referred to the piece as "Her Waltz, His Waltz, Their Waltz").

The Dresden locale gave Gershwin the opportunity to compose several waltzes, including the first-act opener, "In Three Quarter Time." There is a long, fine choral number, "Dancing in the Streets," unfortunately neglected as were virtually all choral pieces from Broadway of the period. Other neglected songs are the ballad "Where You Go I Go" and the rhythmic "I've Got to Be There."

Three songs have become favorites in nightclubs and recording studios: the mildly bawdy "The Lorelei" (who hoped to bite her "initials in a sailor's neck"), the strident "My Cousin in Milwaukee" (specially written for Lyda Roberti, who appears to have been celebrated for the peculiar pronunciation of "h" sounds; songs created for her inevitably employed the word "hot"—there are two in this song's chorus). The third song, "Isn't it a Pity," is the excellent example of what Ira Gershwin meant when he suggested that a good lyric should be "simple, colloquial, rhymed, conversational." The Gershwin melody is as lean as it is supple, perfectly attuned to the rhymed conversation.

Another superior lyric, though the song was eliminated somewhere along the road, is that for the satiric "Freud and Jung and Adler."

The quick failure of *Pardon My English* resulted in the score's being packed into cartons, stored in a warehouse and, while not actually lost, as was implied widely in newspapers, forgotten even by the Gershwins. [This score, and others by others, were recovered, if not rediscovered—for how is something found that was never lost? Even so, Ira was chary about letting the "rediscovered" songs be heard or in any way exploited. Through most of his last years he harbored the traditional view—almost a superstition—that if a show flopped, it was best to forget its songs. Though he was proud of the three known songs, he felt the others were better left forgotten. For years he refused to permit publication of the contrapuntal waltzes ("Hers, His, Theirs") because it was based on the song "Tonight." He feared that it would somehow be confused with the better-known Leonard Bernstein–Stephen Sondheim song of the same title from *West Side Story.*]

The litigation by the creditors that followed the expiration of *Pardon My English* contributed to the shambles. With the producers on the run, no one appears to have attended to the usual after-closing details. In the helter-skelter even the orchestrations (by William Daly, Adolph Deutsch and Robert Russell Bennett) were also misplaced. A pity indeed, for this show revealed George Gershwin's mastery of the waltz. Unfortunately, his next musical, endowed with one of his finest scores, would suffer the same fate as *Pardon My English.*

V

Soon after the closing of Aarons and Freedley's last musical Gershwin resumed discussions (but did no work) on the projected opera with DuBose Heyward, most of it by mail. His next assignment was the *Of Thee I Sing* sequel, *Let 'Em Eat Cake.* But before he began concentrated work on that, he moved out of his penthouse on Riverside Drive.

In the spring of 1933 he took a splendid duplex (of fourteen rooms) at

132 East Seventy-second Street, the ultimate bachelor apartment. It was tastefully decorated, spacious, with discreet lighting and even a trunk room.

It housed his by then extensive art collection—a modest gallery of modernity—which included a few Gershwins. A room was stocked with art materials. His musical workroom's central feature was the twin Steinways plus an ingenious self-designed desk. It was built to his own specifications with the work surface tilted just so and with a bar underneath as a footrest. It had special drawers for manuscript paper, sliding shelves and a pencil sharpener that disappeared when not in use.

The Ira Gershwins also left Riverside Drive and took an apartment directly across the street.

When a third piano, a Steinway grand (A-Ebony #275,916) was delivered on June 13, the furnishing of George's apartment was complete. It was his last Manhattan address; here he would complete his opera. But first he had to get to *Let 'Em Eat Cake*.

In their libretto Kaufman and Ryskind took up the further adventures of their *Of Thee I Sing* protagonists, which reunited Victor Moore (Throttlebottom), William Gaxton (Wintergreen) and Lois Moran (Mary Wintergreen).

The Gershwins spent the hot months of 1933 working on the new musical; on September 23, George wrote George Pallay: "The summer is over, thank God, as it was a tough one for the Gershwin frères. However, most of the hard work (I hope) is over now that the show is nearing the opening. I leave next Thursday night for Boston—the show opens the following Monday.

"There's a lot of good stuff in the new show and it is funny to beat hell but it seems to me it still lacks a little love interest. If the show is funny enough people won't mind that and Boston will tell us everything. After all, this is an entirely new kind of show and it is very hard predicting what the audience's reaction will be."

"If *Strike Up the Band* was a satire on War," Ira Gershwin wrote years later, "and *Of Thee I Sing* one on Politics, *Let 'Em Eat Cake* was a satire on Practically Everything. Straddling no fence, it trampled the Extreme Right one moment, the Extreme Left the next. Kaufman and Ryskind's libretto was at times extremely witty—at other times unrelentingly realistic in its criticism of the then American scene."

In the almost two years since *Of Thee I Sing* had opened, the national as well as the international scene had soured. The Depression shook American confidence in the Hoover administration and Hoover was overwhelmingly voted out of office; he was not stupid, corrupt or inept —the joyride of the twenties had simply caught up with him. When

Franklin D. Roosevelt was inaugurated in March of 1933, Kaufman and Ryskind had plenty of Practically Everything to shoot their barbs at. In that month alone, after Roosevelt had declared a Bank Holiday and promised to end the crime-inducing Prohibition, there were some fifteen million unemployed in the United States and six million on relief. Many lost their homes to settle in ramshackle "Hoovervilles," shacks built of tin, cardboard and materials salvaged from city dumps. There were protests, marches, strikes; the nation was in an ugly mood.

From abroad came intimations of things to come. The name of a man called Adolf Hitler began appearing regularly on the front pages of newspapers. In the last week of March he officially became Germany's Chancellor, with dictatorial powers, for reasons that few in America (or even in Europe) understood. Soon dispatches came from Germany of public demonstrations of anti-Semitism. There were references, too, to one Benito Mussolini, the Fascist dictator of Italy. The Japanese had begun moving into China. But all these events were, it seemed, a good distance from America—and there were plenty of problems at home.

Kaufman and Ryskind adapted these problems and blended them with the disconcerting dispatches from Europe and Asia. Anticipating novelist Sinclair Lewis's *It Can't Happen Here* by two years, the librettists predicted an American dictatorship. This is accomplished by connivance among politicians, industrialists (even a large newspaper chain) and the military.

In the beginning of *Let 'Em Eat Cake* the old *Of Thee I Sing* gang is voted out of the White House. Stunned, the inept Secretary of Agriculture (the consummate New Yorker, he knows nothing about his office or duties), says of this, "An election we had to have. Everything was going along smooth and we have an election."

When it is pointed out elections occur every four years because "It's in the Constitution," he retorts with, "Who reads the Constitution? They'd never have noticed it."

Out of work, like millions of other Americans, they converge on New York (except for the newspaper publisher, who switches his loyalty to the new administration) and eventually go into the shirt business, manufacturing "Maryblue" shirts (the inexpensive creation of Mary Wintergreen) in a building on Union Square. At the time this was the major gathering place for radicals, malcontents and rabble-rousers. When the revolution comes they are ready for it. Wintergreen, in fact, sets out to start one aided by the arch-radical Kruger.

His reasoning is impeccable: "Italy—black shirts! Germany—brown shirts! America—blue shirts. By God, if the American people want a revolution we can give it to them! We've got the shirts for it!"

With the connivance of a remarkably stupid general, they get control of the Army and march on Washington, overthrow the administration of President Tweedledee and take over the White House. The dictatorship of Wintergreen gets into trouble because he promises to pay off the Army with the World War I war debts—if he can collect them.

When the nine nations owing the United States this money balk, Dictator Wintergreen suggests that they form a baseball team. America's team is made up of the nine Supreme Court Judges. If the League of Nations wins it will pay nothing; if the Supreme Court wins, the United States will get double its money. Unfortunately for Wintergreen the Official Umpire is honest Throttlebottom. When one of his calls gives the game to the League, he is arrested by the radical Kruger, who has taken over the Army.

Throttlebottom is sentenced to be beheaded. The French Ambassador, who ran off with Throttlebottom's wife (the "beautiful blossom" of *Of Thee I Sing)* sends a special gift for the ceremony, a guillotine. This distresses Throttlebottom until he learns he will go down in history in the company of Marie Antoinette and Louis XVI, who had similarly lost their heads.

To round matters out, the treacherous Kruger includes Wintergreen and several of his henchmen in the execution ceremony, since the dictator had not come up with the promised war-debt money. (In the final scene of *Let 'Em Eat Cake* the stage is ominously dominated by the guillotine, and the comedy palls.) As in *Of Thee I Sing,* Mary saves the day. She stages a fashion show before the executions (the new Paris styles were on the same ship that brought the guillotine).

The women are so impressed with the new styles—and tired of the blue they've been wearing since the revolution—that they have a revolution of their own. As long as Kruger is dictator, having rid himself of Wintergreen and company, they will be forced to wear the same old blue.

A counterrevolution is incited by Trixie, the general's girlfriend, who has the Navy on her side. Kruger in turn is overthrown (Trixie soon also controls the Army) and is not shot because he reveals he owns a factory in Brooklyn and can produce dresses even cheaper than Mary. The gang decides to return the White House to Tweedledee and go into the dress business. Kruger leaves plotting a strike in the factory.

Tweedledee refuses because he has a better offer, the presidency of Cuba (in 1933 there was a real revolution there, but anyone of Tweedledee's mentality would not have known that). Throttlebottom, because Tweedledee seems to have no Vice President (or can't remember his name), finally becomes President of the United States.

This plot and the form it took in the hands of Kaufman and Ryskind is blamed for the early demise of Let 'Em Eat Cake; it lasted a mere ninety performances. Another reason: sequels to successes inevitably fail; another, it came at the wrong time, because the ominous news from abroad and the hard times at home alienated audiences when they were reminded of these realities in an expected "musical comedy."

The sour mood and the comic but malicious characters (most of them, at least) made audiences uncomfortable; some students of the theater have suggested that the sight of the lovable Victor Moore with his head on the guillotine was not especially droll. In this scene he even fixes the guillotine (the blade won't descend because of wedges inserted during its shipment).

"Now we got it," he says with pride.

"On behalf of the boys (awaiting execution)," Wintergreen says without conviction, "I want to congratulate you."

The book does not hold up dramatically. Brooks Atkinson found Let 'Em Eat Cake "more like a rowdy improvisation in one bitter, hysterical mood than a stage entertainment." Of the librettists he said, "Their hatreds have triumphed over their sense of humor."

A truncated tour of the show (and a revival in 1978) appear to back up the original views.

The score of Let 'Em Eat Cake is one of the Gershwins' finest, a still unrecognized landmark of the American musical theater. If the word "operetta" implies little opera, then Let 'Em Eat Cake is a remarkable collection of eight little operas. It marks George Gershwin on the threshold of opera with an authentic American accent: his.

That this musical was unconventional was evident from the first strains of the overture—ominous, militaristic; drums (with darker undercurrents from the low strings), a strident trumpet (quoting the bugle call popularly known as "There's a Soldier in the Grass"), grinding harmonies in the orchestra (in the brass and strings). All is agitation and discord until momentary melodic tranquillity is introduced by the theme of "Mine," the single love ballad of the show. Shreds of melodies and rhythms tangle as other themes are woven into the overture's texture: the haunting but lyrically chilling "Comes the Revolution," the elegant, very thirties "Blue, Blue, Blue" and the magisterial, at times discordant, title song. The overture is rounded out with restatements of "Mine" and "Let 'Em Eat Cake."

As with his previous political operettas, Gershwin did not settle for the conventional medley overture. He worked closely with orchestrator, Edward Powell, also a Schillinger student. Gershwin's friend Bill Daly conducted Let 'Em Eat Cake, their last professional collaboration.

Working from the libretto, the Gershwins blocked out the musical sequences to blend into the plot; there are few conventional songs, all are subordinate to the structure and movement of story. Nor was it a case of music first, lyrics later. George worked from his brother's conception of what at any point in the musical, the mood, the focus, should be. Music and lyrics grew out of this, for the Gershwins, an unconventional approach. A listing of song titles is misleading. As in opera the melodies vary in length, there is scant dependence on the thirty-two bar popular song form.

Each of the two acts is made up of four extended self-contained musical sequences, preceded by the usual but unconventional opening chorus. Thus Act I has this form:

> *Opening*
> 1. Union Square
> 2. The Store
> 3. The Union League
> 4. The Revolution

Like *Of Thee I Sing, Let 'Em Eat Cake* begins with a noisy political parade with "Wintergreen for President" from the first show, sung contrapuntally against his opponent's "Tweedledee, Tweedledee, He's O.K." Each is initially sung individually and then by two choral groups; the effect is of a striking dissonance. Once the scene is set the setting shifts to the White House and a long stretch of dialogue as Wintergreen's administration is voted out. (This second scene opens on the bemedaled General Snookfield and the redheaded Trixie "in an evening gown that begins where other evening gowns leave off, or vice versa." Her first words: "So this is the White House! What a dump!")

The next musical scene, set in Union Square, consists of a long choral section, beginning and ending with the sweet "Our Hearts Are in Communion." In between the radical Kruger, with chorus, proclaims the theme of the musical, in Ira Gershwin's estimation, "Down with Everything That's Up." His denunciation is all-inclusive: the House of Morgan, the Roxy organ, music by Stravinsky, with shows "except by Minsky" (the burlesque producer).

This leads to a shouting and punching match as the singing becomes discordant ("To hell with you and you and you!"). Police break up the rioting and the crowd returns to "Our Hearts Are in Communion."

Another long stretch of dialogue and the next musical scene consists of four units (two repeated) and a coda: A-B-A$_1$-C-B$_1$-D-coda. Most of the scene is done chorally, opening with "Orders, Orders," which in-

forms the audience that the scheme to produce Maryblue shirts is pay-
ing off ("Good God! how the money rolls in!").

The B section is not much more than a greeting as various characters
make their entrances. In the C section Throttlebottom, a floorwalker in
the store, sings the beautiful melody, "Comes the Revolution!/ Everything is jake!/ Comes the revolution/ We'll be eating cake!" But the
words in the middle section, with its lovely harmonies are "When the
streets and rivers run with red/ I'll be underneath the bed." This extraordinary melody was not designed for popularity.

The D section is introduced by the B's "Good morning/ How do you
do?" which leads to "Mine," sung by the Wintergreens and the chorus.
In the coda Mary leads the chorus in advice on climbing up the social
ladder with membership in "The New D.A.R."

In the Union League scene, Throttlebottom seeks to enlist its membership in their Revolution; if he succeeds, he is assured of Snookfield's
army. The members sing a weary song about membership in the Union
League and about being "Cloistered from the noisy city." All are languid, bearded, superannuated and lethargic (Throttlebottom thinks one
is dead). He convinces the League to join the revolution (the ancients
have the wrong one in mind, they assume they are to fight George III).
The scene concludes with a reprise of Throttlebottom's "Comes the
Revolution" and a grotesque dance by the Union League.

The final musical scene of Act I, The Revolution, is complex in construction and in many aspects the most reminiscent of Gilbert and Sullivan. The march "On and On and On" weaves through the scene as
Wintergreen and his forces with Snookfield's army converge on the
White House during a Fourth of July celebration. Tweedledee makes a
speech revealing monumental ignorance of the country's history.

The general sings the Gilbert-and-Sullivanish, "I brushed my teeth,"
after which he disappears with Trixie; they have a party to attend. The
finale is a cornucopia of reprises, new themes, patter songs and rhythms
undreamed of by Sullivan. Three are outstanding. The general being
AWOL, the Army finds it difficult to make up its mind, should it remain
loyal to the President or join Wintergreen's revolution? Mary steps
forward with a beautiful aria, in which she is hauntingly joined by the
women's chorus, "All the mothers of the nation/Can tell you who your
leader ought to be." She bases her argument on the fact that, unlike her
husband, Tweedledee is a bachelor. (Here Gershwin intensified the rising line of the melody so that the last word sounds like an unflattering
epithet.)

Another outstanding musical invention is the solo and choral
"What's the Proletariat?" It opens solo, by Mary again, who is joined

by the crowd. As Gershwin stated in an interview before *Let 'Em Eat Cake* opened, he had "written most of the music for this show contrapuntally, and it is that very insistence on the sharpness of a form that gives my music the acid touch it has . . ." He felt too that this underscored the thrust of the lyrics, "in keeping with the satire of the piece." "What's the Proletariat?" is one of the many examples in the score of Gershwin's approach. (Later, in 1934, his longtime admirer Gilbert Seldes would say of the maturing Gershwin that his "work gets more complicated and interesting and brittle and unmelodious every year . . . So he composes to be heard, not to be sung." Seldes was obviously thinking of the complexities of *Pardon My English* and, especially, *Let 'Em Eat Cake.* Both overflow with melody, but in the operetta few could be defined as popular song in the conventional sense.)

The scene, and Act I, end with "Let 'Em Eat Cake" sung by Wintergreen and the chorus.

Act II follows the form of the first: musical sequences alternating with dialogue; both advance the plot. An orchestral introduction reprises the title song and alludes briefly to "Blue, Blue, Blue" (the new color of the former White House). The song begins the second act, in the first musical scene of four:

1. The Blue House
2. The Ball Park
3. The Tribunal
4. The Guillotine

"Blue, Blue, Blue" is a fine melody. From Ira Gershwin Lawrence D. Stewart learned that it had been in one of George's Tune Books for some time. He thought it would make a fitting Act II opener. George felt he could develop the theme into a very good song, but deferred to his brother, and this excellent ballad became a song about painting the White House blue (it is sung by a women's chorus in the show). Another good song, a rhythm number, "Why speak of money, when there's love, love, love," is used in this sequence.

The next scene, The Ball Park, is virtually all exposition, with one major tune, "Up and at 'Em, On to Vict'ry," plus a few reprises all seamlessly woven into the fabric of the show. One of the reprises is the song of the Supreme Court judges from *Of Thee I Sing.*

The Tribunal is devoted to the trial of Throttlebottom; he is accused of calling a foul ball fair and replies with the plaintive "I know a foul ball when I see one" with the chorus joining in. Kruger, now head of the Army, insists that they "Throttle Throttlebottom" and then, when he realizes his army is not to be paid, decides to include Wintergreen and his aides in the execution.

The final scene opens with a sober recitative, "Whereas . . ." intoning the events of the day in legalese: "Part A will consist of seven beheadings." Then one of Ira Gershwin's most ingenious lines:

> *Part B:*
> *There is no Part B.*

This is followed by the sale of autographed photographs of the new dictator, Kruger, then a hymnlike dirge—and finally some superlative choral writing—"Oh, they're hanging Throttlebottom in the morning!" In this scene Kaufman and Ryskind lost whatever audience remained after the preceding searings of Practically Everything. Kruger, for example, in a show of benevolence, arranges for the relatives of the condemned to have front row seats, children half price. Executioner Snookfield is to be paid "ten dollars a head" for his work. However, Mary Wintergreen saves the day with her fashion show and the indomitable Trixie incites a counterrevolution, toppling Kruger. With Throttlebottom President, the scene, and the show, closes with a reprise of "Let 'Em Eat Cake."

The year ended as it began for the Gershwins, with a flop show. Of their collaborations, *Pardon My English* was their greatest failure with its forty-six performances; it is followed by *Treasure Girl* (68), and *Let 'Em Eat Cake* (90). These shows have something else in common besides financial fiasco: superlative scores.

The cynicism and pessimism of the libretto to *Let 'Em Eat Cake* may have alienated audiences, but the miniature opera scenes hold up on their own. It is the Gershwins' meridian in their writing for the lyric theater. It is George Gershwin's giant step toward a full-scale opera.

13

Porgy and Bess

Less than a week after *Let 'Em Eat Cake* moved in for the short stay at the Imperial, George Gershwin signed a contract with the Theatre Guild to compose the music for an opera based on the play *Porgy*, which the Guild had successfully produced in 1927.

The date on the contract is October 26, 1933; it had been long in coming. (Not publicized was the fact that Gershwin had rejected Otto Kahn's offer of five thousand dollars for a Metropolitan Opera premiere.)

The play had been inspired by the novel written by the Southern poet DuBose Heyward. It was in its original form that Heyward's story of a crippled beggar had excited Gershwin in 1926. He had been given the book by Emily and Lou Paley. (In an interview a year later he told the writer that his favorite "modern literary piece" was *Porgy.)*

Caught up in Heyward's story he dashed off a letter to Heyward suggesting an operatic treatment of *Porgy*.

Heyward was very much interested indeed and in discussing Gershwin's idea with his wife, Dorothy, he learned that she had not been writing a detective story as he had thought, but had been converting his novel into a play. He could not disappoint her and so informed Gershwin. It placed *Porgy* out of Gershwin's reach for the moment. The Guild production the next year did well: 217 performances, a tour and a return in 1928 for an additional 150 performances.

Gershwin apparently had been talking a lot about his idea. In one of the few dissenting reviews of the play, Gilbert Gabriel wrote in the *Sun,* "It seems all bits and pieces, and nothing but. Or else nothing but the beginnings of the opera George Gershwin hopes to make of it." Finally, after seven years, the Theatre Guild contract meant that something would come of that hope.

I

Dorothy Heyward (a young graduate of the famous "Harvard 47 Workshop" conducted by George Price Baker for, as she put it, "would-be playwrights"), recalled the initiation of the opera.

The "day came when George Gershwin, who was then very young, but already very famous, wrote that he had picked up the novel *Porgy* one night to read himself to sleep but instead read himself wide awake —and how about making the story into an opera? DuBose was greatly excited about the idea. It seems that his objection to a Negro play did not apply to a Negro opera with music by Gershwin. He and George arranged a meeting.

"By that time, after nearly seven months of covert work, I had an almost finished play. It was a great moment when George said there was plenty of room for both play *and* opera. And plenty of time. He wanted to spend years in study before composing his opera. DuBose joined me in the collaboration I had hoped for while secretly toiling on the play, and we rewrote it in two whirlwind weeks."

The Gershwins and the Heywards met briefly in Atlantic City in the summer of 1927. The Gershwins were then occupied with the first *Strike Up the Band;* the Heywards had come North for the production of *Porgy.* Like his wife, Heyward was impressed by the dynamic New Yorker. Gershwin was then not yet thirty; Heyward was over forty.

"My first impression of my collaborator remains with me and is singularly vivid," he recalled eight years later. "A young man of enormous physical and emotional vitality, who possessed the faculty of seeing himself quite impersonally and realistically, and who knew exactly what he wanted and where he was going. This characteristic put him beyond both modesty and conceit. About himself he would mention certain facts, aspirations, failings. They were usually right.

"At that time he had numerous Broadway successes to his credit, and his *Rhapsody in Blue,* published three years before, had placed him in the front rank of American composers. It was extraordinary, I thought, that, in view of a success that might well have dazzled any man, he could appraise his talent with such complete detachment.

"And so we decided then that some day when we were both prepared we would do an operatic version of my simple Negro beggar of the Charleston streets."

And so, with a spontaneous letter, an informal meeting and talk was formed one of the most creative collaborations in the American musical theater. It was a union based on a remarkable mutual respect, free-and-easy give-and-take, devoid of show-business vanity and blatant self-interest endemic to such enterprises.

The collaboration of George Gershwin and DuBose Heyward (and later, Ira Gershwin), is unique. Over a period of close to two years (once the actual work had begun), they not only created a masterwork but were still speaking to one another on opening night. They made a curious pair: a New York Jew and a Southern aristocrat. Heyward trusted Gershwin's creative instincts, artistic judgment and theatrical experience. He realized, too, that Gershwin indeed knew exactly what he wanted to do and how he would accomplish it. Though the senior member, Heyward depended upon and now and then deferred to his younger collaborator.

II

Heyward (1885–1940) knew his subject. Born in Charleston, South Carolina, he spent most of his early life there. From a venerable aristocratic family (one ancestor, Thomas Heyward, was a signer of the Constitution), he suffered through some harrowing years as a youngster. When he was two, the death of his father left the family destitute; the death of his mother, seven years later, virtually put Heyward on the streets. He sold newspapers in Charleston and tried to acquire some schooling. Like Gershwin he left high school while still in his teens (he had, in fact, even less formal schooling than Gershwin). He was fourteen when he began working as an errand boy for an ironmonger.

Two years later he was stricken by poliomyelitis which left him with a crippled right arm. During a long period of convalescence Heyward did a great deal of reading, literally educating himself. Once recovered —though he would always be frail and often in poor health—he found work on the Charleston wharves as a cotton checker; it was there that he came in daily contact with the black dock workers and fishermen who people his novel.

Under this influence he became a student of the folklore and mores of these people and began writing short stories drawing upon this material and the language of the people with whom he worked. Around the same time Heyward began writing poetry and eventually founded the Poetry Society of South Carolina.

In 1922, in collaboration with novelist Hervey Allen (best known for

Anthony Adverse, 1933), he published his first collection of verse, *Carolina Chansons,* which made his name known beyond the limits of Charleston.

It earned him a summer's stay at the famous MacDowell Colony in Peterboro, New Hampshire, which provided artists, writers and musicians with a setting for work free of money worries. It was there he met an aspiring playwright from Canton, Ohio, Dorothy Hartzell Kuhns. They were married the following year (1923); that same year the new Mrs. Heyward received an award for her play *Nancy Ann.* The Heywards had one child, Jenifer, who became an actress and, later, a talented artist.

After publishing another poetry collection, *Skylines and Horizons* (1924), Heyward sold his business, a moderately successful insurance company, at Dorothy's urging and devoted all of his time to writing. *Porgy* was published the next year, followed by a second novel, *Angel.* Another novel, *Mamba's Daughters* was published in 1929 and ten years later was converted by the Heywards into a successful play, one year before Heyward died of a heart attack.

The hero of *Porgy* is actually, if very loosely, based on an individual Heyward had regularly encountered in the streets of Charleston named Samuel Smalls, but popularly known as "Goat Sammy." Smalls had lost the use of his legs and traveled around Charleston in a small cart (fashioned from a wooden soapbox) drawn by a goat. It was regarded as ironically amusing that imprinted on the box was the legend, "Pure and Fragrant," for everyone who remembered Goat Sammy also recalled that his transportation was via "a malodorous billy goat."

"The fumes," recalled Mrs. John Bennett, a friend of the Heywards, ". . . lent a certain piquancy." Smalls, she remembered as "a very powerful man, though as he aged he put on weight. But he had a broad chest and conspicuously powerful arms . . ."

Heyward, like most Charlestonians, initially saw Goat Sammy only as the beggar on King Street; that he might have had another life had never occurred to him until he read about a Samuel Smalls in the *News and Courier,* reporting that he had been jailed "on an aggravated assault charge.

"It is alleged," the article continued, "that on Saturday night he attempted to shoot Maggie Barnes at number four Romney Street. His shots went wide of the mark. Smalls was up on a similar charge some months ago and was given a suspended sentence." He eventually succeeded in shooting one Sally Singleton, whom he accused of stealing his watch. Later, he vanished from King Street and little else is known about him or his fate.

It struck Heyward that Goat Sammy, "the object of public charity by day, had a private life of his own by night. It was a tempestuous life and in it were the seeds of human struggle that make for drama."

He found the setting for his drama practically next door. After their marriage the Heywards rented a house at 98 Church Street. Numbers 89–91, known as "Cabbage Row," had once been a counting house and later an office building. By 1924 it was a black tenement consisting of three interconnected buildings built around a courtyard. The servants and employees of Charleston's white families were crowded into these buildings. While no longer the well-kept elegant structure it had been in antebellum Charleston, Cabbage Row was not a slum. Its post-Civil War name derived from the vendors who came there to sell vegetables, fruits and other edibles. Because his story involved fishermen, Heyward simply moved his locale two blocks east, to Vanderhorst Wharf and rechristened it Catfish Row.

There was another alteration. As he wrote at the MacDowell Colony, he used the name "Porgo" for that of his protagonist. Where that had come from Heyward was never certain, but before he submitted the novel for publication he changed the name to "Porgy," after a species of fish that flourished in the Atlantic off the coast of South Carolina.

When Dorothy questioned him about the unusual character he had chosen as the hero of his novel, Heyward told her, "But of course I got the idea from Goat Sammy. You must have seen him dozens of times. He's always around. Everyone in Charleston knows Goat Sammy." But Dorothy had never seen Smalls. When they returned to Charleston she made a search but never found him.

Once *Porgy* became a bestseller, Porgy became a local legend; he was no longer remembered as Goat Sammy. When the book went into a second printing in 1928, Heyward attempted to set the record straight. "As one with a profound respect for the authentic in folklore," he wrote in a preface, "I desire to record the exact point at which fact ends and the unfettered hand of the story writer takes up a tale.

"To Smalls I make acknowledgment of my obligation. From contemplation of his real and deeply moving tragedy sprang Porgy, a creature of my imagination, who synthesized for me a number of divergent impressions and emotions, and upon whom, being my own creature, I could impose my own white man's conception of a summer of aspiration, devotion, and heartbreak across the color wall."

It was this humane integrity, the sympathetic, rich characterizations and the natural possibilities for the placement of music and song (folk songs and spirituals appear in both the novel and the play) that so captivated Gershwin early one September morning in 1926. He would

endow Heyward's Porgy with a mythic immortality that neither could
have dreamed of in 1928, when Heyward hoped to separate fact from
fiction.

III

After initiating the idea of transforming *Porgy* into an opera and being
gently rebuffed, Gershwin set it aside for six years. Then, after returning
from his Cuban vacation, he became restless and while waiting for Aarons and Freedley to come up with a suitable libretto, turned again to
thinking about an opera.

He again wrote to Heyward, then at his home, Dawn Hill, in Hendersonville, North Carolina. In his letter, dated March 29, 1932, Gershwin
told Heyward that he was planning to leave for Europe (conductor
Albert Coates had invited him to tour as soloist with an orchestra to
perform in London, Paris, Berlin, Barcelona and Moscow). Before leaving Gershwin hoped to discuss the opera with Heyward. He asked Heyward to phone him (collect) or telegram his phone number.

"Is there any chance," Gershwin inquired, "of your being abroad in
the next couple of months?" Heyward, who had begun to feel the pinch
of the Depression, was not considering a European vacation. As it
turned out the Gershwin-Coates tour did not materialize.

On April 12, Heyward wrote to let Gershwin know how "pleased" he
was to know that Gershwin had "returned to your original idea of
doing a musical setting of Porgy . . . I have some new material that
might be introduced, and once I get your ideas as to the general form
suitable for the musical version I am sure that I could do you a satisfac-
tory story."

It was more than a month before Gershwin wrote again. It could not
have pleased Heyward to read that though Gershwin was "very glad"
to know "that the operatic rights to *Porgy* are free and clear" there was
"no possibility of the operatic version's being written before January
1933." He planned to remain in New York for the summer (to prepare
for his Lewisohn Stadium concert and to work on *Rumba)* during
which he would "read the book several times to see what ideas I can
evolve as to how it should be done. Any notions I get I shall forward to
you." He felt, too, that they should meet several times "before any real
start is made."

That done, Gershwin attended to completion of *Rumba,* worked with
Schillinger and, after his triumphant first All-Gershwin Concert at the
Stadium, took a vacation in the Adirondacks. When he returned early

in September, he found a jolting letter from Heyward. His agent, Audrey Wood, had received a peculiar offer that could only be described as having come out of left field.

Al Jolson wanted to portray Porgy.

"I cannot see brother Jolson as Porgy," Heyward told Gershwin, emphasizing that it did not "shake" him in his "desire" to collaborate with him on an opera. But he realized, considering Jolson's interest, that he had "an asset in Porgy, and in these trying times that has to be considered." He had assumed that Gershwin, whose every work went into immediate production, had a specific producer in mind; if so, Heyward would withdraw the dramatic and film rights and reserve them for Gershwin. In financial trouble, Heyward hoped that they might be assured a production of the opera by the spring of 1933, or at the latest by early autumn. He even had a suggestion: "Would it be possible to use Jolson, and arrange some sort of agreement with him, or is that too preposterous?"

Gershwin found it "very interesting that Al Jolson would like to play the part of Porgy, but I really don't know how he would be in it.

"Of course he is a very big star, who certainly knows how to put over a song, and it might mean more to you financially if he should do it— provided that the rest of the production were well done. The sort of thing that I should have in mind for Porgy is a much more serious thing than Jolson could ever do."

Still, he assured Heyward, if "you can see your way to making some ready money from Jolson's version I don't know that it would hurt a later version done by an all-colored cast." He wrote too that he would not even attempt to compose the opera until he had "all the themes and musical devices worked out" and that it "would be more of a labor of love than anything else."

As to Heyward's question about a prospective producer, Gershwin admitted that he had not approached anyone. In fact he preferred completing the work and then decide who might be the most suitable producer. There was slight encouragement for Heyward. "I know that [Herman] Shumlin," Gershwin told him, "the producer of Grand Hotel, is very much interested in the idea."

In late September or early October, Heyward made one of his rare visits North to meet with his agent and Gershwin. They discussed the Jolson incident and how they might transform the play into an opera. On his return to Hendersonville, Heyward learned that Jolson had arrived in New York and had called Audrey Wood to inquire on the availability of Porgy. She immediately called Gershwin.

On October 17, Heyward wrote a letter that encapsulates their unique collaboration; in it, for the first time, he uses the informal first-name salutation. Before that it had begun with "Mr." and later "My dear Gershwin." This is Heyward's complete letter:

Dear George:

Miss Wood of the Century Play Company writes that Jolson has been hot on her trail for the Porgy book, and that in a 'phone conversation with you, she was advised by you that his use of the story for his particular sort of musical play would not kill it for an eventual opera.

As a matter of fact, upon my return here after my talk with you I learned of circumstances that have put me in a tight spot financially, and that alone, has prompted me to write Miss Wood as per enclosed carbon. Of course what I would like to be able to afford would be to wait indefinitely for your operatic version, and to work with you myself without the least thought of the commercial angle.

It is not my idea to work in any way upon a possible Jolson musical, but merely to sell the story. Later I shall hope to work with you as we outlined in our recent conversation.

Please let me tell you that I think your attitude in this matter is simply splendid. It makes me all the more eager to work with you some day, some time, before we wake up and find ourselves in our dotage.

Please feel free to call Miss Wood and insist upon conditions in the contract which will assure the proper release of the book for your use.

With all good wishes,
Sincerely,
DuBose

And there, for the moment, the project rested. Gershwin was then embroiled in *Pardon My English* and its problems. Around this time too Kaufman and Ryskind came up with their libretto to *Let 'Em Eat Cake,* a project impossible to ignore. This work would necessitate postponing the start on *Porgy* even beyond his projection of early 1933. In the interval, both he and Heyward would find outside work, so to speak (Gershwin in radio and Heyward in Hollywood) to sponsor their collaboration until the right producer, with backers, materialized.

Jolson did not give up easily and continued to talk with Audrey Wood. Gershwin, at least in the beginning, was unaware of the formidable talents that had become linked with Jolson's plans: Jerome Kern and Oscar Hammerstein II. These two songwriters (with Hammerstein as librettist) could very readily have written a musical that might have rivaled what Gershwin had in mind. Their *Show Boat* is close to opera.

Luckily for Gershwin and Heyward, they too had other things to do. Even as Jolson called Wood, they were completing their *Music in the Air* which opened in November 1932. Both then went on to other projects; Kern did *Roberta* the following year and Hammerstein went to London to work on *Ball at the Savoy.* Then both reunited in London in the spring of 1934 to collaborate on *Three Sisters.*

With no librettist, since Heyward would not become involved, no composer and no lyricist, Jolson abandoned his pursuit. Whether he approached other songwriters or not is not known; he may simply have grown tired. Even so, the ultrapatient Heyward would have to wait almost a year and a half from the time of his letter just quoted (dated October 17, 1932) before Gershwin started composing the music for their opera.

IV

A full year passed from the time Heyward had resigned himself to permit Jolson to portray Porgy in blackface and the signing of the contract with the Theatre Guild in October 1933. Even so, Gershwin could not get down to the actual composing of their opera because of immediate commitments and, his move from Riverside Drive to East Seventy-second Street.

While Heyward sent him the libretto scene by scene, wrote letters and chafed a little, Gershwin was talked into making a tour celebrating the tenth anniversary of the *Rhapsody in Blue.* For this he composed a piece for himself and orchestra, *Variations on "I Got Rhythm."*

The idea for this tour originated with Harry Askins, a Gershwin admirer from the early Tin Pan Alley period; it was Askins who, impressed with Gershwin's playing during the *Miss 1917* rehearsals, introduced him to Max Dreyfus. Gershwin and Askins entered into a partnership for the tour with Askins serving as the manager.

Askins blocked out a strenuous itinerary: twenty-eight concerts in twenty-eight cities in as many days. The program began with the *Concerto in F,* followed by Gershwin's solo playing several songs. Then, inexplicably, tenor James Melton appeared to sing non-Gershwin cowboy songs ("Home on the Range," "Hills of Home" and "Carry Me Back to the Lone Prairie"); the *Rhapsody in Blue* came next.

After the intermission the orchestra presented *An American in Paris;* this was followed by a group of a couple of spirituals and "Shortnin'

Bread" by Melton. The *Variations on I Got Rhythm* came next, followed by "Wintergreen for President" by the orchestra. The program closed with Bill Daly's song medley by the orchestra, with Gershwin at the piano.

Entitled A Program of Gershwin Successes, the tour featured, besides Gershwin and Melton, the "Reisman Symphonic Orchestra," conducted by Charles Previn (who had been conductor of *La-La-Lucille!* in 1919 and *Of Thee I Sing* in 1931). The Symphonic Orchestra was the popular Leo Reisman Band, whose leader had had to drop out of the tour because of a leg injury he suffered in an accident.

The *Variations* had been largely written at Emil Mosbacher's home in Palm Beach, Florida, in December 1933. Gershwin left New York with Mosbacher on December 2; they arrived the next day in Charleston to remain a couple of days to talk things over with Heyward. "I hope," Gershwin had written, "you can arrange it so as to spend most of the time with me. I would like to see the town and hear some spirituals and perhaps go to a colored cafe or two."

After the short visit Gershwin and Mosbacher proceeded on to Palm Springs where Gershwin spent a little more than three weeks working on the *Variations,* completing his usual two-piano version and beginning the orchestration. Upon returning to Manhattan on January 4 (after an overnight stay in Charleston on the second) Gershwin told an interviewer he had completed more than fifty pages of the orchestration and, "before the night's over I've got to wash up twenty-five more." The date at the end of his manuscript is January 6, 1934. The tour began in Boston on the fourteenth, a Sunday. The dedication reads, "To my brother Ira."

The *Variations,* unarguably a light and lighthearted work, is intricately written and highly polished in its orchestration (Dorothy Heyward recalled that while Gershwin stopped over in Charleston he worked on it without a piano, since they had none there). Gershwin's study with Schillinger is evident throughout the work. At the same time, it is all Gershwin.

Before he began the composition Gershwin sketched out the form:

1. Simple
2. Orch melody—piano chromatic variation
3. Orch rich melody in 3/4
4. Chinese variation interlude
5. Modal variation
6. Hot variation finale

When he later performed the piece on his radio program he had this to say about it: "After the introduction by the orchestra the piano plays the theme rather simply [he demonstrated by playing a couple of bars of the song]. The first variation is a very complicated rhythmic pattern [in the score he marks it *bitingly* and *with metronomic precision]* played by the piano while the orchestra takes the theme. The next variation is in waltz time. The third is a Chinese variation in which I imitate Chinese flutes played out of tune, as they always are . . . Next the piano plays the rhythmic variation in which the left hand plays the melody upside down and the right plays it straight, on the theory that you shouldn't let one hand know what the other is doing. Then comes the finale." (Unfortunately, much of the wit and charm of this work is smothered in the reorchestration by William C. Schoenfeld published in 1953.) While not a grand work, it is inventive in its working within the framework of a single theme.

The tour was successful on all counts except the financial; Gershwin estimated that he and his troupe traveled some twelve thousand miles in the United States (with one stop in Canada). Both Askins and Gershwin seem not to have realized that they had booked themselves into what even on paper would appear to be suspect sites: City Hall Auditorium (Portland, Maine), Central High School (Syracuse, New York), West High School (Madison, Wisconsin), Technical High School (Omaha, Nebraska), etc.

Some of these auditoriums had so little audience room that the one-night stands lost money in seven towns; the tour ended with a deficit that cost Gershwin several thousand dollars. Though he considered Askins "foolish" for having booked them into these towns, as he wrote Heyward at the end of the tour, he regarded it as "a fine artistic success . . . and a very worthwhile thing for me to have done and I have many pleasant memories of cities I had not visited before." In this same letter he told Heyward that he had finally begun composing music for the First Act. He had, in fact, begun on an early version of "Summertime" while staying with the Mosbachers and working on the *Variations.* So Heyward learned late in February, 1934, that his collaborator had begun composing their opera. But not before another interruption.

V

His radio show was called "Music by Gershwin." The first series, two fifteen-minute shows a week on Monday and Friday evenings, was broadcast for the first time on February 19, 1934, nine days after his tour played its final date in Brooklyn's Academy of Music. It was aired until May 31 and was so popular that the sponsor, Feen-A-Mint, signed him on for a second series, a half-hour show Sunday nights which ran from September 30 to December 23.

Gershwin, in an "as told to" article in *Radio Guide,* explained the show's intent and a little on how it was put together. "First of all, in building my programs, I strive for informality and balance . . . We can be sure that we achieve balance because that can be worked out carefully from a purely musical standpoint. The matter of achieving informality—well, that is something else.

"When I set out to build a program, Finas Farr, a writer from the William Esty Agency, and Edward Byron, the agency production man, drop up to my apartment. I run over a few of the tunes on the piano. Then we'll pick out one of my songs for discussion. Farr very quietly pulls a notebook from his pocket and starts to ask questions about the 'birth' of the song." As an example, he told how he and Farr worked out the script on how "Liza" was written for Ziegfeld and Jolson's part in launching the song.

After which ". . . we decide on what overture we'll use in the program. Next is the song I'm to talk about . . . After the song I pick out some contemporary composer and choose one of his works, which the orchestra then plays. After that I select another song I wrote, and with very little description about it we program that. Then I have to pick out the song for the next program so we can play a few bars of it just like they use trailers in movie houses.

"After rehearsal we wait [for the program's time] when Don Wilson takes his place at the microphone—and from there on, you hear in fifteen minutes what I've been talking about four times that long!"

He enjoyed the new experience. As he wrote his friend Pallay, "I am having a lot of fun doing my radio broadcasting," informing him that seven stations on the Pacific Coast had taken it and suggesting that he tune in to "hear some Gershwin music and find out all about Feen-A-Mint laxatives—not that you need it but maybe some of your girls do!"

The program's conductor was Louis Katzman, violinist-trumpeter-conductor, who had been leading dance bands in New York since the early twenties. Besides dance music, he performed light classics in the Whiteman manner and Latin American specialties. He made many recordings in the twenties and thirties with several for Vocalion, Brunswick and Decca Records.

His son, Henry M. Katzman, served as his assistant and played piano in the orchestra for "Music by Gershwin." He recalled working on the show during its second series.

"It was on the CBS network every Sunday at 6 P.M.," he wrote. "The sponsor was Feen-A-Mint with, of course, the standing joke being when would George finish the 1st or 2nd movement of the Feen-A-Mint concerto.

"The caliber of both instrumentalists and arrangers or orchestraters was superb. For instance, among the brass were Harry Glantz (1st trumpet N.Y. Phil.), Manny Klein (top jazz trumpet), Hymie Farberman (great), Bob Effros (Paul Whiteman 1st trumpet), Tommy Dorsey, 1st trombone, Jack Jenny, 2nd trombone, Louis Raderman, violin, Vladimir Zelinsky, violin, Antonio Caffarelli, viola, Verle Mills, harp, Harry Goodson, vibes & xylophone, Charles Magnante, accordion, Andy Sanella, sax, Jimmy Dorsey, sax, Charles Evans, flute & piccolo, etc (N.Y. Phil.)"

Among the arrangers, Katzman recalled the names of his father, Morton Gould, Leith Stevens, Arthur Gutman, Cesare Sodero and others.

"Each week," he continued, "George had a guest composer on and we met and played Irving Berlin, Cole Porter, Richard Rodgers, Vernon Duke, Ray Henderson, etc. [Others: Harold Arlen, Rube Bloom, Dana Suesse, Arthur Schwartz.] By the way, this action gave the lie to the rumor that George would neither play nor listen to anyone else's music but his own."

The one conspicuous absence is that of Kay Swift, who attended all the rehearsals as well as the broadcasts. Gershwin explained that it would be too obvious a display of favoritism at that time.

"Our rehearsals," Katzman recalled, "were the in place to be and, led by Elsa Maxwell, the Broadway/Park Avenue jet set of that era filled the theater (CBS's 45th Street Theatre studio) till 3, 4, & 5 A.M.

"Because the radio show's time element was so short, we could only do bits and pieces or cuts and paste ups of George's major works . . . the *Concerto in F,* the *Rhapsody in Blue, I Got Rhythm Variations, An American in Paris, Cuban Overture . . .*"

Katzman and Gershwin became good friends and in time Gershwin hired him to "annotate and systematize his own works; his printed or published works as one unit and his manuscripts and his little work booklets into a separate unit. For this purpose I had the run of his place [the East Seventy-second Street apartment].

"Oscar Levant and I had keys to the apartment as did about a dozen other persons—his brother, mother, Japanese houseboy and any current amour.

"One last item for posterity. My wife and I were married Oct. 27, 1934 and George threw a wedding reception party for us at Delmonico's to which he invited the whole orchestra & their wives as well as a host of his friends and relations. If you check the calender you'll find that the date was a Saturday and we were married earlier that evening and then our wedding party came . . . to the rehearsal that night."

During this same period—the *Rhapsody* anniversary tour and the radio broadcasts—Heyward was very active on *Porgy* and Gershwin continued to work when he could. Once after one of the broadcasts he and Harold Arlen walked up to the East Side (Arlen then lived on East Eighty-sixth Street). Arlen had been a guest on the first half-hour program on September 30, 1934. Gershwin was obviously annoyed with some of the criticism he was getting because of the radio show. Some friends looked upon it as a kind of selling out—others made jokes about his sponsor, considering his perennial "composer's stomach." While the show kept him quite busy, it also provided him with the extra income to be able to write an opera in a time when royalties from shows and sheet music were down. On his time away from the studio, during the summer break, he performed at concerts and during one would spend a good period with Heyward.

In their book *The Gershwins* Alfred Simon and Robert Kimball quote Arlen quoting Gershwin, "What do they want me to do? What are they criticizing me for?"

"Those were bad times," Arlen summarized, "and what George was doing on his radio show was helping all of us." And it helped him to write his opera.

VI

What is unique about the Gershwin-Heyward collaboration is that the two spent so little time together. Gershwin's agreement with the Feen-A-Mint kept him in New York for most of 1934, and Heyward, once he began concentrating on work, preferred staying home. When Gershwin suggested that he and his family join him at the Mosbachers' in Palm Beach, Heyward declined, saying, ". . . I find my creative ability practically paralyzed in a new environment. I am just getting into my stride here now, and I do not want to risk breaking it."

In fact, Heyward had already been working on *Porgy* for more than three months. As soon as he had returned to Hendersonville from New York and the signing of the contract with the Theatre Guild, he went to work. Within a week he wrote Gershwin on November 12, 1933, "I enclose two copies of the first scene which I have worked over for you to start on.

"I have cut everything possible, and marked a couple of possible further cuts in pencil on ms. As a matter of fact, this is now a very brief scene considering that it carries all of the exposition of the play."

Heyward was working from his and Dorothy's dramatic version. Her contribution to the final form of the play and, consequently, the opera, was considerable though rarely recognized. (In the published vocal score only Heyward is credited with the libretto; a page condensing the plot notes that the opera is based on the play by both Heywards.)

Dorothy Heyward, in her dramatization of the novel, sharpened its impact with several ideas of her own; the most important change was in the play's ending, which Heyward retained for the opera. In the novel Bess runs off to Savannah with a group of stevedores believing that Porgy was facing a long jail sentence for murder. When he is freed, Porgy returns to Catfish Row to learn that Bess is gone. Broken, he ages before the eyes of his friend, Maria, and just gives up. In the play and opera he learns that Bess has gone to New York with the slippery drug dealer Sporting Life, whereupon he calls for his goat cart and sets out for New York in search of Bess. Thus opera and play have a more upbeat conclusion.

In transforming the novel into the play the Heywards did a good deal of character shifting as well as moving the sequence of plot incidents. Heyward wrote the novel in six parts; Bess does not appear until the second. The important pivotal character Sporting Life not only appears late in the novel but is ejected from Catfish Row long before the novel ends, by Maria, the wise strong woman of the book. Her role is greatly compressed in the opera; so is that of the kindly Peter who becomes the doddering "Honey Man" in the opera. While they are important to the plot, compressing their roles enabled the roles of Bess, Sporting Life and the villainous Crown to be expanded.

In his letter enclosed with the opera's first scene, Heyward told Gershwin, "I have been thinking a lot about this job and have a pretty definite feeling about the treatment which I submit for your consideration. I feel more and more that all dialogue should be spoken. It is fast moving, and we will cut it to the bone, but this will give the opera speed and tempo.

"This will give you a chance to develop a new treatment, carrying the orchestration straight through the performance (as you suggested) but enriching it with pantomime and action on the stage, and with such music (singing) as grows out of action. Also, in scenes like the fight, the whole thing can be treated as a unified composition drawing on lighting, orchestra, and the wailing of the crowd, mass sounds of horror from people, etc., instead of singing. It can be lifted to a terrific climax. That fight was treated with a great deal of noise in the play. That is not my idea of best art in handling it."

There is little dialogue in the novel but much poetic description and stream-of-consciousness revelations of the thoughts of the people in Catfish Row. For example, Heyward's introduction to the critical crap game reads: "One Saturday night in late April, with the first premonitory breath of summer in the air, Porgy sat in a gaming circle that had gathered in Catfish Row, and murmured softly to his gods of chance. All day he had been conscious of a vague unrest . . ." This game and the fight it leads to will change his life; in the play and opera this had to be clearly presented in action and dialogue, not rumination.

Heyward used little dialogue in the novel, but his treatment of the African Gullah dialect spoken by the blacks in and around Charleston would have been puzzling on stage. Some lines in the book require a knowledge of the dialect or a second reading:

> *Well; git on de wharf early, an' gib um two dollar. Tell um w'en de boat done git to Ediwander Islan' at eight tuhmorruh night, tuh go right to Lody cabin, an' tell she tuh mek a conjer tuh cas' de debbil out Bess.*

The subject of dialogue, how much, how spare, sung or spoken, was the one major source of what little disagreement the collaborators had and, of course, Gershwin prevailed. Heyward stood by his views but was the least egoistic of collaborators. As early as 1932, when Gershwin revived the project, he graciously suggested, "As to the lyrics, I am not so sure until I know more definitely what you have in mind. Perhaps your brother Ira would want to do them. Or maybe we could do them together . . ."

More than a year later Heyward contributed dramatic as well as musical suggestions. In his November 12 letter he told Gershwin, "I am offering a new idea for [the] opening of scene (1) as you will see from the script. The play opened with a regular riot of noise and color. This makes an entirely different opening, which I think is important. What I have in mind is to let the scene, as I describe it, merge with the overture, almost in the sense of illustration, giving the added force of sight and sound. I think it would be very effective to have the lights go out during [the] overture, so that the curtain rises in darkness, then the first scene will begin to come up as the music takes up the theme of jazz from the dance hall piano. The songs which I have written for this part will fall naturally into the action and mood of the separate flashes of negro life."

Deferentially he added, "You may have entirely different ideas about

this, but we will be able to discuss this when we meet in Charleston."
Porgy and Bess opens virtually as Heyward describes in this letter. Heyward ends the letter with a request of an autographed photograph of Gershwin for his study.

Some time passed before he heard from Gershwin who had been in Pittsburgh with Oscar Levant for performances of the *Rhapsody in Blue* and the *Concerto in F*. Originally Bill Daly was to have conducted but couldn't make it, so Gershwin gave over the piano to Oscar Levant and conducted the rehearsals and the concert. On returning to New York he replied to Heyward's letter.

"I have been reading through the first scene," he wrote, ". . . and think you have done a swell job, especially with the new lyrics. There may be too much talk, but I can't tell until I start composing just how that will work out.

"On account of many things I have to do at the present I haven't actually started composing. I want to do a great deal of thinking about the thing and the gathering in of thematic material before the actual writing begins. So, until my *[Rhapsody in Blue* anniversary] tour is ended I don't expect I will have much finished but after that I shall devote all my time to *Porgy.*"

He then left for Florida with Mosbacher to complete the *Variations on "I Got Rhythm"* and composed "Summertime." In his novel Heyward quoted several lyrics from folk songs and in the play he used these lines from the old song, "All My Trials":

> *Hush, lil' baby, don' yo' cry,*
> *Hush, lil' baby, don' yo' cry,*
> *Fadder an' mudder born to die.*

From the novel he took part of a line from Crown's speech to Bess, "Den soon de cotton will be comin' fas', an' libbin' be easy." In his reworked first scene mailed to Gershwin he has Clara sing a lullaby:

> *Summer time, an' the livin' is easy,*
> *Fish are jumpin', an' the cotton is high.*
> *Yo' Daddy's rich, chile, an yo' ma's good-lookin',*
> *So hush, little baby, don' yo' cry.*

In setting the lyric Gershwin made slight changes, eliminating the contractions in the first three lines for a better rhythmic flow and, in the third, dropping Heyward's "chile" and beginning the line with "Oh." Similar minor changes were made in the remaining four lines.

It is possible that Ira assisted in the editing, though if he did it was never mentioned by him or anyone else. When George began actual work on the opera, late in February, 1934, Ira was collaborating with lyricist E. Y. Harburg and composer Harold Arlen on what would be a successful revue, *Life Begins at 8:40*. After its premiere in August he would be free for full-time work on *Porgy*. However, as early as March George tells of his helping on some words for the first act.

While Gershwin toured, Heyward worked; on the day Gershwin played in Pittsburgh, February 6, Heyward mailed off two more scenes for Gershwin's consideration.

"Act 2, Scene 1 may still be a little long to you," he wrote, "but I have reduced it from 39 pages in the talking script to 18 for the opera, and it is strong on humor and action. Let me know how you feel about it and if you think it needs more lyrics.

"Act 2, Scene 2 ought to be good. I have cut out the conventional Negro vaudeville stuff that was in the original play and incorporated material that is authentic and plenty 'hot' as well. I have discovered for the first time a type of secular dance that is done here that is straight from the African phallic dance, and that is undoubtedly a complete survival. Also I have seen that native band of harmonicas, combs, etc. It will make an extraordinary introduction to the primitive scene of passion between Crown and Bess.

"I think maybe the composition on the lyrics I have done better wait until we get together. I have in mind something for them that I cannot well suggest by writing, especially in the boat song ["It Take a Long Pull to Get There"]. But don't let that stop you, if you feel moved with ideas of your own."

He closed the letter with an appeal: "Please let me know your plans as soon as you perfect them, and I cannot urge you too strongly to plan to come to Charleston at the earliest convenience for your visit. You really haven't scratched the surface of the native material yet. This secular stuff, for instance."

Gershwin had already decided that all the music in the opera would be his, not adaptations of folk music; while his work would be inspired by the music he might hear in Charleston he would not incorporate into his score. Only the "Street Cries" were variants of the real thing.

Although Heyward had to wait almost three weeks for Gershwin's reply, it was worth it, for in that letter Gershwin told him that he had begun composition on the opera. The delay in answering was caused by the preparations for the first two broadcasts of "Music by Gershwin" on Monday and Friday, February 19 and 23.

"I received your Second Act's script," he wrote, "and think it is fine. I really think you are doing a magnificent job with the new libretto and I hope I can match it musically."

As for Heyward's plea for his coming to Charleston, Gershwin countered with, "I am hoping you will find some time to come up North and live at my apartment—if it is convenient for you—so we can work together on some of the spirituals for Scene 2, Act I. Perhaps when the weather grows a little warmer you will find time to do this [the frail Heyward was sensitive to cold and New York in February that year was having a hard winter].

"I cannot leave New York to go South as I am tied up with the radio until June 1st; then I have a two-month vacation—which time I shall devote entirely to the opera. Of course I would prefer you to come North to stay with me long before June 1st and we could do a lot of work together."

He assured Heyward about an all-black opera that might have taken some of the luster off their work. Gershwin told him, "I saw *Four Saints in Three Acts,* an opera by Gertrude Stein and Virgil Thomson, with a colored cast. The libretto was entirely in Stein's manner, which means that it has the effect of a 5-year-old child prattling on. Musically, it sounded early 19th Century, which was a happy inspirtion and made the libretto bearable—in fact, quite entertaining. There may be one or two in the cast that would be useful to us."

Thomson recalled the first New York performance of *Four Saints* on a February night when the "cold was still intense, the streets were icy, and there was a taxi strike. But everybody came, from George Gershwin to Toscanini . . ." Later, Edward Matthews from the cast was selected to sing the role of Jake the fisherman in *Porgy and Bess* and its conductor, Alexander Smallens, would conduct Gershwin's opera.

Heyward was disappointed that Gershwin had contracted himself into staying in New York for so long. "I believe," he wrote, "that if you had gotten down for a reasonably long stay and gotten deep into the sources here you would have done a bigger job.

"I am not criticizing your decision. I know well what an enormously advantageous arrangement the radio is [Gershwin reportedly received two thousand dollars a week], and I know, also, how this tour of yours and the broadcasts are rolling up publicity that will be good for us when the show opens, only I am disappointed. There is so much more here than you have yet gotten hold of.

"Anyway, this can be offset to a great extent by my going on and working with you, and I shall do this, availing myself of your invitation and stopping with you with pleasure. I don't know now [March 2] just when I can go. It will take me adjustments here, but it will possibly be around the middle of April . . ."

Listening to "Music by Gershwin" in his Folly Beach, South Carolina, home, Heyward found the "reception so good it seemed as though you were in the room. In fact, the illusion was so perfect I could hardly keep from shouting at you 'Swell show, George but what the hell is the news about PORGY!!!' It is a good show. You have managed to give it a charming informality, and, in spite of the brevity, a definite impress of your own personality."

He enclosed a copy of the third scene of Act II, pointing out that in the lyrics he had "managed to get the lyrical parts to conform to the rhythms of ordinary speech, and also the idiom, and what I have hoped to do is ease these passages in so that there will be no consciousness of a break in the flow, and no feeling of a set song in the conventional operatic sense."

He admitted at that point he had come to "a deadlock" in the libretto. "The storm scene [which concludes the scene] must stand about as is with very few cuts in dialogue. Musically it must be done when we are together. It must carry itself on the big scene when Crown sings ["A Red Headed Woman"] against a spiritual, and I can't do the lyrics until I get your ideas as to time. Then I am doing a lyric for Porgy just before the curtain as he gets ready to drive out for Bess. Have you any thoughts about any of this last section of the play?"

Heyward was anxious to let the Guild have some idea as to the completion of their work so that a date could be set for an early opening. He was hoping for summer rehearsals and then the premiere soon after, that is, in the autumn of 1934. "Frankly," he told Gershwin, "it is financially quite important to me, as I have been letting everything else go, counting on it for early fall. If it is going to be late, I will have to get at something else, myself, to carry me over. Reassure me about this some time. Also, please, reassure the Guild."

That week Gershwin went to the Theatre Guild's offices on West Fifty-second Street, where he met with the business manager, Warren P. Munsell, to describe the opera's opening scene—Heyward's idea for merging the overture with what has come to be called the Jazzbo Brown piano music, which in turn leads into "Summertime."

"He seemed very excited about it," Gershwin told Heyward, "in fact he asked me to come upstairs and tell some of the other directors what I told him. They all seemed very interested but I must say that Lawrence Langner came through with some pretty stupid remarks. I have heard from several sources that he is on the dull and thick side so I shall probably have to ask him in the future to keep out of my way.

"Munsell was charming and I believe he has written to [Paul] Robeson to find out whether he is available [for Porgy]. I see in the papers where [Jules] Bledsoe [who had sung "Ol' Man River" in the original

Show Boat]—my choice for Crown—has made a sensational hit in the opera *Emperor Jones* in Amsterdam."

With his letter asking for reassurances Heyward had enclosed Act II, Scene 3, which Gershwin found "very interesting and touching . . . although a bit on the long side. However, I see one or two places that do not seem terribly important to the action and which could be cut. You must make sure that the opera is not too long as I am a great believer in not giving people too much of a good thing . . ."

He asked for a little help. "I would like to write the song that opens the second act ["It Take a Long Pull to Get There"], sung by Jake with fish nets, but I don't know the rhythm you had in mind—especially for the answers for the chorus, so I would appreciate it if you would put dots and dashes over the lyric and send it to me."

He was "delighted" to know that Heyward had decided to come North so they could work more closely. He told him, too, in this letter, dated March 8, 1934, that "Ira and I have worked on some words to music in the very opening, in Jazzbo Brown's room while the people are dancing, and I finished it up with a sort of African chant." This was the first mention of Ira Gershwin as a participant in the creation of *Porgy and Bess*. The words were not used, but George Gershwin's only known lyric contribution to the opera, "Da-doo-da/Da-doo-da/Wa-wa . . . wa . . . etc." remained.

It was days before Gershwin heard from Heyward, who had been seriously ill with influenza, but who on March 19 had mailed off another packet containing Act II, Scene 4. As for Gershwin's query about Jake's song, Heyward answered with, "I have done my best to convey my own rather vague idea for the rhythm on the enclosed copy . . . If you will imagine yourself at an oar and write the music to conform to that rhythm that will give you a better idea than anything I can write."

He felt that the just completed scene would present Gershwin with the "greatest musical opportunity of the show. I bank on it heavily to top the big effect in Act I, Scene 2 [the burial scene, highlighted by the affecting 'My Man's Gone Now']. The scene builds rapidly to the climax of Crown's jazz song ['A Red Headed Woman'] being done against the spiritual of the crowd ['Lawd, Lawd, Save Us'].

"I have made no effort to suggest words for these songs, because the music is the basic value. I should think it would be best for you to work out the two tunes and musical effects, then get Ira to work with you on the words as this is a job calling for the closest sort of collaboration. I enclose words suggested for the opening spiritual of that scene ["Oh, Doctor Jesus"; Gershwin would develop this into the remarkable "Six Prayers"]. I have not notated them, as I will be with you in several weeks and can give you a much better idea then, if in the meantime, you have not hit upon you own idea of time for it. The spiritual 'Somebody knocking at the door,' used in the old version will, I think, have to be retained even if varied, as it is a part of the entrance of Crown."

At the end of March, recovered, Heyward completed the first draft of the last act (in the original form *Porgy and Bess* was in three acts; some recent versions have tightened it into two). "Do not be alarmed," he assured Gershwin, "about any inclination toward too much length. There are many places where we can cut in conference without disrupting the story. For instance: the opening episode in Act III, Scene 2, with the detective and the women. This is swell comedy, and the audience loved it, but if necessary, it can be moved out entirely and the detective can go right to Porgy." This scene remained in the final version of the work.

Some time, perhaps in mid- or late April Heyward came to New York to actually collaborate, finally, with his collaborators. He marveled at the Gershwin working method: the brothers, he later wrote, "in their extraordinary fashion, would get at the piano, pound, wrangle, swear, burst into weird snatches of song, and eventually emerge with a polished lyric. Then too, Ira's gift for the more sophisticated lyric was exactly suited to the task of writing songs for Sporting Life, the Harlem gambler who had drifted into Catfish Row."

During these conferences George sensed that a lighter song might be placed between Jake's "It Take a Long Pull" and Maria's "I Hates Yo' Struttin' Style" castigation of Sporting Life.

"Something like this," he demonstrated at the keyboard. The colyricists listened as he played it again, then Ira suggested an opening phrase that fit: "I got plenty o' nothin'." Then he balanced that, in conformance with the tune, "An' nothin's plenty for me." He regarded these lines nothing more than a dummy lyric, temporary words that matched the rhythm and emphasis of the melody.

Heyward, who had for about six months been writing the lyrics for Gershwin's musicalization was anxious, for once, to write a lyric to a completed melody. All agreed it was a fine idea and Ira said, "Fine, I'll get to work on it later."

"Ira," Heyward said, "would you mind if I tried my hand at it? So far everything I've done has been set by George and I've never written words to music. If it's all right with you I'd love to take the tune along with me to Charleston." It was all right with Ira, and two weeks later, after returning to the South, Heyward mailed in his lyric. With some polishing by Ira it went into the opera as the Banjo Song "I Got Plenty o' Nuttin'."

Not long after Heyward left, Gershwin had finished all of the music for the first scene. A week later, on May 31, 1934, that season's final "Music by Gershwin" was broadcast. He was now free to visit the setting of his opera and to meet with the people about whom Heyward had written.

VII

Accompanied by his cousin, the artist Henry Botkin, Gershwin set out from Pennsylvania Station for Charleston on June 16; the departure was festive, as usual, for they were seen off by a crowd of relatives and friends.

Gershwin's man-of-all-work, Paul Mueller, preceded them in Gershwin's Buick, which was loaded down with extra luggage, art materials, other essentials—including Gershwin's golf clubs—necessary to a five-week stay. Mueller would meet them at the station in Charleston and they would then travel by car and ferry to Folly Island, where Gershwin had rented a four-room cottage with a large screened-in porch on Folly Beach. The Heywards had taken a somewhat more elaborate place nearby.

Once settled in their crowded, ramshackle quarters, Gershwin found himself in a totally foreign environment. His earlier vacation settings—Florida, Canada, the Adirondacks—had not prepared him for Folly Beach.

It "looks like a battered, old South Sea Island," he wrote his mother. The weather for the first three days had been pleasant and then it turned hot, which brought an insect invasion. "There are so many swamps in the district that when the breeze comes in from the land there's nothing to do but scratch." There was other wildlife—sand crabs, giant turtles, alligators (which could be heard bellowing from the swamps).

"There was a storm 2 weeks ago which tore down a few houses along the beach & the place is so primitive they just let them stay that way. Imagine, there's not *one* telephone on the whole Island—public or private. The nearest phone is about 10 miles away [in Charleston]."

The Heywards arrived five days later for a two-week stay. The librettist was happy that his collaborator could now steep himself in local color and the raw musical materials. "Under the baking sun," he wrote later, "of July and August [it was in fact, June and July] we established ourselves on Folly Island, a small barrier island ten miles from Charleston. James Island with its large population of primitive Gullah Negroes lay adjacent, and furnished us with a laboratory in which to test our theories, as well as an inexhaustible source of folk material.

"But the most interesting discovery to me, as we sat listening to their spirituals, or watched a group shuffling before a cabin or country store, was that to George it was more like a homecoming than an exploration."

He was especially delighted when he and Gershwin attended a prayer meeting at a church on a nearby island. There were no instruments and the congregation provided its own accompaniment, "a complicated rhythmic pattern beaten out by feet and hands . . . indubitably an African survival." This was called "shouting," by its practitioners. Heyward never forgot the night that Gershwin joined in the "shout" and to the great amusement of the congregation, "stole the show from their champion 'shouter.' "

Word soon spread that Gershwin was at Folly Island and the Charleston *News & Courier* sent a young reporter, Ashley Cooper, to interview him. Not finding anyone at the cottage, Cooper went in search of Gershwin. "I found him speeding along the beach in an open car, grinning like a kid. I waved him down and told him I was a reporter."

Gershwin invited Cooper into the car and told him, "I've never ridden on a beach before. It's exciting, eh?" (Probably, for one of these rides ended with, as he put it, "an auto in 4 feet of Atlantic.")

"I've never lived in such a back-to-nature place," he told Cooper when they reached the cottage. "At home I get up about noon. Here, I get up every morning at 7:00—well, at 7:30 anyway." Cooper reported also that Gershwin served a jolt of a local product known as "Hell Hole Swamp" corn whiskey.

"He couldn't talk about music very long without wanting to play the piano," Cooper recalled. "There was an old upright [which had been shipped in from Charleston] in the cottage on which he had been composing, and he sat down at it and said, 'Here's a good one.'

"Then he grinned and batted out the first couple of bars of 'I Got Rhythm.' Then he played 'The Last Roundup,' singing with it. Although I've always had a voice which has been known to frighten crows, I joined in. As for George, he wasn't Bing Crosby either. But before you knew it, two black servants, back in the kitchen, were beating time. And George was playing. And he and I were singing.

"He paused for a minute to apologize for his playing—which, just the same was superb. He held up the taped index finger of his right hand and explained that he had cut it trying to make a hole in one of his suitcase straps.

"It was well after dark when I finally left. By that time, 30 or 40 people—mostly servants from nearby cottages—were sitting out front. George kept playing, and the people out front were swaying to the music.

" 'Don't know who that man is playing the piano,' said one of the listeners, 'but that man really can play!' "

Mrs. Joseph I. Waring, a friend of the Heywards, then living with her family on another barrier island, Sullivan's, remembered that summer of 1934 affectionately.

"He was very happy," she said of Gershwin. "He used to take off his shirt and walk up and down the beach, and in the evening we would walk and sing spirituals . . . We used to have seven little houses where the help would live on the plantation, and from the day I was born my dah used to put me to sleep singing spirituals. George liked that. He loved to walk on the beach; he was nearly burned black because he loved the sun. He learned a lot of spirituals by going to churches around the area.

"DuBose would take him to the colored churches and schools. Someone told me of his playing in a colored school with a big picture of Robert E. Lee over him . . . One evening we got the Society for the Preservation of Spirituals together. It was in the summer. And that was fine, except that the Society . . . didn't sing very long, because George began to play. Everybody said, 'Play this. Play that.' We had a glorious evening, listening to George play the piano, rather than singing, as we should have been doing for him.

"He was very accommodating. He used to come to Sullivan's Island to see us; my mother was staying with me and the children. He was very, very dear to the children. They were devoted to him.

"One night he invited my mother and me to Folly to have dinner with him. He had a cousin staying with him, an artist who was a Frenchman [Botkin's Hercule Poirot mustache and goatee misled her]. Everything was very nice. He had a maid who served supper. And afterwards he said, 'Now I am going to play these pieces for you that no one has ever heard before. I want you always to remember that you were the first to hear these songs. DuBose hasn't even heard them.'

"DuBose had written the lyrics, but he hadn't heard the finished music. 'You will someday be very proud of this, because this is going to be a classic, it's going to be terrific, something wonderful.'

"And then he played. One was 'A Woman Is a Sometime Thing,' and I've forgotten what the other was. It might have been 'Summertime,' but I think I would have remembered that. Anyway, he was so confident about this, about how important it was going to be.

"When we were driving home, my mother said, 'How can you stand that? That is the most conceited man I've ever known in my life. How can he say all those things about his music and what he's going to do?'

"I said, 'But you know, I think he's right, and we should remember this. It's very important.' "

Her final comment, "George was not conceited. He was confident. He knew it was good music and he knew it was destined to be a great opera.

"He got around," she added. "Of course when you're writing all that music you don't have much time to spare. He spent a lot of time walking and swimming; he tried to be an athlete, a real he-man. And he really looked great."

"Bare and black above the waist," one reporter described him early in July, "habitually wearing only a two-inch beard and a pair of once white linen knickers." Gershwin wrote Emily Paley about this new way of life, "We go around with practically nothing on, shave only every other day (we do have visitors, you know, eat out on the porch not more than 30 feet from the ocean at high tide, sit out at night gazing at the stars, smoking our pipes (I've begun a pipe). The 3 of us, Harry [Botkin], Paul [Mueller] and myself discuss our two favorite subjects, Hitler's Germany & God's women."

Despite his activities, the new friends he had made, Gershwin was lonely. He sensed that many of his neighbors were suspicious of him as "a Yankee from the North" as being "a bit slick."

The solitude and contrasts generated an unusual philosophical side of him and he confided to Emily Paley that he had begun to give a great deal of thought to "my present and future plans & have come to a few decisions." Unfortunately he did not go into detail.

He missed some of the excitement of Manhattan and, except for the rich musical experiences, was not getting much work done. A New York *Herald Tribune* article, dated July 21, on the eve of his departure from Folly Island, has him still referring to "the first scene." He began work on the second, but admitted that it was "very tough for me to work here as the wild waves, playing the role of siren, beckons me every time I get stuck, which is often, and like a weak sailor turn to them causing many hours to be knocked into a thousand useless bits."

Another friend, Kay Halle, wrote and he told her that her letter was "like a drink to a thirsty man . . . so anxious was I to hear what my Yankee friends are up to, because they are still talking about the war—the Civil War—down here," but he was "fascinated by the beaches, the black bambinos, the crabs and turtles with 160 egg nests. There is music in the turtles, in the rhythm of their eggs, first one, then two, then one and two at a time . . ."

He was anxious to tell Emily Paley about the "grand" sermons he had heard, then returned to his nature study with the report that he had found a turtle nest containing "164 eggs about the size of a silver dollar." He had managed to play golf only twice during his stay. And, oh yes, he had been drafted to serve as a judge in a local beauty contest. Two days later they would begin driving back to New York, making stops en route, one of them in Hendersonville to see Heyward, who had left Folly Island about two weeks before.

They arrived in Hendersonville about July 19; he and Heyward that evening attended a religious service in a cabin in the nearby hills. As they were about to enter, Gershwin stopped, took Heyward's arm, beckoned him to listen. Heyward had heard such singing before, many times, but had taken it for granted. He was now hearing it as Gershwin heard it.

Gershwin was obviously excited by something and then Heyward, as he remembered it, "began to catch its extraordinary quality. It consisted of perhaps a dozen voices raised in loud rhythmic prayer. The odd thing about it was that while each started at a different time, they formed a clearly defined rhythmic pattern and that this, with the actual words lost, and the inevitable pounding of the rhythm, produced an effect almost terrifying in its primitive intensity."

Gershwin would re-create this effect in the opera's storm scene (Act II, Scene 4), at its beginning and close. Marked "ad libitum," and entitled simply "Prayer," it rises to an almost disturbing climax, as the six individual prayers intertwine, separate, and clash with an intensity indeed. Gershwin resolved the tension with an orchestral double fortissimo, then introduced a more traditional spiritual, "Oh, de Lawd Shake de Heavens," sung in harmony by the chorus.

Arriving back in New York around July 21, he had a little time before "Music by Gershwin" was scheduled to go on the air again. He devoted this time to *Porgy,* moving between Manhattan and Mosbacher's country home in Westchester. *Life Begins at 8:40* opened in August; Ira could now devote all of his time to working on the opera.

VIII

The second "Music by Gershwin" series began on September 30, 1934; the major difference from the first was that it was a weekly show of a half hour, which made Gershwin's life a little simpler. Gershwin's guest on the premiere broadcast was Harold Arlen, whose "You're a Builder Upper" (lyric by Ira and E. Y. Harburg) from *Life Begins at 8:40* was sung by Katzman's regular vocalist, Dick Robertson. Besides several of his songs and the *Rhapsody in Blue,* the program featured an Arthur Schwartz-Howard Dietz medley.

Even as he worked on the radio show with its preliminary conferences with Farr and Byron, the rehearsals and finally the broadcasts, Gershwin continued working on *Porgy.* By September he had begun orchestrating the second scene (the Saucer Burial) of Act I. Henry Katzman recalls that he would occasionally bring in bits of the score to the radio program's rehearsals for a reading. It was "mostly the incidental music, such as the crap game" . . . because it was "tricky" and "he wanted to hear if he were on the right track." By November he started on the second scene of Act II (in which the detectives investigating Crown's murder take Porgy away to identify the body). In his letter to Heyward of November 5, Gershwin outlined his plan for the opera's production; by this time Heyward and he agreed that they should not rush and that a production should not be done until the end of the 1935 season.

"First, I would like to set a tentative date for rehearsals," Gershwin wrote. "Second, I would like to have auditions started during January or February so that those people we choose for parts can be learning the music and save us so much time. I do hope that you can come to New York for these auditions as your knowledge of certain types will be of great value in picking characters."

He told Heyward of having the director Ernst Lubitsch over one evening and played "bits of the opera. He gave me some interesting slants, such as having the scenery just a bit off realism with very free use of lighting to enhance dramatic events. These ideas of Lubitsch's coincide with my feelings—how about yours?

"Ira has written the lyrics for *Porgy and Bess*'s first duet and I really think that this bit of melody will be most effective." (It was, for it was "Bess, You Is My Woman Now." The published sheet music credits both Ira and Heyward with the lyric; this was only fair, Ira maintained, since he had plucked the idea out of Heyward's libretto, suggested to his brother that it be developed musically and then wrote the lyric.)

Gershwin told Heyward too that he was leaving that afternoon to stay with the Mosbachers to get some work done on Act III, Scene 2, and that he had completed all of Act II. "Incidentally," he wrote, "I start and finish the storm scene with six different prayers sung simultaneously. This has somewhat the effect we heard in Hendersonville as we stood out side the Holy Rollers Church."

Not having heard from Heyward in more than a month—Heyward's work was virtually finished by this time and their correspondence was less regular—Gershwin, on December 17, decided he would bring him up to date on what was happening. "Theresa Helburn [a board member] came up for lunch the other day with Sam Behrman to hear some of the *Porgy* music and I must say they were most enthusiastic and excited.

"Also, I played some of the music for Deems Taylor, whose judgment I respect highly, and he was so enthusiastic and flattering that I blush to mention it. If the opera is so successful as these people think we have an exciting event ahead of us."

Another visitor around this time was music critic Irving Kolodin, who had met Gershwin through Oscar Levant. When Kolodin inquired whether he had ever considered reworking the *Rhapsody in Blue*, Gershwin said he had, then added, "But people seemed to like it the way it was, so I left it that way."

"Having people 'like' what he did was a necessary part of Gershwin's functioning, even more perhaps than with most creative artists," Kolodin wrote in his autobiographical *The Musical Life*. "Aside from the question of royalties, and how long a show ran, and earning power generally, he needed a quick affirmative reaction from his listeners, no matter how few or how many there were."

Kolodin had been invited to Gershwin's East Seventy-second Street duplex one Sunday around noon. "I was taken up to the penthouse and was soon admiring its suavely modish (not garish) interior, the view to the west from the spacious living room, with piano(s), and pictures, and books. Lunch time was at hand. I found myself at the table with Gershwin and Gertrude Niesen, a cafe singer of the girl-baritone variety who was seeking advice on lesser-known Gershwin songs for her act.

"It soon developed that Gershwin was as interested in interviewing me as I was in interviewing him, though for a quite different reasons.

"I would not attempt to reproduce verbatim a conversation nearly twenty-five years after it happened, but it went something like this: 'Oscar tells me you were at the Venice Festival in 1932 when my Concerto in F was played.' 'That's true,' I said. 'Fritz Reiner conducted, and Harry Kaufman was the soloist.' 'Tell us about it,' prompted Gershwin. 'I never had a chance to hear about it from anybody who was there.' 'Well,' I said, 'Reiner had a lot of trouble with the Scala Orchestra, which was playing the festival, especially with the trumpet-in-the-hat effect in the slow movement. But you know Fritz. By the time of the concert he had a really fine performance. It went so well Kaufman had to repeat the finale.'

" 'Think of it,' said Gershwin. 'They had to repeat the finale.' Turning to Miss Niesen, he said: 'The only other time that ever happened was when Von Bülow played the Tchaikovsky Concerto for the first time in Boston in 1875, and he had to repeat the finale.'

"She seemed duly impressed; I frankly was astounded. Where had Gershwin acquired this bit of esoteric information," Kolodin wondered. "When I had the opportunity, I looked it up, and by George, Gershwin was right."

Kolodin noted too Gershwin's impressive art collection and his books which "ranged widely through the current lot, with novels of Huxley, Virginia Woolf, and Hemingway juxtaposed to Rudy Vallee's *Vagabond Lover.*" Other favorites: George Bernard Shaw and Max Beerbohm.

On a second visit, Kolodin found Gershwin in his work room "on the upper level, at an intricate desk of his own design, which was large enough for oversized orchestral paper, and was fitted with ingenious racks and bins, sliding pigeonholes, etc., for the tools of the composer's trade." After a tour of the fourteen-room apartment, Kolodin sat beside Gershwin at the piano to hear the *Porgy* music, which was then intensely occupying him, as were the matter of casting and the right director.

"I spoke of possible producers," Gershwin wrote Heyward later, "and I think the Guild leaned heavily toward [Rouben] Mamoulian [who had directed the 1927 stage version of *Porgy*, several fine Hollywood musicals and, earlier, several operas]. They feel that he knows more about music than any other producer and might do a beautiful thing with the musicalization of the book. They feel John Houseman might be somewhat inexperienced to handle so huge a task. Hearing the music gave them quite a different impression than they had.

"I told them that you are prejudiced a little against Mamoulian and that you would rather have someone else. They seemed surprised at that as they had thought the two of you had worked without friction. The Guild feels that the opera is by far the most ambitious thing they have ever done."

Early in their collaboration, when Heyward began preparing the libretto from the play, he made references to the elimination of the "Negro vaudeville stuff" and changing the first scene because he did not like the handling in the dramatic form which had "opened with a regular riot of noise and color." This and other frictions perhaps during the play's rehearsals led to Heyward's wish not to work with Mamoulian again. With a little pressure from the Guild and Gershwin, he withdrew his objections and Mamoulian was contracted to be producer-director of *Porgy and Bess.*

A week after George posted the newsy letter to Heyward, on December 23, 1934, the final "Music by Gershwin" was broadcast. Gershwin could now devote all his energies to his labor of love.

IX

Before the end of 1934 Gershwin was certain he had found his Porgy in Todd Duncan, who had been suggested to him by Olin Downes. The critic had heard the baritone sing the role of Alfio in an all-black production of *Cavalleria Rusticana* at the Mecca Temple in New York.

Duncan was then teaching voice at Howard University, Washington, D.C., and was head of the Music Department. Between semesters he gave recitals of the standard repertory: Schubert, Schumann, Brahms. A graduate of Columbia University, with a master's degree in voice, Duncan approached Gershwin somewhat prejudicially; he was not fond of popular music or jazz and to him George Gershwin stood for both.

Still, he could not gracefully ignore an invitation to sing for Gershwin on Downes's recommendation and, curiously, the composer had mentioned an opera, not a musical comedy. He traveled up from Washington on a Sunday and was admitted into Gershwin's apartment by the composer himself. Duncan had come alone, so Gershwin was drafted to be his accompanist.

Duncan placed the music on the rack: "Lungi dal caro bene" by an obscure early Italian composer, Secchi, and Mussorgsky's "The Song of the Flea." Gershwin later said he had found this audition refreshing after several earlier Porgy candidates whose repertory seemed to consist only of spirituals or "Ol' Man River." Duncan remembered that first meeting with Gershwin warmly: "Imagine a Negro, auditioning for a Jew, singing an old Italian aria."

Gershwin observed Duncan closely as he sang, his movements, his facial expressions, then stopped playing midway through the Secchi and said, "Will you be my Porgy?"

Duncan wasn't so sure. He wanted to hear some of the music; if he liked it then he might take the part. Gershwin liked his blunt honesty and laughed. He would arrange for him to hear the *Porgy* music if he could return the following Sunday and sing for some of the Guild people, and then he and Ira would present a program of *Porgy* songs. Duncan, on his teacher's salary, wasn't too happy about that and admitted he couldn't spend his time (and little money) traveling between Washington and New York. Gershwin wrote a check which enabled Duncan to return the next week, during the Christmas holiday season, with his wife.

Gershwin then wrote to Heyward: "Here is an exciting piece of news: I heard about a man singer who teaches music in Washington and arranged to have him come and sing for me . . . In my opinion he is the closest thing to a colored Lawrence Tibbett I have ever heard. He is about six feet tall and very well proportioned with a rich booming voice. He would make a superb Crown and, I think, just as good a Porgy . . . I shall ask the Guild to take an option on his services."

Duncan and Mrs. Duncan arrived in time for the one o'clock audition. In the lobby they encountered a very nattily dressed man—with cane—and a woman. The man obviously had spotted Duncan and guessed who he was. He opened a conversation with, "Who are you?" Then he added, "You gotta be goddam good; are you the genius from the South that George has been telling us about?"

"He made me angry," Duncan told Berthe Schuchat later in a radio interview, but decided to hold his tongue. The bumptious interrogator was Lawrence Langner; his companion was Theresa Helburn—both were important members of the Guild's board. Apparently Gershwin and Langner had patched up their differences, or Langner was staying out of his way. For all his brusque manner and a gift for making enemies, Langner was the catalyst in the Guild's success as an important force in the American theater. But he could be a problem. As Brooks Atkinson has written, "The board meetings [degenerated] into dogfights . . . A Guild rehearsal was something to fear."

Summoned from his country home by Gershwin, Langner was disgruntled and he annoyed Duncan. Although Duncan was supposed to sing a few songs, "I sang a whole program" to Gershwin's accompaniment again—"no show tunes, I didn't know any," but lieder, chansons, even a few spirituals. That December Sunday afternoon it was agreed that Todd Duncan would be Gershwin's Porgy.

The two formed a close and some times bantering friendship. Gershwin insisted that Duncan was more Jewish than he and Duncan countered with the suggestion that Gershwin was more Negro than he. They agreed that the conservatory-trained Duncan would have to learn something about the quasi-folk dialect of the lyrics and that he might learn much by studying the speech on the spot.

One weekend he and Gershwin traveled to Charleston; they could not stay with Heyward, then in Hendersonville, so they had to find separate quarters. Duncan recalled for Mrs. Schuchat that he roomed with "a wonderful Negro family—a doctor. Gershwin wanted to stay there too, but he didn't. The races then were too far apart—they didn't want him. I couldn't stay at the white hotel and they didn't want him." Gershwin, Duncan concluded, "didn't have any of that in him."

Porgy was set. The casting of Bess was simpler. Anne Wiggins Brown, a twenty-year-old voice student at the Juilliard School of Music, wrote a letter to Gershwin asking for an audition. The daughter of a Baltimore physician, she sang for Gershwin and got the part. Another Juilliard graduate, Ruby Elzy, gifted with a remarkable soprano voice, was cast as Serena.

Finding the more experienced singers for some of the other parts and the chorus was made easier by Heyward's friend J. Rosamond Johnson, a composer, arranger and authority on black music; in addition, he was selected to appear in the opera as the slightly fraudulent Lawyer Frazier. Also assisting in the casting was Robert Wachsman, who was familiar with black singers because of his association with Harold Arlen from the Cotton Club days. Gershwin himself had already chosen Edward Matthews, after hearing him in *Four Saints in Three Acts;* he would be Jake, the hardworking fisherman.

His wife, Clara, was to be Abbie Mitchell, a veteran vocalist as well as dramatic actress. She had sung with Duncan in the Mecca Temple's *Cavalleria Rusticana;* in real life she was the wife of composer-arranger Will Marion Cook.

An especially interesting casting was the part of Maria, the matriarchal keeper of a Catfish Row cookhouse. Georgette Harvey, primarily a dramatic actress, had portrayed Maria in the original play in 1927; she would play her again in *Porgy* (when the opera was revived in 1942, she played the role again).

As the powerful, sometimes nasty (but not truly evil) stevedore Crown, Boston-bred and -educated Warren Coleman was chosen; he had had a career as a concert singer and was the discovery of Harold Arlen's friend Bob Wachsman. The other major role, that of the wily Sporting Life, was given to the one nonmusical member of the cast, John W. Bubbles of the popular vaudeville team Buck and Bubbles. He would prove to be a source of trouble.

Alexander Smallens was the conductor, and the musical coach was composer-pianist-conductor Alexander Steinert. A Prix de Rome recipient, Steinert had been Gershwin's choice since the winter of 1934, when he was coaching the Russian Opera Company. J. Rosamond Johnson was appointed Steinert's assistant. The well-known Eva Jessye Choir— some forty voices—would sing as residents of Catfish Row. All were under the direction of Rouben Mamoulian.

Within a month after Duncan's Christmastime visit, Gershwin had sent him copies of some of the completed music, which the singer had good things to say about, pleasing Gershwin. By this time two acts had been completed and he prepared for a visit with the Mosbachers in

Florida. In his letter, dated January 24, 1935, he told Duncan, "I just finished a trio ["Where's My Bess?"] in the last scene for Porgy, Serena and Maria which I think will interest you very much." It is the penultimate song in the opera, followed by the finale, "I'm On My Way." Gershwin's major work now was on the orchestration, and that he planned to do much on in Palm Beach as he told a reporter from the Charleston *News & Courier* on January 30 during a stopover to meet with Heyward.

In Palm Beach he stayed with the Mosbachers and their three children in a spacious house Mosbacher had rented for the winter. Early in February he wrote to Ira about an unusual cold spell that had kept him indoors but once the weather turned warm he worked on the patio and worked "slowly, there being millions of notes to write." He expected to complete the scoring of the second scene of Act I that week, after which he tackled Scene 1.

The work went well and he acquired a deep tan and was "rapidly getting to look like the Indian I was accused of being when I was young —working in the sun and golfing." He took time out to visit his mother in Miami to have dinner with her. "Four people last night thought that she was my wife," he told Lou Paley in a postcard. "Don't tell [gossip columnist] Winchell."

After a morning's work he often relaxed on the patio to write letters. He wanted to tell his brother how much Heyward had admired his lyrics and even touched on business matters. He suggested to Ira that, based on a projected production cost of forty thousand dollars, he and Mosbacher would contribute four thousand dollars and Ira two thousand dollars for a 25 percent investment in the opera. But then he learned that the Guild did not want an outside investor—they had their own roster of potential backers—and preferred not having Mosbacher. Gershwin felt then that he and Ira would settle for a 15 percent share. It "would not be risking too much & yet we'd have a good interest in the undertaking. What do you think?" He predicted too that the production costs could go higher (he was right, they almost doubled). So they and Heyward invested in *Porgy*—all were destined to lose their financial contributions to the opera.

In March, back in New York, he continued with the orchestration and, as usual, shared his work in progress with his friends. One was Kay Halle (of the Cleveland department store family) whom he had met in Cleveland after a concert. Interested in music, she was drawn to Gershwin during a period when she served as intermission commentator for the Cleveland Orchestra's radio broadcasts. In 1935 she was living in New York in the Hotel Élysée. Gershwin liked to play her

Steinway baby grand, which Arthur Rubinstein had selected for her. He had a standing invitation to play it whenever he wished and the desk clerk was instructed to give him the key to Halle's room anytime "so that he might 'draw inspiration' from my piano.

"George could not retreat to the country to compose as he 'became too aware of the rhythm of the insects and other sounds of nature.' " His Folly Island back-to-nature experience had affected him. During one of the many preproduction interviews he told a reporter that "the ideal room for composing would be one with four bare walls and no windows."

But, the reporter pointed out, that his walls decorated with modern art and the view from his workroom windows hardly qualified.

"The buildings are fixed and still," Gershwin replied. "They don't disturb you."

Halle recalled being invited with her friend Gloria Braggioti (sister of the pianist) to hear some of the new music as it was completed. On the way to East Seventy-second Street, they stopped first at "Reuben's delicatessen to bring the salami and pumpernickel bread George loved."

She found his large gatherings impressive because of their intermingling of his array of friends, from philosopher-architect Buckminster Fuller to sculptor Isamu Noguchi, as well as musical friends. "Most enjoyable were George's cozy luncheons of six to eight guests, with his fox terrier, Tony, always at his side. George was fascinated by new inventions, and surprisingly knowledgeable about scientific matters. I remember one occasion when he asked his butler to go out and bring back six copies of *Popular Mechanics,* his favorite magazine—one for each guest."

During the period of the creation of *Porgy and Bess* Gershwin did get away from work now and then. Kay Halle believed that the event that most moved Gershwin was an invitation from President Franklin D. Roosevelt to attend a party at the White House with her on December 29, 1934.

"As we reached the entrance hall leading to the East Room, George's joy and excitement were so unbounded that he shot away from the receiving line to stand under the great glittering chandelier, joyfully crying out, 'If only my father could see me now!'

"After dinner, the President directed that the Lincoln piano be rolled nearer to him, motioning George toward it. With stars in his eyes, and a salute in the direction of the President, George sat down and played 'Wintergreen for President' from his musical *Of Thee I Sing,* with all the guests joining in song. Though the President's legs were in steel braces, he managed to move them ever so slightly in rhythm with the cascade of tunes that poured from George's fingers."

Another regular visitor to Gershwin's apartment at this time was Mabel Schirmer. "George did not like to be alone," she told a friend, "not even when he was working. In 1935 I lived nearby, on East Seventy-eighth Street.

"Often he would call me in the morning and invite me to lunch. After lunch we would settle in his workroom and, while I did petit point, he would work. It must have been on the orchestrations—I don't recall his playing the piano very often. After he'd finish for the day we'd go for a walk in Central Park. He was a very strenuous walker!"

The same vigor applied to his work, and the nearer he came to its completion the more carefully he dated each finished section in his score of the orchestration:

Sept. 1934, Act I, Scene 2 (this was completed in Palm Beach in February, 1935)

Feb. 1935, Palm Beach, Fla. Act I, Scene 1

July 22, 1935. (finished) Act III, Scene 1

Aug. 4, 1935, Act III, Scene 2

Finished August 23, 1935, George Gershwin, Act III, Scene 3

Orchestration begun late 1934—finished Sept. 2, 1935. G.G.

There were but twenty-eight days remaining before the Boston premiere. A battery of copyists was assigned to prepare the orchestral parts. Eva Jessye, the choral director, remembered visiting him and seeing a group of men at a long table feverishly working from Gershwin's score, preparing it for rehearsals and the Boston opening.

Even before all of the orchestration was completed, Gershwin decided he would test some of it with several members of the cast—Anne Brown, Todd Duncan, Abbie Mitchell and Edward Matthews. William Paley of CBS arranged for the use of one of their transcription studios for the run-through. Gershwin, the cast and an orchestra squeezed into the studio on July 19, 1935, to see and hear how *Porgy* sounded. During the rehearsals, engineer John V. Gromback recorded portions of the proceedings, preserving a rare example of Gershwin conducting one of his own works (the only other is the rough run-through of the *Second Rhapsody*). From this recording it is evident from the singing and the handling of the orchestra that Gershwin meant his *Porgy*, as it was still being called, to be an opera.

Three days after he marked the last act of *Porgy* "finished," rehearsals were under way.

X

Heyward, who had come North in April for auditions, returned in August for the rehearsals. He was especially impressed with Steinert, who had the cast "ready to read the difficult score from beginning to end."

All except one: John W. Bubbles (né John William Sublett).

He was casual about rehearsal schedules and kept the company waiting, to the indignation of conductor Smallens and director Mamoulian and even some members of the cast. Duncan particularly resented Bubbles's raffish ways.

Also, Bubbles did not read music. A born improvisor and a marvelous dancer (whose work Fred Astaire studied and admired), he had a disturbing tendency to change note values, change his lines and miss cues, depending on his mood.

"I hated him," Duncan confessed years later, but admitted, too, that while Bubbles was impossible before and after performances, he was a "genius" onstage. Once he learned his part he created one of the classic performances of the American musical theater. As Duncan put it, he was "electric!"

His indifference to promptness infuriated Smallens. One day, as the company awaited the arrival of Bubbles, the conductor threw down his baton and shouted to Mamoulian, "I'm sick of this waiting! We'll have to throw him out and get somebody else!"

Gershwin shot out of his seat and hurried to the pit. "You can't do that," he said. "Why, he's—he's the black Toscanini!" This was a rare intervention for him; he rarely meddled in the politics of a show. Bubbles stayed, but would prove to be a nettlesome presence during the run of *Porgy and Bess,* as a result of his cavalier way with the score and with some of the women in the cast and the cities which they toured. (Duncan remembered his coming onstage for a curtain with his fly unzipped: "He was giving a performance," Duncan believed, "in his dressing room.")

By early 1935, with "Music by Gershwin" off the air, Gershwin was well along on the completion of his opera. In February he stayed with the Emil Mosbachers in Palm Beach, Florida, where he worked on the orchestration of Act I. (Gershwin Collection)

In his duplex apartment on East Seventy-second Street, Gershwin completed the orchestration of *Porgy and Bess* in September 1935, about three weeks before his thirty-seventh birthday. (Gershwin Collection, Courtesy of Don Rose)

Mabel Schirmer, a nearby neighbor, frequently came to Gershwin's apartment and kept him company while he orchestrated *Porgy and Bess*. While he wrote, Mabel did petit point. When he finished for the day, they took vigorous walks in Central Park. (Gershwin Collection)

DuBose Heyward, librettist and co-lyricist of *Porgy and Bess,* and Ira Gershwin collaborating on the opera. The collaboration was one of the most gracious, mutually respectful and ultimately most richly productive in the history of the American theater. It was unique in its meshing of temperaments and freedom from ego clashes. (Gershwin Collection)

Porgy and Bess, Act I, Scene I, Catfish Row: the killing of Robbins (Henry Davis, on knees) by Crown (Warren Coleman). Porgy (Todd Duncan) observes from the window of his room. Bess (Anne Brown) on the steps, and Sporting Life (John W. Bubbles, with bowler hat), also watch. (Gershwin Collection)

Anne Brown and Todd Duncan in the duet, "I Loves You, Porgy," Act II, Scene 3. (Gershwin Collection)

Bubbles (whose given name was John William Sublett) as the troublemaker and narcotics and whiskey peddler Sporting Life. His performance, though erratic, was a classic. (Gershwin Collection)

George Gershwin's pencil portrait of DuBose Heyward. (From the collection of I. H. Asper, Q.C., Winnipeg, Canada)

Porgy and Bess, opening-night curtain call, Alvin Theatre, New York, October 10, 1935, Gershwin up front. Behind him from left to right are Georgette Harvey (Maria), Ruby Elzy (Serena), Anne Brown (Bess), director Rouben Mamoulian, DuBose Heyward (over Gershwin's shoulder), Warren Coleman (Crown). (Gershwin Collection)

George Gershwin in his studio after the premiere of *Porgy and Bess;* the painting, by him, is of the daughter of his cook. (Gershwin Collection)

Rehearsing, Alexander Smallens conducting, in Lewisohn Stadium, July 9, 1936, for his last All-Gershwin Concert there. (Gershwin Collection, Courtesy of Louise Kerz)

Soon after settling into Beverly Hills, Ira Gershwin revised the lyric to "Strike Up the Band" for the University of California in Los Angeles. The result was the football song "Strike Up the Band for U.C.L.A." In the house on North Roxbury Drive, Gershwin demonstrates for members of the faculty and the student chorus. Their royalty was two tickets for every home game for many years. (Associated Students, U.C.L.A., Norm Schindler)

Studio publicity shot of George, 1936. (Courtesy Glenn Barr)

Because RKO was not expeditious in coming up with the screenplays for their Astaire musicals, Gershwin had time on his hands; even as he scored his last three films, he conducted part of an All-Gershwin Concert in Los Angeles in February 1937, during which he first experienced signs of his fatal illness. (Gershwin Collection)

During 1936–37 Gershwin toured extensively along the West Coast, playing in Los Angeles, San Francisco and Seattle. Photo shows him in his hotel in Seattle. (Gershwin Collection)

Demonstrating songs written for *Shall We Dance* on the set at RKO. Fred Astaire and Ginger Rogers are seated to George Gershwin's right; behind him are Ira Gershwin (with pipe) and musical director Nathaniel Shilkret. Standing behind Rogers and Astaire are dance director Hermes Pan and director Mark Sandrich. (Gershwin Collection)

Almost immediately after completing the *Shall We Dance* songs, the Gershwins went to work on *A Damsel in Distress,* which starred Astaire without Rogers. Photo was taken in the spring of 1937. (Gershwin Collection)

The Gershwins did not Go Hollywood (i.e., frequent the In places, cultivate producers and stars, etc.). Instead they gathered with the songwriters and writers they had known in New York. Among them were Irving Berlin (photo by Gershwin), Jerome Kern, with another friend, lyricist Dorothy Fields, and E. Y. (Yip) Harburg, a boyhood friend from their Lower East Side years (photo by Gershwin). (Gershwin Collection)

A new friend was composer-theorist Arnold Schoenberg, whose recondite music Gershwin admired (in return, Schoenberg admired Gershwin). This portrait, completed in December 1936, was one of George's last works in oil. (Gershwin Collection)

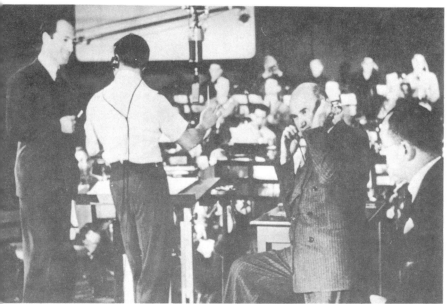

On the sound stage at the *Goldwyn Follies,* 1937; George Gershwin confers with musical director Alfred Newman while Samuel Goldwyn listens to a playback. Ira Gershwin is to Goldwyn's left. (Gershwin Collection)

Gershwin's last photograph taken at the RKO Studies at the end of June 1937. (Gershwin Collection)

After his brother's death, Ira Gershwin rested for a time and then began collaborating on songs with Jerome Kern, Harry Warren and others. (Gershwin Collection)

Unlike his brother, Ira Gershwin liked Hollywood and chose to remain there to work on an occasional show or film. One of his favorites of all Gershwin-scored movies was *An American in Paris* (1951), starring Gene Kelly. Here they hobnob on the set of another film musical, *Singin' in the Rain,* which had songs by his friend Arthur Freed (lyrics) and music by Nacio Herb Brown. (Gershwin Collection)

One of Ira Gershwin's favorite hobbies was making wild bets on the races, most choices based on fanciful word associations. Here, in 1958, he discusses a bet with his secretary, Lawrence D. Stewart, in his box at Hollywood Park. (Gershwin Collection)

In June 1966 Ira Gershwin was presented with the honorary degree of Doctor of Fine Arts by the University of Maryland. With him are Homer Ulrich, head of the Department of Music and the University's president, Dr. Wilson H. Elkins. (University of Maryland)

When he returned to Broadway, Ira Gershwin's most important Broadway collaborator was Kurt Weill; their first collaboration, *Lady in the Dark* (1941), was Ira's first major work since the death of George Gershwin. (Gershwin Collection)

With Harold Arlen, Ira Gershwin wrote the songs for the film *A Star Is Born* (1954), starring Judy Garland; it was Ira's most impressive original film score. (Gershwin Collection)

In his later years Ira Gershwin virtually retired from songwriting, became more reclusive and spent his time annotating Gershwin materials for deposit in the Gershwin Archive, Library of Congress. During this time he was assisted in this by a young enthusiast from Ohio, Michael Feinstein. After Ira's death, Feinstein was launched on a remarkable and successful career as a vocalist-pianist in Los Angeles, New York and London. Photo was taken in 1980. (Photo courtesy of Donald Smith)

Portrait of George Gershwin by Judy Cimaglia.

Gershwin was, Eva Jessye remembered, quite unobtrusive during rehearsals, venting his tensions by cracking and eating peanuts and keeping out of the way until asked to clarify a musical passage or make changes. He believed in his opera and that it represented the best of him and that all would be well.

Mamoulian wrote about his own feelings after the first day's rehearsals: "It is like breaking mountains of ice. The end of it leaves one completely exhausted and usually a little depressed. Everything seems awkward, disorganized, almost hopeless." He returned to his hotel and fell on the bed, "indulging in rather melancholy and misanthropic thoughts," when the phone rang. It was Gershwin.

"Rouben," he said, "I couldn't help calling you . . . I just *had* to call you and tell you how I feel. I am so thrilled and delighted over the rehearsal today."

Mamoulian began to rally; his outlook brightened.

"I tell you," Gershwin went on enthusiastically, "after listening to the rehearsal today, I think the music is so marvelous—I really don't believe I wrote it!"

This was typical and Mamoulian cautioned that such objectivity was "apt to be misunderstood by people who did not know him well. Like a proud parent with a gifted child he praised his creations "without any self-consciousness or false modesty . . . Conceit is made of much sterner stuff—it was not that with George."

Vernon Duke, then collaborating with Ira on songs for the next *Ziegfeld Follies,* remembered coming to a rehearsal to find Gershwin savoring his orchestrations. He "grinned with delight at the well-organized sounds that emerged from the pit. I was sitting quietly in a seat in the last row when George startled me by suddenly appearing from the back and grabbing me by the shoulder.

" 'Hey, Dukie!' he whispered fiercely. 'Just listen to those overtones!' "

Before the company left for Boston a full-scale run-through took place in Carnegie Hall, with family, friends and colleagues as audience. To all it was obvious that *Porgy and Bess* was George Gershwin's greatest achievement.

The Boston reception on September 30, 1935 (four days after Gershwin's thirty-seventh birthday), had been promising indeed. Serge Koussevitzky hailed it as "a great advance in American opera." The distinguished critic of the *Evening Transcript,* Moses Smith, observed that Gershwin "has traveled a long way from Tin Pan Alley. He must now be accepted as a serious composer." The New York *Herald Tribune* had dispatched music critic Francis D. Perkins to Boston for the event and he reported that he considered *Porgy and Bess* "a notable achievement in a new field. It tells of unusually effective craftsmanship; it reflects a marked advance in Mr. Gershwin's progress." The reviewer for the *Christian Science Monitor* called the opera "Gershwin's most important contribution to music." J. Rosamond Johnson called him "the Abraham Lincoln of Negro music." After one performance, the audience concurred with a fifteen-minute ovation.

This triumph was followed by deflation. Some members of the Theatre Guild, as well as director Rouben Mamoulian, felt that the opera's three-hour running time was excessive. Cuts would have to be made; so much for the "unusually effective craftsmanship." Gershwin's most carefully crafted work had to be reworked, abridged, in the name of showmanship and, in one instance, simple practicality. In the first scene of the second act, for example, Porgy was assigned three songs (arias, in fact, though Gershwin did not call them that) in succession: "I Got Plenty o' Nuttin'," "Buzzard Song" and the duet "Bess, You Is My Woman Now." Unlike recent productions of *Porgy and Bess*, the 1935 production had but one Porgy. So "Buzzard Song" was among the first cut, in order to provide Duncan with a chance to breathe between songs.

With applause and praises still ringing in their ears, a small group walked in the snow-covered Boston Common to decide on the excisions: Gershwin, Mamoulian, Alexander Steinert (himself a distinguished composer) and Kay Swift. The atmospheric *Jazzbo Brown* piano music went out, so did the lacerating "I Hates Yo' Struttin' Style," the remarkable "Six Prayers" went—and more. Gershwin tried to understand the practicalities, but when it was suggested that what had been conceived as a trio could be abbreviated into a solo for Porgy, he put up an argument. He wanted "Where's My Bess" to remain as it was, but finally conceded on that too, and it was changed to a Porgy solo.

"Very few composers, if any," Steinert observed, "would have stood by and witnessed with comparative calm the dismemberment of their brain-child until it had been reduced by nearly a quarter! He was quite philosophical about it . . ."

The *Porgy and Bess* that opened at the Alvin Theatre in New York City on October 10, 1935, with its burden of advance publicity and expectation, was not the opera that had been acclaimed in Boston on September 10.

During the final rehearsals in New York for the October 10 premiere, Kay Swift was very busy with preparations for the opening-night party. With a guest list of more than four hundred, she talked Condé Nast into letting her use his Park Avenue apartment for the celebration. It was capacious enough to accommodate not only the guests, but the entire cast and two orchestras—one specializing in Latin rhythms, and Paul Whiteman's. It was daylight before the party ended, although by then, what with the divided reviews, some of the celebrants had little to celebrate. The audience reception had been as enthusiastic as it had been in Boston, but it was the reviews that made the difference at the box office.

"Gershwin does not even know what an opera is," was the verdict of Virgil Thomson in the November/December 1935 issue of *Modern Music.* That he closed the sentence with ". . . and yet Porgy and Bess is an opera and it has power and it has vigor," hardly tempered the impact of the opening phrase, and what followed. The tone of his appraisal was condescending—and surprisingly uninformed. He admitted an unfamiliarity with Gershwin's concert works and named two that did not exist. Thomson's assessment of the opera, however, reflected a consensus of the "intellectual" music Establishment of the time as well as the mixed (predominantly negative) opinions of the press.

This was a mix of drama and music critics; the drama men were generally favorable, the music men were, in most cases, not. Gershwin's former champion, Samuel Chotzinoff, then writing for the New York *Post,* condemned *Porgy and Bess* as "a hybrid"; true to form, Paul Rosenfeld, probably the most distinguished music critic of the "modern" period, and never a Gershwin admirer, dismissed it as "an aggrandized musical show." And so it went, although the music critic for the New York *American,* Leonard Liebling, with certain prescience, called *Porgy and Bess* "the first authentic American opera."

It is speculative whether the mixed critical reception, the perplexity of audiences at an operatic Gershwin or the poor economic climate of the mid-1930s affected the box office. Soon after *Porgy and Bess* opened ticket sales fell below operating costs; while it was kept running on the advance ticket sales that had resulted from early publicity and word from Boston, attempts were made to keep it alive.

Soon after the premiere Gershwin wrote an article for the drama section of the Sunday New York *Times* in which he attempted to define what he meant by "folk opera," explain why he did not offer it for production by a bona fide opera company and answer those critics who had accused him of writing a song-filled opera.

It was a "folk opera," he explained, because *"Porgy and Bess* is a folk tale. Its people would naturally sing folk music" [except he would create his own spirituals and folk songs]. "But they are still folk music— and therefore, being in operatic form, *Porgy and Bess* becomes folk opera."

As for all the songs in an opera, he said, "It was my idea that opera should be entertaining—that it should contain all the elements of entertainment. Therefore, when I chose *Porgy and Bess,* a tale of Charleston Negroes, for a subject, I made sure that it would enable me to write light as well as serious music and that it would enable me to include humor as well as tragedy—in fact, all the elements of entertainment for the eye as well as the ear, because the Negroes, as a race, have all these qualities inherent in them. They are ideal for my purpose because they express themselves not only by the spoken word but quite naturally by song and dance . . .

"No story could be more ideal for the serious form I needed than *Porgy and Bess.* First of all, it is American, and I believe that American music should be based on American material. I felt when I read *Porgy* in novel form that it had 100 percent dramatic intensity in addition to humor. It was then that I wrote to DuBose Heyward suggesting that we make an opera of it.

"It is true that I have written songs for *Porgy and Bess.* I am not ashamed of writing songs at any time so long as they are good songs. In *Porgy and Bess* I realized I was writing an opera for the theatre and without songs it could be neither for the theatre nor entertaining, from my viewpoint.

"But songs are entirely in the operatic tradition. Many of the most successful operas of the past have had songs. Nearly all of Verdi's operas contain what are known as 'song hits.' *Carmen* is almost a collection of song hits. And what about 'The Last Rose of Summer,' perhaps one of the most widely known songs of the generation? How many of those who sing it know that it is from an opera?

"Of course, the songs in *Porgy and Bess* are only part of the whole. The recitatives I have tried to make as close to the Negro inflection in speech as possible, and I believe my songwriting apprenticeship has served invaluably in this respect, because the song writers of America have the best conception of how to set words to music so that the music gives added expression to the words. I have used sustained symphonic music to unify entire scenes, and I prepared myself for the task by further study in counterpoint and modern harmony."

He mentioned several who had helped him to realize his operatic dream: Todd Duncan, Anne Brown, even the incorrigible Bubbles, Mamoulian and Smallens and especially Heyward and Ira, emphasizing the great emotional range and poetry of their work.

Clarification did not help the box office. An attempt to keep expenses down was blocked by the Musicians Union, which would not permit a reduction in the size of the orchestra. The admission price was lowered from the $4.40 top to $3.30, but to no avail; by December it was decided to close and to attempt to diminish the losses with a tour. After 124 performances *Porgy and Bess* closed in New York and was scheduled to begin its tour in Philadelphia on January 27, 1936.

Despite the generally negative reception, Victor Records went ahead with plans to record *Highlights from Porgy and Bess* in a four-record (78 rpm) album. It was curiously cast. Instead of Duncan and Brown, Porgy was sung by Lawrence Tibbett and Bess by Helen Jepson; the Jessye Choir sang and Smallens conducted all but one side (Nathaniel Shilkret conducted "My Man's Gone Now"). Obviously Tibbett and Jepson were bigger names than Duncan and Brown.

The sessions, with Gershwin present, took place on October 14, four days after the opera opened. Soon some of the songs began to be heard on the radio. But as the opera floundered at the box office, plans were hastily made for the tour. Even so, Gershwin was certain he had created a work of lasting value.

His affection and respect for Heyward was deepened by their experience and he looked forward to setting another work by his librettist friend. Heyward's mother, Jane Heyward, had written him a letter after the opera's premiere; he thanked her and called her ". . . indeed a great mother of a great son."

Neither would live to see the eventual recognition of their achievement, but they had nothing to regret. Ira Gershwin best expressed the feelings of all in a letter to Heyward written after his brother's death.

"To the end of my days," he began, "I shall never forget the exciting and thrilling period of *Porgy and Bess*. George had, not only a great respect for you, but also a deep affection, and I assure you, though I believe you must have known, I felt the same way about you and considered it a great honor to be associated with you, however small my contribution."

14

The Goldwyn Coast

A postpartum letdown set in after the exhilarating weeks of rehearsals and the gratifying reception, except from too many critics, of *Porgy and Bess*. The rather sour, even sour-grapes, reviews were unsettling to Gershwin, who generally handled criticism with nonchalant grace. He had put twenty intensive months of work into his opera. After *Porgy and Bess* opened he was wrung out and, worse, had nothing to do. Gershwin decided he needed a rest. Late in November he left New York for Mexico accompanied by an old friend, Edward Warburg, director of the American Ballet and the "arts and society" analyst, Dr. Gregory Zilboorg. It would not be a happy experience for Gershwin.

Zilboorg, a Russian-born psychiatrist who fled during the Bolshevik revolution of 1917, was by the thirties established in New York as a most fashionable analyst of the Freudian persuasion. Erudite, and with artistic pretensions, he attracted an affluent and sizable clientele from the arts.

Gershwin had heard about Zilboorg from Kay Swift who, along with her husband, financier-lyricist James Paul Warburg, was seeing Zilboorg (so was Edward Warburg, James Warburg's cousin). Gershwin expressed an interest in psychiatry (about which he confessed he knew little) and, besides, since he suffered from what he called "composer's stomach," maybe Zilboorg could trace that to some form of emotional stress and strain in an otherwise vibrantly healthy personality. Swift believed that a few sessions with Zilboorg might prove instructive and salubrious for Gershwin.

"It was a mistake," she has since admitted. Zilboorg often exhibited an envious hostility toward his successful, celebrated, "patient." To her dismay, the analyst frequently discussed Gershwin's sessions with her. Gershwin was blithely unaware of Zilboorg's resentment until the Mexican trip.

Besides resting after the *Porgy and Bess* travails, Gershwin hoped to make a study of indigenous music in Mexico. Through a friend in Mexico City, Estrella Elizaga, he had arranged to meet Mexican musicians and artists. According to Vernon Duke, Elizaga was not only "beautiful" and "gifted," she "played piano, composed songs, was equally at home at bullfights and the ballet, spoke French like a native and had the most tremendous chic, envied by women and admired by men." She also had access to money which from time to time she provided for the production of ballets with music by Duke (as Vladimir Dukelsky) and Mexico's Carlos Chavez.

In Gershwin's honor she assembled an impressive group one evening: Chavez, the American sculptor Isamu Noguchi (who had recently designed a magnificent garden in Mexico City and who had done a superb bust of Gershwin in 1929) and Mexican artists Miguel Covarrubias and Diego Rivera. Warburg and Zilboorg were also invited.

Mexico's politics were in ferment in 1935 and under its newly elected President, Lazaro Cardenas, was undergoing transformations and changes that a political conservative like Zilboorg could condemn as Bolshevik. Rivera and Covarrubias were important in Mexico's reformations. As a precaution in the event of a political argument with the firebrand Rivera, Zilboorg came to the party carrying a loaded gun.

While he did not have to defend himself from Mrs. Elizaga's friends, Zilboorg, on that occasion and others, badgered Gershwin. That evening, Gershwin told Kay Swift, he had felt "left out of it." Zilboorg knew that Gershwin's knowledge of Spanish was minimal and made a point of speaking it frequently, which indeed left Gershwin out of the conversations, standing around to his chagrin with nothing to say.

The Mexican vacation (except for Gershwin's time at the piano, which left Zilboorg out in the cold), like the New York reception of *Porgy and Bess,* was a disappointment. He had even found the music "monotonous." When his ship docked in New York in mid-December, the cast of the opera was there to welcome him with songs—a Theatre Guild publicity ploy. But business had not improved during his aggravating "vacation" and his labor of love was about to close.

I

After returning from the frustrating Mexican vacation George found something to occupy himself. That *Porgy and Bess* was in box-office trouble was obvious; in December ticket prices were reduced, from a top of $4.40 to $3.30, but to no avail. But, what with the recalcitrance of the Musicians Union, the costs could not be reduced accordingly.

When *Porgy and Bess* closed the weekly income was about $15,000; musicians' salaries, not counting conductor Smallens's, $3,780—with Smallens it added up to more than $4,100. This left little for cast, chorus (who were willing to take cuts), Mamoulian, Heyward, the Gershwins and, not least, the Theatre Guild. Under these conditions, the management decided to get out of town, where the size of the orchestra could be controlled (once Gershwin had established the size of the original orchestra and then reduced it as much as possible and yet sustained the integrity of the score, the Guild would still have to pay for a full complement of musicians whether they performed or not).

Therefore, the Guild projected a five-city tour of the opera, beginning in Philadelphia on January 27, 1936. To excite interest in that opening, Gershwin, serving as a kind of advance man, appeared as piano soloist there in the *Concerto in F,* with Smallens conducting. For the concert Gershwin prepared a suite from *Porgy and Bess* (it was retitled *Catfish Row* by Ira Gershwin in 1958 when rediscovered by Lawrence D. Stewart after a long period of neglect. It was retitled to avoid confusion with an already popular suite arranged by Robert Russell Bennett).

Though a scissors-and-paste job, Gershwin's suite is a carefully thought out musical précis of the score. He extracted five sections and bridged them skillfully in an impressive compendium including many instrumental passages that had been jettisoned in Boston Common.

These, with his titles, are:
I. *Catfish Row*
   Consisting of the entire opening, from the *Introduction,* through *Jazzbo Brown* for piano and "Summertime."
II. *Porgy Sings*
   a. "I Got Plenty o' Nuttin' "
   b. "Bess, You Is My Woman Now"
III. *Fugue*
   The murder of Crown, Act III, Sc. 1
IV. *Hurricane*
   a. Orchestral introduction, Act II, Sc. 3
   b. *Hurricane,* Act II, Sc. 3

v. *Good Morning, Brother*
    a. Occupational Humoresque, Act III, Sc. 3
    b. "Good Morning, Brother"
    c. Children's song, "Sure to Go to Heaven"
    d. "I'm On My Way" (Finale)

Most of the work consisted in transcribing the vocal lines into the orchestra, illuminating Gershwin's mastery of the orchestra, a feature often obscured in performance and even modern recordings. The importance of the piano in the score is evident in the suite; there is a generous portion of the purely orchestral music—and three of the best-known songs were used. The fugue, an intimation of which is heard immediately after "Summertime" in the first act and, in the suite, as a bridge into the "Porgy Sings" section erupts violently in the fight between Porgy and Crown. It is terrifyingly effective and Gershwin was proud of it. "Get this," he exclaimed to Vernon Duke. "Gershwin writing fugues! What will the boys say now?"

The last two sections are unified with a leitmotif, a thematic fragment from a song in Act I, "Lord I is tired this night"; it opens both the *Hurricane* section and *Good Morning, Brother*. The first is a powerful musical evocation of a tropical storm and the second a Debussyian tone painting of the serene dawning of morning in Catfish Row (in the opera there is no singing, but there is action; a man sweeps, two others enter with a hammer and saw, this section was entitled *Occupational Humoresque*).

The final two parts of the last section were ensemble numbers in the opera, greetings exchanged by soloists who are joined by the full chorus, with a lively children's song and dance adding to the gaiety; the chorus returns and the scene is set, the music having served to bring out the entire company. As he had at the beginning of his suite, Gershwin lifted an entire section from the opera and placed it intact into the suite—all of it had been ejected in Boston.

The result is a finely proportioned work, not a collection of the most popular songs. While the music is programmed almost identically to its place in the opera (except for the *Fugue*, which follows the *Hurricane* in *Porgy and Bess*), the musical interest and development does not depend on any knowledge of the plot. Unfortunately, after only a few performances, some of which Gershwin conducted, the suite was set aside in 1937.

In the wake of a successful revival of *Porgy and Bess* in 1942, Fritz Reiner, conductor of the Pittsburgh Symphony, unaware of the existence of Gershwin's own suite, commissioned Robert Russell Bennett to prepare *A Symphonic Picture of Porgy and Bess.* Premiered by Reiner and the Pittsburgh Symphony in 1943, it has since become the standard *Porgy and Bess* suite. While his effort was commendable, and true to the spirit of Gershwin—even to the orchestration—Bennett tended to ignore the purely orchestral passages in favor of the popular songs. He did use the hurricane music, but its performance is optional. However, he did adapt a couple of the Street Cries. Bennett's is a good representation of the score, but it lacks the unity and flow of Gershwin's *Catfish Row*, in effect Gershwin's last orchestral work.

After the Philadelphia concert and opening of *Porgy and Bess*, Gershwin returned to New York for the first night of his brother's revue *Ziegfeld Follies*, out of which came "I Can't Get Started," music by Vernon Duke. Drained by his work with the kinetic Duke, Ira took a vacation accompanied by Leonore and their friend Vincente Minnelli.

While his brother rested on the ship to and from Trinidad, Gershwin grew restless. Kay Swift, who had divorced James Warburg in 1934 and was then working as staff composer at the Radio City Music Hall, introduced him to her lyricist, Albert Stillman. (He is best known for his lyric written to Ernesto Lecuona's *Andalucía,* "The Breeze and I.") George and Stillman wrote a few songs of no great distinction, though one, "The King of Swing," was sung by Buck and Bubbles onstage at the Music Hall. It must have been the only song on the program for the advertisements read "With Entire Musical Score by George Gershwin." Obviously inspired by Benny Goodman, the impending coronation in Britain and maybe the film showing onscreen, *The King Steps Out,* "King of Swing," though published quickly went into obscurity.

By February, after Ira had returned from his cruise, word had begun to trickle eastward that Hollywood was interested in the Gershwins. This initiated a period of several months best described as one of haggling and offers from several Hollywood-based agents to represent them, submitting such name inducements as Eddie Cantor, Bing Crosby and Harold Lloyd (in a film adaptation of *Strike Up the Band*).

Gershwin did not sell himself short, but Hollywood was not prepared to be munificent to a writer of popular songs who dabbled in opera. When he was approached initially Gershwin told his first representative to ask for one hundred thousand dollars and a percentage of the film's profits. Another representative—they were hardly agents, since they came to Gershwin and he authorized them to approach the studios for a specified time—had gotten to Pandro S. Berman, head of production at RKO, who offered sixty thousand dollars for an Astaire-Rogers score; the Gershwins countered with a demand for seventy-five thousand dollars for twenty weeks or sixty thousand dollars for sixteen.

So nothing happened, except for telegrams and phone calls; February, March, April and May slipped by. Ira did not mind the enforced leisure, but his brother was anxious to get going. The April highlight for him was the exhibition of paintings at the Society of Independent Artists for which two of his were chosen for display. He was booked for another All-Gershwin program at the Stadium on July 9 and 10; at the end of the month he was scheduled to perform with the Chicago Symphony at the Ravinia Festival. These appearances were something to look forward to but were not quite work.

Then on June 11, another "representative" emerged, Archie Selwyn, brother of producer Edgar. He found that he encountered some resistance in offering the Gershwins to the studios whose heads were afraid of Gershwin: he had gone "highbrow." This provoked Gershwin into replying with ". . . rumors about highbrow music ridiculous . . . am out to write hits."

As far as RKO was concerned, the problem was money, for Berman chided with a jocular message, "I think you are letting a few thousand dollars keep you from having a lot of fun and when you figure the government gets eighty percent of it do you thinks its nice to make me suffer this way?"

Sparing Pandro Berman hardly concerned the Gershwins, but writing songs for an Astaire-Rogers musical did. At the end of June they accepted a contract, via Arthur Lyons, although his option had run out and other agents were negotiating to represent them. They agreed to work for sixteen weeks at RKO for fifty-five thousand dollars, with an option for a possible second film at seventy thousand dollars; then Selwyn informed them that Samuel Goldwyn, aware of their contract, was anxious to have them score one of his musicals, whenever they were available. By June 26, 1936, it was definite: the Gershwins were set for the Coast. After all the wrangling and hand-wringing over Gershwin's high brow, it appeared that the brothers had a good year ahead of them.

They planned to leave for Hollywood in August, after the two All-Gershwin nights at Lewisohn Stadium in mid-July and George's appearance at the Ravinia Festival on the twenty-fifth.

II

During the fateful, remarkably prolific, year, Gershwin would learn, after a promising beginning, that Hollywood like Gertrude Stein's Oakland was elusive, equivocal, that "When you got there, there isn't any there there."

Leonore, Ira and George left for California by air on August 10. They were escorted en masse to Newark Airport by cars and cabs of family and friends, among them Bill Daly, Kay Swift and Mabel Schirmer. None would see Gershwin again. During the Hollywood year Daly would die of a heart attack in New York (and his death would affect Gershwin deeply); Mabel Schirmer was on an extended European tour and was aboard ship returning to New York when the ship's newsletter was blown into her lap. She had tossed it away, and when it flew back she thought, "This paper wants to tell me something." Its single sheet carried the news of Gershwin's death.

The farewells to Kay Swift were difficult and complex. Since first meeting about a decade before they had become very close, first primarily in the professional sense. By the late twenties their friendship deepened and they saw much of one another. They had more than music in common, both were gifted and ambitious and each understood the other's dedication to work.

Still it is evident that Kay was willing to assist George to the negligence of her own work. She was a ready musical secretary, happy to take down one of his pieces—a *Prelude*, "In the Mandarin's Orchid Garden" is partly in her hand and his. And she was always delighted to take her place at the second piano whether to play Bach or Gershwin. By 1928, the duo of Swift and Gershwin was "serious." They saw much of each other during the final preparations of *An American in Paris* and, of course, during the creation of *Porgy and Bess*, by which time Warburg and Kay were divorced.

But during the marriage there was no talk of divorce and remarriage. During this time, too, each dated others and Gershwin's letters reveal an almost adolescent longing for Rosamond Walling. Gershwin loved and needed the companionship, but marriage seemed to him a rather drastic final step—and he idealized it. He apparently did not want the kind of marriage that his parents endured.

Some biographers have intimated that Kay Swift's three daughters constrained him, that he was not ready for a readymade family. Although he was relaxed with the Mosbachers' children, and Mrs. Waring of Folly Island reminisced about how "devoted" her children were to him, he was less at ease with Kay's. April, as a teenager, resented him and attributed the breakup of her parents' marriage to him.

Gershwin tried to ingratiate himself by bringing gifts and often asking the youngest, Kay, then about six, "Do you like me?" Younger than April, but older than Kay, Andrea adored him.

So it was that as the chatting, laughing party gathered at the airport, George and Kay had already agreed that they would not communicate, not even by phone, for the year the Gershwins would be away; only then would they decide upon their future.

In Beverly Hills, the Gershwins took a suite in the Beverly-Wilshire Hotel and ordered a piano. Leonore went house-hunting in the neighborhood. The brothers immediately went to work. They had a sketchy outline of the plot to a film entitled *Watch Your Step* in which Fred Astaire is cast as an alleged Russian ballet dancer, "Petrov," though he is really Peter P. Peters from the American Midwest. In their outline, in the opening scene, he is in Paris where he sees the likeness of a popular American musical comedy star, Ginger Rogers as "Linda Keene" all over Paris, on every kiosk and wall. With that cue, the Gershwins came up with a long opening musical sequence in which Astaire declares to everyone he sees that at last he's found his love.

An extraordinary song, more Broadway than Hollywood, it was not considered too highbrow—in fact, director Mark Sandrich on first hearing it, told the Gershwins he thought it was "real $4.40 stuff" (that was the top price then for a Broadway musical). Gershwin's manuscript runs to seven pages with a thirty-eight measure repeat in the music.

"Hi-Ho! At Last!" sparkles with interior rhymes and Gershwinisms with piano passages between lines in the lyric as well as around the words. One musician playing it through for the first time remarked, "It's a miniature piano sonata!" Not quite, but it is a remarkable song and, in a word, "high-brow." Despite studio enthusiasm, "Hi-Ho!" was discarded before filming began, not because of its cerebral content, but, what with its length and its need for an elaborate set, because of its cost. It went back into the trunk (and was finally published in 1968; a home recording, with Ira Gershwin singing and Harold Arlen at the piano, was recorded at a party given by screen writer Sonya Levien Hovey in 1938. Ira permitted its release in a collection of recorded Gershwiniana, *Gershwin by Gershwin;* it remains the best, and only authentic, performance to date).

Even as they fashioned "Hi-Ho!" they received a wire from Vincente Minnelli in New York asking them, please, to complete and send him a waltz parody they had played for him before leaving for California. Still awaiting a script they decided to work up Minnelli's waltz.

The completed song was "By Strauss" and was introduced in *The Show Is On* by Gracie Barry and Robert Shafer and danced by Mitzi Mayfair. The revue, which starred Beatrice Lillie and Bert Lahr, opened late in December; it had a composite score by such composers as Harold Arlen, Vernon Duke, Richard Rodgers and Arthur Schwartz, with lyrics by E. Y. Harburg, Ted Fetter, Lorenz Hart and Howard

Dietz. Only one song, the sentimental "Little Old Lady," lyric by Stanley Adams, music by Hoagy Carmichael, achieved any kind of popularity at the time.

After dispatching "By Strauss," they returned to work on the film and to looking for a house. After ten days of "going practically crazy," in George's phrase, they found "a nice spacious, cheery house" that would "serve beautifully" as their home and work place. While they would have to do something about the furniture, the property had such Beverly Hills appurtenances as a swimming pool and a tennis court.

The large house—Hollywood-Spanish in design—was situated at 1019 North Roxbury Drive, a couple of blocks from Sunset Boulevard. It was a good neighborhood, dotted with equally spacious homes; the wide drive was lined with palm trees and the lawns and flower beds were beautifully kept. The Eddie Cantors lived across the street; an old friend from the early New York–Paley days, Edward G. Robinson, lived nearby, as did Sigmund Romberg (two doors up), Irving Berlin, Jerome Kern, Harold Arlen and Yip Harburg. It was more a reunion than a move into a strange new land, but the Gershwins had much to learn.

Five days after moving into Roxbury Drive, George wrote to their publisher, Max Dreyfus (on August 27), to tell him that he and Ira had performed "a few songs for Pandro Berman and Mark Sandrich . . . and the boys seemed delighted with our stuff. It makes us happy that we are working with people who speak our language."

The songs included "Hi-Ho!" plus "Let's Call the Whole Thing Off," which they had brought with them from New York. Since every Astaire-Rogers film so far had had a misunderstanding and a reconciliation scene, the song was bound to fit into the script somewhere. Soon after, they were ready with "They All Laughed," but after a full month, there was still no script to speak of.

Though he was accustomed to waiting for a libretto or a script, this unusual wait concerned Gershwin, who mentioned the delay frequently in his letters East. Six of their sixteen weeks slipped by with no action—then three months. As late as October 13, he complained that while they continued writing, "in true Hollywood fashion the script is not ready yet . . ." The bright side was that "so far no real pressure has been put upon us." It was to be very different from their theater experience; not intense concentration of a score, no frenzied out-of-town tryout—just a languid day-to-day (and night) of writing letters, tennis games, meeting friends and from time to time a little work—at first.

George took advantage of the temporary tranquillity by sending for his painting equipment and some of his favorite paintings. He considered studying with a new friend, the celebrated composer-theorist-teacher Arnold Schoenberg, who had a standing invitation to use the

Gershwin tennis court. Frequently he and Gershwin challenged one another on the court. Gershwin hoped too to study with another new friend, the Austrian composer and refugee Ernst Toch, whom he had met at an anti-Nazi meeting. But once the studio geared up, he studied with neither. After weeks of irritating delay the frenetic, pressured activity began. George temporarily set aside an idea that he had had during the period of calm, for an extended composition, "either for orchestra and piano or orchestra alone. I'm leaning towards the idea of a bright overture." He was planning ahead for the following year's Ravinia concert.

Until a nearly final script for *Stepping Toes* materialized about mid-October, Gershwin managed to adapt to Hollywood ways, with some reservations, "There's nothing like the phony glamour in Hollywood to bring out the need for one's real friends," he wrote to Mabel Schirmer in New York. Still, he found working conditions had improved since their *Delicious* experience six years before. "There are many people who talk the language of smart showmen," he told her, "and it is therefore much more agreeable working out here. We have many friends here from the East, so the social life has also improved greatly."

He alludes to the great times with "the Jerome Kerns, Sam Behrmans, Moss Hart, Oscar Levant, Harpo Marx, Yip Harburg and dozens of our old cronies," he informed her. "Would certainly be lovely if you could also be here."

He touched on a theme that would run through his letters to Mabel during that Hollywood year: "Have you seen Kay? I haven't written to her nor have I heard from her. I should like to know if you ever see her?" He was eager to hear about "all that goes on in little old New York," knowing that Mabel was a regular gallery visitor and concertgoer.

He kept her up on his activities, writing about parties, dinners, even meetings with members of the American Society of Composers, Authors and Publishers. He was concerned about events in Europe and wrote at the dinners and parties there were "depressing moments, too, when talk of Hitler and his gang creep into the conversation. For some reason or other," he concluded, "the feeling out here is more acute than in the East."

And he reported, "Our work is going along slowly because the script for the picture is not completely finished; however, with a few songs that we have, we feel that we will be ready with our part."

While waiting, he and Ira wrote the one song that, to a slight degree could be called "integrated." Its composition was an example of the give-and-take, the close collaboration of the brothers. To Ira it exemplified George's cooperative understanding and respect for Ira's musical suggestions and of his "never being dogmatic" (this in answer to an interviewer's question: Was George easy to work with?).

George had an idea for a melody, a simple but haunting rhythmic manipulation of a single tone: three eighth notes and one quarter note. He played it for Ira a few times. Ira suggested, "If you can give me two more notes in the first part, I can get, 'The way you wear your hat . . .'"

George tried that, liked it—he raised the melody a third in the first phrase and lowered it a third in the second; simple and most effective. "He was always obliging that way," Ira told the interviewer, "it didn't hurt his melodic scheme."

George felt the song "had distinct possibilities of going places," and soon after, the happiest plugger of Beverly Hills was playing it for his many friends. A favorite stopover was the home of Anya and Harold Arlen, one of his own favorite songwriters. He hurried in one afternoon, went to the piano and played "They Can't Take That Away from Me." The Arlens loved it as much as he did. While he played it again, Arlen worked up a little obbligato for Anya. (In *Life Begins at 8:40* she sang a contrapuntal melody to one of the Arlen-Gershwin-Harburg songs in the show.)

"He loved it," Arlen remembered, "and every time he played it he asked Annie—in her little voice—to sing."

He would not love the song's treatment in the final print of the film, in which, though affectingly sung by Astaire, the song simply vanishes, or as Gershwin put it it was "literally throw[n] . . . away without a plug." (When the song was published both Gershwins signed a copy for Arlen.) In his bold script George wrote: "For Harold, with much affection, George." Ira commented in rhyme to the tune on his perennial knack for picking the wrong baseball or football team whenever he bet with Arlen—a knack that lasted a lifetime. Under his brother's salutation he wrote:

> *The way you get those gets—*
> *And bet me 6 to 3—*
> *The way you win those bets*
> *They can't take that away from me.*
> > *And I can't take it away from you*
> > > *With love,*
> > > *Ira*

A full month had gone by since he had written to Mabel. His October 28th letter was newsy, for by then a good deal of his time for the future was under contract: two more film musicals and a concert tour.

"Hollywood," he began, "is a place of great extremes—when it rains, it pours—when it's cloudy, it's cloudy the whole day—and when the sun shines, well, you know about that.

"Naturally I miss New York and the things it has to offer . . . and will probably miss it more as time goes on, but I must say that California has many advantages; for example, I am writing this letter . . . sitting in a pair of shorts with no top, in a hot sun around our pool. That sounds almost like a moving picture scenario, but it's true. We play quite a lot of tennis and the work so far seems easy . . ."

He was wrong, as he would learn soon. He told Mabel that it "looks as though the three Gershwins will be out here for a longer period than they first anticipated. Samuel Goldwyn is constructing a contract right now for our services for a picture to start around the fifteenth of January [1937]. And, now, RKO has piped up with talk of their option, which was originally in our agreement. They would like us to start on the next Astaire picture shortly after this contract is over. If Goldwyn doesn't have a story ready for us in three weeks, he may put his date back so we could do the next Astaire vehicle, otherwise we go to work for Goldwyn on that date."

Gershwin also wrote Mabel that he had "agreed to do several concerts out here: the first taking place in Seattle on December 15, and in San Francisco on January 15, 16 and 17. Also probably in Los Angeles late in January."

He closed with his customary appeal for her to come out for a visit and, "Have you seen anything of Kay? I think about her a great deal and wonder if she is all right."

Within two weeks he and Ira were at work on the film's final song, "Wake Up, Brother, and Dance" and a concluding ballet; he believed all would be over "in about a week. We haven't a title for the picture as yet, but we are all struggling hard to find the right phrase." Someone found it—*Shall We Dance,* and so the Gershwins were expected to write a suitable title song; "Wake Up, Brother" went out to make room for the new song.

George was about to experience what happened when he worked with Hollywood's "smart showmen." The film's musical director was his friend Nathaniel Shilkret, who had gone to Hollywood in 1935 and had been music director of the previous Astaire-Rogers film, *Swing Time,* with songs by Kern and Dorothy Fields. Shilkret believed that once work on *Shall We Dance* began it proved to be "a horrible mixup for George."

The screenplay he termed as "vague," and recalled director Sandrich asking Gershwin for a finale along the lines of *An American in Paris* (the studio had hired ballerina Harriet Hoctor to dance with Astaire in this sequence). "George came in with something in Latin-American tempo," Shilkret told interviewer Milton A. Caine in 1951, "which no one cared for. Astaire and Sandrich ganged up on Gershwin for a better ballet." Shilkret could not understand why Gershwin did not simply walk out on them, but Gershwin was always "very sweet."

Someone else (there was no paucity of cooks to stir this broth) came up with the idea of adding Jimmy Dorsey's orchestra to the RKO studio orchestra for some kind of jazzy finale. By this time there was more than enough indecision, disguised as decisiveness, prevalent. Gershwin offered to write whatever they wanted provided they could tell him what they wanted.

Although Shilkret was not present and was not certain whether Gershwin was there at this session (he thinks not), Astaire and Sandrich decided that Dorsey's saxophonist Fud Livingston, also an arranger, might take two themes—the title song and "They Can't Take That Away from Me"—and work *them* into a ballet.

When the completed job came to Shilkret, he rehearsed it with his orchestra. He walked off the sound stage saying, "I can't make anything of that." That closed the Dorsey episode; nor did the band appear in the film.

Finally, Gershwin, Shilkret and Robert Russell Bennett, one of the film's orchestrators, worked through a night to concoct an acceptable ballet score, *Hoctor's Ballet.* The opening is in Gershwin's best big-city style—propulsive, nervous, bustling with modern harmonies; it might easily have been developed into a full-scale composition except that time was growing short. This characteristic Gershwin music—even to the orchestration—then segues into a more typical Hollywood medley-finale of "Shall We Dance," a snatch of "Wake Up, Brother, and Dance," "They Can't Take That Away from Me" and "They All Laughed."

The initial sixteen weeks were up in early December and the second began without letup. Early in December George informed Mabel Schirmer that he had begun practicing on the fourteenth for his concert with the Seattle Symphony, the first of a series of concerts that would take him as far east as Detroit.

The concerts were spaced so that he could return to Beverly Hills to work on the new Astaire film and to spend time with his family. George told Mabel that he had toyed "with the idea of coming to New York for about two weeks around the holidays, but for some reason New York has always been a depressing place to me at that time . . ." Perhaps after the first of the year.

He inquired about Kay Swift: "Have you seen anything of Leonore in New York? She wrote saying she called you. She also made some mention about wanting to go see Kay with you and your making some remark about Kay considering the whole thing a closed book. That sounds very much as though you have some items of great interest to me." Despite a crowded schedule, and crowds of friends, he was homesick and he was lonely. He confided in her, "Have not yet found a steady girl out here—you may be interested to know. The girls are surprisingly selfish, stupid & career conscious."

Around this time he was seeing quite a bit of the young French actress, Simone Simon, then about twenty-six years old, British actress Elizabeth Allan, and others. The Simon attachment was for the moment the most serious, for she presented him with an initialed gold key to her West Los Angeles mansion. She would later claim that Gershwin planned to launch her on a career in "light opera." If so, he never appears to have mentioned this to anyone else and certainly not to his closest confidante during his Hollywood year, Mabel Schirmer.

After his appearances in Seattle, where he performed with the handicap of a cold, he returned to Beverly Hills to spend Christmas and begin the New Year with his family; Rose Gershwin had come in from New York and Frankie and Leo Godowsky from Rochester. It was during this holiday visit that George told his sister that he had come to Hollywood to make the money that would enable him to do what he hoped to do in the future, that he "hadn't scratched the surface" in music yet.

"Like old times," he wrote Mabel. "We've managed to squeeze them all into our house & comfortably. We all spent New Year's Eve together at the Clover Club, which was a really gay spot.

"The family is quite amazed at my ability to stay home quietly for many evenings with no urge to go to parties & live the gay life. I am getting to be a home body—and loving it."

As for the new year, 1937, he wrote, "Perhaps, dear Mabel, this is our year. A year that will see both of us finding that elusive something that seems to bring happiness to the lucky. The pendulum swings back, so I've heard and it's about due to swing us back to a more satisfying state. 1936 was a year of important changes to me. They are too obvious to you to mention here [an allusion to Kay Swift]. So, sweet Mabel, lift your glass with me & drink a toast to two nice people who will, in a happy state, go places this year."

He continued to invite her to California and continued to long to return to New York himself. "I have a strong desire to come to New York for a visit but don't see where I can find the time. We start work on the next Astaire picture on the 13th of Jan. & that means 16 weeks of R.K.O. contract to fill out here . . . Please tell me some news about yourself & the town. Do you hear from Kay? How is she?"

On January 9 George wrote to Emily Paley and told her of his visit to the RKO studios to watch the filming of *Shall We Dance*. "The Astaire picture is being 'shot,' " he told her, "& is most interesting to watch as I have never really seen a picture made before. It fascinates me to see the amazing things they do with sound recording, for instance. And lighting. And cutting. And so forth."

It may have been exciting and so forth, but he was not entirely pleased with the final result. He felt that "They Can't Take That Away from Me" was all but wasted. Even so, of the eight songs written for the film, six were used: "Slap That Bass," "I've Got Beginner's Luck," "They All Laughed," "Let's Call the Whole Thing Off," "They Can't Take That Away from Me" and "Shall We Dance." In addition there were several instrumental sequences that he wrote, most notably *Walking the Dog* in which, instead of dancing, Rogers and Astaire do walk dogs. Since Astaire was cast as a classical ballet dancer Gershwin composed a good deal of background music (despite his interview in which he claimed he would not "bother" with it).

The film's cue sheets credit him (with Shilkret as co-composer or arranger) with *French Ballet Class* for two pianos; *Dance of the Waves; Graceful and Elegant; Balloon Ballet* and *Hoctor's Ballet*. Another orchestral sequence, *Valse Arabesque,* was composed by Robert Russell Bennett, who also arranged the opening credits music in which a snatch of the *Rhapsody in Blue* was used (RKO was not taking any chances). There are no fewer than fifty-three musical cues. Among the non-Gershwin items are Shilkret's orchestral *Ballet Eternal* and *The Queen Mary,* Waldteufel's *The Skaters Waltz,* Val Burton and Will Jason's "Isn't This a Night for Love?," Max Steiner's *On the Beach* and Oscar Levant and Dorothy Fields's "Got a New Lease on Life"; even snatches of "For He's a Jolly Good Fellow" and "Sidewalks of New York." On paper the score for *Shall We Dance* looks like a hodgepodge.

In *Shall We Dance* George and Ira Gershwin provided Rogers and Astaire with one of their best scores. It was the seventh Rogers and Astaire film and by this time a certain stylization had set in, a pat formula in plot and characterization. Though the film was generally bright, even sophisticated and crackling with witty dialogue, there were few surprises except in the musical numbers—the unique *Walking the*

Dog sequence, an engine room of a ship as a setting for "Slap That Bass," the roller-skating dance "Let's Call the Whole Thing Off" and the finale in which there appear to be several Ginger Rogerses. The dances were undoubtedly conceived by Astaire and dance directors Hermes Pan and Harry Losee. As Gershwin learned, like a Broadway musical, a film musical was a group effort—only more so. Once he had finished his job, he was expected to stay out of the way.

III

Despite Hollywood's method of assembling a musical film, Gershwin was not totally disenchanted with *Shall We Dance*. He could have contributed more had Hollywood work habits, studio bureaucracy—"front office," producer, director, musical director, et al.—not to mention pecking order, permitted. The studio had staff orchestrators; George was not consulted much on orchestration (even Astaire, the star, had more to say about the final orchestrations than he). Even so, the scoring of *Shall We Dance* is Gershwinesque enough to please the purist.

That the studio took up the option on a second Astaire film pleased both Gershwins. Ira had readily settled into the leisurely pace of life in Beverly Hills; he relished working on a mere handful of songs and, as the studio forces took them over, turned to other activities: reading, playing cards with his friends—George wrote of "seeing a great deal of Irving Berlin and Jerome Kern at poker parties"—and going to the racetrack.

Resigned to a stay of a year, and to the Hollywood routine, George decided to adapt. Though mystified that he was not consulted on some aspects of the production, as he had been in New York, he realized that the approach was indeed different. Ira especially appreciated this aspect of working for films.

George took up palette and brushes to do portraits of an old friend, Jerome Kern, and of a new one, Arnold Schoenberg (which would be his last painting). As at Folly Beach, he spent a good deal of time out of doors.

He discovered a then unique Hollywood institution: the trainer. "This was a select professional group," S. N. Behrman explained in his memoirs, "they upheld the 'Cult of the Body,' a necessary religion for the stars of course, but the executives, producers and Name Writers were acolytes too, as impassioned as the stars." Trainers often doubled as masseurs, who pummeled and stretched their clients—and were the most efficient purveyors of gossip in Beverly Hills. (Ernst Lubitsch learned from his trainer that he had been fired as head of Paramount Pictures before he heard from Paramount itself.)

While gossip never interested the Gershwins, George's trainer introduced him to another of California's pleasures. "Recently," he wrote to Emily Paley, "my masseur suggested a hike in the hills. I acquiesced & have become a victim of its vigorous charm. For the past week, every day, hot or cold, we walked back in the hills & really, Em, I feel as I have discovered something wonderful. It is refreshing & invigorating. Better than golf, because it eliminates the aggravation that comes with that pastime." The hiking kept him in trim for his concertizing.

En route to San Francisco for the concerts with the Symphony under Pierre Monteux, George and Ira stopped off at the Palo Corona Ranch, near Carmel, which belonged to his friends Olga and Sidney Fish. They were joined there by Pandro Berman, director George Stevens, and P. J. Wolfson, who had adapted *Shall We Dance*. Amid the restful surroundings they began discussions of the next Astaire film.

Four days later he arrived in San Francisco for the first concert under Pierre Monteux on January 15, an event made more festive because his mother, Leonore, the Kerns and their daughter, Betty, and others had traveled north for the concert. After his concert at the university in Berkeley on the seventeenth, he boarded an American Airlines DC-3 for the flight to Detroit. The concert on the twentieth was so successful that George was invited to return during the next season. From Detroit he mailed to Mabel Schirmer a card he had written on the plane— which carried but one passenger, Gershwin. Ira recalled that two or three recent crashes had discouraged air travelers at the time. To "Mabe" he wrote that he was "Tired, but happy."

Back in Beverly Hills he went, as he put it, "back to Astaire," at least until his next series of All Gershwin concerts in Los Angeles the next month. Of these he wrote to DuBose Heyward, "I am giving two concerts on February 10 and 11 with the Philharmonic Orchestra in Los Angeles and we are doing some of the *Porgy* music. We are having Todd Duncan come out to sing a few of the songs and Alexander Smallens to conduct.

"This might whip up some enthusiasm for picture possibilities on the part of the studios who, as you know, are keen about it, but slightly afraid on account of the color question. However, I'm sure it's only a matter of time when the opera will be done in that form as the music is constantly being played and the enthusiasm for it great on all sides."

Although he had been approached with three offers for a Broadway musical, all of which intrigued him, he closed his letter to Heyward with this idea: "How about planning another opera or operetta for the future? I am sure you could turn out a grand book and I am very anxious to start thinking about a serious musical. So, put your mind to it, old boy, and I know you can evolve something interesting."

(The other, never written, musicals were one with an American history background with a projected book by Robert E. Sherwood; Kaufman and Hart had an idea in which they as well as the Gershwins would appear—true to form, Ira backed out, shy of appearing onstage. The concept was changed though the plot had something to do with the making of a musical. The third was to have been an operalike setting of Lynn Riggs's *The Lights of Lamy*, a *Porgy*-like ethnic mix, American and Mexican. But George was most inclined toward the Kaufman-Hart musical—as an offstage voice—and a new Heyward work).

Besides the work on the Astaire film, Gershwin had other future works on his mind: possible new compositions for the Chicago concert later in the year, perhaps another for Detroit and, off and on, perhaps because of his friendship with Schoenberg (the recording of whose string quartets he had helped to finance), a string quartet. Oscar Levant told of the day Schoenberg had come over for a tennis match, when Gershwin said offhandedly "I'd like to write a quartet some day. But it will be something simple, like Mozart."

Schoenberg mistook this for a comment of his own work, for the evening before, George, Ira and Oscar had attended a concert to hear the Kolisch Quartet perform Beethoven and all four of Schoenberg's quartets.

"I am not a simple man," Schoenberg said, "and, anyway, Mozart was considered far from simple in his day." Unfortunately, Gershwin did not compose his string quartet. During the period of preparations for the Los Angeles concerts he discussed the quartet with the concert's producer and impresario, Merle Armitage. He frequently picked up Armitage in his "new Cord car, a front-drive vehicle of great chic, one of the earliest streamlined cars. He loved to drive it.

"My interest, though," Armitage recalled, "was in his conversation, for Los Angeles being a huge sprawling community we spent hours crossing town to our various engagements [they were auditioning singers for the chorus for the *Porgy and Bess* portion of the concert].

"George and I talked art. Or we talked music. One of the things we discussed was the string quartet on which he was working at the time . . . He talked of the form his quartet would take, a fast opening movement, followed by a very slow second movement, based on themes he had heard when visiting Folly Island off the Carolina coast with DuBose Heyward. The sounds of the dominant themes were so insistent that he had not bothered to write them down."

"It's going through my head all the time," Gershwin told Armitage, "and as soon as I have finished scoring the next picture, I'm going to rent a little cabin up in Coldwater Canyon, away from Hollywood, and get the thing down on paper. It's about to drive me crazy, it's so damned full of new ideas!"

He was excited over the concerts, both sold out a week before they took place. His letter of February 9 to Mabel Schirmer reflects some of his delight. "I'm sorry," he told her, "that you can't be here to witness the excitement that is going on about the two concerts . . . You know, I have brought out Alexander Smallens and Todd Duncan to sing and they tell me that they've seen nothing like the excitement for a concert in years.

"My friend Arthur Lyons is taking a room at the Trocadero and has invited about 250 people to come after the concert. He's going to great trouble to decorate the room and there will be two orchestras—one American and one Russian. I wish I could send a magic carpet for you, Emilie [sic] and Lou so you could all be here for the occasion."

He told her too that he had heard from Kay Swift. In her letter she told George that she had begun seeing a good deal of Edward Byron, whom she had met when "Music by Gershwin" was being produced. Kay "seemed in good spirits . . . I am very happy for her sake that she was able to adjust herself so soon."

The concerts, in the word of Armitage, were "sensational." Even the rehearsals were "inspired, and George beamed and played with a special *élan."* He also experienced the first serious intimation of an illness —this a month almost to the day after he had written Emily Paley about how refreshed and invigorated he had felt after hiking in the hills. As early as November 1936, he had casually told his friend George Pallay that while he was having his hair trimmed, he had had a moment of dizziness in the barber's chair. During rehearsals on February 10, he suffered another spell while conducting the chorus. Paul Mueller, who had followed him out to California, and who had driven him in from Beverly Hills and was taking photographs of him as he conducted, noticed that Gershwin seemed to stumble and was about to fall from the podium. He caught him and Gershwin assured him that he was all right, and went on with the rehearsal.

During the concert on the second night, he blacked out momentarily and played a few wrong notes in the *Concerto in F.* He spoke later of vertigo and an unpleasant odor, something like burning rubber. A thorough physical examination revealed no serious illness, and a week later he wrote to Daily Paskman, a radio producer, who had inquired about his doing another radio series. George had to turn him down, saying that having completed one Astaire film, he and Ira had the new Astaire film, entitled *A Damsel in Distress* to finish, after which they would begin on *The Goldwyn Follies.*

There was little work done on the film after the initial conferences at the Palo Corona Ranch early in January because of the several concerts in January and February. Some of March was consumed in talks with Armitage about a revival of *Porgy and Bess* the next year. Then Gershwin was free for the second Astaire musical.

A Damsel in Distress starred Fred Astaire without Ginger Rogers; both had let it be known that they would like a separation as a film couple for a while. Appearing opposite Astaire was the nonsinging, nondancing Joan Fontaine; the script was based on an early novel of the same title by their old collaborator P. G. Wodehouse. In 1928, Wodehouse and Ian Hay had converted it into a play. Wodehouse did not come into the project until plans were well along and an early treatment had been prepared by studio staff writers. This was discarded, for about all that had been retained was the title.

Then Wodehouse was summoned to put his story back into its original madcap, delightfully illogical form. He was assisted by two staff writers, Ernest Pagano (who had written the *Shall We Dance* screenplay) and S. K. Lauren. Like Gershwin, Wodehouse was about to be educated in the ways of Hollywood. He produced what he thought was a script that "would make a good picture." But, after the experience, his last word on film writing was, "what uncongenial work picture-writing is. Somebody's got to do it, I suppose, but this is the last time they get me."

They got Gershwin, but the second time around at RKO he would prove to be less generous with his talents. Since so much of his instrumental music, except for *Walking the Dog,* had been virtually thrown away in *Shall We Dance,* he decided he would leave the bridges and incidental music to the studio "hacks." (He was fortunate in that the main arranger-orchestrator was the dependable Robert Russell Bennett, who provided most of the background music with such titles as *The Swans, Damsel Chase, Lady Alyce* theme, *Tunnel of Love,* etc.)

The Gershwins supplied only the songs, songs specifically tailored to Astaire's voice and dancing; Joan Fontaine did not sing, but Gershwin believed that since the casting called for a singing group, he and Ira could come up with a couple of songs that would highlight their gifts. As he wrote to Goldberg, they had "written two English type ballads for background music so the audience will get a chance to hear some singing besides the crooning of the stars." In the same letter, dated May 12, he informed Goldberg that they had completed eight songs for *A*

Damsel in Distress and that the Goldwyn contract, soon to go into effect, would necessitate postponing the "Kaufman-Hart opus until next year."

The quasi-madrigals were "The Jolly Tar and The Milk Maid," sung by the madrigal group and Astaire, and an adaptation of a contrapuntal choral piece Gershwin had been calling "Back to Bach," and for which Ira wrote the lyric, "Sing of Spring." An interesting and quite amusing piece, it was wasted in the film, sung as background to dialogue.

The last song heard in the film, "Nice Work If You Can Get It," was one of the first completed. It dated back to c. 1930 as nine measures of a song entitled "There's No Stopping Me Now."

Since the songs were not locked into the script, the Gershwins had a pretty free hand in their work. Ira recalled the genesis of one of the songs: "Early in 1937," he wrote, they "had finished three or four songs which had been accepted.

"One night I was in the living room reading. About 1 A.M. George returned from a party full of life, took off his dinner jacket, sat down at the piano and said, 'How about some work? Got any ideas?'

"Well, there's one spot Fred is in where we might do something about a fog, and there's never been a song about a fog I know of—how about 'a foggy day in London' or maybe 'foggy day in London Town'?"

"Sounds good to me," George said, "I like it better with 'town.' "

And, Ira continued, ". . . he was off immediately with the melody. We finished the refrain, words and music, in less than an hour. This is quite an achievement on my part, as I'm not too fast a worker and for the most part I was accustomed to struggling with completed tunes (it took me three weeks to get a lyric for 'I Got Rhythm'). Next day the song still sounded good so we started on the verse (which took two days)."

"A Foggy Day" was not wasted in the picture; director George Stevens, special effects supervisor Vernon L. Walker and cameraman Joseph H. August handled its scene with imagination and sensitivity. As Stanley Green has written, the song was not sung "in the city of its title, but rather incongruously, by Fred Astaire in white tie and tails perched on a fence on the castle grounds. The scene remains a pictorial gem: the fog enveloping Fred as he strolls through the grounds puffing a cigarette, with the moonbeams creating shimmering, lacy patterns through the trees."

In the film Astaire is on the grounds of Totleigh Castle, home of Lady Alyce, with whom he had fallen hopelessly in love at first sight upon seeing her in London. An American dancer (in the novel and play the leading man is a composer) with a false reputation as a ladies' man, he follows her to the castle, where the usual complications and misunderstandings arise. Instead of the usual Astaire-Rogers stock company (Eric Blore, Edward Everett Horton, et al.), RKO signed the comedy team of George Burns and Gracie Allen as, respectively, his press agent and the press agent's scatterbrained secretary. Comedian Reginald Gardner appeared as a conniving British butler and band leader Ray Noble as the classic English silly ass of yore. There wasn't too much plot to get in the way of the musical numbers, which employed Astaire mostly, as well as Burns and Allen. This team was extraordinary in the film and revealed a fine flair for musical comedy. Allen was especially delightful in the satiric "Stiff Upper Lip" and the fun-house scene with Astaire and Burns, a variation on the classic Fred and Adele Astaire runaround.

Joan Fontaine danced tentatively with Astaire in one scene to "Things Are Looking Up." It might be noted that when *A Damsel in Distress* was released in November, it was criticized primarily because it did not co-star Ginger Rogers.

The tensions that had marred the Gershwins' work on *Shall We Dance* did not afflict *Damsel*. In March George wrote Mabel that he had spent so much time watching the shooting of the first film that "Ira and I are a little behind on the second one. Can you imagine that we've been on the second Astaire picture for eight weeks already. Time has a special way of flying out here. It just zooms past. Someone once said that when time hurries by, you are happy. If that is true we've been in heaven."

He reported on a dinner party given by Edward G. Robinson, like George an avid art collector, for Stravinsky. "Many celebs were there. Chaplin, Goddard, Fairbanks, Dietrich, Capra & others." Stravinsky and Samuel Dushkin played violin-piano pieces for the guests "& very interesting too." George was seated next to Paulette Goddard, then rumored to be Mrs. Charles Chaplin (though no one was certain). As for Goddard, George told Mabel, "Mmmmm. She's nice. Me likee." He would see more of her.

He was excited about two new paintings he had acquired, one by the Austrian modernist Oskar Kokoschka and the other, *Black Venus,* by the American John Carroll.

He planned to go to New York as soon as the Astaire and Goldwyn assignments were completed. Friends from New York had called a few days before and he got "all the latest information about Kay & was glad to hear that she is working & is happy. Isn't it amazing how things turn out?"

A month later, on April 20, he wrote to Mabel again with a curious report. He had become more than ever conscious of his receding hairline, a preoccupation not uncommon in Hollywood. "I am lying comfortably on a chaise longue with a new gadget on my head" he told her. "You would probably scream with laughter if you could see me. The machine is a new invention put out by the Crosley Radio Company and has been recommended by several people out here as a positive grower of hair. It's an entirely new principle and you know me for new principles." The "gadget" was a helmetlike device that fit over the head and, when activated, vibrated vigorously to massage the scalp. Paul Mueller doubted its efficacy and even cautioned his employer that it might very well be doing harm. Gershwin dismissed that immediately.

They hoped to be finished with *A Damsel in Distress* in three weeks and after a week off he and Ira would begin on the Goldwyn film ". . . so you see that the collaborators Gershwin have been extremely active and shall continue to be until the middle of September. After that, maybe New York for a few months. How is the old burg these days?"

But there was no vacation for the Gershwins. George informed Isaac Goldberg that, by May 12, they had completed all eight songs for *A Damsel in Distress* (plus one extra, "Pay Some Attention to Me" for Gracie Allen which was not used) and instead of a week in Arrowhead Springs, they started on *The Goldwyn Follies* that week. In the letters to the East at this time George began mentioning feeling tired.

IV

During May the Gershwins were occupied with the Goldwyn songs, often to George's annoyance with the man he referred to, rather sarcastically, as the "Great Goldwyn" and the "super, super, stupendous, colossal moving picture extravaganza" they were working on and which he would never complete. Concurrently he experienced a fruitless infatuation and brief fling with Paulette Goddard and talked a great deal about marriage with his friends. In addition, by the end of the month or early in June, he mentioned to his friend George Pallay, that he suffered brief spells of dizziness once while reading and again on the tennis court. Then there were the headaches and fatigue.

"Ira and I have had to literally drag ourselves to work the last few days," he wrote Mabel on May 19, "as we have just finished the second Astaire score and have to start right in on *The Goldwyn Follies*. Even the Gershwins can't take that kind of routine.

"It's too bad our contracts followed one another so closely as we both could use a month's rest. Anyway, the silver lining on this cloud is that after *The Goldwyn Follies* we are going to take a long vacation, come to New York and perhaps I may even go to Europe" (there were offers of European concert tours; and he knew Mabel planned to travel there).

He had soon learned that working for the Great Goldwyn was mostly cloud with no silver lining.

Samuel Goldwyn (1881–1974), one of Hollywood's pioneers (he co-produced *The Squaw Man* in 1914), by the spring of 1937 had achieved the reputation of star-maker and independent producer of films of distinction and quality. He accomplished this by his shrewd selection of writers, directors, stars, technicians et al., rather than an ability to actually make the film; he left that to the others, his hired hands. Such important films, up to that time, as *Arrowsmith, Dodsworth, Barbary Coast* and an Eddie Cantor musical made Goldwyn a name to respect and reckon with.

The word went out that *The Goldwyn Follies* was to be the first of a series of three-hour, all-star, all-color lavish productions. The delay caused by the Gershwins' prolonged work on *A Damsel in Distress* gave publicists even more time to broadcast the promised riches of Goldwyn's first *Follies.* Significantly, there never was a second.

Not that the great man stinted. Besides the Gershwins he signed Ben Hecht to write the screenplay—and to cover himself, three other writers for special comedy sequences. There was George Marshall to direct (he was a dependable but curious choice; up to that time he was best known as director of Harry Carey Westerns).

Edward Powell, a former Schillinger student and good Gershwin friend, who spent a lot of time at the Gershwins' was assigned the orchestrations. Alfred Newman, who had conducted Gershwin's first two *Scandals,* was musical director. All other technical categories were filled with equally qualified people, from Technicolor (Natalie Kalmus) to cinematography (Gregg Toland).

The casting, however, was peculiar. Except for Adolphe Menjou, who portrayed a film producer, the cast was made up primarily of radio personalities: the Ritz Brothers, comedian Phil Baker, ventriloquist Edgar Bergen and his dummy Charlie McCarthy. Bobby Clark had left Broadway for this, his one film appearance. The juvenile lead, tenor Kenny Baker, had also come out of radio (where he played a naïve foil for comedian Jack Benny) and was considered promising as a second Dick Powell. The relatively unknown Andrea Leeds was cast opposite Baker as the typical small-town American girl—bright, unaffected, honest—who was found by the producer and who had all the qualities that would enable him to fashion the Great All-American Movie based on her views.

Into this mélange Goldwyn poured Culture: Metropolitan Opera soprano Helen Jepson and tenor Charles Kullman; choreographer George Balanchine, who would prepare a ballet—Gershwin's *Swing Symphony* —for his wife, Vera Zorina, assisted by William Dollar and the American Ballet of the Metropolitan Opera—and the Goldwyn Girls. *The Swing Symphony* was to combine these forces in a ballet depicting the clash between the classical and popular (i.e., jazz).

By early June the Gershwins had completed five songs, forcing themselves to hurry along so that Gershwin would have time for the *Symphony*. These weeks were harrowing for George, not only because of what appeared to be a sudden unexpected deterioration of his health, but because of the treatment he was subjected to at the Goldwyn studio.

Most of the songs were finished when Goldwyn summoned the Gershwins to his office. They found him surrounded by, as Oscar Levant put it, "his full staff of loyal, well-paid amanuenses (stooges)." The Great Goldwyn then insisted that George and Ira perform the songs for the panel. Gershwin, Levant recalled in "one of the few occasions in my experience, was genuinely offended." He believed he had long passed the demonstration phase of his career.

Goldwyn, who was not celebrated for his musicality, was not impressed. He did like the rhythmically insistent release to "I Was Doing All Right"; that was all. In the final film it was thrown away, sung by the film's only other popular singer, Ella Logan, against dialogue. Ira was somewhat amused at Goldwyn's musicological opinions and George quickly dismissed them. However, when he later showed signs of atypical moodiness and fatigue, complained of headaches and vertigo, his friends and family attributed them to his Goldwyn experience.

The songs had come quickly, considering the sketchy plot—the rivalry of producer and juvenile over the All-American girl—which was regularly interrupted for a star specialty number, including an elephantine excerpt from *La Traviata,* featuring Jepson and Kullman.

For Baker the Gershwins dipped into the 1930–31 Tune Book, expanded a twenty-four-measure "Brahmsian" theme, as Gershwin thought of it, into "Love Walked In." For Logan, they retrieved a song intended for Astaire (possibly the rejected Latin-American piece for the *Shall We Dance* finale), "Just Another Rhumba." It is an unusual, intricate and long song. Although rehearsed, it was not filmed and was dropped from the picture. A delightful word-play number, "I Love to Rhyme," was assigned to Phil Baker to sing to his own accordion accompaniment; he never got to sing it through, for his singing was constantly interrupted. It was a repeat of the *Shall We Dance* experience: a rejection ("Rhumba") and a throwaway ("Rhyme"). Goldwyn's almost-favorite, "I Was Doing All Right," remained mired in talk and distraction.

George Gershwin's last song was also thrown away. "So little footage was given to 'Love Is Here to Stay'—I think only one refrain—that it meant little in *The Goldwyn Follies,*" Ira Gershwin ruefully recalled years later after the song came into its own when beautifully presented in the film, *An American in Paris* in 1951.

Only the music to the refrain had been written down; George had not gotten around to the verse, though he had an initial idea for it. Oscar Levant recalled that on hearing the song for the first time he "complained of its lack of breathing space in the second eight bars, its too-long contours . . ." George, as usual, listened and then, according to Levant, "spent two days trying to rephrase the melody and simplify the line, eventually returning to the original form of it. Ira was quite annoyed with me . . ." (Later, when a verse was needed for the film, Ira and Oscar recalled what George had had in mind.)

During this period Gershwin continued seeing a good deal of Paulette Goddard; there are snapshots and home movies of her at the Roxbury Drive swimming pool. "Paulette would emerge from her cabana [there were several near the pool] in the scantiest of bathing suits and lie à la Cleopatra along the side of the pool," Merle Armitage recalled. "As she stretched out a languid hand to ruffle the hair of the swimming George, the anatomical display was superb."

It was an understandable infatuation, for Goddard, then about twenty-six, was attractive and, as George told Mabel Schirmer, he had "found her the most interesting personality I've come across since arriving in Hollywood. You would be crazy about meeting her as she has one of the most alert minds you can possibly imagine.

"On the other hand, she is married to the 'famous Charlie' and under such circumstances I am not allowing myself to become too involved."

They met surreptitiously after a suspicious Chaplin began to have Paulette followed, particularly after Walter Winchell linked their names in a column. A method was devised to throw the shadow off the trail. According to Paul Mueller, Paulette would drive to a spot where Paul was waiting in his car. She would leave hers and duck down in the back seat for the drive to Roxbury Drive. On another occasion they went off to Palm Springs together, where Alexander Steinert filmed them for his home movies.

Gershwin talked with Steinert about marriage, even to Goddard, but his friend bluntly told him that it was pointless. If she had to make a choice, Steinert told George, Paulette Goddard would remain with a big film star rather than take up with a composer-songwriter. George brought up the subject of marriage with Harold Arlen, who told him he was simply not the type to marry, that he would always "play the field." This angered George and he dropped the subject.

In those latter days of May he became unnaturally moody. He lost his temper at times and as, Pallay, noticed, he became "critical of things, people and events . . . Then he complained of headaches and fatigue." The headaches became so severe that, rather than dismiss his complaints as hypochondria, Leonore and Ira suggested that he should have a physical examination—although most of his friends continued to believe he was suffering from Goldwyn phobia.

V

On June 9 a battery of physicians examined George at home, giving him as thorough a checkup as was possible under the circumstances; they found nothing. A week later he appeared at an RKO convention to play Gershwin, including songs from the forthcoming *A Damsel in Distress,* with his usual verve and precision. When Oscar Levant brought Aaron Copland, who had come to Hollywood hoping to score films, he was in good spirits, complimented Copland on a recent broadcast of his opera for youngsters, *The Second Hurricane,* and asked for a copy of the score. He also graciously offered to sign Copland's application for membership in the American Society of Authors, Composers and Publishers.

On the twelfth, George and his agent-friend Arthur Lyons took a brief breather in Coronado, in Southern California; the stay on the beach seemed to refresh him. After returning, he had dinner with the Berlins on the twentieth; the headaches returned. One physician described these as "severe, pounding" episodes. One was so acute as he walked home from a dinner party that he sank to the curb, his head in his hands.

On June 22, George had lunch with Paulette Goddard and Lyons; his demeanor—detached, distracted, uninterested—indicated that something was seriously wrong. He agreed to undergo another examination. The next day, June 23, he was admitted into Cedars of Lebanon Hospital in Los Angeles for a series of tests. George Pallay wrote of this stay: "Ex-Rays. eye specialist, lung specialist, brain specialist, etc. All found no symptoms of any organic or physical illness. All agreed that his condition showed every proof of nervous affliction, perhaps self induced by worry, overwork or general emotional geographic unhappiness or something."

When Gershwin was released on the twenty-sixth the final words on his medical form read, "most likely hysteria."

However, one neurologist, Dr. Eugene Ziskind noted that Gershwin was suffering from photophobia (an extreme sensitivity to light) but no other abnormalities. This was the onset of a condition known as papilledema, a swelling in the retina where the optic nerve from the brain joins the eye, a definite indication that there is an abnormal increase of pressure somewhere in the brain. When it was suggested at the time that he undergo a spinal tap (which would have revealed he was suffering from a brain tumor), he refused because he had heard it was a most painful procedure. (It might also have proved fatal; surgeons today would not have a patient undergo a spinal tap in the presence of papilledema because of the possibility of herniation of the brain. However, this was not known in 1937.)

After Gershwin returned to his home, his cousin Henry Botkin visited one day and found him in a room with the shades drawn because of the pain sunlight caused him.

The consensus of the examining physicians unwittingly, but unfortunately, contributed to Gershwin's agony. Their "hysteria" diagnosis merely assured some of his skeptical friends that he was responding neurotically to the pressures of work and the annoyances he associated with it. On one occasion, he suffered a dizzy spell while leaving the Brown Derby restaurant and fell to the sidewalk. One member of the party was not impressed.

"Leave him there," she snapped, "all he wants is attention."

Once the "medical" verdict was in, it was decided that George should seek psychiatric help. Pallay tells of this new development: "Immediately the greatest psycho-analyst [Dr. Ernest Simmel] was employed to search out the cause of this apparent mental illness. The man was the best in America. He studied and studied George . . . but the headaches continued. Yet all during these headaches there was no change from normal to subnormal of pulse, appetite, temperature, respiration, blood pressure, etc. Just headaches. And each day physical doctors examined George watching his physical reactions for improvement or unimprovement.

"All during this period there were days when he indicated [he was] on the way to recovery," Pallay wrote. "This by fewer headaches, moments of cheerfulness, clear thinking, planning for his comfort and work. Always most optimistic of not only his recovery but the fact that nothing physical was the matter."

Except that Dr. Simmel sensed that Gershwin's illness was organic, not emotional.

Despite the discomforts and disruptions, George and Ira continued work on *The Goldwyn Follies.* During one of the better periods, they visited the Goldwyn studios, where George enjoyed listening to conductor Alfred Newman record some of the score. Other times he spent a great deal of time asleep, night and day, the headaches controlled somewhat by sedatives.

But there were periods of impaired coordination; his playing was poor; he dropped utensils on the table; he spilled water; he fell on the stairs. These inexplicable occurrences upset his sister-in-law. Once, after spilling food, he was asked to leave the table. Ira helped him upstairs to his room. For a moment their eyes met at the doorway. "I'll never forget that look," Ira later told a friend, "as long as I live."

George's friends were shocked by his appearance, especially S. N. Behrman, who had not seen him for a brief time. Accompanied by Oscar Levant and screenwriter Sonya Levien, Behrman dropped by the Gershwin house with tickets for his play *Amphitryon 38,* scheduled to open in Los Angeles on July 5. Though he had seen George only a few weeks before, he was shaken by the change in his friend.

Behrman remembered the earlier visit vividly because George had played him new recordings of music by Shostakovich, with the observation that the Russian ingeniously worked with short motifs and that he might try that approach himself. He then suggested they go for a drive in his Cord.

"There was something odd about him that day," Behrman noticed. "He was subdued, shadowed. I edged about in my mind, to account for this. I had heard that George had fallen seriously in love with a film star and that it had not been going well. George said nothing. Neither did I." Behrman then asked about the latest songs, and would he sing some? Gershwin complied with renditions of "A Foggy Day" and "They Can't Take That Away from Me."

They both agreed "on how extraordinary Ira was." Behrman was particularly impressed with how Ira, in the last song, had added "singing off-key to the heroine's list of perfections."

It was on the second visit, Saturday, July 3, when Behrman, Levien and Levant saw Gershwin. Before visiting the Gershwins, Behrman phoned ahead and tried to learn what the problem was and was told by Ira that George had "not been feeling well for the last few weeks" and that it seemed "to be some nervous disorder." Levant then suggested that "the general opinion was that George had been frustrated by his lukewarm reception in Hollywood, and by the mild success of the films he worked on." (Actually at this time only *Shall We Dance* had been released. But its success was indeed mild; like the previous Astaire-

Rogers musical, *Swing Time,* it did not do as well at the box office as the earlier five films).

When Gershwin came downstairs, accompanied by a male nurse, Paul Levy, an assistant to Dr. Simmel, Behrman realized he was not seeing a man suffering from a "nervous disorder."

"He was very pale," Behrman wrote of this. "The light had gone from his eyes. He seemed old. He greeted me mirthlessly. His handshake was limp, the spring had gone out of his walk."

Gershwin went unsteadily to a sofa near the chair in which Behrman sat. He did not sit, but lay down on the sofa and attempted to adjust his head in a pillow. Behrman asked if he was in pain.

"Behind my eyes," he said, "behind my eyes."

Berhman left his chair to kneel beside him, took George's head in his hands and asked if he felt like playing the piano. "He shook his head. It was the first such refusal I'd ever heard from him."

He then spoke with not much enthusiasm about the proposed revival of *Porgy and Bess* that Merle Armitage planned for February of 1938. This, too, was uncharacteristic, for he would ordinarily have been excited over such a prospect—and he had been when Armitage initially brought it up earlier in the year. Gershwin's eyes focused on Behrman.

"I had to live for this," he said, "that Sam Goldwyn should say to me: 'Why don't you write hits like Irving Berlin?' "

When Behrman asked if he planned to come to the premiere of *Amphitryon 38* on the following Monday, Gershwin merely shook his head, No. Behrman removed his hands. "He looked at me with lusterless eyes. I had a sinking feeling: he is no longer with us."

Gershwin spoke to Levy. "I want to go back to my room." They slowly ascended the stairs. From Leonore Gershwin, Behrman learned that he was usually worse at night. "Maybe it's seeing you," she suggested, "[it] reminds him of the past."

"In the car," Behrman later remembered, "Sonya, Oscar and I rode in silence." Levant broke that silence.

"You think George is very sick, don't you?"

"Yes," Behrman replied, "I think he is *very* sick."

Disturbed, he believed that George needed medical attention. When he proposed he take George back to New York with him on Tuesday, Levien cautioned him with, "You can't take the responsibility." Behrman strongly believed that George Gershwin needed a surgeon, not an analyst.

The next day, Sunday July 4, Behrman learned that George was no longer in the house on Roxbury Drive. To ease the strain, he had moved into E. Y. Harburg's house nearby. Harburg and his wife were leaving for New York with the Arlens, where the writers were to work on the score for an antiwar musical, *Hooray for What!*

The Arlens dropped in to say goodbye and were as shocked as Behrman to see the drastic change in Gershwin in just a few days. They found him on the sofa, inanimate, listless, his once bronzed, vital face ghastly pale. His one comment was, "All my friends are leaving." As soon as the Harburgs vacated, Gershwin, Mueller and Levy moved into their house.

As soon as they arrived, George asked Mueller to pull the shades and give him a wet towel for his eyes. He was more alone than ever. The flowers Paulette Goddard sent were received with indifference. But Leonore Gershwin's chocolates incited an abnormal reaction: he kneaded the contents of the box and spread the mixture over his body.

He spent the next few days in the darkened room, much of the time sleeping. Levy remained in the room with him constantly and visitors were discouraged. According to Pallay, Simmel wanted to keep George out of the reach of Hollywood's parlor psychiatrists.

Ira Gershwin, and apparently Pallay, were permitted in. On Thursday, the eighth of July, Ira came by to discuss some of the songs they had done for Goldwyn. By then Goldwyn had been told there would be no *Swing Symphony* or additional songs for a while. George was released from the contract.

On Friday Ira and Pallay came by around four in the afternoon and were told that George was asleep, the first time in a long time without the aid of medication. It seemed like a good sign. The two men left and, around seven, George awakened wanting to be helped to the bathroom. He suddenly began trembling and shaking. Levy and Mueller got him back into bed immediately "and his eyes seemed to swell" (the first obvious indication of papilledema).

George's doctors were called; after an examination, they had him readmitted to Cedars of Lebanon around midnight. Dr. Carl Rand, a neurosurgeon, and Dr. Ziskind suspected a brain tumor, although none was visible on an X ray. By this time George was in a deep coma. Various tests were undertaken and around nine-thirty in the morning of Saturday, July 10, "the family was notified and a guarded prognosis was given." Dr. Rand suggested additional consultation.

At three in the afternoon a spinal tap was made; the removal of the fluid reduced the pressure from 400 mm. to 220. As Gershwin's condition worsened a "tentative diagnosis of an expanding brain tumor was made," according to a study made by Dr. Louis Carp in 1979. A not-so-tentative decision was made, after further consultation, to send for the country's leading neurosurgeon, Dr. Walter E. Dandy of the Johns Hopkins Medical School in Baltimore, for further consultation.

Finding Dandy was a problem; it was the weekend and a call to his home by Pallay found that he was spending the weekend in Chesapeake Bay on the yacht of Maryland's governor, Harry W. Nice. According to a letter written soon after by George Pallay to Irene Gallagher, secretary to Max Dreyfus in New York, "The governor's secretary assured me that short wave broadcast by the Maryland Police to the boat would be employed. Then I phoned Emil Mosbacher [in White Plains], told him of the life and death importance of getting Dandy. He got the White House Secretary McIntire and McIntire ordered out the Navy."

According to Mosbacher, it was Leonore Gershwin who had called and urged him to find an outstanding neurosurgeon to fly into California for an urgent consultation. He first thought of a famous surgeon in Boston, Dr. Harvey Cushing, but on phoning learned that Cushing had retired from operative surgery; he suggested that Mosbacher find Dandy. When he learned that Dandy was away from Baltimore, Mosbacher called the White House for aid in finding him on Chesapeake Bay. When the governor's yacht was reached by radio and its position known, a Coast Guard cutter was dispatched to pick Dandy up. A police escort then sped him to the airport at Cumberland, Maryland, where Mosbacher had a chartered plane awaiting him. For the moment it was believed that Gershwin was not in immediate danger and the plan was to fly Dandy to Newark Airport from which he would proceed on to Los Angeles.

Meanwhile, the doctors on the scene took a precautionary step: they sought out and found (vacationing on Lake Tahoe, Nevada) another eminent surgeon, Dr. Howard C. Naffziger. He flew in and arrived at the hospital around nine-thirty in the evening of July 10; after examining Gershwin he felt immediate surgery was necessary. When Dandy called from Newark and conferred with the doctors at Cedars of Lebanon Hospital he agreed with Naffziger. His flight to California was canceled and Gershwin was prepared for surgery.

It was after midnight when the five-hour surgical procedure began. Leonore and Ira, Harry Botkin, the Paleys, Oscar Levant, Alexander Steinert and others, waited on the hospital's fourth floor. George Pallay, according to his own account, established himself at a desk "ten feet away from the [operating] room." He functioned as liaison between the medical team and family and friends.

With Naffziger as consultant, Dr. Rand performed the operation. After trephining, he found "that the right ventricle [of the brain] was compressed and displaced to the left beyond the midline. The left ventricle was enlarged and displaced laterally. Both these findings suggested that there was a tumor in the right temporal lobe."

"The anguish of the family downstairs is indescribable," Pallay wrote of the Saturday night and Sunday morning within a week of the event. "I reported for all to pray that it [the tumor] would be soft and not hard. Then at four-thirty [A.M.] great cheerfulness spread over the doctors as they viewed a formation known as a cyst." However, after they had removed the cyst, they found below it "the root of the tumor embedded deep in the brain." They found too that it was an extremely malignant type of tumor, glioblastoma.

From the beginning Gershwin never had a chance. (Even today glioblastoma is difficult to treat.) An earlier diagnosis would have made little difference in the final outcome. In 1937 there was no sophisticated CAT-scan X ray nor were steroids available to reduce the swelling in the brain. The former would have probably detected and located the tumor and the latter would have reduced the headaches—and might have prolonged Gershwin's agony for six months, perhaps two years. Had it been possible to remove the tumor, or the bulk of it, it would have recurred.

Around six-thirty Sunday morning, July 11, a distraught and weary group returned to Roxbury Drive. Only Pallay appears to have been aware of the inevitable. "I could not get myself to tell them it was hopeless. I did tell Lee Gershwin that even if he lived, he could expect at its best that George's left side of face and arm, side and leg, would be forever paralyzed, that he'd never be able to play again . . ." According to Pallay's letter, there were more than twenty people involved in the surgery and that he was able "to talk constantly with the nurses, internes, doctors, etc. I asked thousands of questions." His description of what went on and particularly of the cyst, its removal and the discovery of the tumor is harrowing and remarkably authentic.

In a letter written to Dr. Gabriell Segal, one of the participants, Dr. Dandy agreed with Pallay. "I do not see what more could have been done for Mr. Gershwin," he wrote. "It was just one of those fulminant tumors. There are not many tumors that are removable, and it would be my impression that although the tumor in large part might have been extirpated and he would have recovered for a little while, it would have recurred very quickly since the whole thing fulminated so suddenly.

"I think the outcome is much best for himself, for a man as brilliant as he with a recurring tumor, it would have been terrible; it would have been a slow death."

Around seven that morning Gershwin was returned to his room where, according to Pallay, "his pulse and respiration rallied wonderfully." It was temporary and a false sign of hope. A few minutes after nine his temperature rose swiftly to 106.5; his pulse was 180 and respiration 45. George Gershwin, aged thirty-eight, died at 10:35 A.M., Sunday, July 11, 1937. He never emerged from the coma he had lapsed into on Friday evening.

VI

Ira was devastated by the death of his brother; family and friends became very concerned. One, Paul Berman, began talking about immediately teaming him up with Jerome Kern to keep him occupied. Goldwyn told him he could select any composer he wished to complete the *Follies* score. But Ira could not consider these suggestions, there was too much to do. An elaborate funeral service was held in New York at Temple Emanu-El on Thursday, July 15. Fifth Avenue, as well as the temple, was crowded that gray, rainy day. There were tributes, spoken and musical.

Following the services and interment, Ira returned to Beverly Hills. He selected Vernon Duke to assist in fulfilling the Goldwyn contract. Since George had not written the *Swing Symphony,* it was suggested that Balanchine choreograph *An American in Paris;* while Goldwyn felt it would be "very beautiful" and "artistic," the "miners in Harrisburg" would not understand it.

So Duke composed the music for two ballets, *Romeo and Juliet* and *Water Nymph* (in which Balanchine had Zorina rising out of a pool of water). They completed two songs, "I'm Not Complaining" and "Spring Again"; only the last remained in the completed film. Released in February 1938, *The Goldwyn Follies* was a shambles, a variety show— a throwback to the first musical films of the late twenties—without focus. Its skimpy plot—the unconvincing romance—was generally lost, as it served to move from one specialty act to another.

None of the songs were presented well, with "Spring Again" coming off best. In April Ira had the pleasure of hearing "Love Walked In" played for the first time on *Your Hit Parade,* where it remained for fourteen weeks, four times in first place. It was not one of his favorite lyrics, and he believed his brother's "Brahmsian" melody deserved a better one. Ira felt that the use of the word "right" in the first line of the refrain was an "obvious padding word." When the song was published he eliminated the offending word from the title.

In addition to writing two songs for the *Follies,* Duke later claimed that he had composed the verses to three of the George Gershwin songs, "Love Walked In," "I Was Doing All Right" and Gershwin's last completed song, "Love Is Here to Stay." If so—and there is reason to doubt him—he must share credit with Oscar Levant and Ira Gershwin. Both heard George play possible verses for these songs, and though they had not written them down they remembered how Gershwin had played them. Levant recalled the distinctive Gershwin harmonies of "Love Is Here to Stay." Ira, of course, was familiar with the intended verses, for he had written his lyrics to them and sang them for Duke to put on paper.

Duke's problem in later life, when he made these claims in interviews, was that he believed he had never been sufficiently recognized in New York or Hollywood, despite the excellence and originality of his work. His forceful personality often precluded his working with the same lyricist twice.

Gershwin's last Hollywood songs are graced with a classical simplicity; they are not lowbrow. They are, to sum up, refined, unpretentious but turned out by the hand of a master. They served their films well, even if the films did not consistently do the same for them. Even the most complex, which of course were not used, "Hi! Ho! At Last!" and "Just Another Rhumba" are readily accessible though experimental and unconventional. If performed without vocals they become piano gems in the mode of the *Piano Preludes*.

The Hollywood songs (as well as the Broadway songs, of course) are alive a half century after they were conceived. There was no diminishing of quality and invention, unusual in that their creator was suffering from a fatal, often excruciatingly painful, illness.

George Gershwin's death truncated a gift that would have continued to grow in popular music as well as the concert hall. The songs for the Kaufman-Hart musical, the music for a new Heyward opera, the symphony, the concerto, the overture, the ballet, the string quartet of which he spoke during his last year, were never written. It is fruitless, though tempting, to conjecture what his accomplishments might have been had he not died so young.

Kay Swift, on being asked this almost inevitable question by a radio interviewer, replied, "We'll never know, will we? But it would have been important."

Epilogue
The Myths of Ira
Gershwin

During George Gershwin's lifetime—and after—the popular misconception was that Ira's talent was almost totally dependent on his brother's genius. The death of George, it was rumored along Broadway and around Hollywood, would be the professional end of Ira Gershwin.

Another tale had him going into seclusion refusing to work and not coming out of it for several years.

He was shaken and depleted when he returned from New York after George's funeral; he was also distressed by guilt. Like everyone else, including batteries of doctors, he had believed, perhaps fervently wanted to believe, that his brother's illness was psychosomatic. That the nature of the tumor was such that George had been doomed from its onset ameliorated some of the guilt, but it was empty consolation. Something vital had been torn out of his life.

Work with "my excitable friend" Duke helped; the volatile composer, so unlike his brother, kept him occupied for a few weeks to finish *The Goldwyn Follies* score. When he learned that *A Damsel in Distress* was still in production, he remembered a song he and George had written for Astaire; he completed the lyric, "Heigh Ho the Merrio" and offered it to RKO. Though Astaire liked it, it was not used. (Almost a decade later, when he and Kay Swift prepared a posthumous Gershwin score for the film *The Shocking Miss Pilgrim,* Ira remembered the song again and revised it as "The Back Bay Polka," sometimes called "But Not in

Boston"). Once Ira had finished with Duke, the Gershwins decided it was time for a vacation.

I

In the spring of 1938 Ira and Leonore spent a weekend driving in California and Nevada. One Saturday evening—May 14, 1938—as they rounded the top of Donner Pass, their vehicle was sideswiped by another. Ira described the driver of the other car as being "higher than the Pass." While there were no injuries, the fender of the Gershwins' car was so buckled that it was impossible to drive. A passing motorist stopped, then drove off, promising to send a tow truck from the next town.

While waiting, Leonore and Ira stayed in their car. It was quite chilly at nine thousand feet, even with overcoats. To while away the wait, Ira turned on the radio, listened to a local commercial, then, searching for something more listenable, tuned in to "Your Hit Parade." This interested him, for "Love Walked In" had been one of the Top Ten songs for the previous six weeks. (The Goldwyn Follies had been released in February). The Gershwin song had joined the Top Ten in ninth place, then fluctuated between third and seventh.

But he was disappointed; he checked with his watch and realized the program was drawing to a close and "I supposed we had missed finding out if the song was still on the list or not." It was: in the Number 1 spot (always performed last, with fanfare). This, Ira felt, "more than made up for a badly busted fender." The remainder of their little motor jaunt was uneventful, but Ira returned to Beverly Hills happy in the thought that their work was widely appreciated despite the burden of a dull film. Having completed "Heigh Ho the Merrio," he took comfort in knowing there were dozens of his brother's songs, some with, some without, lyrics that would prolong their collaboration. He would also collaborate with others.

The first was Jerome Kern, with whom, in 1938, he wrote several songs, among them "Once There Were Two of Us" and "Now That We Are One" designed to be sung serially. Since they went unused and unpublished at the time, it was assumed that Ira had stopped writing after his brother's death (the two songs were published in 1968). Later in the year he joined with Yip Harburg to write a song with Johnny Green, "Baby, You're News," which was published but did not become popular. Later, in 1939, he and Harold Arlen wrote the delightful "I'll Supply the Title (You'll Supply the Tune)." That same year, with the help of Kay Swift, he dipped into his store of unpublished George Gershwin melodies to concoct "The Dawn of a New Day," as the theme song for the 1939 New York World's Fair, out of three melodic fragments.

There were also a few songs written with Harry Warren during this period, but Ira was rarely comfortable with writing single songs; he preferred working on a production, a film or a show, in which the songs were written for a specific point for a specific talent. He bided his time.

Nor was Ira the recluse of legend; the Gershwin parties resumed after a while, with Leonore as one of the most popular hostesses in Beverly Hills. Ira's poker parties went on. He even ventured out of 1019 Roxbury Drive to attend the (mostly) songwriter gatherings at Sonya Levien's home. There are home recordings, c. 1938–39, of Ira singing such Gershwin rareties as "Hi-Ho!," "Stiff Upper Lip" and "Put Me to the Test" with Harold Arlen at the piano. At another session he joined a friend, "Doc" McGonigle, a film writer, and Yip Harburg in good-naturedly harassing Harold Arlen as the composer attempted to sing his and Ted Koehler's, "You've Got Me Sittin' on a Fence." He had not stopped working, or gone into retreat, but merely waited for the right libretto or screenplay to come along. It would come on the first day of 1940.

II

The myth of Ira Gershwin's dependency should have evaporated long before 1937. As early as 1921, with his and Vincent Youmans's *Two Little Girls in Blue,* he enjoyed his first (mild, it is true) Broadway success before his brother had his. Even after the Gershwin collaboration began, Ira worked with other songwriters: with Phil Charig on the popular "Sunny Disposish" (1926) and Harry Warren on and even more popular "Cheerful Little Earful" (1930), both written for revues.

There were full and important scores. First, a revue, in which Ira joined his old East Side friend and college literary collaborator, E. Y. Harburg, to work with Harold Arlen, then at the brilliant beginning of his career. The show was *Life Begins at 8:40* (1934) out of which came such songs as "You're a Builder Upper," "Fun to Be Fooled," "What Can You Say in a Love Song?" and "Let's Take a Walk Around the Block." There are also the witty and mildly salacious "Quartet Erotica," with its telling play on the name of Balzac, and the ineffably inarticulate "Things," sung by Bert Lahr, parodying the mannerisms of a concert hall baritone.

The other important show, also a revue, was an exhausting one with Vernon Duke, the *Ziegfeld Follies of 1936*. The producer had died in 1932 and the new production was purportedly being presented by his widow, Billie Burke—it was, in fact, a Shubert brothers production. They were hard taskmasters; Gershwin and Duke wrote no fewer than twenty-eight songs for the *Follies*, of which fifteen were used. Among them were many good songs: "Island in the West Indies," "That Moment of Moments," "Five A.M.," "Words Without Music" and the evergreen "I Can't Get Started." Ira was especially proud of "The Gazooka," a satirical comment on the rash of songs that had come out of recent film musicals, i.e., "The Carioca," "The Continental," "The Piccolino," etc.

These songs with composers other than George Gershwin established Ira as an outstanding lyricist on his own; the songs with his brother merely enhanced his stature.

III

It was almost three years after George's death before Ira found a book for a musical that interested him. Moss Hart, determined to write a play without George Kaufman, decided he would base one on his analysis with the ubiquitous Gregory Zilboorg. Late in 1939 he completed a play entitled *I Am Listening,* conceived with Katharine Cornell in mind for the lead. But as the work progressed he sensed that it might become the libretto for an unusual musical.

Around this time he was approached by composer Kurt Weill. The refugee from Hitler's Germany was still best known in the United States for his *Threepenny Opera;* two early American musicals, the antiwar *Johnny Johnson* (1936) and the antidictator *Knickerbocker Holiday* (1938) had not proved to be popular although they were admired for the fine work that had gone into them. Nor, at that time, had his Hollywood career prospered. Weill was anxious to work with Hart and over lunch brought up an idea, something entitled *The Funnies,* the script of which he had been told needed rewriting. He hoped that Hart would do the job.

Hart told him he was occupied with work on what he believed would make a good musical; before lunch was over Weill was convinced he would have to write the music for Hart's musical play. Hart was no lyricist, and as they talked the name of Ira Gershwin came up. Weill had wanted to work with him since he arrived in New York in 1935. Hart and Ira were long-time friends. On New Year's Day 1940, Hart called Gershwin and outlined his plot. To his surprise, Gershwin agreed to collaborate on *I Am Listening*. As Ira recalled it, it was he who had approached Hart, feeling that he had been inactive long enough. This may have been even before Hart had decided to turn his play into a play with music. When the call came, he was ready.

The play, now a musical in which the musical sequences revealed the heroine's subconscious anxieties during analysis, required a singer-actress. Hart forgot Katharine Cornell and, having seen Gertrude Lawrence perform at a Sunday night British War Relief program, was determined to have her for his play with music. Not interested, she put him off with a story about having been warned by her astrologer not to make any decisions at that time. When the right moment, according to the stars, arrived, she conferred with her longtime friend and confidant Noël Coward, who managed to materialize at the right time, with a little coaxing from Hart, who had given him a copy of the script. Coward loved it. "Gertie ought to pay you to play in it," he told Hart.

With Coward's blessing, and with her zodiacal signs in place, Lawrence agreed to appear in Hart's play. The two men left and Hart walked Coward to his hotel. As he was about to enter, Coward turned to Hart and said, "Uncle Moss, now your troubles are really beginning."

Perplexed, Hart said, "But Gertie said yes, didn't she?"

"That's just the point, my boy," Coward said airily as he turned and went into the hotel. He was right. It took Hart about three months to get Lawrence to sign a contract, during which time he had threatened to get Irene Dunne instead.

Early in May, Ira boarded the City of Los Angeles for New York, where he began working on *I Am Listening*, soon retitled *Lady in the Dark*. He remained away from Beverly Hills until late August and spent some of the more uncomfortable weeks away from Manhattan's heat at Hart's splendid home in Bucks County, Pennsylvania.

Hart and Weill had blocked out four "little one-act operas" (Weill's term) for the protagonist's dream sessions with her analyst. They were eventually pared down to three by the cost-conscious management. The excised act was the complete "Hollywood Dream," comprised of three individual but musically linked songs. To the additional dismay of Weill and Ira, another of their efforts, "Song of the Zodiac," one of their most worked-over and a favorite, would be jettisoned along the way.

Ira realized he was back on Broadway: long hours, long discussions and extensive cuts. Near the end of his stay he recalled in a letter the working conditions he had almost forgotten while toiling in comparatively serene Hollywood. "For instance," he wrote, "13 days in the Essex House in N.Y. that I spent during the hottest spell they'd known when I used to work until 4 or 5 in the morning and then try to sleep in a half-filled bathtub for a few hours, then go back to the grind again to find a new rhyme."

Relieved that he had finished his part, he returned to Beverly Hills, fairly certain that he and Weill had done good work. But as production neared and cuts left holes in the score, telephone calls came from producer Sam H. Harris. It had been decided that Lawrence needed a song in place of "Song of the Zodiac," which Harris did not find amusing. The star, he maintained, should have a really lively, funny song to brighten the "Circus Dream." Hart, who was staging the book, and Hassard Short, who was staging the musical sequences, both felt that the Zodiac song was too contemplative, not amusing. They hoped for a showstopper for Gertrude Lawrence.

Reluctantly, Ira boarded a train again. "At one conference," he recalled, "Moss had a suggestion that we do a number about a woman who couldn't make up her mind. That sounded possible; and after a week or so of experimenting with style, format, and complete change of melodic mood from the Zodiac song, we started 'Jenny,' and Liza's new defense about ten days later." Gertrude Lawrence, who portrayed Liza Elliott, the brilliant editor of a posh magazine who could not make up her mind about the men in her life, or even the cover of the next issue of *Allure,* had her showstopper in "The Saga of Jenny."

Despite several years as a patient of Zilboorg, Hart treated the play's psychological theme quite simply (and Freudianly). Although psychoanalysis was an innovative subject for a musical, the dream sequences that explained Liza's problem was a kind of childhood father fixation and rejection presented no problem, in turn, to the audience.

Musically, *Lady in the Dark* was also innovative. It is described as a musical play, but has no overture and, in fact, no music until after several pages of dialogue between Liza and the analyst. Hart described Liza as "plain to the point of austerity": severe skirt and jacket, no makeup, no jewelry. Her first session on the couch, "Glamour Dream," begins with a fragment of a childhood song that haunts Liza (it is the play's leitmotif, "My Ship," which is not heard in its entirety until the final dream). In the first dream the plain Liza imagines herself as the toast of New York's social and intellectual world.

The second musical sequence is the "Wedding Dream," with its memorable "My Ship," and the third is the "Circus Dream," which was to have been a "Minstrel Dream," but was switched to the circus setting because of the colorful costume opportunities.

The "Circus Dream" was a problem during rehearsals. Neither Gershwin nor Weill felt that Lawrence's "Jenny" was more than adequate and no substitute for "Song of the Zodiac." Uneasy when the tryout began in Boston on December 30, 1940, Ira Gershwin observed unobtrusively from the back. "We were playing to a packed house, and the show was holding the audience intensely. It was working out. I was among the standees at the back of the house; next to me was one of the Sam Harris staff."

The "Circus Dream" was in progress. At one point a relative newcomer to Broadway, a young comedian named Danny Kaye, took the spotlight. In Liza's real life he was a fussy, effeminate fashion photographer; in her dream he is the ringmaster of the circus as well as the presiding judge in the trial in which Liza is accused of indecision.

In one of her replies, she sings a pretty little melody, which is echoed by the chorus. The ringmaster asks the name of the composer. "Tchaikowsky!" he is told. With the declaration "I love Russian composers!" Kaye launched into a speedy *Allegro barbaro* recitation of forty-nine tongue-twisting Russian names in about thirty-nine seconds. (The song was based on Ira's "The Music Hour," which had been published in the first *Life* in 1924, when he was known as Arthur Francis).

When Kaye finished his tour de force, applause resounded through the Colonial Theatre for, in Ira's estimate, "at least a solid minute." Kaye had stopped the show.

"Christ," Ira heard the Harris man say, "we've lost our star," and fled to the lobby. The applause obscured the next few lines of dialogue as Kaye stepped out of the limelight and Lawrence began "The Saga of Jenny." Then Ira noticed: "She hadn't been singing more than a few lines when I realized an interpretation we'd never seen before at rehearsals was materializing." It was an animated, earthy, rendition with bumps and grinds right out of burlesque, which as Ira watched, completely stunned the audience. Lawrence's ovation, following immediately after Kaye's, actually lasted twice as long. The two show-stoppers remained. They had not lost their star; had "Jenny" not worked as it did, it was likely that Lawrence would have had Kaye's Russian recitation eliminated; that is show business.

Lady in the Dark premiered at the Alvin Theatre in New York on January 23, 1941, to universal critical approval. Ira, happy in the knowledge that he had a Broadway hit, left as soon as possible for the more placid precincts of Beverly Hills. Having decided to remain in California, he bought a large house immediately next to the one they had rented when they had come to work for RKO. The address was 1021 North Roxbury Drive, from whose spacious comforts Ira would emerge from time to time to do a show or film—or to visit the nearby racetrack.

As time went by, his excursions became fewer; he managed to run things nicely from where he was. The size and luxury of the house, and Ira's preference for staying close to home, inspired Harold Arlen to dub the new quarters the Gershwin Plantation.

With the show running healthily in New York, Ira tended to the things he loved, his correspondence, reading—advance copies of books written by friends, *The New Yorker*, from which he tore out all extraneous material (advertisements) before he read it, and the New York *Times* and *Herald Tribune*. There were also the late-night poker parties, and golf, generally with two favorite collaborators, Harry Warren and Harold Arlen.

Four months after *Lady in the Dark* was solidly into its 467-performance run, the Plantation's serenity was disturbed when Gertrude Lawrence asked Weill for a new song to replace "One Life to Live." This surprised Ira, since the song was popular with audiences, third after "Jenny" and "Tchaikowsky." Still, she was the Star. It reminded him of the time, during rehearsals, when she got a lyric change. It was while singing "My Ship," when she came to the release:

> *I can wait for years*
> *Till it appears,*
> *One fine day one spring . . .*

She stopped, stepped forward and glared at Gershwin seated in the orchestra and demanded to know, "Why *four* years, why not five or six?" Nonplussed, he realized he had overlooked an obvious "aural ambiguity." He immediately changed the "for" to "the"; the Star crisis was solved.

Now she demanded an entire new song to replace one that was going well. Weill, who was on the scene, was willing, but Ira did not fancy mail collaboration and even less another trip East. Letters from and to Weill crossed the continent, but Gershwin, who could when necessary be very resolute, procrastinated. The show closed for a summer recess and, when it reopened in September, Lawrence returned to the saga of "One Life to Live," dismissing it as a mere "ice-breaker," an opening number of little significance; she wanted a funnier number. This raised the Gershwin ire.

Lawrence blew up and told Weill that any other star in her position would simply have *demanded* a new song, not *requested* one. It was not her fault that he could not get together with his lyricist, etc., etc. (Weill did not translate the "etc.'s" for Ira).

Gershwin waited twenty days before replying, "I figured," he told Weill, "that the longer I took answering you—or rather, not answering you—the more louse I would be and the more you could blame me. Of all the thankless jobs in show business—to be asked to write a new song for a hit which is in its second season." He suggested shortening the song or eliminating it completely. Then he relented. If Lawrence continued to agitate he would think about a new song idea in a week or so unless he heard from Weill that she had stopped demanding or "forgotten the issue."

By October, when there was no further word from Weill, he was free again to attend to his Plantation work—he was a trustee of the Gershwin Estate—reading scripts for plays and films, whimsical betting at Hollywood Park.

There was a sequel to the "One Life to Live" episode two years later. *Lady in the Dark* was on a successful tour and booked for a run in Los Angeles, where Ira attended its first night. Gratified and happy, he went backstage to congratulate and greet "Gertie." He found her reception "so reluctant and lukewarm" that he quickly slipped out of the theater and fled to the sanctuary of Beverly Hills. Gertie had not forgotten the issue; neither had she forgiven.

IV

Having worked as hard as he had ever worked on a show, Ira felt he could take time out to attend to other matters. In April of 1941 he had begun to talk with Warner Brothers, who were interested in a film biography of George. The process of rights clearances took time, for which Ira was grateful. In May he wrote, "The law department of Warner Brothers has got in touch with me this week—so I imagine they really mean business and that the contract will be drawn up soon and in a month or six weeks I'll probably be working on that picture." This eventually became *Rhapsody in Blue,* on which in fact he did very little work.

Except for consulting from time to time with the staff at Warner Brothers Ira did little else but read, answer letters and turn down scripts. With the Japanese attack on Pearl Harbor, Hollywood became war conscious and Ira became a member of the editorial committee of the Lunch Time Follies—he helped to select the music and songs as entertainment for defense workers in California factories. It was almost two years since he had returned to Beverly Hills in the glow of *Lady in the Dark*'s success, before he told a friend that he might "have a little work to do on the new Russian picture Goldwyn is going to produce—probably a folk song or two."

This turned out to be *The North Star*, a film sympathetic to Russia (the Soviets were America's ally then) in wartime under the Nazis. The screenplay was by a longtime friend, Lillian Hellman. Aaron Copland composed the music and scored the film (he had impressed Hollywood, finally, with his music for *Of Mice and Men* and *Our Town*). The music was written between February and September 1942, while Copland was in Hollywood. In October Ira wrote that "I did quite a lot of work on *The North Star* early this year although I felt very little would be used as songs tend to hold up the action in a more or less documentary melodrama. Haven't seen it yet but am told what little is used is quite effective. Understand Aaron Copland's musical accompaniment is superb. I wasn't around when he got down to the scoring but I'm sure he's done a good job."

The songs are folkish, especially "No Village Like Mine" and the charmingly witty "Younger Generation." A patriotic Soviet song, "Song of the Fatherland," by the Russian songwriters V. Dunayevsky and I. Lebedev-Kumach, was adapted for the film and other appropriate songs, "Song of the Guerrillas" and "Workers of All Nations," were written. The pro-Russian sentiments of such songs, expressing the beliefs of the film's characters and not necessarily those of Gershwin and Copland, would be held against them later during the Tenney Un-American Activities Committee's witch hunts among Hollywood figures.

When Ira saw the finished film after its release early in 1944, he found it "a little dated. Had it been done earlier it would have been a much more important picture." By this time the tide had turned against the Germans in Russia. And Goldwyn's war-torn Soviet Union with its happy, singing, well-scrubbed folk in beautifully tailored peasant costumes did not ring true. Within a decade it would be damned as propaganda (insofar as it may have expressed Hellman's political point of view, it was).

Ira never considered it one of his important efforts; and since the Cold War there have been few requests for choruses in praise of Mother Russia. By the time of the release of *The North Star*, Ira was looking forward to the completion and release of his first important film score since the death of his brother.

Like the Goldwyn epic, this one began early in 1943, when producer Harry Cohn met with composer Arthur Schwartz in New York and asked him to produce and write the music for the next Rita Hayworth film, *Cover Girl*. Surprised, Schwartz reminded Cohn that he had never produced a movie before. Cohn understood, then agreed to finance the project if Schwartz took on the job, still assuming Schwartz would write the music too.

It was a difficult project to reject. Hayworth was the reigning glamour queen of Hollywood, with two successful film musicals, both with Fred Astaire, to her recent credit—*You'll Never Get Rich* (songs by Cole Porter) and *You Were Never Lovelier* (Jerome Kern and Johnny Mercer). She was a fine dancer; that she did not sing was immaterial; her singing voice was dubbed by others. And she was at the peak of popularity, a pinup favorite of the American GI.

Schwartz agreed, provided he handle only the production end of *Cover Girl* and that Cohn let him hire "the very best" to write the songs. Who, Cohn inquired, did he have in mind?

"Jerome Kern and Ira Gershwin."

Schwartz called Kern first at his home in Beverly Hills. The fifty-seven-year-old composer was in a good mood; he and Oscar Hammerstein had won an Academy Award for their song "The Last Time I Saw Paris" (for a song that had not actually been written for a film, but happened to be in one); and *You Were Never Lovelier* had done well. Several of the songs—the title song, "Dearly Beloved" and "I'm Old Fashioned"—had become popular; and his recent effort, *Can't Help Singing,"* with E. Y. Harburg as lyricist and starring Deanna Durbin, showed promise.

He had not done a Broadway musical since the unsuccessful *Very Warm for May* in 1939 and was aware of the growing power of Richard Rodgers on the popular music scene. Kern was competitive and wished to keep his name and songs in the public ear. He consented to write the music for *Cover Girl.*

Schwartz called Ira, who was not very busy. The songs for *The North Star* were nearly completed. He and Kern had worked well together on the few songs they did after George's death—he said yes.

Schwartz had known the Gershwins for years, but he was not acquainted with Kern. He had heard that Kern could be difficult. And, as Schwartz soon learned, hypersensitive.

Once both writers had agreed to write the *Cover Girl* score, Schwartz flew in from New York to call first on Kern at his home on Whittier Drive. The composer was ready for the neophyte producer and brought him to the piano where he played a melody in his lush, embellishment-encrusted style. Schwartz did not evince the proper enthusiasm; grimly Kern marked the song "ADL" (Arthur Doesn't Like). Though a composer himself, Schwartz had trouble in finding the melody in all the rich harmonic decoration.

He had an idea. Would Kern, one-finger style, pick out the tune only?

Hidden among the luxuriant chromatics was the lovely song that would eventually be known as "Long Ago and Far Away."

And so Arthur Schwartz brought together the Emperor of Whittier with the Squire of Roxbury. It would prove to be a long haul.

Work on *Cover Girl* began in the spring of 1943; in June, Ira wrote to an army friend (to whom he faithfully wrote personal and professional news as well as about events in the musical, film and theatrical world) that he was "struggling with ideas for *Cover Girl*. This has been a tough assignment because outside of the star the company seems to have no luck in getting the other actors (I mean actors the producer would like to have), also there have been many changes in the script—so that instead of being finished with this job which I should have by now I'm only about half through."

July brought more of the same: *"Cover Girl* is taking far longer than we expected—mostly script and casting troubles. Naturally with every shift in the cast the number written for one situation usually has to be changed so that in spite of lots of work there's still lots of work to be done."

October: "My troubles on *Cover Girl* are finally over—I hope. This job took twice the time it should have and I grew stale the past few weeks. But I think Kern and I have done some very interesting things for it and the producer assures me the results are going to be good."

Working with Kern, while an honor, was not easy. Each preferred working in his own surroundings (neither liked working at the studios). Kern expected Gershwin to come to him—they lived only a block and a half apart. True, the Roxbury Drive block was rather a long one. But Ira felt more comfortable with his reference volumes around him (whether he consulted them or not; he was a stickler for spelling and grammar). Still Kern insisted and the bulk of the work was done on Whittier Drive. This was a minor cause for irritation in their otherwise productive collaboration—as was Kern's often imperious manner. Once, however, they agreed upon a melody, Ira would take a dummy lyric to Roxbury Drive to complete the song away from Kern.

Among the first completed songs were two that dated back a few years. Ira brought out a copy of "Put Me to the Test," which he and George had written for *A Damsel in Distress.* Since it had not been used, he felt free to use the lyric again. Kern liked it—but, strangely, he also liked George's tune. As Ira reflected years later, "I gave him the lyric, I didn't think he'd take the tune too."

Ira recalled a song he and Kern had worked on during their early collaboration, c. 1939. "I tried to remind him of a lovely tune of the earlier period by humming a snatch of it. But he had never put it on paper, and couldn't recall it. Ira then recalled that Kern's daughter, Betty (then Mrs. Artie Shaw), had been very fond of the melody also. Between them Betty Kern and Ira aided Kern in reconstructing the melody.

"Good tune," he said. "What about it?"

Ira told him that the tune had been haunting him that morning and that if Kern would divide the first note into two shorter notes, he had a good idea for a title of a song that could be used in one of the film's flashback sequences, set in a turn-of-the-century racetrack scene. Kern liked that and split the note and Ira had the tune for "Sure Thing," a ballad with its several clever racing references, which pleased him. While he did not like writing ballads, since they afforded little opportunity for wit and adroit rhymes, he enjoyed the offbeat kind, such as "Sure Thing."

It happened that Kern presented him with a ballad early in the collaboration. It was a beauty, but Ira resisted getting around to writing a lyric for it, although he tried. Among the early attempts were "Just a whisper, soft and low," in response to a dummy lyric an exasperated Kern had sent: "Watching little Alice pee . . ."

Kern rather liked the last line of Ira's lyric, "The moment midnight music made you mine"; the alliteration, he felt, was fine, but Schwartz and others disagreed and Ira kept trying. There were about a half-dozen songs finished when Schwartz called Ira for the ballad lyric. The search for a leading man had finally ended when Columbia borrowed Gene Kelly from MGM; in one of the film's most touching scenes he and Rita Hayworth (with voice dubbed by Martha Mears) sang a ballad.

Gershwin admitted that he had written another lyric for Kern's "Alice" ballad.

"Fine," Schwartz said, "let's have it."

"Now? On the telephone?"

"Sure."

Of all the lyrics he had written to that moment, this was the one he did not really care for, but, reluctantly, he read it to Schwartz, who wrote it down. It began *"Long ago and far away . . ."*

Dictating a lyric over the phone was not the Gershwin method, but Ira was relieved because he knew he would not have to go to the studio to "face anyone with that lyric," which he considered too obvious and commonplace.

After *Cover Girl* opened in New York in April 1944, Ira reported with some surprise and much pleasure that the picture was "a big success (breaking house records at Radio City Music Hall) . . . One of the songs . . . ('Long Ago and Far Away') is on its way to popularity and the jukeboxes. It isn't my favorite lyric but it's an adequate job and the tune is Kern at his best. The other lyrics are better."

Of the eleven songs written for the film, seven were used (there was one non-Kern–Gershwin song interpolated, an old English musical hall number, "Poor John," in the flashback sequence). *Cover Girl* had begun shooting before Gene Kelly joined the cast (leading men were hard to come by during the war) so that four of the songs were discarded. It was Ira who suggested "Put Me to the Test" for Kelly in one of the better musical numbers.

There was, inevitably, a title song, featuring some of the nation's best-known models, among them Anita Colby and Jinx Falkenburg, in an elaborate production number. "The Show Must Go On" was right for its small nightclub setting (in *Cover Girl,* Kelly appeared as the owner of the club; Hayworth was one of the dancers who went on to greater things as a model).

Two songs were timely—"Who's Complaining?," with allusions to wartime rationing and shortages ("My legs will be forgotten/In cotton") and the uplifting "Make Way for Tomorrow," which was written with the help of E. Y. Harburg. Ira enjoyed the film's success and even that of his current least favorite lyric.

He wrote of it in a letter to his army friend, who had just landed in New Guinea. "You sound as if, outside of the mosquitoes," Ira observed, "you're getting along all right. Or, as all right as one gets along in that part of the world. From all reports the attractions aren't such that one becomes a beachcomber. Hawaii?, yes; Cuba?, yes; New Guinea?, no.

"Matter of fact, one of the minor casualties of the war has been the utter demolishment of previously romantic places (on the map) for songwriters. On the blacklist is practically every dot on the atlas. Maybe that's why an innocuous title like 'Long Ago and Far Away' has been Number 1 on the Hit Parade for the past three weeks. There isn't the competition of 'Himalaya Mamma' and 'Nagasaki Polka You Send Me.' Of course it's barely possible that J. Kern wrote a tune in 'L.A.A.F.A.' that the bands like."

As for the "Hit Parade," he had typical reservations. "Actually [it] is an institution that makes for many false values. Many publishers and writers decry it as it tends to point up the commercial and popular consideration of a song rather than quality. But there it is and I imagine there isn't a publisher or writer who doesn't try and/or hope to make it."

"Long Ago and Far Away" is one of Jerome Kern's most haunting melodies—his "last great masterpiece," in the words of his biographer,

Gerald Bordman. But in his modesty Ira overlooked his contribution to the song's staying power and popularity. In the conferences, during which the early versions of the lyric were anything but enthusiastically received, he was advised by Schwartz and others to "keep it simple." Later, after the fatigue wore off he realized it was in fact "a good simple lyric."

Like Irving Berlin's "White Christmas," "Long Ago and Far Away" became a favorite of servicemen and their families. In his lyric, as had Berlin, Gershwin expressed an honest, simple sentiment. In 1944, to American servicemen, most of them very young and many of whom had entered the service fresh out of high school, prom time and graduation time, after nearly three years of war, seemed "long ago" and Britain, France, Italy and stretches of the Pacific, "far away." His "Miss Simplicity" (as he called it) of a lyric had proved timeless and true.

There was little time for reflection or contemplation of the Zeitgeist; no sooner were his *Cover Girl* "troubles" ended than he began working on another film musical, this with the easygoing Kurt Weill. The tentative title was *Where Do We Go From Here?*

Weill had come in from his home in New City, New York, to finish work he had begun, earlier that summer, on the screen versions of *Knickerbocker Holiday* and *Lady in the Dark* (both of which were appalling and butchered his scores). When he arrived in Hollywood early in November 1943, he had left New York with a second hit musical, *One Touch of Venus,* on Broadway. Between November 1943 and February 1944, Ira and Weill scored *Where Do We Go From Here?* and planned their second Broadway musical (which would be *The Firebrand of Florence).*

Weill was disappointed with what he saw happening to his earlier film musicals—interpolations, reorchestrations (Weill was a rarity: he did his own orchestrations), peculiar casting—so he looked forward to working on an original screen musical; at least, whatever the cuts, the score that remained would be his. And working with Ira Gershwin was pleasurable.

Where Do We Go From Here? was a product of the moment: a young patriot desperately yearns to enlist in some branch of the military but cannot because of his 4-F classification. What was unique about this film was its imaginative treatment and innovative use of song.

The screenplay by Morrie Ryskind was based on a story by him and Sid Herzig, blended fantasy and reality: the 4-F Bill (Fred MacMurray) does his part for the war effort by collecting scrap metal and doing dishes at the USO (United Service Organization, a kind of open-house club for servicemen). There he can see his girlfriend, Lucilla (June Haver), dance with the men in uniform, while the girl who truly loves him, Sally (Joan Leslie), subtly pursues him.

While polishing a lamp on the scrap pile, Bill unleashes a genie (Gene Sheldon), who promptly offers to grant three wishes. Bill has but one: to get into uniform. But the genie, perhaps after centuries of inactivity, is rusty. There is a puff of smoke and Bill, indeed, finds himself in uniform —in Washington's army at Valley Forge.

Ira outlined the fantasy portions of the film:

> The 1776 sequence is the first in the fantasy. [in which] our hero becomes a spy for Gen. Washington and this number ["Song of the Rhineland"] is what he hears the Hessians singing in a Trenton Bierstube.
> The next [sequence] is in 1492 on Columbus's flagship, the *Santa Maria*. The 3rd sequence is Manhattan also 1492. The 4th is New Amsterdam in 1664 or thereabouts. The last is where our hero, plus girlfriend, plus genie, ride the carpet through the centuries back to today.

Like Weill, Ira was happy with their work. "A lot of effort and imagination has gone into this film and I hope the results warrant it," he wrote. "It's the first movie musical I know that has some of the flavor of 'Of Thee I Sing' in the writing and the music." He was particularly proud of the 1492 Columbus sequence, a miniature opera that required twelve minutes of screen time, the longest nondancing musical number filmed up to that time.

Weill believed that the musical portions of *Where Do We Go From Here?* were "frankly an experiment in opera form, in which the music and lyrics are integrated with the story, advancing it rather than retarding it as is the case with most musical films. To a friend in New York he wrote, "I have turned out a job here which I can be proud of," and looked forward to even more such film experiments.

By the time of its release in May 1945, the outcome of the Second World War was no longer in doubt; superpatriotism and scrap drives were passé. Military audiences found it rather ludicrous that anyone would be so eager to get into uniform. The charm of the movie lay in its unique musical sequences, but the public had tired of war movies despite the originality of this one. Ira was "quite pleased" with it and, characteristically, let it go at that. Uncharacteristically, even before the release of *Where Do We Go From Here?* he and Weill had begun work on an operetta for Broadway.

V

In their letters, and during Weill's infrequent trips to California over the years since the production of *Lady in The Dark,* Ira and Weill discussed a new musical, possibly in collaboration with Ira's friend playwright-screenwriter Edwin Justus Mayer. (His major claim, c. 1942, when the discussions began, was a very successful play based on the exploits of Benvenuto Cellini, *The Firebrand,* produced in 1924.

Near the close of 1942 the three would-be collaborators, anxious to do an operetta set in another time, came close to beginning one about Nell Gwynn, the mistress of Britain's Charles II; they abandoned that, as well as a musical about Cinderella following her story after she and her prince marry. They then turned to *The Firebrand,* for whose original production Ira had written words to its one song, "The Voice of Love" to the music of Robert Russell Bennett and Maurice Nitke.

Weill, initially, resisted, but Ira's participation as lyricist as well as co-librettist changed his mind. As soon as their work was done on *Where Do We Go From Here?,* they began blocking out their approach to their operetta. Early in August, 1944, Gershwin wrote, "If you haven't heard from me in some time I've been starting on the new opus (the operetta to be done based on *The Firebrand)* and it's always tough getting started." It was Ira's first Broadway musical not set in the twentieth century; Weill saw it "more as a light opera than a musical comedy."

After about four months of work, Ira reported that there was still much to do and planned to leave for New York for the finishing touches. "We have set ourselves quite an ambitious task," he wrote, "so there are many new problems especially as this is the first time I am doing a costume piece." By this time the opening date had been postponed. A month later, on December 12, the Gershwins checked into the Hotel Dorset for a long, and ultimately disappointing, stay.

By the end of January, 1945, with all but one lyric completed, he wrote of the work's progress: "What with finishing my job on *Much Ado About Love* (which is the title of the operetta so far), auditions, conferences, relatives and what not—we've been having a pretty busy time of it. We went into rehearsal a couple of days ago and, on the whole, I'd say things look pretty good with this opus . . . It's been a lot of hard work (we started last July) but also a lot of fun, as being in period, I could do a lot of things in form that I'd hesitate to experiment with if the show were placed in modern times.

"And Kurt Weill has done, I believe, the best job he's ever done—it's a more rounded score than *Lady in the Dark* or *One Touch of Venus*—

also it's going to have the best singing I've been connected with since the original *Porgy and Bess* company.

"Naturally lots of things can go wrong before the opening and lots more after, but at the moment we're all pretty optimistic and know we're connected with something worth while doing artistically—and (this we hope) financially."

A lot went wrong. After rehearsals, the newly titled *The Firebrand of Florence* opened in New Haven, then in Boston, where Ira suffered "a tough session with the elements" requiring dosages of "sulfa and whatnot." There were no cures for what ailed the show despite the ministrations in Boston of play doctor George S. Kaufman. It opened at the Alvin in New York on March 22, 1945; on April 9, taking a little time out from packing for his return to California, Ira wrote that *"Firebrand of Florence* received a couple of good notices but mostly they were bad so it looks as if nine months of hard work has been shot to hell. I doubt that we can survive the oncoming warm weather.

"All I can say is that Weill and I have had a most interesting and exciting time working on the score and feel we have done nothing to be ashamed of—in fact we're still rather proud of our contribution."

The failure of this abundant operetta, which closed after only forty-three performances, has been attributed to its contrived libretto, which even Kaufman could not fix, to the staging by John Murray Anderson (or so believed actress Lotte Lenya, Weill's wife). The consensus, however, was that *The Firebrand of Florence* was hopelessly miscast and the most hopeless was Lenya herself. As Billy Rose put it, "The script called for a sexy duchess, someone with the full-blown charms of Irene Bordoni or Vivienne Segal. Kurt handed this plum to the sensitive Lotte."

The leading roles, that of Cellini and his Angela, went to the relatively then unknown Earl Wrightson and Beverly Tyler; their voices were perfect, but they lacked authority and presence. British comedian Melville Cooper was cast opposite Lenya as Duke Alessandro the Wise, who also pursues Angela. The duchess, in turn, pursues Cellini. Originally Walter Slezak was to have portrayed the Duke, but he soon withdrew. This, Lenya insisted, threw off her performance. "My style," she told an interviewer, "would never ever jell with Melville Cooper's." The feud was on. To replace Lenya was out of the question because Weill was determined to have her appear in one of his American musicals.

One other criticism was that the lavish costumes and settings, by Jo Mielziner, were too ponderous for the tongue-in-cheek score, for all its operetta embellishments. And the often contemporary lyrics were jarringly modern in the sixteenth-century Florentine setting. *The Fire-*

brand of Florence was extinguished after only forty-three performances. [When Ira sent a friend a brochure of the operetta's lyrics, the title page read: *"Much Ado About Love" (working title:),* and under this he inscribed "Lyrics from *The Firebrand of Florence* (non-working title)."]

Only four of the songs were published, all ballads. "There'll Be Life, Love and Laughter," is a typical operetta song; so is "You're Far Too Near Me," but the latter has a more distinctive, more memorable melody. "Sing Me Not a Ballad" is one of the show's best songs, both music and lyrics. It was written at Ira's suggestion and based on a few bars of some rather astringent music, "The Entrance of the Duchess." Expanded, its harmonies sweetened, it is a mock love song of the amoral, amorous duchess.

That *The Firebrand of Florence* was not intended to be a conventional Never-Never Land operetta, should have been obvious. But the anachronistic blend of contemporary satire in a heavy operatic setting did not work and Gershwin was happy to get back to Beverly Hills for a while. But after working hard on a film musical (of which more later) during the summer of 1945 and into the next year, he returned to Broadway in 1946 for his last stage musical.

He was talked into doing it by George S. Kaufman, who in collaboration with Nunnally Johnson, concocted a tale about multiple marriage in the Smart Set, entitled *Park Avenue.* Arthur Schwartz was to supply the music. By May Ira and Schwartz had completed four or five songs of the fifteen or so the plot required. "Hope to have most of them completed," Ira wrote, "by the time we're to go to NY—sometime in July."

He was not looking forward to a summer in an overcrowded, hot New York, especially after he had heard from a friend who had spent ten days there in five different hotels. Some of the work, however, was done at Kaufman's home in Bucks County. The show premiered in New Haven; it did not impress the critics and it was obvious that Kaufman would have to be his own play doctor for a change. The hopeful company moved on to Philadelphia where it opened to unenthusiastic reviews at the Shubert on October 7. A week later, Ira and Schwartz were holed up in the latter's suite in the Warwick, rewriting.

"*Park Avenue* is better than it was when it opened in New Haven," Ira believed. "we're still working hard trying to get it in first-rate shape. The principal trouble was, and is, vocal. However, two or three numbers (comedy) do get over very well and there are some amusing episodes in the story so there's a chance we'll get by when we open in New York."

Park Avenue, as the title implies, had a stylish setting, but as the critics decried, it was extended thinly over a single joke: the marriage/ divorce/remarriage propensities of its natives. Ira agreed with Kaufman and Johnson that Broadway was ripe for a "smart" show after years of period musicals like *Oklahoma!, Up in Central Park, Bloomer Girl* and *Carousel.* Schwartz wasn't so sure and, when they reached Boston, realized they were in trouble. He had invited a friend to see it and was perplexed to find her in tears through most of what was supposed to have been a brittle, sophisticated comedy. Then he learned she had been recently divorced.

The show opened at the Shubert in New York on November 4, 1946; in December Ira reported that *Park Avenue* continued to do quite well (a heavy advance sale, obviously because of the names Gershwin, Schwartz, Johnson and Kaufman, even more than the cast members). But he felt once the momentum of the advance sale ran out business would fall off—"I think it's too much of a task to overcome the reviews."

Several critics attacked the book and its single joke; Schwartz's music was considered disappointing and few in the cast could sing. Of the female lead, Leonora Corbett, Wolcott Gibbs said in *The New Yorker* that she was "wonderful in *Blithe Spirit,* but ought to be restrained from using her voice in public." The one vocalist who was warmly greeted was ex-big-band singer Martha Stewart, who sang the show's best, but not very distinguished, ballad, "There's No Holding Me."

The Gershwin lyrics were generally admired, with special mention going to the before-its-time feminist message, "Don't Be a Woman If You Can" and a calypso number proclaiming the advantages of the United States of America, "Land of Opportunitee." But after nine weeks, and its seventy-two performances, as Ira put it, "there were no longer any audiences." Like his brother, if he liked something he had written he was not shy about admitting it. When a friend praised "Don't Be a Woman," Ira wrote, "I, too, liked it and it went to a really big hand in the show . . . There was another lyric in the show that was quite different, 'The Land of Opportunitee' (calypso), but it too is forgotten by now, unfortunately. Heigh ho—guess I can't afford to do any more flops—two in a row is about six too many."

He decided after *The Firebrand of Florence* and *Park Avenue* that it would take a very extraordinary project to get him out of Beverly Hills again. Meanwhile, he would stay close to home with his encyclopedias, dictionaries and recondite reference volumes and attend to Estate matters. He did write, shortly after the obvious fact that *Park Avenue* was closing, that "Am reading a couple of stories for possible musicalization (if there is such a word) but I hope I don't like them as I think I deserve a long rest." As far as Ira Gershwin was concerned, it was goodbye Broadway.

VI

Between the two Broadway flops, Ira worked on a unique film musical, *The Shocking Miss Pilgrim.* When he first mentioned it in a letter of July 5, 1945, after a news release announced that 20th Century-Fox was planning a Betty Grable film musical, he said it was to be "a musical-technicolor-Boston 1870-Betty Grable-women's rights etc." picture, "but no composer has been assigned. If I can get Harry Warren or Harold Arlen I'll probably go ahead with it. Perhaps I'd better go to work anyway—I just can't break 100 at golf and waste 2 or 3 days a week trying."

There was some social news: "I was a groom once but never been a best man. Vincente Minnelli asked me to be his best man when he married Judy Garland so it was I who handed over the ring and now nobody can say I've never been a best man." [Subsequently the Minnelli's named their first child for a Gershwin song, "Liza".]

Soon after, in the summer of 1945, Ira was at work on the Grable musical; neither Arlen nor Warren was free at the time so he would be working with an unexpected composer, George Gershwin.

It was generally known that there were several never used, unpublished musical fragments among the Gershwin papers; some were songs, some dances. For years Ira had chosen to fend off various offers to use some of his brother's melodies for a show or film score. In 1942, for example, it was announced that a show, *Birds of a Feather,* with a book by Samuel and Bella Spewack, was to be produced and would use a score made up of unpublished Gershwin songs. It never came off. "It was decided," Ira explained, "by the Estate and myself that when a show of film is done with the posthumous music it ought to have a more romantic background than the one *Birds* presents. This is, of course, no reflection on the contemplated offering by the Spewacks, who are most talented writers." (Apparently this project did not work out either; the Spewacks eventually wrote a hit libretto for Cole Porter's *Kiss Me, Kate* in 1948.)

When Ira mentioned the unpublished Gershwin music to producer William Perlberg, the idea of a new Gershwin film score intrigued him. Since it promised to be a big production, besides starring Betty Grable, the Gershwin Estate was also interested—and its Boston period setting seemed to add the right touch of romance.

Since Ira was not a musician, he suggested that Kay Swift be employed as his musical assistant. They spent ten weeks sifting through the manuscripts and their own memories and ended up with more than a hundred songs. Of these, Ira estimated that close to fifty of these were complete. From the remaining fragments—some mere lead sheets of the melody without harmonies—it was possible to stitch together a song, verse, chorus and release, from various sources as they had done when they worked out the 1939 World's Fair song, "Dawn of a New Day." Which, incidentally is how George worked from his Tune Books.

Not all of the songs could be considered for the score of *The Shocking Miss Pilgrim,* because of the film's period setting. As Ira explained, "I can't use some of the rhythmic and modern stuff and have to go in more for charm, etc."

After the ten weeks of transcription, another ten were devoted to preparing or arranging fragments into the songs for the film. Three had been completed years before, with different lyrics; from *Funny Face* (1927) came the cut-out "Blue Hullabaloo," transformed into "Demon Rum." The other dated from 1934, a song about a Depression couple, "Aren't You Kind of Glad We Did?" In its original form it was a duet between two penniless people who marry despite their financial situation. Ira kept the title and in the new version the couple is happy to have flouted stuffy Boston conventions and gone, unchaperoned, for a carriage ride.

"Back Bay Polka" had once been "Heigh-ho the Merrio," written for Fred Astaire but not used in *A Damsel in Distress.* Kay was especially partial to Gershwin Melody No. 51, which she called "a gold mine." It was then fashioned into the refrain of "For You, For Me, For Evermore." By mid-September (1945) Ira reported that they were about halfway through the score and pleased to say that "the producer seems to like very much what's been done so far." But a month later: "Have bogged down a bit on the job the past two or three weeks. Bronchitis or something akin got the better of me and slowed me down. Feel much more alive today and will get to work and hope to finish the job in a couple of weeks. Have a ballad to do and some extra verses, etc." Exactly a month later (November 18), he wrote, "Have just finished the score of *The Shocking Miss Pilgrim.* The studio is quite excited about it. But then studios are always excited. Rare is the new score (at any studio) of which it isn't said, 'Best we ever had,' 'Out of this world,' etc., etc. However, I will say it's a very good Gershwin score . . ."

Ira looked forward to the release of the movie by late spring of 1946, but during the shooting phase there were problems. George Seaton, who had written the screenplay and had begun directing "was told by his doctor that he was a sick young man and had to go to Nevada for a long rest. It was tough on him as he was trying to do (and doing) a fine job. Edmund Goulding has taken over. Goulding has had a lot of successes in his time but I don't know how he'll be on a musical. Seaton, before he left, told me he thought Goulding would work out fine. Could be and hope so."

Seaton finally received the credit for directing, even though a third (anonymous) director replaced Goulding, who also had become ill. There were other delays caused by a Technicolor strike, so that *The Shocking Miss Pilgrim* was not released until January 1947. Ira, however, saw a screening at 20th Century–Fox's New York offices while he was in town working on *Park Avenue* in the summer of 1946. He found it more than passable, as did a couple of friends he had taken with him.

But its reviews were not good and the film was not a success at the box office. "The film was sternly rejected by Grable fans," film historian Miles Kreuger wrote later, "because it violated their rather restricted (and somewhat uncomplimentary) prejudice about how their favorite star should appear and behave on the screen. Now that Betty Grable is gone, it may very well turn out that *The Shocking Miss Pilgrim* contains her most gracious performance."

Betty Grable's Boston-1870 long dresses and severe office coiffure were not in keeping with her image as the wartime pinup girl or as the luscious, leggy singing-and-dancing star of 20th Century-Fox's garish musicals of the war years, which exploited her physical attributes. "The gorgeous Grable gams," Kreuger declared, were as much "an American wartime classic" (as) "Spam and bubble gum cards . . ."

Baritone Dick Haymes starred opposite Grable; the two, pleasant, likable but hardly effervescent, endowed the film with a certain blandness. *The Shocking Miss Pilgrim* bubbled with charm rather than sparkle and deserved a better reception. The problem of multiple directors may have contributed to the stretches of insipidity; worse, the songs could have been presented with more sparkle.

The cool reception of *The Shocking Miss Pilgrim* not only by Betty Grable fans but also the critics and public made Ira more cautious than before about the disposition of his brother's unpublished music. Not one song became popular, though a couple were recorded. It would be years before Ira returned to the Gershwin Archive for musical material; he tended to discourage, even block, interest in the unpublished Gershwin. Nearly twenty years after *The Shocking Miss Pilgrim* he again released some of the songs for another production, the unfortunate, aptly titled *Kiss Me, Stupid*, a much more egregious miscalculation than *The Shocking Miss Pilgrim*.

After the *Pilgrim* experience, and the one immediately following *(Park Avenue)*, Ira was determined to rest—and to remain in Beverly Hills. He played golf and spent a lot of time in his box at Hollywood Park racetrack. His "method" was whimsical as he would select the horses on which he bet by wild word association that only he understood; at times he might bet on every race to see how it all came out. He also waited until the last moment before dashing to the betting window, placing his bets and hurrying back before the race began. When a friend asked about this, Ira replied, "It is my doctor's idea."

"What do you mean?"

"It's the only exercise I get."

He wrote about this period of inactivity. "The horses are treating me very well since the meet closed three weeks ago. And I'm going to give up poker for a while. It's much too costly for the debatable pleasure of being topped almost every hand, staying up all Saturday night, eating questionable food and being a physical wreck for the following two days. This is a resolution I hope to keep. For a few weeks anyway."

In this period after the *Park Avenue* debacle, he spent nearly a year and a half doing little else than answering letters, attending to Estate matters, reading, playing golf and "marking time until some movie or other turns up lacking verse and chorus."

During this time, in March 1948, Ira was incensed by the power of the Tenney Committee and its destructive effect on the film industry. (This was the California Fact-Finding Committee on Un-American Activities, under the chairmanship of ex-Communist and failed musician Jack B. Tenney.) Because of the havoc wrought by Tenney on California schoolteachers and film and theater workers, a Committee for the First Amendment had been formed by director-actor John Huston and director William Wyler, both longtime friends of the Gershwins. The Gershwin house was turned over to the committee for a meeting late in 1947. Over a hundred people attended, among them (as later named by actor Sterling Hayden before the committee) Humphrey Bogart and his wife Lauren Bacall.

Because of his participation, Ira was eventually summoned before the Tenney Committee. He wrote of how the "town is in a turmoil over the movie investigation and everyone is concerned over the harm it has done" (many film people lost their jobs, some were jailed). He referred to the Thomas Committee, the national investigative group under which Tenney's local organization operated with ineptitude and arrogance. No proved subversives were found; those who were jailed had been uncooperative and had taken the Fifth Amendment. Tenney eventually ruined himself politically by falsely smearing his rivals for office and running for Vice President with presidential hopeful Gerald L. K. Smith, a notorious anti-Semite and hatemonger. Thomas, in an example of ironic poetic justice, ended up in jail for taking kickbacks from his staff and falsifying his expenses.

"The Thomas Committee," Ira was certain, "discovered a publicity gold mine but I have yet to see anything subversive about any American movie I ever saw . . . it's pretty bad that these committees have the power to drag you to them just because someone's uncle said he thought you were wearing what seemed to him a red tie at a football game one day last fall. Or because you subscribe to the New York *Herald Tribune* which *calls* itself Republican but—"

When the Tenney Committee summoned Ira before it because of the meeting at his home—with a glamorous roster of Hollywood names—he dutifully appeared. But like other witnesses that made Tenney and company look like fools (among them actor Lionel Stander and comedian Zero Mostel), he proved an unsatisfactory witness. When it was demanded of him to tell the Committee if he was, or ever had been, a member of the Communist Party, the question seemed so ludicrous that he replied by giggling (unusual for Ira, for he generally mustered a quiet chortle when amused). That closed his experience with Un-American activities.

Not long after, he finally found a suitable film script and began working on it in the late spring of 1948. After a long period of silence, he brought a friend in New York up-to-date on his regular activities. "I thought you knew I'd been working on a film at Metro but evidently I hadn't written you about it.

"The film . . . is *The Barkleys of Broadway*. It was intended for Astaire and Judy Garland, but Judy's illness prevented her from starting and Ginger Rogers replaced her. (Oscar) Levant is also in the picture. I worked with Harry Warren about 4 months and we wrote a dozen or more songs. But they won't all be used as Rogers isn't the vocalist that Garland is. But I hear Rogers is doing very well and there seems to be tremendous interest in the Astaire-Rogers reunion. I thought I was all finished with my end a month ago [August] but the producer called me yesterday and I may have to do another number in the next few days." (This was "Swing Trot," a title suggested by Astaire early in the talking phases, but Ira didn't care for it and dismissed it. After the score was completed Astaire continued to demand it, so Ira gave in. Astaire purportedly wanted to promote his dance studios with the song.)

Judy Garland in fact had begun rehearsing for the film when it was still known as *You Made Me Love You*. In the second week of rehearsals she exhibited emotional problems and a dependence on medication to enable her to sleep. Producer Arthur Freed conferred with her physician, and taking his advice, dropped Garland and approached Ginger Rogers. With this change three songs, "The Courtship of Elmer and Ella" (a hillbilly song), "Natchez on the Mississip" and "Poetry in Motion," written especially for Garland, were eliminated. And an interesting one was added.

"By the way," Ira continued, "there is one interpolation: for nostalgic reasons and practical showmanship, Freed (the producer), has put in an old song that Astaire and Rogers did in *Shall We Dance*—'They Can't Take That Away from Me.' The studio is very pleased with the score that Warren and I turned out but since only one or two of the numbers have been shot so far I don't know how what we turned out will turn out. But when one has Astaire and Rogers one doesn't worry too much about the outcome."

It was in fact associate producer Roger Edens who had suggested the interpolation. "I would never have suggested it," Ira told writer Hugh Fordin years later. "But I guess it was all right with Harry."

Not quite. "I didn't take kindly to this," Warren told his biographer, Tony Thomas, "not that I didn't like the song, but there isn't a composer alive who likes having a song by someone else interpolated into his score." It was especially nettling because so much of Warren's work was eliminated: of the fourteen songs he had composed only six remained in the final print, and the final "Swing Trot" was used as under-the-titles music during the opening credits and not as a special number at all.

During the shooting of *The Barkleys of Broadway*, Judy Garland appeared in costume and made the round of the set, ready for work. "She was very friendly with the crew and posed in front of the camera," Fordin has written. "Ginger Rogers put up with the charade until she couldn't stand it any longer and ran into her dressing room. No one had the courage to tell Judy to leave. When [director Charles] Walters finally asked her to go she refused, so he took her by the arm and escorted her out while she hurled insults at Rogers."

The rest of the filming continued without incident, by which time Ira had returned to the quiet of Roxbury Drive.

The screenplay, by Betty Comden and Adolph Green, took up where the successful *Easter Parade* left off, casting Garland (then Rogers) as the wife and Astaire as the husband in a singing-dancing team; a musical equivalent to the theater's Lunt and Fontanne. They bicker; she, encouraged by a French playwright, aspires to Greater Things: she hopes to act in meaningful dramas, not bounce around in musicals. She proves her mettle (in one of the most embarrassing scenes ever filmed) by impersonating Sarah Bernhardt reciting "La Marseillaise" in French. This misfortune appears to have been the suggestion of associate producer Edens. Since Rogers's last film with Astaire, *The Story of Vernon and Irene Castle* (1939), she had appeared in several dramatic roles and in 1940 won an Academy Award for *Kitty Foyle*.

In *The Barkleys*, once she has proved to herself—at least in the film—that she is a great actress (worthy of stepping into Bernhardt's shoes), she returns to her estranged husband and the musical stage.

"It may not be the most robust musical made," Ira felt, "but it has enough novelty and charm to make it entertaining." Of the half-dozen Warren-Gershwin songs retained, he felt that only four counted: "My One and Only Highland Fling," "Shoes with Wings On," "You'd Be Hard to Replace" and a trio, "Weekend in the Country," presented by Rogers, Astaire and Levant. "Swing Trot" remained a nonfavorite.

"My One and Only Highland Fling" was a dialect song *(very Scotch,* according to the sheet music), which leads into a dance with Rogers and Astaire in kilts. To Ira's perturbation, when the song was published, an editor had laundered out all of the idioms. He was especially bothered by what he called a "Brooklynese" substitution of "spoke real soft" for his "spoke me soft." He shot off one of his rare angry letters, which resulted in a final publication of the song with its dialect intact.

The idea for a song about dancing came to Ira while leafing through a copy of Bullfinch's *Mythology;* a drawing of Mercury suggested "Shoes with Wings On" to him. The finished song provided Astaire with his most imaginative dance in the film, a variation of *The Sorcerer's Apprentice* theme. In this sequence, instead of bucket bearing brooms, shoes come to life to dance with Astaire. (A cobbler, he steps into the shoes left at his shop by a dancer and finds that he can dance; the other shoes—with an invisible Astaire wearing them—join in.)

Although the title had come at a glance, it took a lot of work—"maybe ten days' worth"—to fit a lyric to Warren's sprightly tune, every second bar of which ended on two emphatic beats (as does the title). Ira solved this challenge by a sequence of three double rhymes:

> The Neon City glows up;
> My pretty Pretty shows up.
> We'll dance until they close up—
> (Got my Guardian Angel working overtime.)

"You'd Be Hard to Replace" is a typical Warren ballad, simple, appealing and memorable. Sung by Astaire in a reconciliation scene, it is graced by a gentle conversational lyric that complements the melody.

Rogers and Astaire had three outstanding dance scenes together: a rehearsal to a Warren instrumental, "Bouncin' the Blues," the evocative, simply staged "They Can't Take That Away from Me" and the finale, "Manhattan Downbeat." After twelve years "They Can't Take That Away from Me" finally got the plug George had thought it merited but did not get in *Shall We Dance*. The dancers were formally dressed in white gown and white tie and tails as in a thirties RKO film.

The Barkleys of Broadway, while not "robust" (Astaire was fifty and Rogers thirty-eight when it was filmed), was well received (except for the "Bernhardt recitation scene"). The reunion of Astaire and Rogers was cause for critical rejoicing. "Age cannot wither the enchantment of Ginger and Fred," was the conclusion of Bosley Crowther in the *Times*. And it did well at the box office where, ultimately, all things counted. The final word on *The Barkleys of Broadway* to the historian of Arthur Freed films, Hugh Fordin: "The picture went on to gross in excess of $5,421,000." It was also the tenth and last Fred Astaire–Ginger Rogers musical film.

The final word had a good deal to do with Freed's next MGM project, a lavish all-Gershwin musical. Discussion began before the *Barkleys* was released in May 1949. Gene Kelly had once told Freed that he would like to do a musical about an American, an ex-soldier, who chose to remain in Paris after the war to paint. In April Ira wrote a friend: "Re *An American in Paris*—yes, we are negotiating with Metro not only for the title piece but also for about a dozen songs ('I Got Rhythm,' 'Liza,' etc.) to be used in the proposed film."

The "we" included not only himself, but the Gershwin Estate, in which he was one of several trustees, two different and not always congenial and cooperative publishers and countless lawyers for the Estate, the publishers and Metro-Goldwyn-Mayer. Preoccupied with these matters Ira had no time for original work.

Months after negotiations began, he answered a query of a friend in a letter dated November 16, 1949, "About the film at Metro, you ask whether it's been finished. I must sorrowfully tell you that it hasn't even been started. And won't be for some time to come. Matter of fact not even the contracts have been settled. The publishers have put up all sorts of arguments about the restrictions Metro wants. It's all very complicated and negotiations have been going on for nine (count 'em) nine months.

"I'm hoping matters can be adjusted soon and it's quite possible they will be by the end of the month . . . Other than headaches because of the Metro deal and other Estate matters I'm fine and have no complaints . . ." Another half year went by before all the legalities were straightened out and the casting completed before rehearsals began in early June 1950. "I haven't had much to do (outside of lots of conferences) other than change a line here and there in the old songs. So far no indication that any new song will be used. One number ('By Strauss') though, isn't generally known and may sound new. The film's director Vincente Minnelli recalled the song the Gershwins had completed at his request in 1936.

While *An American in Paris* was being shot (August 1, 1950–January 8, 1951), the Gershwins spent most of the time abroad. Leonore had succeeded in prying Ira out of the Gershwin Plantation for an extended tour. He wrote a pithy travelogue reporting that they had been in France and Italy during "Sept., Oct. and part of Nov.

"It never stopped raining in Paris and everything's rather run down but it still contains more beauty than any other town. In Rome I caught a cold in the Catacombs which held on and so I had to spend a good deal of time in bed there (in the hotel I mean—the Catacomb beds wouldn't have been cozy). Venice, even though I retained the cold, was lovely. Stayed there two weeks. Went to Lake Como for a day, then drove to Cannes where we took it easy for ten days. Toured Normandy for 4 or 5 days. Never did get to England or Israel, but all in all, spent an exciting 10 weeks. We flew NY to Paris (Air France) smooth trip, but returned by boat, *Liberté,* a grand ship with wonderful food and *très gai* atmosphere."

He admitted that he had "done little song work the past two years. Spent a lot of time on Estate matters and did give a lot of time to *American in Paris* consultations [for which he had received $56,250]." Which he considered time well spent for he was impresssed with the results.

"The picture is being scored now [January 1951; the orchestrations were by Conrad Salinger and Johnny Green, who was also musical director] and should be ready in about six weeks. Everyone connected with the piece has outdone himself. A lot of integrity and ingenuity has gone into the making and I'll be very surprised if all this isn't recognized by the critics and public. The ballet, which runs 18 minutes [unfortunately edited and with an overblown orchestration by assistant musical director Saul Chaplin] is not only beautiful but fascinating and there's a sequence in which Levant plays part of the concerto magnificently against a comedy idea which I think will be hilarious. Some of the songs like 'By Strauss,' 'Love Is Here to Stay,' 'Tra-La-La' and a couple of others aren't well known but will be easy to take. All in all, quite a picture—so far anyway."

The stunning musical climax—in fact, the finale—was a ballet based on the Gershwin tone poem with backgrounds in the stylings of Van Gogh, Utrillo, Dufy, Toulouse-Lautrec, et al. This was a daring manner in which to conclude the film and upset the money men in Metro's offices in New York when they first saw a rough cut of *An American in Paris* (they were also upset over the high costs). Ending the picture with only music and dancing? No dialogue? No final song medley? (There is a happy ending immediately after the ballet as Gene Kelly, in the final scene, dashes down a flight of simulated Montmartre stairs and co-star Leslie Caron runs up to him.)

After the screening, Dore Schary, then head of production at MGM, received a call from Nicholas Schenck, president of Loew's Consolidated Enterprises, which controlled the finances of MGM. He and a group of yes-men had sat silently through the screening and left, still silent, after it was over. Schenck admitted he rather liked *An American in Paris,* but why was the ballet so long? "Can't you cut it?" he asked. Whatever Schary's reply, the ballet was not cut. Producer Arthur Freed, with many a profitable musical to his credit, would not hear of it.

The *Concerto in F* sequence Ira found hilarious was actually Oscar Levant's idea, not scriptwriter Alan Jay Lerner's. Concerned about his part in the picture, playing himself, cracking wise and accompanying Gene Kelly in Gershwin songs, he hoped to expand the role and play some of the concert music. He was especially bothered when Freed told him early in the production that there would be no other extended piece except the tone poem. "There'll be no lulls in this film," Freed told him. Levant soon evidenced signs of more than customary depression.

Two weeks or so afterward, Levant approached director Minnelli (not Freed, who intimidated him) and outlined his "Ego Fantasy." Minnelli thought it was ingenious and brought it to Freed, who agreed. In the sequence, Levant performs the third movement of the concerto—not only as piano soloist, but also as conductor (his sometime double in this spot was lyricist-screenwriter Adolph Green) and appeared to play every instrument in the orchestra. At the movement's conclusion, he appears in a box applauding himself and exclaiming "Bravo!" The scene ends with Levant the pianist coming onstage to shake hands with Levant the conductor. It had worked.

There were no lulls in *An American in Paris.* In March the Gershwins went to "a sneak of *American in Paris* in Pasadena . . . There were some mechanical difficulties with the theatre's projection machines [the sound volume was too low] so we got only about a 70% performance. But it didn't seem to matter except to us, for the picture got over in a big way. A few minutes have to come out and in one spot a bit of recording has to be redone. This accomplished, I think the studio is going to have everything it hoped for when the project started. It's really one of the best ever."

Among the excisions were Kelly's "I've Got a Crush on You" and Levant's Gershwinesque renditions of "My Cousin in Milwaukee" and "Half of It, Dearie, Blues." After its release in November 1951, *An American in Paris* was unanimously, even ecstatically, acclaimed, a triumph for all concerned. Not only did it do well with critics and the box office, it was voted best film of the year by the Academy of Motion Picture Arts and Sciences; Vincente Minnelli won an Oscar nomination for direction (though the statue went to George Stevens for the drama *A Place in the Sun*). Alan Jay Lerner did get an Oscar for story and screenplay; the cinematography award was shared by cameramen Alfred Gilks and John Alton (who shot the ballet sequence). Johnny Green and Saul Chaplin were honored for the scoring. In the Art Direction/Set Direction category, the year's award went to Edwin B. Willis and Keogh Gleason; Irene Sharaff, Orry-Kelly and Walter Plunkett received the Academy Award for Costume Design (Color).

In addition, Arthur Freed was honored that year with the special Irving G. Thalberg Memorial Award "for his extraordinary accomplishment in the making of musical pictures"; Gene Kelly received an Honorary Award for his "brilliant achievements in the act of choreography on film" (his assistant on *An American in Paris* had been Carol Haney before her Broadway debut in *The Pajama Game*). At the evening's end, *An American in Paris* had netted seven Oscars, six for the several contributors and Best Picture. It was only the third musical to win in this category since the Academy Awards were first given (in 1929) and the first since *The Great Ziegfeld* in 1936.

That year, as a Christmas gift to Freed, Ira turned to painting briefly to do an oil, *The Smug Winner*, a portrait of a grinning Freed, cue in hand, standing by the pool table in the Gershwin basement. Ira explained that it was his way of getting even with Freed for "having beaten the hell out of me at pool all year."

In his note he wrote, "I hope you like it. I know two potential purchasers who will pay a handsome price for it—myself being one of them."

The new year, 1952, opened brightly for Ira; *An American in Paris* was doing well and, in that glow, he felt it was time to get back to work. And he was kindly disposed toward Metro, so that when he got a call from his agent, Irving (Swifty) Lazar, suggesting he go back to work, he surprised Lazar by saying yes.

The project had begun with earlier phone calls. The success of the film *Royal Wedding*, with music by Burton Lane and lyrics by Alan Jay

Lerner, encouraged Metro-Goldwyn-Mayer to follow it with another Lane-scored musical (Lerner was busy elsewhere). Lazar, who was also Lane's agent, called him about another film musical for Metro; Lane agreed. When asked about his choice for lyricist, his first was Ira Gershwin, but he felt a few other names should be borne in mind; he was aware of the myth of Gershwin sloth and deft avoidance of work (there was the two-year gap while *An American in Paris* was discussed, legalized and finally produced).

Burton Lane, like Lazar, was surprised with Ira's quick agreement; then Lane began to fret. He was about sixteen years Ira's junior and had been a friend of the Gershwins since the late twenties, when he was a teenage pianist hoping to become a song writer. By 1951 he was a successful veteran composer for films as well as for Broadway (his best-known stage score at the time was for *Finian's Rainbow).* Despite a good number of successful film songs—"Everything I Have Is Yours," "Moments Like This," "The Lady's in Love with You," etc., and the recent *Royal Wedding*—Lane was nervous about working with his long-time friend for the first time. Like other younger composers he was in awe of Ira Gershwin, "a giant."

When they met for the first time to begin discussions of the songs for *Give a Girl a Break,* Lane confessed to Ira that he was so apprehensive that he had prepared himself for their first professional meeting by taking a sedative. To which Ira replied, "So did I." (Lane was certain he said that to put him at ease.)

Give a Girl a Break, based on a backstage musical story by Vera Caspary (best known for her mysteries, among them *Laura),* had a screenplay by Albert Hackett and Frances Goodrich. It was to be directed by one of Arthur Freed's most trusted aides, Stanley Donen, who had directed *On the Town* and *Royal Wedding* with great flair; Jack Cummings served as producer (Freed was then busy with a new production of Kern's *Show Boat).* Cummings too had impressive credentials: *Born to Dance, Three Little Words,* etc. And there was a sparkling, youthful cast: Marge and Gower Champion, Debbie Reynolds, Bob Fosse. It may not have been a Minnelli-Freed film, but it held promise— as had *Park Avenue.*

Lane and Ira, by early August, 1951, were working very hard on *Give a Girl a Break;* simultaneously Ira had reworked many revisions on lyrics for *Of Thee I Sing* which was to be revived the following year.

Once work began in early August, 1951, and Lane found working with Ira easy, the collaboration went well and they were happy with it; Ira went so far as to pronounce it "very good." He went further: he presented Lane with a fraction of a lyric and a title, "Applause, Applause." The film revolved around show people working on a revue and audience appreciation nurtured them. Ira felt they might do a song about the performer's love of recognition. Lane took the song home—they generally worked afternoons at the Gershwins'—and played it for Ira the next day. Ira listened to the new Lane music and asked him to play it again. As he played, Lane felt an arm on his shoulder; he looked up, and there was Ira in a rare demonstrative moment, beaming down with appreciation and approval. And so it went until they completed eight songs, of which five were used. Two, the amusing "Ach, Du Lieber Oom-Pah-Pah," containing some of Ira's most nimble lyrics—and most atrocious puns—and "Dream World," one of Burton Lane's finest melodies, were among the rejects. A good melody, "It Happens Every Time," and one of Ira's prized lyrics, "In Our United State," remained.

Shot against the United Nations building at night (in one of the rare imaginative sequences in *Give a Girl a Break)*, the scene fit Ira's political allusions in an off-beat love song: "state of the union," "foreign entanglements," "House of cute Representatives," etc.

Finally, after many delays during the shooting, when Ira was concerned with various Estate matters, the revival of *Of Thee I Sing*, which required lyric revisions, and helping a small recording company, Walden Records, get started, the studio held a screening. As he and Lane watched they wondered what had happened to their songs, which were thrown away, poorly done, wasted. They were disappointed, but said nothing to producer Jack Cummings, who was there with his wife, Betty Kern; what could they say?

As they headed back to the Gershwins', the Gershwins and Lane in one car and the Cummingses following, the two collaborators were speechless. Lee Gershwin broke the silence first, "Do you have any stock in Metro, Ira?"

"Yes, I bought several hundred shares last year."

"Sell it!" (He did and lost about five hundred dollars in the transaction.)

Then Lane and Ira began to discuss the possibility of having their names removed from the film's credits; Lane suggested that it be retitled *Give a Song a Break.* But they calmed down and chalked it up to experience. Their apprehensions were confirmed even by MGM, which slipped *Give a Girl a Break* into a Brooklyn theater, bypassing Manhattan, when it was released early in 1953. This did not dupe the critics, who trounced it, with most unfavorable attention given to the screenplay, which obscured the charm of the songs. Years later, Ira felt though it got "few breaks from the press," it was not as bad as they said it was; Burton Lane feels a title change would have been in order.

Having divested himself of Metro, even as *Give a Girl a Break* was sneaked into Brooklyn, Ira began the new year, 1953, with a little gambling foray into Las Vegas. On the twentieth he mentioned a new film project: "I meant to write you just after the New Year when we returned from Las Vegas. But the flu (Spanish style) got me and a doctor and nurses and that new antibiotic—Ilotycin—kept me from being busy. I'm much better now and have even started to work with H. Arlen. We've had 4 or 5 afternoons together and I think we'll get along fine."

Although they had known one another since 1929, they had not collaborated on a major work since 1934's *Life Begins at 8:40* (although in 1943 they wrote a wartime song, "If That's Propaganda"). In the interim Arlen had written the classic screen score, lyrics by E. Y. Harburg, for *The Wizard of Oz,* as well as several popular movie songs, "Blues in the Night," "That Old Black Magic," "Happiness Is Just a Thing Called Joe," "My Shining Hour," "One for My Baby," etc. He had also composed the songs, with Harburg, for the successful Broadway musical *Bloomer Girl.* Since 1936, when the Gershwins moved to California, Arlen had been a frequent visitor, guest, golf companion and good friend.

They had been approached by Sid Luft, then married to Judy Garland, who planned to produce a musical version of *A Star Is Born.* Originally it had been done—with great success—in 1937, starring Janet Gaynor and Frederic March. Gaynor was cast as a young actress on the rise and March as Norman Maine, an established actor on the way down, partially because of alcoholism. Their marriage helps her career but not his; the film ends with his suicide and her triumph as the winner of an Academy Award, who, upon receiving it, announces herself as "Mrs. Norman Maine" instead of "Vicki Lester." The plot, based on a real-life Hollywood tragedy, was initially done in 1932 as *What Price Hollywood;* the Gaynor-March movie followed five years later. The Luft production, with Moss Hart revising the 1937 screenplay by Dorothy Parker, Alan Campbell and Robert Carson, was to be backed by Warner Brothers.

It was to be Judy Garland's first film in four years. She had been dismissed from *The Barkleys of Broadway,* had begun *Annie Get Your Gun,* then dropped out; she completed *Summer Stock,* released in 1950, after which Metro terminated her contract. She had not been idle during her absence from Hollywood. There were triumphant concerts at London's Palladium and New York's Palace. There were also many television appearances that kept her name public; so, unfortunately, did her emotional problems and drinking. Her problems during the making of *A Star Is Born* would prolong production, which ultimately cost well over ten million dollars.

The Gershwin-Arlen collaboration went smoothly, for the pair knew that their score would be tailored to the Garland voice and delivery style. They began working late in January and finished their part of the work by the end of April, 1953, except for some minor additions the following year. (There was an interruption in their work because of the illness and death of Arlen's father.)

Wise to Gershwin's aversion to ballads, Arlen began the collaboration with a lively rhythm number, which evolved into "Gotta Have Me Go with You." Next he brought in a characteristic Arlenesque "tapeworm," a long sixty-two-bar refrain with no verse that he had written while working with Johnny Mercer. Since the song had not been used, he thought he would try it on Ira. Not exactly a ballad, it was bluesy with a hypnotic, rhythmic undercurrent. Gershwin's title was "The Man That Got Away" (he was aware of its ungrammatical pronoun, and its angler's connotation).

Garland was at her peak when the song was filmed; she was slender (her weight had fluctuated a good deal during the protracted making of the film), her voice was fine and her every move was assured. The scene is a smoky nightclub after hours; the musicians have gathered to play just for themselves with the still "Esther Blodgett" joining in, beginning with Ira's despairing opening lines:

> The night is bitter,
> The stars have lost their glitter;
> The winds grow colder
> And suddenly you're older—
> And all because of the man that got away.

It was an exceptional song, beautifully done with direction by George Cukor, choreographic movement by Richard Barstow and fine camera work by Sam Leavitt. "Everything about *Star Is Born* looks and sounds great," Ira reported after he had finished his part of the job and the film went into production, recording and editing. Evidently Cukor felt the same when he finished his work on *A Star Is Born*. But the work was not done; Warner Brothers had provided Luft with the backing, literally banking on the comeback of Judy Garland. The time spent on making the film, the delays—the money!—gave the backers pause and the tampering began with the process of what is known as "Trims and Deletions."

Almost a year after Ira had thought he was done with *A Star Is Born* (and during which he and Arlen had completed the score for another film, *The Country Girl,* of which more later), he wrote on March 30, 1954, that the concerned at Warners wanted more: "what to do about a production number that's to wind up the first half (the showing is to have an intermission—the picture runs about three hours so far). Have no idea what's going to happen to this spot. Arlen and I wrote two songs for it ("Dancing Partner," "Green Light Ahead"), both good, by anyone's standards, but it seems the choreographer [Richard Barstow] couldn't get any production ideas.

"Could be they may even interpolate an outside number which would be a shame. However, there's still a chance that Arlen may be able to leave N.Y. for a week or so and we'll try to give them what they want." The composer, who had settled in New York, was then deep in work on his musical *House of Flowers.*

Ira and Arlen did try, and created an effective, unusual song with a bluesy verse and a rhythm refrain, "I'm Off the Downbeat," but They didn't want it.

In April, with some resignation, Gershwin wrote, "Know no more about possible interpolation in *Star.* With Arlen in hospital (he's on the mend but it'll be weeks before he'll be able to leave) and with an over four million investment in the film, naturally producer and management are nervous—especially about a spot where they aren't certain a number is needed or not. I certainly won't like it if an outside number is interpolated but I'm not going to lose any sleep over it; there's too little sleep left as is."

Management concluded that the film required a Judy Garland tour de force to end the first half of the picture. Two of her friends, lyricist Leonard Gershe and composer-arranger Roger Edens, obligingly concocted a "specialty" they called "Born in a Trunk." The attractive *ritornello* melody, with maudlin biographical lyrics—telling the Garland story—linked a half-dozen songs, ranging from "Swanee" to "The Peanut Vendor," in a whirlwind medley of Garlandiana. It also added fifteen minutes to an already long film. To Cukor's later (and too late) dismay, it necessitated the Trims and Deletions that disrupted the rhythm of the drama.

Philosophically, Ira accepted this misfortune and praised the "fine acting, singing, [and] beautiful production." He was not happy about "Born in a Trunk," but understood that Warners and Luft had "decided that any one new number wouldn't be socky enough . . . they feel it's some kind of insurance and with 4½ mill. invested so far I hope they will find these additional costs worthwhile . . . Anyway, La Garland does right by 'Man That Got Away,' 'It's a New World' and 'Lose That Long Face' so can't complain."

Except for rumor and gossip—word of Cukor's unhappiness with the final cut of the film—none of the problems that had dogged *A Star Is Born* concerned an appreciative public and critics when the film was released in October 1954 (by which time the intermission had been eliminated). However, exhibitors, despite the good attendance, complained of the film's length, not because it had dull spots, but because it restricted the number of showings per day. A few weeks later Warner Brothers had seventeen minutes deleted; among the deletions were two Arlen-Gershwin songs, "Here's What I'm Here For" and "Lose That Long Face." It was no longer the film that the critics had hailed.

When Cukor and Garland saw it, Cukor said they were so disappointed that "neither of us could ever bear to see that final version."

A Star Is Born received six Academy Award nominations that year, including one for James Mason, who had done a fine job as the doomed Norman Maine; the Award went to Marlon Brando *(On the Waterfront);* "The Man That Got Away" was nominated as best song; the Award went to "Three Coins in the Fountain" (Jule Styne and Sammy Cahn). Arlen's citation found a suitable spot on the wall of his bathroom.

Judy Garland was also nominated as Best Actress; the Award, ironically, went to Grace Kelly for *The Country Girl,* a dramatic film with songs by Harold Arlen and Ira Gershwin.

VII

Soon after they finished *A Star Is Born,* or thought they had, Arlen and Gershwin began working on a few songs for *The Country Girl.* Not a musical, it was a George Seaton adaptation of a 1950 Clifford Odets play about an alcoholic singer (Bing Crosby) and his faithful but embittered wife (Grace Kelly). Around the time he fretted over the "Born in a Trunk" interpolation, Ira wrote to tell a friend that the Crosby film was to be finished shooting within a week. "The four songs Arlen and I did for it are well liked but since the picture is a strong psychological study the result won't be a musical even though one number ('The Land Around Us') is given a stage setting." Gershwin did not think enough of a satirical beer commercial he and Arlen had written to mention it.

Neither writer considered *The Country Girl* songs among their most important, although Ira was pleased with the bluesy "Dissertation on the State of Bliss," whose original title was "Love and Learn" (and still is parenthetically). A little research on his part revealed that there were already three songs with that title, "and when the creators of one of them objected, it was a simple matter to make the phrase the subtitle and to decorate the number with the rather impressive 'Dissertation on the State of Bliss!' "

A fine, lucid ballad, "The Search Is Through," was recorded by Crosby, but nothing came of it. Two rather long musical episodes, portions of the stage musical in which Crosby was appearing—also entitled *The Country Girl*—were not particularly inspired: "The Pitchman (It's Mine, It's Yours)" and "The Land Around Us." The first had something to do with a peddler of dreams and the second came off like an uninspired excerpt from *Oklahoma!* In recalling this score, Arlen once said, "We didn't give it our best," though he conceded that the blues and "The Search Is Through" were not bad. He would go on to other things.

But for Ira, *A Star Is Born* and *The Country Girl,* both released in 1954, represent his final professional words as a songwriter. Ten years later he did release three more songs from the Gershwin Archive for a tasteless movie, *Kiss Me, Stupid;* he combined fragments of two: "Phoebe" and "All the Livelong Day," to create a song with the last title. He revised "Wake Up, Brother" from the film *Shall We Dance* and converted it into a less memorable "Sophia." "I'm a Poached Egg" was an expansion of a song he and his brother had begun in the twenties; it, too, is a hybrid, borrowing from yet another song for its bridge. However, *Kiss Me, Stupid* was a most insignificant film and its songs, purportedly written by amateurs, were hardly noticed, although "All the Livelong Day," *sans* "amateur" lyrics—"do-oo-oo" "you-oo-oo"—is fine early Gershwin. Ira Gershwin quit as a songwriter in 1954.

He still had plenty to do, among them to write a book, dabble in the record industry, tidy up the Gershwin Archive and generally look after things Gershwin.

Even as he worked on his last two film scores he became a kind of (unpaid) consultant to friends who had formed a small—and as it eventuated, nonprofit—record company in the beginning of the longplaying era. The company specialized in recording the lesser-known, though not necessarily lesser, songs of the great American songwriters, among them Cole Porter, Jerome Kern, Harold Arlen, Arthur Schwartz. Ira liked the idea and was free with suggestions and introductions; both Schwartz and Arlen appeared on their own albums. When Gershwin albums were programmed he suggested (but did not demand) songs and supplied, even revised, extra lyrics.

When an album highlighting his lyrics was released (and a good one it was) he sent a telegram:

JUST RECEIVED ALBUMS AND COVER TEXT AND PHOTO-
GRAPHS. MANY THANKS FOR A WONDERFUL BIRTHDAY
PRESENT. CONGRATULATIONS TO EVERYONE CONCERNED
IN THE MAKING OF THE ALBUM. YOU HAVE ALL DONE A
SUPERB JOB AND I AM PROUD OF EACH ONE OF YOU. MAT-
TER OF FACT YOU MAKE ME RATHER PROUD OF MYSELF
TOO.

Against the advice of his attorney/advisor and one of the company's founders, he invested a modest amount of money in the never sufficiently financed firm. When its most ambitious album, a two-record Harold Arlen collection was recorded, it was found that while the sessions had been paid for, the set could not be released because there was no money for pressing the records and printing the album. When Gershwin heard of this he sent money—no strings—to have the album released. Arlen, who had contributed his services as vocalist and pianist, was never told that Ira Gershwin had helped to finance his album.

Ira relied on his "partners" in matters concerning the record industry; because it took several weeks for a new recording he had read about in *Variety* or *The New Yorker* to appear in Beverly Hills, he asked a favor now and then.

One year he requested that they gather up several recordings: the *St. Matthew Passion* (conducted by Fritz Lehmann), his album *Lyrics by Ira Gershwin* and another, *Tryout,* in which he and Kurt Weill demonstrated several songs From their *Where Do We Go From Here?* (Weill also sang and played songs from *One Touch of Venus.)* These were to be packaged and addressed:

> Father Louis Merton, OCSO,
> Abbey of Our Lady of Gethsemani,
> Trappist, Kentucky.

(Father Louis was better known outside the walls of the monastery as Thomas Merton, author of the bestselling spiritual autobiography, *The Seven Storey Mountain;* a Trappist since 1941, he was head of the Abbey at this time, 1953.)

"The initials OCSO are a must after the name," Ira explained. "Trappists are supposed never to hear lay music but Merton is special and through him my friend Frater M. Matthew [and old Hollywood friend, Doc McGonigle] can sneak a few minutes now and then of other than Gregorian stuff. Please keep it all quiet. It wouldn't do my friend any

good if W.W. [Walter Winchell] or Earl Wilson [another gossip colum-
nist] wrote: 'What's 'The Saga of Jenny' doing at the Cistercian-Trap-
pist Abbey in Ky.?' "

In the spring, Frater Matthew was permitted to write a letter;
pleased, Ira informed New York: "My Trappist friend was delighted
with the records. (I gather the younger [monks were] permitted to hear
the Bach and only Father Louis and Frater Matthew the *Lyrics By* and
Tryout!)"

As the next Christmas approached, another request came from Ira in
November, this time for *The Goldberg Variations*, "any Purcell harpsichord and Byrd harpsichord compositions [English-born Father Louis
must have submitted his requests too], and the *Concerto in F.* Ira urged
expedition: ". . . the records have to get to Ky. in the next 10 or 12
days (deadline Nov. 30) otherwise they'll be held at the gate until Easter
or something."

The deadline was met and he was happy to report that "the two
monks were thrilled with what you picked. Received a letter not only
from Frater (Doc) Matthew but also from Father Louis (Thomas to
you) Merton. Fr. Matthew manages to be quite alive despite somber
surroundings. His letter winds up with: 'Again, dear Ira, a zillion
thanks. Prayers, love & xxxx from fr m matthew—Doc; & Good Yon-
tiff!' "

Less clandestine schemes occupied Ira during this same period. In
October 1953 he mentioned that he had "started, with the assistance of
Lawrence D. Stewart (English Dept. UCLA) to get all the scrap books
about George in some sort of order. Big job. What with the letters,
photographs, records, etc., looks like a year's work, on and off." Thus
began the final formation of the Gershwin Archive, begun in 1945 when
Kay Swift and Ira had started through the unpublished music. It was a
bigger job than Ira had estimated; Lawrence D. Stewart remained as
assistant archivist, friend and private secretary until 1968, when he decided to return to teaching.

The fruits of this work, which including the rediscovery of several
manuscripts, were eventually deposited in what became known as the
Gershwin Collection in the Library of Congress in Washington, D.C.
Before shipping anything—a song, a painting, letters—Ira carefully annotated each item. The original manuscript scores to all of the concert
works, the sketches, manuscripts and the orchestration manuscripts to
Porgy and Bess, as well as shows and individual songs are in the Collection. Over the years this has been added to by friends with the gift of
manuscripts and letters.

To his surprise Ira learned that his own works had been placed in a collection named for him; he continued to believe that George Gershwin was the immortal Gershwin.

As the collating continued, he set out on another big job. In December 1954 he announced, "Am thinking of having a go at a book of lyrics." As usual he did not leap, but began mulling it over, assisted by Stewart, who had become by then practically a member of the household.

In this playful spirit he finally began the job of writing a book. "He began work on August 3, 1955," Stewart has written (based on a carefully kept diary), by dictating a note for "The Babbitt and the Bromide." Thus the noncommerciality of the project was assured from the beginning, for no hit song that! . . . Three years later, by mid-1958 Ira was still revising the original note—though, admittedly, he had been writing and rewriting dozens of other notes as well. And four years to the day, August 3, 1959, the index and corrected proofs were dispatched to Knopf. "If it were a child, he could talk on his own by now," said Ira.

Lyrics on Several Occasions was published by Knopf late in 1959; it is a whimsical, erudite, informative collection of Ira's lyrics enhanced with brief essays on semantics, songwriting, and biographical and autobiographical tidbits. All is conveyed with the characteristic gentle Gershwin charm. Ira maintained that song lyrics were not to be regarded, or treated as poetry (light verse maybe); he also claimed a special distinction for his effort: ". . . if nothing else, this book is unique in that the author isn't looking forward to another."

Ira's final years were devoted to preparing his and his brother's papers, memorabilia and other items for deposit in the Library of Congress, the University of Texas and the Museum of the City of New York. Always a conscientious correspondent, Ira not only attended to business mail but also the worldwide influx of fan mail, the bulk of it pertaining to George Gershwin. He was especially attentive to correspondence from young admirers, often answering them in handwritten letters. When a friend published a young people's biography of George Gershwin, Ira immediately put in an order for a dozen "to send to 11-up-ers who write me (usually from small towns) asking for information about George for their term essays or whatever."

He enjoyed these communiqués from the outside world, though some could be rather bizarre. A spiritualistic medium wrote offering to serve as a link between him and George, with whom she said she was in communication. For a price she promised to revive their collaboration —only she promised to provide *lyrics.* Or a letter might be innocently bemusing: a young girl asking George's height (five feet nine and a half). There were autograph requests, his as well as his brother's; he had limited supplies of George's signature on canceled checks, which he doled out carefully to the deserving. He also used the checks for signatures when he framed one of George's pencil doodles to present as a gift to friends.

The most disturbing correspondence came from a man (who had begun writing as a fan long before) who, with a name change, claimed to be George Gershwin's illegitimate son. Eventually he went public and items and articles began appearing in newspapers, a sensationalist magazine, a planned appeal on the widely popular Ed Sullivan television show. This greatly troubled Ira, whose friend and attorney, Leonard Saxe, a distinguished teacher and former judge, did some quiet, meticulous research. He found the "imposter's" (Ira's term) birth certificate and military record. He claimed to have been born in California (he was born in Brooklyn) and said the courthouse in which his birth certificate had been stored burned, destroying the record of his birth. He also claimed that his "father" had taken him around and that he had met, among others, Ethel Merman and Oscar Levant (neither ever saw George with a child). He never made it to the Sullivan show.

On Saxe's advice, Ira and the Estate elected not to prosecute, for it would appear that an affluent, powerful Estate was persecuting a helpless, perhaps deluded, man. But it did not please Ira to get letters, usually from New York's music world, like one from Leopold Stokowski demanding that he do something for "George's son."

Ira would have done something, had the illegitimacy been legitimate, but he knew the full story; nor would he pay to have the "son" go away. He ignored the issue, which generally lay dormant until a Gershwin anniversary occurred, at which time the imposter would appear to sign autographs, etc. Ira also ignored a "George Gershwin" listed in the San Francisco telephone book; that too went away. Soon after, someone claiming to be "Ira Gershwin's son" began wheeling and dealing in New York. Among those he pestered was Celeste Holm with a play he had written especially for her; he accumulated large phone bills, appeared—and was welcomed—at fashionable parties and was rumored to have ordered a yacht. He eventually dropped out of sight.

Inured, after a while, Ira found other things to do. After the publication of *Lyrics on Several Occasions* he made only two excursions East (incidentally, he came to New York for the publication of his book, but, except for a radio interview or two, could not bring himself to push it). In June 1966 he was guest of honor at the Library of Congress and on the same day, June 4, he received an honorary degree, Doctor of Fine Arts, from the University of Maryland. Several friends gathered to witness the event. When Ira's name was announced, he stood up in his flowing gown, walked from his seat in the auditorium to the front to the speaker's platform, got his degree (smiling broadly), then made his way through the center aisle and back to his seat. A friend, *Newsweek*'s Allan Chellas, observed this and said, "I'll bet that's the longest walk Ira ever took."

Later, taking a breather on the steps of the university's art gallery, where a reception was held in his honor, Ira turned to a friend and said, "Did you ever think you'd see the day that Ira Gershwin would be a guest of honor at the Library of Congress?"

In May of 1968 he returned to New York for an impressive exhibition of Gershwiniana at the Museum of the City of New York: paintings, photographs, manuscripts, sheet music, memorabilia (George's piano, his portable practice keyboard, pens, a dressing gown, necktie, etc.). Family, relatives and friends gathered at the museum for a preview before the opening on the sixth. Even Ira enjoyed the beautifully planned exhibit, the work of curator Sam Pearce, assisted by Melvin Parks—both greatly assisted by Lawrence D. Stewart. As he passed from one imaginatively mounted display to another, Ira stopped before one filled with pages of yellow legal paper with various versions of one of his lyrics. He studied it for a moment then said, "That guy Gershwin uses up a lot of paper."

Two years later he suffered a mild stroke ("what my doctor is pleased to call a slight spasm"), which affected his right side, face, arm and leg. This made him more reclusive than ever, although he eventually made a good recovery. After 1970, he rarely left the house, let alone Beverly Hills. He began thinking about the publication of some of his brother's Archive music and arranged to have several pieces published, some as piano pieces (though most, like *Impromptu in Two Keys,* were songs or instrumentals initially). For a time he considered publishing a dozen of these pieces in a collection, *Gershwin in New York,* but abandoned that idea.

During the final year of his life Ira returned to the project, although a more ambitious one, for a larger folio of Gershwin songs and instrumentals. This would have included a reproduction of his brother's manuscript and the printed music opposite it. Among the items would have been the alleged "other prelude," the song without words "Sleepless Night."

He was thrilled in 1976 when the Houston Grand Opera presented a stunning production of *Porgy and Bess* with the original score and orchestration intact. The production was a triumph which brought the shock of recognition: *Porgy and Bess* was a real opera. Ira rejoiced in this, his brother's vindication. (He did not live for that ultimate endorsement, a production at the Metropolitan Opera House during the spring of 1985, nor the greater triumph at Glyndebourne, England, in the summer of 1986.)

Near the close of his life Ira was delighted, too, with a "new" Gershwin hit on Broadway, *My One and Only* (1983). It had begun as a revival of *Funny Face,* but eventually, after much agony on the road, ended up as a simpleminded little musical (the plot was no sillier than the original's, on which to some degree it was based). Songs ranging from the early "Boy Wanted" (1921) through one of the last, "Just Another Rhumba" were assembled into a Gershwin cornucopia. It was welcomed in New York, to the surprise of many who had heard of its road troubles and stayed a long time and then went on a successful road tour.

Almost simultaneously with the production of *My One and Only, Porgy and Bess* returned to play to sold-out performances at cavernous Radio City Music Hall (it would sell out completely, too, at the Metropolitan). Although he was pretty much bed-bound at this time, Ira took pride in the Gershwin renaissance.

To the end he was the keeper of the Gershwin keys, with the emphasis on George. Many, with a Freudian turn of mind, have wondered about this unique fraternal collaboration. Was Ira Gershwin envious, or jealous, of his brother's greater celebrity? Did he resent being the "other" Gershwin?

No.

While preferring to stay out of the public eye, Ira was no shrinking violet; nor did he suffer from false modesty. He was aware of who he was, that he was a special practitioner with a high place in a very special profession. He enjoyed recognition and resented being sold short by critics. He was nettled when he felt one of his songs was done wrong. Incensed by the casual singing of one of his lyrics by a popular singer, he commented, "He missed not only the boat but the ox-cart too on 'That Certain Feeling.' Leaving out the word on each sixteenth note in the refrain puts him in that inferno where singers go who insist on 'It's Wonderful' instead of ' 'S Wonderful.' On top of which he gets real chummy with all the ings. I'm no snob but at my age I see no reason to become intimate with 'feelin',' 'stealin',' and 'appealin','. Oh well, these things happen. And it's 4 A.M. Monday morning and I can't be bothered."

He preferred having his songs done as they had been conceived. He was even more careful about George's work and set in motion a plan to restore all of the Gershwin concert works to their original form and orchestrations.

There was at times conventional sibling friction, natural in two such different personalities; there was also true understanding, respect and devotion, but no rivalry; the spotlight belonged to the dashing George.

Although he rarely answered letters personally in the last year of his life, he loved to hear from friends and the usual youthful correspondents. Once upon receiving a scrawled letter (written on three-ring notebook paper by a high school student; it was, though addressed to him, virtually a posthumous fan letter to George Gershwin), Ira responded with: "I understand perfectly. I feel that way about him too. And there are many like us. I still get letters about him from places as far as New Zealand. Yes, in New Zealand there's a man [the late Carl Williams] who has collected over 400 recordings of my brother's music and has designed a special cover for each with a drawing of my brother printed on each. And there's a girl in England who recently sent me a record my brother made in London in 1926. What was wonderful was that she found it while rummaging about in a second hand furniture store during an air raid alarm. So you see you're not alone . . .

"Why I am seemingly grown so expansive when all you request is a short receipt for your letter is because a letter like yours, expressing such admiration of my brother and his work, warms me."

The final years of his life were spent in enjoying that warmth and in overseeing the preservation of his brother's musical legacy.

Ira Gershwin died quietly, sitting up in his bed, on August 17, 1983; he had just enjoyed some of his favorite chocolates.

Compositions by George and Ira Gershwin

I

GEORGE GERSHWIN

Following is a list of all known Gershwin songs and concert works. Some Gershwin songs, though published, are out of print and some are coming back into print. Only five complete scores were (and are) published: *Primrose, Strike Up the Band* (second version), *Girl Crazy* and *Porgy and Bess.* More complete scores, from *Lady, Be Good!* on through *Let 'Em Eat Cake,* deserve publication.

The first section of this listing is devoted to juvenilia, early songs, study pieces (some composed after Gershwin had begun publishing) that he had not intended to publish. The name in parenthesis following the song title is that of the lyricist. Reminder: Ira Gershwin wrote under the name of "Arthur Francis" c. 1920–24.

JUVENILIA

c. 1913

Since I Found You (Leonard Praskins)

Ragging the Traumerei (Leonard Praskins)

1914

Tango, for solo piano

c. 1919

Lullaby for string quartet (published 1968)

c. 1920, probably later

Piece for Four Strings
NOTE The Gershwin Collection in the Library of Congress lists a *Figured Chorale* among its acquisitions. Eight measures long, it is written for two bassoons, two horns, viola, cello and bass and dates from c. 1921; it is not a Gershwin piece but an exercise in orchestration of Bach's *Freu' dich sehr, O meine Seele.*

1916

When You Want 'Em, You Can't Get 'Em, When You've Got 'Em, You Don't Want 'Em (Murray Roth).

Interpolated into *The Passing Show of 1916:*
Making of a Girl (Harold Atteridge; music attributed to Sigmund Romberg and Gershwin).

My Runaway Girl (Murray Roth; not used in *The Passing Show).*

Good Little Tune (Irving Caesar)

1917

Rialto Ripples for piano (written with Will Donaldson)

You Are Not the Girl (Ira Gershwin)

We're Six Little Nieces of Uncle Sam (Lou Paley)

1918

A Corner of Heaven with You (Lou Paley)

Interpolated into *Hitchy-Koo of 1918:*
You-oo, Just You (Irving Caesar)

When the Armies Disband (Irving Caesar)

Interpolated into *Ladies First:*
The Real American Folk Song ("Arthur Francis")
Some Wonderful Sort of Someone (Schuyler Greene)

HALF PAST EIGHT

Revue, lyrics by Fred Caryll. Produced by Edward B. Perkins, Empire Theater, Syracuse, New York, December 9, 1918. Cast: Joe Cook, Sybil Vane, Roy Stever, Mildred Lovejoy, Ruby Loraine, Clef Club Jazz Band.
There's Magic in the Air (Ira Gershwin)
Hong Kong
Cupid
Half Past Eight
Little Sunbeam

1919

Novelette in Fourth for piano

Interpolated into *Good Morning Judge:*
I Was So Young, You Were So Beautiful (Irving Caesar and Al Bryan)
There's More to the Kiss Than X-X-X (Irving Caesar)

O, Land of Mine, America (Michael E. Rourke)
Interpolated into *The Lady in Red:*
Something About Love (Lou Paley)

LA-LA-LUCILLE!

Lyrics by Arthur Jackson and B. G. De-Sylva; book by Fred Jackson. Produced by Alex A. Aarons and George Seitz, Henry Miller Theater, May 26, 1919. 104 performances. Cast: Janet Velie, John E. Hazzard, J. Clarence Harvey, Helen Clark. Conducted by Charles Previn.
When You Live in a Furnished Flat
The Best of Everything
From Now On
It's Hard to Tell
Tee-Oodle-Um-Bum-Bo
Nobody but You
It's Great to Be in Love
Somehow It Seldom Comes True
The Ten Commandments of Love (same song as There's Magic in the Air)
Oo, How I Love to Be Loved by You (Lou Paley)
NOT USED: The Love of a Wife; Our Lit-

tle Kitchenette; Money, Money, Money!, Kisses

Interpolated into *The Capitol Revue:*
  Swanee (Irving Caesar)
  Come to the Moon (Ned Wayburn and Lou Paley)

MORRIS GEST'S MIDNIGHT WHIRL

Lyrics by B. G. DeSylva and John Henry Mears; book by DeSylva and Mears. Produced by Morris Gest, Century Grove, December 27, 1919. 110 performances. Cast: Bessie McCoy Davis, Bernard Granville, Helen Shipman, Rath Brothers. Conducted by Frank Tours.
  The League of Nations
  Doughnuts
  Poppyland
  I'll Show You a Wonderful World
  Limehouse Nights
  Let Cutie Cut Your Cuticle
  Baby Dolls

1920

Yan-Kee (Irving Caesar)

Interpolated into *Dere Mable:*
  We're Pals (Irving Caesar)
  Back Home (Arthur Francis)
  I Don't Know Why (Irving Caesar)

  I Want to Be Wanted by You (Ira Gershwin)

GEORGE WHITE'S SCANDALS OF 1920

Lyrics by Arthur Jackson; book by Andy Rice and George White. Produced by White, Globe Theatre, June 7, 1920. 134 performances. Cast: Ann Pennington, Lou Holtz, "Doc" Rockwell, Ethel Delmar, Lester Allen, George White, the Yerkes Happy Six. Conducted by Alfred Newman.
  My Lady
  Everybody Swat the Profiteer

On My Mind the Whole Night Long
Tum On and Tiss Me
Scandal Walk
The Songs of Long Ago
Idle Dreams
NOT USED Queen Isabella; My Old Love Is My New Love

Interpolated into *The Sweetheart Shop:*
  Waiting for the Sun to Come Out (Arthur Francis)

Interpolated into *Broadway Brevities of 1920:*
  Spanish Love (Irving Caesar)
  Lu Lu (Arthur Jackson)
  Snow Flakes (Arthur Jackson)

Interpolated into *Piccadilly to Broadway:*
  On the Brim of Her Old-Fashioned Bonnet (E. Ray Goetz)
  The Baby Blues (E. Ray Goetz)

1921

Interpolated into *Blue Eyes:* Wanting You (Irving Caesar)

A DANGEROUS MAID

Lyrics by Arthur Francis; book by Charles W. Bell. Produced by Edgar MacGregor, Atlantic City and Pittsburgh, where it closed in April 1921. Cast: Vivienne Segal, Amelia Bingham, Johnnie Arthur, Vinton Freedley, Juanita Fletcher, Creighton Hale.
  Just to Know You Are Mine
  Boy Wanted
  The Simple Life
  Dancing Shoes
  True Love
  Some Rain Must Fall
  The Sirens
NOT USED Anything for You; Pidgee Woo; Every Girl Has a Way

Interpolated into *Selwyn's Snapshots of 1921:* Futuristic Melody (E. Ray Goetz)

GEORGE WHITE'S SCANDALS OF 1921

Lyrics by Arthur Jackson; book by Arthur "Bugs" Baer and George White. Produced by White, Liberty Theatre, July 11, 1921. 97 performances. Cast: Ann Pennington, Charles King, Bert Gordon, Theresa Gardella, George White. Conducted by Alfred Newman.

Mother Eve
I Love You
South Sea Isles
Drifting Along with the Tide
She's Just a Baby
Where East Meets West at Panama

Interpolated into *The Perfect Fool:*
My Log Cabin Home (Irving Caesar and B. G. DeSylva)
No One Else But That Girl of Mine (Irving Caesar)

Tomale (I'm Hot for You) (B. G. De-Sylva)

Dixie Rose (Irving Caesar and B. G. DeSylva; revised and published as Swanee Rose).

In the Heart of the Geisha (Fred Fisher)

Phoebe (Ira Gershwin and Lou Paley; revised, with a new lyric, as "All the Livelong Day" for film, *Kiss Me, Stupid,* 1964).

1922

Interpolated into *The French Doll:*
Do It Again! (B. G. DeSylva)

Interpolated into *For Goodness Sake:*
All to Myself (Arthur Francis)
Someone (Arthur Francis)
Tra-La-La (Arthur Francis)

Mischa, Yascha, Toscha, Sascha (Arthur Francis, pub. 1932)

GEORGE WHITE'S SCANDALS OF 1922

Lyrics by B. G. DeSylva and E. Ray Goetz; book by George White and W. C. Fields and Andy Rice. Produced by White, Globe Theatre, August 28, 1922. 88 performances. Cast: W. C. Fields, Winnie Lightner, Jack McGowan, Lester Allen, George White, Paul Whiteman's Orchestra. Conducted by Max Steiner.

Just a Tiny Cup of Tea
Oh, What She Hangs Out (DeSylva only)
Cinderelatives (DeSylva)
I Found a Four Leaf Clover (DeSylva)
I Can't Tell Where They're from When They Dance
I'll Build a Stairway to Paradise (DeSylva and Arthur Francis)
Across the Sea
Argentina (DeSylva)
Where Is the Man of My Dreams?
Blue Monday, Opera Ala Afro-American (Orch: Will Vodery):
Blue Monday Blues
Has Anyone Seen My Joe?
I'm Going to See My Mother

OUR NELL

Music also by William Daly; lyrics by Brian Hooker. Book by Hooker and A. E. Thomas. Produced by Ed. Davidow and Rufus LeMaire, Nora Bayes Theatre, December 4, 1922. Cast: Mr. and Mrs. Jimmy Barry, Emma Haig, Olin Howland, John Merkyl. Conducted by Charles Sieger.

Gol-Durn!
Innocent Ingenue Baby
The Cooney County Fair (Gershwin only)
Names I Love to Hear
By and By (Gershwin)
Madrigal
We Go to Church on Sunday (Gershwin)

Walking Home with Angeline
(Gershwin)
Oh, You Lady!
Little Villages
NOT USED: The Custody of the Child

The Yankee Doodle Blues (Irving
Caesar and B. G. DeSylva)

The Flapper (B. G. DeSylva)

1923

Rubato for piano

Interpolated into *The Dancing Girl:*
That American Boy of Mine (Irving
Caesar)

THE RAINBOW

Lyrics by Clifford Grey; book by Albert
de Courville, Edgar Wallace and Noel
Scott. Produced by de Courville, Empire
Theatre, London, April 3, 1923. 113 per-
formances. Cast: Grace Hayes, Stephanie
Stevens, Earl Rickard, Ernest Thesiger,
Jack Edge, Lola Raine, Fred A. Leslie.
Conductor, Kennedy Russell.
Sweetheart (I'm So Glad That I Met
You)
Good-Night, My Dear
Any Little Tune
Moonlight in Versailles
In the Rain
Innocent Lonesome Blue Baby (same
song as Innocent Ingenue Baby,
with revised lyric by Grey)
Beneath the Eastern Moon
Oh! Nina
Strut Lady with Me
Sunday in London Town
All Over Town (same melody as
Come to the Moon)
NOT USED: Give Me My Mammy

The Sunshine Trail (Arthur Francis;
theme song for film of same title).

GEORGE WHITE'S
SCANDALS OF 1923

Lyrics by B. G. DeSylva, E. Ray Goetz
and Ballard MacDonald; book by

George White and William K. Wells.
Produced by White, Globe Theatre, June
18, 1923. 168 performances. Cast: Winnie
Lightner, Tom Patricola, Lester Allen,
Richard Bold, Beulah Berson, Johnny
Dooley, Olive Vaughan, Tip Top Four.
Conducted by Charles Drury.
Little Scandal Dolls
You and I
Katinka
Lo-La-Lo (DeSylva only)
There Is Nothing Too Good for You
(DeSylva and Goetz)
Throw Her in High! (DeSylva and
Goetz)
Let's Be Lonesome Together (De
Sylva and Goetz)
The Life of a Rose (DeSylva)
Look in the Looking Glass
Where Is She? (DeSylva)
Laugh Your Cares Away
(On the Beach at) How've-You-Been
(DeSylva)
Garden of Love

Interpolation into *Little Miss Bluebeard:*
I Won't Say I Will and I Won't Say I
Won't (B. G. DeSylva and Arthur
Francis)

Interpolation into *Nifties of 1923:*
At Half Past Seven (B. G. DeSylva)
Nashville Nightingale (Irving Caesar)

1924

SWEET LITTLE DEVIL

Lyrics by B. G. DeSylva; book by Frank
Mandel and Laurence Schwab. Produced
by Schwab, Astor Theatre, January 21,
1924. 120 performances. Cast: Constance
Binney, Marjorie Gateson, Irving Beebe,
Franklyn Ardell, Ruth Warren, William
Wayne. Conducted by Ivan Rudisill.
Strike, Strike, Strike
Virginia
Someone Believes in You
The Jijibo
Quite a Party
Under a One-Man Top

The Matrimonial Handicap
Just Supposing
Hey! Hey! Let 'Er Go!
Hooray for the U.S.A.
Mah-Jongg
Pepita
NOT USED My Little Duckie; Sweet Little Devil; Be the Life of the Crowd

RHAPSODY IN BLUE, for Jazz Band and Orchestra. Orchestrated by Ferde Grofé. Aeolian Hall, New York City, February 12, 1924. Gershwin, piano, Paul Whiteman and his Palais Royal Orchestra.

GEORGE WHITE'S SCANDALS OF 1924

Lyrics by B. G. DeSylva; book by William K. Wells and George White. Produced by White, Apollo Theatre, June 30, 1924. 192 performances. Cast: Winnie Lightner, Tom Patricola, the Elm City Four, the Williams Sisters, Will Mahoney, Richard Bold, Helene Hudson, Helene and Dolores Costello. Conducted by William Daly.

   Just Missed the Opening Chorus
   I Need a Garden
   Night Time in Araby
   I'm Going Back
   Year After Year
   Somebody Loves Me (DeSylva and
     Ballard MacDonald)
   Tune In (to Station J.O.Y.)
   Mah-Jongg
   Lovers of Art
   Rose of Madrid
   I Love You, My Darling
   Kongo Kate

PRIMROSE

Lyrics by Desmond Carter and Ira Gershwin; book by George Grossmith and Guy Bolton. Produced by Grossmith and J. A. E. Malone, Winter Garden Theatre, London, September 11, 1924. 255 performances. Cast: Margery Hicklin, Percy Heming, Leslie Henson, Claude Hulbert, Heather Thatcher, Muriel Barnby, Guy Fane, Vera Lennox. Conducted by John Ansell.

   Leaving Town While We May (Carter
     only)
   Till I Meet Someone Like You
     (Carter)
   Isn't It Wonderful?
   This Is the Life for a Man (Carter)
   When Toby Is Out of Town (Carter)
   Some Far-away Someone (Gershwin
     and B. G. DeSylva; same melody
     as Half Past Seven)
   The Mophams (Carter)
   Can We Do Anything?
   Roses of France (Carter)
   Four Little Sirens (Gershwin)
   Berkley Square and Kew (Carter)
   Boy Wanted
   Wait a Bit, Susie
   Isn't Terrible What They Did to
     Mary, Queen of Scots? (Carter)
   Naughty Baby
   It Is the Fourteenth of July (Carter)
   Ballet
   I Make Hay While the Moon Shines
     (Carter)
   That New-Fangled Mother of Mine
     (Carter)
   Beau Brummel (Carter)
   NOT USED The Live Wire; Pep! Zip! and Punch! (both Carter)

LADY, BE GOOD!

Lyrics by Ira Gershwin; book by Guy Bolton and Fred Thompson. Produced by Alex A. Aarons and Vinton Freedley, Liberty Theatre, December 1, 1924. 330 performances. Cast: Fred and Adele Astaire, Walter Catlett, Kathlene Martyn, Cliff Edwards, Gerald Oliver Smith, Patricia Clark, Alan Edwards, Phil Ohman and Victor Arden, duo-pianists. Conducted by Paul Lannin.

   Hang on to Me
   A Wonderful Party
   The End of a String
   We're Here Because
   Fascinating Rhythm

So Am I
Oh, Lady be Good!
The Robinson Hotel
The Half of It, Dearie, Blues
Juanita
Little Jazz Bird
Swiss Miss (Gershwin and Arthur
  Jackson)
NOT USED: Seeing Dickie Home; The
Man I Love; Will You Remember Me?;
Singin' Pete; Evening Star; The Bad, Bad
Men; Weather Man; Rainy Afternoon
Girls; Laddie Daddie; Leave It to Love.
ADDED TO LONDON PRODUCTION, 1926:
Something About Love (Lou Paley); I'd
Rather Charleston (Desmond Carter);
Buy a Little Button (Carter)

1925

SHORT STORY, for violin and piano
(arr: Samuel Dushkin). Samuel Dushkin,
The University Club, New York City,
February 8, 1925.

TELL ME MORE

Lyrics by B. G. DeSylva and Ira Gersh-
win; book by Fred Thompson and Wil-
liam K. Wells. Produced by Alex A. Aar-
ons, Gaiety Theater, April 13, 1925. 100
performances. Cast: Alexander Gray,
Lou Holtz, Emma Haig, Phyllis Cleve-
land, Andrew Tombes. Conducted by
Max Steiner.
Tell Me More
Mr. and Mrs. Sipkin
When the Debbies Go By
Three Times a Day
Why Do I Love You?
How Can I Win You Now?
Kickin' the Clouds Away
Love Is in the Air
My Fair Lady
In Sardinia
Baby!
The Poetry of Motion
Ukulele Lorelei
NOT USED Shop Girls and Mannikins;
Once; I'm Somethin' on Avenue A; The
He-Man.

ADDED TO LONDON PRODUCTION, 1925:
Murderous Monty (and Light-Fingered
Jane); Love, I Never Knew (both: Des-
mond Carter)

CONCERTO IN F, for piano and orchestra. Carnegie Hall, December 3,
1925. Gershwin, piano; New York Symphony Society, Walter Damrosch conducting.

TIP-TOES

Lyrics by Ira Gershwin; book by Guy
Bolton and Fred Thompson. Produced
by Aarons and Freedley, Liberty The-
ater, December 28, 1925. 194 perfor-
mances. Cast: Queenie Smith, Allen
Kearns, Harry Watson, Jr., Andrew
Tombes, Jeanette MacDonald, Gertrude
McDonald, Robert Halliday, Lovey Lee,
Amy Revere. Conducted by William
Daly.
Waiting for the Train
Nice Baby!
Looking for a Boy
Lady Luck
When Do We Dance?
These Charming People
That Certain Feeling
Sweet and Low-Down
Our Little Captain
Harbor of Dreams
Nightie-Night
Tip-Toes
NOT USED: Harlem River Chanty;
Gather Ye Rosebuds; We; Dancing Hour;
Life's Too Short to Be Blue; It's a Great
Little World.

SONG OF THE FLAME

With Herbert Stothart; lyrics and book
by Oscar Hammerstein II and Otto
Harbach. Produced by Arthur Hammerstein, Forty-fourth Street Theater, December 30, 1925. 219 performances. Cast:
Tessa Kosta, Greek Evans, Dorothy
Mackaye, Hugh Cameron, Guy Robertson, Russian Art Choir. Conducted by
Stothart.

Midnight Bells (Gershwin only)
Far Away
Song of the Flame
Woman's Work Is Never Done
The Signal (Gershwin)
Cossack Love Song (Don't Forget
  Me)
Tar-Tar
You Are You
Vodka

1926

Interpolated into *Americana:*
  That Lost Barbershop Chord (Ira
  Gershwin)

OH, KAY!

Lyrics by Ira Gershwin; book by P. G.
Wodehouse and Guy Bolton. Produced
by Aarons and Freedley, Imperial The-
ater, November 8, 1926. 256 perfor-
mances. Cast: Gertrude Lawrence, Oscar
Shaw, Victor Moore, Betty Compton,
Harland Dixon, Constance Carpenter,
Gerald Oliver Smith, the Fairbanks
Twins, Ohman and Arden, duo-pianists.
Conducted by William Daly.
  The Woman's Touch
  Don't Ask!
  Dear Little Girl
  Maybe
  Clay Yo' Hands
  Bride and Groom
  Do-Do-Do
  Someone to Watch Over Me
  Fidgety Feet
  Heaven on Earth (Gershwin and
    Howard Dietz)
  Oh, Kay! (Gershwin and Dietz)
  NOT USED: Show Me the Town;
    What's the Use?; When Our Ship
    Comes Sailing In; The Moon Is on
    the Sea (The Sun Is on the Sea);
    Stepping with Baby; Guess Who
    (same melody as Don't Ask!); Ain't
    It Romantic; Bring on the Ding
    Dong Dell.

PRELUDES FOR PIANO

Hotel Roosevelt, December 4, 1926,
Gershwin, piano.

1927

STRIKE UP THE BAND

Lyrics by Ira Gershwin; book by George
S. Kaufman. Produced by Edgar Selwyn,
Shubert Theater, Philadelphia, Septem-
ber 2, 1927; closed there. Cast: Vivian
Hart, Roger Pryor, Edna May Oliver,
Morton Downey, Lew Hearn, Jimmy
Savo. Conducted by William Daly.
  Fletcher's American Cheese Choral
    Society
  Seventeen and Twenty-One
  Meadow Serenade
  The Unofficial Spokesman
  Patriotic Rally
  The Man I Love (The Girl I Love)
  Yankee Doodle Rhythm
  Strike Up the Band!
  O, This Is Such a Lovely War (The
    Knitting Song)
  Hoping That Someday You'll Care
  Military Dancing Dancing Drill
  How About a Man Like Me
  Homeward Bound
  The War That Ended War

FUNNY FACE

Lyrics by Ira Gershwin; book by Fred
Thompson and Paul Gerard Smith. Pro-
duced by Aarons and Freedley, Alvin
Theater, November 22, 1927. 244 perfor-
mances. Cast: Fred and Adele Astaire,
Victor Moore, William Kent, Allen
Kearns, Gertrude McDonald, Betty
Compton, Ohman and Arden, duo-pi-
anos. Conducted by Alfred Newman.
  We're All A-Worry, All Agog
  When You're Single
  Those Eyes
  Birthday Party
  High Hat
  Let's Kiss and Make Up
  Funny Face

'S Wonderful
The World Is Mine
Come Along, Let's Gamble
If You Will Take Our Tip
He Loves and She Loves
The Finest of the Finest
My One and Only
Tell the Doc
Sing a Little Song
In the Swim
The Babbitt and the Bromide
Dance Alone with You

NOT USED: How Long Has This Been Going On?; Acrobats; Once; Aviator; When You Smile; Dancing Hour; Blue Hullabaloo.

ADDED TO LONDON PRODUCTION, 1928: Look at the Damn Thing Now.

1928

ROSALIE

Lyrics by Ira Gershwin and P. G. Wodehouse; book by William Anthony McGuire and Guy Bolton. Produced by Florenz Ziegfeld, New Amsterdam Theater, January 10, 1928. 335 performances. Cast: Marilyn Miller, Jack Donahue, Gladys Glad, Frank Morgan, Bobbe Arnst, Oliver McLennan, Margaret Dale. Conducted by Oscar Bradley.

NOTE Sigmund Romberg also composed music for songs and ballets; only the Gershwin music is listed.

Show Me the Town (Gershwin only)
Say So!
Let Me be a Friend to You (Gershwin)
Oh Gee! Oh Joy!
New York Serenade (Gershwin)
Setting-up Exercises (instrumental)
How Long Has This Been Going On? (Gershwin)
Ev'rybody Knows I Love Somebody (Gershwin; same melody as Dance Alone with You)

NOT USED: Rosalie (Gershwin); Beautiful Gypsy (Gershwin; same melody as Wait a Bit, Susie); Yankee Doodle Rhythm

(Gershwin); When Cadets Parade (Gershwin); Follow the Drum (Gershwin); I Forget What I Started to Say (Gershwin); The Man I Love (Gershwin); You Know How It Is; True to Them All; When the Right One Comes Along.

TREASURE GIRL

Lyrics by Ira Gershwin; book by Fred Thompson and Vincent Lawrence. Produced by Aarons and Freedley, Alvin Theatre, November 8, 1928. 68 performances. Cast: Gertrude Lawrence, Clifton Webb, Mary Hay, Walter Catlett, Paul Frawley, Ferris Hartmen. Conducted by Alfred Newman.

Skull and Bones
I've Got a Crush on You
Oh, So Nice
According to Mr. Grimes
Place in the Country
K-ra-zy for You
I Don't Think I'll Fall in Love Today
Got a Rainbow
Feeling I'm Falling
Where's the Boy? Here's the Girl!
What Causes That?

NOT USED: This Particular Party; Treasure Island; Goodbye to the Old Love, Hello to the New; A-Hunting We Will Go; Dead Men Tell No Tales; I Want to Marry a Marionette.

AN AMERICAN IN PARIS, tone poem for orchestra. Carnegie Hall, December 13, 1928. New York Symphony Orchestra, Walter Damrosch conducting.

1929

SHOW GIRL

Lyrics by Ira Gershwin and Gus Kahn; book by William Anthony McGuire and J. P. McEvoy. Produced by Florenz Ziegfeld, Ziegfeld Theater, July 2, 1929. III performances. Cast: Ruby Keeler, Eddie Foy, Jr., Frank McHugh, Jimmy Durante, Lou Clayton, Eddie Jackson, Barbara Newberry, Harriet Hoctor, Duke Ellington and his Orchestra. Conducted by William Daly.

Happy Birthday
My Sunday Fella
How Could I Forget
Lolita
Do What You Do!
One Man
So Are You!
I Must Be Home by Twelve O'Clock
Black and White
Blues Ballet (from *An American in Paris)*
Home Blues
Follow the Minstrel Band
Liza
Harlem Serenade

NOT USED: Feeling Sentimental; At Mrs. Simpkin's Finishing School; Adored One; Tonight's the Night; I Just Looked at You; I'm Just a Bundle of Sunshine; Minstrel Show; Somebody Stole My Heart Away; Someone's Always Calling a Rehearsal; I'm Out for No Good Reason Tonight; Home Lovin' Gal (Man).

Songs written for Ziegfeld's never produced *East Is West:*

Sing Song Girl
Embraceable You
We Are Visitors
In the Mandarin's Orchid Garden
Yellow Blues (Published as a piano solo, *Impromptu in Two Keys);* also known as Blues in Two Keys.
China Girl
Lady of the Moon (eventually: Blah, Blah, Blah)
Under the Cinnamon Tree

1930

STRIKE UP THE BAND

Lyrics by Ira Gershwin; book by Morrie Ryskind, based on Kaufman's original 1927 version. Produced by Edgar Selwyn, Times Square Theater, January 14, 1930. 191 performances. Cast: Bobby Clark, Paul McCullough, Blanche Ring, Dudley

Clements, Gordon Smith, Kathryn Hamill, Helen Gilligan, Doris Carson, Jerry Goff. Conducted by Hilding Anderson.

Fletcher's American Chocolate Choral Society Workers
I Mean To Say
Soon
A Typical Self-Made American
A Man of High Degree
The Unofficial Spokesman
Three Cheers for the Union!
This Could Go on for Years
If I Became the President
Hangin' Around with You
Finaletto: He Knows Milk
Strike Up the Band!
Opening: In the Rattle of the Battle
Military Dancing Drill
Mademoiselle in New Rochelle
I've Got a Crush on You
How About a Boy Like Me?
I Want to Be a War Bride
Unofficial March of General Holmes
Official Resume: First There Was Fletcher
Ding Dong

NOT USED: There Was Never Such a Charming War

Interpolated into *Nine-Fifteen Revue:*
Toddlin' Along (same melody as The World Is Mine)

GIRL CRAZY

Lyrics by Ira Gershwin; book by Guy Bolton and Jack McGowan. Produced by Aarons and Freedley, Alvin Theater, October 14, 1930. 272 performances. Cast: Ginger Rogers, Allen Kearns, Willie Howard, William Kent, Ethel Merman. Conducted by Earl Busby.

The Lonesome Cowboy
Bidin' My Time
Could You Use Me?
Broncho Busters
Barbary Coast
Embraceable You
Goldfarb! That's I'm
Sam and Delilah
I Got Rhythm

Land of the Gay Caballero
Mexican Dance (instrumental)
But Not for Me
Treat Me Rough
Boy! What Love Has Done to Me!
When It's Cactus Time in Arizona
NOT USED: The Gambler of the West;
And I Have You; You Can't Unscramble
Scrambled Eggs; Something Peculiar
(Lou Paley).

c. 1930

Ask Me Again

1931

DELICIOUS

Lyrics by Ira Gershwin; screenplay by
Guy Bolton and Sonya Levien. Produced
by Winfield Sheehan, Fox Film Corporation. Released December 1931. Cast: Janet Gaynor, Charles Farrell, El Brendel,
Raul Roulien, Mischa Auer, Manya
Roberti, Virginia Sherrill, Olive Tell,
Marvine Maazel, Jeanette Gegna. No
musical director credited. Maazel
dubbed Roulien's piano solos.

Delishious
Welcome to the Melting Pot (Dream
   Sequence)
Somebody From Somewhere
Katinkitschka
Blah-Blah-Blah
New York Rhapsody (Instrumental)
You Started It
NOT USED: Mischa, Yascha, Toscha, Sas-
cha; Thanks to You.

OF THEE I SING

Lyrics by Ira Gershwin; book by George
S. Kaufman and Morrie Ryskind. Produced by Sam H. Harris, Music Box, December 26, 1931. 441 performances. Cast:
William Gaxton, Victor Moore, Lois
Moran, Grace Brinkley, Dudley Clements, Ralph Riggs, Florenz Ames,

George Murphy, June O'Dea. Con-
ducted by Charles Previn.
   Wintergreen for President
   Who Is the Lucky Girl to Be?
   The Dimple on My Knee
   Because, Because
   Never Was There a Girl so Fair
   Some Girls Can Bake a Pie
   Love Is Sweeping the Country
   Of Thee I Sing
   Here's a Kiss for Cinderella
   I Was the Most Beautiful Blossom
   Hello, Good Morning
   Who Cares?
   Garçon, S'il Vous Plaît
   The Illegitimate Daughter
   The Senatorial Roll Call
   Jilted
   I'm About to Be a Mother
   Posterity Is Just Around the Corner
   Trumpeter, Blow Your Golden Horn
NOT USED: Call Me Whate'er You Will

1932

SECOND RHAPSODY, for orchestra
with piano. Symphony Hall, Boston, January 29, 1932. Gershwin, piano, Boston
Symphony Orchestra, Serge Koussevitzky conducting. This work, an expansion of the *New York Rhapsody,* was
completed on May 23, 1931.

   Written for the first film version of
      Girl Crazy:
   You've Got What Gets Me

CUBAN OVERTURE, for orchestra.
Lewisohn Stadium, August 16, 1932. New
York Philharmonic-Symphony Orches-
tra, Albert Coates conducting.

PIANO TRANSCRIPTIONS
OF 18 SONGS

Published as *George Gershwin's Song
Book* by Simon and Schuster, September
1932. Illustrations by Constantin
Alajalov. The volume printed the original sheet music of the songs, plus Gershwin's own party version: Swanee; No-

body But You; I'll Build a Stairway to Paradise; Do It Again; Fascinating Rhythm; Oh, Lady Be Good!; Somebody Loves Me; Sweet and Low-Down; That Certain Feeling; The Man I Love; Clap Yo' Hands; Do-Do-Do; My One and Only; 'S Wonderful; Strike Up the Band; Liza; I Got Rhythm; Who Cares? In May a limited, signed edition was published (300 copies); this included a copy of Mischa, Yascha, Toscha, Sascha. The *Transcriptions* are in print in a folio entitled "Gershwin at the Keyboard."

1933
PARDON MY ENGLISH

Lyrics by Ira Gershwin; book by Herbert Fields (et al.). Produced by Aarons and Freedley, Majestic Theater, January 20, 1933. 46 performances. Cast: Lyda Roberti, Jack Pearl, George Givot, Carl Randall, Josephine Huston, Barbara Newberry. Conducted by Earl Busby.

In Three Quarter Time
Lorelei
Pardon My English
Dancing in the Streets
So What?
Isn't It a Pity?
My Cousin in Milwaukee
Hail the Happy Couple
The Dresden Northwest Mounted
Luckiest Man in the World
What Sort of Wedding Is This?
Tonight (also main theme of *Two Waltzes in C*)
Where You Go I Go
I've Got to Be There
He's Not Himself
Deep in the Heart of Me
He's Oversexed, He's Undersexed (He Hasn't Any Sex at All)
NOT USED: Freud and Jung and Adler; Together at Last; Bauer's House; No Tickee, No Washee; Poor Michael! Poor Golo!; Fatherland, Mother of the Band.

LET 'EM EAT CAKE

Lyrics by Ira Gershwin; book by George S. Kaufman and Morrie Ryskind. Produced by Sam H. Harris, Imperial Theater, October 21, 1933. 90 performances. Cast: William Gaxton, Victor Moore, Lois Moran, Philip Loeb, Florenz Ames, Ralph Riggs. Conducted by William Daly.

Wintergreen for President
Tweedledee, Tweedledee
Union Square: Our Hearts Are in Communion; Down with Everything That's Up
Orders, Orders
Comes the Revolution
Mine
Climb Up the Social Ladder (The New D.A.R.)
Cloistered from the Noisy City
The Union League
On and On and On
What More Can a General Do?
What's This/Where's the General?
The General's Gone to a Party
All the Mothers of the Nation
He's a Bachelor (to the melody of Union League)
There's Something We're Worried About
What's the Proletariat?
Let 'Em Eat Cake
Blue, Blue, Blue
No One Greater
Who's the Greatest?
The Welcome
No Comprenez, No Capish, No Versteh!
Why Speak of Money?
No Better Way to Start a Case
Up and At 'Em! On to Vict'ry
Oyez, Oyez, Oyez
That's What He Did
I Know a Foul Ball When I See One
Throttle Throttlebottom
It Isn't What You Did but What You Didn't
We're in a Hell of a Jam
I'm About to Be a Mother
Hanging Throttlebottom in the Morning
Let 'Em Eat Caviar

NOT USED: First Lady and First Gent

Till Then

1934

VARIATIONS ON "I GOT RHYTHM", for piano and orchestra. Symphony Hall, Boston, January 14, 1934. Gershwin, piano, the Reisman Symphonic Orchestra, Charles Previn conducting.

1935

PORGY AND BESS, opera in three acts. Lyrics by DuBose Heyward and Ira Gershwin; libretto by Heyward. Produced by the Theater Guild, Alvin Theater, October 10, 1935. 124 performances. Cast: Todd Duncan, Anne Brown, Warren Coleman, Ruby Elzy, Abbie Mitchell, Georgette Harvey, Eddie Matthews, John W. Bubbles, Ford L. Buck, Henry Davis, Gus Simons, J. Rosamond Johnson, Olive Ball, Helen Dowdy, Jack Carr, John Garth, Ray Yeats, George Lessey, Alexander Campbell, Harold Woolf, George Carleton, Eva Jessye Choir, the Charleston Orphans' Band. Conducted by Alexander Smallens.
Introduction (orchestra)
 Jazzbo Brown (piano; piano and orchestra, chorus)
ACT I, SCENE I
Summertime
CRAP GAME Seems like these bones . . . ; I been sweatin' all day . . . ; Lord, I is tired this night . . .
 A Woman Is a Sometime Thing
 Here Come de Honey Man (Street Cry)
 Evenin' Ladies (entrance of Porgy)
 They Pass By Singin'
CRAP GAME: Yo mammy's gone . . . ; Crown cockeyed drunk . . . ; Oh, little stars . . . *Robbins's murder* (orch.)
SCENE 2
 Gone, Gone, Gone
 Overflow
 My Man's Gone Now

 Leavin' fo' the Promis' Land (Train Song)
ACT II, SCENE I
 It Take a Long Pull to Get There
 I Got Plenty o' Nuttin'
 I Hates Yo' Struttin' Style
 Mornin', Lawyer (Entrance of Frazier)
 Lord, Lord, Listen What She Say
 'Course I Sells Divorce
 Woman to Lady
 Buzzard Song
 Bess, You Is My Woman Now
 Oh, I Can't Sit Down
SCENE 2
 Allegretto barbaro (percussion)
 I Ain't Got No Shame
 It Ain't Necessarily So
 Shame on All of You Sinners
 What You Want with Bess?
SCENE 3
 It Take a Long Pull to Get There (reprise)
 De White Folks Put Me In
 Oh, Doctor Jesus (Time and Time Again)
 Street Cries: Strawberry Woman, Honey Man, Crab Man
 I Loves You, Porgy
 Hurricane (orchestra)
SCENE 4
 Prayers, for Six Voices
 Oh, de Lord Shake de Heavens
 Summertime (reprise) [Lonely Boy, a duet for Bess and Serena, was originally written for this spot].
 Oh, Dere's Somebody Knockin' at de Do'
 A Red Headed Woman
 Lawd, Lawd, Save Us (counterpoint to Red Headed Woman)
 Prayers (reprise)
ACT III, SCENE 3
 Clara, Clara, Don't You Be Downhearted
 Summertime (reprise by Bess)
 Fugue (the death of Crown, orchestra)
SCENE 2
 Scene with detective: Serena been

very sick . . . ; We ain't seen
nothin' Boss . . . ; You knows
me, boss . . .

There's a Boat Dat's Leavin' Soon
for New York

SCENE 3

Moderato commodo (Occupational
humoresque)

Good Mornin', Sister

Sure to Go to Heaven

How Are You Dis Mornin'

Thank Gawd, I's Home Again! (Return of Porgy)

Here, boy look what I brought for
you/ Here gal, hol' up yo' head/
Here Mingo, what's de matter wid
you all?

Where's My Bess?

I'm on My Way

NOT USED: Lonely Boy

Eliminated in Boston: *Jazzbo Brown;*
Buzzard Song; I Hates Yo' Struttin'
Style; I Ain't Got No Shame; Prayers;
Good Mornin', Sister; Sure to Go to
Heaven; How Are You Dis Mornin'.

1936

PORGY AND BESS SUITE, for orchestra. Academy of Music, Philadelphia,
January 21, 1936. The Philadelphia Orchestra, Alexander Smallens conducting.

1. Catfish Row
2. Porgy Sings
3. Fugue
4. Hurricane
5. Good Morning, Brother

NOTE: Ira Gershwin retitled this suite
Catfish Row in 1958.

King of Swing (Albert Stillman)

I Won't Give Up Till You Give In to
Me (Stillman)

Doubting Thomas (Stillman)

Interpolated into *The Show Is On:* By
Strauss

1937

SHALL WE DANCE

Lyrics by Ira Gershwin; screenplay by
Allan Scott and Ernest Pagano (based on
a story by Lee Loeb and Harold Buch-
man). Produced by Pandro S. Berman
for RKO Radio Pictures; released, May
1937. Cast: Fred Astaire, Ginger Rogers,
Edward Everett Horton, Eric Blore, Jerome Cowan, Ketti Gallian, Harriet
Hoctor. Musical director, Nathaniel
Shilkret.

French Ballet Class (orchestra)
Dance of the Waves (orchestra)
Ginger Rhumba (orchestra)
Graceful and Elegant (orchestra)
Slap That Bass
Walking the Dog (orchestra), pub-
lished for solo piano as *Promenade.*
I've Got Beginner's Luck
They All Laughed
Balloon Ballet (orchestra)
Let's Call the Whole Thing Off
They Can't Take That Away from
Me
Hoctor's Ballet (orchestra)

NOT USED: Hi-Ho! At Last; Wake Up,
Brother, and Dance.

A DAMSEL IN DISTRESS

Lyrics by Ira Gershwin; screenplay by
P. G. Wodehouse, Ernest Pagano and
S. K. Lauren (based on a book by Wode-
house). Produced by Pandro S. Berman
for RKO Radio Pictures; released No-
vember 1937. Cast: Fred Astaire, Joan
Fontaine, George Burns, Gracie Allen,
Reginald Gariner, Ray Noble, Constance
Collier, Montagu Love, Harry Watson.
Musical direction by Victor Baravalle.

I Can't Be Bothered Now
The Jolly Tar and the Milkmaid
Put Me to the Test (instrumental)
Stiff Upper Lip
Things Are Looking Up
A Foggy Day
Sing of Spring

Nice Work if You Can Get It
NOT USED: Pay Some Attention to Me

THE GOLDWYN FOLLIES

Lyrics by Ira Gershwin; screenplay by
Ben Hecht. Produced by Samuel Gold-
wyn; released, February 1938. Cast:
Adolph Menjou, the Ritz Brothers, Vera
Zorina, Kenny Baker, Andrea Leeds,
Edgar Bergen and Charlie McCarthy,
Ella Logan, Bobby Clark, Helen Jepson,
Charles Kullman, William Dollar, the
American Ballet, the Goldwyn Girls.
Musical direction by Alfred Newman.
Love Walked In
I Was Doing All Right
I Love to Rhyme
Love Is Here to Stay
NOT USED: Just Another Rhumba

POSTHUMOUS WORKS

1938

Dawn of a New Day (New York
World's Fair, 1939)

1946

THE SHOCKING MISS PILGRIM

Lyrics by Ira Gershwin; screenplay by
George Seaton (based on a story by Er-
nest and Frederica Maas). Musical assis-
tant to Ira Gershwin, Kay Swift. Pro-
duced for 20th Century-Fox by William
Perlberg; released, January 1947. Cast:
Betty Grable, Dick Haymes, Anne Re-
vere, Allyn Joslyn, Gene Lockhart, Eliz-
abeth Paterson, Elisabeth Risdon, Ar-
thur Shields. Musical direction by Alfred
Newman.
Sweet Packard
Stand Up and Fight
Aren't You Kind of Glad We Did?
Changing My Tune
Back Bay Polka
Demon Rum
One, Two, Three
For You, For Me, For Evermore
NOT USED: Tour of the Town; Welcome
Song

1964

KISS ME, STUPID

Lyrics by Ira Gershwin; screenplay by
Billy Wilder and I. A. L. Diamond. Pro-
duced by Wilder for United Artists; re-
leased, December 1964. Cast: Kim No-
vak, Dean Martin, Ray Walston, Felicia
Farr. Musical direction by Andre Previn.
All the Livelong Day
I'm a Poached Egg
Sophia

Additional posthumous publications:
The Real American Folk Song (1918;
pub. 1959)

Just Another Rhumba (1937; pub.
1959)

Promenade, for piano (1937; pub.
1960)

Hi-Ho! (1936; pub. 1968)

Harlem River Chanty, choral arr. by
Ross Hastings (1925; pub. 1968)

Dear Little Girl (1927; pub. 1968)

Lullaby for string quartet (1919; pub.
1968)

Two Waltzes in C, for piano (1933;
pub. 1971)

Merry Andrew for piano (Gershwin Melody No. 43, *Comedy Dance*, c. 1928, pub. 1974).

Three-Quarter Blues for piano (Melody No. 32, "Irish Waltz," pub. 1974).

II

IRA GERSHWIN

c. 1920

Kiss Me, That's All (music, Philip Charig)

1921

TWO LITTLE GIRLS IN BLUE

Music by Vincent Youmans and Paul Lannin; book by Fred Jackson. Produced by A. L. Erlanger, Cohan Theater, May 3, 1921. 135 performances. Cast: Madeline and Marion Fairbanks, Oscar Shaw, Olin Howland, Julia Kelety, Fred Santley. Conducted by Charles Previn.
We're Off on a Wonderful Trip
Wonderful U.S.A. (Lannin only)
Two Little Girls in Blue
The Silly Season
Oh Me! Oh My! (Youmans)
You Started Something (Youmans)
We're Off to India
Here, Steward
Dolly (Youmans; co-lyricist Schuyler Greene)
Who's Who with You? (Youmans)
Just Like You (Lannin)
There's Something About Me They Like (Youmans; co-lyricist Fred Jackson)
Rice and Shoes (Youmans; co-lyricist Greene)
She's Innocent
Honeymoon (When Will You Shine for Me?) (Lannin)
I'm Tickled Silly
NOT USED: Summertime (Lannin); Happy Ending (Lannin); Make the Best of It; Little Bag of Tricks; Utopia (Youmans); Slapstick (Lannin); Mr. and Mrs. (Youmans).

1922

Interpolated into *Pins and Needles:*
The Piccadilly Walk (Edward A. Horan; co-lyricist, Arthur Riscoe)

Interpolated into *For Goodness Sake:*
French Pastry Walk (William Daly and Paul Lannin; co-lyricist, Arthur Jackson)

Interpolated into *Molly Darling:*
When All Your Castles Come Tumbling Down (Milton E. Schwartzwald)

Written for silent film *Fascination:*
Fascination (Louis Silvers; co-lyricist, Schuyler Greene)

What Can I Do? (Maurice Yvain; co-lyricist, Schuyler Greene)

Hubby (William Daly)

1923

Interpolated into *Greenwich Village Follies:*
Hot Hindoo (Lewis Gensler)

Interpolated into *Nifties of 1923:*
Fabric of Dreams (Raymond Hubbell; co-lyricist, B. G. DeSylva)

The Nevada (William Daly and Joseph Meyer)

Little Rhythm, Go 'Way (Daly and Meyer)

Singing in the Rain (Daly and Meyer)

Tell Me in the Gloaming (Irving Caesar and Niclas Kempner)

Mary Louise (Richard Meyers)

1924

BE YOURSELF

Music by Lewis Gensler and Milton Schwarzwald; book by George S. Kaufman and Marc Connelly. Produced by Wilmer and Vincent, Sam H. Harris Theater, September 3, 1924. 93 performances. Cast: Jack Donahue, Queenie Smith, Georgia Caine.

I Came Here (Gensler; co-lyricists, Kaufman and Connelly)

Uh-Uh! (Schwarzwald; co-lyricists, Kaufman and Connelly)

The Wrong Thing at the Right Time (Schwarzwald; co-lyricists, Kaufman and Connelly)

All of Them Was Friends of Mine (co-lyricist, Connelly)

They Don't Make 'Em That Way Any More

Interpolated into *Top Hole:*
Imagine Me Without You (And You Without Me) (Lewis Gensler)

Cheerio! (Gensler)

Interpolated into *The Firebrand:*
The Voice of Love (Robert Russell Bennett and Maurice Nitke)

1925

Interpolated into *Captain Jinks:*
You Must Come Over Blues (Lewis Gensler)

Interpolated into *A Night Out:*
I Want a Yes Man (Youmans; co-lyricists, Clifford Grey and Irving Caesar)

1926

Interpolated into *Americana:*
Blowin' the Blues Away (Philip Charig)

Sunny Disposish (Charig)

1928

THAT'S A GOOD GIRL

Music by Joseph Meyer and Philip Charig; book by Douglas Furber. Produced by Moss Empires Ltd., Hippodrome, London, March 19, 1928. 363 performances. Cast: Jack Buchanan (co-producer), Elsie Randolph, Dave Fitzgibbon, William Kendell. Conducted by Leonard Hornsey.

What to Do?

The One I'm Looking For (co-lyricist, Furber)

Chirp-Chirp

Sweet So-and-So (co-lyricist, Furber)

Let Yourself Go! (co-lyricist, Furber)

Week-end

NOT USED: Before We Were Married; Day After Day; Why Be Good?; There I'd Settle Down

1930

Interpolated into *Garrick Gaieties:*
I'm Only Human After All (Vernon Duke; co-lyricist, E. Y. Harburg)

Interpolated into *Sweet and Low:*
Cheerful Little Earful (Harry Warren; co-lyricist, Billy Rose)

In the Merry Month of Maybe (Warren; co-lyricist, Rose)

1931

Interpolated into *The Social Register:*
The Key to My Heart (Lou Alter)

1934

LIFE BEGINS AT 8:40

Music by Harold Arlen; co-lyricist, E. Y. Harburg. Sketches by David Freedman. Produced by the Shuberts, Winter Garden, August 27, 1934. 237 performances. Cast: Bert Lahr, Ray Bolger, Luella Gear, Frances Williams, Dixie Dunbar, Adrienne Matzenauer, Brian Donlevy, the Charles Weidman Dancers. Conducted by Al Goodman.

Live Begins
Spring Fever
Shoein' the Mare
You're a Builder Upper
I'm Not Myself
Fun to Be Fooled
Quartet Erotica
C'est La Vie
My Paramount-Publix-Roxy Rose
What Can You Say in a Love Song?
Let's Take a Walk Around the Block
Things
The Elks and the Masons
I Couldn't Hold My Man
It Was Long Ago
Life Begins at City Hall
NOT USED: Will You Love Me Monday Morning? (Weekend Cruise); I'm a Collector of Moonbeams; I Knew Him When.

1936

ZIEGFELD FOLLIES OF 1936

Music by Vernon Duke; sketches by David Freedman. Produced by the Shuberts, Winter Garden, January 30, 1936. 227 performances. Cast: Fannie Brice, Josephine Baker, Gertrude Niesen, Eve Arden, Judy Canova, Bob Hope, Harriet Hoctor. Conducted by John McManus.

Time Marches On!
He Hasn't a Thing Except Me
My Red-Letter Day
Island in the West Indies
The Economic Situation
Fancy, Fancy
Maharanee
The Gazooka
That Moment of Moments
Sentimental Weather
Five A.M.
Modernistic Moe (co-lyricist, Billy Rose)
I Can't Get Started
Dancing to Our Score
NOT USED: Please Send My Daddy Back Home; Does a Duck Love Water?; I'm Sharing My Wealth; Wishing Tree of Harlem; Why Save for That Rainy Day?; Hot Number; The Last of the Cabbies; The Ballad of Baby Face McGinty; Sunday Tan; It's a Different World; The Knife-Thrower's Wife; Save Your Yesses.

I Used to Be Above Love (Vernon Duke)

1937

Written for *The Goldwyn Follies:*
Spring Again (Vernon Duke)
NOT USED: I'm Not Complaining (Duke)

1938

No Question in My Heart (Jerome Kern)

Once There Were Two of Us/Now That We Are One (Kern)

1939

Baby, You're News (Johnny Green; co-lyricist, E. Y. Harburg)

1941

LADY IN THE DARK

Music by Kurt Weill; book by Moss Hart. Produced by Sam H. Harris, Alvin Theater, January 23, 1941. 467 performances. Cast: Gertrude Lawrence, Macdonald Carey, Danny Kaye, Victor Ma-ture, Bert Lytell, Margaret Dale, Evelyn Wyckoff, Natalie Schafer, Ann Lee Jeanne Shelby. Conducted by Maurice Abravanel.

Oh, Fabulous One
Huxley
One Life to Live
Girl of the Moment
Mapleton High Chorale
This Is New
The Princess of Pure Delight
The Greatest Show on Earth
The Best Years of His Life
Tschaikowsky
Jenny
My Ship

NOT USED: Unforgettable; It's Never Too Late to Mendelssohn; No Matter Under What Star You're Born; Song of the Zodiac; Bats About You; The Boss Is Bringing Home a Bride; Party Parlando; In Our Little San Fernando Valley Home.

Honorable Moon (Arthur Schwartz; co-lyricist, E. Y. Harburg)

1943

NORTH STAR

Music by Aaron Copland; screenplay by Lillian Hellman. Produced by Samuel Goldwyn, released by RKO, October 1943. Cast: Walter Huston, Walter Brennan, Erich von Stroheim, Anne Baxter, Farley Granger, Dana Andrews, Jane Withers.

Can I Help It?
Loading Song (From the Baltic to the Pacific)
Loading Time at Last Is Over
No Village Like Mine
Song of the Guerrillas
Wagon Song
Younger Generation

NOT USED: Workers of All the Nations

If This Be Propagand (Harold Arlen)

1944

COVER GIRL

Music by Jerome Kern; screenplay by Virginia Van Upp. Produced by Arthur Schwartz; released by Columbia Pictures, April 1944. Cast: Rita Hayworth, Gene Kelly, Phil Silvers, Lee Bowman, Eve Arden. Musical director, Morris Stoloff.

The Show Must Go On
Who's Complaining?
Make Way for Tomorrow (co-lyricist, E. Y. Harburg)
Put Me to the Test
Long Ago and Far Away
Cover Girl

NOT USED: What I Love to Hear; Tropical Night; Time: The present; That's the Best of All.

1945

WHERE DO WE GO FROM HERE?

Music by Kurt Weill; screenplay by Morrie Ryskind. Produced by William Perlberg; released by 20th Century–Fox, May 1945. Cast: Fred MacMurray, Joan Leslie, June Haver, Gene Sheldon, Herman Bing, Fortunio Bonanova, Carlos Ramirez, Alan Mowbray, Anthony Quinn. Musical director, Emil Newman.

Where Do We Go From Here?
Morale
All at Once
If Love Remains
Song of the Rhineland
The Nina, the Pinta, the Santa Maria

NOT USED: Telephone Scene; That's How It Is (In My Country 'Tis); It Happened to Happen to Me; Manhattan.

THE FIREBRAND OF FLORENCE

Music by Kurt Weill; book by Edwin Justus Mayer and Ira Gershwin. Produced by Max Gordon, Alvin Theater, March 22, 1945, 43 performances. Cast: Earl Wrightson, Beverly Tyler, Lotte Lenya, Melville Cooper, Ferdi Hoffman. Conducted by Maurice Abravanel.

One Man's Death Is Another Man's Living
Come to Florence
My Lords and Ladies
There'll Be Life, Love and Laughter
You're Far Too Near Me
Alessandro the Wise
I am Happy Here
Sing Me Not a Ballad
When the Duchess Is Away
Cozy Nook Song
The Nighttime Is No Time for Thinking
Dizzily, Busily
The Little Naked Boy
My Dear Benvenuto
Just in Case
A Rhyme for Angela
The World Is Full of Villains
You Have to Do What You Do Do
Love Is My Enemy
Come to Paris
NOT USED: I Had Just Been Pardoned; Master Is Free Again.

1946

PARK AVENUE

Music by Arthur Schwartz; book by George S. Kaufman and Nunnally Johnson. Produced by Max Gordon, Shubert Theater, November 4, 1946. 72 performances. Cast: Byron Russell, Ray Mc-Donald, Martha Stewart, Arthur Margetson, Leonora Corbett, Robert Chisholm, Marthe Errolle, Mary Wickes, David Wayne. Conducted by Charles Sanford.

Tomorrow Is the Time
For the Life of Me
The Dew Was on the Rose
Don't Be a Woman If You Can
Nevada
There's No Holding Me

There's Nothing Like Marriage for People
Hope for the Best
My Son-in-Law
The Land of Opportunitee
Good-bye to All That
Stay As We Are
NOT USED: Heavenly Day; The Future Mrs. Coleman; Dinner Song.

1949

THE BARKLEYS OF BROADWAY

Music by Harry Warren; screenplay by Betty Comden and Adolph Green. Produced by Arthur Freed; released by MGM, May 1949. Cast: Fred Astaire, Ginger Rogers, Oscar Levant, Billie Burke, Jacques François, George Zucco. Musical director, Lennie Hayton.

Swing Trot
You'd Be Hard to Replace
Bouncin' the Blues
My One and Only Highland Fling
Weekend in the Country
Shoes with Wings On
Manhattan Downbeat
Interpolation: They Can't Take That Away from Me (George and Ira Gershwin)
NOT USED: These Days; There Is No Music; The Poetry of Motion; Call On Us Again; Natchez on the Mississip'; The Courtin' of Elma and Ella; Taking No Chances with You; Second Fiddle to a Harp; Minstrels on Parade.

1953

GIVE A GIRL A BREAK

Music by Burton Lane; screenplay by Albert Hackett and Frances Goodrich. Produced by Jack Cummings; released by MGM, January 1953. Cast: Debbie Reynolds, Marge and Gower Champion, Bob Fosse, Kurt Kasznar. Musical director, André Previn.

Applause! Applause!
Give a Girl a Break
In Our United State
It Happens Every Time
Nothing Is Impossible
NOT USED: Ach, du Lieber Oom-Pah-Pah; Dream World; Woman, There Is No Living with You.

1954

A STAR IS BORN

Music by Harold Arlen; screenplay by Moss Hart. Produced by Sidney Luft; released by Warner Brothers, October 1954. Cast: Judy Garland, James Mason, Tommy Noonan, Charles Bickford, Jack Carson. Musical director, Ray Heindorf.

Gotta Have Me Go with You
The Man That Got Away
Here's What I'm Here For
It's a New World
Someone at Last
Lose That Long Face
The Commercial (Calypso)
NOT USED: I'm Off the Downbeat; Green Light Ahead; Dancing Partner.

THE COUNTRY GIRL

Music by Harold Arlen; screenplay by George Seaton. Produced by William Perlberg; released by Paramount Pictures, December 1954. Cast: Bing Crosby, Grace Kelly, William Holden. Musical director, Joseph Lilley.

It's Mine, It's Yours (The Pitchman)
Beer Commercial
Dissertation on the State of Bliss
  (Love and Learn)
The Search Is Through
The Land Around Us

1959

LYRICS ON SEVERAL OCCASIONS. A selection of Stage & Screen Lyrics Written for Sundry Situations; and Now Arranged in Arbitrary Categories. To Which Have Been Added Many Informative Annotations & Disquisitions on Their Why & Wherefore, Their Whom-For, Their How; And Matters Associative. New York: Alfred A. Knopf, 1959.

Bibliography

I

Books directly about the Gershwins and their works:

Armitage, Merle, ed., *George Gershwin*. New York: Longmans, Green and Co., 1938.

Ewen, David, *George Gershwin—His Journey to Greatness*. Englewood Cliffs, New Jersey: Prentice-Hall, Inc., 1970.

Gershwin, Ira, *Lyrics on Several Occasions*. New York: Alfred A. Knopf, 1959.

Goldberg, Isaac, *George Gershwin*. New York: Simon and Schuster, 1931. Reprint with supplement by Edith Garson. New York, Ungar Publishing Co., 1958.

Jablonski, Edward, and Lawrence D. Stewart, *The Gershwin Years*. Garden City, New York: Doubleday & Company, Inc., 1958; revised edition, 1973.

Kimball, Robert, and Alfred Simon, *The Gershwins*. New York: Atheneum, 1973.

Schwartz, Charles, *Gershwin, His Life and Music*. Indianapolis: Bobbs-Merrill Co., 1973.

II

Volumes pertaining to the times or other aspects of the Gershwins' lives:

Adams, Franklin P., *The Diary of Our Own Samuel Pepys* (1911–1934). New York: Simon and Schuster, 1935.

Astaire, Fred, *Steps in Time*. New York: Harper and Brothers, 1959.

Beach, Sylvia, *Shakespeare and Company*. New York: Harcourt, Brace & Co., 1956/59.

Behrman, S. N., *People in a Diary*. Boston: Little, Brown & Co., 1972.

Bordman, Gerald, *American Musical Theater*. New York: Oxford University Press, 1978.

———, *Jerome Kern, his Life and Music*. New York: Oxford University Press, 1980.

DeLong, Thomas A., *Pops: Paul Whiteman, King of Jazz*. Piscataway, New Jersey: New Century Publishers, 1983.

Dietz, Howard, *Dancing in the Dark*. New York: Quadrangle Books, 1974.

Duke, Vernon, *Passport to Paris*. Boston: Little, Brown & Co., 1955.

Dunn, Don, *The Making of No, No, Nanette*. Secaucus, New Jersey, 1972.

Eells, George, *The Life That Late He Led—A biography of Cole Porter.* New York: G. P. Putnam's Sons, 1967.

Ellington, Duke, *Music Is My Mistress.* Garden City, New York: Doubleday & Company, Inc., 1973.

Fordin, Hugh, *The World of Entertainment.* Garden City, New York: Doubleday & Company, Inc., 1975.

Gaines, James R., *Wit's End.* New York: Harcourt, Brace, Jovanovich, 1977.

Goldberg, Isaac, *Tin Pan Alley.* New York: The John Day Co., 1930.

Green, Abel and Joe Laurie, Jr., *Show Biz—from Vaude to Video.* New York: Henry Holt & Co., 1951.

Green, Stanley, *Encyclopedia of the Musical Film.* New York: Oxford University Press, 1981.

———, *Encyclopedia of the Musical Theater.* New York: Dodd, Mead & Co., 1976. Paperback edition, with additions, Da Capo Press, 1976.

———, and Burt Goldblatt, *Starring Fred Astaire.* New York: Dodd, Mead & Co., 1973.

———, *The World of Musical Comedy* (4th ed.). San Diego: A. S. Barnes & Co., 1980.

Hutcheson, Ernest, *The Literature of the Piano.* New York: Alfred A. Knopf, 1948.

Kimball, Robert, ed., *The Complete Lyrics of Cole Porter.* New York: Alfred A. Knopf, 1983.

Lawrence, Gertrude, *A Star Danced.* Garden City, New York: Doubleday & Company, Inc., 1945.

Levant, Oscar, *A Smattering of Ignorance.* New York: Doubleday, Doran & Company, Inc., 1941.

Mason, Daniel Gregory, *Tune In, America.* New York: Alfred A. Knopf, 1931.

Nichols, Beverly, *Are They the Same at Home?* New York: George H. Doran Company, 1927.

Orenstein, Arbie, *Ravel, Man and Musician.* New York: Columbia University Press, 1975.

Osgood, Henry O., *So This Is Jazz.* Boston: Little, Brown & Co., 1926.

Perrett, Geoffrey, *America in the Twenties.* New York: Simon and Schuster, 1982.

Rosenfeld, Paul, *Discoveries of a Music Critic.* New York: Harcourt, Brace & Co., 1936.

Sanders, Ronald, *The Days Grow Short, the Life and Music of Kurt Weill.* New York: Holt, Rinehart and Winston, 1980.

Saylor, Oliver, ed., *Revolt in the Arts.* New York: Brentano's, 1930.

Slonimsky, Nicolas, *Music Since 1900.* New York: W. W. Norton, 1938.

Stravinsky, Vera and Robert Craft, *Stravinsky.* New York: Simon and Schuster, 1978.

Waters, Edward N., *Victor Herbert.* New York: The Macmillan Co., 1955.

Whiteman, Paul, and Mary Margaret McBride, *Jazz.* New York: J. H. Sears & Co., 1926.

Wilder, Alec, *American Popular Song.* New York: Oxford University Press, 1972.

Wilk, Max, *They're Playing Our*

Song. New York: Atheneum, 1973.

Wodehouse, P. G., and Guy Bolton, *Bring On the Girls.* New York: Simon and Schuster, 1953.

The WPA Guide to New York City. New York: Pantheon Books, 1982 (reprint of original 1939 volume).

Notes on Sources

PREFACE

The O'Hara quote appeared in *Newsweek*, July 15, 1940; The Jacobi and Thomson quotes appeared in *Modern Music*, the former's after Gershwin's death and the latter's after the production of *Porgy and Bess*. The Gershwin quotes were lifted from two sources: "Gershwin on Music," assembled by me for *Musical America*, July 1962, and from *Theater Magazine*, c. June 1926, for which Gershwin purportedly wrote an article, "Jazz Is the Voice of the American Soul"; it reads more like an interview or may have been ghostwritten.

1 THE NEW AMERICAN GERSHVINS

Gershwin's letters to Goldberg are the major source; secondary: Goldberg's *George Gershwin*. Others: Ira Gershwin in the Armitage book, conversations with Frances Gershwin Godowsky and an interview with Nathaniel Shilkret by Milton A. Caine, May 1, 1951. The Gershwin quote appeared in the 1926 article, "Jazz Is the Voice . . ."

2 FROM TIN PAN ALLEY . . .

Major sources: Goldberg's *Tin Pan Alley*, Abel Green and Joe Laurie, Jr.'s *Show Biz—from Vaude to Video* and Stanley Green's *The World of Musical Comedy;* also Ben Yagoda's "Lullaby of Tin Pan Alley," in *American Heritage*, Oct/Nov, 1983. Ira Gershwin's early Journal is a good source also, as are Gershwin's letters to Max Abramson and Goldberg. The names of the lyricist and cast of *Half Past Eight* were taken from an advertisement and article in the Syracuse *Post-Standard*, December 8, 1918; the *Variety* review appeared in the December 11, 1918 issue.

3 . . . TO BROADWAY

Letters from both Gershwins to Emily and Lou Paley are a good source on the early musicals; Ira Gershwin's *Lyrics on Several Occasions* is also. Besides his insights and stories behind the writing of songs, Gershwin's book is refreshingly free of show biz anecdotes. On the other hand, Astaire's autobiography is not very informative about the great songwriters with whom he worked. The Green-Goldblatt book on Astaire is invaluable. My interviews with Jules Glaenzer in 1957 were disappointing in that he appeared to be ignorant of Gershwin's work and re-tailed (repeatedly) the same two or three stories. The Frances Gershwin Godowsky interview appeared in the New York *Times*, June 6, 1984. Before and since we have spoken frequently about her brothers.

4 "EXPERIMENT IN MODERN MUSIC"

The basic sources are Goldberg's affectionate biography, *A Study in American Music*, and the letters Gershwin wrote to him c. 1929–31. The *Zeitgeist* is represented by Osgood's *So This Is Jazz* and the Whiteman-McBride *Jazz* and contemporary accounts. These books prove that neither had any idea as to what jazz was. The story of Victor Herbert's suggestion re: the *Rhapsody in Blue* appears in Waters's biography and also in Goldberg. Ira Gershwin's and Ferde Grofé's recollections appear in the Armitage compilation.

5 1924

Gershwin's quotes in this chapter were taken from his radio broadcast of February 19, 1934, his introduction to Goldberg's *Tin Pan Alley* and an article, "Jazz Is the Voice . . ." *Theater Magazine*, June 1926. The Carl Van Vechten diary notes were first printed as part of his Introduction to *The Gershwin Years*. Gershwin's comments on jazz, the effects of music on people, on the "composer who writes music for himself," etc., were written for a collection *Revolt in the Arts*, edited by Oliver Saylor, and published as

"The Composer and the Machine Age."

6 MODERN ROMANTIC

Gershwin's comings and goings were regularly documented in Franklin P. Adams's column, many of which were republished in book form as *The Diary of Our Own Samuel Pepys*. S. N. Behrman's "Profile" appeared in *The New Yorker*, May 25, 1929. Abram Chasins's recollections of Gershwin were published in *The Saturday Review*, February 25, 1956; I also interviewed him and Philip Charig in 1958. A good deal of firsthand information on Gershwin with emphasis on the music appears in Osgood's *So This Is Jazz*. Walter Damrosch and Lester Donahue prepared their pieces on Gershwin for the Armitage memorial volume, *George Gershwin*. Rosenfeld's critical "No Chabrier" appeared in *The New Republic*, January 4, 1933.

7 INTERLUDE AND PRELUDES
8 HITS AND MISSES

The Levant and Duke observations were drawn primarily from their books *A Smattering of Ignorance* and *Passport to Paris* respectively. Levant's later books (ghostwritten) repeated most of the same stories, but not as well. In later life he rather resented being typed as a Gershwin specialist. Other comments from both Levant and Duke come from radio interviews. Although I knew Levant, we rarely talked about Gershwin in our few meetings. The Gershwin at the piano description by Beverly Nichols originally appeared in *The Sketch* as "George Gershwin or a Drunken Schubert." The signed photo of Gershwin, which dates his consideration of *An American in Paris* to April 1926 is in the collection of Mabel Schirmer; as are Gershwin's letters to her (some of which are in the Library of Congress). Gershwin's royalty statements are also deposited in the Gershwin Collection, Library of Congress. DuBose Heyward's first impressions of Gershwin appear in "Porgy and Bess Return on Wings of Song," *Stage Magazine,* October 1935. Gershwin's remarks to Rudy Vallee were made on the latter's radio show, November 10, 1932.

9 AMERICANS IN PARIS

Ira Gershwin kept a detailed Journal of the Gershwins' 1928 European trip. Interviews with Mabel Schirmer and Frances Godowsky supplied extra details. Ravel's whereabouts during this period are chronicled in Orenstein's *Ravel.* Braggiotti's recollections were published in *Étude,* February 1953, under the title, "Gershwin Is Here to Stay." Specifics of Frankie Gershwin's appearance in a Cole Porter revue singing Gershwin may be found in Eells's Porter biography and Robert Kimball's *The Complete Lyrics of Cole Porter.* The exchange between Gershwin and Stravinsky is footnoted in Vera Stravinsky and Robert Craft's *Stravinsky,* page 647, No. 48. Sylvia Beach mentions Gershwin's purchase of *Ulysses* and the grand party in her *Shakespeare and Company.* Kay Swift is the source on the first performance of *An American in Paris.*

10 TRANSITION: BROADWAY TO HOLLYWOOD

Most of this chapter is based on Gershwin letters, Ira Gershwin's *Lyrics. . . .* Ellington's impression of Gershwin is in his autobiography, *Music Is My Mistress.* Edward Kilenyi's "George Gershwin as I Knew Him" was published in the October 1950 *Étude;* his letters to Milton A. Caine were also drawn upon.

11 MANHATTAN RHAPSODY

As before, Gershwin's letters to Isaac Goldberg, George Pallay and Rosamond Walling form the basis of this chapter. Frank Campbell-Watson's *Preamble* was published in the full score to *Variations on "I Got Rhythm,"* 1953. Daly's "Gershwin as Orchestrator" was published in the New York *Times,* January 15, 1933.

12 SONG BOOK

Based on recollections of Kay Swift and Ira Gershwin, as well as his *Lyrics. . . .*

13 PORGY AND BESS

This section is largely based on the exchange of correspondence between Gershwin and DuBose Heyward, copies of which were given to me by Dorothy Heyward. Her recollections were published in the *Harper's Magazine* article, "Porgy's Goat," December 1957, and in her introduction to the Bantam Books edition of the novel, *Porgy,* 1957. Heyward's article on the writing of

Porgy and Bess appeared in *Stage Magazine*, October 1935. Henry Katzman's letter was written in July 1976. Copies of the Charleston *News & Courier* articles are from Frances Gershwin Godowsky's collection. The Todd Duncan interview, conducted by Berthe Schuchat, was broadcast over WMAV-FM, Washington, D.C. 1976. Kay Halle's recollections appeared in the Washington *Post*, February 5, 1978. Contemporary reviews by Virgil Thomson et al. of *Porgy and Bess* are generally identified. The Steinert opinions appeared in the Armitage compilation; we met several times, also, in his apartment, where he showed me film he had taken during the production and tour of *Porgy and Bess*, as well as during Gershwin's final year in California. Kay Swift and I have discussed *Porgy and Bess* and Gershwin for many years. The Kay Halle interview appeared in the Washington *Post*, February 5, 1978.

14 THE GOLDWYN COAST

Letters, again, are the basis of this chapter, particularly those Gershwin wrote to Mabel Schirmer. The Shilkret quotes are taken from an interview by Milton A. Caine, May 1, 1951. Interviews with Mabel Schirmer, Frances Gershwin Godowsky, Ira Gershwin, Harold Arlen, Alexander Steinert, Henry Botkin contributed to this chapter. Additional quotations from taped radio interviews by Kay Swift, Ira Gershwin,

Vernon Duke, Simone Simon. Pallay's letter about Gershwin's final days was written to Irene Gallagher, then secretary to Gershwin's publisher, Max Dreyfus. The medical material is based on a study by Dr. Louis Carp, "George Gershwin—Illustrious American Composer: His Fatal Glioblastoma" published in *The American Journal of Surgical Pathology*, October 1979; a somewhat less technical study is Dr. N. D. Fabricant's "George Gershwin's Fatal Headache," *The Eye, Ear, Nose and Throat Monthly*, May 1958.

EPILOGUE: THE MYTHS OF IRA GERSHWIN

Two major sources: Ira Gershwin's letters of some forty years and his book, *Lyrics on Several Occasions;* interviews, conversations and telephone communication also provided material. The Kurt Weill references are mostly based on Ronald Sanders's biography of the composer, *The Days Grow Short*. Stanley Green's *Encyclopedias—Musical Theater* and *Musical Film*—were especially helpful. Interviews, or rather conversations, with Harold Arlen, Arthur Schwartz and Burton Lane contributed a great deal too, professionally as well as personally. While all respected Gershwin as one of the major lyricists, their affection for the man was rather unusual in the world of popular song, film and the lyric theater.

Acknowledgments

I am most grateful to the many who have contributed to this work in various ways, ranging from suggestions to questions, from interviews to the loan of mementos, clippings, letters, to insights and enthusiasms. Thanks then to Harold Arlen; I. H. Asper, O.C., Winnipeg, Canada; Paul M. Bailey, Theater Arts Library, University of Texas, Austin; Glenn A. Barr, Indianapolis, Indiana; Peggy and Jack Barrington, Jean and John Bartel, Bay City, Michigan; Irving Berlin, New York; Andrew Berner, Library, University Club, New York; Ken Bloom, New York; Jon Bogdon, New York; Robert Bolles, New York; Gene Bruck of Wurlitzer-Bruck, New York; Milton A. Caine, Melville, New York; Judy Cimaglia, New Haven, Conn.; Kevin Cole, Bay City, Michigan; Cathy Coyne, New York; Dorian Dale, New York; Alan Dashiell, New Hope, Pa.; Bleu Deen, New York; Shelly and Norman Dinhofer, Brooklyn, New York; Michael Feinstein, Hollywood, California; Kurt Fewer, New York; Judy Gershwin, New York; Marc Gershwin, New York; Frances Godowsky, New York; Leopold Godowsky III, Clinton, Connecticut; Stanley Green, Brooklyn, New York; Julie Holtzman, New York; Frances (Veri) and Michael Jamanis, New York; Julie and Jay Judge, New York; Carl Johnson, The Whiteman Collection, Williams College, Williamstown, Massachusetts; Michael Kerker, ASCAP, New York; Chester Kopaz, Bayonne, New Jersey; Tommy Krasker, New York; Burton and Lynn Lane, New York; David Lassman, Syracuse, New York; Lynn Lavner, Brooklyn, New York; Sandy MacLean, New York; David Menard, Brooklyn, New York; Alice Owen, Librarian, Neighborhood Playhouse, New York; Dorothy Peterson, Maryland Center for Public Broadcasting, Owings Mills, Maryland; Patti Pippen, New York; Steven Richman, New York; Don Rose, Miami, Florida; Guy St. Claire, Library, University Club, New York; Wayne D. Shirley, Music Division, Library of Congress, Washington, D.C.; Mabel Schirmer, New York; Berthe Schuchat, New York; George Schultz, New York; Karen Sherry, ASCAP, New York; Alfred Simon, New York; Wanda and Jerry Simpson, Saginaw, Michigan; Lawrence D. Stewart, Beverly Hills, California; Kay Swift, New York; Nadia Turbide, Westmount, Quebec, Canada; Arthur Whitelaw, New York; Marianne Wurlitzer of Wurlitzer-Bruck, New York.

A special mention should be made of the contribution of Eric Smith, Sydney, Australia, and Bert Whelen, Turramurra, Australia. Beginning in 1968 they collected all possible copies of Gershwin music, published as well as unpublished; in this they were assisted by Ira Gershwin as well as Gershwin devotees around the world. Pianist-organist Eric and engineer Bert then began recording the music beginning with "When You Want 'Em . . ." and proceeding through the unknown songs from *Half Past Eight* on to *The Goldwyn Follies*, finishing in February 1982. Not counting *Porgy and Bess* (or the concert pieces), the collection amounts to more than four hundred songs. This many-reeled compilation enabled me to hear Gershwin's songs in the order of their publication as well as in sequence as heard in the musicals and films. Eric's fine musicianship, not to mention devotion to Gershwin, made the listening most pleasurable, as were his adventurous visits to these parts. New York has not been the same since. It might be mentioned that Bert's determined and dedicated research has also assembled a large collection of Gershwin's piano rolls.

From the same part of the world comes Ed Wilson of Auckland, New Zealand. After the death of "the charming and knowledgeable" (Ira Gershwin's words) Carl Williams, his sister Gretchen (Dunedin, New Zealand) presented Carl's vast collection of Gershwiniana (begun in Gershwin's lifetime) to Ed. From this, and his own comprehensive collection, Ed taped rare early performances, film scores, radio and television interviews, which he generously sent to me. As a film projectionist and recording engineer, Ed has supplied me with material long unavailable or never available here.

Anyone who has dealt with collectors (especially the obsessively acquisitive and possessive) can appreciate the thoughtful, selfless generosity of Eric, Bert and Ed.

A longstanding and special debt is owed by me to Ira Gershwin; it is personal and I won't dwell on it, except to say after my parents and my wife, Edith, he most shaped my professional life. Besides, he created some of my very favorite songs.

Members of my family also contributed to the shaping of this study: my sister, Mary Birdsall, Saginaw, Michigan; our children (no longer children, of course), Emily, Carla and David, have grown listening to the music of Gershwin (and Arlen, Berlin, Bartók, and Vaughan Williams and others). At various stages their views, I think, and ideas sharpened my perceptions.

Harold Kuebler, friend and editor (in that order), suggested that I do this book several years ago; we talked about it a good deal and finally, here it is. I only hope it is worthy of the subject and of him.

An Informal Discography and Videography

(1998 Edition)

What follows is a selective, often opinionated listing of recordings (available on compact disc only) of the works of George and Ira Gershwin—George first, as usual. Since the original publication of *Gershwin* a decade ago, several of the performances on long-playing records have gone out of print, while others have been transferred to CD with improved sound quality.

Since that earlier, now obsolete discography appeared, so have new recordings, further spurred by the celebration of the Gershwins' centennials —Ira's (1996) and George's (1998)—with concerts, revivals, recitals, and recordings. A definitive Gershwin discography is a daunting undertaking. The listing for *Rhapsody in Blue* in the Schwann *Opus* runs to nearly fifteen inches of fine print, a good reason for recommending selective recordings rather than extensively cataloging their work. The significant recordings are included and briefly discussed. There is inevitable duplication and inadvertently a worthy candidate may be slighted.

The complex numbering of CDs will be avoided; the record label should be sufficient. All record shops have Gershwin sections for the concert works, shows, and films—plus, in larger shops, computerized search systems. Addresses for independent companies with limited distribution are provided.

GEORGE GERSHWIN

1. GERSHWIN BY GERSHWIN

George Gershwin Plays George Gershwin. Vols. 1 & 2 (MASTERSOUND). These two CDs contain all of Gershwin's studio recordings, including those made with Fred and Adele Astaire in London in 1926, a couple of radio appearances on the "Rudy Vallee Hour," and a rehearsal recording of the *Sound Rhapsody* with Gershwin conducting from the piano. Volume 1 includes the electric (i.e., with microphone) recording of *Rhapsody in Blue*; Volume 2 includes the first acoustic (playing into a large horn). Gershwin is at the piano while Paul Whiteman conducts his Concert Orchestra. By the time the second recording was made in 1927, several of the original musicians had left White, some to form their own bands. So the first, made in October 1924, was probably the original cast of Whiteman's "Experiment in Modern Music," held the previous June. (By this time Ross Gorman, who had played the electrifying opening clarinet glissando, had left to form his own band). On the first volume there is a performance of "Swanee" made sometime in 1919 in Montreal with the Fred Van Eps Trio; the leader was a celebrated banjoist at the time. Gershwin is purportedly at the piano, but is difficult to discern through the banjo. The discs do not carry the address of MASTER-SOUND, but they are distributed by Allegro (14134 Northeast Airport Way, Portland, Oregon, 97230-3443). These excellent, reasonably priced discs provide a well-rounded, almost complete collection of Gershwin performing his works.

Gershwin Performs Gershwin (MUSIC MASTERS, 1710 Highway 3, Ocean City, New Jersey, 07712). The disc includes two of Gershwin's fifteen-minute radio programs: "Music by Gershwin" (1934) and an appearance of the Vallee show a couple of years earlier (some of which has been lifted from the MASTERSOUND discs; no matter, the broadcasts are in public domain). The prize of this collection is a rehearsal recording of the not-yet-complete *Porgy and Bess* with the original cast: Todd Duncan, Anne Brown, Ruby Elzy, Abbie Mitchell, and Edward Matthews. Gershwin conducts, speaks, and even contributes a little vocalizing in the introduction to "Summertime" by Mitchell, who never recorded her song commercially.

Elzy's "My Man's Gone Now" is stunning. Producer Russell L. Caplan reworked the old MARK 56 recordings, using the originals from the Gershwin Archive for the radio shows and the *Second Rhapsody* rehearsal. Considering the age and condition of the recordings, this collection is a remarkable job of reconstruction.

George Gershwin Plays George Gershwin (PEARL, two discs). This release covers the same territory as the MUSIC MASTERS and the MASTER-SOUNDS collections (the *Rhapsody in Blue* recording, the *Second Rhapsody* rehearsal, etc.). The major difference is the inclusion of excerpts from *Porgy and Bess* recorded under Gershwin's supervision four days after the opera's premiere. It is a curious effort: the singers are Lawrence Tibbett and Helen Jepson with their white Metropolitan-Opera voices. The Eva Jessye Choir and conductor Alexander Smallen from the opera were on hand for the sessions. But Duncan and Brown were too little known at the time, while Tibbett, especially, was riding high. An interesting novelty, but for the devoted specialist.

2. THE "SERIOUS" GERSHWIN

Lullaby (ca.1919). Gershwin's original exists in the form of a fragment for piano and as a string quartet prepared during his study with Edward Kilenyi (1919–21). In her CD **Gershwin Rediscovered, Vol. 2** (CARLTON CLASSICS), Alicia Zizzo performs the solo piano version based on the extant Gershwin manuscript. It is beautifully done in a distinguished collection. The string quartet is available as performed by the Kohan Quartet in **American String**

Quartets, 1900–1950 (VOX BOX, two discs). The performance is a bit slow, missing the work's rhythmic flow, although the melody comes through, as do the harmonies (this being a study in harmony). The fine recording by the Juilliard Quartet, the group that premiered the composition at the Library of Congress in 1967, is at this writing unfortunately out of print, but will probably be back. The string-quartet *Lullaby* is not Gershwin's orchestration but one prepared by the publisher; it is available on several discs.

Rhapsody in Blue (1924). The result of painstaking research, **Gershwin Rediscovered, Vol. 2** (originally **Gershwin by Gershwin**, CARLTON CLASSICS) brings together works by Gershwin performed according to original manuscripts. For years the bulk of the recorded performances were the edited versions of the publishers. This resulted in unnecessary deletions, "improved" orchestrations, and other corruptions by less talented musicians who believed they knew more about Gershwin than Gershwin. In this compilation the *Rhapsody in Blue* is played as Gershwin wrote it and as he played it at Aeolian Hall in 1924; several bars of the piano part have been restored. The *Concerto in F*, which suffered the least tampering, has also been corrected to reflect Gershwin's intention to balance the piano, orchestra, and tempos. The disc opens with the *Cuban Overture*, recorded for the first time with all the music intact. For years performances and recordings were lacking three bars that bring the overture to an exciting close. Conductor Michael Charry achieves an idiomatic performance with the Budapest Symphony. The recording spotlights the Cuban instruments that Gershwin featured by having the percussionists stand directly in front of the orchestra. Ms. Zizzo's sensitive reading of *Lullaby* rounds out the disc.

There appears to be no end of *Rhapsody* recordings, but a few should be mentioned. Gershwin's acerbic friend and favored interpreter Oscar Levant virtually built a career—concerts, recordings, recitals—as a Gershwin pianist who had been close to the source, a role of which he tired near the end of his unhappy life. He is at his peak in **Levant Plays Gershwin** (CBS) in performances recorded in the mid- and late-Forties under the direction of sympathetic conductors: Eugene Ormandy (*Rhapsody in Blue*, Philadelphia Orchestra), Andre Kostelanetz (the *Concerto in F*, New York Philharmonic), and Morton Gould (the *Second Rhapsody* and the *"I Got Rhythm" Variations*, the Columbia Symphony). Particularly valuable is the fact that these interpretations are based on Gershwin's own orchestrations before the tampering got under way. This is critical in the *Second Rhapsody* and *Variations*. As an encore Levant plays the *Three Preludes*. Another fascinating disc (taken from radio broadcasts mainly) is **Oscar Levant Plays Levant and Gershwin** (DRG RECORDS, 130 West 57th St., New York City, 10019). Compiled and produced by Gershwin devotee Michael Feinstein, the disc lets us hear Levant talk about Gershwin (from a World War II V-Disc) and perform the *Rhapsody in Blue* (Kostelanetz, cond.) as well as the final movement of the *Concerto in F* with another good Gershwin friend (William Daly) conducting. The reproduction of the 1934 broadcast transcription is less than excellent, but authoritative and historic. Levant's own works include quasi-operatic songs from the film *Charlie Chan at the Opera* as well as the splendid *Piano Sonatina* and the spiky Piano Concerto (proof positive that Levant studied with Arnold Schoenberg). Particularly treasurable are Levant's performances of several Gershwin songs (outtakes from the *An American in Paris* soundtrack) played in the style of Gershwin.

More radio broadcasts are the source for **Toscanini dirige Gershwin** (an Italian release, HUNT PRODUCTIONS, readily available). The *Rhapsody* with Earl Wild at the piano and Benny Goodman on clarinet (opening with the blooper of the year) was broadcast in 1942. Levant is the pianist in the 1944 broadcast. Toscanini conducts the NBC Symphony (as he does in the other works) in *An American in Paris* (recorded commercially for RCA). When Ira Gershwin heard about Toscanini's broadcast of the *Rhapsody*, he remarked, "Pretty enterprising of the old boy." The "old boy" was then 75. Enterprising indeed, for Toscanini performed, and recorded, little American music. Besides *An American in Paris*, he did Grofé's *Grand Canyon Suite* and Samuel Barber's *Adagio for Strings.*

Economical and excellently performed, **The Complete Gershwin** (VOX BOX, two discs) collects all the works for orchestra and piano and orchestra, from *Rhapsody in Blue* through *Catfish Row*, Gershwin's own suite from *Porgy and Bess*. Included also are *Promenade* (the "Walking the Dog" sequence from the film *Shall We Dance*) and the *Lullaby for Strings*. The idiomatic performances are conducted by Leonard Slatkin; the pianist is the very able Jeffry Siegel, accompanied by the St. Louis Symphony Orchestra. An extremely good buy.

There are several other performances of *Rhapsody in Blue* that can be recommended, particularly André Previn's (EMI CLASSICS, coupled with the *Concerto in F* and *An American in Paris*). Likewise, the performances conducted by Eric Kunzel and Andrew Litton, full of verve and authority, are superb, as are Earl Wild's performances with the Boston Pops (RCA, along with the *Concerto in F*, "*I Got Rhythm*" Variations, and *An American in Paris*). For years Leonard Bernstein's reading of the *Rhapsody* has been a favorite (though, in my view, it is mannered and overwrought); the disc (SONY) also contains *An American in Paris* and Bernstein's *Candide Overture*. Then, too, there is the old Boston Pops version conducted by Arthur Fiedler, with Jesus Maria Sanroma at the piano (RCA CAMDEN CLASSICS, along with the *Concerto in F*). The problem is not in finding fine—even extraordinary—readings of Gershwin's concert works, but in the profusion. This brings to mind the comment made by Oscar Levant's mother. In the early phase of Levant's concert career he was often asked to perform the *Rhapsody*. He hardly played anything else. When his mother heard he was scheduled to perform the work, she sighed and said, "Again the *Rhapsody*?" Levant was happy when he heard Gershwin had composed a concerto. "It doubled my repertoire," he quipped. The Marous Roberts interpretation in the CD *Portraits in Blue* is not the *Rhapsody* but a parody. The *Rhapsody* is a composition—not a pop tune. This performance is merely an improvisational arrangement.

Concerto in F (1925). Although not as frequently recorded as the *Rhapsody*, there are more than enough versions of the *Concerto*. Since every Gershwin devotee has the *Rhapsody*, the chances are excellent that he has the work that followed in its wake of noteriety and success. The releases of the Zizzo-Charry, Levant-Kostelanetz, Ormandy-Gould, Kunzel, and Litton recordings as well as the bargain Siegel-Slatkin compilations (and Slatkin's later re-recordings) are all admirable. The Wild-Fiedler disc is fine, as is the Previn-Previn. There is an especially involving performance of the *Concerto* by pianist Gwenneth Pryor, with Richard Williams conducting the London Symphony (PICKWICK). Eugene List and Howard Hanson, with the Eastman-Rochester Orchestra (MERCURY), is also notable.

Piano Preludes (1927). The must-have CD here is Alicia Zizzo's **Gershwin Rediscovered, Vol. 2** (CARLTON CLASSICS), in which she plays the six preludes Gershwin performed in his recitals with Marguerite D'Alvarez. Zizzo also includes a fragment, the seventh, which Gershwin used to open the final movement of the *Concerto in F*. The preludes were revised according to Gershwin manuscripts as well as radio and other recorded performances. There are two versions of the legendary "lost" prelude "Sleepless Night." The first is the intended, and probably performed, prelude from Gershwin's manuscript and Kay Swift's arrangement at a time when Ira Gershwin planned to use it for the song "Sleepless Night" (but never did). The performance is exemplary. Other Gershwin treasures fill out the collection. The three published *Piano Preludes* are well represented in renditions by Levant, David Buechner (CONNOISSEUR

SOCIETY), Richard Glazier (CENTAUR), Paul Bisaccia (VISTA, 41-C Willard St., Hartford, Connecticut, 06105), and Dorothy Lewis-Griffith (ETCETERA).

An American in Paris (1928). The same recommendations apply to recordings of this work as to those of the *Concerto in F*. If you have a well-performed *Rhapsody in Blue*, you probably have a fine *An American in Paris*. But here are some additional remarks. Leonard Bernstein has recorded the composition several times. Recently reissued, **Leonard Bernstein, The Early Years** (BMG-RCA GOLD SEAL) is one of his most exciting. This was his first recording, made in 1947, when he was adventurous in respect to repertoire, as evidenced in the other pieces that fill out this CD: Ravel's *Piano Concerto in G*, Bernstein's ballet *Facsimile*, and the *Jingo* section from Copland's *Statements for Orchestra*. A disc to treasure.

Bernstein is present as well in Gerard Schwartz and the Seattle Symphony's **Bernstein/Barber/Gershwin** (DELOS). Barber's *School for Scandal Overture* and Bernstein's final composition (orchestrated by Bright Sheng), *Airs and Barcarolles*, are coupled with *An American in Paris*. What makes this rendition special is that Schwartz uses Gershwin's original manuscript for the recording and performs it as written, restoring some three minutes to the score. It would appear that conductor Walter Damrosch excised them before the premiere, and Gershwin let the deletion stand for the recording by Nathaniel Shilkret, with Gershwin on hand and at the celeste for the session.

Dayful of Song (DELOS) brings together *An American in Paris*, *Cuban Overture*, *Rhapsody in Blue*, and *Lull-*

aby. The Dallas Symphony is conducted by Andrew Litton, who also supplies the piano wherever needed. The title track, *Dayful of Song* (Lawrence D. Stewart, Gershwin estate archivist, suggested the apposite title from an Ira Gershwin lyric), is a suite of seven unpublished Gershwin melodies arranged and orchestrated by Sid Ramin for piano and orchestra. One could only wish for more. The performances are outstanding and the sound quality is stunning.

Second Rhapsody (1931, premiered January 1932). There are excellent performances by Levant-Gould, Siegel-Slatkin, Goodyear-Kunzel (TELARC), and Michael Tilson Thomas conducting the Los Angeles Philharmonic (CBS). This last disc includes the *Rhapsody* and several unpublished songs from the Gershwin Melodies Collection. Thomas arranged these for the recording and could not avoid touching up the little pieces with his own "realizations." Gershwin is better served by Alicia Zizzo. Unfortunately Arthur Fiedler's recording on LONDON's Phase 4 Series uses the reorchestrated version of the *Second Rhapsody*, made by Robert McBride after Gershwin's death.

Cuban Overture (1932). The performances conducted by Michael Charry and Andrew Litton, from Gershwin's manuscript, are complete and well done. Kay Swift, who was familiar with Gershwin's works, was partial to the earlier recording (available again on CD) in which Howard Hanson conducts the Eastman-Rochester Orchestra (MERCURY). The Litton recording is exceptionally vibrant and idiomatic; besides, it comes with the delightful *Dayful of Song*.

George Gershwin's Songbook (1932). When Ira Gershwin compiled a list of his brother's works, his title for this collection of Gershwin arrangements was *Piano Transcriptions of 18 Songs*. Several recorded versions use the other title. My favorites are those by Richard Rodney Bennett (PICKWICK; along with the *Preludes, Jazzbo Brown* from *Porgy and Bess*, and several songs arranged by the pianist); Paul Bisaccia (VISTA RECORDS, 41-C Willard St., Hartford, Connecticut, 06105); and William Bolcom (ELEKTRA/NONESUCH). These discs contain several other piano pieces and songs.

"I Got Rhythm" Variations (1934). Gershwin's radio introduction and performance have been noted in the "Gershwin by Gershwin" section. The outstanding, most modern recordings are those by Levant-Gould, Siegel-Slatkin, Tritt-Kunzel, and Wild-Fiedler. In this little composition, written for Gershwin's 1934 cross-country tour marking the tenth anniversary of *Rhapsody in Blue*, and dedicated to "My Brother Ira," the composer manifests a mastery of pianistic pyrotechnics and a sparkling wit. It reveals that George had taken his study with Joseph Schillinger seriously.

Catfish Row (1936) is Gershwin's own *Porgy and Bess* suite, renamed by Ira Gershwin to distinguish it from Robert Russell Bennett's *Symphonic Picture*. The composer's is longer, virtually a précis of the score; Bennett's is in the form of highlights, skillfully bridged and faithful to Gershwin's orchestration. Gershwin's suite is fuller, beginning with the introduction and closing with "I'm on My Way." *Catfish Row* retains the highlights, but incorporates some music and songs eliminated during the Boston tryout—the *Jazzbo Brown* piano music, "I Hates Yo' Struttin' Style," the wild "I Ain't Got No Shame," and the atmospheric "Occupational Humoresque" from Act III.

Again, there is an embarrassment of riches, but you can't go wrong with Kunzel, James Levine (DEUTSCHE GRAMOPHONE), and Slatkin. Bennett's *Symphonic Picture* is fine in its way, and all that we had for several years (till Lawrence D. Stewart found *Catfish Row*, ca.1958, while assembling the Gershwin Archive for the Library of Congress). Possibly, had its existence been known when Fritz Reiner commissioned Bennett's *Symphonic Picture*, it would have been Gershwin's suite that would have been done. It was originally conducted in 1936 by Gershwin and *Porgy* conductor Alexander Smallens in concerts following the tour of *Porgy and Bess*, and forgotten after that tour ran out of steam following Gershwin's death a year later. Recordings of Bennett's suite exist, including a version he conducts; it is generally coupled with works by Bernstein, Grofé, and others.

3. THE OPERAS

Blue Monday (1922). There are three recordings of Gershwin's first venture into opera. The earliest recording by Gregg Smith and his chorus, first issued on a long-playing disc, has not been reissued on CD. Marin Alsop conducts her Concordia Orchestra and soloists for the ANGEL-label version. It also includes Ferde Grofé's occasionally unfortunate reorchestrated version of the *Concerto in F*, which was issued in Gershwin's lifetime and which he did not like. Equally unfortunate is the fact that Ms. Alsop used the orchestration created by George Bass-

man for an early presentation of the opera on television. At that time, the original orchestration by Will Vodary was "lost." The later reworking by Ferde Grofé for a 1925 performance at Carnegie Hall was well received critically and exists in a copy at the Lincoln Center Library. In all fairness, I must admit that, as customary, Alsop's conducting is superb (in her concerts she reveals a flair for adventurous repertoire); that the middle movement of the *Concerto in F* is quite beautiful in Grofé's treatment; and that the inclusion of the brief (about $8^{1}/_{2}$ minutes) yet fascinating *Caprice for Orchestra* by Oscar Levant is worth the price of admission.

Now the good news. Gershwin lover Erich Kunzel found the original Will Vodary orchestration of *Blue Monday* (it was, rather mysteriously, already there when the Alsop recording was made). Kunzel's recording of the opera was issued on the TELARC label. Needless to say, the performance is impeccable, flavorful, and idiomatic. The disc is filled out with selections from *Porgy and Bess*, includ- ing the "lost" duet "Lonely Boy."

Porgy and Bess (1935). In order of appearance, there are three complete recordings of this classic in which all the deleted songs and music are restored and Gershwin's original orchestration is used. All are beautifully accomplished and admirably recorded. The first to be released (1986) was based on a concert performance of *Porgy and Bess* (LONDON, three discs) by the Cleveland Orchestra and Chorus, conducted by Lorin Maazel. I confess it is my favorite, because of its musical understanding and because Gershwin comes first throughout. The following year the Houston Grand Opera's production, conducted by John DeMain (RCA, three discs), engendered much excitement in theaters and in the record industry. The recording was produced by theaterwise Thomas Z. Shepard and the result is a more theatrical—dice rolling, cotton hook flung to the floor—adaptation than Maazel's. The most recent is the widely praised Glyndebourne Festival Opera version with the London Philharmonic, conducted by Simon Rattle (EMI, three discs). London Philharmonic? The Glyndebourne Chorus? And Simon Rattle? Yet, it sounds great. (Interestingly, Willard White is the "Porgy" on this recording as well as on the early Maazel-Cleveland version). All the leads are American-trained singers; the British chorus has their Americanisms down pat. And Rattle is definitely a Gershwinite. Incidentally, this set was used (with lip-synching) for the video (PICTURE MUSIC INTERNATIONAL). If you get the video, you get the album.

There are numerous collections, including single CDs, of "selections" from the complete opera. Take your pick. Here are mine. The recording by members of the successful revival of *Porgy and Bess* (MCA CLASSICS) dates back to the early Forties. From the 1935 production there are several veteran performers—Todd Duncan, Anne Brown, Edward Matthews, and Georgette Harvey (who appeared in the original play, the original opera, and this revival). Also present are the Eva Jessye Choir and conductor Alexander Smallens. The transfers are excellent—maybe a little hiss, but not intrusive. These artists, along with the Gershwins and DuBose Heyward, made history with this masterwork.

Another revival—a joint effort by Blevins Davis and Robert Breen, who also directed—resulted in an extraordinary album, **Porgy and Bess–Highlights** (RCA VICTOR). The leads of that production (which virtually toured the world), Leontyne Price and William Warfield, recreate their roles as "Bess" and "Porgy." The RCA Victor Orchestra is conducted with fine understanding by Skitch Henderson, and the Chorus by Leonard de Paur. Baritone McHenry Boatwright sings the songs of "Crown" and the original "Sportin' Life," John W. Bubbles, makes a special appearance. Altogether, a set to cherish.

Cherishable also is the endearing **Porgy & Bess/Ella Fitzgerald and Louis Armstrong** (VERVE). A bit offbeat perhaps for the purist (although this set, when initially released on LP, pleased Ira Gershwin), the whole undertaking exudes warmth, affection, and a supreme imaginative musicality. Russell Garcia conducts his reorchestrations (without doing violence to Gershwin) to complement the vocals and Armstrong's trumpet. This is an album to own.

Further afield is **Miles Davis–Porgy and Bess** (COLUMBIA). Gil Evans conducts his special orchestration with a band of nineteen musicians (including composer Gunther Schuller on the French horn) in some of the most inventive interpretations of Gershwin themes ever recorded. (Surprisingly, considering the bold variations, Ira Gershwin admired these performances, too.) Davis seems to play slightly to the left of the melody, but with an appealing tone and wondrous turns of melody and rhythm. And the first-rate band follows adroitly with great musicianship.

4. BROADWAY

Lady, Be Good! (1924). This is one in a series of five Gershwin musicals produced under the aegis of Leonore Gershwin and the Library of Congress (before her death Ira Gershwin's widow set up a fund to establish the joint project) and released by NONESUCH RECORDS. All shows were restored—so far as it was possible—to their original complete form, and used the original orchestrations (if they existed) or authentic restorations (in the case of *Lady, Be Good!*, Larry Wilcox and Russell Warner). The search for the score, parts, and lyrics was accomplished by Tommy Krasker. The result is a close approximation of the original production; conductor Eric Stern firmly but gently, and with proper verve, sets the jazzy tone. An added touch is the use of duo-pianos in the orchestra, as Gershwin had in several of his shows. A youthful cast captures the spirit of the Gershwin brothers' first major Broadway musical. It is especially pleasurable to hear such neglected, unpublished gems as "We're Here Because," "Little Jazz Bird" (recreating Cliff Edward's rendition—this time with John Pizzarelli on the ukulele), and the instrumental "Carnival Time." The wonderful choral work reminds us that Gershwin was a master of writing for groups. An important contribution.

Oh, Kay! (1926) is, in my view, the prize of the series. It owes much to the presence of Dawn Upshaw (performing Gertrude Lawrence's songs); Kevin Cole for his vocal arrangements and the reconstruction of Gershwin's two-piano scoring; and Eric Stern for conducting the Orchestra of St. Luke's. Fine voices, solo and choral, do full justice to the score. It is a pleasure to hear such standards as "Someone to Watch Over Me," "Do, Do, Do," "Clap Yo' Hands," "Dear Little Girl," "Don't Ask," and "Ain't It Romantic." There are also delightful appearances by television-star Susan Lucci and actor Fritz Weaver (who, as a judge, never sounded stuffier!).

Strike Up the Band (1927/1930) is the most ambitious of the series, combining the scores of the productions of both shows; the first flopped, but the second became the first Gershwin hit of 1930. In this two-disc set John Mauceri conducts a fine orchestra and vocalists. Most of the 1927 score is intact, bringing back the ingenuous "17 and 21," the mock pastorale "Meadow Serenade" (with the verse set to music by Gershwin friend and Ira-collaborator Burton Lane; the original music to the verse having been lost), and the plaintive "Homeward Bound." The second disc consists of songs fashioned for the 1930 revision/revival, including the lovely "Soon."

Girl Crazy (1930) was the Gershwins' final fling with the Jazz Age musical and minimal plot, but contains plenty of laughs and some wonderful songs. Because the show was a success, the orchestrations by Robert Russell Bennett survived. The instrumental and choral numbers highlight Gershwin's genius, a musical instinct not taught in conservatories. When hearing these songs and Gershwin's transitions, it is a mystery that listeners at the time were confounded to learn that he also wrote works for symphony orchestras and an opera. *Girl Crazy* was a hit-rich musical, but Gershwin's more experimental creations—"Could You Use Me?," "Sam and Delilah," "But Not for Me," and "Boy! What Love Has Done to Me!"—have long been favorites among connoisseurs of fine song writing. John Mauceri conducts the cast.

Pardon My English (1933) was a major Gershwin flop, but also one of the brothers' most inventive scores. Only two songs achieved circulation among the cognoscenti—"My Cousin in Milwaukee" and "Isn't It a Pity?"—in a score that ripples with waltzes, some written with tongue-in-*both*-cheeks ("In Three-Quarter Time" and "Dancing in the Streets," for example). There are also contrapuntal waltzes, "Tonight" and "Deep in the Heart of Me," sung both separately and together. Gershwin performed these pieces with Kay Swift at the second piano, which led Ira to call the first "His Waltz," the second "Her Waltz," and the final chorus "Their Waltz." There is a sunny ballad, "Luckiest Man in the World," as well as superior rhythm numbers like "Where You Go, I Go" and "I've Got to Be There." A good deal of the score is plot-related (what plot survived by the time the musical arrived in New York to linger for only a month). The witty, at times wicked, "Freud and Jung and Adler" ("He's oversexed/ He's undersexed/He hasn't any sex at all") must have mystified what little audience remained. The Gershwins took on this job reluctantly. Ira did not like the book at all and was upset when he learned that the long-lost score had been rediscovered in Seacaucus, New Jersey. Despite their reluctance they produced a spirited score. Eric Stern does well by it. This release, like the other NONESUCH discs, is boxed and includes a substantial booklet of the lyrics (researched and restored by Tommy Krasker), essays, and photos.

Of Thee I Sing (1931)/**Let 'Em Eat Cake** (1933) form a two-disc set conducted by Michael Tilson Thomas (CBS RECORDS), as restored by Tommy Krasker for presentation at the Brooklyn Academy of Music in 1987. It is a must for every Gershwin collection, with every word clear and well sung, pointing up again Gershwin's mastery of choral and orchestral writing. The political operettas (which include *Strike Up the Band),* though comedic, are a satiric view of American politics, made palatable by the freshness and wit of the words and music. Although *Of Thee I Sing*'s sequel—employing the same characters, including the peerless "Throttlebottom"—was a failure with a limited run and with only one song (the contrapuntal "Mine") that survived the show, it is one of the Gershwins' most dazzling scores. The "Union Square" scene is worthy of Gilbert and Sullivan. "Blue, Blue, Blue" is melodic Gershwin at his most sophisticated, while the sequence in which Throttlebottom is to be guillotined is a marvel of choral writing. Ira Gershwin attributed the failure of *Let 'Em Eat Cake* to the bitterness of the Kaufman-Ryskind book, "a satire on practically everything. Straddling no fence, it trampled the Extreme Right one moment, the Extreme Left the next—at times unrelentingly realistic in its criticism of the American scene." Where are those guys now when we need them?

5. HOLLYWOOD

George and Ira Gershwin in Hollywood. This two-CD set (TURNER CLASSIC MOVIES) compiles soundtrack excerpts from more than a dozen films (plus a track from a short by Artie Shaw) and includes a generous selection from *Shall We Dance*—songs performed by Astaire and Rogers as well as the "Walking the Dog" instrumental. The first of their Hollywood musicals, *Delicious*, is represented by "Delishious." From *A Damsel in Distress* Astaire sings several songs; from *The Goldwyn Follies* Ella Logan sings the complete "I Was Doing All Right," and we hear "Love Walked In" but not as used in the final film. Keeping track of the tracks is a fascinating education in itself, considering the extensive outtakes and extended versions. Gene Kelly partially redeems the *Goldwyn* flop with the classic "Love Is Here to Stay." There are excerpts from two filmings of *Girl Crazy*, neither of which quite recreates the original Broadway show. For the first, the Gershwins wrote an additional song, "You've Got What Gets Me," sung by a trio from the original film. The later *Girl Crazy* starred Judy Garland and Mickey Rooney performing songs from the show. There are other excellent tracks like the selections from *Rhapsody in Blue* (beginning with the unheard orchestral overture), Jolson singing his "Swanee," and a condensed *Blue Monday*. Important, too, are the excerpts from *An American in Paris* (including Oscar Levant's cut *Third Prelude*). The many fine touches include a couple of examples of Ira's later work with Harry Warren ("You'd Be Hard to Replace," sung by Astaire from *The Barkleys of Broadway*) and with Burton Lane ("In Our United State," as interpreted by Bob Fosse in *Give a Girl a Break*). The elaborate, annotated, illustrated booklet accompanying the two-disc set keeps all the contents straight.

A cognate, though not all-Gershwin, anthology is **Starring Fred Astaire** (COLUMBIA, two discs). His interpretations of songs from *Shall We Dance* and *A Damsel in Distress* were recorded around the time the films were shot. Accompanied by the piano and band of Johnny Green, the selections are evocative, stylish, and exactly right. Extra bonuses include songs from the Irving Berlin and Jerome Kern films in which Astaire appeared.

Other Gershwin-scored soundtracks filmed after the composer's death include, in order of release, **Girl Crazy** (RHINO), **An American in Paris** (RHINO, two discs), and **Funny Face** (VERVE). *Girl Crazy* stars Judy Garland and Mickey Rooney with help from the Tommy Dorsey Orchestra. The complete score of seven songs is augmented with outtakes, alternate versions, and extended sequences. Especially recommended are the dazzling pianistics of Mickey Rooney, playing with the Dorsey Orchestra, in "Fascinating Rhythm," which was borrowed from *Lady, Be Good!*. The same format and value found in the *Girl Crazy* release apply to *An American in Paris*. The film is a recognized classic, Arthur Freed's highpoint at M-G-M (though one must not overlook *Singin' in the Rain* and *The Band Wagon*). Gene Kelly, George Guetary, and Oscar Levant supply the musical moments— Levant even sings a bit. There are also band instrumentals by the Benny Carter Orchestra. Especially venerable are several solos by Levant, some of which were eliminated from the final cut of the film. As usual, the accompanying booklet is replete with stills, set photos, recording dates, and other information. *Funny Face*, in its way another classic film, brings us Fred Astaire, who reprises a few of the songs he sang in the original *Funny Face* of 1927, including the lovely "He Loves and She Loves," which segues into one of the film's outstanding dances between Astaire and a radiant Audrey Hepburn. Kay Thompson lends her voice to some of the Roger Edens–Leonard Gershe interpolations, while Hepburn's "How Long Has This Been Going On?" is enchanting.

6. SONG COLLECTIONS

Preeminent in this category is **Ella Fitzgerald Sings the George and Ira Gershwin Songbooks** (VERVE, three discs), a 59-song treasury released in 1959. The collaboration between Fitzgerald and arranger-conductor Nelson Riddle sets a standard rarely matched in this kind of undertaking. Little more need be said than that this was one of Ira Gershwin's favorite collections, and he could be quite exacting, though he was rarely publicly critical. He liked Lee Wiley's singing, but not when she sang "It's Wonderful" instead of "'S Wonderful." Ira's comment on a male singer who waywardly dropped the final "g" in verbs (comin', treatin') was "He's too cozy with the endings."

A Gershwin alumnus, Michael Feinstein has recorded **Pure Gershwin** (ELEKTRA) and **Nice Work If You Can Get It** (ATLANTIC), two collections that bring to light several lesser-known or unpublished Gershwin songs (this is especially so in the ATLANTIC release). His attention to the lyric (no coziness here) and respect for the melody and harmonies are true to the Gershwin tradition. These are *not* reverential interpretations; the Gershwinesque fun is present, the wit and playfulness that too often gets lost in a display of stylized distortion (Ira usually termed this "taking liberties"). Feinstein has a deep affection for this music (and the words, too), as he also demonstrates in his recordings of songs by Burton Lane and Hugh Martin.

Frances Gershwin's **For George and Ira** (AUDIOPHILE RECORDS, 1206 Decatur St., New Orleans, Louisiana, 70116) was reissued in time for her 80th birthday (December 1996). It is difficult to believe that the youthful voice heard in this supreme song collection belongs to a woman of 66. Frankie Gershwin had a brief fling in show business as a little girl, accompanied by a tough stage mother, and later in Paris and New York. She gave this up for marriage, motherhood, and painting; luckily for us, she was talked into doing this album, which may possibly be one of the most charming Gershwin recordings ever made. She is accompanied by Gershwin friend Alfred Simon (who heard Gershwin accompany sister Frankie at their now legendary parties) and Jack Easton.

Lee Wiley Sings (AUDIOPHILE) collects her recordings, originally released in 1940 on 78-rpm shellac discs that became instant collector's items. She devoted one album to the songs of the Gershwins and another to those of Cole Porter. Her accompanists include legendary jazz musicians of the period: Pee Wee Russell, Joe Bushkin, Bud Freeman, Max Kaminsky, Bunny Berigan, and even Fats Waller (using the *nom de disque* of "Maurice" —he was under contract to another recording company). Gershwin was an admirer of Lee Wiley and so was Ira—except for Wiley's slow-tempoed "I've Got a Crush on You" and the previously mentioned "'S Wonderful."

Another vocal collection worth exploring is **He Loves and She Loves** (KOCH INTERNATIONAL), featuring the resplendent voices of Judy Kaye and William Sharp with the gifted pianist-arranger Steven Blier. This is an intelligently inclusive disc with a good sampling of some Gershwin rarities, fine duets, and solos.

The husband-wife team of Joan Morris and William Bolcom sing and play Gershwin with a delightful period flair in **The George Gershwin Songbook** (NONESUCH). Ms. Morris, with her trained mezzo-soprano voice, charmingly evokes the musical-comedy soubrette of the Twenties. Her husband's attentive and apposite accompaniment is admirable.

These are but a handful of Gershwin song anthologies, of which there are more than enough, especially of the "standards." Now that the Gershwin Melodies Collection is being explored and full scores are being recorded, there will be an even *wider* selection from which to choose.

7. KEYBOARDS

The Authentic George Gershwin (ASV, three discs, boxed, also available singly), taken as a whole, is nothing less than a comprehensive survey of the works of Gershwin—songs and concert works—from 1918 to 1937. The young English pianist Jack Gibbons, a latecomer to Gershwin, became enamored with the American composer on hearing a recording of Gershwin himself performing one of his own works. Gibbons neglected Chopin and Alkan, among others, to delve into Gershwin. He studied recordings, broadcasts, and piano rolls; transcribed Gershwin's performances; and then performed

them in successful recitals, from London's Royal Albert Hall to New York's Merkin Hall. He is an astonishingly prodigious pianist; his Gershwin performances are impeccable and authentic. There are more than three hours of music on these discs—all played with flair, relish, and Gershwinesque virtuosity. The collection begins with "Swanee" and closes with "Our Love Is Here to Stay" (which Gershwin did not record; Gibbons provides his own true-to-Gershwin arrangement). All the large works are included, from *Rhapsody in Blue* to Gibbons's astonishing transcription of *Catfish Row*. The *Second Rhapsody* is likewise stunning. The *Concerto in F* is represented by only the slow second movement—the pianist concluded that the outer sections of the work required an orchestra. Some of the lesser-known songs are "Come to the Moon" (1918), "When Do We Dance?" (1925), "Jilted" (1931), and "Meadow Serenade" (1927).

In its initial release Kevin Cole's brilliant performances of Gershwin's work—especially his uncanny emulation of Gershwin himself—were titled **Lady Be Good or The Unknown George Gershwin** (PRO-ARTS, 1984). In 1997, in time for the Gershwin centennial, it will be re-released by CARLTON CLASSICS. This is one of my favorites among Gershwin releases (and I am not alone). Many who had known Gershwin, heard him play, or shared keyboards with him were astonished when they heard a teen-aged pianist from Michigan who had never heard a Gershwin performance—not even on records—play the music (songs as well as concert works) so much like Gershwin himself. The point of this CD was to collect some of the lesser-known works, ranging from the *Lady, Be Good!* overture to such discarded efforts as "Wake Up, Brother, and Dance" and "Just Another Rhumba" (one of Gershwin's last compositions). There is also a medley from *Primrose*, the British musical never produced in the United States, as well as a Cole-arranged waltz medley. After eliminating the violin portion of *Short Story*, which had been arranged by Samuel Dushkin from two of Gershwin's early novelettes for piano and violin, Cole performs the *Novelette in Fourths* and *Rubato* (later incorporated into Gershwin's *Preludes* performances, though not published). The booklet credits me as "Production Supervisor"; true, I dug up some of the musical material and helped plan the program, but Kevin did the rest. (I did turn pages when needed). Anton Kwiatkowski, who recorded the excellent sound, also contributed several suggestions, which Kevin took with his customary good humor and grace.

Gershwin Rediscovered, Vol. 2 (CARLTON CLASSICS). Another treasure. Pianist Alicia Zizzo has devoted the past several years to discovering unpublished Gershwiniana and restoring concert work to their original form as conceived by Gershwin. All six *Preludes* were found in manuscript form, on recordings, or from radio broadcasts. The works performed on this disc are a revelation: the *Blue Monday Suite*, which fares better without the DeSylva lyrics; *Rhapsody in Blue*; the several Gershwin Archive pieces (most intended as possible songs), including the lovely "Three Note Waltz"; and Kay Swift's arrangement of "Sleepless Night," based on a *Prelude*. Anton Kwiatkowski is again

responsible for the superlative sound. American music, musicians, and just plain Gershwin lovers are in debt to Alicia Zizzo for dedicating herself to the genius of George Gershwin.

George Gershwin–A Piano Solo Album (ETCETERA) is just that—but with a difference. Pianist Dorothy Lewis-Griffith transcribed *Rhapsody in Blue* and the *Concerto in F* for solo piano and performs them with poetry, vivacity, and a sense of style. Her *Preludes* (released before Zizzo's) are fine. She rounds out the collection with Cy Walter's stylization of "Bidin' My Time." Frankly, I had some initial doubts that this approach, especially in the case of the *Concerto*, would work. It does indeed.

Rhapsody in Blue–Gershwin's Complete Solo Piano Music (VISTA, 41-C Willard St., Hartford, Connecticut, 06105) is a neat collection of the solo piano music known up to the time of the recording (1994). Besides the *Rhapsody*, there are the *Three Preludes*, the *Two Waltzes in C*, *Merry Andrew*, *Promenade* ("Walking the Dog"), *Impromptu in 2 Keys* ("Yellow Blues"), *Rialto Ripples*, and the complete *Song Book* (stylishly and idiomatically played by classically trained Paul Bisaccia).

Another brilliant, classically trained pianist, David Buechner, has recorded **George Gershwin–Original Piano Works and Transcriptions for Solo Piano** (CONNOISSEUR SOCIETY). He plays not only the first but also the *Second Rhapsody*, several songs (including the Gershwin-Swift "Sleepless Night"), and the *Preludes*.

Rhythmic Moments (PREMIERE RECORDINGS, Box 1214, Gracie Station, New York, 10028-0008), though not all-Gershwin, is valuable, in part, because of the non-Gershwin activity. Like all the trained pianists already discussed, Joseph Smith is familiar with the standard concert repertoire and, like them, plays compositions that fall between those artificial categories of "popular" and "serious." In this collection he plays Gershwin's *Novelette in Fourths*, *Rubato* (from Gershwin's manuscript), and "Sleepless Night." There are also wonderful excursions into the "serious" Stephen Foster; contributions from Victor Herbert, Scott Joplin, and James P. Johnson; Bix Beiderbecke's delightful *In a Mist*, *Flashes*, *Candlelight*, and *In the Dark*; Harold Arlen's early rag, *Rhythmic Moments*, and his later ones, *Ode* and *Bonbon*; an interesting Ellington work; and Oscar Levant's prickly *Sonatina*. Even without Gershwin, this would be a fetching collection of Musical Americana.

8. PIANO ROLLS

There are several recordings of Gershwin's early piano rolls of his compositions and those by Jerome Kern and Irving Berlin. The rolls were punched before Gershwin was known as a songwriter and celebrated as a bright, young, teenaged pianist. He was soon discovered and actually cut rolls of his first song, "When You Want 'Em," in 1916 when he was eighteen, and the early *Novelette in Fourths* in 1919. Until he began making rolls for the more sophisticated Duo-Art piano, Gershwin's rolls had a mechanical, rushed sound. The notes are his, as are the arrangements; some rolls were made with a second pianist or Gershwin himself cutting over the original recording. In the early Twenties one activated parlor pianolas by pumping

one's foot and adjusting the tempo with a lever; a piano roll sounded like a piano roll and *not* a pianist performing in your living room. It was close, however, when the Welte or Duo-Art systems made the use of dynamics possible. The more primitive sound of Gershwin performing may be found on the KLAVIER and PRO-ARTS labels.

The most remarkable re-creation of Gershwin's rolls began in 1993 and concluded in 1995 with the releases of **Gershwin Plays Gershwin–The Piano Rolls** and **George Gershwin–The Piano Rolls, Volume Two** (both NONESUCH). Pianist Artis Wodehouse spent years "realizing" the transfer of Gershwin's performances from paper to computerized disc for reproduction on the Yamaha Disklavier (she explains this in her literate notes). The result is an unusually life-like sound. The first disc is all-Gershwin: the *Novelette in Fourths*, *Rhapsody in Blue*, several songs, and *An American in Paris* (cut in 1933, and performed, four-hands, by Frank Milne). The second disc contains a couple of Gershwin pieces, "From Now On" (1919) and the instrumental *Rialto Ripples* (1917); the rest re-creates the Tin Pan Alley phase of Gershwin's career with songs or instrumentals by Schonberger, Akst, Conard, Robinson, Lewis, Young, and Matthews—sixteen selections altogether. Quite an accomplishment for the indefatigable Artis Wodehouse.

The Smithsonian recently issued a comprehensive collection of Gershwin that could serve as *the* single source for his works. **I Got Rhythm–The Music of George Gershwin** (SMITHSONIAN INSTITUTION, 7955 Angus Court, Springfield, Virginia, 22153-2846; four discs or cassettes). This set is perfect for the

Gershwin devotee who does not wish to wallow in specialization. There are plenty of vintage recordings by Gershwin himself; vocals by Irene Bordoni, Gertrude Lawrence, Fred Astaire and Ginger Rogers, Judy Garland, Lena Horne, Bing Crosby, and Ella Fitzgerald; and jazzy interpretations by Duke Ellington, Tommy Dorsey, Benny Goodman, and Miles Davis. Those who want a thoughtfully selected overview will find this collection the ideal choice.

IRA GERSHWIN—MOSTLY WITHOUT GEORGE

At the top of the list is **Delicious–Lyrics by Ira Gershwin** (OAKTON RECORDINGS, 70 Allston St., Boston, Massachusetts, 02134). Although not "all-Ira *sans* George," this is a, well, delicious program conceived and amicably served by vocalist Benjamin Sears and pianist Bradford Connor (lending his voice to a couple of songs as well). What is outstanding—besides the knowing performances—is the comprehensiveness of the program, which opens with the instrumental *Rialto Ripples*, leading into the first Gershwin collaboration, "The Real American Folk Song." There are other rare Gershwin efforts—"Just to Know You Are Mine," "Blah, Blah, Blah," and "Just Another Rhumba." There is a quintet of "Arthur Francis" lyrics with music by the likes of Lewis Gensler, Paul Lannin, and the great Vincent Youmans. Later songs are by Harold Arlen, Vernon Duke, Kurt Weill, Jerome Kern, Arthur Schwartz, and Aaron Copland. It makes one wish for a Volume Two; meanwhile, treasure this intelligent and beautifully presented tribute to Ira.

There are four "Ladies in the Dark." The first **Lady in the Dark**, starring the original performers Gertrude Lawrence and MacDonald Carey, is taken from a radio broadcast ca.1941. There is dialogue and a good selection of songs, though not the complete score. The prize is Gertrude Lawrence in her role as Liza Elliot, the lady who could not make up her mind. This release is available from the AEI label (P. O. Box 21036, Los Angeles, California, 90006). The next version (also AEI) stars Ann Southern in a 1954 television production. It contains more of the songs as well as several of Gertrude Lawrence's renditions from the 1941 RCA VICTOR album and from the radio broadcast. More comprehensive than the others, the third *Lady in the Dark* (COLUMBIA SONY CLASSICAL) stars a radiant Rose Stevens and costars John Reardon and, in the role originated by Danny Kaye, lyricist Adolph Green. Virtually the complete score uses Weill's orchestration. This was one of the outstanding albums issued by Columbia Records during its rich Goddard-Lieberson years. Produced by Jim Fogelsong and Thomas Z. Shepard with careful attention to musical and lyrical detail, this album is, to borrow a phrase, pure delight, and there is much more (particularly Danny Kaye's 1941 recordings of six songs from the show, including "Tschaikowsky and Other Russian," which made him a Broadway star). Gershwin and Weill are very well served in this beautifully packed CD. Lastly, a truly complete *Lady in the Dark* (JAY PRODUCTIONS) was re-released in the spring of 1998, featuring the superb cast from the Royal National Theatre production presented in London the year before. All the music is here, as are all the lyrics and Kurt Weill's orchestrations. The cast is excellent. One of the better show albums of the year—or any year.

Tryout (DRG RECORDS, 130 West 57th Street, New York City, 10019). Primarily a Kurt Weill collection in which he sings and accompanies himself in songs from *One Touch of Venus*, lyrics by Ogden Nash. These recordings were taken from acetate demonstration records ("demos") that had been made privately for producers, casts, and directors by the songwriters as an aid in setting tempos, lyric emphasis, and even pronunciation. A better pianist than vocalist (in fact, no vocalist at all), Weill makes a good case for his songs. Non-vocalist Gershwin joins him in songs from their imaginative film *Where Do We Go From Here?*, such as their opera spoof, "The Niña, the Pinta, the Santa Maria" (one of the longest musical sequences filmed at that time), and the anti-Nazi "Song of the Rhineland." (The film was released in 1945, near the close of World War II.)

A more generous collection of demos was available on an album released by MARK 56 RECORDS, a label that no longer exists. Titled **Ira Gershwin Loves to Rhyme**, it contains all of *Where Do We Go From Here?* ("All at Once" and "If Love Remains," which are not on *Tryout*); songs from *The*

Firebrand of Florence (Weill), and *Give a Girl a Break* (Burton Lane, who also plays piano and sings—quite well); and Harold Arlen's deft performances of "If That's Propaganda" and "The Man That Got Away." A two-LP set, .the album may still be found in collector shops at what may be considered a decidedly *un*pretty penny.

Kurt Weill on Broadway (ANGEL) features the big-but-flexible voice of Thomas Hampson, assisted by Elizabeth Futral, Jerry Hadley, Jeanne Lehman, and the London Sinfoniette Chorus and Orchestra (directed by American musical theater scholar and devotee John McGlinn). There are songs with lyrics by Paul Green, Maxwell Anderson, Ogden Nash, and Alan Jay Lerner. The Ira Gershwin section brings together generous portions (the entire first scene of Act I and excerpts from Act II) from their great failure *The Firebrand of Florence* —finally sung by voices that the music deserves. McGlinn, in his meticulous way, presents the music in Weill's own orchestrations to recreate the feel of the original production. The singing is on an equally high level throughout. Miles Kreuger's essay tells you everything you need to know about the shows and Weill to appreciate this impressive collection.

Cover Girl (CURTAIN CALLS), the 1944 Hollywood musical with music by Jerome Kern, and starring Gene Kelly and Rita Hayworth (whose voice was dubbed by Martha Mears), was a popular wartime hit. This is a transfer from the soundtrack with vocals by Kelly, Mears, and Phil Silvers. The second portion of the CD is devoted to Kern's score for *You Were Never Lovelier*, with lyrics by Johnny Mercer, and starring Hayworth and Fred Astaire; again it is based on the soundtrack. Anyone seriously interested in obtaining this CD can write to FOOTLIGHT RECORDS, 113 East 12th Street, New York City, 10003.

A Star Is Born (COLUMBIA) was the final major film score by Ira Gershwin with music by Harold Arlen; it was also Judy Garland's last musical (except for her voice in *Pepe*, the cartoon *Gay* *Pure-ee*, and the dramatic *I Could Go on Singing* in 1962). Although difficult during the filming of *A Star Is Born* in 1953–54, she was in top vocal form. This recording contains the full score, from the *Overture* to "Lose That Long Face" and, of course, the interpolated "Born in a Trunk" by Roger Edens (not credited) as well as Leonard Gersh in a medley of songs associated with Garland. Fine listening.

VIDEOGRAPHY

All three of the final films have been transferred to video, and are very well done, too. They are **Shall We Dance, A Damsel in Distress** (both TURNER HOME ENTERTAINMENT), and **The Goldwyn Follies** (HBO VIDEO). Their first, **Delicious**, has not been released commercially, but bootleg copies of the film are in circulation, at least in Australia and New Zealand.

Ira's work without George is well represented on video: **Cover Girl** (RCA/COLUMBIA PICTURES HOME VIDEO), **The Barkleys of Broadway, Give a Girl a Break** (both MGM/UA HOME VIDEO), **A Star Is Born** (WARNER HOME VIDEO; the fully restored film), and **The Country Girl** (PARAMOUNT; not a musical, but with songs by Arlen and Gershwin).

Other notable videos include: **Rhapsody in Blue** (MGM/UA HOME VIDEO), an excellent presentation of the music and songs; **An American in Paris** (MGM/UA), a classic and a must; and **Funny Face** (PARAMOUNT HOME VIDEO), exquisitely filmed, and gracefully performed by Astaire and Audrey Hepburn. There are several songs from the 1927 show (in which Astaire starred), one from *Oh, Kay!* ("Clap Yo' Hands"), and additional songs by Roger Edens and Leonard Gershe that are quite good—"Think Pink" and "Bonjour, Paris!."

In the early 1960s Ira Gershwin reworked and released some songs in the Gershwin Archive for a film to be produced and directed by his friend Billy Wilder. The result was a quasi-musical, *Kiss Me, Stupid* (MGM/UA), starring Dean Martin and Kim Novak. Purportedly, aspiring rather than professional songwriters wrote the songs in this comedy, so Ira had to write down a bit. He refashioned "Wake Up, Brother, and Dance" (from *Shall We Dance)* as an Italianate waltz, "Sophia," and dipped into the Gershwin Melody Collection to come up with "All the Livelong Day" and the witty "I'm a Poached Egg." That is the extent of the Gershwin "score" for the film. Ira was not happy with the result, though there are some moments.

Porgy and Bess, complete on two video cassettes from EMI CLASSICS, contains the complete score beautifully sung by the cast and conducted by Simon Rattle. Trevor Nunn (who did the same for the Glyndebourne Festival Opera) directed the video. As I pointed out in the recordings section, the video production uses the original recording, which is then dubbed, though the effect is hardly noticeable.

A well-made documentary, **George Gershwin Remembered** (LONDON) was a joint production of the British Broadcasting Company (BBC) and the American WNET. Peter Adam wrote and directed. In roughly ninety minutes Gershwin's story is told, from his childhood until his death. Still photos, film (some with sound), and interviews with friends and his sister Frances Gershwin Godowsky are woven skillfully into an excellent biographical study, part of the superb *American Masters* series. There is plenty of music with Gershwin himself performing some of it; the home movies of Gershwin are extraordinary.

A FINAL WORD

Fairly recent quasi-Gershwin musicals came to Broadway and enjoyed much success. In 1983 **My One and Only** (ATLANTIC RECORDS) began as a revival of *Funny Face*, starring Twiggy and Tommy Tune. After severe roadsickness and the firing of eccentric director Peter Sellars (the first of four to go), a new book, having nothing to do with the original (no less actually), and a score lifted from several Gershwin sources invigorated *My One and Only*, which was a hit in New York and on the road. The recording is an interesting example of Gershwin brought up to date and, in general, the songs are well done.

Crazy for You (ANGEL) approximated *Girl Crazy*, using a half dozen songs from the 1930 show, but fleshed out the evening with over a dozen other numbers—including a quotation from the *Concerto in F.* There were no big name stars (at least not in 1992), but the melody-and-rhythm-rich musical took off for a long run on Broadway and abroad. Jody Benson and Harry Groener are endearing as the leads. The true-to-Gershwin orchestrations by William D. Brohn are affectionately conducted by Paul Gemignani. The authentic Broadway sound of the CD was assured by the show's producer, Thomas Z. Shepard.

New York City
July 1998

Index

Other titles of interest

**THE COMPLETE LYRICS
OF IRA GERSHWIN**
Robert Kimball
448 pp., 10 1/2 × 11 3/8, 54 photos
80856-0 $35.00

DOO-DAH!
**Stephen Foster and the Rise of
American Popular Culture**
Ken Emerson
416 pp., 34 illus.
80852-8 $16.95

AS THOUSANDS CHEER
The Life of Irving Berlin
Laurence Bergreen
704 pp., 51 photos
80675-4 $18.95

BENNY: King of Swing
Introduction by Stanley Baron
208 pp., 250 photos
80289-9 $14.95

BEYOND CATEGORY
**The Life and Genius of
Duke Ellington**
John Edward Hasse
Foreword by Wynton Marsalis
480 pp., 119 illus.
80614-2 $15.95

**BILLIE'S BLUES: The Billie
Holiday Story, 1933–1959**
John Chilton
272 pp., 20 photos
80363-1 $13.95

BLACK BEAUTY, WHITE HEAT
**A Pictorial History of
Classic Jazz, 1920–1950**
Frank Driggs and Harris Lewine
Foreword by John Hammond
360 pp., 1,516 illus.
80672-X $29.95

**THE BOOKS OF AMERICAN
NEGRO SPIRITUALS**
Two volumes in one
James Weldon & J. R. Johnson
384 pp.
80074-8 $15.95

BROWN SUGAR
**Eighty Years of America's
Black Female Superstars**
Donald Bogle
208 pp., 183 photos
80380-1 $17.95

CALL ME LUCKY
Bing Crosby as told
to Pete Martin
New introd. by Gary Giddins
384 pp., 64 photos
80504-9 $13.95

A CENTURY OF JAZZ
**From Blues to Bop, Swing to
Hip-Hop: A Hundred Years
of Music, Musicians,
Singers and Styles**
Roy Carr
256 pp., $9^5/_8$ × $11^1/_2$
350 illus., 200 in color
80778-5 $28.95

COLE PORTER
A Biography
Charles Schwartz
364 pp., 33 photos
80097-7 $14.95

**THE COMPLETE LYRICS
OF COLE PORTER**
Edited by Robert Kimball
535 pp., 13 illus.
80483-2 $22.50

**THE COMPLETE LYRICS
OF LORENZ HART**
Expanded Edition
Edited by Dorothy Hart and
Robert Kimball
367 pp., 47 illus.
80667-3 $25.00

DUKE ELLINGTON IN PERSON
Mercer Ellington with
Stanley Dance
236 pp., 25 pp. of photos
80104-3 $11.95

ELLA FITZGERALD
**A Biography of the
First Lady of Jazz**
Stuart Nicholson
368 pp., 29 illus.
80642-8 $15.95

**THE ESSENTIAL
JAZZ RECORDS**
Volume I: From Ragtime to Swing
Max Harrison, Charles Fox
and Eric Thacker
605 pp.
80326-7 $14.95

FACES IN THE CROWD
**Musicians, Writers, Actors &
Filmmakers**
Gary Giddins
288 pp.
80705-X $13.95

GEORGE GERSHWIN
Edited and designed by
Merle Armitage
New introduction by
Edward Jablonski
261 pp., 36 illus.
80615-0 $16.95